Sustaining Life on Earth

Advance Praise for *Sustaining Life on Earth*

"This book is a powerful attempt to prove that human intelligence, and the institutions it has created, possess power enough to blunt the force of our ecological destructiveness. It provides a light for the path, one that is badly needed." —**Bill McKibben**, author of *Deep Economy*

"For those who still believe that we can have our current lifestyles based on the current model of unlimited growth, *Sustaining Life on Earth* is a revelation; for those who already know that we have hit the earth's limits, this book is a guide. Many thanks for this lovely but challenging collection." —**Maude Barlow**, author of the upcoming book *Blue Covenant: The Global Water Crisis and the Coming Battle for the Right to Water*

"This collection of state-of-the-art summaries of what ails planet Earth offers prescriptions for the effective treatment, care, and maintenance of the home we all share. Scientists and scholars from many disciplines and countries have collaborated to compile this timely statement of what we as individuals and as societies and nations must do about the precariously unstable state of the world's life-support systems. In short, we need a system of global governance to deal effectively with environmental and ecosystem deterioration. The whole work is set out clearly and concisely in language accessible to non-specialists, and is supported by rich reference lists to guide concerned readers toward sources of further information. This book should be on the high priority list of required reading for everyone who is concerned about the world and its future." —**John M. Last**, emeritus professor of epidemiology, University of Ottawa

"I plan to use this textbook in my seminar next spring, and look forward to studying it more deeply along with my students. It is a fine collection of subjects and authors." —**Herman E. Daly**, professor, School of Public Policy, University of Maryland, College Park

"Like Cassandra of Troy, according to Homer's *Iliad*, experts in environmental matters—including biology, ecology, economics, law, public health, and social sciences—have come together as 'doomsayers, destined to tell the truth, but never to be believed.' This book brings together experts from relevant disciplines and, under the shrewd pen of its editors, the text is distilled to read as if from a single author. The idea of bridging, and thereby reconnecting the role of humans and their institutions to the global ecology, is shown to be critical if solutions are to be found that will help us to preserve ecosystems and thus ensure a more sustainable future for human populations. Assembling such varied information from multiple authors is the very kind of contribution needed for policymakers and students alike to help save us from ourselves. The contribution of this book to sustaining life on Earth is unique. Reading it is an enlightening experience and I strongly advise it to anybody." —**Roberto Bertollini**, director, Special Programme on Health and Environment, World Health Organization (WHO) Regional Office for Europe

Sustaining Life on Earth

Environmental and Human Health through Global Governance

EDITED BY COLIN L. SOSKOLNE

COEDITED BY LAURA WESTRA,
LOUIS J. KOTZÉ, BRENDAN MACKEY,
WILLIAM E. REES, AND RICHARD WESTRA

LEXINGTON BOOKS

A division of
ROWMAN & LITTLEFIELD PUBLISHERS, INC.
Lanham • Boulder • New York • Toronto • Plymouth, UK

LEXINGTON BOOKS

A division of Rowman & Littlefield Publishers, Inc.
A wholly owned subsidiary of The Rowman & Littlefield Publishing Group, Inc.
4501 Forbes Boulevard, Suite 200
Lanham, MD 20706

Estover Road
Plymouth PL6 7PY
United Kingdom

The opinions, facts, and figures contained within the individual chapters of this book
remain the responsibility of the respective chapter authors. In all single-authored
chapters, the "Royal Plural" has been adopted to be consistent across all chapters, and
also as a mechanism for being more inclusive of the reader.

British Library Cataloguing in Publication Information Available

Library of Congress Cataloging-in-Publication Data

Sustaining life on earth : environmental and human health through global governance /
edited by Colin L. Soskolne ; coedited by Laura Westra . . . [et al.].
   p. ; cm.
  Includes bibliographical references and index.
  ISBN-13: 978-0-7391-1729-3 (cloth : alk. paper)
  ISBN-10: 0-7391-1729-7 (cloth : alk. paper)
  ISBN-13: 978-0-7391-1730-9 (pbk. : alk. paper)
  ISBN-10: 0-7391-1730-0 (pbk. : alk. paper)
  1. World health. 2. Environmental health. 3. Medical policy—International
cooperation. I. Soskolne, Colin L. (Colin Lionel) II. Westra, Laura.
  [DNLM: 1. World Health. 2. Ecology. 3. Environment. 4. Health Policy—legislation
& jurisprudence. 5. International Cooperation—legislation & jurisprudence. WA 530.1
S964 2008]
  RA441.S87 2008
  362.1—dc22   2007032754

Printed in the United States of America

♾™ The paper used in this publication meets the minimum requirements of American
National Standard for Information Sciences—Permanence of Paper for Printed Library
Materials, ANSI/NISO Z39.48–1992.

Dedication

To my mother, Lily Soskolne (nee Slabe), and *my late father, Mike (Myer Lipe) Soskolne,* parents who provided me with the fortitude to "do good in the world," to "do the right thing for the right reason," and to "call a spade a spade"; and

To parents around the world who work toward similar goals, and the children who will come after them; and

To my colleagues who have contributed to this text, as well as to those who are often cited throughout and on whose shoulders this contribution now stands, thank you for your collegiality, insights, nurturing, and mentoring over the years.

In particular, this book could not have materialized without *Laura Westra*'s vision and influence in founding and steering the Global Ecological Integrity Group (GEIG) over the past fifteen years. It is from the GEIG's strong network of accomplished scholars and thinkers that we were able to draw for contributions to this focused collection.

In Memoriam

We reflect with sadness on the fact that *James J. Kay* died from cancer on May 30, 2004. Many of the basic ideas on which Chapter 9 is based were conceived of and, indeed, developed by him. This book, and in particular, Chapter 9, are dedicated to his memory. His legacy is an enduring one, and his premature loss immeasurable to the field.

As editor, my mother's late sisters, *Anita Ray (Ann)* and her late husband, *Shmuel (Sam) Gotz,* as well as *Sophie Brenner,* were relatives who played a formative role in my personal development.

Table of Contents

Figures, Tables, and Text Boxes

Figures

Tables

xi

Text Boxes

Foreword

Anthony J. McMichael

Should we worry about sustaining life on Earth? There may once have been life on Mars. If so, there appears to be none there now—and, of course, no one to tell the tale. And, if we earthlings were to discover remains of extinct life forms on the Red Planet, we would certainly be fascinated scientifically, but probably not moved emotionally, spiritually or morally. And so, the grand saga of the universe unfolds.

But, wait! We earthlings—humans as well as all other species—are genetically programmed for survival. The Darwinian theory of evolution tells us that marginal differences in living organisms, through adaptation to environmental stress and change, keep life in step with its physical and biological environment. So, at least at that basic organismal level, we are designed for survival on planet Earth—in its current condition.

Yet there is a reason why we actually can, and do, worry about sustaining life. That same evolutionary process has conferred a large and complex brain on *Homo sapiens*. Among all species, we have an unprecedented capacity for abstract thought, for imagining distant and very different futures. We have a "moral" sense (which may or may not be grounded, deeply, in nuances of self-interest). Hence, we also feel a moral obligation to our fellow species and to this planet's complex and wonderful ecosystems of which they (and we) are part.

This book has a prime focus on "health": the health of ecosystems and of the human species. That these two entities are interdependent is a central message of this book. Yet, with typical self-centeredness, we generally imagine—particularly in modern, urbanized human cultures—that our health largely reflects personal behaviors, consumer choice, access to health care, heredity, and a dose of good or bad luck. However, we are beginning to sense a few impending rude shocks in relation to these comfortable assumptions. As we continue to change the world's climate, disrupt ecosystems, wipe out entire species, degrade the soils, and otherwise assault nature's delicate balance, so it becomes clear that we are actually weakening Earth's life-support systems. These are the very systems that, until recent times, most smaller, simpler, human societies had been able to take more or less for granted.

At both regional and global levels it is now becoming evident that we have overplayed our hand, both in terms of human numbers and in the type and intensity of economic activity through the use of natural resources. Increasingly, we are operating in ecological deficit—and the manifestations of that are becoming apparent through the weakening of life-supporting ecosystems.

This takes us to the core of that somewhat elusive concept: sustainability.

Much recent talk about "sustainability" has focused on questions of whether we can shore up those things that, more immediately and tangibly, we value and depend on: economic productivity, local environmental conditions (and the iconic species that symbolize nature), and cohesive social structures and relations. These are all important. Misleadingly, however, they are referred to as the "triple bottom line"—an optimized balance of economic, social, and environmental conditions. Yet those things are not the bottom line; they are the next-to-last line. The reason we want to sustain them is because they are, in fact, the basis for long-term population well-being and health. We cannot see in advance just how that course will be maintained by future societies. But, our task is to set today's societies in the right direction. Sustainability is not a destination; it is an endless journey.

There have been various attempts to define sustainability. In 1987, the World Commission on Environment and Development, the Brundtland Commission, wrote of meeting the needs of the current generation without compromising the needs of future generations. The report stated: "We all depend on one biosphere for sustaining our lives." However, the Brundtland Commission focused predominantly on how to manage the environment in the interests of conventional economic development. That view is defensible if the natural environmental base is not being overloaded. Two decades on, however, we can see more clearly the mounting evidence of overload. Clearly, it is no longer just the technical and economic management of the environment that we should be stressing; we must now reassess the values, priorities, and activities of people and populations that are overloading the environment and harming ecosystems—since these are the upstream determinants of population health and well-being.

The Internet's Wikipedia offers an attractively simple description of sustainability as a system of parallel care and respect for the world's ecosystems and the people within it—recognizing the interdependence between these. Definitions are important, but we need good examples. They help our understanding and they assist communication to ill-informed policy-makers. The story of the mounting pressures on the world's fisheries is a compelling one.

The global wild fish catch peaked in the mid-1980s, and has since declined. This includes the well-known story of the collapse of the Grand Banks cod fishery off Newfoundland, Canada. Following the post-World War II escalation of industrialized fishing, vast quantities of fish were scooped from the ocean, and that prodigious bounty collapsed. Some other fisheries are showing signs of doing likewise. These fish stocks have long been a crucial source of high-quality protein for many of the world's populations, particularly in lower-income countries, and also a source of sustenance for other species in the oceans.

Further, recent studies have reported that the warming of the oceans is causing displacement of fish populations to higher latitudes, as they seek to retain constant temperature. Also, there have been recent reports (including from the United Kingdom's Royal Society and the German Advisory Council on Global Change) that the oceans' increasing uptake of atmospheric carbon dioxide is acidifying those waters. The Royal Society's report estimated that, if this were to continue for another three or four decades, it would seriously jeopardize the calcification processes underlying the marine food web.

This modern combination of human-made environmental pressures (over-fishing, ocean warming, and acidification) on the oceans' ecosystems illustrates well how we—mostly unintentionally, yet more and more inexcusably—are jeopardizing the sustainability of life on Earth. It reminds us of the real interdependence between the health of ecosystems and the health of the human species, as well as of our greater moral obligation to this planet and the generations to come. That combination of self-interest and moral necessity must now become integral to our societal objectives, our value systems, and the way we administer this invaluable inheritance that is Earth.

That is the essential message from this book.

Anthony J. McMichael
National Centre for Epidemiology and Population Health
The Australian National University

Preface

Colin L. Soskolne

Being part of the intelligent species, we consider ourselves to be smart. Yet, how smart are we? Both collectively and individually, we move into environments, and then we proceed to modify them, and in so doing, we erode the natural world's ability to provide us with our daily sustenance. We push the boundaries of common sense in all that we do in the name of progress, approaching system-level thresholds, and even exceeding the tipping points of these living systems.

And, why do we behave in these destructive and potentially suicidal ways? Is it because we are defective in some way? Is it greed that drives us to, on the one hand, achieve remarkable excellence, and yet, on the other hand, behave with such short-sightedness? Why have we failed to appreciate the consequences of our actions and see the connectedness between the world in which we live and our own health and well-being? What about that connected-ness and the health and well-being of our children and their children, and of their children's children?

Indeed, if not only for our own immediate good, our economy is signifi-cantly dependent on the natural world for maintaining its vibrancy. Our liveli-hoods and, in fact, life itself, fundamentally depend on the ability of ecosystems to function, producing goods and services, the sources of which we have, for far too long, taken for granted. So, with a track record of wanton destruction, how smart are we?

And, if not for our own good, what about the good of the species with whom we share life on Earth? Again, as we push other biological life forms to extinction, so too do we place our own futures in grave jeopardy. We undermine the diversity and vitality of all that is living. So, with this track record of neglect and abuse, how smart are we?

Sadly, we—certainly collectively—are a seriously dumb species. Any spe-cies that persists in fouling its nest we would label as being pretty dumb. And, so it is that we are pretty dumb. Further, we are fickle by the way in which we are so easily seduced, be it by technology, or by the perception of security. It is the lack of collective wisdom that dominates our species. Despite vast amounts of data, measuring everything measurable on Earth and from which knowledge derives, it is the absence of collective wisdom that contributes heavily to our decline and to our ultimate demise under current trends.

This book provides diverse and critical perspectives on several key "busi-ness-as-usual" ways of doing things; indeed, of conducting our affairs in the world. "Business as usual," we argue, is no longer an option if we wish to steer a course that stops fouling our collective nest (i.e., Earth), and one that places us on a course that is more likely to result in a future, a future secure in health and happiness; health and happiness not only for ourselves, but also for the genera-tions of children to come.

Time and again, we demonstrate our profound inability to act wisely. Acting wisely would, in our collective view, see us implement policies that would recognize that for every right that we have

- to populate the world,
- to consume and dispose of our waste,
- to spread technological innovation for better or worse, and
- to exploit renewable and nonrenewable resources,

we also have a duty

- to conserve, and
- to consider the implications of current actions on the health and well-being of other species and of other people, now and into the future.

Why have we not embraced this notion in the past? And how should we go about changing our behavior to accommodate this notion in the future? This book provides some of the answers.

Now, time is of the essence: we need to implement policies that will help us to cleanse our nest, and to maintain it as we change our approach from being one that is wantonly destructive of life on Earth, to one of being good stewards of the grand bounty of which we are a part.

We must reconnect ourselves with the very essence of life. Our duty to protect Earth's capacity to sustain life, not only for our own enjoyment, but also for the enjoyment of the generations of children to come, is to be recognized.

How to achieve such a lofty goal? First, we need, individually and collectively, to embrace the *Earth Charter* (see the Appendix) as *the* set of values and principles that will guide us, globally, onto a future path that provides for just, sustainable, and peaceful ways of living. Second, in the Teacher's Guide, we explain how the content of this book can be conveyed to students at both the undergraduate and the postgraduate levels of education. Now, more than ever, future leaders in all fields of endeavor need to understand and embrace the message of this book.

Colin L. Soskolne
Editor

Acknowledgments

The Global Ecological Integrity Group (GEIG) includes more than two hundred scholars and independent researchers worldwide, from diverse disciplines, including ecology, biology, philosophy, epidemiology, public health, ecological economics, and international law. The mandate of the GEIG is to push the boundaries of scholarly endeavor through inter- and transdisciplinary engagement on matters affecting and governing the sustainability of life for both present and future generations.

This book is based on papers presented at three successive annual conferences of the GEIG, the first held in Urbino, Italy, in 2003, the second held in Montreal, Canada, in 2004, and the third held in Venice, Italy, in 2005. Each chapter has been updated to reflect current thinking. The editors owe the following a debt of gratitude:

- **Social Sciences and Humanities Research Council of Canada (SSHRC)** grant, awarded to W. E. Rees (University of British Columbia), entitled "Controlling Eco-Violence: Linking Consumption and the Loss of Ecological Integrity to Population Health, Eco-Justice and International Law" (co-applicant C. L. Soskolne) provided partial funding for student assistance and technical editing support.
- **Dany Gagnon** of META E-editing, Montreal, Quebec, Canada, took responsibility for the technical editing, followed by taking charge of the book layout, typesetting, and technical production of the camera-ready copy for publication. Mr. Gagnon's diligence, attention to detail, and commitment to the task are greatly appreciated.
- **Frank Giorgilli** of Philadelphia, Pennsylvania, in the United States, assisted early on in the formative stages of the book prospectus.
- **Valerie Brown** of Canberra, Australia, provided encouragement throughout, and valued editorial assistance with several of the chapters.
- **Lee E. Sieswerda** of Thunder Bay, Ontario, provided valued editorial assistance with one of the chapters.
- **Luc Quenneville**, Reprographic/WordPro Operator, University of Windsor, Ontario, brought his technical editor skills to bear, ensuring the standard use of reference material throughout.
- Last, but not least, **Jennifer Rushing-Schurr** brought her expertise to bear in creating an extensive index.

As editor, I thank my team of co-editors, each of whom has played a significant role, from formulating the book's prospectus and selecting its title, to helping to ensure the excellence of each chapter.

On a personal note, I am grateful to my massage therapist, Don Desrosiers, who managed to keep me physically functional throughout the process of producing this book.

Teacher's Guide

Great need exists to teach about *sustainability* at the university, college, or tertiary level of education. In our view, it is a disservice to permit any student in any discipline to emerge from an education without a deeper understanding of *sustainability*.

This book can be used either as a complement to any existing curriculum materials, or as the foundation for teaching a full course in any way related to *sustainability* at any level, from the undergraduate level, through the postgraduate level of education and training. How can a single text serve all purposes?

This book has been written from a broad range of interdisciplinary perspectives (with twenty-seven contributed chapters), each bridged with single-page summaries in language designed for access and understanding by the nonspecialized reader. Further, the book is organized in eight parts and each part has a summary written in nonspecialist language. Finally, the Preface and Foreword, and the Introduction and Concluding chapters also are written in nonspecialist language.

At the undergraduate level, the student would be expected to assimilate content from the Preface and Foreword, the Introduction, all Part pages, the summary for each and every chapter and, finally, the Concluding chapter for examination purposes. In addition, the teacher should expect each student to review any one chapter of choice as a function of that student's or group of students' specialization interest/focus, for deeper critique and on which to base an essay. This essay should be written in groups of at least two and at most a few students to stimulate discussion within each group. The group would submit the joint essay under the names of those making up the group. After the halfway point in the course, each remaining class/session would include at least one group presentation of its critique to ensure that cross-disciplinary perspectives are discussed by the entire class of students.

At the graduate level, all that is expected of those at the undergraduate level (see above) would be required. In addition, each student making up a group for an essay would select not only one chapter, but they would connect at least two chapters (from 1 through 27), and tie these into the concluding chapter to provide a deep critique of transdisciplinary thinking from the perspective of at least two selected chapters that have common content, whether that be biology, ecology, economics, health, law, theology, and so on. Seminar and group learning are encouraged to enhance the transdisciplinary nature of the learning that this book is designed to stimulate.

Introduction

Global and Local Contexts as Evidence for Concern

**Colin L. Soskolne, Laura Westra, Louis J. Kotzé,
Brendan Mackey, William E. Rees, and Richard Westra**

How to convey a complex topic in an understandable way? This book is designed to be readable by non-specialists. In fact, the editors have gone to considerable lengths to make the opening sections here, as well as the opening section to each part and the summary for each and every chapter, as understandable as they could make them. Also, the concluding chapter that distills and synthesizes the book's contents and points the way forward for our individual and collective thinking about sustainability has been written in less specialized language. This book therefore is intended to be accessible to anyone interested in making the world a safer place, both for ourselves and for future generations.

In 2005, the Millennium Ecosystem Assessment declared that life-supporting ecosystems are in danger, and the effects are being felt by people globally. To prevent an escalation in catastrophic harms to human health and well-being in the years ahead, human-created institutions are urgently needed to protect us from ourselves. These would include institutions of governance, structured to steer us onto a sustainable course that would offer more hope than the present one for ensuring not only our own survival, but also that of our children and of our children's children.

How to steer such a course? The grave nature of ecological degradation demands that sustainability be approached in a new way, one that can be found only by bringing together people of competence in the public interest from a broad range of academic disciplines and real-world circumstances. This group must have the capacity to think about complex problems beyond each of their own more narrow perspectives. To rely on only one type of expert would be to maintain the *status quo*, conveying falsely that simplistic approaches will be sufficient to deal with the complex problems that we face. Given the seriousness and the broad range of challenges ahead, entirely novel approaches must be adopted if solutions for sustainability are to be found.

The needed shifts in policy to questions of sustainability that reconnect human behavior to ecological integrity will benefit both present and future generations. Through the existence over the past fifteen years of the Global Ecological Integrity Group (GEIG), interdisciplinary scholars have come together annually to discuss these matters. The opportunity realized by this Group results in this book that brings together the Group's collective and most current insights.

Anthropocentric (human-centered) perspectives—in addition to biocentric and ecocentric (biologically- and ecologically-centered) worldviews—are discussed throughout this book to ensure that concerns about the sustainability of life on Earth are understood from a shared-values perspective for greater appreciation in the collective public mind. It is primarily through demonstrating the

1

ongoing negative consequences to humans from continuing ecological degradation that new policies will be introduced at the local, national and inter-/supra-
national levels. Based on specific topics, mechanisms are identified throughout
the book for the implementation and enforcement of new policies critical to a
sustainable future for life on Earth.

This book reinforces the view that concern about ecological degradation
cannot be addressed solely through one academic discipline, but rather requires
a variety of experts willing to think beyond the traditional confines of their individual disciplines. Chapter content is organized to reflect that sustainability must
be addressed in the context of shared values and human rights. The range of
topics to address this broader goal includes an in-depth look at current international legal mechanisms and institutions, stressing their failures and incomplete-
ness, with negative consequences for a sustainable future. Legal and extralegal
mechanisms that aim to entrench sustainability and ethics, such as the *Earth
Charter* and other soft law instruments, are also investigated. Scientific ways of
linking issues and of measuring their impacts are presented. The book also contains, for example, topics addressing food and water security, catastrophic
events, and the influence of the media on the education of children—illustrating
current directions that are informative for motivating and justifying changes to
achieve sustainability.

The book emphasizes that the burdens and dangers imposed by biological
impoverishment are by no means limited to one region, let alone to one country.
International and supranational understandings and agreements must be pursued
if current trends are to be reversed. We further clarify that economic and social
considerations are unavoidably connected to terrestrial (i.e., land), marine (i.e.,
ocean), freshwater (i.e., lakes and rivers), and atmospheric (i.e., air) conditions.
We stress that with the spread of famine, the expansion of deserts and disease
affects present children and those yet-to-be born. These problems result in disproportionately greater harms to developing countries (i.e., the global South)
and in all less-developed economies that cannot buffer themselves because of an
absence of resources, including social infrastructure. Here lies the core of our
challenge.

A theme throughout this book is for the need to examine and understand existing global governance systems, of what passes for "justice" as trade continues
to supersede the right to life and health everywhere, and to re-examine the
meaning of democracy. We note the interface between all of these harms and
their interconnections with the broader environment. It is not sufficient to point
to moral principles and past paradigms (i.e., previous worldviews) to help redirect the present global situation. The extensive array of topics and issues included in this book speak to the necessity for a novel approach to how we do
things, both collectively and individually, that is both holistic and comprehensive. A change in our collective worldview is urgently needed. This is also one
of the primary imperatives of the *Earth Charter*.

This book endorses and promotes the *Earth Charter*, adopted in November
2004 as policy of the International Union for the Conservation of Nature

(IUCN). The Charter is a set of values and principles that can help us move from current, unsustainable approaches not only to our individual behavior, but also in local, national, and supranational ways of governance. These approaches help us to reconnect the environment both to the economy as well as to social issues, which are the drivers of health and well-being. Theoretically-grounded values embodied in the *Earth Charter*, as well as the Universal Declaration of Human Rights and other international law mechanisms, are used by the contributors to this book to promote transdisciplinary approaches to finding solutions to complex, systems-wide problems for a sustainable future through appropriate legal means.

In this book, we bring together a broad selection of preeminent scholars and achievers, from a variety of academic disciplines and in a format accessible to civil society as well as to policy-makers. It thus should serve as a book basic to any inter- and transdisciplinary university course concerned with issues of sustainability because it exemplifies communication among many specialist groups. It combines their specialist knowledge to reach beyond the confines of their individual areas of expertise in thinking "outside the box" in pursuit of sustainable solutions.

This book has been written because the authors believe that people worldwide will be interested in it. Indeed, we reckon that it is imperative for the public to be informed about our perspectives.

The book lays out clearly constructive opportunities for change toward sustainability. It provides much to think about and to seriously consider. It is organized into five parts, each addressing different dimensions of sustainability.

Part I of the book ties governance to ecology, economy, and human well-being. Bosselmann and Engel, in their respective chapters, address modern theories of governance, which are shown to be inherently incapable of arresting continuing declines in the human condition and render little hope of sustainability, owing to their exclusion of ecological justice. To achieve the shift to ecological justice, a true covenant is needed to serve as a sacred agreement that will enable change. Richard Westra cogently argues that economic growth, under the current capitalist model of a market society, is incompatible with the maintenance of ecological integrity. Burkhardt creatively demonstrates how integrity indicators that extend beyond classic economic measures of gross domestic product are more helpful measures of social well-being.

Part II of the book links globalization and human rights with broader recognition of the human condition and the way we make individual and collective policy decisions. Huynen and Martens nicely conceptualize and clarify the linkages among globalization, human rights, and health. The chapter by Rees, and then that by Karr, reveal how unsustainable and self-destructive our existing ways have been. Each of these chapters points, from different perspectives that resonate strongly with intuition, to the critically urgent need for us to redirect our collective self-destructive paths of the past to achieve a new path of sustainability with justice. Serious ongoing threats to biological systems globally serve to justify needed shifts away from the manner in which we conduct our lives today. Their analyses extend nicely from the linkages identified in the previous chapter. To conclude this part of the book, the notion of "strong sustainability," presented by Ott and Döring, is invoked as the necessary justification for moving toward sustainability.

Part III of the book clarifies how governance determines the viability of life-sustaining ecosystems, and how these are foundational to people's health and well-being. First, Manuel-Navarrete, Kay, and Dolderman provide critical insights into the debate around ecological integrity. After all, the ability of ecosystems to provide their various services to the planet, from clean air and water, to aesthetic and cultural diversity, is foundational to the question of a sustainable future for life on Earth. Val Brown's perspective is essential for deconstructing current knowledge that has led to our present unsustainable way of life. She also shows us how collective decision-making can be achieved to help us redirect ourselves toward sustainability. Kotzé articulately explains how fragmented decision-making relating to sustainability, across levels of government, has led to broad systems' degradation from which lessons for integrated governance can be learned. Finally, the Rainham, McDowell, and Krewski analysis shows us that although most of the healthy societies globally consume relatively vast amounts of natural capital to sustain their high levels of general health, some societies achieve high levels of general health on relatively less natural capital. Lessons from what other societies have achieved with smaller footprints should help pursuing sustainability.

In Part IV of this book, we examine the role of covenants that, in the pursuit of sustainability, respect all life forms, the public-good, and traditional knowledge. The *Earth Charter* is examined as *the* covenant that will guide us toward sustainability. Mackey's arguments resonate strongly with all of us in the Global Ecological Integrity Group. He shows that the value system espoused through the *Earth Charter* provides an enabling set of sixteen principles. Adoption of these principles will help us achieve a more just, sustainable, and peaceful world. Crabbé uses the context of global public goods in order to help us understand the significance of the *Earth Charter* (within the history of preceding official declaratory documents with the same purpose) when matched against a recent official document of the Ecological Society of America and the Copenhagen Consensus. His argument is that strong differences in the underlying ethics of these documents do not much affect the resulting pragmatic ranking of policies (as offered by the Copenhagen Consensus), and that these documents, despite their ethical differences, are actually mutually reinforcing. Finally, Oke provides a strong case for embracing diversity through the strength of traditional (or, indigenous) knowledge as applied to questions of ecological sustainability. The strength of his arguments lies both in their practicality, and their likelihood for success, using Africa as a model.

Part V brings the preceding four parts together in the form of a broad array of topics specific to sustainability in which the theories and approaches identified in the earlier chapters are drawn upon. These topics are grouped into four categories of focus.

Part V(a) of the book is devoted to an examination of governance amid ideological influences in a globalizing world. Don Brown demonstrates the role of think tanks whose role is to protect the position of powerful financial interests. To implement the shifts needed to achieve sustainability, the explicit ethical examination of issues around sustainability is necessary to counter these ideological biases. The policy debate would thereby become transparent, making clear for all concerned the values underlying policy alternatives. Two related examples are provided. The first, by De Leo and Gatto, points out that while Russia's ratification of the Kyoto Protocol provided a successful step toward achieving the Protocol's targets for carbon dioxide emission reductions, many countries, including several European ones, have fallen behind in adopting new non- or less-polluting technologies. Even more regrettably, the two countries that contribute most to greenhouse gas emissions, the United States and China, are still resistant, for different reasons, to adopt any binding target to limit their emissions. Until local governments understand better the direct and indirect impacts of greenhouse gas emissions, little movement will be seen nationally. Analogously, and from a governance perspective, Taylor argues that, in the case of Genetically Modified Organisms (GMOs), new forms of ecological governance are required. These new forms of governance involve the sharing of competence between national and local governments, empowering local jurisdictions to control or prohibit GMO release.

In Part V(b) of this book we examine the rights to food and water. First, David and Marcia Pimentel provide sobering facts, noting that with world population projected to double in the next fifty-eight years—to reach thirteen billion—and with over half of the world's current population suffering from deficiencies of calories, protein, or critical nutrients such as iron, iodine, and vitamins, the rate of deficiencies will become even more extreme. Because we expect agricultural systems to provide sustenance for the world's ever-increasing population, the interrelated availability and functioning of cropland, freshwater, energy, and biodiversity resources is critical. Population growth must be slowed and basic resources conserved for our future food security. Concerning water per se since 1996, Dellapenna summarizes, in the next chapter, how the International Law Association undertook to reformulate the Helsinki Rules to incorporate international environmental law and international human rights law resulting, in 2004, in the Berlin Rules on Water Resources. These rules provide a new holistic approach for addressing international water law. In the next chapter, Rajepakse describes how the UN Committee on Economic, Social and Cultural Rights issued General Comment No. 15 of 2002, which recognizes the constraints on States from limited water resources, declaring inappropriate resource allocation and unaffordable pricing to be forms of discrimination. Sri Lanka's experience provides a rich practical example of how traditional concepts relating to water have blended with modern human rights jurisprudence. As a final example, Witbooi examines the need for cooperation in promoting integrity and socioeconomic justice in marine fisheries. Guided by the *Earth Charter* principles, the European Union's new fisheries partnership approach could facilitate the necessary transition from serving the socioeconomic self-interests of the parties involved, to progressively promoting ecological integrity and socioeconomic justice toward sustainable fisheries management.

In Part V(c) of this book we examine the social forces (or, drivers) at play in environmental and human catastrophes. In the first chapter, Goodland exposes the extent to which economic development projects depend on the forced displacement of people and whole communities to make way for large-scale projects such as highways, mines, irrigation schemes, and power plants. This constitutes institutionalized violence. The notion of "prior fully informed consent" is relevant to economic development projects where the forced displacement of communities dislocates cultural and economic norms, and indigenous knowledge is lost. In the second chapter in this part of the book, Manno and Vo discuss the findings from their study comparing the degradation of rural livelihoods between Vietnam and Mexico under globalized trade liberalization. They demonstrate the decline in rural livelihoods where development projects have been implemented, indicating that rural livelihood decision-making is strongly influenced by trade policies. Local indigenous knowledge is central to guide us to live within the limits and productive capacities of the ecosystems on which we depend and of which we are a part. In the final chapter in this part of the book, Ladd and Soskolne show how the science of epidemiology is recognizing the sub-specialty of ecoepidemiology for studying complex and systemic problems affecting the health of communities. Public health cannot ignore the warnings from other sciences that point to damage to the ecosystems on which communities depend for their sustenance. So, new tools and the application of existing tools, under-utilized in the past, need to be brought to bear in this area of science, traditionally oriented toward informing policy.

In Part V(d) of the book we examine two focused areas that relate primarily to children. First, Dyson argues that the cultural environment is formative for children as future voters. Media programming of violence and consumer-driven value systems are especially harmful to children and hence also to the democracies into which these children will be socialized. While the debate about the harmful effects of media violence and the impact of advertising has raged for decades, this chapter addresses the persistent obstacles to meaningful change. In the second and final chapter in this part of the book, Laura Westra identifies that the right of children to both physical and mental health is possible only through national, international, and supranational law. Only by world bodies, such as the World Health Organization, taking a more proactive stance, will the mechanism for change toward the sustainability of life on Earth by enabling the health and survival of future generations be more assured.

The final chapter draws upon all of the preceding material to challenge us, individually and collectively, to make our way forward with policies that inspire both hope and promise. Some members of the Editorial Team conclude with policy recommendations, distilling and synthesizing the foregoing arguments and examples into a coherent case for changes needed to sustain life on Earth. The collective will to continuously strive toward sustainability is our goal.

Part I:
Tying Governance to Ecology, Economy, and Human Well-Being

Modern theories of how we are governed are proving to be incapable of supporting shifts to sustainable ways of living. The way that we are presently governed excludes fairness in how societies around the globe share the very life-sustaining services that support all life forms. Life-sustaining services include the air we breathe, the water we drink, and the soil that provides the food that feeds us. Without good quality air, water and soil, people cannot survive for long. Our utter dependence on the vitality of all forms of life, and not only on that of humans, is paramount if solutions to our very survival are to be implemented.

The principal focus of the first part of this book is on ecological justice. Here, we concern ourselves with fairness toward the community of life; fairness not only among the present generations of people globally, but also in how we serve as stewards of Earth's bountiful but depleting resources and beauty for the survival of future generations.

The ability of life-supporting ecosystems to continue to sustain life is under grave threat and, under the current market driven and globalizing world, is destined to collapse. To see governments adopt sustainable policies, a true covenant is needed to serve as a sacred agreement that enables required shifts to ecological justice. Such a covenant is provided by the *Earth Charter* (see the Appendix), a document with sixteen primary principles that, if embraced in our governance, would lead us to sustainable paths for both present and future generations. For this to be achieved, each society will need to reform its individual covenant in light of the *Earth Charter* covenant so that the world is governed by a new "covenant of covenants."

The *Earth Charter* can assist in this and other ways in the task of reformulating the way in which we govern ourselves. It can help us to better recognize what we do as individuals and in what we expect from our governments for the continuance of both life and civilization. Current approaches of externalizing costs reduces market efficiencies, highlighting the need for integrity indicators that extend beyond classic economic measures of gross domestic product (GDP) to better ways of measuring social well-being. Current integrity indicators reveal global disparities that are profoundly unjust in our modern world.

Chapter 1

Institutions for Global Governance

Klaus Bosselmann, Ph.D. (Law)
Professor of Law
Director, New Zealand Centre of Environmental Law,
University of Auckland, New Zealand

Contact Information: Private Bag 92019, Auckland 1142 *NEW ZEALAND*
Phone: +64 9 373 7599 ext. 87827; Fax : +64 9 373 7471
Email: k.bosselmann@auckland.ac.nz

Summary

Most legal theories of global governance consider the nation-state as a pillar of international law. While there is scope for developing new global governance structures around the notion of international or transnational law, there is a strong case to be made for a different approach.

Nation-states have, after all, lost many of their traditional powers, surrendering to global corporate power. So, instead, we propose an ecologically-derived theory of global governance. This theory does not consider either the state or any institution, other than the maintenance of ecological integrity, as the focal point for governance. This theory is invoked because people globally have realized the need to adopt strategies for preserving Earth's ecological integrity.

Global governance can no longer be delayed, given the ongoing failures of states and institutions to contribute to a sustainable future. Ultimately, all life, including human beings and their institutions, depends on ecological integrity (i.e., on the ability of life-sustaining ecosystems to withstand perturbations).

How then can we link the concern for ecological integrity with the concern for appropriate governance? The short answer is through adoption of the *Earth Charter*, a document that addresses both the ethical principles of caring for ecological integrity and the legal principles of governance. The long answer is that people, through states and global civil society, need to adopt a credible concept of governance driven by global ecological concern.

In this chapter, we identify relevant driving forces of global ecological governance. These forces are found in existing institutions and in the changes that they are currently undergoing. By recognizing these changes, we are helped in formulating a concept of global governance based on ecological citizenship, the values of a global civil society, and a new role for nation-states. This approach, if adopted, could usher us into an era more supporting of global peace, democracy, and sustainability.

Introduction

From the legal perspective and of most relevance to a sustainable global society are its institutions and their guiding norms. A lawyer can ask: what functions do institutional structures (such as: citizenship, civil society, states, and international organizations) have for the governance aspect of a sustainable society?

In response, we can distinguish between two kinds of institutions. The first kind is the concept of citizenship in both of its manifestations: individual citizenship, and civil society. The second kind of institution relates to the legal constructs derived from citizenship. One of these constructs is the nation-state; the other constructs are the international institutions created by states. Following a "bottom-up" approach to global governance, we can think of individual citizenship as core, emerging civil society as its collective manifestation, and the state as the ultimate creation of citizens. Because none of these categories are static, each can be examined both in terms of its dynamics and ability to preserve ecological integrity under our proposed new approach to global governance.

Insofar as citizenship and civil society have a global component, they form part of global governance. Global governance can be perceived as taking many shapes and forms. However, any realistic concept would include states. States are at the center of the current architecture of international governance; they are not likely to disappear simply because they may have failed to provide global ecological stewardship. The question then is not whether, but how states can contribute to a new approach to global governance. Equally, international organizations, such as the United Nations, are not per se unsuitable; they need to be assessed in terms of their ability to change and transform. The *Earth Charter* (see the Appendix) resonates with people and can be used to enable the changes needed at each of the above two identified levels of institutions to achieve ecologically sound global governance.

With respect to the first level, the *Earth Charter*'s Preamble states: "We are at once citizens of different nations and of one world in which the local and the global are linked. Everyone shares responsibility for the present and future well-being of the human family and the larger living world." Second, the Preamble proclaims: "The emergence of global civil society is creating new opportunities to build a democratic and humane world. Our environmental, economic, political, social, and spiritual challenges are interconnected, and together we can forge inclusive solutions."

This last notion implies the recognition and legitimacy of states. Global civil society is not diametrically opposed, but complementary to states and established institutions. This is visible in the Preamble's plea for a "global partnership to care for the Earth" and spelled out in the concluding statement ("The Way Forward"):

The partnership of government, civil society, and business is essential for effective governance. . . . In order to build a sustainable global community, the nations of the world must renew their commitment to the United Nations, fulfill their obligations under existing international agreements, and support the implementation of the Earth Charter principles.

Our aim in this chapter is to reveal the potential that traditional institutions have for transformation. In the current age of globalization, calls for global governance are already in a stage of transformation because they are simultaneously losing and increasing their relevance and importance. To achieve global ecological stewardship, the challenge is to minimize the "negative" and maximize the "positive" influences on this transformation.

Transforming Citizenship

Essentially, citizenship confers rights and duties as instruments of the political community to generate internal security, stability, and identity; create a sense of loyalty; and, through taxation and military service, provide the resources necessary for the survival and functioning of the community.[1] International Law has always respected the State's sovereign right to exclusively decide on questions of citizenship, i.e., to define under which conditions someone may or may not be a citizen.[2]

Under our new approach to global governance, we explore the dynamics and changing rules of citizenship. There is much to suggest that citizenship has lost its original function, i.e., to define people's rights and duties in their community. We need to remind ourselves how crucially important this function remains. Without a mechanism that guarantees people the essential right to life in their community, individuals and communities would lose all sense of security. The core idea of citizenship is, and will remain, to provide legal security and political identity.

a) Globalization and Citizenship

Globalization and migration have posed a fundamental challenge to identity, humanitarian law, and human rights.[3] More people than ever before are faced with their greatest fears, i.e., losing their political identity and sense of belonging. Ironically, the more open and globalized the world becomes, the greater the need for the protection of citizenship.

Citizenship is challenged by a host of political threats, including international migration and mobility, nationalism, intolerance, religious fundamentalism, loss of social and environmental security, democratic deficits, voter apathy, and worldwide restructuring of welfare systems to accommodate demographic changes. More than ever, human rights depend on active, vigilant citizenship: *"The institutions of constitutional freedom are only worth as much as a popula-*

tion makes of them."[4] Individuals can no longer simply turn to the state for the fulfillment of their basic aspirations because citizenship has become "less organically connected to an individual's search for security and meaning in life."[5]

Proliferation of Identity

In a globalized world, states cannot rely on their citizens' national identity. Instead, they are faced with a proliferation of identities in one person, the multi-belonging citizen. We are all part of a "global culture"[6] with an internationalization of values. Both are facilitated through globally consumed Hollywood entertainment, fast food and big cars, ironically preaching the gospel of individualism and hedonism.[7]

The counterforces of economic globalization are disloyal identities and different worldviews. Global culture consists of competing paradigms, i.e., the modern paradigm of "economism" vs. the post-modern paradigm of "ecologism." The ecological paradigm fits a world embracing diversity with unity. We encounter this new world on an almost daily basis. Most of us live in societies in which many people travel all over the world and encounter other people from all over the world. To some extent, it becomes impossible to ascertain how much foreign culture is "absorbed" with each encounter. The foreign becomes the familiar, and what was familiar becomes foreign. As a result, national identity is being replaced by a multinational identity more akin to global citizenship.

Shifting Loyalty

Closely connected to identity is loyalty as its emotional, intellectual, or psychological prerequisite. It forms a bond of allegiance with a set of values encapsulated in a social system. Loyalty to a nation, however, has become either weak or multiple and frequently expresses critical commitment rather than blind obedience.[8] Loyalty can expand as well as shrink depending on the point of reference. It can apply equally to one's family as to humanity as a whole, depending on the sphere or layer of moral obligation. Loyalty is often accompanied by a feeling of moral obligation and responsibility because, with loyalty comes the desire to protect and worship the ideals to which one subscribes. This can go so far as to elicit an altruistic readiness of self-sacrifice for a "higher cause." With respect to global problems such as poverty, war, ecological decline, social injustice, and human rights violations, loyalty can be the ferment for a sense of global justice uniting humanity in often unpredictable ways.

Changing Citizenship Laws

Responding to non-national, or multinational identity and loyalty are those legal concepts that promote the transfer of political powers. This is happening with all kinds of supranational or transnational and international organizations, such as the European Union,[9] the World Trade Organization, the World Bank, and the United Nations, to name but a few. Other forms of political connections include economic free-trade zones (such as APEC and NAFTA), military alliances (such as NATO), cultural and educational programs (such as UNESCO), but also groupings of a different kind such as "Western industrialized countries," "the Arab countries," the "Middle" and the "Far East"—even the infamous "Axis of Evil," or the "Old Europe."

In this sense, political and legal perceptions of identity and loyalty have become more closely connected to broader concepts.[10] They also demonstrate the potential for multiple and multi-layered, extra-national forms of citizenship, with European integration being the most advanced model.[11] In combination with the principle of "subsidiarity," regional arrangements such as the EU are conceived of as a new federal structure replacing the representative nation-state system.[12] Moreover, the individual has been given procedural rights, such as access to the European Court of Justice, and to take legal action before national courts to enforce the realization of EU guidelines.[13] It is this novelty that is interpreted as an indicator of the emergence of a new layer of citizenship.[14] EU citizenship is sometimes considered the precursor to global citizenship.

Considering the darker side of European integration ("Fortress Europe"), some say that European citizenship "may in fact prove to be a hindrance to global citizenship" because many of the policies of EU citizenship run counter to the idea of cosmopolitan citizenship.[15] So far, Union citizenship has not succeeded in uniting different nationalities. It relies on traditional notions (such as nationality itself), and while a European identity may be emerging, it comes with a sense of exclusion.[16] Some warn of a real danger that the EU population will be divided between citizens and an underclass of "foreigners."[17]

Nevertheless, the European experience represents a helpful reference for global citizenship.[18] Whereas different ideologies form the basis of these types of citizenship, namely with regard to the degree of institutionalization and inclusion or exclusion respectively, some features resemble each other, such as the idea that citizenship, aside from state citizenship, could be complementing national citizenship.

b) Toward Global Citizenship

The strongest justification for global citizenship is the globalized world we live in; more precisely, the global dimension of national and local issues that most people encounter on a day-to-day basis. None of these issues can be solved by states or their citizens alone. States, like citizens, are almost forced into the (eco-)logic of global citizenship. At least, traditional citizenship needs to be transformed to a new model of multilayer citizenship.

There is little that is revolutionary about a global dimension of citizenship. Even political liberalism has acknowledged this—either in practical terms ("free movement of capital, goods and services") or in theoretical terms, observing the "changing face of citizenship."[19] Bart van Steenbergen promotes the "global ecological citizen,"[20] and Ralf Dahrendorf stresses the "complications" when a citizen owes duties not only "to her home country, but to the world community, to the earth, to humankind."[21]

According to *Nigel Dower*, global citizenship consists of three components: normative, existential, and aspirational.[22] The normative aspect is based on the conviction that, as global citizens, we all share certain duties, and that we all have a moral status of being worthy of moral respect.[23] In its existential meaning, the idea acknowledges that we are all part of a global community, be it an institutional or quasi-political one. The aspirational side is based on a long tradition of thought and feeling about the ultimate unity of the human experience.[24] It rests upon the other two in striving for a world in which basic values become fully realizable through a strengthening of the community and its institutions and building a legal framework.

Notwithstanding philosophical differences between the various proponents of ecological citizenship,[25] they all agree on some key prerequisites: the normative idea of a community of humankind, the assumption of a community of life, the existential recognition that the future of the human species depends on the functioning of its surrounding ecosystems, and an aspiration of an increasing sense of responsibility that will lead to action on behalf of the environment.

If it is true that transforming individual attitudes and ideas precedes the transformation of institutions, we can describe some characteristics of citizenship that is ecologically centered. First, ecologically centered citizenship reflects an extension of individual citizenship. We can imagine ourselves as citizens of a social and an ecological community, and both forms of community can be experienced locally, nationally, regionally, or globally. Thus, ecological citizenship is not global as opposed to national, but relevant at any community level of which we are a part.

Second, a defining aspect of ecologically centered citizenship is the recognition of nonhuman beings as "fellow citizens." The notion of nonhuman citizens is purely metaphoric, but helpful to acknowledge a fiduciary or stewardship relationship between citizenship and nonhuman entities. The ecological steward adopts a guardianship responsibility for entities not represented in the political decision-making process. This role has been described as follows:

> The ecologically aware citizen takes responsibility for the place where . . . she lives, understands the importance of making collective decisions regarding the commons, seeks the common good, identifies with bioregions and ecosystems rather than obsolete nation-states or transnational corporations, considers the wider impact of . . . her actions, is committed to . . . community building, observes the flow of power . . . , and acts according to his or her conviction.[26]

Third, in legal terms, the fiduciary aspect of citizenship first requires wide-reaching procedural and participatory rights. The *Earth Charter* details them in Principle 13 (see Appendix).

A further requirement of the fiduciary aspect is the recognition of duties. As much as there are rights to access and use the environment, there are duties as well. They can translate to either specific duties[27] or to certain limitations of individual rights[28] that are drawn from the fundamental concern for the Earth's ecological integrity.

The *Earth Charter* (see Appendix) expresses such limitations in various respects in Principle 1 (a), Principle 2 (a), and Principle 6 (a).

These and other principles of the *Earth Charter* put self-restrictions on the rights of citizens. In order to exercise our fiduciary responsibility, the right to the use of natural resources, for example, is restricted by the respect for the community of life and the duty to prevent harm.

Consequently, the concept of ecological stewardship is embedded in the *Earth Charter*. Having described the individual component of our approach to global governance, we can now describe the collective component, i.e., global civil society.

Emerging Global Civil Society

When citizens "move" politically, they constitute a citizens' movement. Citizens' movements and civil society groups provide the impetus for social change. The perspective of governments and states defines them in more negative, complementary terms: Non-Governmental Organizations (NGOs) making "important contributions in many fields, both nationally and internationally."[29]

According to April Carter, the concept of civil society evolved in the 1980s when dissident intellectuals in Eastern Europe created a social platform for resistance and political change.[30] If civil society were responsible for the most radical system change in recent times, it is perceivable that it is capable of more. It is certainly recognized today as the main driving force toward global governance.

In International Environmental Law, the pressures of civil advocacy are particularly strong. This legal field would not even exist were it not for the worldwide environmental movement putting global environmental degradation on the agenda of state conferences. The existence and practice of the UN Environmental Programme (UNEP), for example, is largely shaped through the input of environmental groups.[31]

Global civil society builds upon the autonomy of civil society bodies within their own nation-states and links them within a transnational realm independent of all nation-states.[32] It represents the whole network of international relationships and organizations that underlie society outside the sphere of established political institutions.[33]

While globalization has curtailed the nation-states' capacity to regulate key areas, it has also opened up new spaces to be filled by other actors. States are no longer simply tolerating civil society groups, but they depend on them to make up for lost political power.[34] In this respect, globalization thus cuts both ways.

Originating from grass-roots movements, sometimes very powerful NGOs[35] have succeeded to set the international agenda.

However, despite the positive influence that global civil society can have on global governance, it lacks democratic legitimacy and accountability in its classical sense. Ultimately, while its policies might impact on citizens' lives, citizens in turn do not have any democratic means to control civil society.[36] Moreover, civil society has mainly been dominated by Western and Northern states and does therefore carry the imminent danger of endorsing moral concepts entertained by the more privileged parts of global society.[37] Its global expansion could thus bring about the exportation of predominantly Western values, westernization, and cultural imperialism.[38]

Civil society, in its present form, cannot substitute a representative system of governance, but could be legitimized by an emerging global citizenship. To the degree that the concept of global civil society is being associated with global citizenship, its mandate becomes stronger. As Robin Attfield points out, legitimizing and monitoring institutions of global governance could be the main effect of global citizenship.[39] The UN Commission on Global Governance is convinced that global governance without civil society is impossible. Its definition of global governance clearly involves civil society:

> Governance is the sum of the many ways individuals and institutions, public and private, manage their common affairs. It is a continuing process through which conflicting or diverse interests may be accommodated and co-operative actions may be taken. It includes formal institutions and regimes empowered to enforce compliance, as well as informal arrangements that people and institutions either have agreed to or perceive to be in their interest. . . . At the global level, governance has been viewed primarily as intergovernmental relationships, but it must be understood as also involving nongovernmental organizations (NGOs), citizens' movements, multinational corporations, and the global capital. Interacting with these are the global mass media of dramatically enlarged influence.[40]

Redefining State Sovereignty

No matter how global governance may shape up, it is safe to assume that international relations will be dominated by states for many years to come. A central point of interest, therefore, remains the concept of state sovereignty. With respect to our approach to global governance, we need to ask the extent to which the state actually "owns" its own territory.

Historically, territorial sovereignty emerged as a means to protect state boundaries, not the use of territory or resources. When Hugo Grotius (1583-1645) formulated the imperative of international law "that foreign property is respected" (*De jure bellis ac pacis*), he saw the exclusive competence of the state over its territory essentially as the protection of property. With respect to nineteenth century international law theory, Anthony Carty found this link firmly established: "The relationship of a state to its own territory could be described in the same language as that of a private individual toward his own property, i.e. in the sense of a spatial dimension over which he had absolute right of use and disposal."[41] The language may be different in international documents, but economic interests were clearly behind the reasoning for the mid-twentieth-century concepts of the "right to exploit freely the natural resources"[42] and the permanent sovereignty over natural resources.[43] Around the time of the 1972 Stockholm Conference, additional documents[44] broadened the concept to specifically include all economic activities of states and any property rights associated with them.

Property-rights thinking influenced the drafting of Principle 21 of the Stockholm Declaration ("States have . . . the sovereign right to exploit their own resources")[45] and formed the background against which Principle 21 sets some limitations: "the responsibility to ensure that activities within their jurisdiction or control do not cause damage to the environment of other States or areas beyond the limits of national jurisdiction."[46] The International Court of Justice found this responsibility to be "now part of the body of international law relating to the environment"[47] emphasizing the "great significance that it attaches to respect for the environment, not only for states, but for the whole of mankind."[48]

Despite such broad respect for the environment, the actual obligations are much narrower. They are hampered by rigid territorial sovereignty on the one hand, and by legal insignificance of the environment on the other.

Legally, the "environment" exists only as areas within or outside national jurisdictions. Thus, not the environment, but state-owned parts of it, are the referential point for any environmental obligation. Viewing the environment solely from the perspectives of states has an absurd effect: it creates the perception of four categorically different environments. One environment is owned by the individual state, a second environment owned by other individual states, a third environment is owned by all (high seas, Antarctica, super-adjacent airspace), and a fourth, global environment is owned by none. Consequently, the first environment is of concrete, immediate interest (state sovereignty); the second environment of still concrete, but of less immediate interest (state responsibility); the third is of a more abstract interest (a general, but undefined duty not to harm); and, the fourth environment is of an even more abstract, distant interest (mere cooperation).

Correspondingly, we can distinguish between intraterritorial, transboundary, common areas, and global forms of environmental harm or degradation:

1. "*Intraterritorial damages*" are confined to the state's territory[49] where it originates. Essentially, the controls here are an internal affair. International environmental law knows no obligation not to harm the "national" environment.[50]
2. "*Transfrontier*"[51] or "*transboundary*"[52] forms of environmental harm originate in one country with effects on another country. Transboundary pollution may have effects on the air, water and soil, and there are many treaties

covering its various forms of transport and effect.[53] Likewise, several customary rules and general principles with limiting effects on the exercise of territorial sovereignty are applicable.

3.   Transboundary pollution not affecting other states, but areas under no state
jurisdiction, can be categorized as *"common areas pollution."* The areas concerned here are the high seas (including the seabed), Antarctica, and the super-
adjacent airspace (not including outer space).[54] They are distinguished from the
global environment not only by their spatial nature, but also by the fact that international law recognizes them in a specific manner.

The "common areas"[55] are recognized either as humankind's common
heritage (seabed), common concern (Antarctica), or shared resources (high
seas, airspace). The common interest behind each of these concepts varies in
weight and so do the corresponding obligations: the environments of the seabed
and Antarctica are, in theory, better protected, imposing more limitations to
sovereignty and property rights than the high seas and the airspace. The overall
picture, however, shows few signs of a limitation to territorial sovereignty with
respect to common areas. With the exception of a duty to not pollute the marine
environment, no general environmental obligations exist. The reason for this is
that the areas beyond national jurisdictions are not categorized in total, but individually, with differing obligations for each of them.

4.   Finally, *"global environmental harm"* affects the environment that is neither confined to national jurisdictions nor to the areas beyond national jurisdictions. The global environment includes both, but embraces the Earth as a
whole. Any limitations on sovereignty to be considered here would not originate from territorial concerns of states, but from the global environment per se.
It is here where our thinking about global ecological governance needs to start.

The World Charter for Nature of 1982 was the first document to focus on
Earth as a whole. It aims to protect the global environment for its own sake,
independently from jurisdictions or spatial segments. The UN resolution carrying the Charter[56] was opposed by the United States, and its principles were not
developed further in a binding legal instrument. But, it helped considerably to
give international environmental law direction and shape.[57] With its emphasis on
the intrinsic value of nature and the need for humanity to be guided by a code of
ethics, the Charter promoted ecocentrism as a viable alternative to anthropocentrism.[58] Ecocentrism, with its central notion of intrinsic values, increasingly
shaped municipal[59] and international[60] environmental law. Examples of international documents include the 1980 Convention for the Conservation of Antarctic
Living Resources, the 1991 Protocol to the Antarctic Treaty, the 1979 Convention on the Conservation of European Wildlife and Natural Habitats, the 1992
Convention on Biological Diversity, and the 1995 IUCN Draft International
Covenant on Environment and Development. Article 3 of the Draft Covenant
specifically defines the "global environment" as a "common concern of humanity."

However, the clearest expression of responsibility for Earth as a whole is
the *Earth Charter*. With its central reference point (e.g., "Earth, our home, is
alive with a unique community of life" and the recognition of "universal respon-

sibility"), it almost reverses the logic of international environmental law. The central reference point is not the community of nations, but the community of life. Designing global governance around the community of life demands an integration of the natural environment into the concept of territorial sovereignty. The externalized environment becomes internalized.

The internalization of the environment requires certain changes to the concept of territorial sovereignty. Sovereignty over one's own natural resources is to be limited by the fact that the "national" environment is also part of a wider, transnational, or global environment. As a consequence, the state would be transformed from the purely exploitative institution that it is now to accepting a guardianship or trusteeship (or, ecological stewardship) role.

The transformational approach as, for example, advocated by Richard Falk,[61] Günther Handl,[62] or Lynton Caldwell,[63] assumes the existence of state sovereignty, but relates it to the idea of civil society. The perspective shifts from state-centeredness to globality and sets a new agenda. In strategic terms, the functions of state sovereignty are relative to the needs of civil society. In political terms, states are not expected to relinquish sovereignty by means of sweeping changes, but to adjust sovereignty to global realities.

A first step toward transformation would be to see the parallels between property and sovereignty as indicated earlier. Just as private property cannot be defined without its social dimensions,[64] state sovereignty cannot be defined without its international dimensions.[65] Both are neither absolute, nor independent of the system within which they are operating. The international dimension of sovereignty could, therefore, be perceived as an integral component.[66] This conceptual limitation to state sovereignty serves the protection of the international community of states.

The community of states is, however, different from the community of ecosystems. The difference is crucial as the community of states defines any limitations to sovereignty on the basis of mutual expectation. Such reciprocity cannot be expected with respect to the global environment. If the protection of the global environment is determined through the reciprocal expectations of states, states' interests *in* the environment will again prevail over the interests *of* the environment. Global environmental protection would remain derivative and secondary. The recognition of the collective dimension of sovereignty can, therefore, be only the first step.

A second step is to add the ecological dimension to concepts of property and sovereignty, respectively. Just as property is determined by ecological realities, so is sovereignty. The crucial question is, therefore, whether an ecological dimension should be part of the definition of property[67] and of sovereignty.

The justification for taking this step is the indivisibility of the environment. To accommodate environmental indivisibility in international law, two approaches are possible. Either the idea of territorial sovereignty is dismissed altogether on the grounds that the environment cannot be divided into territories.[68] Or, territorial sovereignty is redefined on the grounds that there are use and conservation aspects of the (indivisible) environment to be addressed. Following this approach, territorial sovereignty needs to recognize the dual nature of the environment that it occupies. The dual nature is best understood as consisting of a right to use "territorial" natural resources and an obligation to protect the environment. Territorial sovereignty over natural resources (or "fruits" of the environment) can be perceived, therefore, only as inherently linked to an obligation to protect the environment ("the substance").

In positive terms, the use of resources is covered by territorial sovereignty within the parameters of ecological sustainability. As a result, the current "sovereign right of states to exploit their resources pursuant to their own environmental policy" (Stockholm Declaration, Rio Declaration) converts to the new "sovereign right of states to sustainably use their resources pursuant to ecological governance."

The reference to ecological governance is crucial for the redefinition of territorial sovereignty. There is little merit in restricting sovereignty with reference to the existing state governance paradigm. If the restriction depends on "environmental components" of "global importance" and "the consequences of their potential degradation or destruction for all,"[69] anthropocentric state interests will dictate the content of territorial sovereignty. Not all "environmental components," but only those of assumed "global importance" would be exempted from the sovereign right of exploitation. This would continue the transboundary approach to pollution which assumes an environmental boundary between national territory and areas outside.

Effects limited to national jurisdiction would be seen as covered by territorial sovereignty and transboundary effects as not covered.[70] The ecological reality does not suggest such distinction. Whether or not intraterritorial activities have global effects is not determined by their "global importance." For example, clear-felling of a very small forest might be seen as intraterritorial and not transboundary, thus covered by territorial sovereignty. The cumulative effects of local activities may, however, be of global significance regardless of how insignificant they appear judged on their own. It is, therefore, wrong to distinguish between "environmental components" of "global importance" and those that are not.[71] The focus should be on activities and on the distinction between activities that are ecologically sustainable and those that are not.

The idea that states should act as trustees or guardians (or stewards) underlies both approaches: the ecological governance approach, and the state governance approach to restricted territorial sovereignty. However, it makes a difference whether the trusteeship role is derived from the environment per se or from the community of states. This second form of trusteeship would be limited to environmental components of global importance or global commons.[72] The first form would include the entire environment within territorial jurisdiction. States are trustees of the entire environment, not only of globally important "components."[73] Apart from the ecological importance involved here, there is also a global justice issue to be considered. If trustee functions were limited to globally significant resources, poor states with rich natural resources ("developing" countries) would be more restricted in their sovereignty than rich states with poor natural resources ("developed" countries).

Governance for ecological stewardship requires acceptance that the environment is entrusted to the individual state not by virtue of its sovereignty or any other form of legal entitlement, but by virtue of the laws of physics: any territory exists in an indivisible global environment. It follows that the community of life belongs neither to states nor to humanity, but only to itself through its intrinsic value. States, therefore, can claim sovereignty and ownership over natural resources within the limits of Earth's ecological integrity.

Governance for ecological stewardship conceptually restricts territorial sovereignty leading to a paradigm shift in international environmental law: not from state sovereignty setting the limits to environmental protection, but from environmental protection setting limits to state sovereignty.

Conclusions

The *Earth Charter* assumes the leadership role for global citizens and global civil society. The latter lead where states and state-related institutions must follow. The *Earth Charter*'s ultimate, yet conciliatory message to states is expressed in "The Way Forward": "Life often involves tensions between important values. This can mean difficult choices. However, we must find ways to harmonize diversity with unity, the exercise of freedom with the common good, short-term objectives and long-term goals."

These sentiments leave room for reforms as much as for transformation. However, they do express a commitment toward global governance for ecological stewardship. If states are not and willing and able to support this commitment, ecological dictatorship may well be the consequence. It would be forced upon us either by state and corporate power, or by the power of nature herself. Transforming ourselves and our institutions is the only choice we have.

Notes

1. David Dunkerley, Lesley Hodgson, Stanislaw Konopacki, Tony Spybey, and Andrew Thompson, *Changing Europe: Identities, Nations, Citizens* (London and New York: Routledge, 2002), 10–11.

2. Valeria Ottonelli, "Immigration: What does Global Justice require?," in *Global Citizenship: A Critical Reader*, eds. Nigel Dower and John Williams (Edinburgh: Edinburgh University Press, 2002), 234, speaking of the principle of self-determination of political communities when granting membership; Renaud Dehousse, *Europe after Maastricht: An ever closer Union?* (Munich: Beck Law Books in Europe, 1994), 12.

3. Dower, *Global Citizenship*, 3; Richard Falk, "An Emergent Matrix of Citizenship: Complex, Uneven, and Fluid," in *Global Citizenship*; Chris Hilson, "Greening

Citizenship: Boundaries of Membership and the Environment," *Journal of Environmental Law* 13, no. 3 (2001): 335–48, at 335.

4. Will Kymlicka and Wayne Norman, "Return of the Citizen: A Survey of Recent Work on Citizenship Theory," *Ethics* 104, no. 2 (1994): 352–81, 353, quoting Habermas.

5. Falk, "Emergent Matrix," 16.

6. Engin Isin and Patricia Wood, *Citizenship and Identity* (London, Thousand Oaks, New Delhi: Sage Publications, 1999), 155.

7. Stephen Castles and Alistair Davidson, *Citizenship and Migration: Globalization and the Politics of Belonging* (London: Macmillan Press Ltd., 2000), 8. On the other hand, there are also indications that cultural diversity will prevail because of "rapidity and multidirectionality of mobility and communication" (127).

8. For a summary, see Michael Waller and Andrew Linklater, *Political Loyalty and the Nation-State* (London and New York: Routledge, 2003), 228–29.

9. Kim Economides et al., eds., *Fundamental Values* (Oxford: Hart Publishing, 2000), 116. Speak of a "seepage of power."

10. Dino Kritsiotis, "Imagining the International Community," *European Journal of International Law* 13, no. 4 (2002), at 962, critically refers to the "emerging sense of global community" and at 966–67 and 991–92 questions the term "international community" altogether. Objects of identification may well be the environment, the poor, women, or social movements rather than "Britain" or "Europe."

11. April Carter, *The Political Theory of Global Citizenship* (London and New York: Routledge, 2001), 119, 139.

12. Alistair Davidson, "Democracy, Class and Citizenship," in *Citizenship and Democracy in a Global Era*, ed. A. Vandenberg (London: Macmillan Press Ltd., 2000), 117–18, 120.

13. Economides et al., *Fundamental Values*, 124–5.

14. Castles and Davidson, "Citizenship and Migration," in *The Condition of Citizenship*, ed. Steenbergen (London: Sage Publications, 1994), 176; Dehousse, *Europe after Maastricht*, at 147, observes a significant departure from the traditional link between nationality and citizenship of the nation-state, a loosening of the metaphysical ties between persons and a state, and forming a symptom of cosmopolitization of citizenship.

15. Bart van Steenbergen, "Towards a Global Ecological Citizen," in *The Condition of Citizenship*, 148; Carter, *Political Theory*, 141, 235, for reasons why regional bodies may obstruct as much as support international goals.

16. Dunkerley et al., *Changing Europe*, 19.

17. Dehousse, *Europe*, 146.

18. Dehousse, *Europe*, 148, conceding that European citizenship may be useful as a laboratory for a modern active procedural concept of proto-cosmopolitan citizenship.

19. Ralf Dahrendorf, "The Changing Face of Citizenship," in *The Condition of Citizenship*, 13.

20. Van Steenbergen, "Towards a Global Ecological Citizen," 148.

21. Dahrendorf, "The Changing Face," 13.

22. Dower, *Global Citizenship*, 140.

23. Dower, *Global Citizenship*, 6, 147, 149.

24. Dower, *Global Citizenship*, 7.

25. See such diverse authors as Van Steenbergen, "Towards a Global Ecological Citizen," 148; Richard Falk, "An Emergent Matrix of Citizenship: Complex, Uneven, and Fluid," 16; and generally, Aldo Leopold, *A Sand County Almanac* (Oxford: Oxford University Press, 1949).

26. Presented in Isin and Wood, *Citizenship and Identity*, 117, quoting Mitchell Tomashow, *Ecological Identity: Becoming a Reflective Environmentalist* (Cambridge, MA: MIT Press, 1995), 139.

27. See F. Fracchia, "The Legal Definition of Environment: From Rights to Duties," *ICFAI Journal of Environmental Law* (IJEL) 17 (2006).

28. K. Bosselmann, "Human Rights and the Environment: Redefining Fundamental Principles?" in *Governance for the Environment: Global Problems, Ethics and Democracy*, eds. B. Gleeson and N. Low (London: Palgrave, 2001), 118–34.

29. *Our Global Neighborhood*, Report of the Commission on Global Governance (New York: Oxford University Press, 1995), 32–33.

30. Carter, *Political Theory*, 79. The movement for radical political change has not only created new states, but transformed many governments in Eastern Europe and now South America.

31. Alicia Barcena, "Global, Environmental Citizenship," UNEP 25, *Our Planet* no. 8, (January 1997). Shows how UNEP's Global Environmental Citizenship Programme has developed strategic alliances with parliamentarians, consumers, local authorities, educators, religious groups, media, and other key civil society groups.

32. Carter, *Political Theory*, 80.

33. Robin Attfield, "Global Citizenship and the Global Environment," in *Global Citizenship*, 197.

34. The current oppression of international NGOs in Russia is more a sign of the government's powerlessness rather than proof of its power.

35. Apart from NGOs, civil society consists of various other groups such as trade unions, business associations, religious bodies, academic institutions, student organizations, ethnic lobbies, community groups, and so forth. Similarly defined in Dower, *Global Citizenship*, xxi.

36. Isin and Wood, *Citizenship*, 117.

37. Isin and Wood, *Citizenship*, 121–22.

38. Isin and Wood, *Citizenship*, pointing out to the fact that, so far, globalization has meant westernization.

39. Attfield, "Global Citizenship," 200.

40. *Our Global Neighborhood*, 2–3. The inclusion of "multinational corporations, and the global capital" is, of course, the crux of most political moves toward global governance.

41. Anthony Carty, *The Decay of International Law?* (Manchester: Manchester University Press, 1986), 44; Prue Taylor, *An Ecological Approach to International Law* (London and New York: Routledge, 1998), 119–20.

42. First formulated in UN General Assembly Resolution 523 (VI) of 12 Jan. 1952; United Nations Yearbook 5 (1951), 418; UN General Assembly Resolution 626 (VII) of 21 Dec. 1952; United Nations Yearbook 6 (1952), 390.

43. Beginning with the UN General Assembly Resolution 837 (IX) of 14 Dec. 1954 (United Nations Yearbook 12 [1958], 212) nine further UN resolutions between 1958 and 1974 established this concept as a heritage of newly emerging international environmental law.

44. E.g., Charter of Economic Rights and Duties of States (Art. 2 II), UN General Assembly Resolution 3281 (XXIX) of 12 Dec. 1974 (International Legal Materials 14 [1975], 251).

45. Taylor, *Ecological Approach*, 119–20. The desire of the new developing states for greater economic independence was, of course, the other driving force behind the concept of permanent sovereignty over natural resources.

46. Repeated in Principle 2 of the 1992 Rio Declaration and Art. 3 of the 1992 Convention on Biological Diversity.

47. *Legality of the Threat or Use of Nuclear Weapons*, Advisory Opinion, 1996, I.C.J. 241–42, para. 29.

48. *Judgment concerning the Gabcikovo-Nagymaros Project*, 1997, 37 I.L.M., 162, para. 53.

49. Including territorial land and territorial seas together with the airspace (of ca. 90 km) above.

50. Alexander Kiss, "Nouvelles tendances en droit international de l'environnement," *German Yearbook of International Law* (1989), 241, at 258; Rüdiger Wolfrum, "Purposes and Principles of International Environmental Law," *German Yearbook of International Law* (1990), 308 (328).

51. E.g. OECD, Implementation of a Regime of Equal Right of Access and Non-Discrimination in Relation to Transfrontier Pollution, Recomm. C (77) 28, 1977.

52. E.g. Convention on Long-Range Transboundary Air Pollution, Geneva, 13 Nov. 1979, 18 I.L.M. 1449.

53. Alexander Kiss and Dinah Shelton, *International Environmental Law*, 2nd ed. (New York and London: Transnational Publishers, 2000), 266–94, 395–432, 527–58. A notable exception to an otherwise broad coverage is the protection of soils; apart from the 1994 UN Convention to Combat Desertification, UNEP guidelines for national soil policies and a FAO Code of Conduct on the Distribution and Use of Pesticides there are no agreements controlling transboundary effects on soils.

54. The exclusion of the outer space (beyond an altitude of 90-100 km) is justified because there is no measurable evidence of pollution originating from countries. Debris and chemical emissions originate from activities within space; other chemical or radioactive pollution has not been found.

55. This term is preferable to the term "global commons" which is sometimes understood as a plural term for the various areas and aspects beyond national jurisdiction (including atmosphere or global biodiversity), sometimes as a singular term for all these areas, and sometimes in the sense of "common areas" as defined here. For an analysis see Taylor, *Ecological Approach*, 165–69.

56. UN General Assembly Resolution 37/7 of 28 Oct. 1982.

57. Kiss and Shelton, *International Environmental*, 65.

58. Taylor, *Ecological Approach*, 300.

59. E.g., New Zealand Resource Management Act 1991, sections 2 and 7; Klaus Bosselmann, "Justice and the Environment: Building Blocks for a Theory on Ecological Justice," in *Environmental Justice and Market Mechanisms*, eds. Klaus Bosselmann and Benjamin Richardson (London: Kluwer International, 1999) 30, at 52.

60. Klaus Bosselmann "Ecological Justice and Law," in *Environmental Law for Sustainability: A Critical Reader*, eds. Benjamin Richardson and Stepan Wood (Oxford: Hart Publishing, 2006), 129, at 160.

61. E.g., Richard A. Falk, *Revitalizing International Law* (Iowa State University Press, 1989).

62. E.g., Gunter Handl, "Environmental Security and Global Change: The Challenge to International Law," in *Environmental Protection and International Law*, eds. W. Lang et al. (London: Graham & Trotman/Martinus Nijhoff, 1991), 59.

63. Lynton Keith Caldwell, *International Environmental Policy: Emergence and Dimensions* (Durham, NC: Duke University Press, 1984).

64. As expressed, for example, in continental European constitutions.

65. Bruno Simma, "Does the UN-Charter Provide an Adequate Legal Basis for Individual or Collective Responses to Violations of Obligations *erga omnes*?" in *The Future of International Law Enforcement: New Scenarios—New Law?* ed. Joachim Delbrück (Berlin: Duncker & Humblodt, 1993), 125 (129).

66. Philip Allott, *Eunomia. New Order for a New World* (New York: Oxford University Press, 1990), 296; R. Bernhardt, "Ungeschriebenes Völkerrecht," *Zeitschrift für ausländisches öffentliches Recht und Völkerrecht* 36 (1976), 50 (58).

67. As, for example, developed in Klaus Bosselmann, *Ökologische Grundrechte* (Baden-Baden: Nomos, 1998), 100–124; Prue Taylor, "From Environmental to Ecological Human Rights: A New Dynamic in International Law?" *Georgetown International Environmental Law Review*, 10/2 (1999), 309, 384–85; Michael Schröter, *Mensch, Erde, Recht. Grundfragen ökologischer Rechtstheorie* (Baden-Baden: Nomos, 1999), 246–53; David Hunter, "An Ecological Perspective of Property: A Call for Juridical Protection of the Public's Interest in Environmentally Critical Resources," *Harvard Environmental Law Review* 12 (1988), 311; Alison Rieser, "Ecological Preservation as a Public Property Right: An Emerging Doctrine in Search of a Theory," *Harvard Environmental Law Review*, 15 (1991), 393.

68. Such approach may be accused of "throwing the baby out with the bath water." The total abolition of territorial sovereignty, even if conceivable, may render states (even more) defenseless against interventions from states, terrorists, multinational companies, etc.

69. Kiss and Shelton, *International Environmental Law*, 150.

70. E.g. Nico Shrijver, *Sovereignty over Natural Resources, Balancing Rights and Duties* (New York: Cambridge University Press, 1997), 290–92.

71. U.S. American public trust doctrine, although helpful, carry this inherent flaw. See e.g. Taylor, "From Environmental to Ecological Human Rights," 386–92; Hunter, "An Ecological Perspective," 317–19 and 375–76.

72. "States having under their jurisdiction such (i.e. globally important) environmental components should be considered as trustees in charge of their conservation"; Kiss and Shelton, *International Environmental Law*, 150.

73. Taylor, "From Environmental to Ecological Human Rights," 394; Karin Odendahl, *Die Umweltpflichtigkeit der Staaten* (Berlin: Duncker & Humblodt, 1998), 353, 36.

Chapter 2

A Covenant of Covenants:
A Federal Vision of Global Governance
for the Twenty-first Century

J. Ronald Engel, Ph.D. (Ethics and Society)
Professor Emeritus of Social and Environmental Ethics,
Meadville/Lombard Theological School,
(University of Chicago affiliate), Chicago, IL, U.S.A.
Senior Research Consultant, Center for Humans and Nature,
New York, NY, U.S.A.
Contact Information: P.O. Box 717, Beverly Shores, IN 46301 U.S.A.
Phone: +1 219 874 0067; Fax: +1 219 874 0067; Email: ronengel@humansandnature.org

Summary

New forms of democratic global governance are needed to ensure fair access to and protection of global ecological resources. Global governance also must address the fact that global integration is occurring simultaneously with global decentralization. More just and sustainable forms of global governance are attainable through covenants, which have often provided ethical norms for human societies in times of constitutional crisis.

At their best, covenants offer a way for different individuals and communities to retain their identities and "walk together" in mutual respect and peace. They also offer a way of understanding our obligations to future generations as a sacred trust. Contrary to contemporary belief, a covenant is implicit in every form of effective human relationship, including the global market. The only meaningful choice is between covenants that are closed and life-denying, and covenants that are inclusive and life-affirming.

A federal (covenantal) model of global governance that joins self-rule (autonomy) with shared rule (communal policy-making) is well suited for the governance of human relationships, including those to the rest of nature, and is congruent with the principle of "common but differentiated responsibilities" in international law. The federal model requires two complementary processes of covenant making: going beyond differences in the quest for common principles, and building on differences to enrich the world community.

The *Earth Charter*, launched in 2000, is a landmark covenantal expression of the common principles for a just, sustainable, peaceful, and democratic world community. It now needs to be supplemented with the covenants of local communities that make explicit the ways in which they can be stewards of the shared global heritage. In this way, the world will become joined in a covenant of covenants.

27

The Challenge of Global Governance

The Constitutional Crisis of the Twenty-first Century

In the opening years of the twenty-first century, the world is in a constitutional crisis. Economic globalization erases borders, identities, and claims to national sovereignty. The United States of America continues its post-September 11, 2001 bid for global hegemony. India and China emerge as goliaths on the world stage. Warring religious fundamentalisms in the Middle East threaten a clash of civilizations. Progress in international treaty law built up at great cost over many generations stalls. Civil society mounts massive protests to claim its voice in world assemblies. The Westphalian world order, the order of sovereign states with clear boundaries between "domestic" and "foreign" affairs that has served as the de facto world constitution since 1648, is fraying. And, there is no new pattern on the horizon that appears acceptable to the majority of world leaders.

The question of global governance is a source of profound anxiety. We find meaning in life through our worldviews, our pictures of the origin and destiny of the world that we inhabit, and our place within it. Like the young East Berliner in the movie *Good Bye Lenin!* who tries to fool his invalid socialist mother into believing that the fall of East Germany never happened, and has to explain away the huge red Coca-Cola banner now draped outside her apartment window, we will often go to great lengths to retain worldviews.

The question of global governance is therefore existential as well as political. Systems theorist Roland Robertson attests that for increasing numbers of persons "globalization constitutes a major—perhaps the major—site for the contemporary generation of concern for the sacred." (Robertson, 1985)

It took two world wars to force the nations of the world to seriously address the question of what form of global governance should prevail in the modern era.

The United Nations did not seriously question the Westphalian settlement, but it did acknowledge in its Charter and in the Universal Declaration of Human Rights that we are all now bound up in the vicissitudes of a single world history that requires shared ethical principles. Beginning with the World Conference on the Human Environment in 1972, there has been growing recognition that all of the great issues of contemporary life—the sustainability of ecological systems, the health of present and future generations, the security and freedom of our persons and communities, the distribution of the wealth and benefits from economic production—depend for their resolution upon the answer we give to the question of what is an effective, fair, and environmentally responsible system of global governance. (Falk, 1975)

The Challenge of Double Democratization

Democratic self-government is not only the aspiration of most of the world's peoples (however it is betrayed in practice), but a necessary means to achieving the preservation and just distribution of ecological resources. Personal dignity, mutual respect, social well-being, self-actualization, public deliberation, freedom for dissent—these are essential values in any but the most thin or procedural understandings of democracy. Without these values there is little hope that the changes in consumption, reproduction, and production required for the "great transition" to more just and sustainable living will come into being.

Yet prospects for a democratic world community in the twenty-first century are highly problematic. Increasing global integration is occurring simultaneously with increasing decentralization, leading to what Anthony Giddens calls the challenge of "double democratization." (Giddons, 2003) How are we to govern radically increased integration at the international level and, at the same time, support local communities that bear so much of the burden of rapid social and environmental change? This challenge is compounded by the fact that many influential post-modern thinkers suspect that universalisms in any form, even that of human rights, are dogmas of the Western mind, new forms of imperialistic ideology. Life and meaning are viewed as irreducibly culture-based, relative, and resistant to any necessary or obligatory order, scientific or ethical.

We therefore have a two-fold task:

> "Global citizenship"—the idea that we are citizens of the world as a whole—a theme in democratic thought since the Radical Enlightenment (Israel, 2001)—will need to take on a concreteness that it has not so far achieved. And, the customary rights and obligations of citizenship that follow from membership in a particular territory, community or nation-state, will need to be redefined. (Dower and Williams, 1999)

A Covenant Model of Global Ethics

The Covenant Idea

With the above as background, we must understand the calls by international figures, such as United Nations Director Generals Javier Perez de Cuellar and Kofi Anan, for a "new global covenant," or "compact." There is hope abroad that a covenant, a time-honored form of social relation that has served human societies in times of constitutional crisis, will provide the moral, political, and spiritual foundations for democratic and ecological global governance. (Held, 2004)

Although there is an immense literature on covenants, there is as yet no comprehensive model of covenant that has proven adequate for both descriptive and prescriptive purposes. Daniel Elazar's four volume study, *The Covenant Idea in Politics*, traces the covenant notion from ancient Israel through succeeding notions of natural law, commonwealth, constitutional republicanism, and civil society. (Elazar, 1998) Elazar's work, however, needs to be supplemented by a range of theological, philosophical, sociological, and comparative cultural studies. (Engel, 2004)

"Covenant" is one of the great mother worldviews in human history with diverse cultural expressions that share certain generic traits. In contrast to either hierarchical or organic models of reality, a covenantal model sees the world as constituted by individuals-in-community. Elazar uses the image of the "matrix" to suggest how covenants may hold together freedom among equals and still satisfy the needs for coordination, cooperation, and mutual relationships. Covenant and compact are often used interchangeably to describe public agreements that are of unlimited duration and consequently require mutual consent to be abrogated. A covenant differs from a compact in that its morally binding dimension takes precedence over its legal dimensions. Even more importantly, in covenant the moral dimension is assumed to be authorized by a higher or "ultimate" authority—whether understood as God, nature, or the will of the people. A compact rests more heavily on a legal, though still ethical, grounding for its politics.

Elazar uses the term "theo-political" to suggest the transcendent reference in the idea of covenant. Bernard Meland, a theologian working in the process or naturalist metaphysical tradition, speaks of the "communal matrix" out of which all life has emerged as a "covenant of being." (Meland, 1976)

The most ethically developed understandings of covenant see a radical gap between the promise of a world composed of free and equal individuals in just and mutually enhancing relationships, and the communities which have actually emerged over the course of human history. Not only does life evolve, but we have betrayed the life entrusted to us. We are called to make new relationships and to repair the relationships we have broken—to explicitly renew the original promise of the covenant of being. Theological ethicist Douglas Sturm writes: "The idea of a social covenant bespeaks a world in which we already belong together, but are called repeatedly to acknowledge that fact anew and to determine what the forms of our life together shall be." (Sturm, 1988)

At their best, the special covenants of history are voluntary, principled, unconditional agreements that enable free, equal, and different individuals or communities to "walk together" in mutual care and respect. They seek the common good of the whole community of life with which they are internally related. Through covenant we affirm our entrustment of one another and of generations past and generations to come. We become bearers of the public trust. John O'Neill employs the contrast between covenant and contract to establish the moral obligations of trust between the generations:

Children are born into social membership of families and nations, whose traditions and commitments shape their life prospects. Children inherit the conditions of their sustenance and, in turn, are expected as adults to guard and enhance the bestowal of legacies to succeeding generations. These are not the market relations of trade and contract, but the civic ties of transmission and covenant. (O'Neill, 1994)

A morally mature covenanted people acknowledges its responsibilities for the character of all dimensions of its common life as an integrated whole; and it engages in dialogue, debate, and argument about how this should best be accomplished. Such covenants stipulate practices that have been found over generations to enable free, different, and equal individuals and communities to live in reciprocally beneficial ways. They involve long-standing covenantal virtues such as hope, respect, care, humility, truthfulness, steadfastness, frugality, and loving kindness; principles such as righteousness, equity, justice, shared economic well-being, and mutual accountability; and peace as wholeness of being. Broken covenants are renewed and new covenantal beginnings are made possible by gifts of forgiveness, repentance, and remembrance.

The Power of Covenant

Contemporary individualist culture dismisses covenant as too fraught with the exclusive and repressive dogmas of the past to ground a truly liberating and Earth-caring constitution. But, we are born into covenants and find ourselves in covenant whether we choose to be so or not.

Because covenant is inherent in every form of effective human governance, it provides an entry into the inner dynamics of human history, and therefore a way of changing it. Our choices are not between having covenants and not having covenants, but between covenants that are closed and life-denying and covenants that are inclusive and life-affirming. Our ability to make our implicit covenants explicit, and to criticize, reform, renew, or begin again on the basis of deliberate moral reflection and choice is the surest way to break the deadly chains of exclusivity, aggression, and vengeance.

There is a vast covenantal substratum of our lives that we take for granted and rarely acknowledge. The whole array of institutions to which we look for moral guidance and leadership, from families to congregations to schools to responsible businesses and professions to voluntary associations gathered on behalf of special social purposes to legislative and government agencies, are covenant-bound. As the Earth spins and the seasons return, people show up for work, friends respond to our requests for help, teachers conscientiously teach students, and the food we eat nurtures us. Our societies are cross-hatched with expectations of mutual trust.

Unfortunately, modern capitalist industrial culture both hides and erodes this reality. Capitalism forces social relations into private contracts—limited agreements that seek a utility of direct benefit to the consenting individuals only, and are dissolved when that utility is achieved. But, the market itself only functions because of covenantal expectations. Indeed, this may help explain popular acceptance of the global market ideology. It is appealing to think that if we each uphold our contractual responsibilities and buy or sell honestly and fairly, we can connect directly to the "ultimate" agency—the invisible hand—that is governing the global economy, and together, with our neighbors near and far, fulfill the promise of ever-growing material prosperity. The failure to see the global market as the perpetuation of a vast covenant that could be otherwise is surely one of the greatest challenges of global governance today. (Engel, 2005; McMurty, 1998)

The persons we acknowledge with admiration are those who have broken the walls of such oppressive and alienating covenants by reaching out to others with simple gestures of ordinary human care and respect. Nelson Mandela made such gestures to his jailers on Robben Island and was able to lead the covenanted community of the African National Congress to make similar gestures toward the Afrikaner community and, in this way, facilitate a new democratic covenant for all the citizens of South Africa. His 1994 inaugural address was an explicit attempt to re-found his country on the basis of a new covenant of universal solidarity between land and people:

> I have no hesitation in saying that each one of us is as intimately attached to the soil of this beautiful country as are the famous jacaranda trees of Pretoria and the mimosa trees of the bushveld. Each time one of us touches the soil of this land, we feel a sense of personal renewal. . . . That spiritual and physical oneness we all share with this common homeland explains the depth of the pain we all carried in our hearts as we saw our country tear itself apart in a terrible conflict, and as we saw it spurned, outlawed and isolated by the peoples of the world. . . . We enter into a covenant that we shall build the society in which all South Africans, both black and white, will be able to walk tall, without any fear in their hearts, assured of their inalienable right to human dignity—a rainbow nation at peace with itself and the world. (Mandela, 2003)

Can this now happen across the whole world?

A Federal Model of Global Governance

The Federal Idea

The form of global governance that is called for by a covenantal worldview is suggested by the Latin word for covenant, "foedus," from which the English word "federal" derives. A federal structure is one composed of equal confederates that freely bind themselves to one another in a common whole that retains their respective identities.

The main lines of federalist thinking in the West are undoubtedly indebted to Greco-Roman, Hebrew, and Christian theo-political traditions. But other cultural influences are important as well, and in recent years there has been special interest among environmental philosophers in the "covenantal" aspects of the traditions of native peoples. In the "Thanksgiving Address" that founded the Haudenosaunee (Iroquois) Confederacy of Native Americans each person and each being (animals, plants, the earth, the wind, and the sun) is assumed to be free to assume, or neglect, its unique responsibilities to others and for the flourishing of the whole community of life. The original "covenant of being" is renewed each day as thanksgiving is offered for all those who have fulfilled these responsibilities (Haudenosaunee Environmental Task Force, n.d.).

Global federalism is also a confederacy. It is "the covenant idea" extended across the political and physical landscape of the planet as the organizing principle for the relationships between citizens within, between, and among societies, and therefore is especially apt for meeting the "challenge of double democratization." Global federalism is being discussed today in terms of "pluralist/commonwealth" (Alperovitz, 2005); "cosmopolitan regionalism" (Donnelley, 1998); "solidarity/pluralism" (Dower, 1998); and "differentiated solidarity" (Young, 2000).

Federalism affirms that ultimate political authority is vested in the hands of the people, who by covenant or compact constitute a body politic, and decide what powers, competences, and jurisdictions are required for their mutual well-being and good governance. This is the core doctrine of government by consent, and of pluralist theories of democratic constitutional government. Another way to describe the federalist model is that civil society is a matrix of associations, with the institutions of government being only some among the many institutions that the people empower to undertake their diverse tasks of political, religious, social, cultural, and economic expression and governance. Governance is multiple and divided, although the state exercises under the constitution a certain monopoly of coercive power to enforce the rule of law.

Federal constitutions are necessarily constitutions of limited government. Political power between communities is generated in the same way as political power within each community: by joining self-rule with shared rule. The power of each party is self-limited in order to permit others to freely exercise their capacities and responsibilities. At the same time, all parties join with one another in common deliberation and decisions on shared issues and concerns. Pacts are built upon pacts, from the ground up. The world is governed as a community of communities by a covenant of covenants.

As the Haudenosaunee Confederacy suggests, the federal model can also be a model for the governance of human relationships to the rest of nature. Polities can be expanded to include the place-based "civil ground" of every community, the "commons" inclusive of land, ecosystems, plants, animals, and people—

globally, the biosphere as a whole. If the power of human beings is self-limited in order to permit the rest of nature to flourish, then nature's multiple agencies can participate in determining the constitutional order. Shared rule is exercised through the competencies and jurisdictions that enable just and sustainable ways of life for all. It is this kind of federalist understanding of the eco-political order that French thinkers Michel Serres and Bruno Latour appear to be calling for when they speak (in English translation) of a new "natural contract," and a new "politics" conceived as the "progressive democratic composition of a common world." (Serres, 1990; Latour, 2004) William James anticipated a similar federalist vision for the governance of the biosphere a century ago when he wrote, in *A Pluralistic Universe*, that the Earth is a "pluralism of independent powers that enables each other's preservation and salvation." (James, 1909)

Common, but Differentiated Responsibilities

An indication that the nations of the world may be groping toward some such bioregional federalism is the fact that the principle of "common, but differentiated responsibilities" has moved from a "soft law" principle to an increasingly robust component of international law. The first note taken of the different capacities—and hence responsibilities—of nations to contribute to the achievement of agreed-upon standards of global economic development and environmental protection was at the Stockholm Conference in 1972. Difference was interpreted in terms of equity between developing countries and industrialized states.

The 1992 United Nations Framework Convention on Climate Change (UNFCCC) was more explicit in stating that parties should protect the climate system for the benefit of present and future generations on the basis of equity "and in accordance with their common, but differentiated responsibilities and respective capabilities." Subsequent negotiations have broadened the meaning of "responsibility" to cover the differential contributions that developed nations make to emitting greenhouse gases in addition to their differential capabilities for addressing it. (Harris, 1999)

A more flexible line of interpretation also began in 1972, with the ratification of the World Heritage Convention. State members of UNESCO agreed to hold in trust for the rest of humankind those special parts of the World Heritage that were found within their boundaries, support each other in discharging this trust, exercise the same responsibility to the works of nature as to works of humankind, and grant to cosignatories the right to observe the degree to which each met its obligations under the Convention. (McNeely and Miller, 1982)

The principle of "common, but differentiated responsibilities" suggests that two complementary processes of covenant making are required to underwrite a federal system of global governance. One seeks covenantal bonds that are essentially blind to differences in the quest for common principles. The other seeks covenantal bonds that are built on differences in the quest for ways in which these differences can become mutually enriching.

The first involves a process of ethical universalization. Since we are members of one moral community by virtue of our powers of reason, and are interdependent with one another and the rest of nature by virtue of the global character of the world, we have both the capacity and the need to develop, through rational deliberation and consensus, a set of shared values by which to order our global existence. This set of principles is then applied to particular situations to arrive at proper actions—for example, obligating developed nations to help lesser developed ones.

The second approach involves a process of building ethical complementarity. Its logic is summarized by Charles Taylor when he writes:

> People can also bond not in spite of, but because of differences. They can sense
> . . . that their differences enrich each party, that their lives are narrower and less
> full when they are alone than when they are in association with each other. In
> this sense, the difference defines a complement. . . . Humanity is something to
> be realized, not in each individual human being, but rather in communion be-
> tween all humans. (Taylor, 1998)

It follows that we each have the obligation to do what is required to maintain the "common heritage" of the world community given our special legacies, capacities, and relative place within that community at any particular time.

Making the Global Covenant

The Earth Charter as a Universal Covenant

The Charter of the United Nations and the Universal Declaration of Human Rights were catalysts for an ambitious agenda of global covenant making in the post-World War II years. Two of the most important international treaties were explicitly named "covenants"—the International Covenant on Economic, Social and Cultural Rights (1976), and the International Covenant on Civil and Political Rights (1976). In 1995, the World Conservation Union Commission on Environmental Law proposed the Draft International Covenant for Environment and Development as a negotiating text for a further step in this process. Complementing these "hard law" covenants are the many "soft" or aspirational charters and declarations adopted by the United Nations and various organizations of civil society over the past half century, such as the World Charter for Nature adopted by the UN General Assembly in 1982 (Burhenne and Irwin, 1986); the Earth Covenant circulated in 1988 by Global Education Associates (translated into twenty languages, signed by nearly two million people in over one-hundred countries); the texts generated by the World Council of Churches' program on

"Covenanting for Peace, Justice and Integrity of Creation" in the early 1990s; and the numerous people's treaties negotiated during the 1992 Rio Earth Summit. (Commonweal Sustainable Futures Group, 1992)

Launched in 2000, the *Earth Charter* (see the Appendix) is a landmark in the ongoing process of global covenant making. It was intentionally drafted as a "people's treaty" through a series of international and regional consultations, beginning with the Rio+5 conference in 1997, and as a distillation of the leading ethical principles of human rights, economic justice, environmental sustainability, and peace and security articulated in previous international documents. (Rockefeller, 1996) These two dimensions of the drafting process provided both legitimation and justification for the final text.

A similar document, The Charter of Human Responsibilities, was prepared in 2001 by the Alliance for a Responsible, United, and Plural World (www.fgf.be/pdf/charte_en.pdf, accessed 20 May 2007). The global covenant-making process now taking place across the planet is larger than any single movement or text.

The *Earth Charter* is a covenant in all important senses of the word. (Sturm, 2000)

- It is covenantal in form—written in the voice of the first person plural, to make clear that it is a binding enactment of free individuals and groups with the capacity to choose their future together, and to mutually commit to enduring and comprehensive purposes.
- It is covenantal in worldview: "Recognize that all beings are interdependent and every form of life has value regardless of its worth to human beings."
- It is covenantal in its overarching moral principle and promise: "Respect and Care for the Community of Life."
- It is covenantal in grounding its moral vision in the "ultimate" authority of the gift of life and the reverence we share for the "mystery of being."
- It is covenantal in its assumption that human beings have betrayed the beauty and promise of the community of life and must therefore "seek a new beginning."
- It is covenantal in its justifications, drawing on the "wisdom" of contemporary science, international law, the world's great religious and philosophical traditions, and global ethics.
- It is covenantal in its federal model of "partnership" for global governance: "We are at once citizens of different nations and of one world in which the local and global are linked." The *Earth Charter* does not explicitly affirm the principle of "common, but differentiated responsibilities," but, it does affirm its implications for the meaning of equity: "Affirm that with increased freedom, knowledge, and power come increased responsibility to promote the common good." (Brenes, 2005)
- It is covenantal in its moral content, reflecting long-standing covenantal values including the protection of Earth's vitality, diversity, and beauty as a trust for present and future generations; respect, compassion, and love for Earth and life in all its diversity; a precautionary approach when

knowledge is limited; the eradication of poverty; equality and equity as prerequisites to sustainable development; and universal access to education, health care, and economic opportunity. It recognizes that "peace is the wholeness created by right relationships with oneself, other persons, other cultures, other life, Earth, and the larger whole of which all are a part."

- It is covenantal in membership. The *Earth Charter* Initiative, based in San Jose, Costa Rica, keeps records through its Web site (www.earthcharter.org, accessed 27 May 2007) of all the organizations and individuals who have taken the "pledge" of commitment to the Charter and coordinates the international movement seeking to embody these principles in education and public policy. (www.earthcharterinaction.org, accessed 27 May 2007)

But, while the *Earth Charter* proposes a universal narrative of world history and common principles to guide its future, the covenant it bears is far from being a global social reality.

Local Frontiers of Global Covenant Making

There is good reason to believe that we are now crossing a promising new frontier of global covenant making—enabling local citizens to make the special covenants which will articulate the visions, needs, rights and responsibilities of each of the world's communities in a common but differentiated understanding of world covenant.

We come to consciousness of our participation in the creativity of the "covenant of being" through our experience of particular places, people, and cultures. The roots of a shared covenant for the flourishing of the global community as a whole lie in the love we have for these very different and particular places and the loyalties they engender. Our hopes for the planet are tightly bound to our hopes for these communities. They are not only the roots, but the branches and leaves of the common covenantal tree.

The metaphor of the "covenantal tree" is a way of acknowledging the fact that the Earth community cannot flourish apart from the flourishing of its constitutive members, and no member can flourish apart from the flourishing of the Earth community as a whole. The new word "glocal" was invented to communicate this relational, global-local reality.

The areas of environmental law in which greatest progress is presently occurring are at local, state, and regional levels rather than at the international level. Indeed, there is increasing recognition of the contributions that local communities have made to the development of international law (Rajagopal, 2003; Santos, 2005). Environmental rights are now written into seventy-two national constitutions, most of which make appeal to a "higher authority." Indeed, a "plethora of unilateral, subglobal government actions to address the global commons problem of climate change" has emerged in the absence of an unambiguous international regulatory framework with global scope. (K. Engel and S. Saleska, 2005) More than 500 cities worldwide and more than 150 in the United States (the world's largest emitter of greenhouse gases) are participating in the Cities for Climate Protection Campaign sponsored by the International Council for Local Environmental Initiatives (ICLEI).

If the *Earth Charter*'s self-ascribed authorship, "we, the peoples of Earth," is to have validity, the global covenant must be firmly grounded in the capacities for moral self-government exercised by the world's citizens in their local and national communities as well as in the alliances they build through international organizations. The *Earth Charter* affirms the importance of local commitment and action in its imperative: "Strengthen local communities, enabling them to care for their environments, and assign environmental responsibilities to the levels of government where they can be carried out most effectively" (Brenes, 2005); and in its closing acknowledgment, "Our cultural diversity is a precious heritage and different cultures will find their own distinctive ways to realize the vision." It is instructive that the most positive current developments in the Earth Charter Initiative are being made by local and national organizations as evidenced, for example, through recent decisions by the governments of Delhi, India, the city of Sao Paolo and the Brazilian ministry of the environment, and the Mexican ministries of the environment and education, to incorporate the Earth Charter into their educational programs.

If local citizens are to create a just and sustainable community and fulfill their responsibilities as global citizens, they must themselves draft the covenants that they need. Each region of the world has its unique geography, history, civic, and spiritual culture, its distinctive vision of health and justice and human rights, and a special portion of the world natural and cultural heritage it is called to steward. The strength of the global covenant depends upon critical transformations of the covenants that govern us locally and nationally in light of the needs of the world as a whole.

How can we expect that justice and human rights will be honored in the common Earth covenant without solidarity and commitment to one another in the joint political projects of our local community life and the conviction that these commitments are worthy and enduring because they are grounded in the highest authorities recognized by our religious and secular cultures? How do we expect sustainability will be achieved without shared love of a particular place and loyalty to its past and future? What reason is there to think that we have the power to embody universal principles of global ethics if we are not able to work together for the common good of the places closest to us? What hope is there that an alternative global covenant can change the world without our unlimited promises to our neighbors that we will be loyal to truth as we see it, and not bear false witness against them?

Furthermore, how can we realistically anticipate that the world's urban centers, the engines of global economic production and consumption, environmental degradation, and of inequity, can become sustainable and healthy environments for all their citizens without this kind of covenant making? How else can poor nations hope to find strength to resist the forces placing them under such great environmental and social stress? How can indigenous peoples retain the integrity of traditions and land-use practices in the face of cultural and economic globalization?

Political philosopher Hannah Arendt describes how compacts have been the source of positive liberty throughout modern history. (Arendt, 1963) But, rarely did these compacts take note of the ecological components of our shared life. This is now changing. Political power is increasingly shown to depend upon sustaining relationships between people and nature as well as among people. Internationally celebrated figures such as Wangari Maathai organizing the Green Belt movement to plant trees and empower women in Kenya, and Vandana Shiva founding the Jaiv Panchayat, an alliance of two hundred Himalayan villages, to assert their sovereign rights over their vital natural resources, are making this clear.

Hope for the achievement of a federal form of global governance in the twenty-first century, founded on principles of ecological stewardship and justice, depends on our adopting a global covenant that is a covenant of covenants. We will never deal with the planetary issues that threaten to overwhelm us until we learn how to govern ourselves in ways that reinforce our local and global commitments rather than pitting them against one another. It is a revolutionary prospect. But, the new and greater covenant is already taking shape, and it awaits only our recognition and commitment.

References

Alperovitz, Gar. *America Beyond Capitalism*. Hoboken, NJ: J. Wiley, 2005.

Arendt, Hannah. *On Revolution*. New York: Viking, 1963.

Brenes, Abelardo. "Universal and Differentiated Responsibility." Pp. 35–37 in *The Earth Charter in Action: Toward a Sustainable World*, edited by Peter Blaze Corcoran, with Mirian Vilela, and Alide Roerink. Amsterdam: KIT Publishers, 2005.

Burhenne, Wolfgang, and Will Irwin. *The World Charter for Nature: A Background Paper*. Berlin: Erich Schmidt Verlag, 1986.

Commonweal Sustainable Futures Group. *The People's Treaties from the Earth Summit*. Bolinas, CA: Common Knowledge Press, 1992.

Donnelley, Strachan, ed. "Nature, Polis, Ethics." *Hastings Center Report, Special Supplement*, 28/6 (Nov.–Dec. 1998).

Dower, Nigel. *World Ethics: The New Agenda*. Edinburgh: Edinburgh University Press, 1998.

Dower, Nigel, and John Williams, eds. *Global Citizenship: A Critical Reader*. Edinburgh: Edinburgh University Press, 1999.

Elazar, Daniel J. *The Covenant Tradition in Politics*. 4 vols. New Brunswick, NJ: Transaction Publishers, 1998.

Engel, J. Ronald. "A Covenant Model of Global Ethics." *Worldviews: Religion, Culture, Ethics* 8/1 (Winter 2004): 29–46.

———. "The Moral Power of the World Conservation Movement to Engage Economic Globalization." George Wright Forum 22/3 (Sept. 2005): 58–71.

Engel, Kirsten H., and Scott R. Saleska. "Subglobal Regulations of the Global Commons: the Case of Climate Change." *Ecology Law Quarterly* 32, no. 2 (2005): 183–233.

Falk, Richard A. *A Study of Future Worlds.* New York: Free Press, 1975.

Giddens, Anthony, ed. *The Progressive Manifesto.* Cambridge, MA: Polity Press, 2003.

Harris, Paul G. "Common but Differentiated Responsibility: The Kyoto Protocol and United States Policy." *New York University Law Journal* 7, no. 1 (1999): 27–48.

Haudenosaunee Environmental Task Force. *Worlds that Come Before All Else.* Cornwall Island, ON: Native North American Travelling College, n.d.

Held, David. *Global Covenant: The Social Democratic Alternative to the Washington Consensus.* Cambridge, MA: Polity Press, 2004.

Israel, Jonathan I. *Radical Enlightenment: Philosophy and the Making of Modernity 1650–1750.* New York: Oxford University Press, 2001.

James, William. *A Pluralistic Universe.* London: Longmans, Green, and Co., 1909.

Latour, Bruno. *Politics of Nature.* Cambridge, MA: Harvard University Press, 2004.

Mandela, Nelson. *In His Own Words.* New York: Little Brown and Company, 2003.

McMurty, John. *Unequal Freedoms: The Global Market as an Ethical System.* West Hartford, CT: Kumarian Press, 1998

McNeely, Jeffrey, and Kenton R. Miller, eds. *National Parks, Conservation and Development: the Role of Protected Areas in Sustaining Society.* Washington, DC: Smithsonian Institution Press, 1982.

Meland, Bernard E. *Fallible Forms and Symbols: Discourses on Method in a Theology of Culture.* Philadelphia: Fortress Press, 1976.

O'Neill, John. *The Missing Child in Liberal Theory: Towards a Covenant Theory of Family, Community, Welfare and the Civic State.* Toronto, ON: University of Toronto Press, 1994.

Rajagopal, Balakrishnan. *International Law from Below: Development, Social Movements and Third World Resistance.* Cambridge, UK: Cambridge University Press, 2003.

Robertson, Roland. "The Sacred and the World System." Pp. 347–58 in *The Sacred in a Secular Age,* edited by Phillip E. Hammond. San Francisco: University of California Press, 1985.

Rockefeller, Steven C. *Principles of Environmental Conservation and Sustainable Development: Summary and Survey.* Middlebury, VT: Earth Council, 1996.

Santos, Boaventura de Sousa, and César A. Rodriguez-Garavito, eds. *Law and Globalization from Below: Towards a Cosmopolitan Legality.* Cambridge, UK: Cambridge University Press, 2005.

Serres, Michel. *The Natural Contract.* Anne Arbor: University of Michigan Press, 1990.

Sturm, Douglas. *Community and Alienation: Essays on Process Thought and Public Life.* Notre Dame, IN: University of Notre Dame Press, 1988.

———. "Identity and Alterity: Summons to a New Axial Age." *Journal of Liberal Religion* 1 (Apr. 2000): http://www.meadville.edu (27 May 2007).

Taylor, Charles. "Living with Differences." Pp. 212–26 in *Debating Democracy's Discontent: Essays on American Politics, Law, and Public Philosophy,* edited by Anita L. Allen and Milton C. Regan, Jr. New York: Oxford University Press, 1998.

Young, Iris Marion. *Inclusion and Democracy.* New York: Oxford University Press, 2000.

Chapter 3

Market Society and Ecological Integrity: Theory and Practice

Richard Westra, Ph.D. (Political Science)
Division of International and Area Studies
Pukyong National University, Pusan, South Korea

Contact Information: 599-1 Daeyeon 3-Dong, Nam-gu Busan 608-737 REPUBLIC OF S. KOREA
Phone: +82 51 620 6695; Cell: +82 10 7595-6695; Email: westrarj@aim.com

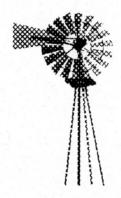

Summary

The quest for ecological integrity to sustain life on Earth demands that we revisit questions of the optimal institutional vehicles to more ensure wise environmental stewardship. In this chapter, we focus on the limits to capitalist markets in realizing key tenets of integrity as expressed in the *Earth Charter*.

We argue that correcting markets to internalize mounting ecological and social externalities necessary to achieve ecological integrity increasingly compromises the profit motive that drives market operations. This fact is reflected in the global trend of neoliberalism to abdicate responsibility for managing environmental externalities and hence for its poor environmental stewardship.

Moreover, we argue from a political economy perspective that sustaining life on Earth will actually require more than policy reform and a bolstering of existing governance structures. Human beings must fundamentally reconfigure their economic and political systems.

We conclude by suggesting institutional alternatives for future societies to live in integrity that deepen popular democracy and restrict markets in reorganized economic communities.

Introduction

The evidence is undeniable. In a comprehensive landmark study extrapolating current environmental trends to 2020, the OECD (2001) adopts a traffic signal system to vividly illustrate the preponderance of red and yellow lights on roads to the future in virtually every area of human economic endeavor. As part of a gathering environmental movement responding to robust analyses of this sort, the Global Ecological Integrity Group (GEIG) and *Earth Charter* Initiative (ECI, see the Appendix) offer an ethical vision and set of policy principles designed to foster a sustainable, equitable, and humane future for all on Earth.[1]

For GEIG, the concept of integrity is used as the touchstone for gauging sustainability at the interface of human beings and nature. Integrity captures the properties of autopoiesis (i.e., self-perpetuation) and reciprocal articulation of natural processes characteristic of natural ecosystems. To live in integrity requires human beings to organize their society in ways that simulate the productive and reproductive modalities of ecosystems and that lead to the combined sustainability of the eco/social system as a whole.

Achieving integrity is perceived as a goal for the future that will likely take generations to attain. To set humanity on the journey, however, the *Earth Charter* offers a set of sixteen principles that its authors hope will ultimately yield the integrity outcome. Of these, we view Principle 7—"Adopt patterns of production, consumption, and reproduction that safeguard Earth's regenerative capacities, human rights, and community well-being"—as particularly significant because it speaks directly to the reorganizing of human economic existence. Principle 7 as well as sub-principles 5 and 6 (demanding sustainable use of non-renewable resources and addressing "long distance, and global consequences of human activities") suggest that GEIG and the *Earth Charter* expect sweeping changes in current economic practices.

The overarching focus of this chapter is upon the optimal economic vehicle to sustain life on Earth. While we concur with GEIG and the *Earth Charter* on the issue of major change, our concern is whether the changes that are sought can be realized within the contours of a market economy. We argue that to the extent human economic endeavors are organized on a capitalist basis they will remain inherently unsustainable. (Rees, 2002) The argument unfolds in two parts:

First, we detail the fundamental anti-environmental bias in the operation of the market economy.

Second, we argue that while state policies to manage market externalities demonstrate a range of flexibility and responsiveness, there are limits to what can be realistically achieved; something compounded by the increasingly global thrust of neo-liberalism. Finally, this chapter concludes with suggestions as to how human economic life might be institutionally configured to realize GEIG and *Earth Charter* goals.

Eco-sustainability and the Abstract, Quantitative Operation of Markets

Economic historian Karl Polanyi (1977) captured the historically peculiar character of market society with his view of the economy "disembedding" itself from society—its politics, culture, and religion—with which human economic existence had been intermeshed since the dawn of time. Interestingly, though less acknowledged, Karl Marx also understood that there was something unique in the way economic life is reproduced in market, or what he designated as capitalist, society. He referred to this variously as the "upside-down," "inverted," "one-sided" character of capitalism. If we draw together insights of both Marx and Polanyi, we can see that, in the historical emergence of capitalism, manufacturing was taken out of the hands of peasants—who had plied it as a supplementary operation—and was converted first into cottage industry, then factory production—even as peasant life itself was uprooted through commons enclosures. The latter facilitated the transfer of labor power from rural areas to factories, completing the disembedding of industry from its agricultural base. As explained by Sekine (1992), this led to the further disembedding "of human beings from their natural environment, of technology from ecology, of science from knowledge" and so forth, to yield the one-sided society of capitalism.

It would fall to the Japanese political economist Kozo Uno (1980) to develop Marx's indictment of capitalism as an upside-down, inverted social order, and in a way that also most convincingly exposes the unsustainable predisposition of capitalism. As Uno maintained, the survival of any human society is predicated upon the satisfaction of what he dubbed "general norms of economic life." The key norm is that the society in question must have at its core a principle to ensure that social demand for basic goods is met with a minimal waste of resources. If resources are chronically misallocated such as, for example, supply of available labor power being continuously devoted to iron production while people are clamoring for grain, the respective society will become extinct. And, human history is replete with examples of societies that could not meet that essential test.

What particularly challenged Uno was to demonstrate how it is possible for capitalism to satisfy the general norms of economic life in the first place. After all, as Marx, Polanyi and Uno observe, capitalism dissolves the face-to-face interpersonal economic relations of the past, replacing them with the impersonal operation of systems of society-wide self-regulating markets. It was as if—to paraphrase Marx—abstract "relations among things" are substituted for concrete human social relations. For Uno then, to explain the economic viability of capitalism, under conditions where the economy appeared to take on a "life of its own," required exploring the phenomenon of what economists refer to as the market reaching a state of equilibrium.[2]

When economists praise the efficiency of markets over alternative institutional arrangements for an economy, they are alluding to the "cost-less" transmitting of economic information by markets in the form of market prices. From the perspective of business actors, prices act as signals indicating where profitable investment opportunities exist. The ability of capitalism to shift rapidly to the production of any good in response to changing patterns of demand and possible profit is rooted in the existence of the aforementioned class of "free laborers" uprooted from ties to the land and available in the market for businesses to purchase as but another input into the production process. To arrive at an equilibrium where demand for both the means of production and the product is supplied at prices that ensure profitability, and that goods are purchased by both workers and business investors, the market must perform a series of abstract calculations based upon quantitative value/price criteria.

In achieving market equilibrium, capitalism simultaneously realizes its goal of augmenting wealth and profit-making, and meets the test of economic viability necessary for the survival of all human societies (ensuring that social resources have not been chronically misallocated). But, capitalism passes this test under conditions where human beings essentially transfer their responsibility for reproducing their own economic life to an "extra-human" force—self-regulating, unfettered markets that manage economic existence according to abstract, quantitative, value/price determinations. This process helps explain how augmenting wealth in capitalist society produces so many questionable goods and noxious substances, things that threaten the existence of life on Earth. Paradoxically, while unimpeded, abstract market calculations constitute the taproot of capitalism's economic viability, they are also the source of capitalism's profaning of the world. In this sense, capitalism is an inverted social order, the extra-human, abstract, quantitative modus operandi of which conflicts fundamentally with concrete, qualitative, human needs and goals.

Eco-sustainability, State Policy and Neo-liberal Globalization

If the above depicts the anti-eco-sustainability of capitalism in its most fundamental incarnation, the question remains whether capitalism is transformable. Uno's insight was to see that while capitalism aspires to materialize an objective, impersonal commodity-economic society, real capitalism never operates in such a "pure" fashion. That is, capitalist market economies always produce a range of externalities—aspects of economic life which self-regulating markets are unable to manage—that the capitalist state is called forth to manage or "internalize" through public policy. Uno argued that to best comprehend the capitalist management of externalities, demanded analytically breaking down capitalist history into epochs or stages of development. These are based upon historic types of capitalist economy characterized by differing major policy initiatives in support of capital accumulation.[3] In doing this, Uno recognized that following the capitalist stage of liberalism—represented by the mid-nineteenth-century economy of Britain, where capitalism most closely approximated the small-business, price-competitive, "pure" market economy captured in theory—subsequent stages of capitalism demonstrate a clear movement away from self-regulating market operations.

Consumerism (Albritton, 1991), the post-war stage of capitalism, aptly named for its characteristic economy of mass production and consumption of consumer goods, supported by state policy, constitutes the most dramatic shift of capitalism away from its self-regulating market modus operandi. Massive investment costs of producing goods such as the automobile engender a business structure of joint-stock corporations that undermines the entrepreneurial basis of capitalism by vesting decision-making in a management technostructure, increasingly coordinates economic transactions through corporate branches rather than markets, eschews price competition, and is deeply involved in extra-market demand management. The internationalization of production and finance characterizing consumerism not only intensifies such trends, but contributes to the corporate need to coordinate each and every arm of business activity on a scale that existed in Soviet-style states. (Korten, 1995, 221)

Paralleling the programming and planning activities of corporate capital is the rise of the consumerist state with a formidable policy arsenal at its disposal to support capital accumulation and internalize market externalities. The social wage, creation of effective demand (military, transportation infrastructure, and so on), monetary, fiscal, labor, and "free trade" policy, are typical policy levers. The upshot of all this is that both profit-making and the economic viability of the capitalist stage of consumerism is largely dependent upon extra-market principles and state support.

Why the "consumer society" emerges as the most environmentally unsound stage of capitalism hardly needs review. The mass consumption of consumer goods upon which corporate accumulation depends, requires that consumer demand for such goods remains virtually insatiable. The result is rapid product obsolescence, an ever expanding and novel assortment of replacement goods, and unconscionable mountains of waste. Further, the accompanying explosion of energy consumption, mainly of petroleum, but also of nuclear power, has ravaged the biosphere and contains the specter of human annihilation. Global pollution has only been compounded by the increasing internationalization of production, both because the latter spreads environmental problems around the world and demands the expansion of hyper-polluting transportation networks. All this, of course, saddles the consumerist state with the burden of managing the externalities of capital accumulation even as they grow to threaten the sustainability of global society.

As we have argued elsewhere (Westra, 2003; 2004a), neo-liberalism as the ideological basis of "globalization" reflects the contradictory path and potential limits of capitalism. On the one hand, its demand for deregulation, off-ground global financialization, the gutting of social wage entitlements, asymmetric wealth distribution and so forth, appears to "free" capitalism from cumbersome extra-market constraints. On the other hand, global corporate business structure with its hugely expensive technology outlays, rising transaction costs, corporate international transfer pricing, growing demand for energy, and ongoing need to stimulate consumer demand, all generate problems that defy correction by markets alone. State intervention in the workings of the global economy is clearly necessary for capitalism to constitute a viable economic order. It follows that abdication by the state of its responsibilities as *capitalist* state to manage the externalities of its capitalist economy, while exhibiting no real measurable diminution in state activity per se, suggests that the current economy is in a period of transition to a yet undetermined world order.

What does this analysis portend for sustainability and realizing the policy aims of GEIG and the *Earth Charter*? At the risk of oversimplification, the mainstream debate over our environmental morass may be divided into two streams. (Dryzek, 1996) On one side, there are enthusiasts of neo-liberalism who believe that sustainability questions are best addressed through the instrumental rationality of free-market actors. On the other side, there are environmentalists, Greens and democrats, including GEIG and the *Earth Charter* Initiative, who believe solutions are best achieved through improved governance and regulatory frameworks.

To neo-liberals, it can be immediately pointed out, as argued above, that the instrumental rationality of self-regulating markets in capitalist society is attuned to the achievement of abstract/quantitative goals, not the concrete qualitative ones necessary to sustain life on Earth. Further, even if neo-liberals were correct in their view that a pure, "perfectly competitive" market would eventually solve its own problems, such a market does not exist outside of economics textbooks. Nor will neo-liberal policy ever bring an economy into existence that even faintly resembles it as long as capitalist accumulation is marked by the modalities of the stage of Consumerism with its perpetual growth imperative, and gross energy (petroleum) dependence, as is the case today. What neo-liberal policy has accomplished is widening global inequality that exacerbates neglect of both population health and the global environment. (Greenhalgh, 2005; Vlachou, 2005) Indeed, inequality fuels denial of environmental concerns as beneficiaries of neo-liberal policy become increasingly protective of and defensive over their gains. (Hornborg, 2003)

The question of global governance has been framed in terms of: a) a "Hobbesian" world order, defended by the United States of America (U.S.A.) which seeks, through its military and economic muscle, to establish regulatory norms that leave what former President George H. W. Bush referred to as "our way of life" intact; and, b) a "Kantian" model, institutionalizing a universal ethic of sustainability, championed by the European Union (EU). (Lipietz, 2004) While in spirit we side with the Kantians, in practice the problem from a political economy standpoint is rather more complex. Though Lipietz (2004) makes clear that EU global governance initiatives have had important impacts in areas such as climate change, the failure to extend these is not just a matter of U.S. recalcitrance. The global spread of neo-liberalism has imposed decisive limits on the adaptive capacities of Europe's post-war "mixed" economy of markets and economic programming. Stamped as they are by the policy incoherence of neo-liberalism, the U.S.A. and major EU economies are similarly inhibited from exacting sweeping changes in environmental practices that would risk the viability of economic life. In fact, globalization offers no template for either an economically viable or eco-sustainable future. (Westra, 2004a) As the breaking down of barriers to the unencumbered, worldwide predatory relocation of production processes and subsequent globe-circling movement of goods, globalization serves only to disembed economic life further from agriculture and nature than did the "national" economic organization induced by early capitalism.

Concluding with a Viable Model?
Re-designing Economic Institutions
to Sustain Life on Earth

If capitalist patterns of production and consumption cannot sustain civilized life, then it is incumbent upon us to think creatively about institutional arrangements for economic life that will help us to live in integrity. What remains of this chapter develops earlier work (Westra, 2002; 2004b) as a contribution to this goal. First, a revolutionary implication of Uno's (1980) political economy is that economic life with its general norms—something without which human society would be impossible—and the historically peculiar form of the capitalist market economy that satisfies those norms, are two different things. Thus, to the extent that the eco-destructiveness of capitalism is rooted in the objective, abstract, quantitative operation of self-regulating markets, an essential task for the eco-sustainable future is prying economic life loose from capitalism's quantitative determinants, and infusing it with qualitative human considerations. The new institutional reconfiguring, however, must satisfy available criteria and standards for economic viability, eco-pedigree, and overall social betterment.

Polanyi (1977) offers us an instructive classification of non-capitalist economies: "Small-m" markets, involving face-to-face exchanges, have existed benignly throughout history as the means for satisfying demand for basic goods in society. Redistributive economies, such as the Asiatic and European models of feudalism, and the failed Soviet-style experiments, all of which relied on largely centralized coercive political apparatuses to reproduce economic life, are another mode. Reciprocity as in aboriginal community life is the third.

Society-wide central planning, as realized in Soviet-style societies, can safely be discounted as a template for economic viability, eco-sustainability, and social betterment. Autarchic (i.e., economically "closed") communities, with "small-m" markets and forms of reciprocity as envisioned by Schumacher (1999), are potentially economically viable, but eco-sustainability might still be compromised if autarchic communities pass their environmental problems on to others. In addition, they offer no solution to the large-scale clean-up operation required following more than a century of capitalist abuse during which time externalities have been permitted to accumulate. And it is not clear whether a world based solely on autarchic communities would achieve social betterment given the positive aspects of cosmopolitan society that would be lost.

What we propose here is to dismantle capitalism and its environmentally disabling residues, giving consideration not so much to geo-spatial scale, but to the logical scale of economic coordination, by breaking down economies into tri-sector communities. A small goods sector might be formed around rural areas and small towns with arable lands and boroughs adjacent to major urban centers. Its production focus, depending on local resources, would be foodstuffs, furniture, apparel, household sundries, and so forth. Its mode of economic coordination would incorporate, reciprocity, "small-m" markets such as current local exchange and trading systems (LETS), and blend communal and individual ownership. A heavy goods sector would assume responsibility for producing machinery and other industrial wares, producer and consumer, as well as environmentally sound forms of mass transportation, energy delivery, and social infrastructure. Its economic coordination would involve regional planning and programming; ownership would be cooperative or public through shareholding by its workers and inhabitants of the local communities that it services. Finally, an administrative sector would be linked to both communities through trade and shareholding.

Economic viability will largely be ensured by the small goods sector. Its lived environment could also be most closely fashioned according to the integrity benchmark. Incentives to maintain the lived environment of all sectors, however, would follow from their interlocking ownership, and the possible democratic rotation of working families through each sector. And, methods of ecological footprinting (Wackernagel and Rees, 1996) could be deployed to identify possible eco-deficits of sectors so that remedial action could be taken. Finally, positive elements of cosmopolitan society and culture would be co-opted to contribute to overall social betterment. Though this will still entail sweeping change from current practices, on the basis of this tri-sector model, and in a global commonwealth of similar economic communities that may or may not adopt the pattern of existing nation-states, we believe that the universal values and commitments espoused by the *Earth Charter* could be realized in full.

At present there exists no organized coalition of groups and social classes able to bring about the sort of social transformation advocated here. However, it is our view that in making models of economically viable, eco-sustainable societies available for public consideration, we can contribute to the building of such a coalition at a time when the future of human life on this planet is dependant on the emergence of one.

Notes

1.   What follows on GEIG draws from L. Westra et al. (2000) and on ECI, www.earthcharter.org.

2. I do not want to burden this chapter with arcane debates within and between economic traditions on the question of equilibrium. For debates within neo-classical economics see Blaug (2003). In the Marxist tradition, see Westra (1999).

3. The literature in this area of political economy is extensive and complex. On the theory of operation of a "pure" capitalist society, see Sekine (1997). On the Uno approach to stages of capitalism, see Albritton (1991); Westra (2006). For debates over how to best theorize stages see the anthology, Albritton et al. (2001).

References

Albritton, Robert. *A Japanese Approach to Stages of Capitalist Development.* Basingstoke, UK: Macmillan, 1991.

Albritton, Robert, Makoto Itoh, Richard Westra, and Alan Zuege, eds. *Phases of Capitalist Development: Booms, Crises and Globalizations.* Basingstoke, UK: Palgrave, 2001.

Blaug, Mark. "The Formalist Revolution of the 1950s." *Journal of the History of Economic Thought* 25, no. 2 (2003).

Dryzek, John, S. "Foundations for Environmental Political Economy: The Search for Homo Ecologicus?" *New Political Economy* 1, no. 1 (1996).

Earth Charter Initiative. www.earthcharter.org (22 May 2007).

Greenhalgh, Christine. "Why Does Market capitalism Fail to Deliver a Sustainable Environment and Greater Inequality of Incomes?" *Cambridge Journal of Economics* 29 (2005).

Hornborg, Alf. "Cornucopia or Zero-Sum Game? The Epistemology of Sustainability." *Journal of World-Systems Research* 9, no. 2 (2003).

Korten, David. C. *When Corporations Rule the World.* West Hartford, CT: Kumarian Press, 1995.

Lipietz, Alan. "Kyoto, Johannesburg, Baghdad." *International Journal of Political Economy* 34, no. 1 (2004).

OECD Environmental Outlook. Paris: 2001.

Polanyi, Karl. *The Livelihood of Man.* New York: Academic Press, 1977.

Rees, William E. "Globalization and Sustainability: Conflict or Convergence?" *Bulletin of Science, Technology and Society* 22, no. 4 (2002): 249–68.

Schumacher, E. F. *Small is Beautiful.* Vancouver, BC: Hartley and Marks, 1999.

Sekine, Thomas T. "Broadening the Scope of Political Economy." *CDAS Discussion Paper No. 74.* Montreal: McGill University, 1992.

———. *An Outline of the Dialectic of Capital.* 2 vol. Basingstoke, UK: Macmillan, 1997.

Uno, Kozo. *Principles of Political Economy.* Atlantic Highlands, New Jersey: Humanities Press, 1980.

Vlachou, Andriana. "Environmental Regulation: A Value-theoretic and Class-based Analysis." *Cambridge Journal of Economics*, 29 (2005).

Wackernagel, Mathis and William E. Rees. *Our Ecological Footprint: Reducing Human Impact on Earth.* Gabriola Island, BC: New Society Publishers, 1996.

Westra, Laura, Peter Miller, James R. Karr, William E. Rees, and Robert E. Ulanowitz. "Ecological Integrity and the Aims of the Global Integrity Project" in *Ecological Integrity: Integrating Environment, Conservation and Health,* edited by David Pimentel, Laura Westra, and Reed F. Noss. Washington, DC: Island Press, 2000.

Westra, Richard. "The Capitalist Stage of Consumerism and South Korean Development." *Journal of Contemporary Asia* 36, no. 1 (2006).

———. "Globalization and the Pathway to Socio-material Betterment." *Review of Radical Political Economics* 36, no. 3 (2004b).

———. "Globalization: The Retreat of Capital to the 'Interstices' of the World?" in *Value and the World Economy Today: Production, Finance and Globalization,* edited by R. Westra and A. Zuege. Basingstoke, UK: Palgrave, 2003.

———. "The 'Impasse' Debate and Socialist Development" in *New Socialisms: Futures beyond Globalization,* edited by R. Albritton, S. Bell, J. Bell, and R. Westra. Innis Centenary Series: Governance and Change in the Global Era. London: Routledge, 2004a.

———. "A Japanese Contribution to the Critique of Rational Choice Marxism." *Social Theory and Practice*, 25, 3 (1999).

———. "Marxian Economic Theory and an Ontology of Socialism: A Japanese Intervention." *Capital & Class*, 78 (2002).

Chapter 4

A Full Spectrum Integrity Index of Nations

Helmut Burkhardt, Ph.D. (Physics)
Professor Emeritus of Physics
Ryerson University
Toronto, Ontario, Canada

Contact Information: 142 Balsam Avenue, Toronto, Ont. M4E 3C1 CANADA
Phone: +1 416 694 8385; Email: burkhard@ryerson.ca

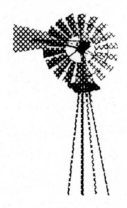

Summary

Integrity is a broad concept that can be applied not only to individuals and physical structures, but also to ecosystems, and to nations.

The "full spectrum" index of integrity proposed here is a summary measure of a system's sustainability. It quantifies both the quality of a system's state and its performance functions. By using state and performance indicators of large systems, it is possible to rank their relative level of integrity. All relevant dimensions of integrity need to be integrated for meaningful relative comparisons of integrity across nations.

In this chapter, we describe a "full spectrum" integrity index of nations. The available specific indicators are first combined into four broader domains: the ecological, societal, individual, and physical indicators of the integrity of nations. The four are then combined by simple multiplication into a single, full spectrum index of integrity.

The results are presented for 106 countries, with New Zealand, Australia, Sweden, Canada, and Finland in the top five. Yemen, Pakistan, Rwanda, Bangladesh, and Tajikistan have the lowest ranks in the "full spectrum" integrity index. These nations are in deep trouble and need help from the global community. The findings are discussed, recognizing the crude nature of summary indicators.

The Concept of Full Spectrum Integrity of a Nation

In this chapter, "national integrity" is the quality that describes a secure, healthy, and just nation. A nation with integrity is likely to be sustainable in the long term.

The integrity of a nation rests on two pillars. The first necessary condition both for sustainability and integrity is the availability of resources to support the nation's way of life in the long term. The second necessary factor for sustainability and integrity is local and global peace; i.e., the absence of destructive forces. The lack of resources, or of peace, will destroy the structural and functional integrity of the nation.

In the past, the integrity of a nation was frequently based on internal resources, including peace through military strength. However, the complete, local, self-reliance of nations is an unlikely future scenario.

Today, many nations have insufficient internal resources to support their lifestyles and must supplement internal resources through trade with other nations. Furthermore, with the possibility of mutually assured destruction (MAD) of nations, and with the potential of terrorists acquiring weapons of mass destruction, military strength of individual nations can no longer guarantee security. The desirable mode of achieving national integrity in our globalized world is enhanced self-reliance, fair trade, and the rule of international law enforced by a multilateral police force under the control of the United Nations. A global government could protect the integrity of nations just as national governments protect their citizens. This modus operandi is a rational option for humanity in the present situation.

Examples of indicators that quantify performance on specific aspects exist and are readily obtainable in the literature. The concept of ecological integrity combines issues of the environment and health. (Pimentel et al., 2000) The notion of ecological deficit is widely accepted as a measure of the extent to which total material consumption exceeds a nation's domestic biocapacity (ecosystems' productivity). (Rees, 1996; Wackernagel and Rees, 1996)

Several indices are available to describe societal integrity. A Corruption Perceptions Index is published and updated annually by Transparency International. The Reporters Without Borders index ranks nations with respect to the freedom of speech. The World Bank, the U.S. Central Intelligence Agency, and the Carleton University Department of Political Science publish lists of the political and economic performance of nations. The United Nations Development Programme publishes a ranking of nations by the quality of life of their citizens.

The full spectrum integrity of a nation (F) is a multidimensional concept that combines the specific aspects of ecological integrity (E), societal integrity (S), individual integrity (B), and physical integrity (P). Local and global justice in each of these four domains is a precondition for a nation to reach a high level of full spectrum integrity.

Rank as a Relative Measure of Integrity

A relative measure of integrity for a nation is achieved by comparison with other nations. An initial step is to rank the nations according to each of the four particular components considered. Then, one way to develop a measure of full spectrum integrity is to take the average of the individual ranks in each of the four domains. A second meaningful overall rank is derived from the "volume" formed by the product of the ranks in each of the four essential dimensions of national integrity. The latter method of ranking is less forgiving of shortcomings in any one of the dimensions of integrity. In practice, the difference in ranking produced by the two methods turns out to be minor.

For this chapter, we compiled a complete set of data for 106 nations from the Internet, and ranked the nations first within the ecological, societal, individual, and physical domains. We then multiplied the ranks for each nation in the four dimensions of integrity and present the resultant re-ranking (the product E*S*B*P) as the full spectrum integrity index of nations.

Ecological Integrity Ranks (E)

The overall ecological integrity of a nation is characterized by the present wellness of the ecosystem. A second aspect of the ecological integrity is the direction and the rate of change in a nation's environmental health.

One aspect of a nation's ecological integrity is the relationship between its ecological footprint and the productivity of its domestic ecosystems i.e., its biocapacity. The difference between a country's ecological footprint and its domestic biocapacity represents that country's ecological surplus or deficit. The ecological footprint is defined as the productive land and water area required to sustain a population at a specific material standard of living. Biocapacity is the nation's actual ecologically productive land/water area. (Rees, 2006; WWF, 2006) Countries whose footprint is bigger than their biocapacity deserve a low ranking in ecological integrity as they destroy their own ecosystem by living off their ecological capital, or by importing goods they contribute to the degradation of other countries' ecosystems.

Another aspect of national ecological integrity is the direction and speed of environmental change. Ranking the trends in ecosystems requires a consideration of the processes that damage the environment. Factors that determine humanity's impact (I) on the environment can be described by a simple formula (Ehrlich and Holdren, 1971):

$$I = PAT,$$

where "P" is the human population, "A" is affluence, or disposable income (consumption) per person, and "T" is the environmental impact per unit of affluence. One approximate measure for P*A is the nation's gross national product.

The size of the T factor depends on the kind of technologies used by the nation. Clearly, too, the change rates of population, affluence, and technology will determine the direction, and the rate of ecological change.

In traditional thinking, growth is a positive value. However, as far as ecosystems are concerned, growth of human populations and affluence beyond identifiable limits is detrimental to ecological integrity. When they breach these limits, ecologically responsible nations will try to reduce their environmental impacts. According to the I=PAT formula this will entail some combination of reducing populations, reducing affluence, and converting of environmentally damaging technologies to "green" technologies. For the sake of ecological integrity, politicians, economists, and the general public must begin to value declining population and consumption as positive trends.

This shift of values will raise many questions of ecological, societal, and individual justice. The concept of "contraction and convergence" of per capita energy use has been developed during the creation of the Kyoto Protocol on CO_2 emissions. This principle states that, for fairness, the energy-squandering rich nations must reduce energy consumption, and allow the energy-poor developing nations to increase energy consumption until both arrive in the long term at a common level that is globally sustainable. Contraction and convergence could and should be applied to all critical resources and pollutants; similar reasoning should determine the desirable direction and speed of change in other factors affecting sustainability, e.g., population, affluence and technology. Only fair change in all relevant factors will produce both global justice and integrity of nations.

What are the implications of these new values? Today's technology still relies heavily on environmentally damaging fossil fuels. Clean renewable energy technologies are still in the early stages of development; a quick implementation of renewable energy technology is needed. Population and economic factors are equally important in determining national and global ecological integrity.

Ranking Ecological Integrity of Nations

The rank of ecological integrity is determined using the ecologically relevant descriptors of nations described above: the nation's ecological surplus (or deficit), population change rate, and affluence (GDP) change rate. Population and GDP declines are valued positively in the ecological domain because they reduce environmental impact. The averages are sorted and a rank between 1 and 100 is assigned. The ranking of the relative ecological surplus of nations is based on data available on the Internet. (Wackernagel et al., 2002; WWF, 2006) The data for the ranking of population and affluence change rates are found in the World Bank's Development Education Program. (World Bank, 2002) The data from these sources are sorted, and ranked. Column 3 in Table 4.1 (see page 57) gives a complete set of ecological integrity ranks for 106 nations in alphabetical order. The approximate population of each country is listed as a convenient reference in Column 2.

The countries with a good score in ecological integrity have a healthy ecosystem, and contribute little to the degradation of the global ecosystem. The countries with a bad ecological integrity score suffer from both an ecological deficit and a tendency to further degrade their own or the global environment. Japan, for example, may protect its own ecosystem, but scores lower on the ecological ranking owing to imports required to maintain its lifestyle. Table 4.1 shows that Uruguay has the healthiest ecosystem and occupies rank 1 in ecological integrity, while Tajikistan has the lowest ecological integrity at rank 100. The ecological integrity rank of the most populous countries is quite low; the rank of the United States is 40, India has the rank 73, and China occupies rank 86 out of 100.

Societal Integrity Rank (S)

The societal integrity of a nation depends to a large degree on internal and external peace. The rank with respect to internal peace is derived from available indicators for political stability, economic justice, the rule of local law or criminality, press freedom, and transparency or corruption. Indicators of a nation's international disputes, degree of support for the United Nations or international treaties, and low military spending relative to their GDP describe external peace.

The United Nations Development Programme's Human Development Report offers several indices relevant to the societal integrity of a nation: the "political stability index," which is an estimate of the life expectancy of the nation; the "rule of law index," which measures the control of criminality within the nation; and the "press freedom indicators." (United Nations, 2002) A worldwide press freedom index is also available on the Internet. (Reporters Without Borders, 2002) Transparency International's "Corruption Perceptions Index" (Transparency International, 2002) is used as another input to determine a nation's societal integrity rank.

Economists use the Gini index to quantify the degree of economic justice—income equity—in a nation. The Gini index of countries is available in the World Bank's World Development Report. (World Bank, 2001) This index measures the deviation from equality in the distribution of wealth. The ideal socialist state, in which citizens have nearly equal wealth, would have a Gini index near zero. The opposite situation is given in the perfect neo-liberal capitalist country where most of the wealth is amassed by a few, and the rest of the citizens are poor. This results in a Gini index tending toward one.

Indices describing various countries' "external peace" can be found in the Carleton University project: Country indicators for Foreign Policy. (Carleton University, 2003) The "international disputes index," which quantifies a country's relationship with its neighbors, is based on the World Fact Book. (U.S. Central Intelligence Agency, 2002) The "UN support index" and the "military expenses relative to the GDP" of a nation are given by the same sources.

The overall societal integrity rank is determined by averaging the ranks of the following eight components of societal integrity: political stability, economic justice, rule of law, press freedom, transparency, international disputes, UN support, and military expenditure relative to the nation's GDP. Each component of the societal indicators is ranked from 1 to 100, with "1" indicating the highest rank, and "100" the lowest. An average of these eight rankings is used to determine the overall societal integrity rank of a nation. The resulting societal integrity rank is shown in Column 4 of Table 4.1.

The countries with the highest societal integrity ranking enjoy inner and outer peace. Those in the lowest ranks need to reorganize internally and improve their relations with their neighbors. Austria occupies the first spot in societal integrity, while Russia is last with a rank of 100. The most populous countries rank poorly in societal integrity, the U.S. being an exception with a rank of 23.

An elaborate study of the societal integrity ranks of nations has recently been published by Vision of Humanity as a Global Peace Index (Vision of Humanity, 2007).

Individual Integrity Rank (B)

The individual integrity rank categorizes nations by the well-being of their citizens. The measure of individual well-being includes three major factors: life expectancy at birth, educational achievements, and standard of living. A combined rank of all these factors already exists in the United Nations Human Development Report. (United Nations, 2002) Those countries with good ranking in this category treat their citizens well with health care, education, and access to clean air and water, food and housing. Those with low individual integrity ranks cannot supply the necessities of life to their citizens. Column 5 in Table 4.1 lists the individual integrity rank for all 106 nations. Norway's citizens top the list of individual integrity; the citizens of Sierra Leone are at the bottom of the list with a rank of 100. Of the most populous nations, the United States of America ranks 6th in this category, China is 57th, and India is 74th.

Physical Integrity Rank (P)

Population, together with geographic and climatic factors, determines the physical quality of a nation. Mineral and fossil fuel resources, availability of solar or wind energy, rainfall, and productive ecosystems, *but also* absence of natural disasters such as earthquakes, storms, floods, droughts, or ozone holes, determine the physical integrity of a nation. The only quantitative analysis that could be found in the literature was the per capita ecological capacity (biocapacity) of nations (Wackernagel et al., 2002; WWF, 2006). Therefore, it was used to rank the nations by their sustainable natural resources as shown in column 6 of Table 4.1.

New Zealand ranks at the top in physical resources, and Jordan is at the low end of the list. Of the most populous countries, the United States' physical integrity is ranked 13th, China is 69th, and India is ranked 84th.

Full Spectrum Integrity Rank (F)

The full spectrum integrity index of nations is determined by ranking the product E*S*B*P for the 106 nations. The overall, full spectrum integrity rank F is given in the last column of Table 4.1. In the full spectrum integrity of nations, New Zealand occupies the top spot, and Yemen is at the bottom of the list. Of the most populous countries, China's full spectrum integrity rank is 83, India's is 92, and the full spectrum integrity rank of the United States is 14.

Table 4.1. Integrity Ranks of 106 Nations
The highest rank is 1, the lowest is 100. Column 1 is a list of the countries in alphabetical order. Approximate population (in millions) in the year 2000 is listed in the second column. The ecological integrity rank E, the societal integrity rank S, the individual integrity rank B, and the physical integrity rank P are listed in columns 3 to 6. The full spectrum integrity rank F, in column 7, is derived from a ranking of the product E*S*B*P.

Country	Pop	E	S	B	P	F
Algeria	30	92	83	62	92	94
Armenia	4	87	96	44	92	90
Australia	19	8	11	5	2	2
Austria	8	14	1	13	29	9
Azerbaijan	8	90	98	52	72	87
Bangladesh	137	88	72	84	98	97
Belarus	10	34	49	35	31	45
Belgium	10	62	6	4	66	19
Bolivia	8	7	75	68	8	20
Brazil	170	5	39	43	10	8
Bulgaria	8	23	28	39	46	44
Burkina Faso	12	91	76	97	73	77
Burundi	6	38	97	99	93	85
Cambodia	13	68	67	75	58	79
Cameroon	15	63	92	79	21	54
Canada	31	15	9	3	3	4
Chile	15	24	25	27	18	13
China	1275	86	61	57	69	83
Colombia	42	9	94	41	34	28
Costa Rica	4	11	17	30	37	8
Côte d'Ivoire	16	6	56	92	42	36
Croatia	5	32	48	31	41	50
Czech Republic	10	27	27	24	38	38
Denmark	5	26	8	12	25	22

Continued on next page

Table 4.1 (Continued)

Country	Pop	E	S	B	P	F
Ecuador	13	52	59	55	32	49
Egypt	68	81	38	69	80	89
El Salvador	6	69	47	60	94	48
Estonia	2	35	26	29	20	29
Finland	5	13	2	8	5	5
France	59	42	20	10	28	26
Gambia	1	95	33	93	74	59
Georgia	5	55	74	48	75	70
Germany	82	19	7	14	50	23
Ghana	19	77	30	75	75	65
Greece	10	58	29	20	39	46
Guatemala	11	66	80	72	63	61
Guinea	8	58	46	92	42	58
Guinea-Bissau	1	70	54	96	19	21
Honduras	7	51	91	70	53	58
Hungary	10	48	14	25	51	41
India	1009	73	58	74	84	92
Indonesia	212	44	62	65	47	64
Ireland	4	61	13	15	9	18
Israel	6	75	51	19	89	66
Italy	58	33	16	17	64	34
Japan	127	28	8	8	85	25
Jordan	5	99	40	58	100	92
Kazakhstan	16	72	66	46	23	55
Kenya	31	25	90	78	67	56
Korea, Republic of	48	41	37	21	86	53
Kyrgyzstan	5	64	69	59	70	76
Lao People's D. R.	5	71	86	82	17	60
Latvia	2	29	31	33	15	30
Lesotho	2	57	65	76	87	71
Lithuania	4	36	32	32	27	40
Madagascar	16	85	73	85	44	78
Malaysia	22	25	64	37	22	37
Mali	11	43	53	95	59	52
Mauritania	3	74	77	89	33	73
Mexico	99	22	35	34	52	27
Moldova, Republic of	4	75	81	61	81	86
Mongolia	3	18	25	67	8	24
Morocco	30	78	63	73	76	93
Mozambique	18	76	42	98	45	69
Nepal	23	79	57	81	90	91
Netherlands	16	56	4	7	82	16
New Zealand	4	4	15	16	1	1
Nicaragua	5	50	88	71	25	51
Nigeria	114	92	84	86	77	80
Norway	5	20	10	1	11	6

Continued on next page

Table 4.1 (Continued)

Country	Pop	E	S	B	P	F
Pakistan	141	89	82	80	97	99
Panama	3	10	36	36	26	17
Papua New Guinea	5	3	60	77	4	11
Paraguay	6	12	70	54	7	15
Peru	26	2	41	49	12	10
Philippines	76	82	78	45	91	75
Poland	39	45	21	26	54	43
Portugal	10	39	12	22	55	25
Romania	22	60	55	40	60	68
Russian Federation	146	17	100	38	14	31
Rwanda	8	93	79	94	78	98
Senegal	9	94	52	91	57	82
Sierra Leone	4	47	58	100	68	62
Slovakia	5	42	34	25	35	47
Slovenia	2	46	19	23	40	39
South Africa	43	54	42	63	36	42
Spain	40	59	18	18	48	35
Sri Lanka	19	37	50	53	95	67
Sweden	9	8	5	2	6	3
Switzerland	7	30	3	9	49	12
Tajikistan	6	100	89	66	99	96
Tanzania, U. Republic	35	80	43	88	62	81
Thailand	63	16	45	42	61	42
Tunisia	10	83	44	58	71	74
Turkey	67	31	85	50	65	63
Turkmenistan	5	97	99	51	43	75
Uganda	23	98	68	87	79	95
Ukraine	50	67	95	47	58	72
United Kingdom	59	53	22	11	56	33
United States	283	40	23	6	13	14
Uruguay	3	1	24	28	16	7
Uzbekistan	25	84	87	56	88	84
Venezuela	24	21	75	42	24	32
Viet Nam	78	65	93	64	83	88
Yemen	18	96	92	83	96	100
Zambia	10	49	71	90	30	57

Discussion and Conclusions

Nations with low ranks in ecological integrity, such as Tajikistan, Jordan, Uganda, Turkmenistan, Yemen, and others need to reduce their population, and their per capita consumption, or decrease their use of non-green technology, whichever factor is most responsible for their low ranking.

Nations with lowest ranks in societal integrity, i.e., Russia, Turkmenistan, Azerbaijan, Burundi, Armenia, and others need to move toward internal peace by improving political stability, and economic justice. Furthermore, they need to enforce the rule of law, increase press freedom, and eradicate corruption. In external affairs, those nations with a low score in societal integrity need to resolve their disputes with other nations, contribute more to the United Nations, and reduce their military spending relative to their GDP.

Nations with a low rank in individual integrity, i.e., Sierra Leone, Burundi, Mozambique, Burkina Faso, Guinea-Bissau and others need to improve their health care, their education system, and the disposable income of their citizens.

Nations with low scores on the physical integrity index—Jordan, Pakistan, Rwanda, Bangladesh, Tajikistan, and others—need to improve their per capita physical resources by lowering their population. A change in technology could also improve the situation. Use of locally available solar or wind energy resources could improve stress due to lack of fuel resources.

The full spectrum integrity index of a nation emerges from a combination of integrity ranks in the ecological, societal, individual, and physical dimensions of a nation. It is a single indicator of the overall health and vitality of a nation, and of how well that nation contributes to the health of the global community of nations.

The top ranking nations in the full spectrum integrity index live within their means in relatively healthy ecosystems. They have a sound social system blessed by inner and outer peace. Their citizens enjoy a good quality life, and they have the physical resources to sustain their nation. New Zealand, Australia, Finland, Sweden, and Canada have the highest rank in the full spectrum index of integrity.

By contrast, those nations with low ranks in the full spectrum integrity index live beyond their means, have poor and decaying ecosystems, a social system in turmoil, their citizens live in misery, and they lack physical resources in poor climatic conditions. Yemen, Pakistan, Rwanda, Bangladesh, and Tajikistan have the lowest ranks in the full spectrum integrity index. These nations need internal reform, and assistance from the global community.

References

Carleton University. "Country Indicators for Foreign Policy—2003." www.carleton.ca/cifp/rank.htm (28 May 2007).

Ehrlich, Paul R., and John P. Holdren. "The Impact of Population Growth." *Science* 171 (1971): 1212–17.

Pimentel, David, Laura Westra, and Reed F. Noss. *Ecological Integrity: Integrating Environment, Conservation, and Health.* Washington, DC: Island Press, 2000.

Rees, William E. "Ecological Footprints and Bio-Capacity: Essential Elements in Sustainability Assessment." Ch. 9 in *Renewables-Based Technology: Sustainability Assessment,* edited by Jo Dewulf and Herman Van Langenhove. Chichester, UK: John Wiley and Sons, 2006.

————. "Revisiting Carrying Capacity: Area-Based Indicators of Sustainability." *Population and Environment* 17 (1996): 195–215.
Reporters Without Borders: Worldwide Press Freedom Index. http://www.rsf.org/article.php3?id_article=4118&var_recherche=index (28 May 2007).
Transparency International. "Corruption Perceptions Index." 2002. http://www.transparency.org/policy_research/surveys_indices/cpi/2002 (28 May 2007).
United Nations. "Human Development Report 2002." Ch. 1. p. 36. http://hdr.undp.org/reports/global/2002/en/ (28 May 2007).
U.S. Central Intelligence Agency. "The World Factbook. 2002." GDP—Real Growth Rate. http://www.cia.gov/cia/publications/factbook/index.html (28 May 2007).
Vision of Humanity 2007. www.visionofhumanity.com/rankings (5 Jun. 2007).
Wackernagel, Mathis, Chad Monfreda, and Diana Deumling. "Ecological Footprint of Nations, November 2002 Update: How Much Nature Do They Use? How Much Nature Do They Have? Redefining Progress." San Francisco: 2002. [available from the author]
Wackernagel, Mathis, and William E. Rees. *Our Ecological Footprint: Reducing Human Impact on the Earth.* Gabriola Island, BC: New Society Publishers, 1996.
World Bank. "Development Education Program." 2002. http://www.worldbank.org/depweb/english/modules/basicdata/datanotbasic.html (4 Jun. 2007).
————. "World Development Report 2000/2001." P. 282, Table 5. http://siteresources.worldbank.org/INTPOVERTY/Resources/WDR/English-Full-text-Report/tab5.pdf (4 Jun. 2007).
WWF. *Living Planet Report 2006.* Gland, Switzerland: World Wide Fund (WWF) for Nature International, 2006.

Part II:
Globalization, Human Rights, and the Human Condition

In the second part of this book, we link globalization and human rights with broader recognition of the human condition and the way in which we make policy decisions. A holistic approach for ensuring the health of populations in a globalizing world is argued from a human rights perspective. Demonstrating the vital aspects of sustainability resonates strongly with intuition.

Because of our collective self-destructive paths of the past, we need to overcome our collective cultural maladaptations. We need to align ourselves on a sustainable path, one that includes respect for the global community of life, ecological integrity, social and economic justice, democracy, non-violence, and peace. These necessary goals are embodied as principles of the *Earth Charter* (see the Appendix).

Serious ongoing threats to biological and life-supporting ecosystems globally serve to justify needed shifts away from existing approaches in the way that business is currently conducted internationally. The notion of "strong sustainability" is invoked to justify these shifts. "Strong sustainability" is rooted in ethics, has a distinctive focus on natural capital, and entails policy suggestions with regard to different aspects of environmental policy.

Chapter 5

Linkages among Globalization, Human Rights, and Health[1]

Maud Huynen, Ph.D. Candidate (Global Health)
International Centre for Integrated assessment and
Sustainable development (ICIS)
Maastricht University, Netherlands

Contact Information: P.O. Box 616, 6200 MD Maastricht THE NETHERLANDS
Phone: +31 43 3884840; Fax: +31 43 3884916; Email: m.huynen@icis.unimaas.nl

Pim Martens, Ph.D. (Mathematics)
Professor of Sustainable Development
Director, International Centre for Integrated assessment and
Sustainable development (ICIS)
Maastricht University, Netherlands

Contact Information: P.O. Box 616, 6200 MD Maastricht THE NETHERLANDS
Phone: +31 43 3883555; Fax: +31 43 3884916; Email: p.martens@icis.unimaas.nl

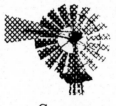

Summary

Over the past decade, global health has been recognized as one of the key challenges in achieving a sustainable form of globalization. However, opinions about the future health effects of globalization are polarized. We need to tackle this deadlock in order to engage in a true dialogue toward a sustainable and healthy globalized world.

Achieving a healthy globalized world concerns not only the right to health, but also requires the fulfillment of other important human rights upon which human health and well-being depend. In this chapter, we use a conceptual framework to suggest that several important human rights considerations (e.g., the right to health care, food, water, and a healthy environment) can help to address the health effects of the globalization processes.

An additional challenge in facilitating the transition toward global health is to enhance the accountability of the increasingly important non-state actors (e.g., the World Trade Organization, and transnational corporations). We demonstrate that, in our effort to promote a healthy globalized world, human rights provide a framework for meaningful discussion and international cooperation.

Introduction

Over the past decade, sustaining good health has been recognized as one of the key elements in achieving a sustainable form of globalization. (Lee, 2003) With globalization, the geographical scale of important health issues is increasing, as was clearly demonstrated by the rapid spread of the Severe Acute Respiratory Syndrome (SARS) in 2003. Additionally, intergenerational equity implied by sustainable development also forces us to think about the right of future generations to a healthy life.

However, opinions about the (future) health effects of globalization differ. "Optimists" argue that globalization will be mostly good for population health, whereas "pessimists" stress that the effects will be primarily negative. In this polarized debate, it is difficult to discuss how globalization should move forward. (Lee, 2001) Still, the deadlock has to be addressed. We demonstrate that a rights-based approach can help to foster true dialogue for a sustainable health-based globalization.

Population Health and Its Determinants

Population health essentially reflects the conditions of our economic, social, and natural environments. (Martens et al., 2000) We define population health as the integrated outcome of the economic, sociocultural, institutional, and ecological determinants that affect a population's physical, mental, and social capacities to function normally. (Huynen and Martens, 2002)

A recent analysis of existing health models concluded that the nature of these determinants and their level of causality can be combined into a basic framework that conceptualizes the complex multi-causality of population health. (Huynen et al., 2005a)

To differentiate among different kinds of health determinants, a distinction across sociocultural, economic, environmental, and institutional factors is made. These factors operate at different hierarchical levels of causality. The chain of events leading to a certain health outcome includes both proximal and distal causes—proximal factors act directly to cause disease or health gains, while distal determinants are further back in the causal chain and act via intermediary causes. (WHO, 2002)

In addition, contextual factors also play an important role. These can be seen as the macro-level conditions shaping the distal and proximate health determinants; they form the context in which the distal and proximate factors operate and develop. (Huynen et al., 2005a)

Table 5.1 shows the wide-ranging overview of the health determinants that can be fitted within this framework.

Table 5.1. Determinants of Population Health

Level/Nature	General Determinants	Detailed Determinants
Contextual level		
Institutional	Institutional infrastructure	Governance structure
		Political environment
		System of law
		Regulation
Economic	Economic infrastructure	Occupational structure
		Tax system
		Markets
Sociocultural	Culture	Religion
		Ideology
		Customs
	Population	Population size
		Structure
		Geographical distribution
	Social infrastructure	Social organization
		Knowledge development
		Social security
		Insurance system
		Mobility and communication
Environmental	Ecological settings	Ecosystems
		Climate
Distal level		
Institutional	Health policy	Effective health policy
		Public health budget
	Health-related policy	Food policy
		Water policy
		Social policy
		Environmental policy
Economic	Economic development	Income/wealth
		Economic equity
	Trade	Trade in goods and services
		Marketing
Sociocultural	Knowledge	Education and literacy
		Health education
		Technology
	Social interactions	Social equity
		Conflicts
		Travel and migration
Environmental	Ecosystem goods	Habitat
	and services	Information
		Production
		Regulation

Continued on next page

Table 5.1 (Continued)

Level/nature	General determinants	Detailed determinants
Proximal level		
Institutional	Health services	Provision and access
Economic	—	—
Sociocultural	Lifestyle	Food consumption patterns
		Alcohol and tobacco use
		Drug abuse
		Unsafe sexual behavior
		Physical activity
		Lifestyle-related endogenous factors (blood pressure, obesity, cholesterol levels)
		Stress coping
		Child care
	Social Environment	Social support and informal care
		Intended injuries and abuse/violence
Environmental	Food and Water	Sufficient quality
		Sufficient quantity
		Sanitation
	Physical living environment	Quality of the living environment (biotic, physical, and chemical factors)
		Unintended injuries (e.g., disasters, traffic accidents, work-related accidents)

Sources: Huynen, MMTE, P. Martens, and HBM Hilderink (2005a and 2005b).

Conceptual Framework for Globalization and Health

Globalization is increasingly perceived as a comprehensive phenomenon, shaped by and comprising a multitude of factors and events, that is rapidly reshaping society. The globalization process is characterized by a growing intensity, extensity,[2] and velocity of institutional, economic, sociocultural, and ecological interactions, resulting in transborder processes and effects. In order to focus our conceptual framework, however, the following important features of globalization are identified (Huynen et al., 2005b):

- *Global governance structures:* globalization increases the interdependence among nations while reducing nation-states' sovereignty, leading to a need for new global governance structures;
- *Global markets:* globalization is characterized by the worldwide integration of economic infrastructures and the emergence of global markets, and a global trading system;

- *Global communication:* globalization makes the sharing of information and the exchange of experiences around common problems possible and necessary;
- *Global mobility:* globalization is characterized by a major increase in the extensity, intensity, and velocity of movement, and by a wide variety in "types" of mobility. Goods and capital, however, often move more freely than people;
- *Cross-cultural interaction:* globalizing cultural flows result in interactions between global and local cultural elements;
- *Global environmental changes:* global environmental threats to ecosystems include global climate change, loss of biodiversity, global ozone depletion, and the global decline in natural areas.

These features all operate at the contextual level of health determination and influence distal factors such as health(-related) policies, economic development, trade, social interactions, knowledge, and the provision of ecosystem goods and services. In turn, these changes have the potential to affect the proximal determinants of health. Figure 5.1 links the above-mentioned features of the globalization process with the identified health determinants. This conceptual framework provides valuable insights in how to organize the complexity involved in studying the health effects of globalization.

Conceptualizing Globalization and Population Health

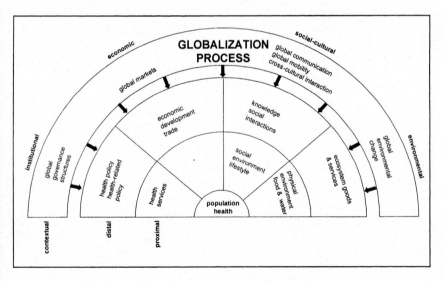

Figure 5.1. Conceptual Framework for Globalization and Population Health (Huynen et al., 2005a; Huynen et al., 2005b)

However, owing to the lack of empirical evidence, the potential pathways from globalization to health are surrounded by uncertainty. (Huynen et al., 2005b) For example, opinions largely differ with regard to the benefits of global markets. "Optimists" state that global markets facilitate economic growth and economic security, which benefits health. (Feachem, 2001) Meanwhile, others worry about possible negative effects. Baum (2001), for example, states that "the current forms of globalization are making the world a safe place for unfettered market liberalism and the consequent growth of inequities . . . posing severe threats to people's health."

The 2005 Human Development Report (UNDP, 2005) argues that one of the prevailing "myths" of economic globalization is that open markets will result in an era of convergence. In fact, and to the contrary, trade liberalization "has done little to slow down the marginalization of certain impoverished regions such as Sub-Saharan Africa."

Linking the Health Effects of Globalization to Human Rights

All states in the world have ratified at least one important human rights treaty such as the International Covenant on Civil and Political Rights (ICCPR), the International Covenant on Economic, Social and Cultural Rights (ICESCR), and the Convention on the Rights of the Child (CRC).

Thus, under international human rights law, states have the legal obligation to respect, protect, and fulfill human rights for all citizens. States also have international and extraterritorial human rights obligations. They have to ensure that their own policies do not impact negatively on the enjoyment of human rights in other countries, and that the activities of the international organizations of which they are a member are human-rights consistent. (Smaller, 2005) Some of the general principles underlying the international human rights framework include universality, participation, transparency, empowerment, accountability, and nondiscrimination.

The Right to Health

The right to health was first recognized in 1946 when the Constitution of the World Health Organization (WHO) stated that "the enjoyment of the highest attainable standard of health is one of the fundamental rights of every human being." (WHO, 1946)

Subsequently, health rights have been recognized in numerous international conventions and declarations (see Table 5.2).

However, the right to health does not imply the right to be healthy, as the complex multi-causality of health makes it impossible to guarantee a specific minimum state of health.

Human rights documents that appear in Table 5.2 can be downloaded from the Treaty Body Database of the United Nations Human Rights Web site at http://www.unhchr.ch/tbs/doc.nsf (last accessed June 16, 2007).

Table 5.2. Examples of "Health" in Human Rights Documents

Human Rights Documents (Year)	Extract Referring to Health
Universal Declaration of Human Rights (UDHR): Article 25 (1948)	*"Everyone has the right to a standard of living adequate for the health and well-being of himself and of his family, including food, clothing, housing and medical care and necessary social services, and the right to security in the event of unemployment, sickness, disability, widowhood, old age or other lack of livelihood in circumstances beyond his control."*
International Covenant on Economic, Social and Cultural Rights (ICECR): Article 12 (1966)	*"The States Parties . . . recognize the right of everyone to the enjoyment of the highest attainable standard of physical and mental health."*
Convention of the Rights of the Child (CRC): Article 24 (1989)	*"States Parties recognize the right of the child to the enjoyment of the highest attainable standard of health. . . . State Parties . . . shall take appropriate measures to . . . combat disease and malnutrition, including within the framework of primary health care, through, inter alia, the application of readily available technology and through the provision of adequate nutritious foods and clean drinking-water, taking into consideration the dangers and risks of environmental pollution."*
United Nations Committee on Economic, Social and Cultural Rights, General Comment on the Right to Highest Attainable Standard to Health (2000)	*"The Committee interprets the right to health . . . as an inclusive right extending not only to timely and appropriate health care but also to the underlying determinants of health, such as access to safe and potable water and adequate sanitation, an adequate supply of safe food, nutrition and housing, healthy occupational and environmental conditions, and access to health-related education and information."*

It is important to note that human rights are indivisible, interdependent, and interrelated. Figure 5.2 illustrates that several important human rights issues mediate the pathways from globalization to health. These include the rights to food, access to safe drinking water and sanitation, access to adequate health care, a safe and healthy environment, work, social security, education, and information relating to health. Consequently, achieving healthy globalization concerns not only the right to health per se, but also the fulfillment of these other important human rights. The next sections discuss how the globalization processes affect access to adequate health care, food security, the access to safe water, and the quality of our environment.

Linking Globalization, Human Rights, and Health

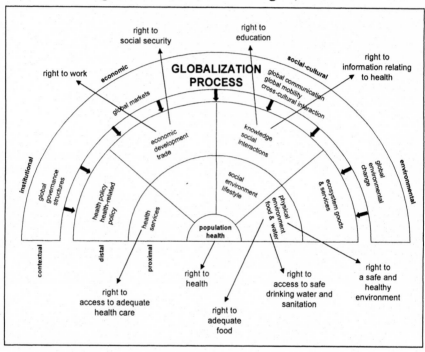

Figure 5.2. The Links among Globalization, Human Rights, and Health

Globalization and the Right to Adequate Health Care

The right to adequate health care is addressed in several important documents like the Universal Declaration of Human Rights (UDHR) (Article 25), the ICESCR (Article 12), the CRC (Article 28), and the United Nations (UN) Committee on ESCR (General Comment 14 on the highest attainable standard of health). The fulfillment of this right is, however, increasingly influenced by globalization processes that affect health care policy, economic development, trade, knowledge, and migration.

Although the WHO aims to assist governments to strengthen health services, government involvement in health care has been decreasing because of persistent challenges from the neo-liberal economic model. This has undermined the financial security of medical institutions which are thus pressured to explore "free-market" alternatives. Some argue that market-based financing will increase health care efficiency, while others are concerned that health will increasingly be perceived as a private good. This, in turn, implies that the marketplace alone should determine the distribution of good health, based on the criterion of whose health is profitable for investment and whose is not. According to Collins (2003), the populations of transitional economies are increasingly left unprotected by centralized universal health-care systems, and some groups are even denied the most basic medical services.

The privatization of, and increasing trade in health services, can obviously have profound implications for the provision of proper health care. Although some argue that global market-based health will improve consumer choice, others point out long-term dangers such as the entrenchment of a two-tier health system, the movement of health professionals from the public sector to the private sector, inequitable access to health care, and the undermining of national health systems. (Hong, 2000) Globalization may also produce a potentially serious "brain-drain" if it fosters the migration of health-care professionals from developing to developed regions.

The spread of technological knowledge resulting from the global diffusion of information has the potential to improve the treatment and prevention of all kinds of illnesses and diseases. However, the illegal trading of drugs and the provision of access to controlled drugs via the Internet constitute potential health risks.

Globalization and the Right to Food

The UDHR states that "everyone has the right to a standard of living adequate for the health and well-being of himself and of his family, including food." Examples of other human rights documents addressing the right to food are the ICESCR (Article 11) and the UN Committee on ESCR (General Comment 12 on the right to food). Additionally, the Universal Declaration on the Eradication of Hunger and Malnutrition (UDEHM) states that "every man, woman and child has the inalienable right to be free from hunger and malnutrition in order to develop fully and maintain their physical and mental faculties." In 1996, the World Food Summit reaffirmed "the right of everyone to have access to safe and nutritious food."

Globalization can affect the fulfillment of the right to food in several ways. Economic liberalization policies are expected to have profound implications both good and bad on food trade and, subsequently, on food security. The FAO argues that free trade could potentially create access to better and cheaper food supplies via food imports and could stimulate more efficient use of the world's resources as well as the production of food in regions that are more suitable to do so. Free trade permits food consumption to grow faster than domestic food production in countries where there are constraints on increasing the latter. Accelerated economic growth can also contribute to food security. (FAO, 1996; FAO, 2003) On the other hand, the FAO acknowledges that increasing dependence on food imports goes hand in hand with a higher vulnerability to shocks arising in global markets, which can affect import capacity and access to food imports. Many food-insecure countries are not able to earn enough with exporting goods to pay for needed food imports. (FAO, 1996; FAO, 2003)

There is an increasing concern about the adverse consequences of food trade resulting from current asymmetric imbalances in the global market (e.g., Lang, 1996; Shiva, 2004; Smaller, 2005; Stevens 2003). At present, the developed countries still impose protectionist trade policies by, for example, subsidizing their domestic agricultural sectors (allowing domestic producers to sell their products more cheaply then their foreign competitors) and imposing relatively high agricultural tariffs on imported goods (making them less competitive with domestic goods). Stevens (2003) argues that the protectionist policies of the OECD countries, together with stricter food standards, are expected to affect Africa's food security. Africa is being "squeezed," as the price of cereal imports could increase, while the volume and price of agricultural exports could decline. Shiva (2004) states that agricultural trade liberalization, facilitated by the policies and rules of the World Trade Organization (WTO), World Bank, and the International Monetary Fund (IMF), has resulted in a declining access to food and an intensification of hunger in India. As a result, food security based on self-sufficiency is a recurring theme among developing-country members of the WTO.

In case of extreme food insecurity and insufficient import capacity, international food aid may be provided in order to supplement the scarce food imports. One can also deal with the mismatch between demand and supply by increasing food production in food-short regions. The globalization process can facilitate the worldwide implementation of better technologies and improved knowledge. At the same time, however, the natural resource base for food production is increasingly threatened by global environmental changes.

Globalization and the Right to Water

The effects of globalization are also raising concerns over the fulfillment of the right of access to water. This right is recognized in the UN Committee on ESCR (General Comment 15 on the right to access to water and in Article 24 of the CRC). On a global scale, there are increasing efforts to set up global guidelines or policies with regard to freshwater. However, none of the international declarations and conference statements requires states actually to meet individuals' water requirements. (Gleick, 2000) The globalization process is accompanied by pressures to privatize the provision of water. Governments and international financial institutions promote privatization, because they believe that it will promote market competition and efficiency. However, others are less optimistic about the effects of privatization. In fact, some cases show that prices and inequalities of access actually increase. (Olivera and Lewis, 2004)

Globalization could also potentially increase water security by facilitating the worldwide implementation of better technologies and improved knowledge. At the same time, the natural resource base is increasingly threatened because, for example, global climate change and deforestation profoundly affect our ecosystems' ability to provide us with sufficient and adequate freshwater.

Note that the virtual trade of water is of increasing importance. The water that is used in the production of a commodity is called the "virtual water" associated with that commodity. Increasing global commodity trade obviously results in an increasing global trade in virtual water. The global volume of crop-related international virtual water flows between nations is estimated at 695 Gm^3 per year for the period 1995-1999 (13 percent of total water use for crop production). (Hoekstra and Hung, 2005)

Globalization and the Right to a Healthy Environment

Both Article 12 of the ICESCR and the UN Committee on ESCR (General Comment 14 on the highest attainable standard of health) address the right to a healthy environment. Additionally, many principles from bioethics, law, and sustainable development are also of direct relevance in discussions about this human right (see except below). Respecting the environmental effects of globalization, the spread of infectious diseases in the living environment is probably one of the most mentioned. Past disease outbreaks have been frequently linked to factors that are related to the globalization process. (Newcomb, 2003) The combination of the movement of goods and people, and profound changes affecting ecosystem goods and services, all contribute to increased risk of disease spread. The outbreak of SARS demonstrates the potential of new infectious diseases to spread rapidly in today's world, increasing the risk of pandemics.

The global diffusion of knowledge and new technologies should improve the surveillance of infectious diseases and monitoring of antibiotic resistance. (Feachem, 2001) Additionally, globalization potentially increases the speed of responses in some cases. Wilson (1995) states that responding to disease emergence requires a global perspective—both conceptually and geographically—as the current global situation favors the outbreak and rapid spread of infectious disease. The policies and actions of the WHO are becoming increasingly important in controlling infectious diseases at a global level. For instance, the WHO played a critical role in controlling SARS by means of global alerts, geographically specific travel advisories, and monitoring.

A Healthy Environment: Integrating Principles from Human Rights,
Bioethics, Law, and Sustainable Development

In 1999-2000, the WHO addressed the issue of healthy indoor air (Mølhave et al., 2000; Mølhave and Kryzanowski, 2001). The working group constructed nine principles relating to the right to breathe healthy indoor air. These principles were derived from not only human rights documents, but also from key articles/principles from bioethics, sustainable development, and law. Although they specifically referred to healthy indoor air, they can easily be reformulated to address the right to a healthy environment in general:

1.   Under the human rights article of the right to health, everyone has the right to a healthy environment.
2.   Under the bioethics principle of respect for autonomy (self-determination), everyone has the right to adequate information about potentially harmful environmental exposures, and to be provided with effective means for controlling at least part of their exposure.
3.   Under the bioethics principle of non-maleficence ("doing no harm"), no agent at a concentration that exposes any person to an unnecessary health risk should be introduced into the environment.
4.   Under the bioethics principle of beneficence ("doing good"), all individuals, groups, and organizations (whether private, public, or governmental), bear responsibility to advocate or work for acceptable environmental quality.
5.   Under the bioethics principle of social justice, the socioeconomic status of persons should have no bearing on their access to a healthy environment, but health status may determine special needs for some groups.
6.   Under the legal principle of accountability, all relevant organizations should establish explicit criteria for evaluating and assessing the impacts of their activities on the health of the population and on the environment.
7.   Under the precautionary principle as articulated at The Earth Summit in 1992, where there is a risk of harmful environmental exposure, the presence of uncertainty shall not be used as a reason for postponing cost-effective measures to prevent such exposure.
8.   Under the legal "polluter pays" principle, the polluter is accountable for any harm to health and/or welfare resulting from unhealthy environmental exposure(s). In addition, the polluter is responsible for mitigation and remediation.
9.   Under the principle of sustainability as conceived at The Earth Summit in 1992, health and environmental concerns cannot be separated, and the provision of a healthy environment should not compromise global or local ecological integrity, or the rights of future generations.

Human Rights Obligations in a Globalizing World

The international human rights framework would seek to oblige governments to promote and protect these human rights, and to strive for a "healthy" globalization. An additional challenge in this globalizing world is the human rights accountability of non-state actors. New actors, such as the WTO and transnational corporations, are gaining importance and power. The policies of the WTO increasingly influence population health. (WHO and WTO, 2002) Fidler (2002) even argues that "from the international legal perspective, the center of power for global health governance has shifted from WHO to the WTO." Opinions differ with regard to whether the WTO agreements provide sufficient possibilities to protect the population from adverse (health) effects associated with free trade. (Singer, 2002) It is a fact that all member countries of the WTO have signed at least one human rights document. So, when negotiating and implementing international trade rules, they should bear in mind their obligation under the international human rights framework. On a cautionary note, Smaller (2005) argues that the World Trade Organization's Agreement on Agriculture promotes the "right to export" over human rights. In addition, protecting citizens against health risks in cases of scientific uncertainty is still difficult, as the WTO is reluctant to accept precautionary trade restrictions. (Mbengue and Thomas, 2005)

Demanding human rights accountability from these new actors will be difficult, but could have profound implications for our future health. The UDHR asserts that "every individual and every organ of society shall promote respect for these rights." The UN Commission on Human Rights (Turk, 1991) has affirmed this broad concept of human rights responsibility in observing that the legal obligations toward the realization of economic, social, and cultural rights affect "national and local governments and agencies, as well as third parties capable of breaching the norms, the international community of States, and intergovernmental organizations and agencies."

In 2003, the UN Sub-commission on the Promotion and Protection of Human Rights adopted the UN Human Rights Norms for Business, recognizing that transnational corporations and other businesses carry responsibilities as well. (UN Committee on Human Rights, 2003) These UN Norms encompass a list of the most important human rights obligations of companies. In addition to setting a standard that business can measure itself against, the UN Norms can be used as an important advocacy tool for non-governmental organizations and as a useful benchmark against which national policies can be judged. Additionally, they provide a comprehensive document that can be referred to by (inter)national tribunals. (ESCR-Net, 2005)

Conclusions

Globalization reflects a historically unprecedented situation that challenges scientists, policy-makers, and other stakeholders worldwide. The conceptual framework presented here provides insights into how to organize the complexity involved in studying the health effects resulting from globalization. However, opinions about the (future) health effects of globalization are still polarized. (Lee, 2001; Huynen et al., 2005b)

The current debate about the pros and cons of globalization must recognize that the forces of globalization should be subject to moral and ethical considerations, and should respect international legal standards and principles. We can use human rights to provide a framework for discussion and international cooperation. A rights-based approach transforms needs into rights, challenges global inequalities in health, draws attention to the most vulnerable members of society, and stresses the interrelationship and interdependence of health with other human rights. In addition, approaching globalization from a rights perspective informs people of their legal rights and entitlements, and empowers them to achieve those rights and prevent future violations. A crucial feature of a rights-based approach is the notion of accountability, which in practice requires the development of adequate laws, policies, institutions, and administrative procedures and practices.

If we want to achieve a sustainable healthy globalization, the international community must stress the human rights obligations and responsibilities of both state and non-state actors. A rights-based approach toward a "healthy" globalization integrates the international human rights norms and principles into the plans, policies, and processes of globalization. It can help to engage in a true debate on a sustainable form of globalization, with health and well-being at the core of this discussion.

Acknowledgments

This work was financially supported by the Netherlands Environmental Assessment Agency (MNP).

Notes

1. Partly based on Huynen et al. (2005a and 2005b).
2. Extensity refers to a widening (geographical) reach.

References

Human rights documents can be downloaded from the Treaty Body Database of the United Nations Human Rights Web site at www.unhchr.ch (24 May 2007).

Baum, Fran. "Health, Equity, Justice and Globalisation: Some Lessons from the People's Health Assembly." *J. Epidemiol. Community Health* 55 (2001): 613–616.
Collins, Téa. "Globalization, Global Health and Access to Health Care." *International J. of Health Planning and Management* 18 (2003): 97–104.
ESCR-Net. *UN Human Rights Norms for Business: Briefing Kit.* New York: The International Network for Economic, Social and Cultural Rights, 2005.
FAO. "Food and International Trade. The World Food Summit Technical Background Document No. 12." Rome: Food and Agricultural Organisation of the United Nations, 1996.
———. "Trade Reforms and Food Security: Conceptualizing the Linkages." Rome: Food and Agricultural Organisation of the United Nations, 2003.

Feachem, Richard GA. "Globalisation Is Good for Your Health, Mostly." *BMJ* 323 (2001): 504–6.

Fidler, David. "Global Health Governance: Overview of the Role of International Law in Protecting and Promoting Global Public Health. Discussion Paper No. 3." London: Centre on Global Change and Health, London School of Hygiene and Tropical Medicine, 2002.

Gleick, Peter H. *The World's Water 2000–2001: The Biennial Report on Freshwater Resources*. Washington, DC: Island Press, 2000.

Hoekstra, Arjen Y., and Pham Q. Hung. "Globalisation of Water Resources: International Virtual Water Flows in Relation to Crop Trade." *Global Environmental Change* 15, (2005): 45–56.

Hong, Evelyne. "Globalisation and the Impact on Health: A Third World View." Issue paper prepared for The Peoples' Assembly, December 4–8, 2000, Savar Bangladesh. 2000.

Huynen, Maud MTE, and Pim Martens. *Future Health: The Health Dimension in Global Scenarios*. Maastricht: ICIS, 2002.

Huynen, Maud MTE, Pim Martens, and Henk BM Hilderink. *The Health Impacts of Globalisation: A Conceptual Framework*. Bilthoven: Netherlands Environmental Assessment Agency (MNP-RIVM), 2005a.

———. "The Health Impacts of Globalisation: A Conceptual Framework." *Globalization and Health* 1, (2005b): article number 14 (12 pages).

Lang, Tim. "Food Security: Does It Conflict with Globalisation?" *Development* 4, (1996): 45–50.

Lee, Kelley. "Dialogue of the Deaf? The Health Impact of Globalisation." *J. of Epidemiol. Community Health* 55 (2001): 619.

———. *Globalization and Health: An Introduction*. New York: Palgrave Macmillan, 2003.

Martens, Pim, Anthony J. McMichael, and Jonathan Patz. "Globalisation, Environmental Change and Health." *Global Change and Human Health* 1 (2000): 4–8.

Mbengue, Makane M., and Urs P. Thomas. "The Precautionary Principle: Torn between Biodiversity, Environment-Related Food Safety and the WTO." *Int. J. Global Environmental Issues* 5 (2005): 36–53.

Mølhave, Lars, Nadia Boschi, Michal Krzyzanowski, Kjell Aas, Jan V. Bakke, et al. "The Right to Healthy Indoor Air." Report of a WHO Meeting. European Health 21 targets 10, 13. World Health Organization Regional Office for Europe, 2000.

Mølhave, Lars, and Michal Krzyzanowski. "The Right to Healthy Indoor Air." Pp. 65–66 in *Proceedings of International Symposium on Current Status of Indoor Air Pollution by Organic Compounds and Countermeasures for Healthy Housing*, eds. Shuozo Murakami, Yukio Yanagisawa, Satoshi Ishikawa, and John Spengler. Tokyo: Architectural Institute of Japan, 2001.

Newcomb, James. *Biology and Borders: SARS and the New Economics of Bio-security*. Cambridge: Bio Economic Research Associates, 2003.

Olivera, Oscar, and Tom Lewis. *Cochabamba! Water War in Bolivia*. Cambridge: South End Press, 2004.

Shiva, Vandana. "The Future of Food: Countering Globalization and Recolonisation of Indian Agriculture." *Futures* 36 (2004): 715–32.

Singer, Peter. *One World*. New Haven: Yale University Press, 2002.

Smaller, Carin. *Planting the Rights Seed: A Human Rights Perspective on Agricultural Trade and the WTO*. Geneva: 3D Publications and Institute for Agriculture and Trade Policy (IATP), 2005.

Stevens, Christopher. "Food Trade and Food Policy in Sub-Saharan Africa: Old Myths and New Challenges." *Development Policy Review* 21 (2003): 669–81.

Turk, Danilo. "Realization of Economic, Social and Cultural Rights. Second Progress Report of the Special Rapporteur." UN Doc. E/CN.4/Sub.2/1991/17. United Nations Commission on Human Rights, 1991.

UN Committee on Human Rights. "Norms on the Responsibilities of Transnational Corporations and Other Business Enterprises with Regard to Human Rights." United Nations Committee on Human Rights, Sub-Commission on the Promotion and Protection of Human Rights. E/CN.4/Sub.2/2003/12/Rev.2, 2003.

UNDP. *Human Development Report 2005: International Cooperation at a Crossroads: Aid, Trade and Security in an Unequal World.* New York: United Nations Development Programme, 2005.

WHO. *The World Health Report 2002: Reducing Risks, Promoting Healthy Life.* Geneva: World Health Organization, 2002.

———. World Health Organization Constitution. Geneva: World Health Organization, 1946.

WHO and WTO. *WTO Agreements and Public Health.* Geneva: World Health Organization and the World Bank, 2002.

Wilson, Mary E. "Travel and the Emergence of Infectious Diseases." *Emerging Infectious Diseases* 1 (1995): 39–46.

Chapter 6

Toward Sustainability with Justice: Are Human Nature and History on Side?

William E. Rees, Ph.D. (Population Ecology)
University of British Columbia
School of Community and Regional Planning
Vancouver, British Columbia, Canada

Contact Information: UBC/SCARP, 6333 Memorial Road, Vancouver, B.C. V6T 1Z2 CANADA
Phone: +1 604 822-2937; Fax: +1 604 822-3787; Email: wrees@interchange.ubc.ca

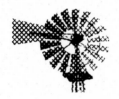

Summary

Techno-industrial society is inherently unsustainable with the root causes being both biological and cultural. Individual and group behaviors that were adaptive in prehistory have become maladaptive today.

Despite forty years of organized environmentalism, two world summits on environment and development, repeated warnings by scientists, and the emergence of "sustainable development" as a mainstream mantra, global society continues its drive toward ecological disaster and geopolitical chaos. The daily news is spiked with stories of accelerating climate change and its immediate threats to, among others, fisheries, agriculture, and coastal cities, while biodiversity losses, land degradation, and tropical deforestation irreversibly disrupt natural life-support functions. Meanwhile, despite unprecedented economic growth and wealth creation, almost a third of humanity still lives in material poverty, and the income gap, both between and within countries, is widening.

The world presently has the wealth, human capital, and natural resources to execute a smooth transition to global sustainability out of mutual self-interest, yet we do not act. Further delay may result in critical resource shortages that shift the survival advantage to those nations that ultimately choose to make war in their *exclusive* self-interest.

To avoid the descent into chaos, the world community must acknowledge the true (human) nature of our collective dilemma and act consciously to override the innate sociobehavioral predispositions that block collective action. Only then will we be able to develop the international institutions, treaties, and other legal instruments necessary to reduce our ecological footprint, avoid shortages, and share the global commons more equitably.

Context: The Present State of (Un)Sustainability

There is general scientific consensus that the present global development path is grossly unsustainable on both ecological and socioeconomic grounds. In 1992 the Union of Concerned Scientists issued the following assessment of the risk posed by prevailing trends to global civilization:

> We the undersigned, senior members of the world's scientific community, hereby warn all humanity of what lies ahead. A great change in our stewardship of the earth and the life on it is required if vast human misery is to be avoided and our global home on this planet is not to be irretrievably mutilated. (UCS, 1992)

More than a decade later, the Millennium Ecosystem Assessment—the MEA is the most comprehensive sustainability assessment ever undertaken—summarized its findings this way:

> At the heart of this assessment is a stark warning. Human activity is putting such a strain on the natural functions of the Earth that the ability of the planet's ecosystems to sustain future generations can no longer be taken for granted. (MEA, 2005)

The MEA's "stark warning" thus is testament to a gloomy fact. Despite forty years of intense debate on the so-called environmental crisis and almost two decades since the World Commission on Environment and Development (WCED)[1] popularized the concept of "sustainable development," little has been achieved in the international and national policy arenas that effectively addresses the immediate cause of our ecological problems—excessive energy and material consumption and the attendant accumulation of noxious wastes. To the contrary, while the governing elites of the market democracies have all joined in singing the sustainability chorus, they reserve their heartiest voices for the main verse that lauds a vigorously growing global economy. Even the WCED argued that while future expansion would have to be qualitatively different from prevailing forms of growth, "a five- to tenfold increase in world industrial output can be anticipated before the population stabilizes [at about twice 1987 levels] sometime in the [twenty-first] century."(WCED, 1987)

This seeming explosion would merely extend existing trends. During the twentieth century:

- The human population almost quadrupled to 6.4 billion.
- Industrial production exploded more than forty-fold.
- Energy use increased sixteen-fold (and CO_2 emissions by seventeen-fold).
- Fish catches expanded by a factor of thirty-five (and 90 percent of the targeted biomass has been removed from the sea).
- Water use increased nine times.

By the beginning of the present century, the scale of human activities had approached the scale of natural processes—industrial activities now fix more atmospheric nitrogen and inject it into terrestrial ecosystems than do all natural processes combined; humans have already directly transformed half of the land-area of Earth; people now use more than half of the planet's accessible freshwater. (Data from Vitousek et al., 1997; Lubchenco, 1998; McNeill, 2000; Myers and Worm, 2003) Even earth scientists agree that human activity has become the most significant geological force altering the face of the planet and the erosive pace is accelerating. *Homo sapiens* var. *economicus* has become a renegade species whose activities threaten its own long-term security by wreaking havoc on the natural world.

And we are not doing much better in our efforts to improve the strictly human world. The primary social goal of development-through-globalization—and the first of United Nations' so-called Millennium Development Goals—is to eliminate poverty and human misery through global economic growth. However, according to the United Nations' 2005 Human Development Report (UNDP, 2005), progress toward satisfying the Millennium Development Goals (MDGs) is dismal.[2] More than one billion people still live on less than one dollar a day and another 1.5 billion people subsist on one to two dollars a day. As a consequence, 850 million people remain calorically malnourished and as many as 3.5 billion suffer from various nutrient deficiencies. "The majority of countries fall behind most of the goals, in some key areas human development is faltering, and already deep inequalities are widening." (Martens, 2005)

Indeed, a major problem is that the benefits of the global economic machine remain grossly maldistributed. The chronically impoverished 20 percent of the world's people survive on just 1.5 percent of world income, while the richest 10 percent take home 54 percent. The richest 500 people in the world enjoy a combined income greater than that of the poorest 416 million and the gap is ever-widening. The average American, who was thirty-eight times richer than the average Tanzanian in 1990, is sixty-one times richer today!

Income disparity is increasing not only between rich and poor countries, but also within nations, including some of the wealthiest. In the United States the gap between the top 20 percent and the bottom 20 percent in 1960 was thirty-fold. Now it is seventy-five to one. Thirty years ago the average annual compensation of the top one hundred chief executives in the country was thirty times the pay of the average worker; today it is one thousand times greater. (Moyers, 2006)

Tellingly, what most affects subjective well-being in the developed world is relative, not absolute, income. Among high-income countries it is not the richest societies that have the best individual and population health, but rather those with the smallest income differences between rich and poor. (Wilkinson, 1996) In other words, the prevailing global development paradigm is driving socioeconomic indicators in the wrong direction.

Purpose: Considering Prospects for Sustainability with Justice

Technical data suggest that sustainability requires an absolute 50 percent reduction in the consumption of energy and material by the global economy over the next few decades. However, because the wealthiest 20 percent of humankind consumes in excess of 80 percent of natural resources, and Earth is already beyond carrying capacity, justice demands that the rich vacate some "environmental space" to make room for the poor. This means that "the richer countries need to dematerialize their technical basis of wealth—or, increase the resource productivity—by at least a factor of ten on the average." (Schmidt-Bleek, 2000) The overall purpose of this chapter is to assess prospects for achieving sustainability with justice in the twenty-first century.

The Human Nature of (Un)Sustainability

H. Sapiens prides itself in being the best evidence for intelligent life on Earth. Our species is uniquely self-aware, capable of great works of philosophy and art, and our modern science is making progress toward abolishing ignorance and superstition and in gaining mastery over the physical world. Why, then, are we allowing the accelerating degradation of our planetary home and why, in this age of unprecedented wealth, are so many members of the human family forced to live in poverty?

Most attempts to answer these questions assume that our problems are temporary, that they can be solved by more environmentally benign technologies, higher resource productivity, greater economic efficiency, and more liberal trading relationships (open world markets). However, the majority of such mainstream approaches to sustainability ignore the evidence that these measures have actually exacerbated both ecological decay and material inequality over the past half-century.

To explain the global predicament, we suggest that at least some of the roots of un-sustainability are much deeper than is usually assumed; we cannot understand the problem, let alone derive valid solutions, until these roots have been exposed. Furthermore, we suggest that the distal causes of human ecological dysfunction and gross social inequity are essentially beneath perception. Our present unsustainable state is the product of individual and group behavior derived, in part, from unconscious genetic predispositions. The evidence suggests that much of the relevant behavior is "bipolar." It is the expression of the uneasy interplay between higher-order conscious activities of the cerebral cortex (e.g., the capacity for rational thought and logical process), and lower order, often unconscious, propensities of the limbic system and reptilian brain stem (e.g., the quest for social status and dominance, jealousy, aggression and violence when provoked, the tendency to tribalism).

Now, consider the unassailable fact that *H. Sapiens*, like all other species, is a product of evolution (natural selection). Consider too that one factor distinguishing humans from other organisms is that the direction of human evolution is determined both by (what appear to be) sociocultural factors and by purely innate biological factors. From this, it is only a short step to accepting that both genetic mutations and cultural missteps are subject to natural selection—both disadvantageous biological variants (bad genes) and maladaptive cultural traits (bad memes) can be "selected out" by a changing environment. It follows that societies operating from a cultural worldview or economic paradigm based on beliefs, values, and assumptions that conflict with ecological reality are societies at risk.

Within this framework, the central premise of our argument is that techno-industrial society is presently *inherently unsustainable* and that this state is an *inevitable emergent property* of the systemic interaction between modern society and the ecosphere. (Rees, 2002) If the world community cannot come to agreement on ways to reconfigure humankind-nature interactions so that humanity can live more equitably within Earth's carrying capacity, global society is likely to be "selected out" by a rapidly changing ecosphere.

The Biological Driver

Let's face it: *Homo economicus* is one hell of an overachiever. He has invaded more than three-quarters of the globe's surface and monopolized nearly half of all plant life to help make dinner. He has netted most of the ocean's fish and will soon eat his way through the world's last great apes. For good measure, he has fouled most of the world's rivers. And his gluttonous appetites have started a wave of extinctions that could trigger the demise of 25 percent of the world's creatures within fifty years. The more godlike he becomes the less godly *Homo economicus* behaves. (Nikiforuk, 2006)

The main biological factor at cause of the (un)sustainability crisis is a natural predisposition that humans share with all other species. Unless constrained by negative feedback (e.g., resource shortages, disease, social conflicts, or other growth-induced factors) populations tend to expand to fill all suitable habitats and to use all the resources prevailing technology makes available to them.

The propensity to reproduce and expand geographic range is, of course, necessary for the survival of any species. Organisms compete for available resources and space and have developed various strategies that ensure the survival of adequate numbers of offspring, thus maintaining their genes in the pool. Humans are what ecologists refer to as "K" strategists. "K" strategists produce few offspring but have relatively high survival rates. They tend to be large, long-lived, and have adapted to compete near the carrying capacities ("K") of their habitats. (The Reverend Malthus' famous essay on population actually recognized humanity's archetypal "K"-strategic behavior of constantly pressing the limits of food availability.)

H. sapiens has several competitive advantages over other K-strategists that have enabled modern humans, to invade all the ecosystems on Earth and gain access to ever more resources. In particular, our capacity for complex language, especially written language, has ensured that our technological competence to exploit nature is cumulative. Today, ecosystems are no match for modern harvesting and other extractive technologies powered by abundant, cheap fossil energy. In effect, our modern techno-industrial mind-set and growth-based economic paradigm reinforce humanity's natural expansionist tendencies (see following section).

As a result, humans have become an "outlier" among ecologically similar species. For example, humanity's consumption of biomass (i.e., exploitation of ecosystems) is almost one hundred times higher than the highest level of biomass appropriation by ninety-six other mammals. (Fowler and Hobbs, 2003) The result? "Although there is considerable variation in detail, there is remarkable consistency in the history of resource exploitation: resources are inevitably overexploited, often to the point of collapse or extinction." (Ludwig, Hilborn, and Walters, 1993) What further proof do we need of humanity's "over-achievement" as a consumer organism!

The Human Ecological Footprint

The equity and geopolitical implications of insatiable human demand are revealed by ecological footprint analysis (EFA). We define the ecological footprint of any specified population as the area of productive land and water ecosystems required, on a continuous basis, to produce the resources that the population consumes, and to assimilate the wastes that it produces. (Rees, 2001; Wackernagel and Rees, 1996) EFA reveals, *first*, that the citizens of many high-density consumer economies have ecofootprints of four to almost ten hectares per capita compared to as little as half a hectare in the poorest countries. Ecofootprint data thus dramatically reflect the growing income disparity between rich and poor.

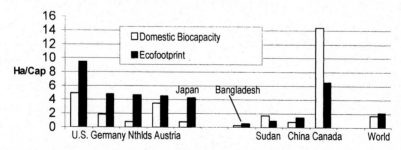

Figure 6.1. Ecological Footprints and Biocapacities of Selected Countries Compared to World Averages

Second, the global average ecofootprint is 2.2 ha/capita while there are only 1.8 ha/cap of available biocapacity on Earth. Thus, the citizens of wealthy market economies like the U.S., Canada, most Western European countries, and Japan appropriate two to five times their equitable share of the planet's productive land/water. Low-income countries like Bangladesh and Sudan—and even burgeoning China—use only a fraction of their equitable population-based allocation.

Third, many wealthy nations, even the most technologically advanced and economically efficient, have national ecofootprints up to several-times larger than their domestic productive areas. Such countries are running large "ecological deficits" with the rest of the world. (Figure 6.1; data from WWF, 2004) Absent trade, many such societies would have long ago stabilized or collapsed. International commerce thus appears to increase local carrying capacity by shuffling resources around, but in the process puts the entire human family at risk as we deplete nature and hit global limits simultaneously. Indeed, with an average ecofootprint of 2.2 ha/cap and only 1.8 ha/cap of available biocapacity, the human enterprise has already overshot global carrying capacity by about 22 percent. (Figure 6.1)

Fourth is an obvious ecological corollary—it is not biophysically possible for all countries to run an ecodeficit. The less-developed countries cannot sustainably follow the developed world's path to material extravagance. To bring the present world population up to North American material standards with prevailing technology would require four additional Earth-like planets!

In sum, ecofootprinting shows graphically that the expanding global economy is on a collision course with ecological sustainability. Geopolitical sustainability too—in a competitive world of climate change and increasing resource shortages, rising material expectations everywhere may well become the greatest threat to human security.

Sociocultural Reinforcement: On Myth and Self-Delusion

A major cultural factor in global unsustainability resides in the fact that techno-industrial society is as unconsciously myth-bound as any more "primitive" pre-industrial culture.[3] The modern mind has difficulty in grasping this paradox only because we have learned to equate myth with falsehood, superstition, and the unscientific beliefs of earlier peoples. But this belies a sterile dismissive view of the role of myth. Colin Grant describes myths not as unfounded superstitions but as "comprehensive visions that give shape and direction to life." He argues that society not only operates from a complex of contemporary myths, but that "the function of our myths might not be as different from that of those ancient stories as we might be inclined to think." (Grant, 1998) One such function is to shield society from unpleasant realities.

I Consume, therefore I Am

Given the ubiquity of mythic visions, it would be surprising if they did *not* play some role in the unsustainability conundrum. In fact, myth commands the world stage like a colossus even as the stage crumbles beneath our feet. On the highest level, most of the world shares a common development myth of uncommon destructive power. Almost all national governments and mainstream international agencies are in the thrall of a neo-liberal economic orthodoxy that unites them in a vision of global development and poverty alleviation centered on unlimited economic expansion fueled by open markets, technological efficiency, and more liberalized trade.

This expansionist myth has been giving "shape and direction" to both political and social life in both developed and developing countries all over the world for the past forty years. (Rees, 2002)

Underpinning the perpetual growth myth is a deliberate consumption myth—astonishingly our reckless throw-away society is actually a purposeful social construct. Following World War II, North America was "blessed" with great industrial overcapacity (war-time factories) and large numbers of under-employed workers (returning soldiers). Meanwhile, the general population, having endured the depression and wartime rationing, was used to living modestly. To take advantage of available labor and break people of their habit of "under-consuming," American industry organized to legitimize profligate consumption, to make of it a spiritual activity. Retail analyst Victor Lebow summarized the rationale as follows:

> Our enormously productive economy demands that we make consumption our way of life, that we convert the buying and use of goods into rituals, that we seek our spiritual satisfaction and our ego satisfaction in consumption. We need things consumed, burned up, worn out, replaced and discarded at an ever-increasing rate. (Lebow, 1955)

One legacy today is a pumped-up, multibillion dollar global advertising sector, a whole industry dedicated to making "consumers" unhappy with whatever they already have, no matter that it is practically new and perfectly functional. Indeed, the consumer myth appeals to so many human traits (e.g., avarice, competitiveness, lust, jealousy, insecurity) and preys so easily upon the spiritual void in peoples' lives left by the "death of God" that it has rapidly colonized the entire world, abetted by the spread of market capitalism and facilitated by sequential waves of emerging communication technologies from radio and television to the Internet. Result: the world consumed as many goods and services between 1950 (when commercial TV was launched) and the mid-1990s as had all previous generations combined. (Motvalli, 1996)

Today, "Consumption, along with the technology that produces it and the advertising that expresses it . . . has become the meaning of life, the chief sacred, the point of morality, the criterion of existence, the mystery before which one bows." (Ellul, 1975) It is no small irony that the same consumption that has lately become "the meaning of life" has now also emerged as the greatest hazard to life.

Discussion: On Prospects for a Just Sustainability

[For humanity to survive the sustainability crisis] we must rely on highly-evolved genetically-based biological mechanisms, as well as on supra-instinctual survival strategies that have developed in society, are transmitted by culture, and require for their application, consciousness, reasoned deliberation and willpower. (A. Damasio, 1994)

We can summarize the sustainability dilemma this way. The world is ecologically full, but grossly inequitable. Contrary to conventional wisdom, we cannot safely grow our way to sustainability, but must instead come to share the world's economic and ecological output more justly. Humanity has arrived at this discomforting juncture through unconscious expansionist tendencies reinforced by the social construction of both a perpetual growth myth and an increasingly global consumer myth. Those who would guide humanity to sustainability are therefore pitted against formidable biological *and* cultural imperatives. In the early years of the twenty-first century, nature and nurture have converged in a dangerous liaison that has rendered modern *H. Sapiens* fundamentally unsustainable.[4]

On the positive side, the world presently has enormous wealth (inequitably distributed as it might be) and we are not yet experiencing serious resource shortages. There will never be a better time to begin the transition to a sustainable, low-throughput steady-state society—it should still be possible to achieve ecological sustainability while maintaining reasonable average living standards and improving the well-being of the majority of humankind. In the best of all possible worlds, therefore, love of nature (biophilia), compassion for the less-privileged members of the human family, and mutual self-interest would be reasons enough for the global community to act assuredly now.

But, this is not the best of all possible worlds. Biophilia has never been a significant political force and we humans are not notably moved by compassion for members of other tribes. (We could cure poverty today, but we don't.) Even mutual self-interest holds no ground if there are risks, and when exclusive self-interest promises a bigger pay-off. As Lynton Caldwell (1990) observes,

The prospect of worldwide cooperation to forestall a disaster . . . seems far less likely where deeply entrenched economic and political interests are involved. . . . The cooperative task would require behavior that humans find most difficult: collective self-discipline in a common effort.

The manufactured values churned out by the contemporary myth machine further confound prospects for a just sustainability. Once entrenched, comfortable myths shield our collective awareness from the painful barbs of contrary data. Our best science may tell us that the consumer society is on a self-destructive tack, but we successfully deflect the evidence by repeating in unison the mantra of perpetual growth. As Jensen (2000) observes: "For us to maintain our way of living, we must . . . tell lies to each other, and especially to ourselves." On the dark side of myth, our shared illusions converge on deep denial.

The mythed-out citizens of modern consumer democracies are simply not prepared to accept significant changes to the economy, particularly if they perceive such changes as requiring sacrifice and diminished material prospects for themselves or their children. Mainstream discussions of sustainability therefore start from the paradoxical assumption that economic growth, materialistic lifestyles, and rising consumption are permanent fixtures of the geopolitical landscape. In the words of British Deputy Prime Minister, John Prescott:

> Modern environmentalism recognises that . . . an efficient, clean economy will mean *more, not less economic growth and prosperity.* . . . Treating the environment with respect will not impede economic progress, it will help identify areas of inefficiency and waste and so unleash whole new forces of innovation. (Prescott, 2003, emphasis added)

In this political climate, Barry (2006) argues that critiquing consumption and materialism on ecological or ethical grounds "is a strategic distraction from aligning a vision for a more sustainable economy and society with the aspirations of people for a better life."

The problem is that not critiquing the consumer myth may prove to be a *tragic* distraction. To the extent that it blinds society both to the scale and causes of our sustainability conundrum, the perpetual growth paradigm could prove fatal to civilization itself. Continuing population and consumption growth will almost certainly accelerate climate change and resource shortages, particularly of energy, water, and food. Resource scarcity will, in turn, increase the probability of violent conflict, particularly if there is already gross social inequity and hoarding by the rich (precisely the conditions being induced by contemporary globalization).

This calls to account yet another innate human behavioral trait—the tendency to tribal affiliation and loyalty. "There is something deep in religious [or linguistic, or nationalist, or ideological or tribal . . .] belief that divides people and amplifies societal conflict," (Wilson, 2005) and nothing has more potential to amplify inter-group tensions than existing inequity aggravated by resource scarcity and economic decline. Violent conflict is virtually certain to break out among self-identifying groups, both between and within nations, if resource scarcity intensifies or some groups appear to be systematically privileged by prevailing social and political institutions (as they increasingly are today). In most such circumstances any appeal to global or national collective interests will almost certainly give way to the defense of strictly tribal or individual interests.

Let us acknowledge, too, that in times of scarcity, violent unilateral action may well seem to be the most (coldly) rational strategy. It is certainly the most appropriate Darwinian survival strategy—those individuals, tribes, or nations that gain what they need by force enhance their own prospects for survival.

But, there is a problem with strict Darwinian logic in the modern era. A strategy that might have been adaptive in human prehistory has become fatally maladaptive in the nuclear age. An all-out nuclear conflagration among self-interested tribes over a declining resource base will leave no winners and few survivors.

This is the ultimate reason for the world community to acknowledge the true (human) nature of our collective dilemma. We must assert our capacity for "consciousness, reasoned deliberation, and willpower," both to override humanity's expansionist tendencies, and to check potentially dangerous tribal passions. Only then can we hope to develop the "supranational survival strategies" (i.e., the international institutions, treaties, and other legal instruments) required to reduce the human ecological footprint and share the global commons more equitably within the means of nature. In effect, we must engage in a global dialogue to re-write the "myths we live by" and articulate the necessary conditions for sustainability. The most likely alternative is a world embroiled in violent confrontation and rapid decline.

Epilogue: Is Societal Collapse Possible?

To those mesmerized by the myth of abundance and rising expectations, the idea that nation-states and even global society may be on the verge of resource shortages, political chaos, and even collapse may seem ludicrous. Nevertheless, as Tainter (1995) observed, "what is perhaps most intriguing in the evolution of human societies is the regularity with which the pattern of increasing complexity is interrupted by collapse" and there is nothing about contemporary circumstances to suggest that modern societies are less vulnerable than ancient ones. To the contrary, the same ecological and sociocultural problems plaguing us today played a central role in the implosion of many earlier human societies from the subtropical paradise of Easter Island to the sub-Arctic outpost of the Greenland Norse. (Diamond, 2005)

Diamond (2005) also found that in exceptional circumstances, societies are able to draw back from the abyss. These resilient societies are nimble societies, capable of long-term thinking and of abandoning deeply entrenched, but ultimately destructive core values and beliefs. This, in turn, would seem to require a well-informed public, inspired leadership, and the political will to take decisions against the established order. In light of these preconditions, we leave it to the reader to ponder whether contemporary society is actually on the road to sustainability with justice.

Acknowledgments

This project is funded in part by a grant from the University of British Columbia's Social Sciences Hampton Fund.

Notes

1. The WCED was also known as "the Brundtland Commission." Its landmark report, *Our Common Future* (WCED, 1987) was the popular background document for the 1992 Rio Summit on Environment and Development.
2. The eight MDGs are: to eradicate extreme poverty and hunger; to achieve universal primary education; to promote gender equality and empower women; to reduce child mortality; to improve maternal health; to combat HIV/AIDS, malaria, and other diseases; to ensure environmental sustainability; to develop a Global Partnership for Development.
3. Worldviews, paradigms, ideologies all have the qualities of myth as described by Grant (1998).
4. As ever, the line between nature and nurture is somewhat blurred. Although there are potentially any numbers of differing cultural myths (nurture), the propensity for myth-making itself is apparently innate (nature).

References

Barry, John. "Towards a Concrete Utopian Model of Green Political Economy: From Economic Growth and Ecological Modernisation to Economic Security." *Post-Autistic Economics Review*, no. 36 (24 Feb. 2006): 2–20. http://www.paecon.net/PAEReview/issue36/Barry36.htm (23 May 2007).

Caldwell, Lynton K. *Between Two Worlds: Science, the Environmental Movement and Policy Choice*. Cambridge, UK: Cambridge University Press, 1990.

Damasio, Antonio. *Descartes' Error: Emotion, Reason and the Human Brain*. New York: Avon Books, 1994.

Diamond, Jared. *Collapse: How Societies Choose to Fail or Succeed*. Viking, 2005

Ellul, Jacques. *The New Demons*. Translated by C. E. Hopkin. New York: Seabury Press (A Crossroad Book), 1975.

Fowler, Charles W., and Larry Hobbs. "Is humanity sustainable?" *Proceedings of the Royal Society of London, Series B: Biological Sciences* 270 (2003): 2579–83.

Grant, Colin. *Myths We Live By*. Ottawa: University of Ottawa Press, 1998.

Jensen, Derrick. *A Language Older than Words*. New York: Context Books, 2000.

Lebow, Victor. *The Journal of Retailing*. (Spring 1955): 7.

Lubchenco, Jane. "Entering the Century of the Environment: A New Social Contract for Science." *Science* 297 (1998): 491–97.

Ludwig, Don, Ray Hilborn, and Carl Walters. "Uncertainty, Resource Exploitation, and Conservation: Lessons from History." *Science* 260 (1993): 17, 36.

Martens, Jens. *A Compendium of Inequality: The Human Development Report 2005*. Berlin: Global Policy Forum (FES), 2005.

McNeill, John R. *Something New under the Sun: An Environmental History of the Twentieth-Century World*. New York: W. W. Norton, 2000.

MEA. "Living Beyond Our Means: Natural Assets and Human Well-Being" (Statement from the Board). *Millennium Ecosystem Assessment*, 2005. http://www.millenniumassessment.org/documents/document.429.aspx.pdf (28 May 2007)

Motvalli, Jim. "Enough!" *E Magazine* (Apr. 1996): 28–35.

Moyers, Bill. "Restoring the Public Trust." TomPaine.com. 24 Feb. 2006. http://www.tompaine.com/articles/2006/02/24/restoring_the_public_trust.php   (8   Jun. 2007).

Myers, Ransom A., and Boris Worm. "Rapid Worldwide Depletion of Predatory Fish Communities." *Nature* 423 (2003): 280–83.

Nikiforuk, Andrew. "At War with Our Planet," review of *The Weather Makers: How We Are Changing the Climate and What it Means for Life on Earth* by Tim Flannery (Harper Collins, 2006). *The Globe and Mail* (Section D), 4 Mar. 2006.

Prescott, John. "Environmental Modernisation." Speech to Fabian Society/SERA Conference, 2003.

Rees, William E. "Ecological Footprint, Concept of." Pp. 229–44 in *Encyclopedia of Biodiversity*, edited by Simon Levin, vol. 2. San Diego: Academic Press, 2001.

———. "Globalization and Sustainability: Conflict or Convergence?" *Bulletin of Science, Technology and Society* 2, no. 4 (2002): 249–68.

Schmidt-Bleek Friedrich. "Factor 10 Manifesto." 20 Jan. 2000. http://www.factor10-institute.org/pdf/F10Manif.pdf (23 May 2007).

Tainter, Joseph. "Sustainability of Complex Societies." *Futures* 27 (1995): 397–404.

UCS. "World Scientists' Warning to Humanity (1992)." Union of Concerned Scientists. http://www.ucsusa.org/ucs/about/1992-world-scientists-warning-to-humanity.html (8 Jun. 2007).

UNDP. *Human Development Report 2005. International Cooperation at a Crossroads— Aid, Trade and Security in an Unequal World.* New York: United Nations Development Programme. 2005. http://hdr.undp.org/reports/global/2005/ (28 May 2007).

Vitousek, Peter M., Harold A. Mooney, Jane Lubchenco, and Jerry M. Melillo. "Human Domination of Earth's Ecosystems." *Science* 277 (1997): 494–99.

Wackernagel, Mathis and William E. Rees. *Our Ecological Footprint: Reducing Human Impact on the Earth.* Gabriola Island, BC: New Society Publishers, 1996.

WCED. *Our Common Future.* Oxford: Oxford University Press (for the UN World Commission on Economy and Environment), 1987.

Wilkinson, Richard G. *Unhealthy Societies: The Afflictions of Inequality.* London and New York: Routledge, 1996.

Wilson, Edward O. "Intelligent Evolution." Forum, *Harvard Magazine* (Nov.–Dec. 2005). http://www.harvard-magazine.com/on-line/110518.html (23 May 2007).

WWF. *Living Planet Report 2004.* Gland, Switzerland: World Wide Fund (WWF) for Nature International, 2004.

Chapter 7

Protecting Society from Itself: Reconnecting Ecology and Economy

James R. Karr, Ph.D. (Zoology: Ecology)
School of Aquatic and Fishery Sciences and Department of
Biology, University of Washington, Seattle, WA, U.S.A.
*Contact Information: 190 Cascadia Loop, Sequim, WA 98382-6704 U.S.A.
Phone: +1 360 681 3163; Email: jrkarr@u.washington.edu*

Summary

Humanity has prospered largely thanks to what it could take from Earth's ecosystems. With advances in technology—from the earliest agriculture ten thousand years ago to a bewildering array of scientific advances in the twentieth century—humans appear to have released themselves from dependence on their surroundings.

But over the millennia, environmental degradation and social inequities have accompanied these perceived advances. Now twenty-first century globalization poses challenges without equal in human history. As a result, human society faces a paradox: as scientific understanding of Earth and of humans' effects on it expand, the threats to Earth's living systems—human and nonhuman—worsen.

How can we be smarter and more knowledgeable and yet ignore so many lessons of that knowledge? If twenty-first century society is to halt or reverse ominous social and ecological trends, humanity must revise its actions in four important ways.

First, we must replace the dominant worldview—which dissociates humans from ecosystems—with one that regains awareness of our dependence on the rest of Earth's complex living systems.

Second, we must temper globalization in its most recent form—runaway industrial capitalism—with policy decisions that recognize the importance of social, ecological, and aesthetic goals.

Third, thoughtful people must not cede all power to politicians and business interests; we must make our voices heard across the full range of professional, social, and civic circles.

Fourth, democratic societies must harness good governance to counterbalance the forces of money and industry.

Background

Humanity owes its prosperity in large part to what it has taken from Earth's ecosystems. But in the ten thousand years since the advent of agriculture, the biosphere has become distorted in ways that harm human health and well-being and even threaten our very existence.

At the beginning of the twenty-first century, we know this much: in the twentieth century, many facts came to light about the relationship between the health of the biosphere as a whole and our own. Scholars from diverse fields—archaeology to epidemiology, history to zoology—have been interpreting historical patterns and current situations to gain new insights about Earth. In addition, thoughtful people concerned about the health of both present and future generations—citizens, business people, and political leaders—recognize that modern human activity so seriously disrupts the biosphere that the quality of human and nonhuman life is at risk.

Yet our ability to alter trajectories set in motion more than ten thousand years ago is limited by the persistence of a skewed worldview, use of misguided and misleading indicators of well-being, and power imbalances fostered by those indicators. We face a paradox: Even though we are more able than ever in the history of human society to understand the present, learn from the past, and take action for a more sustainable future, we do not use what we know, and the state of the biosphere worsens. Four actions are required to reverse present trends.

Recognize the Real Relationship between Ecology and Economy

The dominant worldview assumes that the human economy is separate from the environment and thus free of biophysical constraints. (Rees, 2002) Under what has been labeled the expansionist perspective, the environment is the source of an unlimited supply of resources and a sink for an unlimited quantity of wastes, allowing the human economy to expand without limit. (Figure 7.1.a) The rise of neoclassical economics late in the nineteenth century launched this perspective, effectively decoupling culture and environment. Today "society" and "economy" seem almost synonymous, at least in the minds of many political leaders. We make societal decisions almost exclusively on the basis of narrowly construed economic indicators, unless these indicators are trumped by ideological or political goals.

Expansionists have had faith that, especially under free-market conditions, human ingenuity always has provided and always will provide creative solutions to all challenges society faces. In support of that faith, expansionists assume that we can project previous trends in population and economic growth indefinitely into the future. But predicting the future on the basis of faulty assumptions can be both misleading and dangerous, especially if those assumptions come solely from the past few centuries of European expansion, a small subset of history that took place over a narrow time frame. In reality, the Earth, a finite body, does not continue to grow, so neither can populations or the material consumption of these populations. A dynamic steady-state perspective more accurately reflects the reality of a finite Earth. (Figure 7.1.b)

Two Conceptual Models of the Relationship between Ecological and Economic Systems

a. Expansionist Perspective

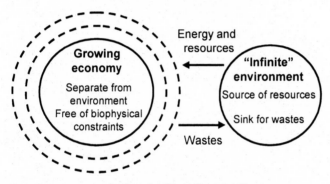

b. Steady-State Perspective

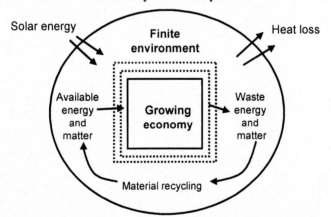

Figure 7.1 (a and b). (a) The expansionist perspective assumes that the economy can grow indefinitely while extracting resources from and discharging wastes to an environment whose capacity to provide resources and absorb wastes is infinite. (b) The steady-state perspective assumes a finite ecosphere enclosing a dependent economic system that cannot grow indefinitely for thermodynamic and other reasons. (Modified from Rees, 2002)

Moreover, even on an uncrowded Earth, faulty assumptions and a failure to acknowledge the impacts of agriculture, population growth, urbanization, and the accumulation of wealth have distorted nature worldwide for at least the last five thousand years. (Chew, 2001; Hughes, 2001) The archaeological record reveals numerous societies that did not live in accord with nature (Redman, 1999), often with serious social and health consequences for the elite as well as for ordinary people. (Fagan, 1999; 2000) From the ancient Middle East to the modern world, societies have collapsed when they were not aware of, or when they ignored, the consequences of their actions. (Diamond, 2005) Ignoring these collapses—as expansionists do in predicting the future—violates a fundamental rule in history and science: responsible historians and scientists consider all the data, even data that do not support the researchers' own ideologies.

During the twentieth century, human population and consumption grew at unprecedented rates, leading to disharmonies between people and their surroundings that may well overshadow the importance of sociopolitical events like the world wars, the rise and fall of communism, or the spread of mass literacy. (McNeill, 2000) Perhaps the most visible disharmony came in the form of increased energy consumption with the burning of fossil fuels. (Crosby, 2006) Consider, for example, "energy" consumption by ancient Roman citizens and citizens in the late twentieth century. In ancient Rome, the wealthy used slaves—directly subjugating members of the current generation—as an inexpensive energy subsidy. Most modern cultures view slavery as repugnant. Yet as of 1990, modern citizens consumed, per capita, the energy equivalent of the work of twenty full-time energy slaves, that is, "twenty human equivalents working twenty-four hours a day, 365 days a year." (McNeill, 2000) Rather than directly subjugating slaves, the average person practices *de facto* slavery. Excessive energy use indirectly subjugates today's powerless, such as indigenous communities in oil-rich areas and people living near refineries, as well as future generations, who will have to contend with human-induced climate change, environmental contamination, and the impoverishment of human and nonhuman living systems. Such short- and long-term consequences make modern rates of fossil fuel consumption and policies that favor present patterns of energy use as morally repugnant as Roman slavery.

Additional disharmonies result from scientific and technological advances that have given humans the power to capture more and more of Earth's bounty. Technologies help us achieve specific objectives, but the benefits are often outweighed by belated, complex, and often disastrous unintended consequences. "Magic bullets" yielded unexpected "ills"; wonder drugs control common pathogens and pesticides kill pests, but both yield resistant pathogens and pests. Hatchery fish bred to augment overharvested wild populations intensified, rather than relaxed, pressure on wild populations. Water reservoirs in the tropics improved the supply of potable water for humans, but they also created ideal environments for human parasites. Water wells in deserts made historically nomadic societies sedentary, undermining regional ecosystems and cultures. Industrialization exposed human society to a remarkable array of natural and synthetic chemicals, such as heavy metals, nutrients, and chlorinated hydrocarbons, with diverse impacts on health. In addition, many engineering and political schemes for managing rivers to benefit one group of people have led to unanticipated problems for others. Clearing land to harvest trees and straightening upstream river channels to reduce local flooding, for example, worsen flooding downstream and destroy downstream and coastal fisheries.

Worst of all, as technology piles upon technology, the expansionist perspective lulls society into self-satisfaction. We come to accept the notion that technologies make people independent of natural systems, while momentum propels us to further ignore our real dependence, and the risks to people and society from environmental distortions grow. Our technical ability to predict consequences improves, yet our willingness, perhaps even our ability, to use that knowledge to inform political decisions lags behind.

As long as modern society accepts the nonoverlapping circles of the expansionist perspective (see Figure 7.1.a), efforts to track societal well-being will be dominated by measures that celebrate economic growth as the primary measure of that well-being. Resource depletion, waste accumulation, and impoverished living systems will remain invisible as we come to value whatever we measure, rather than measuring what is valuable. Perhaps worse, flawed indicators wed us to the dominant expansionist worldview, making us resist change at the same time that they endorse value systems promoting unsustainable lifestyles. The most frequently used economic indicators essentially give people permission to escape responsibility for the social and ecological effects of their actions.

How might we depict an alternative, more realistic worldview? One common depiction is a Venn diagram consisting of environment, economy, and society as three overlapping circles. (Figure 7.2) Although this diagram adds a distinct social dimension beyond economics, it creates a different kind of misunderstanding by illustrating relationships as overlaps. For one, the area of overlap is small, as if the largest area within each conceptual circle were independent of the others. For another, the diagram does not suggest three-dimensional relationships, as among spheres instead of circles.

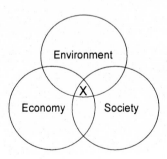

Figure 7.2. Venn diagrams are often inappropriately used to portray relationships among social, ecological, and economic systems.

A more realistic alternative presents social, economic, and ecological systems in three dimensions and as interdependent, much like the layers of a cake. (Figure 7.3.a) The economic system is the top layer, supported by the social system; both are supported by the natural system, the bottom layer. Intensification of human economic activity in recent centuries has eroded the lower layers of the cake, progressively impoverishing the biosphere and destabilizing the very foundations of society, while the frosting on the cake—the economy—expands. (Figure 7.3.b) Each year, for example, humans consume forty percent of Earth's terrestrial and thirty-five percent of its coastal production. (Pimm, 2001) Human and nonhuman dimensions of biotic impoverishment now take many forms (Figure 7.4), including degraded soils, failed fisheries, rising asthma rates, increased food insecurity, and stress syndromes from overcrowding and the pace of modern industrialized life. (Chu and Karr, 2001) Unfortunately, the indicators invoked by the expansionists make it impossible to detect the biotic impoverishment that results from the erosion of the social and natural layers.

The "Layer Cake" Model

a. Three-layer cake

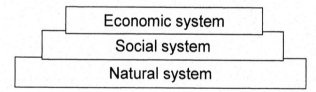

b. Economic frosting on two-layer cake

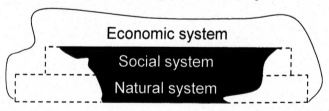

Figure 7.3 (a and b). (a) The key components of Earth's systems and their relationships to one another can be depicted as a layer cake, with economic and social systems resting on top of the natural, or ecological, system that forms the cake's base layer. (b) As human economies (the frosting) expand, they erode the underlying social and ecological systems, destabilizing the foundation and threatening the sustainability of those systems. Indicators of economic vitality, social well-being, human health, and ecological health are needed to understand the true condition of all the layers.

Biotic Impoverishment

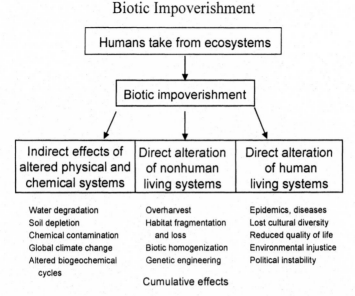

Figure 7.4. The many faces of biotic impoverishment—the result of humans' taking from Earth's ecosystems. (Modified from Karr and Chu, 1995; and Chu and Karr, 2001)

Science and technology in combination with the wisdom of the arts and humanities could turn this juggernaut and rebalance our relationship to the rest of the biosphere. We could replace the expansionist perspective with improved understanding of human dependence on the living systems that have fueled the last ten thousand years of human development.

Moderate the Negative Effects of Global Business Networks

Although humans did not begin as a global species, we became one. Our success came from our ability to adapt to diverse environments, to evolve regional natural histories (a.k.a. societies) with adaptive qualities that vary across ecological regions of the world. Globalization, then, is not a process that began with free trade or the information highway; rather, it is a process with roots in the distant past, a process that is as much ecological and demographic as it is economic and political. (Clark, 2001) Each step in this multiphased globalization has benefited human society while exacting a heavy toll on Earth's living systems.

The first globalization began when humans migrated out of Africa and ended when hunter-gatherers occupied the majority of Earth's terrestrial environments some thirteen thousand years ago. The second round came with the independent regional evolution of domestication and agriculture (the Fertile Crescent, the Americas, China). These regional specializations took advantage of peculiar arrays of plants and animals suitable for domestication. (Diamond, 1997) This domestication—a coevolution involving humans, plants, animals, and diseases (Clark, 2001)—yielded geographically specific packages of inter-dependent life forms (e.g., Fertile Crescent: wheat, cows, horses, and smallpox; the Americas: corn, beans, potatoes, and llamas; China: rice, pigs, chickens, and influenza). Beyond the coevolution of these packages, early agricultural discoveries changed regional land cover, setting off the first round of human-induced changes in climate. (Ruddiman, 2005)

These packages permitted human populations to expand beyond what could be supported by a hunter-gatherer mode of existence. The expansion allowed the packages to disperse outside the geographic range of each component species; regional civilizations interacted, spreading their domesticated species and associated diseases. The third round of globalization included the spread of the potato from South America, rice from Asia and Africa, and wheat from the Middle East—as well as the global spread of diseases such as bubonic plague, smallpox, and others that decimated immunologically naïve cultures. Continuing technological advances increased agricultural production and improved humans' ability to harvest wild fish, game, and trees. The resulting material surpluses led to more expansion in the human population and to increasingly complex social, political, and economic relations in human societies. These advances appeared to release humans from dependence on their surroundings. But as cultural and other constraints—which had long kept societal behavior within environmental bounds—withered under this impression, environmental degradation followed.

The start and spread of industrialization (agriculture, fishing, logging, manufacturing) in the eighteenth and nineteenth centuries, driven by the availability of fossil fuels, initiated a fourth round of globalization, making it possible to move foods, raw materials, manufactured commodities, and societal wastes over distances and at speeds never dreamed of by earlier humans. A fifth round—economic globalization—which included development of global financial markets, the growth of transnational corporations, and their increasing domination over national economies (Soros, 2002), became the dominant event of the twentieth century; industrial capitalism emerged as the victor over centrally planned economies.

The modern industrial system persuaded us that technology and economic growth are always good; that firms must always expand; that consumption is the source of happiness; that nothing should interfere with growth and consumption; and that, in the words of renowned economist John Kenneth Galbraith, the role of the state is to ensure that all these things happen. (Galbraith, 1967) Harvesting more from nature and manufacturing more with raw materials taken from nature constitute the unstated core of capitalism.

Fortunately, not all were persuaded. Galbraith himself made a case for the value of some centralized market oversight to "assert the superior claims of aesthetic over economic goals and particularly of environment over cost." (Galbraith, 1967) He wrote:

The [great] danger is in the subordination of belief to the needs of the modern industrial system. . . . If we continue to believe that the goals of the modern industrial system and the public policies that serve these goals are coordinate with all of life, then all of our lives will be in the service of these goals. . . . We will be the mentally indentured servants of the industrial system. (Galbraith, 1967)

Other thinkers concur, citing unacceptable consequences of uncontrolled capitalism, such as its effects on the natural world, the sprawling ugliness of cities, the polluting effects of industries, massive alterations of rivers, its moral deficiencies, and the political and social consequences of inequality. (Fernández-Armesto, 2001)

Because the forces of capitalism and its associated pressures are the primary drivers of modern globalization, we must assess the extent to which modern capitalism, with its global business networks (Woodbridge, 2004), is an appropriate model for humans to follow. Modern industrial capitalism is driven by an imperative to expand total production locally and geographically to attain two objectives. (Wallerstein, 1999) The first, the endless accumulation of capital (perceived as wealth) by capitalists, is widely understood; the second, the less often discussed "dirty little secret" of capitalism, is that during the accumulation of capital by capitalists, the capitalists do not pay their bills. (Wallerstein, 1999) Indeed, social and environmental consequences, called externalities by economists, are borne by society at large, while the profits accrue to a few capitalists. Like many technologies, industrial capitalism is a two-edged sword.

It has not always been that way. Early economists such as Adam Smith, Thomas Malthus, David Ricardo, and John Stuart Mill regarded long-term economic and population growth as unlikely; limits would eventually slow or stop growth, they believed, and the process would end with most people living at a subsistence level. (Prugh et al., 1995) These early economists understood that capitalism should balance growth with social objectives.

By the 1870s, mainstream economics fostered a different worldview. First, value was said to derive from scarcity, rather than from the land and labor needed to produce a product, further separating the human economy from the natural economy. Second, long-term concerns were replaced with a narrow focus on marginal analysis, the study of the relationships between small changes in prices and quantities as economic activity expands by small amounts. This neoclassical economics cast itself as a value-free, scientific enterprise seeking laws to describe economic activity. (Prugh et al., 1995) Neoclassical economists adopted a deterministic outlook, excluding the importance of contingency and history and largely ignoring the costs of aesthetic, social, and ecological damage. Some economists have expressed concerns about these changes, but the vast majority have either actively promoted materially wasteful economic growth or quietly tolerated it. (Czech, 2000)

As the twenty-first century unfolds, the free-market at the core of industrial capitalism has become a "mythic . . . larger-than-life, quasi-magical, all-

knowing force that can cure most any economic, environmental, or social ill."
(Gardner, 2006) This mysterious and ethereal force (Adam Smith's "invisible
hand") promises much but in reality promotes social inequities and environmental degradation. Market systems weaken social relationships and wreak
environmental havoc because of their narrow favoring of goods and services that
generate profits in the market. (Manno, 2000) Moreover, existing international
financial and trade institutions aid in wealth creation, the first goal of capitalism,
while they fail to provide other public goods, and they damage social and environmental infrastructure. (Soros, 2002) When one combines these flaws with
rampant cheating in the marketplace (think, failed energy company Enron and
other high-profile cases), the tendency of chief executives to worry less about
the long-term health of their companies (shareholder capitalism) and more about
executive stock options (manager capitalism; Bogle, 2005), and today's near-
instantaneous electronic globalization of information, the cheerleading of political and business leaders promises what the market in its dominant form cannot
deliver.

As ten thousand years of history demonstrates, humans can do little to alter
the major trends of globalization. But thoughtful people understand and recognize much of the baggage of globalization, especially the globalization of industrial capitalism. New ways to measure progress, such as ecological footprint
analysis (Rees, 2002), stop assuming the benevolent operation of an imaginary
invisible hand (Stiglitz, 2002) and start accounting for the very real footprint of
human industrial metabolism. Wise use of markets could redirect economic
tools to better serve human needs. Because the biosphere places limits on what
humans can do, better accounting systems and more appropriate markets are
essential if human societies hope to sustain the vitality and diversity of human
culture and the extraordinary richness of Earth's living systems.

Make Our Voices Heard in Professional,
Social, and Civic Circles

Two constituencies—a thoughtful, informed citizenry and scholars or experts—
have the potential to wield considerable power. In early America, a small group
of thoughtful, committed individuals with relevant experience and expertise
came together and founded a new nation. Collectively, they established a set of
principles and a framework of governance to protect both the interests of individuals and the collective well-being. The foundation they laid in the Declaration of Independence and in the U.S. Constitution and Bill of Rights still stands
today.

Twenty-first century citizens, too, should rise to the standards set more than
two centuries ago. A society of committed citizens should assert the importance
of aesthetic over economic goals and the right to a quality environment over
some flawed accounting procedure that misleads citizens about the true cost of

commodities available in the market. For example, an international effort driven largely by citizens in many countries produced the *Earth Charter*. This document is a declaration of interdependence and mutual responsibility to all life, which calls for respect and care for the community of life; for the protection of ecological integrity; for social and economic justice; and for democracy, nonviolence, and peace (see the Appendix).

Scientists and scholars have particular responsibilities to participate in civic life because they have benefited, directly and indirectly, from publicly funded educational institutions and research grants. Moreover, science and scholarship are almost never irrelevant to policy decisions. (Franz, 2001) Neither current events nor policy-making should be off limits to scientists' discourse, as some policy-makers and scientists contend. (Wooster, 1998; Mills, 2000; Sarewitz, 2006) Keeping science at arm's length from policy-making is precisely the sort of practice that results in economic analyses that fail to account for ecological value. When ecological benefits—such as flood control provided by an intact wetland floodplain or crop pollination provided by bees—are ignored and effectively set at zero, the resulting calculations may be precise, but they will be wrong. The benefits accruing from living systems are not zero, and citizens and scholars should say so.

Science is in fact central to policy decisions having immense societal impact. Given the complexity of the twenty-first-century world, scientists and policy-makers would be remiss to ignore or marginalize each other. (Karr, 2006) The public, whose dollars pay for educational institutions and government granting agencies, has a right to expect some public good from action based on scientific findings. In addition, the training scientists receive—to question assumptions and conventions in science—also equips them to challenge the assumptions of public policy, the law, and implementation of the law. Scientists can work within legal and political systems toward ensuring that both science and common sense underpin decision-making. When scientists fail to make a compelling case for decisions based on scientific evidence (or when their recommendations are ignored), the decisions' long-term costs often outweigh any short-term economic benefits put forth to justify leaving science out. When regulations are ignored or not enacted despite the lessons already available to all, money is wasted, human health can suffer, and social and environmental damage can devastate local economies and communities.

Improve Institutions of Local, National, and International Governance

More than a century ago, Henry Demarest Lloyd (1881) wrote that the forces of capital and industry had outgrown the forces of government. More than 125 years after Lloyd, the reality is worse than he could have envisioned. The modern economic system misallocates resources between private goods and public goods, hurting both the environment and other social values.

Local, national, and international government institutions—and the political arrangements they are supposed to invoke to protect the people's interest—have not kept pace with international financial markets, which are amoral. (Soros, 2002) Markets allow individuals to act in accordance with their interests but, Soros contends, do not pass moral judgments on the interests themselves. For that reason alone, financial markets need a guiding hand—in the form of good governance—to moderate their negative influences. Controls must be exercised to balance the provision of public and private goods. (Soros, 2002) The failure of governmental institutions explains the paradox: for the past 150 years, human knowledge has expanded beyond imagination, but we seem incapable of using that knowledge to protect human society from itself. During most of the past two centuries, governance has fostered economic development through a collaboration between capitalists and governments.

The focus of governance in the future must shift to preventing ecological decline. Halting the expansion of the human population and per capita consumption will be essential to such prevention. The provisioning of more than six billion people with the requirements for their survival in a time of ecological scarcity must be job number one for government. (Woodbridge, 2004) Negative, or at least zero, population growth must go hand in hand with provisioning despite scarcity; provisioning an ever-growing and more-consuming population is simply impossible. After all, citizens have a contract with their government: governments are expected to use collected taxes to understand the world and to apply that knowledge to make decisions that will protect the citizens' well-being. In a time when society faces more, and more difficult, decisions, government institutions cannot be allowed to distort or ignore accumulated knowledge or to behave as if that knowledge were irrelevant. (Karr, 2006)

Interdisciplinary scholars strive to understand the present, gain wisdom from the past, and chart a course for the future. Their efforts demonstrate the need to alter the dominant worldview, tune markets to avert the devastating effects of modern globalization, and foster interdisciplinary dialogue to understand and measure social and ecological as well as economic health. Government, bolstered by thoughtful citizens, should serve the public good, not a false idol of industrial capitalism that benefits the few at the expense of the many while eroding both the social and ecological layers of Earth's systems.

Acknowledgments

Special thanks to the members of the Global Ecological Integrity Group (GEIG) and Elena Karr for helping me to see the world in new ways, to Ellen W. Chu for extraordinary editorial insight, and to Bob Hughes and Leska Fore for thoughtful comments on an earlier draft.

References

Bogle, John C. *The Battle for the Soul of Capitalism*. New Haven, CT: Yale University Press, 2005.

Chew, Sing C. *World Ecological Degradation: Accumulation, Urbanization, and Deforestation 3000 B.C.–A.D. 2000*. Walnut Creek, CA: Altamira Press, 2001.

Chu, Ellen W., and James R. Karr. "Environmental Impact, Concept and Measurement of." Pp. 557–77 in *Encyclopedia of Biodiversity*, vol. 2, edited by Simon A. Levin. Orlando, FL: Academic Press, 2001.

Clark, Robert P. *Global Life Systems: Population, Food, and Disease in the Process of Globalization*. Lanham, MD: Rowman & Littlefield, 2001.

Crosby, Alfred W. *Children of the Sun: A History of Humanity's Unappeasable Appetite for Energy*. New York: W. W. Norton, 2006.

Czech, Brian. *Shoveling Fuel for a Runaway Train: Errant Economists, Shameful Spenders, and a Plan to Stop Them All*. Berkeley: University of California Press, 2000.

Diamond, Jared. *Collapse: How Societies Choose to Fail or Succeed*. New York: Viking, 2005.

———. *Guns, Germs, and Steel: The Fates of Human Societies*. New York: W. W. Norton, 1997.

Fagan, Brian. *Floods, Famines, and Emperors: El Niño and the Fate of Civilizations*. New York: Basic Books, 1999.

———. *The Little Ice Age: How Climate Made History, 1300–1850*. New York: Basic Books, 2000.

Fernández-Armesto, Felipe. *Civilizations: Culture, Ambition, and the Transformation of Nature*. New York: Free Press, 2001.

Franz, Eldon. "Ecology, Values, and Policy." *BioScience* 51, no. 6 (June 2001): 469–74.

Galbraith, John Kenneth. "Capitalism, Socialism, and the Future of the Industrial State." *Atlantic Monthly* 219, no. 6 (June 1967): 61–67. (Excerpted in *Atlantic Monthly* 297, no. 3 [April 2006]: 46–47.)

Gardner, Gary. "Marketing Markets." *World Watch* 19, no. 3 (May/June 2006): 14–15.

Hughes, J. Donald. *An Environmental History of the World: Humankind's Changing Role in the Community of Life*. New York: Routledge, 2001.

Karr, James R. "When Government Ignores Science, Scientists Should Speak Up." *BioScience* 56, no. 4 (April 2006): 287–88.

Karr, James R., and Ellen W. Chu. "Ecological Integrity: Reclaiming Lost Connections." Pp. 34–48 in *Perspectives on Ecological Integrity*, edited by Laura Westra and John Lemons. Dordrecht, Netherlands: Kluwer Academic Publishers, 1995.

Lloyd, Henry Demarest. "Story of a Great Monopoly." *Atlantic Monthly* 47, no. 281 (March 1881): 317–34. (Excerpted in *Atlantic Monthly* 297, no. 3 [April 2006]: 44, 46.)

Manno, Jack P. *Privileged Goods: Commoditization and Its Impact on Environment and Society*. Boca Raton, FL: Lewis Publishers, 2000.

McNeill, John Robert. *Something New under the Sun: An Environmental History of the Twentieth-Century World*. New York: W. W. Norton, 2000.

Mills, Thomas J. "Position Advocacy by Scientists Risks Scientific Credibility and May Be Unethical." *Northwest Science* 74, no. 2 (Spring 2000): 165–67.

Pimm, Stuart. *The World According to Pimm: A Scientist Audits the Earth*. New York: McGraw-Hill, 2001.

Prugh, Thomas, Robert Costanza, John H. Cumberland, Herman Daly, Robert Goodland, and Richard B. Norgaard. *Natural Capital and Human Economic Survival.* Solomons, MD: International Society for Ecological Economics Press, 1995.

Redman, Charles L. *Human Impact on Ancient Environments.* Tucson: University of Arizona Press, 1999.

Rees, William E. "Globalization and Sustainability: Conflict or Convergence?" *Bulletin of Science, Technology, and Society* 22, no. 4 (August 2002): 249–68.

Ruddiman, William F. *Plows, Plagues, and Petroleum: How Humans Took Control of Climate.* Princeton, NJ: Princeton University Press, 2005.

Sarewitz, Daniel. "Liberating Science from Politics: The Notion That Science Can Be Used to Reconcile Political Disputes Is Fundamentally Flawed." *American Scientist* 94, no. 2 (March/April 2006): 104–6.

Soros, George. *George Soros on Globalization.* New York: Public Affairs, 2002.

Stiglitz, Joseph E. *Globalization and Its Discontents.* New York: W. W. Norton, 2002.

Wallerstein, Immanuel M. *The End of the World as We Know It.* Minneapolis: University of Minnesota Press, 1999.

Woodbridge, Roy. *The Next World War: Tribes, Cities, Nations, and Ecological Decline.* Toronto: University of Toronto Press, 2004.

Wooster, Warren S. "Science, Advocacy, and Credibility." *Science* 282, no. 1823 (4 Dec. 1998): 1823–24.

Chapter 8

Strong Sustainability and Environmental Policy: Justification and Implementation

Konrad Ott, Ph.D. (Philosophy)

Professor of Environmental Ethics, University of Greifswald
German Environmental Advisory Council, Germany

Contact Information: Dept. of Environmental Ethics
Grimmer Straße 88, D-17487 Greifswald GERMANY
Email:ott@uni-greifswald.de

Ralf Döring, Ph.D. (Economics)

Senior Researcher, Department of Landscape Economics
University of Greifswald, Germany

Contact Information: Dept. of Landcape Economics
Grimmer Straße 88, D-17487 Greifswald GERMANY
Phone: +49 03834 864127; Fax: +49 03834 864107
Email: doering@uni-greifswald.de

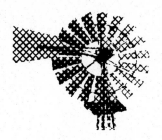

Summary

The term "sustainable development" has been adopted to guide international policy-making. However, this term still lacks specific meaning and clear conceptualization.

We outline an approach toward a conception of "strong sustainability" which is rooted in ethics, has a distinctive focus on natural (or, ecological) capital, and entails policy suggestions with regard to different aspects of environmental policy.

Since its introduction by Herman Daly, this concept has been adopted by the Environmental Advisory Council of Germany, and it has been included in different reports of the Council. Thus, the concept is very much alive, at least in the more theoretical environmental debates in Europe.

In this chapter, we apply the concept of "strong sustainability" to each of climate change, agricultural policy and fisheries. We conclude that the implementation of "strong sustainability" is both feasible and desirable at only moderate cost.

Introduction and Background

The following ideas on an ecologically focused concept of sustainability and its possible implementation are not simply armchair reasoning performed by ethicists. Indeed, they have been adopted by the Environmental Advisory Council (Sachverständigenrat für Umweltfragen or SRU) which counsels the German Federal Government on environmental affairs.[1]

In its report of 2002, SRU (2002a) proposed a slightly modified concept of "strong sustainability" to guide environmental policy-making. Meanwhile, it has published several special reports on the protection of nature (2002b), the protection of marine environments in the Northern and the Baltic Seas (2004), and on traffic and mobility policies (2005). A new report on the sustainable production of biomass for energy supply is in the making. Each report specifies objectives as well as analyses of instruments and feasible strategies, while maintaining the concept of sustainability throughout.

Consequently, an explanatory network has emerged, which has a conceptual core and a set of practical applications. This network can be examined through an epistemological lens. Being a member of SRU since 2000, Konrad Ott has contributed to these reports and thus all claims made in this chapter are close to the recommendations of the SRU reports.[2]

In the two following sections, the concept of "strong sustainability" is justified on ethical grounds. Thereafter, the notion of natural capital is examined. Destruction of natural capital, interpreted as "bio-impoverishment," is deemed morally repugnant. Three policy areas are selected for closer debate: 1) climate change, 2) agriculture, and 3) fisheries. The implementation of "strong sustainability" is shown to be feasible at only moderate cost.

Objective: Toward a Comprehensive Theory of Sustainability

The term "sustainable development" can be traced back to German forestry management of the early eighteenth century ("Nachhalt"). It was coined by the Brundtland-report (WCED, 1987). Twenty years later, the term "sustainability" is often used as a catch phrase without specific meaning. For logical reasons, any concept which has to encompass almost everything (*extension*) must lose meaning (*intension*). SRU argues that sustainable development should be regarded neither as a catch phrase nor as a theory about everything. For purposes of theory formation, it seems helpful to distinguish some layers of the scientific and ethical debate on sustainability (Ott and Döring, 2004, Ch. 1):

1. Idea (intergenerational justice)
2. Concepts ("strong" or "weak" sustainability, intermediate concepts)
3. Rules (constant natural capital rule, management rules)

4. Dimensions of policy-making (e.g., climate change, fisheries, forestry, agriculture)
5. Objectives (targets, time frames, set of instruments, indicators)
6. Processes (e.g., implementation, monitoring).

There is broad agreement that the *idea* of sustainability is based on ethical suppositions about intergenerational equity. It is also agreed that the depletion and the preservation of natural resources is a crucial topic in any theory of sustainability.

Future Ethics[3]

A comprehensive future ethics should be organized around the following topics (Krebs, 2002):

1. Which ethical theory should govern assessments of future events?
2. Are there obligations to future generations at all?
3. Should the ethical approach toward future generations be egalitarian?
4. What kind and amount of goods belong to a fair intergenerational bequest package?
5. Are we permitted to discount future states of affairs?[4]

Ethicists have to incorporate *future ethics* in any overall theory of ethics they wish to defend. Since any ethical theory is focused around some basic principles which constitute the core of the theory, any future ethics must be conceptualized in such terms.

Discourse ethics is a promising approach in ethical theory. (Ott, 1998) From the core of discourse ethics, only weak obligation toward future generations can be derived. However, there is an ongoing debate about intergenerational obligations. This debate entails "no-obligation-arguments" which have been analyzed elsewhere.[5]

The analysis assumes that no-obligation-arguments presented so far do not deserve much ethical credit. On the other hand, it finds some sound arguments which justify intergenerational obligations from different moral perspectives.[6] Therefore, the authors provide an affirmative answer to question no. 2.

A stringent approach toward intergenerational justice combines the idea of practical discourse with the Rawls' veil of ignorance. In the debate between Habermas and Rawls, Rawls restricted himself to a freestanding political theory of justice, "leaving philosophy as it is." (1995: 134) Rawls refused to raise such ambitious philosophical claims as did Habermas, but he neither denied nor rejected them. To Rawls, the ideal discourse situation and the original position are two different "devices of representation." (Rawls, 1995: 132) The devices are not mutually exclusive and do not contradict each other. Based on this, a Habermasian can utilize a theory of justice in a comprehensive discourse ethics. A theory of distributive justice, then, is a solid element in any set of applications of discourse ethics, encompassing intergenerational justice as a special case. We will thus adopt a two-track approach. First, there is real discourse about future ethics. The arguments presented in this discourse serve as focal points ("topoi"). Second, we make use of Rawls' veil of ignorance (i.e., the features of particular persons including their specific positions in the social order, constituting a special situation in reasoning about the principles of justice). A reasonable choice of such principles being made in such situation counts to Rawls as a rationale. The Rawlsian concept of reflexive equilibrium enables us to move between focal points and principles that reasonable persons might adopt behind such veil.

The persons behind the Veil of Ignorance (VOI) are free, rational, and mutually disinterested. They are deprived of information about their individuality, their life prospects, their social status, and their concept of the good life. We hold that persons adopt the well-known Rawlsian principles (system of rights, equal opportunities, difference principle). The VOI can be varied according to different problems. Regrettably, Rawls confused the idea that the original position could be adopted at any time with the idea that the persons behind the veil are contemporaries. Moreover, he modeled them as being representatives of family lines. If these confusions are resolved, it seems consistent with the basic structure of Rawls' theory to modify the VOI in order, *first*, to cover any specific knowledge of one's location in time; *second*, to concentrate on a fair intergenerational saving schedule (i.e., a schedule on goods and endowments a society should save for future generations); and, *third*, to add some general ecological knowledge to the knowledge base.[7] Such a design allows persons to argue from behind the VOI at to which saving schedule they would like to choose. Rawls rightly argued that the persons behind the VOI should debate about a fair intergenerational saving rate.[8]

Rawls' intuitions about how this debate might proceed seem to suppose an egalitarian principle stating that no generation in the overall chain of generations has claim to privileged treatment. Now, we face question no. 3. In many realms of practical reasoning, we accept egalitarian standards, as equal treatment at court, as equal freedom to live autonomously, or as equality of opportunities. In other cases, we accept a presumption in favor of equality, which implies a modest burden of justification for those who wish to distribute certain goods unequally.[9] Intuitively, a presumption of equality seems to be implied in the idea of a chain of generations which constitutes mankind through time.

This intuition is in reflective equilibrium with a reasonable choice that persons would make behind the VOI. A rational person might consider the following option of choice between two options A and B. Option A entails one Welfare Level WL1, which can be sustained indefinitely, while option B encompasses two different Welfare Levels, WL2 and WL3, which are connected by causal relationship, WL2 causing WL3. WL1 is superior to WL3, that only allows for minimally-decent, life-meeting basic needs ("absolute standard"). Thus, WL1 provides better life prospects than an absolute "basic-need" standard. WL2 is high above WL1, so rational persons have the following order of preference: WL2 > WL1 > WL3, but see also the risk in option B. If such persons have a certain degree of risk aversion ("minimax" strategy) and are placed behind the VOI, they probably will prefer the egalitarian option A. If so, persons behind the VOI have a reason to adopt an egalitarian standard of intergenerational justice. Such a standard requires that, other things being equal, future living conditions should at least be as good as contemporary ones if such conditions can be sustained over time. This is a big "if," but it is not unreasonable to assume that a high quality of life for all humans (which has to be distinguished from a high economic standard of living) can be sustained without depletion and overexploitation of natural resources.[10]

Rawls did not sharply distinguish the concepts of saving rate and saving schedule. The concept of a fair intergenerational saving schedule makes more room for environmental concerns than the economical concept of a saving rate. We claim that different concepts of sustainability can be interpreted as proposals for different saving schedules. The arguments which justify specific concepts of sustainability must be found acceptable behind the VOI or in practical discourse. The arguments presented in the following section are considered under these requirements.

The persons behind the VOI share some basic knowledge about how the fabric of society works. From environmental sciences they could adopt some ecological knowledge on how human societies are dependent upon natural endowments ("life support systems"). They can acknowledge that ecological systems provide a lot of functions and services which are of value for the overall well-being of humans, including health. Such services can be distinguished into different types (supporting, provisioning, regulating, cultural). This is general knowledge only, which does not exclude the option to substitute such functions and services artificially.

Approach: Justification of Strong Sustainability

At the *conceptual layer*, distinctions are made between weak, strong, and intermediate sustainability. The struggle between these concepts stems from different assumptions about substitutability between natural and man-made capital, about compensating future generations for losses, and about discounting future events. (Neumayer, 1999). The concept of *weak sustainability* is based on the obligation that present generations should bequeath future generations an undiminished stock of capital. In this concept, however, natural capital can be substituted on an unlimited basis. There is an intuitive element at the conceptual core of weak sustainability, namely an "educated guess" (Solow, 1974) that the degree of substitutability between artificial and natural capital is, in general, no less than unity. Solow's guess implies a Cobb-Douglas function in economic models. Thus, contemporary persons are entitled to "draw down the pool (optimally, of course!) as long as they add (optimally, of course!) to the stock of reproducible capital." (Solow, 1974) Consequently, the saving schedule can be measured by economic means. Most prominent is the genuine-savings approach. (Atkinson et al., 1997)

The concept of *strong sustainability* is based on the assumption that natural capital must be preserved on different scales (global, continental, national) out of moral respect for future generations. It is assumed that the range of substitutability between natural and man-made capital is limited. The loss of natural capital impoverishes the life prospects of future generations. Some management rules and some policy suggestions (as, for instance, to not count the depletion of natural capital as income) are derived from this concept. (Daly, 1997) Strong sustainability has to justify the Constant Natural Capital Rule (CNCR). Because of the distinction between natural capital and cultivated natural capital, a limited range of substitution is left under the CNCR.

CNCR and the principle of unlimited substitutability are incompatible. Intermediate concepts of sustainability leave some room for substitution conceding that some stocks of "critical" natural capital should be maintained. Given either some risk aversion behind the VOI or the precautionary principle in discourse, intermediate sustainability converges toward CNCR. Regardless, the crucial struggle lies between weak and strong sustainability.

Arguments in Favor of Strong Sustainability

The problem of how to justify a choice between competing concepts of sustainability has been addressed by Neumayer (1999) and by SRU (2002: 67). Such justification is not a scientific proof, but a prudent judgment.[11] Substantial arguments that support strong sustainability are given by Neumayer (1999); SRU (2002a, Ch. 1); and Ott and Döring (2004, Ch. 3). The arguments are summarized as follows:

First argument: Weak sustainability is framed by neoclassical economics. In this frame, the general objective is to maximize net present value. Rationality is defined as egoistic utility maximization. Morality is either an external constraint, or a set of altruistic preferences. Intergenerational obligations are reduced to altruistic preferences. Discounting is permitted (often at the rate of interest). Future ethics is transformed into efficient allocation across periods of time. On reflection, this theoretical frame contradicts a genuine future ethic. Many assumptions in economic models (Cobb-Douglas function, Kaldor-Hicks criterion, discounting, value of a statistical life) are repugnant for either epistemic or moral reasons.

Second argument: If we do not know the preferences and interests of members of future generations, we are neither permitted to assume that such preferences will differ from ours, nor to assume their appreciation for life in artificial environments. It could also be the case that their habits, beliefs, and interests will be "greener" than contemporary ones. If uncertainty is seriously considered, there is a reason to maintain options for life according to such habits and beliefs. Strong sustainability is therefore more liberal by allowing more options.

Persons behind the VOI know that they have a specific concept of the good life, but they do not know specifically what it might be. Thus, they do not know whether or not they will be nature-loving environmentalists. They know that many people place high value on "recreation in free nature," on "living lightly in nature," on wilderness experiences, and the like. If persons behind the VOI choose weak sustainability, they might find themselves as naturalists being trapped in a "full world economy" where unspoiled nature has been lost. This situation would be uncomfortable, if not painful. If persons prefer to avoid such a negative outcome, they should opt for a saving schedule which preserves natural capital on a different spatial scale.

Third argument: Many people are searching for a personal environmental morality (as a source of personal identity). There is the so-called *reasoning space of environmental ethics* that comprehends all arguments that may count as rationale for the protection of nature. (SRU 2002, Ch. 2) This intellectual space entails instrumental values, eudaimonistic (i.e., aesthetic, cultural and spiritual) values, and (contested) conceptions of inherent moral values in nature. Since each argument can, in principle, be either adopted or rejected, there is a plurality of reasonable interpretations of this universe of environmental discourse. Obviously, the concept of strong sustainability leaves more room to live according to different interpretations of this universe of discourse. People seeking an environmental morality or even a "deep" ecophilosophy have a good reason to adopt strong sustainability. This is true also for "deep" anthropocentrism.

Fourth argument: If many ecological systems provide several kinds of functions, amenities, and services, adequate substitutes must be found for any single function. Weak sustainability has to assume such findings or design the models accordingly. In reality, however, it is highly uncertain whether such substitutes will be found. Multifunctionality in conjunction with uncertainty provides sound patterns of argument in favor of CNCR.

Fifth argument: The case of the Pacific island Nauru counts as a counterexample against weak sustainability. (Gowdy and McDaniel, 1999) Nauru's inhabitants and its former colonial powers destroyed Nauru's natural environment because of heavy mining. For some decades, Nauru's inhabitants were afforded a high standard of living thanks to the interest from accumulated capital. According to the measures of weak sustainability, Nauru had been the most sustainable place on Earth. Quality of life on Nauru, however, had not increased because of widespread disease and alcoholism. Meanwhile, a huge fraction of the economic capital had been lost in business affairs. If the measure of weak sustainability implies that countries with an impoverished state of the environment, poor health conditions, widespread addiction to alcohol, and a risky and dependent economic base are to be ranked as highly sustainable, there is something at odds with the concept. If so, the Nauru case counts as a refutation (some say, falsification) of weak sustainability.

Sixth argument: In many cases, the relationship between man-made and natural capital is complementary. This has been Daly's main argument (Daly, 1996), which has been supported by some examples (fisheries, forestry). Taken in isolation, Daly's argument is not sufficient for adopting the concept of strong sustainability. (Ott and Döring, 2004) But, if this line of reasoning is regarded as one pattern of argument in an overall judgment formation, the complementarity argument counts in favor of strong sustainability.

Seventh argument: The precautionary principle, the "minimax" criterion, or the safe minimum standard can be used in order to justify CNCR. Under conditions of uncertainty, and in unique cases, a prudent society should rather err on the side of caution (and avoid "false positives" in a pay-off matrix). Risk-averse persons will agree to the precautionary principle behind the VOI, but the argument is also sound in practical discourse.

In the light of these seven arguments, the concept of weak sustainability should be discarded both behind the VOI and in practical discourse. SRU argued that strong sustainability, the CNCR, and some management rules can be justified discursively (2002: 67). In the paradigm of discourse ethics, both concept and rules of strong sustainability specify the sub-case of "future ethics." On the other hand, Rawls' final list of principles of justice can be included. Rawls added the fair saving schedule as a restriction upon the difference principle (section 46 of "Theory of Justice"). The rules of strong sustainability defining the fair saving schedule are restrictions (constraints) to modes of intragenerational distribution.

As a consequence, programs in environmental policy-making should be enacted as either preservation or investment strategies related to natural capital. Such strategies, including objectives, indicators, and standards, cannot be conceived under the VOI. Having chosen the "best" available concept of sustainability, either behind the VOI or in practical discourse, persons now are down to Earth and becoming real citizens who take an interest in environmental policy-making. At the end of this line of reasoning, persons can no longer be conceived as private persons or consumers. If persons have adopted strong sustainability out of reason, they *ipso facto* have taken the roles of both moral persons and prudent citizens.

The Notion of Natural Capital

The notion of natural capital cannot be specified behind the VOI. Natural capital is not a homogeneous stock. Essentially, the very nature of natural capital is its heterogeneity. It includes atmosphere, photosynthesis, freshwater, soils, forests, fisheries, ozone layer, the global climate system, many components of biodiversity (genes, species, ecosystems), and natural units of cultural significance. Many components of natural capital cannot be substituted by others (soil cannot be substituted by clean air). "Natural capital" is a term that denotes different stocks ("Bestände") and different living funds ("Fonds").[12] SRU (2002a) argues that natural capital is to be characterized by its internal dynamics and by a network-like relationship among single components. Any philosophical account of natural capital must address the naturalness of natural capital in all of its specificities.

Natural capital encompasses not only entities, but also relationships and potencies. Thus, it seems impossible to draw a sharp line between critical and non-critical components. Despite scientific work in progress, understanding natural capital in all of its richness is in its infancy.[13] Such understanding has to address, *first*, the relationship between natural capital and cultivated natural capital, *second*, the intertwinement of components, relations, and potencies, and, *third*, the dialectics of human systems being embedded in ecological life-support systems and humans perceiving such systems as resources. The "classical" modern point of view perceived nature as "resource," while reflective modernity takes these peculiar dialectics into account seriously. (The logic of environmentalism will probably be a Hegelian one.)

Application: Selected Realms of Policy-Making

Climate Change

One of the most important realms of environmental policy is *climate change*. The global climate system is part of natural capital on a global scale. Human-induced emissions of greenhouse gases (GHG) use this capital as a common sink and increase the amount of atmospheric GHG concentrations by so doing. Article 2 of the Framework Convention on Climate Change (FCCC) postulates the ultimate goal of the framework convention: stabilizing atmospheric GHG concentrations at a level that would prevent dangerous anthropogenic interference with the climate system. Since the term "dangerous level" is related to questions of risk assessment and value judgments, no interpretation of Article 2 can avoid ethical questions. "Unsafe" levels of GHG concentrations cannot be in accordance with strong sustainability because of the overall negative impacts on human systems and on natural capital.[14] Stabilization at safe levels conforms, first, to Daly's rule that the human pressure on natural systems should be relieved and, second, to the management rule that sink capacities should not be overused. Many scholars argue that beyond 560 ppm of CO_2, the risks of adverse impacts (floods, droughts, heat waves, storms, and diseases) cannot be assessed with confidence. Unexpected phenomena are more likely because of the many positive feedbacks and the nonlinear behavior of ecological systems. The vast majority of scientists recommend stabilizing GHG levels below 560 ppm CO_2. With regard to recent information about probable climate sensitivity, one should favor 450 ppm CO_2 as an upper limit. (Ott et al., 2004) The recent IPCC report provides compelling evidence for stringent goal setting. By making a judgment about limits to atmospheric GHG concentrations, one determines the aspect of "*contraction.*"[15]

The other dimension is about *equity*. From a moral point of view, there is no reason why any person should be entitled to use a global sink resource (as the atmosphere) more than any other person. If the atmosphere is to be regarded as a global common pool good, a per capita principle of the allocation of GHG emission entitlements only seems fair. If both aspects (safety, equity) are seen in conjunction, the *"contraction-and-convergence"* approach (Meyer, 1999) emerges as the result. To SRU, "contraction and convergence" is in accordance with genuine sustainable development and it should serve as the basis for a long-term strategy in climate change policies (2002a: 255).

Ambitious objectives of industrialized countries to reduce GHG emissions are the first decisive steps toward a global climate regime. SRU proposed to reduce the German CO_2 emissions by 40 percent (compared to 1990 levels) by 2020 as a mid-term objective. The former "red-green" German Federal Government had adopted this objective under the condition that the EU would adopt a 30 percent reduction target. The present German government remains determined to continue this policy, but it will become increasingly difficult for any single industrialized country or even for the EU to justify ambitious unilateral leadership roles if other heavy polluters, such as the United States (which is a "rogue state" in international climate policies), are unwilling to contribute to global climate policy in a commensurate (and responsible) way. It will be hard to reach a second commitment period of the Kyoto Protocol if the U.S. continues in its refusal to join the Kyoto Protocol.

Agricultural Policy and Nature Conservation

European biodiversity in forests, marine, and coastal systems; mires and peatlands, on pastures and arable land, is under threat. Many species adapted to low-level nutrients, dead wood in forests, or large and undisturbed space, are close to extinction. Many endangered species depend on the ongoing use of culturally modified landscapes ("Kulturlandschaft"). To follow the CNCR implies severe changes in European land-use systems. Thus, agricultural policy in the EU has been an important topic in different reports of the SRU. In a special report, the SRU (2002a) outlines strategies for the integration of nature conservation into agricultural policy.

The most pressing problem of EU's agriculture policy is the following: most of the subsidy payments to farmers are not combined with a strong incentive to meet ecological standards. Therefore, the intensification of agriculture continues. The agrarian subsidies are divided between the so-called first pillar (90 percent) and second pillar (10 percent). Most of the subsidies to the first pillar are payments for production purposes which depend on the amount of arable land a farmer uses for the production of crops, or for the amount of cattle raised. The second pillar contains payments for rural development, including payments for the provision of ecological services. These financial means are clearly insufficient to meet the goals of biodiversity preservation and to minimize other external effects. Besides the ecological arguments to change subsidization,[16] the regulations of WTO demand reforms because of the trade distortions of many "pillar-one subsidies." Therefore, there are strong arguments for a change in agricultural policies, but also in political barriers, since many countries (Spain, France, new members of EU) benefit the current system.

Two publications have indicated how much land is needed in Germany to preserve biodiversity on the species and ecosystems levels.[17] Both studies indicate that 10-15 percent of the terrestrial land (of which a lot must be used extensively in order to preserve ecosystems adapted to more traditional land-use practices) and 5 percent that connects habitats (buffers, corridors) would be sufficient to preserve Germany's overall biodiversity. Economic studies indicate that the opportunity costs are rather low (1.5 billion euros at time of publication) while contingent-valuation studies strongly indicate that the willingness to pay is much higher. (Degenhardt et al., 1998) Therefore, it seems well justified even on economic grounds that European countries invest in a network of areas in which nature conservation has priority. This seems to be a paradigm case for investment in natural capital.

Fisheries

One of Daly's paradigmatic examples for the complementary relationship between man-made and natural capital is fisheries. In fisheries, we are faced with a situation of over-fishing and destruction of marine habitats. Natural capital has become scarce. Globally, humans are fishing down the marine food web. The FAO estimated that 65 percent of the world's commercially used fish stocks are over-fished, fully exploited, or depleted. (FAO, 1999) And, 70 percent of the stocks from European waters are over-fished. (EU Commission, 2001). Since 1995, the EU has introduced instruments to measure the declining resource base as the Total Allowable Catch (TAC), which is specified by quotas. Since then, we have seen both investments in expensive fishing techniques (such as search facilities), and declining fish stocks (in our natural-capital terminology: "living funds"). Because of EU's policy of credit for investing in larger boats, fishermen are forced to pay back loans and therefore cannot accept drastic cuts in TACs.[18] A vicious circle is created from bargaining quotas, overexploitation of resources, and economic precariousness.

Programs to rebuild different living stocks of fish and to minimize negative effects on marine ecosystems should be implemented. Results of several studies provide clear evidence that an investment in natural capital (fish) will minimize external costs and provide high and truly sustainable yields within safe biological limits in the shorter term. Society should pay fishermen for not catching fish for some years in order to derive sustainable yields in the future. Such payments should be perceived as a long-term investment in a crucial fund of natural capital.

Conclusions and Prospects

A "strong sustainability" strategy seems ethically and conceptually sound, politically feasible, and not over-demanding. To wealthy countries, the opportunity costs are modest in the realms of nature conservation and fisheries. A fraction of money being spent for perverse subsidies would be sufficient to implement strong sustainability with regard to nature conservation, agriculture, and fisheries. In the case of climate change, costs are heavily overestimated by mainstream economists since long-term overall costs are discounted. Effective mitigation will cost only a tiny fraction of future GDP. If the rate of discount is reduced to the rate of long-term average economic growth (less than 2 percent), many mitigation policies are efficient today. If non-market impacts on natural assets are assessed fairly, and if technological progress is modeled endogenously, mitigation costs rapidly decline.[19] Thus, we entertain the hypothesis that transitions toward strong sustainability (which is now the essence of "sustainable development") will be less expensive than what many economists believe— and continue to convince others to believe. Under the concept of strong sustainability, the current system of economic accounting needs to be radically transformed. New visions of the quality of human life (sufficiency) should be added to assessment framework. (Milbrath, 1993; Reisch, 2001) And, things look different if Daly's spiritual proposal to include biblical ways of using land as a gift from God is taken into account. (Daly, 1996, Ch. 14) Detailed explanation of a sufficient lifestyle, sustainable consumption, and a biblical "ethos" of exodus and liberation, stewardship and care, joy and plenty, will require, for some, rather different perspectives in their writings.[20]

One might argue that the ethical arguments are sound, the concept of strong sustainability reasonable, the strategies feasible, and opportunity costs modest. But one might still need to add that imperatives for the accumulation of man-made capital are incompatible with strong sustainability. As long as the return on investments remains higher in the realm of man-made capital, one should not expect the fulfillment of CNCR or even investments in natural capital. Capitalism in its deep structure works toward weak sustainability. It would be a bourgeois illusion to believe that one can choose freely between competing concepts of sustainability in a capitalist world order. This criticism has to be taken seriously. For the time being, we entertain the hypothesis that market-based capitalism can be reconciled with strong sustainability. As scientists, we have to look for evidence which might falsify this optimistic hypothesis.

Notes

1.   Further information is to be found under www.umweltrat.de (accessed 9 Jun. 2007). All reports are available in a highly abridged, electronic, English version.
2.   The usual disclaimer applies.
3.   Notice that the ethical justification given in the following section is not to be found in the SRU's report (2002a). It had been skipped since a majority of members argued that politicians will not be interested in ethical theory.
4.   This question has been addressed by articles in Hampicke and Ott (2003).
5.   A close analysis has been done elsewhere (Ott, 2004). This section relies on this article.

6.   See Narveson (1978), Partridge (1990), Howarth (1992).

7.   We will not address the question whether the VOI can be as thick as to cover the information of species membership.

8.   "In attempting to estimate the fair rate of saving to the persons in the original position, one must ask what is reasonable for members of adjacent generations to expect of one another at each level of advance. They try to piece together a just savings schedule by balancing how much at each stage they would be willing to save for their immediate descendants against what they would feel entitled to claim of their immediate predecessors. . . . When they arrive at an estimate that seems fair from both sides . . . then the fair rate . . . is specified." (1971, § 44, p. 290).

9.   There are, of course, many good reasons for unequal distribution according to criteria as work, merit, contribution, special needs, and the like.

10.   Quality of life can be assessed according to Nussbaum's and Sen's approach to capabilities.

11.   Prudence is, as Aristotle argued, always based on moral virtues.

12.   A theory of living funds is given by Faber and Manstetten and Proops (1995).

13.   Many intuitions about "ecological integrity" can be integrated into the concept of natural capital. There are some philosophical advantages in avoiding the notion of integrity with regard to ecosystems.

14.   Climate change triggers huge impacts upon global biodiversity. From a growing body of literature, see Leemans and Eickhout (2004), Thomas et al. (2004), Erasmus et al. (2002).

15.   According to the IPCC scenarios (Nakicenovic et al. 2000; see also WBGU, 2003) it is still possible to reach such a level.

16.   On a national scale, agriculture can be sustained in the longer run in many German regions only by payments given to farmers for ecological services as ground water recharge, soil fertility, or biodiversity. Such payments are investments in natural capital, not subsidies.

17.   Horlitz (1994) for former West Germany and Kretschmer et al. (1995) for former East Germany.

18.   Other problems of today's fishing practices are external effects of certain fishing methods on ecosystems. By-catch of marine mammals, birds, juveniles, and non-target species is high (Hall, 1999). Another external effect of today's fishing practices is the destruction of marine habitats. (Kaiser et al. 2001) Heavy bottom trawls, dredging of seabeds, etc. destroy marine ecosystems. Climate change puts an additional threat to fish species which are adapted to cold waters.

19.   U.S. economists always exaggerated costs and played down benefits of mitigation in their models. Attempts to calculate an "economically optimal climate path" will fail for many reasons. The "optimal climate path" is real Voodoo economics.

20.   See Crüsemann (1997), Segbers (2002). Thanks to Christof Hardmeier (Greifswald).

References

Atkinson, Giles, Richard Dubourg, Kirk Hamilton, Mohan Munasinghe, David Pearce, and Carlos Young, eds. *Measuring Sustainable Development.* Cheltenham, UK: Edward Elgar, 1997.

Crüsemann, Frank. *Die Tora.* Gütersloh: Kaiser, 1997.

Daly, Herman. *Beyond Growth*. Boston: Beacon Press, 1996.
————. "Reconciling Internal and External Policies for Sustainable Development." Pp. 11–31 in *Sustainability and Global Environmental Policy*, edited by Andrew K. Dragun and Kristin M. Jakobsson. Cheltenham, UK: Edward Elgar, 1997.
Degenhardt, Stefan, Ulrich Hampicke, Karin Holm-Müller, Wolfgang Jedicke, and Christian Pfeiffer. *Zahlungsbereitschaft für Naturschutzprogramme*. Bonn: Bundesamt für Naturschutz, 1998.
Erasmus, Barend F. N., Albert S. van Jaarsveld, Steven L. Chown, Mrigesh Kshatriya, and Konrad J. Wessel. "Vulnerability of South African Animal Taxa to Climate Change." *Global Change Biology* 8 (2002): 679–93.
EU Commission. "Green Paper on the Future of the Common Fisheries Policy." 2001. http://ec.europa.eu/fisheries/greenpaper/volume1_en.pdf (23 May 2007).
Faber, Malte, Reiner Manstetten, and John L. R. Proops. "On the Conceptual Foundation of Ecological Economics: A Teleological Approach." *Ecological Economics* 12 (1995): 41–54.
FAO. *The State of the World Fisheries and Aquaculture*. Rome: 1999.
Gowdy, John M., and Carl N. McDaniel. "The Physical Destruction of Nauru: An Example of Weak Sustainability." *Land Economics* 75 (1999): 333–38.
Hall, Stephen J. *The Effects of Fishing on Marine Ecosystems and Communities*. Oxford: Blackwell Science, 1999.
Hampicke, Ulrich, and Konrad Ott, eds. "Reflections on Discounting. Special Issue." *International Journey of Sustainable Development* 6, no. 1 (2003).
Horlitz, Thomas. *Flächenansprüche des Arten- und Biotopschutzes*. Eching: IHW-Verlag, 1994.
Howarth, Richard B. "Intergenerational Justice and the Chain of Obligation." *Environmental Values* 1 (1992): 133–40.
Kaiser, Michel J., and Sebastiaan J. DeGroot. *The Effects of Fishing on Non-Target Species and Habitats*. Oxford: Blackwell Science, 2001.
Krebs, Angelika. "Wieviel Natur schulden wir der Zukunft?" Pp. 313–34 in *Die Zukunft des Wissens*, edited by Jürgen Mittelstraß. Berlin: Akademie Verlag, 2002.
Kretschmer, Hartmut, Holger Pfeffer, Jörg Hoffmann, G. Schrödl, and I. Fux. *Strukturelemente in Agrarlandschaften Ostdeutschlands*. Müncheberg: ZALF, Bericht Nr. 19, 1995.
Leemans, Rick, and Bas Eickhout. "Another Reason for Concern: Regional and Global Impacts on Ecosystems for Different Levels of Climate Change." *Global Environmental Change* 14 (2004): 219–28.
Meyer, Aubrey. "The Kyoto Protocol and the Emergence of 'Contraction and Convergence' as a Framework for an International Political Solution to Greenhouse Gas Emission Abatement." Pp. 291–345 in *Man-Made Climate Change*, edited by Olav Hohmeyer and Klaus Rennings. Mannheim, Germany: Physica, 1999.
Milbrath, Lester W. "Redefining the Good Life in a Sustainable Society." *Environmental Values* 2 (1993): 261–69.
Nakicenovic, Nebosja, et al. *Special Report on Emission Scenarios*. Working Group III of IPCC. Cambridge: Cambridge University Press, 2000.
Narveson, Ian. "Future People and Us." Pp. 38–60 in *Obligations to Future Generations*, edited by Brian Barry and Robert J. Sikora. Philadelphia: Temple University Press, 1978.
Neumayer, Eric. *Weak versus Strong Sustainability*. Cheltenham: Edward Elgar, 1999.

Ott, Konrad. "Essential Components of Future Ethics." Pp. 83–108 in *Ökonomische Rationalität und praktische Vernunft*, edited by Michael Rühs and Ralf Döring. Würzburg, Germany: Königshausen & Neumann, 2004.

———. "Über den Theoriekern und einige intendierte Anwendungen der Diskursethik. Eine strukturalistische Perspektive." *Zeitschrift für philosophische Forschung* 52, no. 2 (1998): 268–91.

Ott, Konrad, and Ralf Döring. *Theorie und Praxis starker Nachhaltigkeit*. Marburg, Germany: Metropolis, 2004.

Ott, Konrad, Gernot Klepper, Stefan Lingner, Achim Schäfer, Jürgen Scheffran, and Detlef Sprinz. *Reasoning Goals of Climate Protection. Specification of Art 2 UNFCCC*. Berlin: Umweltbundesamt, 2004.

Partridge, Ernest. "On the Rights of Future Generations." Pp. 40–66 in *Upstream/Downstream*, edited by Donald Scherer. Philadelphia: Temple University Press, 1990.

Rawls, John. "Reply to Habermas." *The Journal of Philosophy* 92, no. 3 (1995): 132–80.

———. *A Theory of Justice*. Cambridge: Harvard, 1971.

Reisch, Lucia. "Time and Wealth." *Time & Society* 10, no. 2–3 (2001): 367–85.

Segbers, Franz. *Die Hausordnung der Tora. Biblische Impulse für eine theologische Wirtschaftsethik*. Luzern: Edition Exodus, 2002.

Solow, Robert. "Intergenerational Equity and Exhaustible Resources." *Review of Economic Studies* 14 (1974): 29–45.

SRU (Der Rat von Sachverständigen für Umweltfragen). *Für eine neue Vorreiterpolitik*. Umweltgutachten 2002. Stuttgart: Metzler-Poeschel, 2002a.

———. *Für eine Stärkung und Neuorientierung im Naturschutz. Sondergutachten*. Stuttgart: Metzler-Poeschel, 2002b.

———. *Meeresumweltschutz für Nord- und Ostsee. Sondergutachten*. Baden-Baden: Nomos, 2004.

———. *Umwelt und Straßenverkehr. Sondergutachten*. Baden-Baden: Nomos, 2005.

Thomas, Chris D., and Allison Cameron. Extinction Risk from Climate Change. *Nature* 427 (2004): 145–48.

WBGU (Wissenschaftlicher Beirat der Bundesregierung Globale Umweltveränderungen). *Energiewende zur Nachhaltigkeit*. Berlin and Heidelberg: Springer, 2003.

World Commission on Environment and Development (WCED). *Our Common Future*. Oxford: Oxford University Press, 1987.

Part III:
Governance for Ecological Integrity, Sustainable Ecosystem Function, and Public Health

The ability of ecosystems to provide their various services to the planet, from clean air, water, and soil, to aesthetic and cultural diversity, is foundational to the question of a sustainable future for life on Earth. In this, the third part of the book, we present the background to the concept of "ecological integrity."

Then, to understand how humans have allowed themselves to pursue a path that is as undermining of ecosystem integrity as what our present path is, we introduce the method for deconstructing knowledge to gain insight into how we permit ourselves to continue on such an unsustainable path.

We need collective decision-making as an aid for redirecting ourselves toward sustainability. In fact, it is necessary to move away from fragmented decision-making relating to sustainability across levels of government, and lessons for integrated governance can be applied.

The fact is that most of the healthier societies globally consume relatively vast amounts of the world's resources to sustain their high levels of personal and community health. On close inspection, however, some societies achieve high levels of general health on relatively less natural capital. Lessons from what other societies have achieved with smaller footprints can help us in our pursuit of sustainability.

Because ever-enlarging ecological footprints are unsustainable under a model of global equity, governance for achieving balance is desirable.

Chapter 9

Evolution of the Ecological Integrity Debate

David Manuel-Navarrete, Ph.D. (Geography)
United Nations Economic Commission for
Latin America, Santiago, Chile
Contact Information:
Email: david.manuel_navarrete@kcl.ac.uk

The Late James J. Kay, Ph.D.
(Systems Design Engineering)
University of Waterloo, Ontario, Canada

Dan Dolderman, Ph.D. (Social Psychology)
Department of Psychology,
University of Toronto, Ontario, Canada
Contact Information: 100 St. George St., Toronto, Ont. M5S 3G3 CANADA
Phone: +1 416 978 6057; Fax: +1 416 978 4811
Email: dolderman@psych.utoronto.ca

Summary

Ecological integrity (EI) has become a central concept in conservation policies and programs around North America and in other parts of the world. This chapter narrates the evolution of this concept.

Two main positions in the literature are identified: one emphasizes the normative aspects of conservation; that is, EI is achieved by enforcing policies and laws, which are based on ethical norms and scientific standards.

The second position focuses on transforming society by re-thinking the relationship between humans and ecosystems. That is, EI is achieved through dialogue and negotiation leading to social and cultural transformation.

The origins and evolution of these two broad positions are documented. It is concluded that embracing both positions, rather than promoting one under all circumstances, would be a step toward integrated governance in decision-making for sustainability.

Context

Integrity has been conventionally used to describe the moral standing of human beings. To have integrity is to be dependable and responsible, with a clear sense of what is good and what is not good. In this way, integrity is linked to moral autonomy and refers to questions of moral good. In engineering terms, we speak of a building's structural integrity. That is, it will stand and not collapse. Integrity also implies integration. Specifically, the recent emphasis on integrity has arisen from the emerging postmodern recognition that there are multiple valid perspectives that must be voiced, considered, and integrated. It is the integration of these multiple perspectives that allows progress toward integrated governance to be made.

The Early Origins of the Concept of Integrity

One of the earliest references to integrity in the environmental literature was Aldo Leopold's (1949: 224) famous statement in his essay on land ethics:

> The key-log which must be moved to release the evolutionary process for an ethic is simply this: quit thinking about decent land-use as solely an economic problem. Examine each question in terms of what is ethically and aesthetically right, as well as what is economically expedient. A thing is right when it tends to preserve the *integrity*, stability, and beauty of the biotic community. It is wrong when it tends otherwise. [*emphasis added*]

However, Leopold never explained what he meant by integrity. (Noss et al., 2000) As Sellars (1997) argues, the concept of ecological integrity (EI) was already implicit within Parks Service debates prior to the 1960s. Sellars identifies two groups within the Parks Service: one emphasized recreational tourism and public enjoyment of majestic landscapes, along with preservation of a semblance of wild America; the other, represented mainly by wildlife biologists, focused on preserving ecological integrity in the parks, while permitting development for public use in carefully selected areas. According to Sellars (1997):

> The central dilemma of national park management has long been the question of exactly what in a park should be preserved. Is it the scenery— the resplendent landscapes of forests, streams, wildflowers, and majestic mammals? Or is it the integrity of each park's entire natural system, including not just the biological and scenic superstars, but also the vast array of less compelling species, such as grasses, lichens, and mice?

During the 1960s, the Leopold and Robbins reports (Leopold et al., 1963; NRC, 1963) were very influential in encouraging major commitments to ecological principles among the staff of natural parks. Written by scientists (mostly biologists), these reports gave considerable weight to the scientific perspective regarding national park management. (NRC, 1992) In seeking stronger influence on national park management, the scientists were bolstered by the emergence of the environmental movement and resulting legislation (in particular, the 1964 Wilderness Act). Social and environmental justice movements in the 1960s and 1980s reflected an awakening among many individuals in Western society regarding ideals of justice and equity for all people, regardless of gender, race, nationality, or other distinctions. (Wallerstein, 2000) These movements, and the political and social actions that resulted, were an attempt to recognize and redress perceived inequities between different groups in society, a goal which was also compatible with the emerging concerns for environmental protection and conservation, and the extension of rights to future human generations, as well as to other species. Parallel to the growing desires for social justice were desires for environmental equality, based on the recognition that our current treatment of natural ecosystems will have consequences for the rights of future generations, and an acknowledgment that the basic right to survive should be shared by the rest of the living world in its own natural course of evolution.

In the international environmental arena, an early manifestation of these concerns was the 1968 UNESCO Conference on the Conservation and Rational Use of the Biosphere. This conference launched the Man and the Biosphere (MAB) Program, in which international cooperation led to the creation of 208 biosphere reserves around the world from 1976 to 1981. The World Network for Biosphere Reserves included 283 sites in 1990, 324 in 1995, and 440 in 2002. (Batisse, 1993; Price, 2002) This program was instrumental in explicitly recognizing, at an international level, that the movement toward integrity in the environmental domain required a great deal of cooperation between conflicting interests in society, based on differing economic, social, political, and ethical values. As stated in Bridgewater, 2002: 15:

> From the outset, then, the primary concern of this MAB project was essentially a scientific one, with the designated areas consisting of representative ecosystems and the aim being to achieve the fullest possible cover of the world, ensuring more systematic conservation than before. At the same time, biosphere reserves are more than just protected areas. Their conservation objective is all the better achieved in that it is supported by research, monitoring and training activities, on the one hand, and is pursued by involving systematically the cooperation and the local populations concerned, on the other hand.

Bringing the Concept into Environmental Legislation

During the 1970s, science gained further prominence within environmental management in the United States of America. (NRC, 1992; Sellars, 1997) The 1972 U.S. Water Pollution Control Act Amendments introduced the notion of EI into legislation. (Mackenthun, 1975; Karr, 1991; Noss et al., 2000) The goal of the "Clean Water Act" was stated as: "restoration and maintenance of chemical, physical, and biological integrity of the Nation's waters."[1] Emphasis was placed on the integrity of water systems as an objective property determined by chemical and biological indicators. These 1972 amendments were instrumental in ensuring the inclusion of the EI concept into the environmental discussion; promoting the notion that integrity has to be understood as a holistic quality involving ecosystems as wholes, and suggesting the need to elucidate ecological principles to guide human behavior. (Westra et al., 2000) From the early days then, there has been consensus that EI is fundamentally about the interconnections and interdependencies between humans and the environment. However, it is worthwhile noting that although the discussion of EI may have been stimulated by 1960s social justice movements, the goals of assessing, working toward, and maintaining EI were primarily conceptualized as technical problems to which conservation biology could provide answers and solutions. (Jackson and Davis, 1995) The 1972 U.S. Water Pollution Control Act Amendments had great influence in the efforts to define EI in operational terms. According to Outen (1975: 215), EI was used in the 1972 Amendments to:

> Convey a concept that refers to a condition in which the natural structure and function of ecosystems is maintained. . . . Although man is a "part of nature" and a product of evolution, "natural" is generally defined as that condition in existence before the activities of man invoked perturbations which prevented the system from returning to its original state of equilibrium.

In 1975, the U.S. Environmental Protection Agency convened a symposium to clarify the concept of integrity. (Ballantine and Guarraia, 1975; Karr, 1991) The symposium was designed to interrelate two aspects of integrity: (1) as a measurable characteristic of ecosystems, and (2) as a normative principle to guide policy and regulatory practices. This symposium strongly promoted the role of science as being to provide objective criteria for meeting the integrity needs of ecosystems (e.g., Cairns, 1975). Human activities were mainly depicted as stressors acting over natural ecosystems. At this point in 1975, the discussion of EI revolved primarily around biophysical concerns, and the need for meeting criteria that could "objectively" represent the integrity of natural systems. Issues of social justice and the recognition that human values ultimately underlie any definition of EI remained in the background of the discussion (see Ballantine and Guarraia, 1975).

In the late 1970s, two major events reinforced the incorporation of EI into environmental management in North America. One was a report by the United States National Parks and Conservation Association (NPCA, 1979), which emphasized "external threats" jeopardizing the remaining integrity of the parks' natural conditions. This report called for the collection of baseline biological information needed to permit the identification of incremental changes that could be affecting the integrity of natural resources. (Sellars, 1997) The inclusion of "external threats" represented an important shift toward understanding parks on a broader spatial scale beyond their strict legal limits.

During the same period, the 1978 Great Lakes Water Quality Agreement led to considerable work to operationalize EI as it pertained to the Great Lakes ecosystems. (Regier, 1992) The Agreement, first signed in 1972 and renewed several times since 1978, expresses the commitment of Canada and the United States of America to restore and maintain the chemical, physical and biological integrity of the Great Lakes Basin Ecosystem.

Ecological research on the Great Lakes emphasized systemic approaches to EI, with several conceptual consequences. First, systems theory caused people to question the understanding of traditional, reductionist scientific approaches to knowledge, and to refocus on the value-laden dimension of EI and the interconnections between humans and "natural" systems. (Kay, 1993; Jensen et al., 1996; Kay and Regier, 2000) Second, addressing the complexity of ecosystems highlighted the unavoidable uncertainties of these systems. As a consequence, adaptive strategies were devised to incorporate surprise. (Holling, 1978) Third, attention started to shift to social systems, and the management and influence of human behavior, moving away from a mind-set based primarily on the application of technological fixes. (Francis and Regier, 1995) The net result of this systemic perspective was that discussions of EI began to emphasize:

1.   The need for a cultural shift away from the progress ethic,
2.   A renewed appreciation of the primacy of the relationship between humans and nature in conceptualizing environmental management, and
3.   The need to include the multiple perspectives of those individuals affected by decisions. Thus, by the 1980s, the discussion of integrity had returned to the initial 1960s roots in incorporating the social dimension of conservation.

Late Conceptual and Legislative Developments

During the 1980s and 1990s, the evolution of the concept of EI was heavily influenced by the academic development of environmental ethics, ecophilosophy, conservation biology, and conservation ecology. It is therefore necessary to understand the contributions made by these four disciplines in steering the further development of the EI concept.

Environmental ethics emerged, according to the International Society of Environmental Ethics, from the first Earth Day in 1970 when environmentalists started urging philosophers to do something about environmental ethics.[2] During the 1970s the environmental ethics debate was centered on historical, theological, and religious aspects rather than on purely philosophical ones. (Bakken et al., 1995) In 1973, Norwegian philosopher Arne Naess published a paper on shallow and deep ecology which marked the beginning of the Deep Ecology Movement and the development of Ecophilosophy. (Naess, 1973; Devall and Sessions, 1985; Fox, 1990)

The development of environmental philosophy was catalyzed in 1979 with the creation of the journal *Environmental Ethics*. The first five years of the journal were focused on discussions of animal rights and rights for nature. Aldo Leopold's Land Ethic had a great influence on the discussions regarding both the rights for nature in general, and EI in particular. (Callicot, 1989; Westra, 2001) In 1990, the International Society of Environmental Ethics was established through the efforts of Laura Westra and Holmes Roston III. In 1992 and 1996, two additional refereed journals devoted to environmental ethics were established: *Environmental Values*, and *Ethics and Environment*. In 1997, a second international association was created, the International Association for Environmental Philosophy, with an emphasis on environmental phenomenology. One of the main issues addressed by environmental ethics is the dilemma of anthropocentrism versus biocentrism, and intrinsic versus instrumental or pragmatic values of nature. (Norton, 1995; Callicott et al., 1999; Zack, 2002)

Conservation biology is a specialized discipline which aims to bridge the gap between pure science and practical management by providing guidelines for tackling the complexity of ecosystems. (Soulé, 1985; Western, 1989) Western (1989: 23) describes the goals of conservation biology as being to: (1) provide scientific conservation principles, (2) identify conservation problems, (3) establish corrective procedures, and (4) bridge science and management by making scientists responsive to conservation problems and managers responsive to biological issues. The Society for Conservation Biology was established in 1985. Its mission is: "to help develop the scientific and technical means for the protection, maintenance, and restoration of life on this planet—its species, its ecological and evolutionary processes, and its particular and total environment." (Jules et al., 2002: 2)

Conservation ecology emerged in 1997 with the establishment of the journal *Conservation Ecology*. Holling (1998: 4) defined conservation ecology as a "place" to develop and explore the novel theories, methods, research, and policies that are needed to underpin the conservation, restoration, and maintenance of the natural heritage that sustains life and human opportunity. Conservation ecology can be seen as a complement to conservation biology with a stronger emphasis on socioecological dynamics and complex systems theory (e.g., by acknowledging irreducible uncertainties). At the theoretical level, conservation ecology has been strongly influenced by Holling's Figure-8 adaptive cycle model and cross-scale panarchies. (Holling, 1978; 2001) In the present, conservation ecology is increasing its emphasis on interdisciplinary approaches and the incorporation of humans in the study of ecosystems (e.g., Gunderson and Folke, 2003). Both conservation biology and conservation ecology share the aim of bridging the gap between science and policy.

An important effort to define EI was undertaken during the 1990s. Initiated by Laura Westra in 1992 (Westra et al., 2000), one of the main objectives of this effort was to relate the ecosystem approach and the goal of restoring integrity to moral principles and norms in a way that might serve as a basis for public policy. (Westra and Lemons, 1995; Lackey, 2001) This group of researchers promoted a scientific conceptualization of EI: "the capability of supporting and maintaining a balanced, integrated, adaptive community of organisms having species composition, diversity, and functional organization comparable to that of natural habitats of the region." (Karr and Dudley, 1981) However, the concept of EI was still assumed to carry normative value, or weight. That is, EI possesses intrinsic value, setting an ethical standard of what is "good," with the clear implication being that EI becomes a moral imperative, in the Kantian sense; it becomes something that society must work toward, on the same order as, perhaps, "freedom," "equality," or "truth." This particular way of conceptualizing EI favored a normative perspective leading to efforts to operationalize EI in terms of precise management goals. These goals are to be based on a scientific delineation of the biological parameters of EI, thus providing an objective framework that can be used to guide public policy. In the North American legal context, this approach seems to make the concept of EI quite useful as it can be used to set standards in legislation and regulations.

This approach has also been applied in the European Union by incorporating the notion of EI into the Water Framework Directive of the European Parliament and the Council (2000/60/EC), establishing a framework for action in the field of water policy. Austria was one of the pioneer European countries in incorporating the notion of EI (*ökologische Funktionsfähigkeit*) into water management legislation. Chovanec et al. (2000: 445) describe the methodology that has been developed in Austria for assessing the EI of water bodies:

> Ecological integrity reflects the necessity of considering water bodies as ecological systems. Although ecological integrity of running waters is and must remain a holistic concept, the current Austrian methodology aims at assessing it by investigating a number of key components: hydro-morphological aspects . . . physico-chemical parameters, macroinvertebrate and fish assemblages, biological water quality assessment and ecotoxicological valuations.

EI is also one of the ten basic principles of the Pan-European Biological and Landscape Diversity Strategy developed by the European Council in 1994. The strategy aims to achieve the conservation and sustainable use of biological and landscape diversity in Europe.

Internationally, the concept of EI has been incorporated into regulatory and legislative documents. (Karr, 1991; Miller and Rees, 2000) These include international agreements, national regulations, constitutional texts, reports from advisory boards, and political statements. As stated by Westra (1995: 12):

> From the time of the 1972 Clean Water Act to the recent vision and mission statements following the Earth Summit in Rio de Janeiro, the term and concepts of "integrity" have appeared in the Great Lakes Water Quality Agreement (1978), the Canada Park Services Regulations (1992), the Great Lakes Science Advisory Board Report (1991), Agenda 21, Ascend 21, the draft Montana Environmental Protection Act (1992), Environment Canada's Mission Statement (1992), UNCED documents (1992), World Bank reports (particularly in the

bank's 1992 discussion of biodiversity), and many other documents, including the constitution of Brazil (Ch. 6, *Meio Ambiente*).

In some documents, EI is considered to be the most relevant concept for conservation strategies. For instance, the Canadian National Parks Act, as amended in 1988, and since, requires that maintenance of EI be a first priority when developing a park management plan.

During the last decade, EI has acquired greater significance and new meanings in the international arena through the *Earth Charter* initiative. The *Earth Charter* (see the Appendix) aims to offer a code of ethics by whose principles humans should orient their personal lives and organizations during the forthcoming century. (Brenes, 2002) Four of the sixteen sub-principles of the *Earth Charter* are explicitly related to the concept of EI. A first draft was issued at Rio 92 for its adoption by the United Nations, but the governments did not agree. In 1997, The Earth Council and Green Cross International formed an *Earth Charter* Commission to give oversight to the process. Five co-chairs were selected to represent the regions of the world and a secretariat for the commission was established. (Evie and Glass, 2002) The final version of the *Earth Charter* was issued in March 2000. This version dropped off part of its biocentrism and religiosity in order to adapt the document to the tone of UN's resolutions.

Conclusions

The conceptual construction of EI has evolved considerably since Leopold's (1949) formulation. Despite this evolution, the definition of the term remains remarkably ambiguous and controversial. As indicated by Noss et al. (2000: 1), EI is often used as "an umbrella concept to encompass all that is good and right in ecosystems," or merely considered as "a convenient way to describe and summarize the condition of a biological community or ecosystem." However, this controversial character should not be seen as a disadvantage. Quite the opposite, ambiguity increases the concept's adaptability to the needs imposed by contextual circumstances and realities.

In the above historical overview, a tension can be discerned between (1) those who see the definition of EI as part of a subjective exercise involving the negotiation of values (e.g. Regier, 1992; Francis and Regier, 1995; Kay et al., 1999; Meppem and Bourke, 1999; Morito, 1999), and (2) others who see EI as a largely objective issue (e.g. Karr, 1993; Noss, 1995; Ulanowicz, 1995; Westra, 1995; Barbour et al., 2000; Kurtz et al., 2001). The first perspective revolves around the belief that EI requires understanding how to promote a society based on social and environmental justice principles, where the discussion of integrity itself can unfold in a manner that reflects integrity, and the interests of all are represented and acknowledged. In contrast, the second perspective implies a process of "institutionalization," where EI is defined as an objective property of ecosystems that can be determined through scientific measurement, and therefore, recommendations to promote EI can be incorporated into political agendas without considering or including the perspectives or values of lay people and society in general.

The first perspective leads to more open-ended and flexible definitions of EI, putting it on the same level as other ambiguous concepts such as justice, freedom, love, and democracy. The second perspective leads to centered definitions which try to fix the meaning of EI in order to make it operational (i.e., measurable, and easy to monitor and communicate) so that effective policies can be rapidly implemented.

Rather than engaging in an endless debate over which is the best and most comprehensive definition or approach to EI, we believe it is more convenient to embrace these multiple definitions. This embracement can be seen as a step toward integrated forms of governance. Contextual circumstances can determine which of these possible approaches, or their combination, can be the most effective.

Notes

1. Available at: http://www.epa.gov/watertrain/cwa (30 May 2007).
2. From the Center of Environmental Philosophy Web site. URL: http://cep.unt.edu (30 May 2007).

References

Bakken, Peter W., Joan Gibb Engel, and J. Ronald Engel. *Ecology, Justice, and Christian Faith: A Guide to the Literature 1960–1993*. Westport, CT: Greenwood Press, 1995.

Ballantine, R. K., and L. J. Guarraia, eds. *The Integrity of Water: Proceedings of a Symposium*. Washington, DC: U.S. Environmental Protection Agency, 1975.

Barbour, Michael T., W. F. Swietlik, S. K. Jackson, D. L. Courtemanch, S. P. Davies, and C. O. Yoder. "Measuring the Attainment of Biological Integrity in the U.S.A.: A Critical Element of Ecological Integrity." *Hydrobiologia* 422/423 (2000): 453–64.

Batisse, Michel. "The Silver Jubilee of MAB and Its Revival." *Environmental Conservation* 20, no. 2 (1993): 107–12.

Brenes, Abelardo. "The Earth Charter Principles: Source for an Ethics of Universal Responsibility." Pp. 26–36 in *Just Ecological Integrity*, edited by Peter Miller and Laura Westra. Lanham, MD: Rowman & Littlefield, 2002.

Bridgewater, Peter. "Biosphere Reserves—A Network for Conservation and Sustainability." *Parks: The International Journal for Protected Area Managers* 12, no. 3 (2002): 15–20.

Cairns, John, Jr. "Quantification of Biological Integrity." Pp. 171–87 in *The Integrity of Water: Proceedings of a Symposium*, edited by Richard K. Ballantine and L. J. Guarraia. Washington, DC: U.S. Environmental Protection Agency, 1975.

Callicott, J. Baird, Larry B. Crowder, and Karen Mumford. "Current Normative Concepts in Conservation." *Conservation Biology* 13, no. 1 (1999): 22–35.

Chovanec, Andreas, P. Jäger, M. Jungwirth, V. Koller-Kreimel, O. Moog, et al. "The Austrian Way of Assessing the Ecological Integrity of Running Waters: A Contribution to the EU Water Framework Directive." *Hydrobiologia* 422/423 (2000): 445–52.

Devall, Bill, and George Sessions. *Deep Ecology. Living as if Nature Mattered*. Salt Lake City: Peregrine Smith Books, 1985.

D'Evie, Fayen, and Steven M. Glass. "The Earth Charter: An Ethical Framework for Sustainable Living." Pp. 17–25 in *Just Ecological Integrity*, edited by Peter Miller and Laura Westra. Lanham, MD: Rowman & Littlefield, 2002.

Fox, Warwick. *Towards Transpersonal Ecology: Developing New Foundations for Environmentalism*. Boston and London: Shambhala Publications, 1990.

Francis, George R., and Henry R. Regier. "Restoration of the Great Lakes Basin Ecosystem." Pp. 256–91 in *Barriers and Bridges to the Renewal of Ecosystems and Institutions*, edited by Lance H. Gunderson, C. S. Holling, and Stephen S. Light. New York: Columbia University Press, 1995.

Gunderson, Lance, and Carl Folke. "Toward a 'Science of the Long View.'" *Conservation Ecology* 7, no. 1 (2003): 15.

Holling, Crawford S., ed. *Adaptive Environmental Assessment and Management*. Chichester, UK: John Wiley and Sons, 1978.

Holling, Crawford S. "Two Cultures of Ecology." *Conservation Ecology* [online] 2, no. 2 (1998): 4. http://www.ecologyandsociety.org/vol2/iss2/art4/ (30 May 2007).

———. "Understanding the Complexity of Economic, Ecological, and Social Systems." *Ecosystems* 4 (2001): 390–405.

Jackson, Susan, and Wayne S. Davis. "Meeting the Goal of Biological Integrity in Water Resource Programs in the U.S. Environmental Protection Agency." *Journal of the North American Benthological Society* 13, no. 4 (1995): 592–97.

Jensen, Mark E., Patrick S. Bourgeron, Richard Everett, and Iris Goodman. "Ecosystem Management: A Landscape Ecology Perspective." *Water Resources Bulletin* 32, no. 2 (1996): 203–16.

Jules, Erik S., Thomas V. Dietsch, Aina B. Bernier, Virginia Nickerson, Patrick J. Christie, et al. "Toward a More Effective Conservation Biology: Including Social Equity in the Formulation of Scientific Questions and Management Options." *THEOMAI* 6, no. 2 (2002).

Karr, James R. "Biological Integrity: A Long-Neglected Aspect of Water Resource Management." *Ecological Applications* 1 (1991): 66–84.

———. "Measuring Biological Integrity: Lessons from Streams." Pp. 83–104 in *Ecological Integrity and the Management of Ecosystems*, edited by Stephen Woodley, James Kay, and George Francis. Delray, FL: St. Lucie Press, 1993.

Karr, James R., and Daniel R. Dudley. "Ecological Perspective on Water Quality Goals." *Environmental Management* 5, no. 1 (1981): 55–68.

Kay, James J. "On the Nature of Ecological Integrity: Some Closing Comments." Pp. 201–14 in *Ecological Integrity and the Management of Ecosystems*, edited by Stephen Woodley, James Kay, and George Francis. Delray, FL: St. Lucie Press, 1993.

Kay, James J., Michelle Boyle, Henry A. Regier, and George Francis. "An Ecosystem Approach for Sustainability: Addressing the Challenge of Complexity." *Futures* 31, no. 7 (1999): 721–42.

Kay, James J., and Henry Regier. "Uncertainty, Complexity, and Ecological Integrity: Insights from and Ecosystem Approach." Pp. 121–56 in *Implementing Ecological Integrity: Restoring Regional and Global Environmental and Human Health*, edited by Philippe Crabbé, Alan J. Holland, Lech Ryszkowski, and Laura Westra. Kluwer, Netherlands: NATO Series, Environmental Security, 2000.

Kurtz, Janice C., Laura E. Jackson, and William S. Fischer. "Strategies for Evaluating Indicators Based on Guidelines from the Environmental Protection Agency's Office of Research and Development." *Ecological Indicators* 1 (2001): 49–60.

Lackey, Robert T. "Values, Policy, and Ecosystem Health." *Bioscience* 51, no. 6 (2001): 437–43.

Leopold, Aldo S. *A Sand County Almanac*. New York: Oxford University Press, 1949.

Leopold, Aldo S., Stanley A. Cain, Clarence M. Cottam, Ira N. Gabrielson, and Thomas L. Kimball. "Wildlife Management in the National Parks." *Transcript of the North American Wildlife and Natural Resources Conference* 28 (1963): 28–45.

MacKenthun, Kenneth M. "Legislative requirements." Pp. 5–7 in *The Integrity of Water: Proceedings of a Symposium*, edited by Richard K. Ballantine and L. J. Guarraia. Washington, DC: U.S. Environmental Protection Agency, 1975.

Meppem, Tony, and Simon Bourke. "Different Ways of Knowing: A Communicative Turn toward Sustainability." *Ecological Economics* 30 (1999): 389–404.

Miller, Peter, and William E. Rees. "Introduction." Pp. 19–44 in *Integrating Environment, Conservation, and Health*, edited by David Pimentel, Laura Westra, and Reed F. Noss. Washington DC: Island Press, 2000.

Morito, Bruce. "Examining Ecosystem Integrity as a Primary Mode of Recognizing the Autonomy of Nature." *Environmental Ethics* 21, no. 2 (1999): 59–73.

Naess, Arne. "The Shallow and the Deep, Long-Range Ecology Movement: A Summary." *Inquiry* 16 (1973): 95–100.

Norton, Bryan "Ecological Integrity and Social Values: At What scale?" *Ecosystem Health* 1, no. 4 (1995): 228–41.

Noss, Reed F., Nicholas C. Slosser, James R. Strittholt, and C. Carroll. *Some Thoughts on Metrics of Ecological Integrity for Terrestrial Ecosystems and Entire Landscapes*. Corvallis, OR: Report of the Conservation Biology Institute, 2000.

Noss, Reed F. "Ecological Integrity and Sustainability: Buzzwords in Conflict?" Pp. 60–76 in *Perspectives on Ecological Integrity*, edited by Laura Westra and John Lemons. Kluwer, Netherlands: Kluwer Academic Publishers, 1995.

NPCA (National Parks and Conservation Association). *NPCA Adjacent Lands Survey: No Park is an Island*. Washington, DC: NPCA, 1979.

NRC (National Research Council). *A Report: Advisory Committee to the National Park Service*. Washington, DC: National Academy Press, 1963.

———. *Science and the National Parks*. Washington, DC: National Academies Press, 1992.

Outen, Ronald. "A Conservationist View." Pp. 215–20 in *The Integrity of Water: Proceedings of a Symposium*, edited by Richard K. Ballantine, and L. J. Guarraia. Washington, DC: U.S. Environmental Protection Agency, 1975.

Price, Martin F. "The Periodic Review of Biosphere Reserves: A Mechanism to Foster Sites of Excellence for Conservation and Sustainable Development." *Environmental Science & Policy* 5 (2002): 13–18.

Regier, Henry A. "Ecosystem Integrity in the Great Lakes Basin: An Historical Sketch of Ideas and Actions." *Journal of Aquatic Ecosystem Health* 1 (1992): 25–37.

Sellars, Richard W. *Preserving Nature in the National Parks: A History*. Ann Arbor, MI: Edwards Brothers Inc., 1997.

Soulé, Michael E. "Conservation Biology." *Bioscience* 35 (1985): 727–34.

Ulanowicz, Robert E. "Ecosystem Integrity: A Causal Necessity." Pp. 77–87 in *Perspectives on Ecological Integrity*, edited by Laura Westra and John Lemons. Kluwer, Netherlands: Kluwer Academic Publishers, 1995.

Wallerstein, Immanuel. "¿La globalización o la era de la transición?: Una visión a largo plazo de la trayectoria del sistema-mundo." *Casa de las Américas* 219 (2000): 14–25.

Western, David. "Conservation Biology." Pp. 31–36 in *Conservation for the Twenty-first Century*, edited by David Western and Mary C. Pearl. New York: Oxford University Press, 1989.

Westra, Laura. "From Aldo Leopold to the Wildlands Project: The Ethics of Integrity." *Environmental Ethics* 23 (2001): 261–74.

———. "Ecosystem Integrity and Sustainability: The Foundation Value of the Wild." Pp. 12–33 in *Perspectives on Ecological Integrity*, edited by Laura Westra and John Lemons. Kluwer, Netherlands: Kluwer Academic Publishers, 1995.

Westra, Laura, and John Lemons. "Introduction to Perspectives on Ecological Integrity." Pp. 1–11 in *Perspectives on Ecological Integrity*, edited by Laura Westra and John Lemons. Kluwer, Netherlands: Kluwer Academic Publishers, 1995.

Westra, Laura, Peter Miller, James R. Karr, William E. Rees, and Robert E. Ulanowicz. "Ecological Integrity and the Aims of the Global Integrity Project." Pp. 19–44 in *Integrating Environment, Conservation, and Health*, edited by David Pimentel, Laura Westra, and Reed F. Noss. Washington, DC: Island Press, 2000.

Zack, Naomi. "Human Values as a Source for Sustaining the Environment." Pp. 69–73 in *Just Ecological Integrity*, edited by Peter Miller and Laura Westra. Lanham, MD: Rowman & Littlefield, 2002.

Chapter 10

Collective Decision-Making Bridging Public Health, Sustainability Governance, and Environmental Management

Valerie Brown, Ph.D. (Human Sciences)

Professor Emeritus, University of Western Sydney
Director, Local Sustainability Project
Fenner School of Environment and Society
Australian National University, Canberra, Australia

Contact Information: Building 48, Linneaus Way, Canberra 0200 *AUSTRALIA*
Phone: +61 2 62958650; Fax: +61 2 62958650; Email: valeriebrown@ozemail.com.au

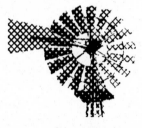

Summary

Collective governance at the interface of public health, sustainability, and the environment is crucial for repairing the breaches in global ecological integrity that stand in the way of a just, humane, and healthy global future. This proposition, however, rests on a paradox: the components to be brought together to generate a solution are the same divided compartments of knowledge credited with leading to the problem in the first place.

Collective decisions among public health practitioners, sustainability advocates, and environmental scientists will need to address this paradox, or they risk becoming enmeshed as part of the problem. Collective decision-making will challenge the well-established assumptions that science, politics and art do not mix, and that science is the only reliable form of knowledge.

In this chapter, we identify five constructions of knowledge involved in the governance of sustainable futures: individual, community, specialized, organizational, and holistic. We explore the synthesis processes required to bring those ways of knowing together, not only to make collective decisions, but also to take collective action. Unless such a synthesis becomes a practicable option and collective social learning takes place, both locally and globally, there is little hope of a system of coordinated global governance capable of sustaining life on Earth.

Background: Losing a Generation

Over the past three decades, international reviews, committees of inquiry, and global conferences have arrived at the same conclusion about one necessary condition for sustainability governance. From the first World Conference on the Environment 1972, and the World Commission on Environment and Development 1987, to the United Nations Commission on Sustainable Development 1998, the United Nations Millennium Development Goals of 2000, the World Summit on Sustainable Development 2002, and the United Nations Millennium Ecosystem Assessment 2005, have come pleas for collective decision-making. They unanimously argue that a more integrative approach, bringing together the knowledge and actions of the specialist disciplines, the powerful organizations, and the affected communities, is essential if we are to achieve systems-based interventions. Community, specialists, and governments are urged to cooperate as a collaborative team in addressing the breaches in global ecological integrity. For over a generation, calls for collective decision-making between these interested parties have continued to increase while the state of the planet degenerates. (McMichael, 2001)

There is no shortage of suggestions on ways to achieve such collaboration. The World Commission on Environment and Development's "Our Common Future" devoted several chapters to avenues for bringing together the professions (for example, law, economics, health, and environmental science) with government and civil service organizations. Influential as the report has been, these suggestions for an integrated response have largely been ignored, and there was little about health (WCED, 1987)

There were some successes, however. In 2000, the World Commission on Dams successfully combined contributions from all the interested parties in a widely-praised report: Dams and Development: A New Framework for Decision-making. Yet, the conclusions were rejected as impractical by the World Bank and the dam-building industry, the very organizations that had been asking for an integrated approach. (World Commission on Dams, 2000)

Further attempts at a practical integration have included the calculation of the Ecological Footprint, the impact of human activities on ecological integrity at the individual, local and global levels. (Rees and Wackernagel, 1996) Progress toward sustainability has been monitored against the "Triple Bottom Line" of economic, social, and environmental accounting. (World Business Council for Sustainable Development, 2005)

Short-term collaboration between the specializations of health, environmental science, economics, education, and political science rarely continues into long-term programs. Responses to environmental issues have been channeled through the separate and often competing decision-making systems of government, industry, and community organizations. Academic disciplines vie for dominance within multidisciplinary teams. There is a need to integrate the integrators.

The continuing fragmentation of effort arising from the divisions between the disciplines, the walls that insulate departments, and the competition between individuals, should not be surprising. The very success of analytic thinking since the eighteen-century Enlightenment has made the division of knowledge into its constituent parts the preferred approach to all decision-making. Consequently, the Western cultural approach to knowledge places multiple hurdles in the way of redressing the fragmentation and polarization of issues and their solutions. (Latour, 1993; Funtowicz and Ravetz, 1993) Rules of analysis and hierarchical structure have become so firmly established that they remain the default option when facing pressures to change. The shift in treating complex issues as open ended and interconnected, rather than as stratified and predetermined, requires no less than a reorganization of our customary patterns of decision-making. (Costanza and Jorgenson, 2002) We go on to consider a program in which this reorganization was introduced in a wide range of contexts over six years.

Proposition: Adopting a Collective Approach to Integration

The calls for an integrative approach to global ecological problems are based on the need for a systemic solution to system-wide disruptions. However, most attempts at integrated sustainability governance involve the synthesis of only one set of interests at a time. They combine a range of disciplines and professions, or unite community interests, or negotiate shared organizational power. This leaves different solutions being advocated by different sectors, and so generating continual conflicts of interest within each group as well as among them. The full set of these interests are seldom brought together to achieve a common goal that will last over time.

A six-year study of the introduction of sustainability initiatives at the interface between health, environment, and governance, the Local Sustainability Project, documented a range of attempts at collective decision-making. (Brown, 2007) The key question posed in the study was whether collective decision-making on sustainability issues was a matter of adjusting current practice, or an actual transformation of the way the decisions were being made.

Preliminary studies suggested that the key contributors to lasting decisions went beyond the familiar trio of community, experts, and government. There appeared to be five sets of key contributors in all long-term constructive decisions. These are: the key individuals, the affected community, the relevant specialists, the influential organizations, and a shared holistic focus. (Brown, 2001)

As Thomas Kuhn demonstrated, each particular construction of knowledge develops its own body of content through its own methods of inquiry, tests for truth, and frameworks for interpretation. (Kuhn, 1970) Each such body he labeled a paradigm, and documented the way in which each paradigm was tightly held by its practitioners. In Table 10.1, it can be seen that each group of contributors to sustainability governance, namely, individuals, community members, specialists, organizational players, and holistic thinkers, meets the conditions for distinct knowledge paradigms, in the Kuhnian sense. Each therefore brings to collective decisions different bodies of knowledge, methods of inquiry, and interpretation of evidence. This diversity can seriously disrupt consequent decision-making. On the other hand, properly managed, it can bring rich diversity and synergy, which produce fresh and effective solutions to the complex issue of sustainability.

The conditions under which the individuals, communities, specialists, organizations, and holistic thinkers can best contribute collectively to sustainability issues were explored in each of the LSP set of ten case studies. (Table 10.2) Now all published in their own right, these studies ranged from a national program to reduce greenhouse gases (Brown and Pitcher, 2000) to a textbook on sustainability and health. (Brown, Grootjans, Ritchie, et al., 2005)

Table 10.1. Five Paradigms of Knowledge

Contributors to Collective Decision-Making

Dimension	Individual	Community	Specialized	Strategic	Holistic
Content:	Personal lived experience	Mutual place-based experience	Academic disciplines, professions	Agendas, regulations, precedents	Symbols, metaphors, images
Inquiry:	Reflection	Dialogue	Observations	Cost/benefit	Imagination
Validation:	Self-reference	Local stories	Generalization	Will it work?	Recognition
Explanatory frameworks:	Sense of identity	Community ethos	Cause-and-effect linkages	Strategic plans	Essence, focus
Role models:	*Personal heroes*	*Eminent citizens*	*Nobel Prize winners*	*Powerful leaders*	*Writers, Artists*

After Kuhn, 1970 (Brown, Grootjans, Ritchie, et al., 2005)

Method of Inquiry: Collaborative Action Research

Between 1996 and 2003, a research team from the Australian-based Local Sustainability Project (LSP) set out to explore a process of collective sustainability decision-making capable of including each of the contributing paradigms listed in Table 10.1. (Brown, 2001) The mode of inquiry was collaborative action research. First, the multidisciplinary team identified leading-edge sustainable development initiatives from each of the contributing knowledge paradigms. They then approached the proponents of the initiatives with an offer to place their research skills at the disposal of the project. In some instances the members of the research team were invited to act as consultants; in others, as observers; and in still others, as external evaluators. In each instance, the research team responded to the needs of the project team.

The inquiry was pursued in the spirit of Kurt Lewin's classic Field Theory (Lewin, 1951) and Foucault's position on the equivalence between the construction of knowledge and power. (Foucault 1970) Field theory was an early recognition of the need to explore solutions to any complex issue within their full social and environmental context. Insights into the integral relationship between knowledge, power, and decision-making are offered by Foucault in his case studies of the justice system and the health industry. (Foucault, 1995; 1988) Foucault follows the century satirist Swift in generating transformational propositions, such as "Why does our society jail the criminals and treat the sick, when it could confine the sick and treat the criminals?"

In each field study of the LSP, the collaborators followed these authors in reporting on the drivers of social change. These included enabling and impeding factors, successes and failures, and intended and unintended outcomes. Overall, each study actively attempted to establish collective thinking in the particular social context in which integrated solutions to sustainability issues were being trialed. These contexts included individuals' transdisciplinary research, community monitoring and engagement, the professions of public health and environmental management, local government initiatives, and holistic professional practices. (Table 10.2)

Table 10.2. Local Sustainability Project Field Studies, 1996–2003

Knowledge Culture	Focus of Study	Outcome of study*
Individual	Collaborative inquiry Transdisciplinary research	Ten Ph.D. theses Textbook: *Social Learning for Environmental Management*
Community	Regional collaboration Regional monitoring	Whole-of-community toolkit State-of-the-region report
Specializations	Professional practice Professional education	Environment and health handbook Textbook: *Sustainability and Health*
Organizations	Whole-of-council change Local government sector	Integrated strategic planning National advocacy group
Holists	Pattern making A pattern language	Social change practitioners Text: *Librating Voices: Living Communication for the Public Sphere*
Collective	Synoptic workshops	Focus activity of each of the above

*Published as: UWS Ph.D. theses; Keen et al., 2005; Aslin and Brown, 2004; Brown et al., 2000; Nicholson et al., 2002; Brown et al., 2005; Paine, 2005; and Schuler, 2006.

The overview of the Local Sustainability Project in Table 10.2 provides details of ten field studies of integrated approaches to sustainability, two from each of the five knowledge paradigms of Western decision-making systems. The projects included individual inquiry, whole-of-community change, professional reorientation, organizational learning, and skills in holistic thinking. Each study was finalized by a synoptic workshop, bringing together teams from each interest group on equal terms. Each initiative has resulted in ongoing change supported by all five paradigms. Each study produced a handbook or textbook describing collective decision-making from the perspective of that particular knowledge culture. In order of mention in Table 10.2, these are Griffith, 2004; Keen, Brown and Dyball, 2005; Aslin and Brown, 2004; WESROC, 2000; Nicholson, Stephenson and Brown, et al., 2001; Brown, Grootjans, Ritchie, et al., 2005; Critchley and Scott, 2005; Brown, 2005; Paine, 2005, Schuler, 2007; and Brown, 2007.

Findings: Living in Parallel Worlds

Some general lessons can be drawn from reflection on the full set of studies. In interviews with key informants from each of the five sets of contributors to sustainability initiatives, major differences emerged. The conditions participants reported as being the basis for their actions differed widely. These included very different resource priorities, sources of authority, and timetable for action, as follows:

— **Resource priorities:**
Individuals: Self-confidence, shared commitment, support from others.
Community: Personal contacts, sympathetic advice, more group members.
Specialists: Funding, support from community and government.
Strategists: Negotiation, legislation, common ground.
Holists: Team-building, linked regulatory and voluntary frameworks.
— **Source of authority:**
Individuals: Own experience; power from belonging to one of the other groups.
Community: Own local history; agencies and experts they feel they can trust.
Specialists: Own reputation; power and authority of profession or discipline.
Strategists: Own organization's power base; legislation, resources, politics.
Holists: Setting the direction, fresh insights.
— **Timescale for action:**
Individuals: Personal tempo of response: leaders and laggards.
Community: Action needed today, if not yesterday.
Specialist: Sufficient time for thorough research.
Strategists: First negotiate the numbers, check the authority.
Holists: Start thinking, begin the dialogue now.

It may be derived from the foregoing that the participants in a collective decision are operating not only within different paradigms, but from different interpretations of reality. Observation of the groups as they face significant change led to the further findings discussed below (see Figure 10.1 on the next page). Each interest group proved to have a different basis for collecting evidence, drawing conclusions and maintaining their own reality. That is, each set of contributors developed their own knowledge culture. (Figure 10.1) Each knowledge culture maintains its boundary by dismissing the other knowledge cultures as subjective, gossip, jargon, unethical deals, and immaterial, respectively. The groups function within a hierarchy reinforced by existing power relationships. Remedial action was clearly necessary to overcome these powerful defenses. But, first it was important to understand the distinctive differences between the knowledge cultures themselves.

Individual Knowledge

Individuals build their knowledge out of their own lived experience, shaped by their social and physical setting. We all tend to reject material that does not match our own version of reality, and thus maintain our own identity. (Berger and Luckmann, 1971) The creation of each person's identity is due to a synthesis of the information sent to them from within their physical body, their society, their biophysical environment, and their intellect.

Polanyi distinguishes between explicit and tacit knowledge. (Polanyi, 1958) Tacit knowledge is the knowledge we draw on all the time, without being directly aware that we hold it. Each individual draws tacitly on all the knowledge cultures, but is likely to identify only one as their explicit source of knowledge. Individual knowledge is represented in Figure 10.1 by the cloud of small dots. In the Local Sustainability Studies, the significant contribution of individuals was their commitment to transformational change to be achieved through the goals of sustainability, the processes of collective decision-making, and to holistic thinking. (Paine, 2005)

Local Community Knowledge

Residents of towns or cities often suggest that newcomers can never be truly "local," even if they have spent many years in the area. They are right. Local communities are cemented by a collection of a diverse body of local knowledge that is legitimized through shared symbols of places and events. Each community member develops a sense of belonging to a people and a place, and holds a body of knowledge common to all other members. This body of knowledge may prove more reliable than that of "outsiders." Wynne, in his classic study of the radioactive fallout around the British Windscale nuclear plant, found that the farmers' commonsense observations proved more reliable than those of research scientists. (Wynne, 1996)

Each community is different, but is linked to others in a network in the local region and across the nation. Hence, local knowledge is represented as a continuous, but changing wavy line in Figures 10.1 and 10.2. It has, up to this point, not really been indicated what benefits an integrated approach may entail/lead to. This may be crucial to support the underlying hypothesis of the chapter. Geertz writes of communities as cultures of common sense, with "the citizens not just using their eyes and ears, but using them collectively, judiciously and reflectively to understand their own locality." (Geertz, 1983) Geertz's words were confirmed in the community-based field study, where twenty-five communities worked to reduce their greenhouse gas emissions. The most successful communities were those that had combined all the knowledge cultures in their local action. (Brown and Pitcher, 2000)

Knowledge Cultures

Knowledge culture	Structure	Sources of truth	Sources of ignorance
INDIVIDUAL KNOWLEDGE Lived experience, Identity	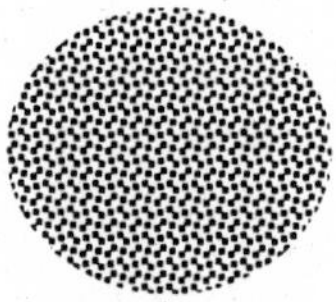	Memory Learning style Five senses	Subjective Limited Vague
LOCAL KNOWLEDGE Share experience of people and place	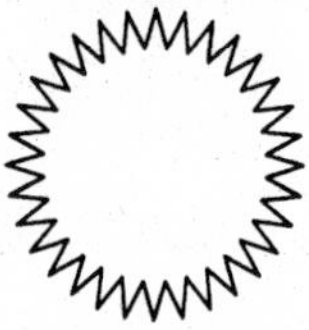	Stories Events Symbols	Gossip Anecdote Inaccurate
SPECIALIZED KNOWLEDGE Mono, multi and transdisciplinarity, the professions		Inquiry Measurements Observations	Jargon Irrelevant Narrow
ORGANIZATIONAL KNOWLEDGE Administration, government, industry, strategic thinking		Agendas Alliances Networks	Deals Buddies Corruption
HOLISTIC KNOWLEDGE Essence, core, purpose		Synthesis Focus Creative leap	Immaterial Impossible Impractical

Figure 10.1. The Knowledge Cultures of Western Decision-Making (Brown, 2001)

Specialized Knowledge

The strength of specialized knowledge lies in its firm focus, set rules of inquiry, and established explanatory frameworks. Each framework, be it in law, literature, history, philosophy, geography, or physics, services a distinct subset of practitioners and practices. Ever since the Enlightenment, the subsets have been proliferating. At Oxford University, in the nineteenth century, philosophy included physics. Today we have analytic, environmental, and moral philosophy, with a separate school of physics—itself divided into astrophysics, geophysics, and more. There is no inherent connection between the disciplinary frameworks, and hence, that specialized knowledge is represented by a disconnected ring of boxes in Figure 10.1.

Each new discipline has tended to adopt the methods of empirical science, including the social sciences, and the humanities. The normal scientific mind-set fosters ideals of regularity, simplicity, and certainty. Science itself has moved on. Methods for managing complex science-related issues include uncertainty, complexity, and recognition of values. (Funtowicz and Ravetz, 1993) From the field studies, we found that the adoption of the principles of sustainability in public health and environmental health required collaboration with other knowledge cultures, as well as their fellow disciplines. The solution was a set of commonsense questions which acts as a translation mechanism between the disciplines and across the knowledge cultures. (Brown et al., 2005)

Organizational Knowledge

Responding to complex issues with a high social and environmental impact calls for management that takes account of political and administrative realities. This dimension of reality is addressed through organizations, which may be government, social services, or industry. Organizational knowledge is strategic, directional, and validated by making progress toward the set goals. This is represented in Figure 10.1 as a closed circle, since organizations and governments usually give priority to self-maintenance and pursuing their own internal goals. This cycle becomes a spiral when there is a need to respond strategically to change.

Organizational or strategic knowledge is discontinuous across geographic scales. Management of a small locality differs in form, not only in size, from that of a region, a nation, or the planet. Strategic knowledge has informed decision-making throughout the centuries through the Chinese *Art of Strategy* by Sun-zhu, Machiavelli's *The Prince,* and even the television series *Yes Minister.* The "normal" form of an organization is increasingly that of the private for-profit organization.

Voltaire defined democratic management as rationality plus the ethical principles of equality and justice. (Voltaire, 1998 [1759]). Saul argues that this makes current forms of governance that claim to be democratic, illegitimate. (Saul, 1992) In the Local Sustainability field studies, local government authorities found that sustainability principles restored legitimacy, and acted as a point of synthesis. (Keen et al., 2005)

Holistic Knowledge

Holistic knowledge is interpreted in two contrasting ways: as the whole of the whole, or the essence of the whole. In the first usage, holistic thinking may be applied to a set of interconnected parts representing the whole of an organizational, a biophysical, or a social learning system. In claiming to encompass all the relevant knowledge of a topic, this use of holism is frequently dismissed as a presumptuous claim to know all about everything.

In its original sense, holism applied to the core rationale, purpose, or essence of a whole. (Smuts, 1936) From the Concise Oxford English Dictionary 1971: "*Holism: a term coined by General J. C. Smuts to designate the tendency in nature to produce wholes (i.e., bodies or organisms) from the ordered groupings of unit structures.*" Holistic knowledge is constructed through the creative leap—the Aha!—that gives access to fresh understandings. Biodiversity is a holistic idea, a sustainable city is another. The creative leap is often regarded as the task of the arts alone. Providing the freedom to take such creative leaps, through visioning, brainstorming, and conviviality, was a factor of successful collaboration in all of our field studies.

Throughout the observations of sustainability initiatives, the parallel worlds became increasingly clear. In standard practice, they have come to be regarded as mutually exclusive. In terms of governance, they have become competitors for resources and priorities for action, not collaborators. In contrast to expectations, in pursuit of sustainability goals, when conditions were provided for synthesis, the result was not a standoff, nor a lowest common denominator. There was synergy between the contributions.

The cross-fertilization that took place between the knowledge cultures before the final synthesis, proved to be the deciding factor in its success. This entailed setting the scene in which the synthesis was to take place. Sustainability initiatives were found to be more likely to offer fresh solutions and to bring about long-term change if they were:

- Future-directed: working toward a shared ideal, rather than tied to repairing past mistakes.

- Collective: finding ways to combine individual, community, specialized, organizational, and holistic contributions to knowledge on equal terms.

- An open learning spiral: providing maximum opportunities for continual collective learning that involve all the contributors.

- A positive sum game: recognizing that each collective decision adds value to the individual contributors and the whole at the same time; and rich with ambiguity and paradox: welcoming these as essential elements of collective change-oriented decisions.

Implications: Connecting the Knowledge Cultures

Achieving the above preconditions for collective decisions on sustainability requires a transformation of traditional mainstream practice. This is not a revolution, rejecting what has gone before. Nor does it require dismissing the valuable contributions of any of the knowledge cultures. It does, however, require establishing patterns of connection which replace the existing hierarchy, and allow for equal respect for all contributions.

One possible pattern of connection is in the form of nested knowledges (see Figure 10.2 on the next page). In this, the knowledge cultures form a holarchy; that is, an arrangement of equally important wholes building sequentially on one another. An underlying pattern of knowledge construction begins with the individual, since all knowledge originates in the human head. Groups of individuals form communities who develop a shared understanding from their mutual experiences. All specialized knowledge draws in some way on these two sources of information. For collective decisions to be effective, the three prior knowledge cultures need to be pulled together in a concerted strategy that takes pragmatic account of power relationships. At the core of the decisions lies a mutual understanding of the essence of the enterprise—holistic knowledge.

If there is one single tool that allowed the communication throughout the nested system, it was the practical application of Bohm's Rules of Dialogue (1995). Throughout the dialogue:

1. Commit yourself to the process.
2. Listen and speak without judgment.
3. Identify your own and others' beliefs and assumptions.
4. Acknowledge the other speakers and their ideas.
5. Respect other speakers and value their opinions.
6. Balance inquiry and advocacy.
7. Relax your need for any particular outcome.
8. Listen to yourself and speak when moved.
9. Take it easy—go with the flow—enjoy.

In the different Local Sustainability Project field studies, this nested system was entered at many different points, depending upon where the projects were based. The key to success was that collective processes were employed by all concerned, whatever the starting point. Thus, research inquiries began with the individual researcher's commitment to exploring the whole of their particular question. Local government organizations struggled with developing inclusive whole-of-community strategic plans. Reorienting the public health profession to include sustainability started with commonsense questions on "What does sustainability mean to us?" as generated among the many disciplines involved. Communities began by talking among themselves until they arrived at shared symbols for their preferred future. Holistic thinkers reflected on all that was going on, and came up with core ideas until they found one that everyone shared.

Nested Knowledge Cultures

Culture and Content	**Key**	**Nested Knowledges**

INDIVIDUAL KNOWLEDGE
Own lived experience, lifestyle, choices, learning style, identity
Content: reflections, learning

LOCAL KNOWLEDGE
Shared lived experience of individuals, families, businesses, communities
Content: stories, events, histories

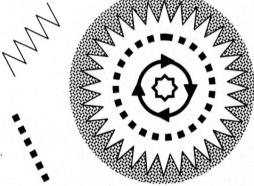

SPECIALIZED KNOWLEDGE
Environment and Health Sciences, Engineering, Law, Philosophy, etc.
Content: case studies, experiments

ORGANIZATIONAL KNOWLEDGE
Organizational governance, policy, strategies
Content: agendas, alliances, plans

HOLISTIC KNOWLEDGE
Core of the matter, vision of the future a common purpose
Content: symbol, vision, ideal

Figure 10.2. Knowledge Cultures as a Nested System (Brown, 2001)

Throughout the inquiry into collective thinking, the collaboration between researchers and practitioners was conducted in the spirit of practicing what you preach; that is, in terms of applying collective approaches to the research process itself. Such a practical purpose for an idealistic enterprise is well expressed in Plato's comment on trying to implement Socratic ideals in his utopian design for The Republic:

Suppose, for instance, that on seeing beautiful creatures, whether works of art, or actually live, but in repose, a man should be moved to desire to behold them in motion and vigorously engaged in some exercise as seemed suitable to their physique. Well, that is the very feeling I have regarding the descriptions of the ideal state. (Plato, on Socrates' *The Republic*, 1962 ed.)

The synthesis of individual commitment, community ethos, specialist commonsense, organizational ethical principles, and holistic focus toward governance for sustainability was alive and working well in the practices described here. These are only individual projects, however. We live in a society whose decisions have long been partitioned into separate disciplines, fragmented organizations, and divided communities. Collective decision-making can only come into more general use through a concerted effort toward developing a collective mind-set, a transformational change.

Conclusions

In this chapter, we highlight the importance of collaborative decision-making (or "integrated" decision-making as opposed to "fragmented" decision-making) in pursuit of united social support for restoring global ecological integrity. The Local Sustainability Project in Australia has developed and demonstrated techniques of integrated decision-making that can be implemented in working toward sustainability governance. Harnessing individual change agents, whole-of-community support, specialist advice, and organizational power in a collective, systemic approach, has proved effective in establishing transformational change toward sustainability practices at the local level. Several of the projects (regional sustainability monitoring, a national-behavior-change program, and internationally published text books) take the same collective approach to higher levels.

In all case studies of the Local Sustainability Project, the adoption of the idea of the contributors—as distinct knowledge cultures working within a cumulative social learning spiral—has led to collective decisions linking environmental management, human health, and sustainability governance. Conducting those activities with the principles of the *Earth Charter* (see the Appendix) for guidance, offers some hope for a future capable of sustaining life on Earth.

References

Aslin, Heather, and Valerie A. Brown. *Towards Whole of Community Engagement. A Practical Toolkit*. Canberra, Australia: Murray Darling Basin Commission, 2004.

Berger, Peter L., and Thomas Luckmann. *The Social Construction of Reality: A Treatise in the Sociology of Knowledge*. Harmondsworth, UK: Penguin, 1971.

Bohm, David. *On Dialogue*. London: Routledge, 1995.

Brown, Valerie A. "Knowing: Linking the Knowledge Cultures of Sustainability and Health." Pp. 131–61 in *Sustainability and Health: Supporting Global Ecological Integrity in Public Health*, edited by Valerie A. Brown, John Grootjans, Jan Ritchie, Mardi Townsend, and Glenda Verrinder. Sydney: Allen and Unwin. London: Earthscan, 2005.

———. *Leonardo's Vision: A Guide to Collective Thinking and Action.* Rotterdam: SENSE Publishers. Forthcoming 2007.

———. "Planners and the Planet: Reshaping the People/Planet Relationship: Do Planners Have a Role?" *Australian Planner* 38, no. 3 (2001): 67–73.

Brown, Valerie A., John Grootjans, Jan Ritchie, Mardi Townsend, and Glenda Verrinder. *Sustainability and Health: Supporting Global Ecological Integrity in Public Health.* Sidney: Allen and Unwin. London: Earthscan, 2005.

Brown, Valerie A., and Jennifer Pitcher, J. "Islands and Beaches." Pp. 123–46 in *Social Learning in Environmental Management,* edited by Meg Keen, Valerie A. Brown, and Robert Dyball. London: Earthscan, 2000.

Commission on Sustainable Development. *Agenda 21: Work Program 1993-98. Meetings on Thematic Clusters.* New York: United Nations, 1998.

Costanza, Robert, and Sven Jorgensen, S., eds. *Understanding and Solving Environmental Problems in the 21st Century: Toward a New, Integrated Hard Problem Science.* Oxford, UK: Elsevier, 2002.

Foucault, Michel. *Discipline and Punish: The Birth of the Prison.* Translated by Alan Sheridan. New York: Vintage books, 1995 (orig. 1978).

———. *Madness and Civilization: A History of Insanity in the Age of Reason.* New York: Pantheon Books, 1988 (orig. 1965).

———. *The Order of Things: An Archaeology of the Human Sciences.* London: Random House, 1970.

Funtowicz, Silvio, and Jerome Ravetz. "Science for the Post-Normal Age." *Futures* (Sept. 1993): 739–55.

Geertz, Clifford. *Local Knowledge: Further Essays in Interpretive Anthropology.* London: Fontana Press, 1983, 75.

Keen, Meg, Valerie A. Brown, and Robert Dyball. *Social Learning in Environmental Management.* London: Earthscan, 2005.

Kuhn, Thomas S. *The Structure of Scientific Revolutions.* Chicago: University of Chicago Press, 1970.

Latour, Bruno. *We Have Never Been Modern.* Cambridge, MA: Harvard University Press, 1993.

Lewin, Kurt. *Field Theory in Social Science: Selected Theoretical Papers,* edited by David Cartwright. New York: Harper & Row, 1951.

McMichael, Anthony J. *Human Frontiers, Environments, and Disease: Past Patterns, Uncertain Futures.* New York: Cambridge University Press, 2001.

Nicholson, Rosemary, Peter Stephenson, Valerie A. Brown, and Kathy Mitchell. *Common Ground and Common Sense: Community-Based Environmental Health Planning.* Canberra: Commonwealth of Australia, 2001.

Paine, Gregory. "Patterns, Wholes and Sustainable Development: Closing the Gap between Concern and Action." Ph.D. thesis. Richmond, Australia: University of Western Sydney, 2005.

Plato, on Socrates' *The Republic* (360 BCE). English translation by R. G. Bury. Cambridge, MA: Harvard University Press, 1962, 73.

Polanyi, Michael. *Personal Knowledge: Towards a Post-Critical Philosophy.* Chicago: University of Chicago Press, 1958.

Rees, William, and Matthias Wackernagel. "Urban Ecological Footprints: Why Cities Cannot Be Sustainable—And Why They Are a Key to Sustainability" [An article from: *Environmental Impact Assessment Review*] [HTML] (Digital) Amazon.com. 1996.

Saul, John Ralston. *Voltaire's Bastards: The Dictatorship of Reason in the West.* Toronto: Viking, 1992.

Smuts, Johann C. *Holism and Evolution.* London: Macmillan, 1936.

United Nations Millenium Development Goals. http://www.un.org/millenniumgoals (2 Jun. 2007).

Voltaire [François Marie Arouet]. "Candide or Optimism" in *Candide and Other Stories,* edited and translated by R. Pearson. London: Oxford University Press, 1998 (orig. 1759).

WESROC (Regional Organisation of Councils: editors Valerie A. Brown, David Love, Rod Griffith, Alan Mossfield, and Marilin Benjamin). *Western Sydney Regional State of the Environment Report 2000* (Text, CD and Web page). Blacktown, Australia: Western Sydney Regional Organisation of Councils, 2000.

World Business Council for Sustainable Development (WBCSD) coalition of 150 international companies. http://www.wbcsd.org (2 Jun. 2007).

World Commission on Dams. "Dams and Development: A New Framework for Decision-Making." *The Report of the World Commission on Dams.* 2000.

World Commission on Environment and Development. *Our Common Future: Report of the World Commission on Environment and Development.* New York: Oxford University Press, 1987.

World Summit on Sustainable Development. "Health and Environment: Supporting Sustainable Livelihoods, Towards Earth Summit 2002." Social Briefing No. 3: Linkages, World Information Transfer.

Wynne, Brian. "May the Sheep Safely Graze? A Reflexive View of the Expert-lay Knowledge Divide." In *Risk Environment and Modernity: Towards a New Ecology,* edited by Scott Lash, Bronishlaw Szerszynski, and Brian Wynne. London: Sage Publications, 1996.

"Yes Minister." Antony Jay and Jonathan Lynn. BBC (UK) television broadcast (1983 and 1984). www.bbc.co.uk/comedy/guide/articles/y/yesminister_7777145.shtml (3 Jun. 2007).

Chapter 11

Toward Sustainable Environmental Governance in South Africa: Cooperative Environmental Governance and Integrated Environmental Management as Possible Solutions to Fragmentation

Louis J. Kotzé, LL.D. (Environmental Law),
Associate Professor, Faculty of Law
North-West University, Potchefstroom Campus
Potchefstroom, South Africa

Contact Information: *Private Bag X 6001, Potchefstroom SOUTH AFRICA*
Phone: +27 18 299 1956; Fax: +27 18 299 1955
Email: louis.kotze@nwu.ac.za

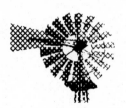

Summary

The South African environmental governance sphere, like most environmental governance regimes in developing countries, is severely fragmented. Fragmentation includes an unconnected environmental law framework consisting of various legislative acts dealing with a variety of environmental media and issues, and uncoordinated governance structures, processes, and governance mechanisms.

We argue that fragmentation may result in unsustainable and inefficient governance practices, including: delayed decision-making; duplication of functions; overlap of mandates, jurisdictions, functions, and use of governance tools; and, ultimately, a confusing and complicated governance regime for both the governed and the government. This may ultimately result in negative impacts on humans and the natural environment.

Fragmentation needs to be addressed as a matter of priority in order to foster and achieve a more sustainable environmental governance strategy. It may be addressed by way of cooperative environmental governance and integrated environmental management. Both should be management or governance strategies aimed at the integration of structures, processes, and mechanisms common to any environmental governance effort.

Background

Environmental governance (EG) in South Africa has come a long way since the entrenchment of an environmental right in the Constitution of the Republic of South Africa, 1996 (1996 Constitution). Section 24 provides that:

> Everyone has the right—
> (a) to an environment that is not harmful to their health or well-being; and
> (b) to have the environment protected, for the benefit of present and future generations, through reasonable legislative and other measures that—
>> (i) prevent pollution and ecological degradation;
>> (ii) promote conservation; and
>> (iii) secure ecologically sustainable development and use of natural resources while promoting justifiable economic and social development.

Virtually all current developments regarding environmental law in South Africa are based on the theory, substantive, and normative content of this right, which essentially follows an anthropocentric approach. The right ultimately seeks to achieve sustainability by placing a positive obligation on government to realize the content of the right through "reasonable legislative and other measures."

Commendable as what the recent developments of the EG effort may be, the EG regime is severely fragmented. (Kotzé, 2006) Fragmentation is evident from the plethora of environmental acts which are environmental media-, or issue-specific. The current legislative framework addresses among other issues, air pollution, water pollution, soil pollution, land-use management, natural resource conservation, and issues of cultural heritage, by way of a fragmented matrix framework of acts which overlap and thereby cause confusion. Legislative fragmentation is exacerbated by the fact that these acts are administered by various departments of state (for example, Department of Water Affairs and Forestry, Department of Environmental Affairs and Tourism, and Department of Minerals and Energy) which are situated in various spheres of government (national, provincial, and local).

In South Africa today, there exists a confusing legislative framework, overlapping and perplexing mandates, and a complex governance structure responsible for executing EG tasks. The various mechanisms employed and processes followed for executing EG mandates are also not uniform and integrated by way of a single environmental act, and executed by a single and integrated environmental agency or department (sometimes referred to as a one-stop EG shop).

The South African scenario is not unique. Fragmentation of EG regimes is especially observed in developing countries, struggling with limited human and financial resources, lacking specialized skills and the political commitment to sustainable EG strategies, all within fragmented government structures previously imposed under colonial regimes.

Hypothesis and Objectives

Fragmented EG regimes may lead to unsustainable governance. This holds true especially insofar as it creates, or in some instances exacerbates, the use of multiple mechanisms to address singular media; turf wars and the protection of mandates in and among government departments and the three spheres of government (national, provincial, and local); uncooperative organizational behavior in the ranks of government; legal uncertainty with regard to jurisdictions and mandates in terms of various environmental acts; duplication of functions; and delayed decision-making. This essentially results in a complicated, time consuming, and confusing governance effort; it may negatively impact on the natural environment and the health and well-being of humans who stand central in the anthropocentric governance effort and who are the ultimate receptors of negative impacts on the natural environment.

Fragmentation also may lead to results contrary to those envisaged in the *Earth Charter* (EC, see the Appendix). The EC does not specifically provide for strategies to address fragmented EG regimes. Some of the provisions of the Charter, however, support a cooperative, integrated, aligned, and collaborative approach. For example, it states that the environment is a common concern, which requires a global partnership, fundamental changes in institutions, and inclusive solutions (preamble). Principle 1 of the EC furthermore recognizes that the environment is an integrated, interrelated, and holistic phenomenon, which must be dealt with in an integrated fashion. While the EC acknowledges the important role of governance through institutions and at all levels (principle 13), it also emphasizes the need to "encourage and support mutual understanding, solidarity, and cooperation among all peoples and within and among nations" (principle 16), through, inter alia, partnerships with government, civil society, and business for effective governance.

In light of this background, this contribution aims to: investigate the theory behind an integrated environmental management (IEM) approach and cooperative environmental governance (CEG). Although both strategies are provided for in South African environmental law, they are not unique to the South African EG effort. One finds, for example, cooperation and integration strategies in the Dutch, Finnish, and German legal systems (Kotzé, 2006). Although the detailed provisions and scope of these strategies may differ, the objective remains the same in each instance, namely, to achieve a more sustainable EG effort through more streamlined and integrated structures, processes, and media. While IEM relates to a specialized management strategy which focuses on streamlining, optimizing, and integrating EG mechanisms, media, and structures and functions of governance, CEG entails a strategy through which cooperation may be achieved along fragmented spheres and various departments of government. These strategies may be employed to address fragmentation by achieving a more streamlined, integrated, and sustainable EG effort.

Framework

We commence with an investigation of the theory underpinning integrated environmental management (IEM), the application of IEM in South Africa, and the manner in which IEM may be employed to achieve integration. We then proceed to investigate the strategy of cooperative environmental governance (CEG), the application of CEG in South African environmental law, and recommendations on how CEG may be utilized to address fragmentation. We conclude with recommendations on how IEM and CEG may be employed to address fragmentation and achieve a more integrated and sustainable environmental governance (EG) effort.

Discussion: Integrated Environmental Management

The theory of Integrated Environmental Management (IEM)

Environmental management (EM) is defined as management skills and techniques implemented to achieve the principles of sustainability at all levels, including the macro-level (government) and the micro-level (private sector). (Bosman, 1999) These principles include, inter alia: the precautionary approach, the preventive principle, the polluter pays principle, the cradle-to-grave principle, the principle of an integrated and holistic approach, the principle that due consideration must be given to all alternatives, and the principles of continual improvement, accountability, liability, transparency, and democracy.

A management strategy necessitates planned controls to ultimately achieve a desired outcome. The execution of planned controls is commonly referred to as "management" in its broadest possible sense. (Fuggle, 1992) When planned controls are applied to aspects directly or indirectly related to the environment, one arguably deals with EM.

It is important to note that EM is not "management of the environment." EM is rather "management of activities within tolerable constraints imposed by the environment itself, and with full consideration of ecological factors." (Beale, 1980) Hence, EM is the management of the activities of people in the environment, and the management of resultant effects of these activities on the environment. This reflects the notion that should guide the activities of people through governance, with the involvement of civil society and industry, to achieve a desired objective, namely that of sustainable EG results, aimed at achieving the optimum benefit for people and the natural environment. It is accordingly evident that EM operates at the public and private levels, the ultimate objective being the achievement of the principles of sustainability, or that sustainable EG ensues.

An integrated approach to environmental management, or IEM, means the optimal alignment of current disjointed and fragmented governance tools, instruments, processes, structures, and procedures to govern development from an environmental perspective in a sustainable fashion. (Nel and Du Plessis, 2004; and Centre for Environmental Management, 2004)

IEM, as an integration strategy, is thus understood to mean:

> The management of the activities of people at micro- and macro-levels to en-sure achievement of the principles of sustainability, notably to ensure the utili-zation of natural resources provided by all environmental media within their carrying capacities, while promoting economic growth as a primary objective, by ensuring the implementation of decision-making and management tools for EM; based on the Deming-management approach, for the different phases of the project life-cycle through the integration of the activities between the dif-ferent spheres of government; and within their various line functions. (Kotzé, 2006)

Integration in Terms of IEM

Integration is fundamental to IEM. Integration primarily includes integra-tion of: the interrelationships between the different spheres of government, envi-ronmental media (land, air, and water), different line functionaries or depart-ments of government, the Deming-management approach, decision cycles, and different mechanisms for environmental management and governance. Figure 11.1 (below) represents an integrated model that illustrates the six different components of IEM for integration (adapted from Nel and Du Plessis, 2004).

Integrated Environmental Management Model

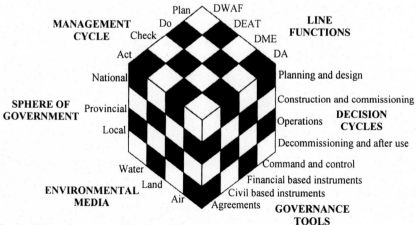

Figure 11.1. A Comprehensive IEM Model

Integration of these various aspects is explained as follows. The South Afri-can government consists of national, provincial, and local spheres (section 40[1] of the 1996 Constitution). Each sphere, in turn, consists of various line functionaries or departments. Environmental line functionaries include, but are not limited to, the Department of Environmental Affairs and Tourism (DEAT), the Department of Water Affairs and Forestry (DWAF), the Department of Minerals and Energy (DME), and the Department of Agriculture (DA). Some of these line functionaries are also represented at the provincial and local levels. Integration of the various spheres and line functionaries of government may contribute to the alignment of EG structures and procedures. Alignment in this context arguably refers to uniform institutional policy, project and decision processes, and structures related to EG tasks.

The traditional Deming-management approach is a generic, outcomes-based management approach that relies on the process of continual improvement. It encompasses four actions that must be performed during the process of executing planned controls. (Kreitner and Kinicki, 2004) These include planning, doing, checking, and acting (PDCA), in this sequence. (Later, 1999 and Global Environmental Management Initiative, 1993) The project life cycle is an additional important element that needs to be integrated, and correlates with the Deming-management approach. The project life cycle is applicable to certain specific projects, be it projects initiated by government, or by industry. It includes certain phases, namely planning and design, construction and decommissioning, the operational phase, and the decommissioning phase. (Centre for Environmental Management, 2004) The PDCA approach should be applied through the whole project life cycle, since it creates the basis for this cycle. Whereas one would employ environmental assessment in the planning and design phases, all relevant environmental authorizations should be considered, applied for, and implemented in the operational and construction phases. The latter may include, for example, air, water and soil pollution permits, as well as building authorizations and waste management authorizations.

All relevant authorizations and actions should also be considered, applied for, and implemented in the decommissioning phase of a project. These may include, for example, rehabilitation actions and remediation commitments in permits. It is argued that consideration, application, and implementation of all these requirements should be done in a holistic and integrated manner throughout the whole life cycle of a project. This, in itself, may already result in a more integrated governance effort.

Various tools are furthermore available for IEM. These tools include, among others, "command and control" tools, fiscal-based tools, civil-based tools, and agreements. (Du Plessis and Nel, 2001) In order to achieve sustainable governance results, decision-makers should not only focus on a single instrument, such as environmental authorizations. Rather, a hybrid use of tools should be considered and employed, which will allow for optimal policy options together with broader discretion in the use of specific tools for specific scenarios. This may arguably enable an integrated and tailor-made EG strategy.

When integrating the various tools for governance it must be remembered that the environment consists of different media, including air, land, and water.

The necessity for integrating the various environmental media is evident from the holistic approach of IEM and the integrated, holistic, and interrelated nature of the environment where one element necessarily influences the other in a symbiotic fashion. In this sense, IEM should not be aimed at shifting pollutants from different environmental media, but rather to address pollutants in an integrated way according to the tolerable constraints of the environment, and within the carrying capacity of natural systems.

It may be inferred from the foregoing that "integration" in relation to IEM includes: integration, or alignment of governance arrangements between the various spheres of government; integration of governance arrangements within the same sphere of government, but between various line functions; recognition of the integrated nature of the environmental management cycle to include all PDCA elements of the Deming-management approach; recognition of the need to address all the phases of a project or development cycle from planning and design through authorization, to construction, operation and decommissioning; integrated use of a hybrid of EG tools and implementation strategies; recognition of the human-environment system as a closed system that requires an integrated perspective on the various environmental media in order to prevent intramedia transfer of impacts; and alignment of administrative practices, procedures, policies, strategies, and instrumentation of autonomous line functions of all spheres and line functions to achieve effective and integrated service-delivery efforts. (Centre for Environmental Management, 2004)

Cooperative Environmental Governance

Cooperative Governance and the Environment

Governance may be defined as "being both the process and structure[s] by which officials are held accountable for executing the fiduciary duty with which they are entrusted to the public." (Turton, 2004) Governance, in other words, refers to the structures of rule making, rule application, and rule adjudication in a given society. (Hatting et al., 2003) Governance may also be directed at the regulation of people's activities within the environment. This is done by way of EG, which is defined as "the collection of legislative, executive and administrative functions, processes and instruments used by any organ of state [including the private sector] to ensure sustainable behavior by all as far as governance of activities, product services, processes and tools are concerned." (Nel and Du Plessis, 2004) Hence, EG encapsulates the regulatory functions of EG bodies, because it implies an endeavor to govern behavior by setting rules, standards, and principles by means of legislation, administrative and executive functions, as well as processes and instruments. (Birnie, 1992)

The fact that different organs of state are sometimes required to cooperate on certain matters during governance activities, necessitates cooperative governance. (Bosman, Kotzé, and Du Plessis, 2004) This necessarily acknowledges the existence of intergovernmental relations. These relations manifest in a vertical and horizontal sense. While the vertical relationship mainly refers to the provision of financial and other aid, the horizontal relationship may be described as a "compact" that permits the:

[J]oint administration of public services; agreements to share information or technical assistance; reciprocal legislation that permits the citizens of one jurisdiction to receive certain services within another jurisdiction [and legislation that permits administrative organs to render certain administrative services in another jurisdiction]; and the membership of governmental officials in organizations that seek to develop solutions for common problems. (Sharkansky, 1972)

In addition, because the environment is a holistic, integrated, and interrelated phenomenon that is not confined by boundaries, problems that may occur with regard to the environment may require solutions, and hence cooperation in problem-solving strategies, from all spheres and line functionaries of government that may be involved with a particular environmental problem. Intergovernmental relationships imply cooperative governance, or, formulated differently, for intergovernmental relations to be successful, cooperative governance is a *sine qua non*. The impetus for cooperative governance in the above context may, therefore, be summarized as including: the desire to create an agreeable and convenient work environment for government officials; concern that programs of other administrative organs may affect in-house programs; the desire to support one's own projects that are funded by other administrative organs; the desire to protect the interests of the public from possible effects of programs initiated by other organs; and the desire to build rapport with other administrative organs. (Sharkansky, 1972)

In more general terms, "the obligations towards cooperative government reconcile the notion of independent spheres with the interdependence between these spheres necessary to ensure the success of the national development project." (Besdziek, 2003)

As such, cooperative governance represents a new governance strategy that is primarily concerned with the growing role of associations, and different agencies and partnerships that reflect the dynamic and interactive nature of coordination. It also includes, among other things: coordination of activities to avoid competition and duplication; development of a multisectoral perspective in the interests of all South Africans; effective dispute resolution; collective harnessing of public resources by way of coordination and support; and a clear division of roles and responsibilities so as to minimize confusion and maximize effectiveness, and ultimately improve service delivery through governance efforts. Given the fragmented nature of the EG regime, cooperative governance, as a specific governance strategy, may be indispensable for ensuring cooperation in the EG regime. This strategy is commonly referred to as CEG.

Defining Cooperative Environmental Governance

CEG is a relatively novel concept in South African environmental law. Few definitions thereof, at least from an academic perspective, exist. CEG has been defined as meaning, inter alia, "the evolution of devolved governance, involving discussions, agreements and a combination of formal and informal regulation between industry, the public/stakeholders and [environmental] government departments." (Boer, O' Beirne, and Greyling, 2003) It is therefore aimed at the promotion of integrated service delivery and stakeholder involvement by government departments, and all other interested and affected parties involved with the environment. In this context, CEG arguably does not only refer to cooperation between the various spheres of government in the execution of their duties. The scope of CEG is far greater than the aforementioned and could be based on the integrated model of IEM. CEG includes not only the narrowly defined concept of governance that refers to mechanisms and relations between state departments. It also includes the public sector, private sector, and all stakeholders that may directly or indirectly be involved with the environment. It encompasses cooperation and coordination between the different spheres of government, at international and interregional levels, as well as on an intra-governmental level. Furthermore, it refers to the alignment of policies, plans, and programs across the different spheres of government, and the different line functionaries within each sphere. It also entails procedures and processes for the empowerment of civil society and industry to actively engage in EG. (Du Plessis and Nel, 2001) The foregoing describes an interactive and all-inclusive process that should ultimately enable cooperation and exchange of information between stakeholders, better decision-making, and the achievement of more outcomes that are acceptable to all. (Bulman, 2003)

The characteristics of CEG reflect the notion that sustainability, as an interdependent, multidisciplinary and interrelated concept, requires a multilateral approach to governance. The characteristics of CEG, which correlate with some of the principles of sustainability referred to above, include: fairness, accountability, responsibility and transparency, participation, rule of law, responsiveness, consensus, equity, effectiveness, efficiency, coherence, integration, responsiveness, and sustainability. Furthermore, these principles correlate with section 41(1)(c) of the 1996 Constitution that requires governance to be effective, transparent, accountable, and coherent. It also highlights the need for CEG to foster a culture of collaboration, internal organizational change, coherence and coordination, as well as flexible approaches to IEM and decision-making. (Govender and Parkes, 2003). One may even go as far as to suggest that many of the characteristics of CEG are also prevalent in some of the most basic provisions of the EC (see also the discussion above).

The integrated nature of CEG is illustrated by Figure 11.2 (on the next page) and may be defined, in light of the foregoing, as:

The integration of the different spheres of government and line functionaries at international, intra-regional and intra-governmental levels; co-operation between individual government officials in each sphere/line functionary; co-operation between government officials in different spheres/line functionaries; integration of policy, regulation methods and tools, service provision and scrutiny; and co-operation with industry and the public in order to achieve the principles of sustainability. (Kotzé, 2006)

Cooperative Environmental Governance Model

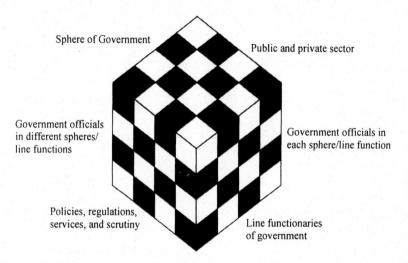

Sphere of Government

Public and private sector

Government officials in different spheres/line functions

Government officials in each sphere/line function

Policies, regulations, services, and scrutiny

Line functionaries of government

Figure 11.2. A Comprehensive CEG Model

CEG and South African Environmental Law

CEG is provided for in chapter 3 of the 1996 Constitution as well as in various provisions of the National Environmental Management Act 107 of 1998 (NEMA) and other sectoral environmental legislation (see, for example, the National Water Act 36 of 1998, the National Environmental Management: Biodiversity Act 10 of 2004, the Mineral and Petroleum Resources Development Act 28 of 2002, the National Environmental Management: Air Quality Act 39 of 2004, and the National Environmental Management: Protected Areas Act 57 of 2003). CEG, as provided for by this legislative framework, is applicable to all EG bodies at national, provincial, and local sphere, as well as to all line functionaries in each sphere. (Bray, 2005)

Section 41(1) of the 1996 Constitution states that:

All spheres of government and all organs of state within each sphere must: . . .
(e) respect the constitutional status, institutions, powers and functions of government in other spheres;
(f) not assume any power or function except those conferred on them in terms of the Constitution;

(g) exercise their powers and perform their functions in a manner that does not encroach on the geographical, functional or institutional integrity of government in another sphere;

(h) co-operate with one another in mutual trust and good faith by—

(i) fostering friendly relations;

(ii) assisting and supporting one another;

(iii) informing one another of, and consulting one another on matters of common interest;

(iv) coordinating their actions and legislation with one another;

(v) adhering to agreed procedures; and

(vi) avoiding legal proceedings against one another.

Chapter 3 of the 1996 Constitution provides for national, provincial, and local spheres of government, which are required to perform different functions unique to that sphere of government. The execution of these distinct governmental functions should, however, be based on the constitutionally entrenched principle of cooperative governance. These principles advocate a cooperative form of "federalism," which preempts sharing of the same responsibilities by different spheres and line functionaries of government. (De Waal et al., 2001)

Apart from the constitutional provisions, certain principles, procedures, tools, and structures are furthermore established by NEMA to give effect to cooperative governance. Chapter 1 of NEMA contains a set of EM principles that constitute the foundation of all activities to be undertaken under the provisions of this environmental framework act. These principles include, inter alia: the polluter-pays principle; the precautionary principle; the duty-of-care principle; the principle of sustainability; the principle of environmental justice; the principle of integrated environmental management and governance; the principle of transparency and public participation; and more importantly for the present purpose, the principle of intergovernmental coordination and harmonization of policies, legislation, and actions relating to the environment (section 2).

These principles may serve as a useful tool to establish integration, since the principles are crosscutting and apply to all sectoral environmental policies and legislation. In the case of actual or potential conflicting interests between organs of state, such conflicts should also be resolved through appropriate conflict resolution procedures [sections 2(4)(l)-2(4)(m)]. Section 7 establishes the Committee for Environmental Co-ordination (CEC). The CEC primarily strives to coordinate and integrate the implementation of all governmental policies pertaining to environmental management and governance. It is proposed that the establishment of the CEC is of special importance for the practical and day-to-day establishment, execution, regulation, and facilitation of cooperative governance at the policy level. It is another example of an institution that could be established in terms of a generically applicable environmental framework act, and which has as its primary objective to facilitate cooperation between fragmented organs and spheres of government.

Chapter 3 of the NEMA deals with procedures for cooperative governance. Section 11 provides for the preparation of environmental implementation and management plans by national departments. In their preparation of such plans, national departments must, in the spirit of CEG, take into consideration all existing plans with a view to ultimately achieving consistency among such plans [section 11(4)]. Environmental implementation plans and environmental management plans address core issues of cooperative governance by aiming to coordinate and harmonize environmental policies, plans, programs, and decisions of various national, provincial, and local organs of state. The coordination and harmonization responsibility specifically strives, inter alia, to minimize duplication of procedures and functions of organs of state; and to promote consistency of governance functions [sections 12(a)-(b)].

Cooperative governance has also been formalized in terms of the Intergovernmental Relations Framework Act 13 of 2005 (IRFA). Specific objectives of the IRFA include: to provide, within the scope of cooperative governance as established by the 1996 Constitution, a framework for the various spheres of government and all organs of state to facilitate coordination in the implementation of policy and legislation—including coherent government, effective provision of service, monitoring and implementation of policy and legislation; and realization of national priorities, including, the achievement of sustainability (section 3).

The Act recognizes that the South African governance framework is fragmented along three autonomous, yet, interdependent and interrelated spheres; and that all spheres must provide effective, efficient, transparent, accountable, and coherent governance in order to secure the well-being of people and the progressive realization of their constitutional rights (Preamble). The Act also recognizes that cooperation in government depends on a stable and effective system of governance for regulating the conduct of relations and the settlement of intergovernmental disputes (Preamble). Furthermore, Chapter 2 provides for a number of intergovernmental structures that may be employed to establish cooperative governance. These include the President's Coordinating Council and intergovernmental forums in the national, provincial, and local spheres of government. These forums act as a platform for intergovernmental consultation and discussion, and although they are not deemed to be executive decision-making bodies, they may adopt resolutions or make recommendations in terms of agreed procedures (section 29).

Conclusions

Fragmentation of the South African EG regime is a serious concern. IEM and CEG are provided for in South African law as possible strategies to address fragmentation. These strategies focus on the integration and alignment of governance structures, processes, procedures, mandates, jurisdictions, and tools by fostering a culture of cooperation, rapport building, and reciprocal and mutually-beneficial relationships between organs of state in different spheres of government. Apart from creating such a cooperative culture, these strategies may also be successfully employed to practically align and integrate the various spheres and line functions of government, the various governance tools, processes in terms of legislation which should deal with environmental media in an integrated fashion, and the various decision cycles. It will be a long and difficult process to achieve integration of the fragmented EG regime in South Africa. As far as political commitment to environmental considerations is concerned, this is currently lacking in South Africa.

Recommendations

Integration may best be achieved by abolishing the various governance structures and various acts dealing with EG, or by establishing a one-stop EG shop. The establishment of a one-stop shop may, however, require unqualified political buy-in and support.

In the absence of such drastic and possibly less feasible measures, it is proposed that all actors in the South African EG effort should aim to rather employ less drastic strategies such as CEG and IEM. These strategies are at the disposal of the public and private sectors and can be utilized as methods to align and integrate the fragmented regime. They need not be invented or legislated on, since they are already provided for in South African law.

A need exists, however, for CEG and IEM to be implemented and operationalized. By integrating the various elements provided for in the IEM strategy, and by employing the cooperative approach provided for by CEG, the fragmented EG regime may ultimately be transformed into a streamlined and efficient system of governance; one that ultimately aims to achieve sustainable EG results based on a holistic premise that is integrative as opposed to being fragmented.

References

Beale, Jack G. *The Manager and the Environment: General Theory and Practice of Environmental Management.* Oxford: Pergamon Press, 1980.

Besdziek, Dirk. "Provincial Government." P. 192 in *Government and Politics in the New South Africa.* 2nd ed., edited by A. Venter. Pretoria, South Africa: Van Schaik Publishers, 2003.

Birnie, Patricia. "International Environmental Law: Its Adequacy for Present and Future Needs." P. 52 in *The International Politics of the Environment,* edited by A. Hurrell and B. Kingsbury. Oxford: Clarendon Press, 1992.

Boer, Annarie, Sean O' Beirne, and Tisha Greyling. "The Quest for Co-operative Environmental Governance: Do Stakeholders Have a Consistent Map and Directions?" Conference Proceedings. Paper presented at the Annual Conference of the International Association for Impact Assessment, George, South Africa, 1–3 Sept. 2003.

Bosman, Carin. *Waste Disposal or Discharge: A Harmonised Regulatory Framework towards Sustainable Use.* Potchefstroom, SA: Potchefstroom University for Christian Higher Education, 1999.

Bosman, Carin, Louis J. Kotzé, and Willemien du Plessis. "The Failure of the Constitution to Ensure Integrated Environmental Management from a Co-operative Governance Perspective." *SA Public Law,* no. 19(2) (2004): 411–21.

Bray, Elmene. "Legal Perspectives on Global Environmental Governance: South Africa's Partnership Role (Part 2)." *Journal of Contemporary Roman-Dutch Law,* no. 3 (2005): 357–73.

Bulman, Janoff R. "Instant Governance: Just Add Civil Society—No Mess, No Fuss." Conference Proceedings. Paper presented at the Annual Conference of the International Association for Impact Assessment, George, South Africa, 1–3 Sept. 2003.

Centre for Environmental Management. *Report on an Environmental Management System for the North-West Province.* Potchefstroom, SA: North-West University, 2004.

Constitution of the Republic of South Africa, 1996.

De Waal, Johan, Ian Currie, and Gerhard Erasmus. *The Bill of Rights Handbook.* 4th ed. Landsdowne, SA: Juta, 2001.

Du Plessis, Willemien, and Johan G. Nel. "An Evaluation of NEMA Based on a Generic Framework for Environmental Framework Legislation." *South African Journal of Environmental Law and Policy,* no. 8(1) (2001): 1–37.

Fuggle, Richard F. "Environmental Management: An Introduction," P. 3 in *Environmental Management in South Africa,* edited by Richard F. Fuggle and Marinus A. Rabie. Kenwyn, SA: Juta, 1992.

Global Environmental Management Initiative. *Total Quality Environmental Management: The Primer.* Washington, DC: GEMI, 1993.

Govender, Kathy, and Lee Parkes. "Bridge over Troubled Waters: The Realities of Cooperative Governance Encountered during the Tyger Falls Development." Conference Proceedings. Paper presented at the Annual Conference of the International Association for Impact Assessment, George, South Africa, 1–3 Sept. 2003.

Hatting, Hanlie, et al. "Obstacles to Successful Implementation of Governance Tools." Conference Proceedings. Paper presented at the Annual Conference of the International Association for Impact Assessment, George, South Africa, 1–3 Sept. 2003.

Kotzé, Louis J. *A Legal Framework for Integrated Environmental Governance in South Africa and the North West Province.* Tilburg, Netherlands: Wolf Publishers, 2006.

Kreitner, Robert, and Angelo Kinicki. *Organizational Behavior.* 6th ed. New York: McGraw-Hill, 2004.

Later, FK. "Vergunning op Hoofdzaken in de Praktijk." P. 29 in *De Milieuvergunning in Ontwikkeling,* edited by Rosa Uylenburg and Corne J. Van der Wilt. Alpen aan de Rijn, Netherlands: Samson, 1999.

Mineral and Petroleum Resources Development Act 28 of 2002.

National Environmental Management: Air Quality Act 39 of 2004.

National Environmental Management: Biodiversity Act 10 of 2004.

National Environmental Management: Protected Areas Act 57 of 2003.

National Water Act 36 of 1998.

Nel, Johan G., and Willemien du Plessis. "Unpacking Integrated Environmental Management—A Step Closer to Effective Co-operative Governance?" *SA Public Law,* no. 19(1) (2004): 181–90.

Sharkansky, Ira. *Public Administration: Policy-making in Government Agencies.* 2nd ed. Chicago: Markham Publishing Company, 1972.

Turton, Anthony R. "The Challenges of Developing Policy in a Multi-country Context." Conference Proceedings. Paper presented at the Seminar on Policy Development and Implementation in the Water Sector: Reflection and Learning. Pretoria, South Africa, 10–12 Feb. 2004.

Chapter 12

A Sense of Possibility: What Does Governance for Health and Ecological Sustainability Look like?

Daniel Rainham, Ph.D. Candidate (Population Health)

University of Ottawa, Ottawa, Canada

Contact Information: One Stewart Street, Ottawa, Ont. K1N 6N5 CANADA
Phone: +1 613 562 5381; Fax: +1 613 562 5380; Email: drain067@uottawa.ca

Ian McDowell, Ph.D. (Epidemiology)

University of Ottawa

Contact Information: Dept. of Epidemiology and Community Medicine, 451 Smyth Road,
Room RGN3229B, Ottawa, Ont. K1H 8M5 CANADA
Phone: +1 613 562 5800 ext. 8284; Fax: +1 613 562 5465; Email: mcdowell@uottawa.ca

Daniel Krewski, Ph.D. (Statistics)

Institute of Population Health, University of Ottawa

Contact Information: One Stewart St., Room 318B, Ottawa, Ont. K1N 6N5 CANADA
Phone: +1 613 562 5381; Fax: +1 613 562 5380; Email: dkrewski@uottawa.ca

Summary

The paths toward sustainability require forms of governance that obligate those governed to prevent declines in, and collapse of ecological integrity. Current trends reveal that disruption to the flows and stocks of natural capital are global in reach, and many problems are directly related to the excessive human appropriation of the global commons.

Previous research examining the relationships between the appropriation of natural capital for both the production of wealth and population health, indicates that more healthy societies tend to consume vast amounts of natural capital. Most technological societies now operate beyond the basic biophysical parameters for sustainability and, in turn, continue to cultivate a culture of conspicuous consumption and irresponsible waste. There are several societies, however, that are able to balance comparably good health outcomes using much less natural capital.

We explore forms of governance characteristic to societies where this balance is being achieved and for societies where it is not. While no society is ultimately sustainable in isolation, it should be possible to develop a form of governance for sustainability that is mutually agreed upon; one that can provide hope of permanence for humanity, recognizing our dependence on the array of species with whom we share the planet.

171

Introduction

The current dominant pattern of resource-intensive and ecologically destructive human development, which Rees (2002) has described as the result of an enormously successful evolutionary strategy, presents a critical challenge. The concepts of sustainability and ecological integrity recognize the fundamental importance of functioning ecosystems as the primary determinant of health for humans and all other forms of life.

Scientific assessments reveal massive alterations to terrestrial, freshwater, and marine ecosystems. (Vitousek et al., 1997; WWF, 2004; Agardy et al., 2005) Paradoxically the intent to improve human well-being may threaten the integrity and thus the permanence of the ecosystems upon which we ultimately depend.

To the degree that unsustainable consumption is a logical consequence of increasingly complex, technological societies, any departure from the current path toward sustainability means that the dominant mode of governance in these societies must come under scrutiny.

The determinants of population health, in addition to the influence of ecological integrity, also comprise socioeconomic and cultural influences such as the distribution of wealth, the development of technology and infrastructure, and the advancement of knowledge. The affirmed support of many states is toward governance for sustainability, to promote social and economic development within the carrying capacity of ecosystems (WSSD, 2002), and is consistent as a basis for improvements in the health of human and nonhuman populations. Global agreements on issues such as climate change, poverty alleviation, and biodiversity loss indicate willingness for states to engage in a transition toward new forms of governance.

Nevertheless, the concept of governance for sustainability and how it supports progress in human health and well-being remains largely understudied. The form of governance adopted by any country affects virtually every aspect of society, including health.

In this chapter, we investigate the associations between governance and human health across a range of societies determined to be more or less sustainable.

First, we discuss the idea of sustainability as a challenge to governance and introduce a form of governance more suited toward sustainability. We then review research that has examined the relationship between human health and measures of governance and sustainability.

Next, we compare a set of governance indicators to health outcomes for 146 countries that have been categorized according to a measure of sustainability.

Lastly, we examine more closely the forms of governance found in three countries that are sustainable from a biophysical context and are distinguished by relatively laudable health outcomes.

From Good Governance to Governance for Sustainability

Sustainability presents a challenge to governance. If societies are to achieve some semblance of permanence, then most would agree that they should be characterized by a willingness to live within the ecological bounds of nature, and that societies should be purposefully equitable, just, democratic, and healthy. This is a rather tall order and it is not entirely clear how, or if specific forms of governance may contribute toward these ends.

Governance as a tool for social administration is both a structure and a process. Lafferty (2004) proposes the notion of governance as the complete mix of mechanisms and instruments designed to alter, channel, and influence social change in predetermined directions. As a structure, governance provides a framework for the initiation and/or reduction of negotiation, compliance, penalty, and/or conflict (Eden and Hampson, 1997), and is characteristic of the traditions and institutions by which authority in a society is exercised. (Kaufmann et al., 2003) As a process, it denotes a combination of approaches used to maintain order and orientation in contemporary sociopolitical systems, including the activities of governments, and other processes of regular societal interaction. (Meadowcroft et al., 2005)

The concept of good governance represents an ideal. Like sustainability, the notion of good governance represents a shift toward more or less ambitious societal objectives. Determining what constitutes good governance leads to debate on values and cultural norms, and on the desired pathways to achieve desired conditions or outcomes. One of the more comprehensive efforts on the study of good governance has been cultivated by the World Bank Institute's research program on governance and anti-corruption. (Kaufmann et al., 2003)

Still, it remains uncertain as to whether the features of good governance will confer the conditions necessary to promote sustainability and health. (Easterly, 2002) Conceptions of good governance prescribe a normative weight that is not always apparent within their description. For example, good governance as observed by the World Bank and OECD is adopted to support an agenda that favors market mechanisms and corporate interests in place of traditional roles of government. (OECD, 1995; World Bank, 1992) Arguably, many of the most unsustainable democratic societies have adopted a form of this agenda as a means of instilling a form of democratic pluralism. This form of pluralism is the means in which the divergent preferences of interdependent actors are translated into policy choices to allocate values. (Eising and Kohler-Koch, 2000) The transition toward ecological disintegrity can be characterized by a fundamental imbalance in pluralistic governance leading to: 1) obsessive focus on growth in productivity and the irrational use of nonrenewable resources, 2) disinvestment from public infrastructure and changes in social policy to maintain class structures, and 3) little consideration of the ecological and social consequences associated with the processes of production and conspicuous consumption. (Demirović, 1994) If ecological disintegrity and unsustainable activities are the logical consequence of liberal-pluralist market societies, then any movement toward ecological sustainability must also scrutinize the dominant character of governance in these societies.

Governance for sustainability is desirable since what currently constitutes good governance fails to acknowledge the primacy of natural capital and associated services for sustainability. Figure 12.1 depicts forty-year trends in human and ecological welfare since 1960. The horizontal line across the figure (value = 1.0) indicates Earth's total ecological capacity or available natural capital. Based on analyses of global consumption (Wackernagel et al., 2002), the demand on natural capital from all human beings rose to equal the supply in about 1986. The absolute number of humans added to the planet is still growing by more than 85 million annually. (Cohen, 1995) The global economy as measured by per capita gross domestic product has increased almost fourfold in the past four decades. This trend should be tempered with an acknowledgment of unequal consumption where a mere 20 percent of total population accounts for more than 80 percent of all consumption. (UNDP, 2002) Human life expectancy has increased more than fifteen years since 1960, and infant mortality rates have been cut in half. Contrary to this phenomenal growth are trends related both to the well-being of other species and in specific measures of good governance. Populations of nonhuman species, as measured by the Living Planet Index, have decreased by almost 40 percent. Measures of freedom in terms of political rights and civil liberties, and subjective well-being (not shown) have actually declined.

Global Trends of Sustainability

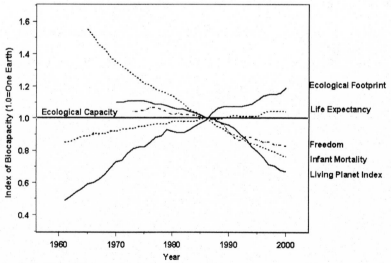

Figure 12.1. Global Trends of Sustainability, Health, and Democracy for 146 Countries, Comprising Approximately 5.6 Billion People

Since the processes leading to ecological disintegrity are complex, the approach to sustainable governance should be adaptive and learning-based, rather than engineered. Governance for sustainability should reflect and serve the dominant functions of complex, ecological systems. Many notions of governance are congruent with the concepts of complexity theory and imply an explicit appreciation of uncertainty, surprise, and a requirement for adaptive capacities. (Kemp et al., 2005)

Local development can have global implications. Governance for sustainability should support the development and implementation of international agreements, as well as strong intergovernmental arrangements (Yencken, 2002) so that the benefits and harms associated with development are shared equitably.

Another dimension of governance for sustainability necessitates processes to increase citizen involvement in deliberations on decisions related to well-being, traditionally relegated to state authorities. (Dorcey and McDaniels, 2001) Commitments made by states to global environmental agreements are rarely discussed in domestic elections, leading to problems of implementation. Furthermore, governance for sustainability must have a degree of authoritativeness on matters in support of ecological integrity so as to prevent interference from political impulse. (Lafferty, 2004) Too often it is assumed that support for democratic ideals will lead to commitments for ecological sustainability. Ironically, the same support may have unintended undemocratic consequences since "rational" democratic decisions may not always be in the best interests of support for ecological sustainability in the absence of commitments to sustainability per se.

Population Health, Governance, and Sustainability

The study of population health is concerned with the study of relationships between health and its determinants. (Health Canada, 2003) Socioeconomic determinants of health such as income, income inequality, and alternative measures of socioeconomic status have received a substantial amount of attention. (WHO, 2001; Wilkinson, 1996) However, mounting evidence suggests that a society's economic status alone cannot fully account for variations in population health outcomes. (Blomley, 1994; Farmer, 1999; McMichael, 2001; Szreter, 2003) Improvements in population health beyond a certain level of wealth provide solid evidence for the shift of capital for social rather than individual gains with negligible detriment to health outcomes. (Soskolne and Bertollini, 1998) Moreover, societies with congruent measures of economic development can have significantly dissimilar health outcomes. Thus, it remains an important task for population health research to extend the analysis to broad structural factors, such as governance and ecological sustainability, to improve our understanding of global variations in health status.

Few theoretical or empirical studies exist associating governance and health. Disentangling the health-governance relationship is complicated by difficulty in identifying independent influences and interactions that comprise governance. For example, democracy has been associated with improvements in life expectancy, infant mortality, and maternal health. (Franco et al., 2004) These associations appear, however, to be highly sensitive to the handling of the raw data in the statistical model. (Sieswerda and Soskolne, 2005) Similar investigation has shown good governance to be associated with low prevalence of HIV infection. (Menon-Johanson, 2005)

More widely studied is the relationship between population health and measures of sustainability. Several measures of ecological integrity and biodiversity have been employed to test the hypothesis that a reduction in integrity and/or biodiversity is detrimental to human health. (Huynen et al., 2004; Sieswerda et al., 2001) In both studies, the strength of the relationship between measures of sustainability and human health was diminished after control for socioeconomic measures. Data from the more recent study showed improving health outcomes in association with declines in biodiversity. Using a similar approach, Rainham and McDowell (2005) demonstrated a small but statistically significant relationship between life expectancy and ecological footprint even after controlling for the influence of economic output. This brings into focus the current dilemma facing humanity and provides direction for further study. If improvements to health arise at nature's expense (and there is only limited nature available given current patterns of development and predicted population levels), then humanity must acknowledge its unsustainable path. Intriguing are the few societies able to attain relatively good levels of population health without threatening long-term sustainability, i.e., a society that is healthy with ecological footprints at or below the value to avoid ecological overshoot. A focus on these "outlier" societies may provide some insight into the forms of governance in support of ecological integrity. (Soskolne and Bertollini, 1998)

We now focus on two objectives. First, we investigate the relationship between population health and measures of governance among countries considered more or less sustainable, determined using the ecological footprint. The analysis proceeds under the hypothesis that there is no relationship between population health and governance between societies classified as either ecologically sustainable or unsustainable. Second, we explore the nature of governance among societies able to balance relatively high life expectancies with sustainable levels of natural capital consumption.

Methods

Aggregate data at the state level were used to achieve the study objectives. Socioeconomic data were excluded from hypothesis testing for several reasons. Measures such as per capita gross domestic product and gross national product are highly correlated with ecological footprint. Wealth is generated from the consumption of natural capital which may then be allocated to appropriate more natural capital or ecosystem services. More wealthy societies use wealth generated from consumption to derive more natural capital from less-wealthy, export-dependent, but resource- (natural and human capital) rich societies. (Hornborg, 2001) Ultimately, the origins of consumption and wealth can be traced to the formation of states and geopolitical boundaries through colonialism and other forms of resource exploration. Nevertheless, there are many ecosystem services, such as water filtration, provided to all populations included in footprint values that are not included in economic indicators.

Selection of Data and Sources

Data to measure sustainability, population health, and governance were collected from multiple international agency databases for 146 countries. (Table 12.1) Two datasets were assembled, the first to examine long-term trends, and the second to perform a cross-sectional analysis on data from 2002.

Table 12.1. Measures, Definitions, Sources, and Summary of Data for 146 Countries

Measures	Definition	Source	Summary (Mean, SD)
Health			
Health-adjusted life expectancy	Health expectancy indicator extends measures of life expectancy to account for the distribution of health states in the population (Years)	WHO (World Health Organization). World Health Report: Annex Table 4. Geneva, Switzerland: WHO, 2004.	56.9 (11.8)
Infant mortality rate	The number of children dying under a year of age divided by the number of live births that year (deaths/1,000 births)	United Nations Children's Fund (UNICEF). The State of the World's Children 2006: Excluded and Invisible. Table 1. New York, NY: UNICEF, 2005.	45.8 (41.8)
Sustainability			
Ecological footprint	The amount of the surface of the Earth needed to support a person or system (hectares in this study)	Global Footprint Network. National Footprint and Biocapacity Accounts, 2005 Edition. Oakland, CA: Global Footprint Network, 2005.	2.4 (1.9)
Governance			
Voice and accountability	Measures of political process, civil liberties, and political rights; citizen participation in governments selection; media independence	Daniel Kaufmann, Aart Kraay, and Massimo Mastruzzi. Governance Matters III: Governance Indicators for 1996-2002. Washington, DC: World Bank, 2003.	-0.12 (1.0)

Continued on next page

Table 12.1 (continued)

Measures	Definition	Source	Summary (Mean, SD)
Political stability	Perception of likelihood that governance may be compromised by unconstitutional and/or violent means, including terrorism		-0.10 (0.98)
Government effectiveness	Quality of public service provision, bureaucracy, competence of civil service, and their independence from political pressures		-0.09 (0.97)
Regulatory quality	Incidence of market-unfriendly policies and perception of burden imposed by excessive regulation		-0.04 (0.96)
Rule of law	Extent agents have confidence in/abide by rules of society		-0.11 (0.98)
Corruption	Perception of corruption defined as exercise of public power for private gain		-0.11 (0.99)
Environmental Governance			
Land protected (percentage)	Protected areas as a percent of total land area (percentage)	UNEP-WCMC. World Database on Protected Areas (WDPA). CD-ROM. 2004.	12.3 (11.8)
Gasoline ratio	Ratio of gasoline price to world average		1.0 (0.4)
Initiatives and organizations	Aggregate measure of IUCN member organizations and Agenda 21 initiatives per million people	World Conservation Union (2006); International Council for Local Environmental Initiatives (ICLEI, 2001)	3.5 (9.0)
Environmental governance	Regulation and enforcement of environmental regulations	World Economic Forum Survey on environmental governance	37.1 (10.5)
Funding, participation and memberships	Contributions to funding of environmental projects, participation in international environmental agreements, memberships in environmental intergovernmental organizations	Yearbook of International Organizations 2003/04; Global Environmental Facility	1.3 (0.4)

Indicator for Sustainability

The ecological footprint is a measure of human impact designed to assess the area of biologically productive land and water required to produce the resources consumed in human activity and to assimilate wastes. (Wackernagel and Rees, 1996; Wackernagel et al., 2002) It comprises an appropriate measure of sustainability for the following reasons. First, international trade allows states to import resources and export wastes. Thus depletion of natural capital may occur beyond traditional economic borders. The usual indicators used to assess ecological integrity and/or biodiversity (air pollution, forest cover, species status, etc.) focus only on ecological impacts within states and ignore the location(s) of actions and decisions leading to ecological disintegrity. Natural capital flows and consumption patterns can be converted into biologically productive land areas for comparison. Second, the ecological footprint includes the overall ecological impact for a specified population which helps to avoid collinearity problems when multiple variables are used. Footprint data for 2002 were obtained from the National Footprint and Biocapacity Accounts, 2005 database developed by the Global Footprint Network (2005).

Indicators for Governance

The World Bank Institute's research program on governance and anti-corruption research group has collated country-level governance indicators covering three time periods since 1996. The concept of governance is represented in six dimensions based on 250 indicators measuring perceptions of governance from twenty-five separate data sources and includes a variety of international organizations, political and business risk-rating agencies, think tanks, and non-governmental organizations. The dimensions of governance include: voice and accountability, political stability, government effectiveness, regulatory quality, rule of law, and corruption. (Kaufmann et al., 2003) Standardized values on each dimension for 2002 are available for all 146 countries. An overall measure of governance was also calculated as the average of the six dimensions of governance.

Five additional dimensions were created in an effort to assess environmental governance. The first dimension represents that total area of protected land (in percent) as a measure of governance for the protection of natural capital and investment in biodiversity conservation. Data for 2002 were abstracted from the World Database of Protected Areas CD-ROM. (UNEP-WCMC, 2004) The second dimension is the ratio of gasoline price to the world average and was selected to represent an approach to the appropriate regulation of nonrenewable resources. These data were taken from the World Bank Development Indicators 2004 database. A third dimension for environmental governance, called Initiatives and Organizations, represents a crude measure of citizen involvement in activities related to the conservation and sustainability of their local environments. It was constructed by aggregating the values from two variables, the number of IUCN member organizations per million people, and the number of local Agenda 21 initiatives per million people. Data were obtained from The World Conservation Union (IUCN) and the International Council for Local Environmental Initiatives (ICLEI) for 2002, and 2001 respectively. The fourth dimension is called Environmental Governance and is a single measure derived from principal component analyses of survey questions addressing several aspects of environmental regulation, policy, and enforcement. These data were made available by the World Economic Forum Survey on Environmental Governance. (WEF, 2004) The final dimension, called Funding, Participation, and Memberships, combines three variables from three separate datasets. The first variable (Funding) represents the contribution of states to international and bi-lateral funding of environmental projects and development aid. (World Bank, 2004) The second variable (Participation) is an indication of a society's partici-pation in international/multilateral environmental agreements. (WRI, 2006) The third variable (Memberships) is based on the number of memberships a country has in environmental intergovernmental organizations. (Esty et al., 2005)

The World Bank governance data are supplied in a standardized form so that each dimension has a mean value of close to zero and a standard deviation of one. Data used in the creation of the environmental governance dimensions were subsequently standardized using a similar method as outlined in Kaufmann et al. (2003).

Indicators for Population Health

Two indicators of population health were selected: the Health-Adjusted Life Expectancy is an indicator that extends measures of life expectancy to account for the distribution of health states in the population (Mathers et al., 2004), and the infant mortality rate per one thousand live births. The data were available for 2002 from the World Health Organization (2004). It is unclear whether these types of health endpoints are sensitive to variations in ecological sustainability. (Grifo and Rosenthal, 1997)

Additional Development Indicators

Supplementary indicators of human development were added to the data-base for a more in-depth description of states observed to be healthy and sus-tainable. The indicators include: Human Development Index (UNDP, 2004), Disability-Adjusted Life Years (WHO, 2003), the number of physicians per hundred thousand population (WHO, 2004), per capita gross domestic product (PPP in US dollars), and the GINI index (World Bank, 2004) to assess income inequality (percentage).

Correlation Analysis and Country Identification

The null hypothesis of no association between health and governance was tested using the following procedure. Countries were assigned to one of three categories based on the measure of per capita ecological footprint. The most recent assessment of global per capita biocapacity is approximately 1.8 hectares (approximately 4.4 acres). This value can be used as a benchmark for assessing the sustainability of all states. Countries with ecological footprints close to or below 1.8 hectares have an ecological impact that, if replicated by all other countries, diminish pressures on ecological integrity, provided that population growth is halted or declines.

There is good evidence from similar cross-sectional studies that nations with very small footprints experience higher domestic levels of particular forms of environmental degradation (Lofdahl, 2002), such as deforestation and organic water pollution. (Clapp, 2002) States with very small footprints are more likely to be underdeveloped in the sense of being unable to supply the minimum resources required for citizens to improve their health. Using a similar rationale, states with large footprints are also unsustainable in that far-reaching pressures on natural capital result in only moderate gains in health and other measures of human well-being. (Rainham and McDowell, 2005) All countries were assigned to one of three categories: those with ecological footprints less than 1.2 hectares (N=50: "unsustainable"), greater than 2.4 hectares (N=48: "unsustainable"), and between 1.2 and 2.4 hectares (N=48: "sustainable"). The first two categories include states with imbalanced approaches to the use of natural capital for human development and are labeled as unsustainable. The remaining countries (N=48), those with ecological footprints between 1.2 and 2.4 hectares, represent a category of consumption to which all nations should aspire if global sustainability and ecological integrity are to be achieved, and are categorized as sustainable. Countries were then further categorized according to levels of good environmental governance. Mean values of infant mortality and health-adjusted life expectancy were then calculated for each level of governance (weak, medium, and strong) within each footprint category so that it is possible to assess variations of health with governance among the categories of ecological footprint.

Kendall's Tau was used to provide a distribution-free test of independence, and to measure the strength of dependence between indicators of health and dimensions of governance. It has been shown to provide a more conservative and accurate estimate of correlation when compared to similar nonparametric statistics. (Arndt et al., 1999)

A scatter plot was created with the Log10 of the ecological footprint on the X-axis, and life expectancy on the Y-axis to identify states that may constitute outliers in the relationship between ecological footprint and health-adjusted life expectancy. States were selected if they placed in the top quartile of life expectancy and had ecological footprints below 1.8 hectares.

Results

The final dataset represents 94.4 percent of the world's population among 146 countries. Summary values of population health, governance (including environmental governance), and sustainability are shown in Table 12.1.

Non-parametric analysis of the association between population health and governance among countries, categorized according to ecological footprint, is shown in Table 12.2. Values with asterisks indicate a p-value of less than 0.05, and many correlations had much smaller values (not shown).

Associations between all measures of governance and health were strongest among states with ecological footprints greater than 2.4 hectares. The strength and significance of these associations declined among states with ecological footprints less than 1.2 hectares. Among sustainable countries, the association between governance and health was weakly, but significantly correlated with infant mortality, and only one dimension of governance was significantly (weakly) associated with health-adjusted life expectancy. The most influential dimensions of governance across all categories were government effectiveness, rule of law, funding, participations and memberships, and gasoline pricing. Mean governance, as measured by the average of the World Bank governance dimensions, was correlated with health outcomes among countries in all categories except for health-adjusted life expectancy among countries with reasonable footprints. Mean environmental governance was positively correlated with health only among countries with the largest ecological footprints.

Table 12.2. Health-Adjusted Life Expectancy (HALE)[a] and Infant Mortality Rate (IMR)[b] Correlations with Governance Dimensions among 146 Countries Grouped by the Size of Their Ecological Footprint (EF)[c]

Dimensions of Governance	Ecological Footprint Groups and Correlation Coefficients					
	EF < 1.2 (N=50)		EF = 1.2 to 2.4 (N=48)		EF > 2.4 (N=48)	
	HALE	IMR	HALE	IMR	HALE	IMR
World Bank Governance Dimensions						
Voice and accountability	0.148	-0.167	0.157	-0.223*	0.584*	-0.549*
Political stability and absence of violence	0.023	-0.091	0.120	-0.160	0.430*	-0.441*
Government effectiveness	0.331*	-0.403*	0.219*	-0.249*	0.621*	-0.558*
Regulatory quality	0.173	-0.229*	0.167	-0.201*	0.561*	-0.519*
Rule of law	0.223*	-0.264*	0.151	-0.180*	0.628*	-0.554*
Corruption	0.121	-0.113	0.217	-0.254*	0.620*	-0.535*
Mean governance	0.203*	-0.248*	0.165	-0.199*	0.613*	-0.558*
Environmental Governance Dimensions						
Land protected	-0.096	-0.070	-0.024	-0.039	0.216*	-0.182
Gasoline price ratio	-0.228*	0.197*	0.112	-0.081	0.485*	-0.561*
Initiatives and organizations	-0.017	-0.129	0.049	-0.122	0.428*	-0.415*
Environmental governance	0.010	-0.060	0.034	-0.052	0.609*	-0.608*
Funding, participation, and memberships	0.208*	-0.217*	0.069	-0.102	0.443*	-0.504*
Mean environmental governance	0.010	-0.043	0.093	-0.130	0.555*	-0.581*

[a] Health-adjusted life expectancy, units in years
[b] Infant mortality rate, units in deaths per 1,000 live births
[c] Per capita ecological footprint, units in hectares (ha), 1ha = 2.47 acres.
* Level of statistical significance, $p < 0.05$

The strength and direction of these associations indicate that governance is significantly correlated with improvements in life expectancy and infant mortality, but is dependent on per capita pressures on natural capital. Figures 12.2 and 12.3 illustrate the change in the relationship between governance measures and population health along strata of ecological footprint. Health performance improves with the strength in governance among countries with footprints larger than 2.4 hectares. As governance improves, infant mortality declines and life expectancy increases. This pattern is less apparent among countries with smaller footprints. Governance does not appear to influence the health of populations among more sustainable states.

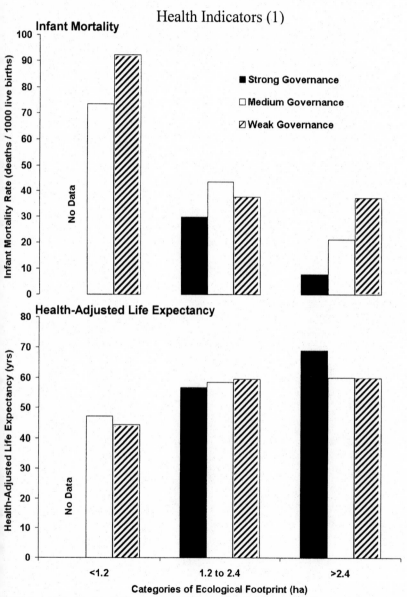

Figure 12.2. Health Indicators in 146 Countries by Classification of Sustainability and Governance (2002)

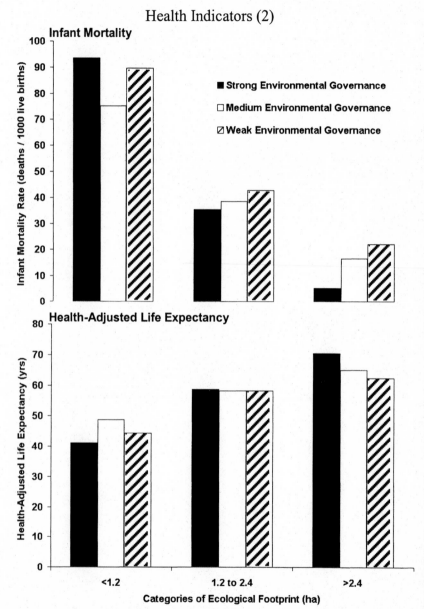

Figure 12.3. Health Indicators in 146 Countries by Classification of Sustainability and Environmental Governance (2002)

Three countries—Cuba, Jamaica, and Panama—were identified as outliers among the 146 countries in terms of their ability to achieve relatively high health-adjusted life expectancies while maintaining sustainable patterns of natural capital consumption as measured by the ecological footprint. Table 12.3 shows values for indicators of health, governance, environmental governance, and development for these three countries and comparison with averages from the top ten healthiest countries in the OECD.

Table 12.3. Health, Governance, and Development Indicators for Countries with "Sustainable" Ecological Footprints and Respectable Health Outcomes Compared to Most Healthy OECD Countries[a]

Indicators	Cuba	Panama	Jamaica	OECD[a]
		Country		
Ecological Footprint	1.7	1.7	1.7	5.4
Health				
HALE (yrs)	68.3	66.2	65.1	72.7
DALY (per 100,000)	14,087	14,748	14,714	11,585
IMR (deaths/1,000 births)	7	19	17	4
Physicians per 100,000 (1990-2003)	590	85	168	~300
Governance[b]				
Voice and accountability	140	43	42	13
Political stability	59	52	74	17
Government effectiveness	65	58	56	13
Regulatory quality	131	43	47	15
Rule of law	118	55	69	12
Corruption	54	62	79	13
Environmental Governance[b]				
Land protected	132	34	47	56
Gasoline price/World average ratio	27	95	91	31
Env. initiatives and organizations	93	32	36	20
Environmental governance	27	72	87	13
Funding, participation, and memberships	65	103	102	36
Development				
Human Development Index	0.81	0.55	0.93	0.83
GDP-PPP ($ per capita)	1,700	6,166	3,982	27,924
GINI Index (1984-2001)	22-41	56.4	37.9	30.6
Literacy rate (in percent, 2000-2004)	99.8	91.9	87.6	99.6
Female literacy (as percent. of male literacy)	100.0	98.6	109.1	99.7

[a] All values derived from average of top ten OECD countries with highest health-adjusted life expectancies. [b] Values are rankings out of 146 countries; smaller values indicate superior performance.

Discussion

An important aspect of sustainability research is an examination of relationships between pressures exerted on the systems that support all life and measures of human development. For most societies, the relationship is paradoxical. Many of the healthiest societies are also the most ecologically unsustainable. (Rainham and McDowell, 2005) The transition toward sustainability will require acknowledgment of the primacy of natural capital, not only for human health, but for the health of all species. Recent global ecological diagnoses have indicated a startling deterioration of ecological integrity and have forecast potentially devastating impacts to human health and development. (Agardy et al., 2005) While population growth and poverty are certainly drivers of this deterioration, few would oppose the notion that technologically-driven industrialized democracies exert a tremendous strain on ecosystem resources and services to support a form of human development exemplified by conspicuous consumption for economic growth.

We have explored whether governance is related to health among countries that exert more or less pressure on natural systems, and have identified specific countries where health is achieved in an ecologically sustainable manner.

Good governance, at least as defined by the World Bank, is typical of most Western democracies. This includes (1) the process by which governments are selected, monitored, and replaced, (2) the capacity of the government to effectively formulate and implement sound policies, and (3) the respect of citizens and the state for the institutions that govern economic and social interactions among them. (Kaufmann et al., 2003) There is nothing inherently faulty with the concept of good governance, except for the failure to acknowledge purpose—that is—governance to what end? Governance for sustainability is a concept akin to good governance with the primary objective of maintaining ecological integrity.

The association between measures of governance and population health was evaluated among societies that place varying demands on natural capital to support human development. This demand was measured using the ecological footprint. The probability of a relationship between governance and health is higher among countries with footprints that are considered unsustainable (unsustainable, if we concur with the principle that natural capital should be shared equitably among the current global population).

For countries with sustainable footprints, the association between governance and health was more tenuous. None of the environmental governance measures was associated with health, and the World Bank measures were associated only with infant mortality. Two indicators that seem to be of particular importance for health are government effectiveness and rule of law. Government effectiveness refers to the inputs, such as bureaucratic quality, competence of the civil service, and other measures, required for government to be able to produce and implement good policy and deliver public goods. (Kaufmann et al., 2003) The rule of law includes several indicators measuring the extent to which agents have confidence in and abide by the rules of society.

There have been few studies of the relationship between governance and population health, notwithstanding how this relationship varies with ecological sustainability. This study represents an exploratory investigation and raises more questions than conclusions. For example, are the measures of governance as used in this study appropriate for sustainability research?

Elite groups often maintain the power to define social goals and, in many instances, redirect the attention of governments and citizens away from the pressing issue of ecological disintegrity toward the concept of economic prosperity at any cost. (Forgacs, 2000) Ultimately it would be prudent to develop measures of governance to account for the extent to which power is centralized and decision-making influenced by the interests of economic elites. Do the measures of governance here consider the role of power, especially military and technological power? Many OECD country budgets for military expenditures have risen 1-2 percent per year over the past decade, while expenditures in countries like Cuba have declined more than two-fold in the past two decades, and are more than four to five times less than the average per capita military expenditures in industrialized states. (Pérez-López, 1996)

Global governance and governance of the global commons are dominated by states with extensive military might. Measures of governance should acknowledge the extent to which national interests disproportionately attain natural capital, thus fostering the creation of global inequalities and economic dependency. Moreover, the general disassociation between governance and health among more sustainable societies is also noteworthy. There is strong pressure from the international community for societies to become more democratic, mainly based on the premise that decisions of the collective majority will lead to improvements in human development. However, democracy is a difficult pill to swallow if equal weight is afforded to those in any society who, for the short-term interest in accruing wealth or material items, would destroy ecological integrity.

The concept of the "democratic trap" (Grumbine, 1992) opens the possibility that efforts to maintain ecological integrity might be justified not for promoting the public interest, but as a constraint on the same objective. If ecological sustainability must take precedence for the survival of our species, then we must be willing to explore potential restrictions to the forms of democracy and governance that dominate highly consumptive societies.

Cuba, Jamaica, and Panama are three countries in the top quintile of health-adjusted life expectancy with per capita ecological footprints at or below the amount required to sustain the current global population (EF=1.8). The purpose of identifying these countries was to explore the forms of governance among countries able to achieve relatively good health outcomes without placing undue pressure on ecological systems.

Table 12.3 shows health, governance, and development indicators. A feature of all three countries is a warm climate. Climate plays an important role in influencing patterns of geographic and economic development. (Diamond, 1997; Freese, 1997) Countries with similar population health measures, but with footprints above 1.8 hectares, include Costa Rica (2.0), Uruguay (2.1), Chile (2.2), Argentina (2.2), and Mexico (2.4). The rate of natural capital consumption is associated with climate, and possibly some bioregional aspect of Latin American lifestyles that may also contribute to longevity. This finding is consistent with theories from human ecology that incorporate biophysical factors, such as climate and biogeography, as contexts in which social factors drive environmental impacts.

The Cuban model of governance may be one to emulate should other countries wish to transition toward ecological sustainability. Most studies of Cuban governance have been oriented toward issues linked to the economic and political situation from a structural perspective. Cuba is considered by many to be undemocratic, its population lacking political rights and freedoms, and civil liberties. However, there is likely just as much propaganda coming from outside Cuba as there is from within.

There is friction between open versus closed systems of governance—this does not infer that one system is better than another, only that one may be more transparent than another. Cuba may actually provide a legitimate model for alternative development, and there is good evidence to show that Cuba is actually more democratic than many "Western" states. From Saney's (2004) analysis of Cuban democracy, several striking characteristics emerge: 1) Cuban governance is responsive to citizen demands as increasing powers have been delegated to local government, 2) public consultation and participation in governance is central to decision-making, 3) consensus and unity form the basis of Cuban political process (as opposed to the adversarial approach found in most Western democracies), and 4) civil society plays a very important role in the processes of new policy formulation and the adoption of legislation.

The strength of Cuban governance has been tested with the collapse of the socialist camp and the crises that ensued in the early 1990s. The collapse provoked a 35 percent reduction in GDP and a severe deterioration in most social indicators: university enrollment dropped 58 percent, maternal mortality jumped 123 percent, mortality at age sixty-five and above increased 15 percent, and the rate of most contagious diseases and child malnourishment rose dramatically. (Mesa-Lago, 2005) The scale of the collapse has been likened to the Great Depression of the 1930s.

Nevertheless, Cuba continues to defy convention by performing well in many areas of human health and development. For example, prevalence of HIV and many other infectious diseases is low in Cuba. Cuba was one of the first countries in the Americas to launch a nationwide HIV policy to contain transmission and care for those people living with HIV/AIDS. (Farmer, 2003) Healthcare is provided free to its citizens by the state and there is strong political commitment toward interventions for health promotion. Infant mortality has continued to decline in spite of tremendous economic hardship. Cuba has also radically transformed many of its industries. Notably, agriculture has transitioned from pesticide-dependent industrial monocultures to intensive, localized organic farms run by small teams that rotate duties in an egalitarian fashion.

By necessity, the country has greatly reduced its dependence on expensive imported oil by encouraging wide use of bicycles and other low-power technologies. Cuba provides a remarkable example of how alternative forms of governance can enhance citizen participation, maintain and even improve population health and development within the constraints of a finite ecology.

A key driver of ecological footprint values is the land required to absorb carbon dioxide emissions. Energy requirements in tropical countries, as long as there is no reliance on air conditioning, would be much less than in countries from more northerly or southerly latitudes where footprints would be driven partially by energy requirements for heating. A smaller ecological footprint does not necessarily mean that ecological integrity is being maintained. Degradation of ecological integrity is especially evident in Panama, for example, and less so in Cuba. (Díaz-Briquets and Pérez-López, 2000; USAID, 2005) Equally important to remember, however, is that there are many examples of large-scale violations of ecological integrity in most industrialized states.

The use of life expectancy and infant mortality do not adequately measure the health of populations, and the study design used here merely portrays relationships at a specific point in time. However, this research does provide some useful contributions. First, measures of good governance have little to do with the production of health in societies with smaller ecological footprints. In addition, it is clear that further research needs to be undertaken to examine why the societies identified in this study are able to foster improvements in human health and well-being without exerting unsustainable pressures on natural capital. Second, measures of governance for sustainability are relatively nonexistent and require development. The measures chosen for this study were selected based on best available data rather than a comprehensive theoretical model. Finally, it appears that any form of governance will have to acknowledge the primacy of ecological integrity and equality if permanence for humanity is the goal.

Conclusions

The way we view governance, democracy, consumption, wealth, and health must change. Many of the healthiest societies are often the most ecologically unsustainable and *vice versa* (e.g., Cuba). We distinguish between good governance and governance for sustainability. Good governance, at least from an environmental and constitutional law perspective, is necessary to achieve sustainability. However, we have argued that sustainability should be the mode by which natural capital, and ultimately human health and well-being could be protected and even enhanced. To do so, we must traverse disciplines and preconceptions, acknowledging the collective goal of maintaining ecological integrity.

Acknowledgments

The author acknowledges the support of the Canadian Institutes of Health Research and the McLaughlin Centre for Population Health Risk Assessment in the Institute of Population Health at the University of Ottawa. The author also thanks Lee Sieswerda and Brian Ladd for their helpful and critical insights during the initial stages of this paper.

References

Agardy, Tundi, Jackie Alder, Neville Ash, Ruth DeFries, and Gerald Nelson. "Synthesis: Condition and Trends in Systems and Services, Trade-offs for Human Well-being, and Implications for the Future." Ch. 28 in *Ecosystems and Human Well-Being: Current State and Trends,* edited by Rashid Hassan, Robert Scholes, and Neville Ash. Washington, DC: Island Press, 2005.

Arndt, Stephan, Carolyn Turvey, and Nancy C. Andreasen. "Correlating and Predicting Psychiatric Symptom Ratings: Spearmans r versus Kendalls tau Correlation." *Journal of Psychiatric Research* 33, no. 2 (1999): 97–104.

Blomley, Nicholas K. *Law, Space, and the Geographies of Power.* New York: Guilford Press, 1994.

Clapp, Jennifer. "The Distancing of Waste: Overconsumption in a Global Economy." Pp. 155–76 in *Confronting Consumption,* edited by Thomas Princen, Michael F. Maniates, and Ken Conca. Cambridge, MA: MIT Press, 2002.

Cohen, Joel E. *How Many People Can the Earth Support?* New York: W.W. Norton, 1995.

Demirović, Alex. "Ecological Crisis and the Future of Democracy." Pp. 253–74 in *Is Capitalism Sustainable?* edited by Martin O'Conner. New York: Guilford Press, 1994.

Diamond, Jared. *Guns, Germs, and Steel: The Fates of Human Societies.* New York: W.W. Norton & Company, 1997.

Díaz-Briquets, Sergio, and Jorge Pérez-López. *Conquering Nature: The Environmental Legacy of Socialism in Cuba.* Pittsburgh, PA: University of Pittsburgh Press, 2000.

Dorcey, Anthony H., and Timothy McDaniels. "Great Expectations, Mixed Results: Trends in Citizen Involvement in Canadian Environmental Governance." Pp. 247–302 in *Governing the Environment: Persistent Challenges, Uncertain Innovations,* edited by Edward Parson. Toronto: University of Toronto Press, 2001.

Easterly, William. *The Elusive Quest for Growth.* Cambridge, MA: MIT Press, 2002.

Eden, Lorraine, and Fen Osler Hampson. "Clubs are Trumps: The Formation of International Regimes in the Absence of Hegemon." Pp. 361–94 in *Contemporary Capitalism: The Embeddedness of Institutions,* edited by J. Rogers Hollingsworth and Robert Boyer. Cambridge, UK: Cambridge University Press, 1997.

Eising, Rainer, and Beate Kohler-Koch. "Introduction: Network Governance in the European Union." Pp. 3–13 in *The Transformation of EU Governance,* edited by Rainer Eising and Beate Kohler-Koch. New York: Routledge, 2000.

Esty, Daniel C., Marc Levy, Tanja Srebotnjak, and Alexander de Sherbinin. "2005 Environmental Sustainability Index: Benchmarking National Environmental Stewardship." New Haven: Yale Center for Environmental Law and Policy, 2005.

Farmer, Paul. *The Pathologies of Power.* Berkeley: University of California Press, 2003.

———. *Pathologies of Power: Health, Human Rights, and the New War on the Poor.* Berkeley: University of California Press, 1999.

Forgacs, David, ed. *An Antonio Gramsci Reader: Selected Writings, 1916–1935.* New York: New York University Press, 2000.

Franco, Álvaro, Carlos Álvarez-Dardet, and Maria T. Ruiz. "Effect of Democracy on Health: Ecological Study." *British Medical Journal* 329 (2004): 1421–23.

Freese, Lee. *Environmental Connections.* London: JAI Press, 1997.

Global Footprint Network. *National Footprint and Biocapacity Accounts, 2005 Edition.* Oakland, CA: Global Footprint Network, 2005. http://www.footprintnetwork.org (24 May 2007).

Grifo, Francesca, and Joshua Rosenthal, eds. *Biodiversity and Human Health.* Washington, DC.: Island Press, 1997.

Grumbine, Edward. *Ghost Bears: Exploring the Biodiversity Crisis.* Washington, DC: Island Press, 1992.

Health Canada (Public Health Agency of Canada). "What Is the Population Health Approach?" Ottawa: Health Canada, 2003. http://www.phac-aspc.gc.ca/ph-sp/phdd/approach/index.html (4 Jun. 2007).

Hornborg, Alf. *The Power of the Machine: Global Inequalities of Economy, Technology, and Environment.* Walnut Creek, CA: AltaMira Press, 2001.

Huynen, Maude, Pim Martens, and Dolf De Groot. "Linkages between Biodiversity Loss and Human Health: A Global Indicator Analysis." *International Journal of Environmental Health Research* 14, no. 1 (2004): 13–30.

ICLEI (International Council for Local Environmental Initiatives). "Second Local Agenda 21 Survey. Background Paper No. 15." Toronto, ON: ICLEI, 2001. http://www.iclei.org/documents/Global/final_document.pdf (4 Jun. 2007).

IUCN (The World Conservation Union). http://www.iucn.org (4 Jun. 2007).

Kaufmann, Daniel, Aart Kraay, and Massimo Mastruzzi. *Governance Matters III: Governance Indicators for 1996-2002.* Washington, DC: World Bank, 2003. http://www.worldbank.org/wbi/governance/pdf/govmatters3.pdf (24 May 2007).

Kemp, René, Saeed Parto, and Robert B. Gibson. "Governance for Sustainable Development: Moving from Theory to Practice." *International Journal of Sustainable Development* 8, nos. 1/2 (2005): 12–30.

Lafferty, William. "Governance for Sustainable Development: Lessons and Implications." Pp. 319–61 in *Governance for Sustainable Development: The Challenge of Adapting Form to Function,* edited by William Lafferty. Cheltenham, UK: Edward Elgar Publishing, 2004.

Lofdahl, Corey L. *Environmental Impacts of Globalization and Trade.* Cambridge, MA: MIT Press, 2002.

Mathers, Colin D., Kim M. Iburg, Joshua A. Salomon, Ajay Tandon, Somnath Chatterji, Bedirhan Ustün, and Christopher J. L. Murray. "Global Patterns of Healthy Life Expectancy in the Year 2002." *BMC Public Health* 4 (2004): http://www.biomedcentral.com/1471-2458/4/66 (24 May 2007).

McMichael, Anthony J. *Human Frontiers, Environments and Disease.* Cambridge: Cambridge University Press, 2001.

Meadowcroft, James, Katherine N. Farrell, and Joachim Spangenberg. "Developing a Framework for Sustainability Governance in the European Union." *International Journal of Sustainable Development* 8, nos. 1/2 (2005): 3–11.

Menon-Johansson, Anatole S. "Good Governance and Good Health: The Role of Societal Structures in the Human Immunodeficiency Virus Pandemic." *BMC International Health and Human Rights* (2005). http://www.biomedcentral.com/1472-698X/5/4 (24 May 2007).

Mesa-Lago, Carmelo. "Cuba's Ranking in the Human Development Index of 2005." *Focal Point* 4, no. 9 (2005): 1–3.

OECD (Organisation for Economic Co-operation and Development). *Governance in Transition: Public Management in OECD Countries.* Paris, France: OECD/PUMA, 1995.

Pérez-López, Jorge F. "Cuban Military Expenditures: Concepts, Data and Burden Measures." *Cuba in Transition*. Proceedings of the Fifth Annual Meeting of the Association for the Study of the Cuban Economy (ASCE). Miami, FL: ASCE, 1996.

Rainham, Daniel G., and Ian W. McDowell. "The Sustainability of Population Health." *Population and Environment* 26, no. 4 (2005): 303–24.

Rees, William W. "Globalization and Sustainability: Conflict or Convergence?" *Bulletin of Science, Technology & Society* 22, no. 4 (2002): 249–68.

Saney, Isaac. *Cuba: Revolution in Motion*. London: Zed Books, 2004.

Sieswerda, Lee E., and Colin L. Soskolne. "Franco et al.'s Results Need To Be Revisited Because Their Analysis Did Not Correctly Model the Relationship between Wealth and Health." *British Medical Journal*. Rapid Responses, 28 Jan. 2005.

Sieswerda, Lee E., Colin L. Soskolne, Stephen C. Newman, Donald Schopflocher, and Karen E. Smoyer. "Toward Measuring the Impact of Ecological Integrity on Human Health." *Epidemiology* 12 (2001): 28–32. http://bmj.bmjjournals.com/cgi/eletters/329/7480/1421#94484 (24 May 2007).

Soskolne, Colin L., and Roberto Bertollini. "Global Ecological Integrity and 'Sustainable Development': Cornerstones of Public Health—A Discussion Document Based on a WHO International Workshop." WHO/ECEH Rome Division, Italy, 3–4 Dec. 1998. http://www.euro.who.int/document/gch/ecorep5.pdf (24 May 2007).

Szreter, Simon. "The Population Health Approach in Historical Perspective." *American Journal of Public Health* 93 (2003): 421–31.

UNDP (United Nations Development Programme). *Governance and Sustainable Human Development: A UNDP Policy Document*. 1997. http://mirror.undp.org/magnet/policy (4 Jun. 2007).

———. *Human Development Report 2000: Developing Democracy in a Fragmented World*. New York: Oxford University Press, 2002.

———. *Human Development Report 2004*. United Nations. New York. http://hdr.undp.org/reports/global/2004/ (24 May 2007).

UNEP-WCMC (United Nations Environment Programme and World Conservation Monitoring Centre). *World Database on Protected Areas (WDPA)*. CD-ROM. Cambridge, UK: UNEP-WCMC, 2004. http://sea.unep-wcmc.org/wdbpa (24 May 2007).

United Nations Children's Fund (UNICEF). *The State of the World's Children 2006: Excluded and Invisible. Table 1*. New York: UNICEF, 2005. http://www.unicef.org/sowc06/fullreport/full_report.php (24 May 2007).

USAID. *Democracy and Governance in Panama*. http://www.usaid.gov/our_work/democracy_and_governance/regions/lac/panama.html (24 May 2007).

Vitousek, Peter M., Harold A. Mooney, Jane Lubchenko, and Jerry M. Melillo. "Human Domination of Earth's Ecosystems." *Science* 277, 1997: 494–99.

Wackernagel, Mathis, and William Rees. *Our Ecological Footprint: Reducing Human Impact on the Earth*. Gabriola Island, BC: New Society Publishers, 1996.

Wackernagel, Mathis, Niels B. Schulz, Diana Deumlin, Alejandro Callejas Linares, Martin Jenkins, et al. "Tracking the Ecological Overshoot of the Human Economy." *Proceedings of the National Academy of Sciences* 99, no. 14 (2002): 9266–71.

WEF (World Economic Forum). *The Global Competitiveness Report 2003–2004*. Edited by Michael E. Porter, Klaus Schwab, Xavier Sala-i-Martin, and Augusto Lopez-Carlos. New York: Oxford University Press, 2004.

WHO (World Health Organization). *Global Health Atlas*. Geneva: WHO, 2004. http://globalatlas.who.int/GlobalAtlas/ (24 May 2007).

———. *Macroeconomics and Health: Investing in Health for Economic Development*. Report of the Commission on Macroeconomics and Health. Geneva: WHO, 2001. http://www.eldis.org/static/DOC6008.htm (24 May 2007).

———. *World Health Report: Annex Table 4*. Geneva: WHO, 2004. http://www.who.int/whr/2004/en/09_annexes_en.pdf (24 May 2007).

———. *World Health Report 2003: Shaping the Future*. Geneva: WHO, 2003.

Wilkinson, Richard G. *Unhealthy Societies. The Afflictions of Inequality*. New York: Routledge, 1996.

World Bank. *Governance and Development*. Washington, DC: World Bank, 1992.

———. *World Development Indicators 2004*. Washington, DC: World Bank, 2004. http://publications.worldbank.org/ecommerce/catalog/product?item_id=631625 (24 May 2007).

WRI (World Resources Institute). "Earth Trends: The Environmental Information Portal". 2006. http://earthtrends.wri.org/index.php (4 Jun. 2007).

WSSD (World Summit on Sustainable Development). "Plan of Implementation of the World Summit on Sustainable Development." *Report of the World Summit on Sustainable Development*. Johannesburg, South Africa, 2002.

WWF (World Wildlife Fund for Nature). *Living Planet Report*, edited by Jonathan Loh and Mathis Wackernagel. Prepared in cooperation with the United Nations Environment Programme's World Conservation Monitoring Centre, and the Global Footprint Network. Cambridge: World Wildlife Fund for Nature, 2004.

Yencken, David. "Governance for Sustainability." *Australian Journal of Public Administration* 61, no. 2 (2002): 78–89.

Part IV:
Covenants and Respect for All Life, Public-Good, and Traditional Knowledge

The ethical framework represented by the *Earth Charter* (see the Appendix) provides an enabling set of principles, and shared values for a more just, sustainable, and peaceful world. Civil society organizations around the world contributed to its drafting and are helping to promote its endorsement and use.

In part four of this book, the *Earth Charter* is examined as a covenant that can guide us toward sustainability. Its sixteen clearly articulated principles provide promise and hope. It is a document that resonates with all that is good in the world.

The concept of the "global public good" is used to help understand the significance of the *Earth Charter*. In particular, when it is compared with other declaratory documents, their differences in ethical expression and focus are actually found to be mutually reinforcing.

Despite the universality of declarations, however, an African perspective points to the need to adapt these declaratory arrangements to the local level where indigenous (or, traditional) knowledge should be embraced. The *Earth Charter* calls for respect of diversity, both cultural and ecological, and has principles that support indigenous rights and acknowledge the contributions of traditional knowledge to advancing sustainability.

Chapter 13

The *Earth Charter*, Ethics, and Global Governance

Brendan Mackey, Ph.D. (Plant Ecology)
Fenner School of Environment and Society
The Australian National University
Canberra, Australia

Contact Information: Building 48, Linneaus Way, Canberra ACT 0200 AUSTRALIA
Phone: +61 2 61254960; Email: brendan.mackey@anu.edu.au

Summary

The *Earth Charter*, if embraced by all, could play a significant role in advancing global governance toward sustaining life on Earth.

A key contribution of the Charter is in promoting a global moral community that calls for and supports the next generation of global governance mechanisms, in accordance with the Charter's values and principles. This, along with any further contribution hinges on the validity of the Charter's claim as an authentic world ethic in theory, and as a social reality.

There are four major reasons in support of this claim: (1) The inclusive, grass-roots nature of the Charter's drafting process and its subsequent uptake; (2) The Charter's explicit attempt to link personal ethics with public ethics; (3) The increasing currency given to "values" in national and international affairs; and (4) The prominence given in the Charter to the ecological integrity imperative.

Some reasons why the *Earth Charter* may fail to attain its full potential include: (1) The length of time needed for it to significantly influence a critical mass in all sectors; (2) Limits to the impact of civil society bottom-up processes on global affairs; (3) Rejection of its ethic on philosophical grounds with respect to either specific principles or in its entirety as an instrument of authoritarian control; and (4) Failure to act as a world ethic bridging civil society, government, and business.

Regardless, the *Earth Charter* will remain an important educational resource, an articulation of civil society aspirations, and an inspirational roadmap for global reform.

Background

The *Earth Charter* preamble claims that:

> We stand at a critical moment in Earth's history, a time when humanity must
> choose its future. As the world becomes increasingly interdependent and frag-
> ile, the future at once holds great peril and great promise. . . . The choice is
> ours: form a global partnership to care for Earth and one another, or risk the de-
> struction of ourselves and the diversity of life. Fundamental changes are needed
> in our values, institutions, and ways of living.

The *Earth Charter* (see the Appendix) is not alone in expressing deep concern about the state of Earth's environment, the connectedness of our ecological,
social, and economic challenges, and the need for global reform in support of a
more just, sustainable, and peaceful world.

There has been a plethora of international ethical statements and commitments over the last decade or so in relation to issues of environment and development. Examples include the Rio Declaration (UN, 1992a), the World Summit
on Sustainable Development Political Declaration (UN, 2002a), and the various
ethical principles (such as the precautionary principle) contained within legal
instruments such as the United National Framework Convention on Climate
Change (UN, 1992b). Given this, what is the added value to global governance
of a civil society document such as the *Earth Charter*?

The relevance of the *Earth Charter* is further challenged by the prevailing
geopolitical situation. Multilateralism appears on the wane as the guiding principle of international relations. National self-interest is apparently on the ascen-
dancy and threatens to reverse the remarkable progress made in redefining international relations since the formation of the United Nations. Yet, the
globalization of the human endeavor continues unabated, with all its intended
and unintended consequences. Economic globalization is proceeding largely
unfettered by environmental and social responsibilities. International affairs are
increasingly dominated by militaristic responses, at least on the part of some
national governments. A lack of international cooperation is evident in the area
of environment and sustainable development, as witnessed by the failure of the
2002 World Summit on Sustainable Development to agree on targets and time-
tables for meeting commitments made at the 1992 Rio Earth Summit.

From an environmental and social justice perspective, current world trends
are deeply worrying and point to the need for a significant improvement in
global governance. The Millennium Ecosystem Assessment (MEA, 2005) provides rigorous scientific assessments of the extent to which current patterns of
production, consumption, and reproduction are ecologically unsustainable. The
UN Millennium Development Goals (UN, 2000) provide a clear reminder of the
extent of human deprivation in the world today and that poverty alleviation
remains our greatest human development challenge. Global governance is
needed that promotes a balance between, among other things:

1. the legitimate rights of nations to self-determination and safeguard national self-interest,
2. the benefits that flow from efficient economic systems,
3. the need to maintain environmental life-support systems, and prevent the loss of biodiversity and associated natural heritage and traditional human-nature relations, and
4. the imperative obligation to alleviate poverty and provide all with life's essentials.

The *Earth Charter* can play a vital role in advancing the global governance structures, instruments, and processes needed to secure a more just, sustainable, and peaceful world. The case in support of this claim hinges on the proposition that if global governance is to advance, there must be a global moral community that calls for and supports the next generation of global governance mechanisms. There needs to be a strong international community of people in all regions and cultures of the world that seeks to have their national interests balanced with a commitment to the well-being and security of all. The root causes of global insecurity are now so interconnected that this commitment must be comprehensive and extend to future generations and other life forms with whom we share Earth as home.

There are four reasons why the *Earth Charter* can contribute to this critical task of building the necessary global moral community in support of advancing global governance for a more sustainable world:

- the Charter's inclusive grass-roots drafting process and subsequent uptake,
- the Charter's explicit attempt to link personal ethics with public ethics,
- the increasing currency given to the primacy of values in national and international affairs, and
- the prominence given in the Charter to the ecological integrity imperative.

Drafting Process and Uptake

The Charter's capacity to influence global reform processes is a function of the validity of its claim to be a world ethic of shared values and universal principles. In addition to the validity of this claim in theory, Dower (1998) argued that, for a world ethic to be a social reality, its values and principles need to be accepted by a significant number of actors in the world, and established in influential international organizations. The evidence in support of the *Earth Charter*'s claim to be a valid world ethic can be found in both the story of its drafting and its subsequent uptake and applications. A brief review of the *Earth Charter*'s history is therefore necessary (see ECIS, 2006).

The *Earth Charter* was conceived in a recommendation from the report of the World Commission on Environment and Development "Our Common Future" (WCED, 1987) and born out of disappointment with the compromised ethical vision of the Rio Declaration from the 1992 Earth Summit. To advance the idea of a "Peoples" *Earth Charter*, a group of eminent civil society leaders were invited to form an *Earth Charter* Commission, and a small secretariat created in Costa Rica through assistance from the Dutch and Costa Rican governments. An international drafting team was formed, chaired by Steven Rockefeller, at the time Professor of Religion at Middlebury College, in the United States of America (U.S.A). However, the final authority for the text lay with the *Earth Charter* Commission.

The drafting process involved three main stages. First, a review was made of values and principles articulated in existing international treaties and declarations such as the Rio Declaration and universal ethical declarations such as the World Charter for Nature. (UN, 1982) A draft Charter was then examined at the 1997 Rio+5 NGO attended by around five hundred civil society representatives. The text was extensively revised from these consultations to produce a Benchmark Draft II.

The *Earth Charter* Commission then embarked upon an ambitious global consultation process to give the document the broadest possible exposure. Over the next four years, the document was considered by groups from different sectors in over forty countries, along with regional consultations. In parallel, international meetings of various expert groups considered drafts of the document. The Charter was redrafted dozens of times in response to the incoming recommendations and comments received from all regions of the world. The global consultation process ended when the Commission launched the Charter in a special event at the Hague Peace Palace in 2000.

The *Earth Charter*'s values and principles are organized around the four pillars of "Respect and Care for the Community of Life," "Ecological Integrity," "Social and Economic Justice" and "Democracy, Nonviolence and Peace." These four major themes contain sixteen major and sixty-one supporting principles, which are preceded by an introductory section called "The Preamble," which summarizes the document in prose form; and these are followed by a concluding comment called "The Way Forward." The document can be found online at www.earthcharter.org (accessed 29 May 2007).

The Charter has been endorsed by around fourteen thousand organizations, along with some national governments (e.g., Mexico). It has been used in various educational programs in many of the world's regions, and formed the basis of a Type II educational partnership at the 2002 World Summit on Sustainable Development. The Charter has been endorsed by UNESCO and ICLEI (International Council for Local Environmental Initiatives), among others, with an international dimension. (ECIS, 2003) It has been presented and debated at numerous international conferences. For example, the 2004 IUCN Bangkok World Conservation Congress; and in 2005 a major international conference was held in Amsterdam, called *Earth Charter +5*. Moreover, an extensive literature now exists about the *Earth Charter* which bears further testimony to its international reach. (ECIS, 2004; Corcoran et al., 2005)

Linking Private and Public Ethics

The second argument in support of the *Earth Charter*'s potential to influence global governance is the link it provides between private and public ethics. Previous international ethical declarations such as the World Charter for Nature and the Rio Declaration were drafted and negotiated as government-to-government documents, identifying the principles to be followed by and the responsibilities of national governments. However, a characteristic of the global sustainability challenge is the diversity of agents in all sectors and levels who must be involved—because sustainability is everyone's business. In addition to the advocacy of international organizations, modern electronic communications is facilitating the connectivity between local and national organizations and global governance issues. Individuals and communities are better informed about globalization and are more able to network in order to advocate reform.

The intergovernmental nature of documents, like the Rio Declaration, dictates their format and language, and limits their relevance to non-national governmental agents. However, declarations of shared values and principles are needed, having a purpose, format, and language relevant to individuals and organizations, as well as to governments at all levels. The *Earth Charter* was specifically drafted as a "Peoples" Charter rather than an intergovernmental agreement. The Charter does not specify who is responsible for giving effect to each principle. While some might think of this feature of the document as a limitation, it has the advantage of making the Charter relevant to everyone in every sector.

Values and Public Policy

The third reason for the *Earth Charter*'s role in global governance reform processes rests on the proposition that it provides a vehicle to address a major impediment to sustainability, namely, the clash of values systems and the lack of a shared ethical framework for their peaceful resolution.

The rise in the political influence of neo-conservative political agendas in the U.S.A. has revived public debate about values, their cultural basis, and their role in public policy. Lakoff (2005) argued that neo-conservative values are defined by a specific set of reinforcing views on, among other things, economics, government, education, nature, regulation, rights, democracy, and foreign policy. More liberal-minded politicians and voters have been taken by surprise by the explicit reference to values systems of neo-conservative political parties and their success at the electoral ballots.

The success of neo-conservative politics in the U.S.A. has spilt over into other conservative governments, such as Australia, where similar "values wars" are now being argued in the public domain. For example, a senior Australian Federal politician was reported as saying in a speech that "radical Muslims

needed to assimilate and accept Australian values, or move to another country."
(NINEMSN, 2006) The use of "values" language has now become common-
place in Australian politics. Where neo-conservative-influenced governments
are winning the values war, it is not necessarily because they have more powerful logic or better-constructed arguments. Rather, it is probably because they
have succeeded in reframing the political debates in terms of their values systems.

The influence of neo-conservative values on global governance can be seen
through the shift in foreign policy and strategy as many nations retreat from
universal multilateral negotiations. Now, international agreements between
select nations are being negotiated outside the UN system. For example, as of
writing, the Australian government has still failed to ratify the Kyoto Protocol it
helped negotiate under the UN Framework Convention on Climate Change
(UNFCCC). Rather, it has negotiated with the U.S.A., and selected governments, a global climate change agreement outside the UNFCCC: the Asia-
Pacific Partnership on Clean Development and Climate. (McKibbin, 2005)

The philosophical basis for a rejection of universal multilateralism lies in
the concepts that:

- the nation-state is the only valid foundation of culture, values, moral responsibility, and law,
- the responsibility of governments is to their citizens and not to citizens of
  other nation-states (nor nonhuman life), and
- the only loyalty their citizens can possess is to their nation-state. (Dower,
  1998)

Neo-conservatives argue that we have gone too far down the road of global
governance as human culture and values are grounded within the nation-state.
From this perspective, there is no global society, culture, and morality and,
therefore, no social reality that can be used to justify global ethics and strong
democratic global governance mechanisms.

The cosmopolitan ethic of the *Earth Charter* is based on a different worldview to that of a neo-conservative worldview (which reflects an extreme libertarian dogmatism). Though, it is important to stress that the *Earth Charter* ethic
is not an anti-free-market ethic. Rather, it explicitly recognizes the positive
contributions of markets, calling for market corrections of various kinds such as
internalizing the full social and environmental costs of production in the price of
goods and services. Nor is the *Earth Charter* in any way "anti-personal freedoms"; quite the opposite—it rather expands upon and champions universal
individual rights. However, it does present the view that personal liberties, while
necessary, are insufficient to bring about the global conditions necessary for the
flourishing of human well-being and life generally. Personal freedoms can only
flourish in a supporting social and ecological environment where global obligations are recognized and the need is accepted for collaboration to address shared
problems.

The Ecological Integrity Imperative

The fourth argument in support of the *Earth Charter's* potential international influence stems from the extent its ethic draws upon a scientific perspective of ecological integrity. It is only since the 1972 Stockholm UN Conference on the Human Environment that global environmental concerns have been on the international policy agenda. (UNEP, 1972) That meeting also set a precedent for the use of scientific-based information about the state of the global environment to inform dialogue and negotiations around international agreements.

Modern, industrialized societies have an odd relationship with science. On the one hand, people are happy to enjoy the material benefits that flow from technological innovations. New technologies are generally now adopted without question, and few pause to query the science underpinning their development and ongoing operation. So long as the product delivers the desired service, the scientific understanding upon which the technology is based is taken for granted. We travel around Earth's atmosphere strapped inside metal cigar-shaped jets, kilometers high, at mind-boggling speeds, without doubting for one second the physics of flight and aero-engineering.

However, a different attitude emerges when application of the same scientific method provides information challenging the *status quo* and confronting people with uncomfortable facts about the state of Earth's environment and the impact of human activities. Evidence of severe global environmental degradation is dismissed as inconclusive, and the messenger declared an emotive scaremonger. Nonetheless, there is now a raft of authoritative scientific assessments of the state of Earth's environment and life support systems. (MEA, 2005; IPCC, 2007) Indeed, the world's nations have in recent years acknowledged the significance of the situation and signed various international treaties concerning climate change, loss of biodiversity, and desertification. (UN, 1992b; CBD-UNEP, 1992; UN, 1994) However, deep political skepticism remains about the scientifically based urgency of the ecological imperative faced by humanity.

Perhaps the skepticism around scientific environmental assessments partly reflects ignorance. Contemporary scientific understanding about the coevolution of Earth's life-support systems has yet to be integrated into educational curricula at any level—with only a handful of courses currently dealing with such themes evident at university level. Indeed, many people still deny biological evolution, let alone scientific understating of cosmology. Consequently, there is a general level of ignorance about the scientific basis to human-nature relations, the dependency of human health and well-being on the continued functioning of natural processes, and the capacity of human endeavors to alter global environmental conditions.

In drafting the *Earth Charter* ethic, in particular the Ecological Integrity theme of section II, scientific-based understanding about the Earth system and associated ecological and evolutionary processes were drawn upon in the formulation of its values and principles. Scientific-based understanding can profoundly alter our perception of the world and our place in it. How humans value the natural environment is influenced by scientific understanding of Earth's life support systems. Knowledge about the ongoing process of biological evolution and the origins of the human species affects how we perceive and value other species. Meeting the challenges of global governance in the twenty-first century demands a world ethic that is informed by the realities of our ecological situation. The *Earth Charter* is uniquely placed in this respect.

Why the *Earth Charter* May Fail

We have suggested four reasons why the *Earth Charter* can contribute to global governance reform. However, all four arguments can be challenged in ways that could cause the *Earth Charter* to fail to meet its potential.

Regarding the first argument, while the *Earth Charter* has achieved considerable international recognition, there is a long road to travel before the *Earth Charter* ethic can claim to be a significant influence on the values systems dominating global governance. A useful analogy is the Universal Declaration of Human Rights (UN, 1948), which, after fifty years, has now reached a point where its ethic does significantly influence national and international policies and programs. Herein lies a guide to the long-term effort needed before the *Earth Charter* can substantiate its claim to be a global social reality.

The second reason can also be challenged, because there are critics who reject the Charter's ethic on philosophical grounds, either with respect to specific principles or in its entirety. The *Earth Charter* ethic calls for, among other things, restraint in consumerist lifestyles, and a recommitment to the UN Charter and nonviolent means (e.g., Principle 16c: "Demilitarize national security systems to the level of a non-provocative defense posture, and convert military resources to peaceful purposes, including ecological restoration").

The Charter challenges policies that promote uni- and bilateral approaches ahead of multilateralism in addressing global problems. Consequently, we can predict that governments of a neo-conservative persuasion may be predisposed to view the *Earth Charter* with skepticism. In any case, many national governments will remain cynical about the role of ethics in international relations, accepting them only up to the point where they are useful and convenient while not a challenge to their sovereignty. National defense advisers will no doubt continue to promote foreign policy that assumes an ongoing state of "war readiness." (Dower, 1998; Machiavelli, 1531; Hobbes, 1651)

Those of an anarchistic philosophical persuasion may view any mechanism related to "global governance" with great suspicion, and see initiatives like the *Earth Charter* as merely reinforcing the existing flawed system and therefore, as part of the problem. Postmodernist constructionists may also be suspicious of documents like the *Earth Charter* that attempt to articulate universal perspectives on the grounds that however well intended such documents are, they will inevitably reflect dominant, Western values at the expense of local cultural diversity.

The *Earth Charter* could also be dismissed by deep green (*sensu* Naess, 1989) environmentalists as being too human focused. Conversely, social justice advocates may find the Charter's attempt to couple human/nature concerns as unhelpful. Pragmatic civil society members, hardened by years of activism in international forums, may agree with the Charter's values and principles, but dismiss the *Earth Charter* on the basis that the "era of declarations" has come and gone, and more time should not be wasted on such things, which merely serve to divert scarce resources from "more urgent and practical problems."

Perhaps the critics are right in that we have already gone too far down the path of globalization, and more action is needed at the local community level. Is the only necessary principle that of subsidiarity? Has not the era of declarations passed and the priority now shifted to *Realpolitik* and to reaching agreement on achievable concrete targets and timelines? Why focus on even more unenforceable (para-) legal instruments when there is scope to implement innovative market-based approaches? In any case, why should the international community take any notice of a civil society declaration like the *Earth Charter*?

The above criticisms and concerns illustrate the point that there are many philosophical and practical impediments to the *Earth Charter* being substantially accepted across sectors and being broadly embraced as a universal world ethic linking civil society, governments at all levels, together with business and industry.

Conclusion and Recommendations

Perhaps we should not expect too much from a world ethic produced by a civil society initiative. However, the *Earth Charter* remains a compelling concept, and its text is a commendable, if not historic, attempt at an integrated world ethic enjoying great resonance in many quarters internationally. Even if the Charter's future as a social reality is limited, it will be for many an aspirational (and, indeed, an inspirational) document, providing a basis for discussion about what remains to be achieved in all sectors and levels of government if a more just, sustainable, and peaceful world is to be established.

It is hard to predict the future of global governance. International relations may simply continue to stagger forth as they have over the last few years, to varying extents involving and being guided by UN-related processes. However, by way of example, the Asia Pacific Partnership on Clean Development and Climate, if it results in participating governments side-stepping the Kyoto Protocol, is a worrying initiative for those who see the future of global governance linked to a strengthening of the United Nations.

As a "cosmopolitan" ethic, the *Earth Charter* does not seek to replace the diversity of values in different cultures with a new, mono-ethic. Rather, it articulates shared values and principles that coexist with more culturally specific values. A critical mass of people is needed in nations throughout the world who have integrated into their values systems the principles of the *Earth Charter* and its related ethical norms.

When this happens, there will be a strong global moral community whose worldview acknowledges universal obligations to promote the flourishing of the entire community of life, and the equitable sharing of the good things of life for present and future generations. This global moral community will demand the democratic and just global governance mechanisms needed to protect and advance these shared values and universal obligations.

Of course, we have the foundations of global society, world ethics, and international law in the great work of the UN since the end of World War II, together with the efforts of earlier endeavors such as the International Labor Organization. (ILO, 1919) But, a next generation of global governance mechanisms is now needed to meet the challenges of the twenty-first century. What these will look like remains to be determined; though from an *Earth Charter* perspective, they will build upon the existing UN system; as promoted in its concluding section (The Way Forward):

> In order to build a sustainable global community, the nations of the world must renew their commitment to the United Nations, fulfill their obligations under existing international agreements, and support the implementation of *Earth Charter* principles.

In the long term, the growth of a global moral community, which respects diversity and includes all life and future generations in the sphere of its moral concern, is an essential prerequisite and foundation of global governance reform. In the short term, and in the absence of substantial new international institutions and mechanisms, the *Earth Charter* can still serve as a source of paralegal principles for national governments to draw upon when drafting and negotiating new international agreements. For example, the *Earth Charter* could be used as a reference document for the negotiation of a new UN-based, international, legally binding instrument on environment and development such as proposed by the IUCN (2004). Finally, the use of the *Earth Charter* in formal and informal education will contribute to an integrated understanding of the world situation, the ethical dimensions of our shared problems, and the need for advancing global governance for sustaining life on Earth.

In parallel with the above, global digital communications point to a future where civil society is connected and empowered like never before. Perhaps the days of "top-down command and control" are changing in ways that we cannot foresee. We should not underestimate the capacity of "bottom-up autocatalytic" people-centered processes, guided by the values and principles of the *Earth Charter* and related world ethics, to help transform the global community toward more just, sustainable, and peaceful ways of living.

References

CBD-UNEP. "The Convention on Biological Diversity." *Convention on Biological Diversity and United Nations Environment Programme.* 1992. http://www.biodiv.org/default.shtml (3 May 2007).

Corcoran, Peter Blaze, Mirian Vilela, and Alide Roerink, eds. *Toward a Sustainable World: The Earth Charter in Action.* Amsterdam: Kit Publishers, 2005.

Dower, Nigel. *World Ethics—The New Agenda.* Edinburgh: Edinburgh University Press, 1998.

ECIS. "The Earth Charter Handbook." San Jose, Costa Rica: Earth Charter International Secretariat. 2006. http://www.earthcharter.org/resources/index.cfm?pagina=categories_display.cfm&id_category=79 (3 May 2007).

———. "Earth Charter Initiative Biannual Report 2002–2003." San Jose, Costa Rica: Earth Charter International Secretariat. 2003. http://www.earthcharter.org/files/resources/Biannual%20Report.pdf (3 May 2007).

———. "Selected Bibliography of Books, Essays, Papers, Magazines and Newsletters Related to the Earth Charter." compiled By Claire Wilson and Betty Mcdermott. San Jose, Costa Rica: Earth Charter Secretariat. 2004. http://www.Earthcharter.Org/Files/Resources/Bibliography2.Pdf (3 May 2007).

Hobbes, Thomas. *Leviathan,* edited by R. Tuck. Cambridge: Cambridge University Press, 1991 (orig. 1651).

ILO. International Labor Organization. 1919. http://www.ilo.org/ (3 May 2007).

IPCC. "Climate Change 2007: The Physical Science Basis—Summary for Policymakers." Intergovernmental Panel on Climate Change, Switzerland. http://www.ipcc.ch/SPM2feb07.pdf (4 Jun. 2007).

IUCN. "Draft International Covenant on Environment and Development" 3rd ed. Environmental Policy and Law Paper No. 31 Rev. 2. Commission on Environmental Law of IUCN—the World Conservation Union in cooperation with the International Council of Environmental Law. 2004. http://www.i-c-e-l.org/english/ EPLP31EN_rev2.pdf (3 May 2007).

Lakoff, George. *Don't Think of an Elephant.* Carlton North, Australia: Scribe Publications, 2005.

Machiavelli, Niccolò. "Discourses." Cited in *The Portable Machiavelli,* edited by P. Bondanelli and M. Musa. Harmondsworth, UK: Penguin Books, 1979 (orig. 1531).

Mckibbin, Warwick. "Climate Pact a Good Beginning." *Australian Financial Review,* 1 Aug. 2005.

MEA, 2005. "Reports of the Millennium Ecosystem Assessment—various." 2005. http://www.millenniumassessment.org/en/index.aspx (3 May 2007).

Naess, Arne. *Ecology, Community and Lifestyle.* Cambridge, MA: Cambridge University Press, 1989.

NINEMSN. "Don't ostracise hardline Muslims: Abbott." *NINEMSN News.* 27 Feb. 2006. http://news.ninemsn.com.au/article.aspx?id=88387 (3 May 2007).

UN. "From Our Origins to the Future." Johannesburg Declaration on Sustainable Development. World Summit on Sustainable Development, Johannesburg. 2002. United Nations Organization. 2002a. http://www.un.org/esa/sustdev/documents/WSSD_POI_PD/English/POI_PD.htm (3 May 2007).

———. "Millennium Development Goals." United Nations Organization. 2000. http://www.un.org/millenniumgoals/ (3 May 2007).

———. "Rio Declaration on Environment and Development." Report of the United Nations Conference on Environment and Development, Rio de Janeiro, June 3–14, 1992, Annex I. United Nations Organization. 1992a. http://www.un.org/cyberschoolbus/peace/earthsummit.htm (3 May 2007).

———. "United Nations Convention to Combat Desertification." United Nations Organization. 1994. http://www.unccd.int (29 May 2007).

———. "United Nations Framework Convention on Climate Change." United Nations Organization. 1992b. http://unfccc.int/2860.php (3 May 2007).

———. "Universal Declaration of Human Rights." United Nations Organization. 1948. http://www.un.org/Overview/rights.html (3 May 2007).

———. "World Charter for Nature." United Nations Organization. 1982. http://www.un.org/documents/ga/res/37/a37r007.htm (3 May 2007).

UNEP. Report of the United Nations Conference on the Human Environment. United Nations Environmental Programme. Stockholm, 1972. http://www.unep.org/ Documents.multilingual/Default.asp?DocumentID=97&ArticleID= (3 May 2007).

WCED. Our Common Future. Report of the World Commission on Environment and Development. Oxford: Oxford University Press, 1987.

Chapter 14

The Copenhagen Consensus: A Global Public-Good Perspective Comparing the *Earth Charter* with Other Recent Declarations

Philippe Crabbé, Doctor of Law

Professor Emeritus, Department of Economics
University of Ottawa, Ottawa, Canada
Contact Information: Institute of the Environment
555, King Edward, Ottawa, Ont. K1N 6N5 CANADA
Phone: +1 613 562 5800 ext. 1430; Fax: +1 613 562 5873
Email: crabbe@uottawa.ca

Summary

The *Earth Charter* and an official document of the Ecological Society of America have one point in common with the Copenhagen Consensus: they each deal with global "public goods." A "public good" (such as, for example, air and water) is a good from which one cannot deny anyone else access to benefits, and one individual's consumption of the good does not deplete it.

The fundamental feature of these goods is that exclusive property rights have not been bestowed on them, either because it is physically impossible to do so, or because institutions have not been designed to make them exclusive.

Public goods are global when they potentially benefit mankind as a whole. This is the case of the *Earth Charter*, which claims to be foundational to sustainability. This is the case of ecosystem restoration, the benefits of which are not limited locally because ecosystems tend to interact with each other.

The Copenhagen Consensus aimed at determining a ranking according to benefit-cost analysis about a suite of institutionally defined, potential global public goods related to the UN Millennium Development Goals. Although the ethics underlying the *Earth Charter* and those underlying Economics are at variance with each other, both can work hand-in-hand when tackling public goods. This is because global public goods provide benefits to all, and because, in many cases, a wider adoption of the public good enhances its social value.

Economics makes sure that services are provided at least cost. Moreover, it contributes to the design of institutions, which restrict overuse and remove incentives to under-provision of the public good.

Introduction: The Economist's Perspective

Three historically independent, but logically related documents appeared recently: the *Earth Charter* (see the Appendix); an ecovision report from the Ecological Society of America (Palmer et al. and ESA, 2004); and, the Copenhagen Consensus. (Lomborg, 2004) We pursue several questions in this chapter:

- Does the *Earth Charter* add something new to previous United Nations (UN) documents of a similar nature?
- Does the *Earth Charter* allow for deliberate tinkering with ecosystems?
- Is benefit-cost a valid criterion to allocate resources, not in a routine fashion perhaps adequate for the selection of investments in marketable commodities, but for relatively exceptional opportunities identified as pragmatic, ethical priorities to further the welfare of mankind, i.e., to invest in global public goods?
- Is the *Earth Charter* itself a global public good?
- Are some natural ecosystem functions or services of a global public good nature?

In other words, we claim in this chapter that the theme of global public goods that we tend to under-provide or overuse, is common to the three issues raised in the aforementioned documents.

Public Goods

Economists define public goods as goods or services, which are indivisible in such a way that they cannot easily be allocated to a given individual, e.g., the grid which supplies electricity to an individual is used by all who use electricity and it is impossible to identify which portion of the grid is used by a given subscriber, except for the last link between the grid and the subscribing household. This indivisibility results in non-excludability: since we cannot determine which portion of the grid is used by a given subscriber, we cannot exclude any subscribed consumer from using a portion of the grid.

Not only are public goods non-excludable, they are non-rival in consumption as well; that is, my usage of the grid does not affect your usage of the grid for electricity consumption up to a point. The usage of the grid does not result in the depletion of the grid; there is sufficient grid capacity for all until the grid is used up at capacity (electricity consumption occurs on peak), i.e., there is no way to accommodate an additional consumer without crowding out, bumping off another one unless one is willing to run the risk of grid collapse. Off-peak grid capacity was free; on peak, grid capacity is scarce, commands a premium, a rent determined by the amount of money the highest bidder is willing to pay for access to the grid, independently of the price of electricity. This is why, on peak, one must, in a free market, pay more for the electricity that one consumes than off-peak.

Public goods, whether they are stocks or services, create three problems if we compare them to private goods:

- They provide an incentive to shirk the responsibility of contributing to the cost of the public good (free-riding) since the delinquent cannot be excluded from the consumption of the good;[1]

- They provide an incentive to underestimate their social benefit since people may be tempted to value the benefit only in terms of the private benefit they alone derive from the grid independently of what benefit others derive from it[2] (prisoners' dilemma);

- They provide an incentive to disguise the true value of one's private benefit in any process attempting to have one reveal one's preference for the public good, because one may wish to deceive a sharing allocation, say by a public utility, of its costs among its consumers in proportion of the consumers' share in its benefits.

Global public goods, such as biodiversity, ozone layer or climate stabilization, nuclear non-proliferation, international court of justice, offer benefits at the planetary level. They tend to be overused beyond their (carrying) capacity when they are natural because their planetary benefits are not internalized by individuals and governments because of the aforementioned problems. When global public goods need to be provided (e.g., through restoration to their carrying capacity), they are under-provided for the same reason. Public goods are, to some extent, social constructs depending upon what political scientists call "regime"; that is, shared principles, norms, rules, rights, decision-making procedures, ways of defining problems and of handling relevant artifacts and persons, all embedded in institutions and infrastructures, which favor cooperation, but cannot be enforced through binding agreements. (Parson et al., 1998; Rip et al., 1998; Kaul et al., 2003)

Examples of social constructs are: what is deemed "dangerous climate change" (Article 2 of the UN Framework Convention on Climate Change), a "public bad," "irreplaceable ecosystem services" (for which no substitutes are deemed to exist). There is a whole slate of culturally determined expectations attached to these social constructs. A traffic light (an artifact) is culturally associated with traffic safety for the automobile drivers and pedestrians, but also with a smooth traffic flow minimizing the time spent in traffic. (Kaul et al., 1999)

The regime associated with an artifact (natural or artificial) has network properties, i.e., the more people or governments subscribe to the regime, the more value the regime has for all of its beneficiaries.

Neoclassical Economics

Economists trained in the British Classical economic tradition, i.e., all the traditional Neoclassical economists, abide by the utilitarian ethic. The latter offers goals (maximization of preferences or well-being) that economists believe motivate most individuals (economic rationality) in most of their behaviors related to exchangeable goods and services. Daly and Cobb (1989) made the point that most environmental (or ecosystem) goods and services (this is true for health goods and services as well) are not exchangeable on markets that work properly because property rights thereon are ill-defined. Moreover, for health and, to a lesser extent, for environment, the asymmetry of information between the provider (e.g., the physician, or the National Parks Service) and the recipient is huge, preventing him/her from making informed and thus rational decisions (in the economic sense).

Besides information asymmetry, these so-called market failures result from the fact that these goods and services are mainly of the nature of externalities (non-excludable)—for which the beneficiaries/victims are not fully compensated (e.g., pollution)—which include public goods, and open access resources (the service is a private good, but the stock has some public good properties such as non-excludability, but not non-rivalry; for example, a high-sea fishery). Environmental goods may similarly be affected by non-environmental government policies resulting in environmental policy failures (e.g., subsidy to a polluting fuel consumed by the least-well-off segment of society).

Society's preferences (or well-being) are maximized if no individual can be made better off by a reallocation of goods and services among individuals or social groups. The corresponding allocation is called "efficient." If it is not efficient, it is wasteful. Aside from market imperfections, inefficiency or waste results from ignorance (about alternatives), transaction costs (barriers affecting behavioral changes and whose removal would bring more benefits than costs), myopia (biasing time horizons to be short) and, of course, market and policy failures.

A policy is a deliberate intervention in the market or in the political arena by a group, whose concern is the well-being of the same interest group or of another group (altruism). A policy is based on a narrative, a story or worldview, which will give basic consistency to a set of policies. Environmental policy is essentially a political choice, a political compromise, i.e., the solution to bounded conflicts among various worldviews including the ones concerning the environment. (Lee, 1992) The generation of public good regimes are an outcome of policies.

The Construct of a Public "Bad"

The urgency for environmental policies results from a perceived "environmental crisis" (a public bad) by a group (e.g., climate change today or, a century ago, the risk of fires resulting from sparks emitted by coal-burning steam engines). Crises, whether they are environmental or public health related, or of another nature, are social constructs. (Gare, 1995) The concept of crisis has an external dimension in terms of policy, and an internal one in terms of perception. As with all policies, there is a top-down and a bottom-up approach to a crisis. In the top-down perspective, focus is on expert-determined physical vulnerability while, in the bottom-up approach, it is on individually or institutionally determined social vulnerability. The internal dimension focuses on social, cultural, and institutional contexts, and social psychology methods. (Dessai et al., 2004) It may also rely on political assessments of the acceptability of the risk—similarly, for global public goods.

Though policies, including economic ones, need not be restricted to the realm of utilitarian ethics and marketable commodities, the choice among policies achieving the same goals must satisfy the highest Benefit-Cost ratio or be cost-effective (minimize costs) if benefits cannot be estimated. This is tantamount to maximizing a flow of consumption coming from a resource investment. Greater weight in benefits can be given to new investments resulting from the original one through a multiplier effect to compensate for investment market imperfections (lack of competition).

Greater weight can be set on who receives the consumption benefits (equity) if equity distortions are not too large to begin with. Intrinsic values on environment, health, and preventing death or illness may be included in the tally of the benefits. Willingness to pay is the criterion for measuring intrinsic value in monetary units. Since intrinsic values are not exchangeable, modifications to the basic economic method must be made and these modifications may not always be satisfactory (e.g., some economists will talk of the "warm glow" resulting from protecting the environment in order to respect utilitarian ethics).

The *Earth Charter*

The *Earth Charter* aims at providing an ethical framework for sustainable development. It is, therefore, a global public good. It was requested in 1987 by the World Commission on Environment and Development, formulated through a worldwide participatory process, and finalized in 2000. It amounts to a declaration of fundamental values and principles for building a just, sustainable, and peaceful global interdependence and shared responsibility for the well-being of humans, their communities and future generations, and of nature. This shared responsibility for the enlarged common good increases with freedom, knowledge, and power.

The *Earth Charter* was preceded by the Stockholm Declaration of the Conference on the Human Environment (1972), the UN Charter for Nature (1982), and the Rio Declaration on Environment and Development (1992). All these non-binding instruments introduced norms of national and international behavior with respect to the management of natural resources, the environment, and development. All of these visionary documents are declaratory in nature and contribute to the development of what is called "soft" law. In 1989, a first draft of a binding Covenant on Environment and Development was produced by IUCN and revised in 1995. It aimed at being the first binding treaty on sustainable development, but the treaty never materialized. (Hassan, IUCN Web site)

The Stockholm Declaration is human-centered and focuses on human responsibility toward the environment and development.

The UN Charter for Nature acknowledges the principle of intrinsic value of life and that over-consumption and human conflicts affect the environment negatively. (Preamble; Rockefeller, 1996) Generally, the Charter for Nature is much more limited to ecosystem health than the *Earth Charter*, which is more focused on the active membership of humans in ecosystems and on sustainability. The Charter for Nature proclaims general principles of conservation "by which all human conduct affecting nature is to be guided and judged." (Preamble) The principles call for:

- nature to be respected and its essential processes not to be impaired;
- for the maintenance of genetic viability, critical population size for species and protection of their habitats;
- for special protection of unique areas and of representative samples of ecosystems and rare and endangered species;
- for management of ecosystems and organisms to achieve and maintain "optimum sustainable productivity" without adversely affecting other ecosystems or species; and
- for the protection of nature against destruction caused by warfare and hostilities.

The Charter for Nature emphasizes the importance to consider natural systems in the planning and implementation of social and economic development activities. Article II stipulates that natural resources shall not be wasted, but used with a restraint appropriate to the principles set forth in the Charter; activities, which might impact on nature, shall be controlled and risks of damage minimized by use of the best available technologies; discharge of pollutants shall be avoided wherever possible; and, natural disaster or disease prevention measures shall avoid adverse side effects on nature.

The Charter for Nature articulates most provisions in a general way. However, since the Charter was adopted by the General Assembly, many of its principles have been developed further in other national and international legal instruments (Article III). (Hassan, IUCN Web site)

Originally, the 1992 Rio Declaration was supposed to be called the *Earth Charter*. It is more pragmatic and less encompassing than the *Earth Charter*, which ventures well beyond environmental territory. As indicated by the NGO preparatory text, the Rio Declaration lacked punch. A similar comment can be made about the *Earth Charter*: "No child will post it on the door of the family refrigerator unless the parents work for a UN agency!" (Quoted in Crabbé, 1992)

According to the *Earth Charter*, responsibility for the well-being of humans is based on the inherent dignity of all human beings and the intellectual, artistic, ethical, and spiritual potential of humanity. It includes the recognition of Universal Human Rights, Economic Justice, and a Culture of Peace. It should enable all to achieve a secure and meaningful livelihood that is ecologically responsible. Responsibility to humans is based on the acknowledgment that human development is about *being* more rather than *having* more, after basic needs are met. Social scientists, not only economists, have great difficulty with the concept of need, as it cannot be objectively defined. (Douglas, 1998)

The Rio Declaration avoided the concept of need (only alluded to in Article 6.2). Economists predicate their concept of welfare on having more since preferences are required in economic theory to increase with greater quantities of goods and services. Responsibility for the well-being of mankind, according to the *Earth Charter*, includes responsibility to future generations through the transmission to future generations of values, traditions, and institutions that support the long-term flourishing of Earth's human and ecological communities, another global public good. (This is vaguer in the Rio Declaration, Article 3.) Responsibility for the well-being of mankind requires acknowledgment that there are currently great sufferings resulting from poverty, ignorance, conflicts, overpopulation burdens (the Rio Declaration talks about the states' responsibility to formulate demographic policies, Article 8.2), ecological systems, and social systems degradation. Environmental, economic, political, social, and spiritual challenges are interconnected, a point also emphasized by the Millennium Development Goals (MDG) that the UN set for 2015. Tools and basic principles are spelled out.

Tools include:

- Ensure universal access to health care that fosters reproductive health and responsible reproduction (this ignores economic and cultural incentives for reproduction and the state's responsibility that is recognized in the Rio Declaration).
- Adopt lifestyles that emphasize quality of life and material sufficiency (anti-consumerism).
- Protect traditional knowledge and cooperate on sustainability with developing countries.
- Maintain in the public domain vital information on human health, environmental protection, and genetic information (limits to privatization not present in the Rio Declaration).

Basic principles deal with social and economic justice (Articles 9 and 10), elimination of discrimination (Articles 11 and 12), democracy (Article 13), education for sustainability (Article 14), peace (Article 16), and animal protection (Article 15).

Responsibility for Nature requires protection of its vitality, diversity, beauty, and integrity, reverence for the mystery of being, gratitude for the gift of life, and humility regarding the human place in nature. It requires furthermore an acknowledgment that every form of life has value regardless of its worth for human beings (Article 1 a.), and to avoid environmental harm.

This principle is at variance with the Rio Declaration which placed anthropocentrism as its first principle. It is also at variance with the Neoclassical approach to valuation, which is based on willingness to pay and, thus, on the principle that there is no intrinsic value except as perceived by humans. It requires acknowledgment that Earth's resources are finite. This is certainly correct in a conceptual thermodynamic sense (Conservation law), but not in a pragmatic economic sense. Economic resources are smaller than the physically available resources because the former are cost- and technology-dependent. Economists hold a Ricardian view of natural resources, i.e., resource quality is declining but economic limits are variable and reached well before physical limits are reached. According to the Charter, dominant patterns of production and consumption cause environmental devastation, depletion of resources (especially renewable), massive extinction of species, undermining traditional communities built on common property, and the inequitable distribution of the benefits of development. Changes in values toward a sustainable way of life, in institutions, which lead to the wrong incentives and lifestyles, are required.

The tools to operate change is to support the Charter with a legally binding instrument on environment and development, i.e., a Covenant, to create more biosphere reserves, prevent organisms harmful to the environment and native species, manage renewable resources to protect ecosystem health, manage non-renewable resources to minimize depletion (a meaningless statement!) and environmental damage, avoid irreversible environmental harm (Precautionary Principle; see Article 15 of the Rio Declaration), place the burden of proof on developers (not in the Rio Declaration), apply full cost principle and full cost pricing (Article 16, also in the Rio Declaration). Other practical tools are: prevent pollution, avoid military activities damaging the environment (Article 24.1), adopt the "Three Rs" (i.e., Reduce, Reuse, Recycle), ensure residual waste is biodegradable, adopt energy efficiency and use renewable energy, promote transfer of environmentally sound technologies, adopt eco-labeling.

The ethical base of the *Earth Charter* is wider than the one of the Rio Declaration; the former is resolutely ecocentric, while the latter is resolutely anthropocentric (Rio Declaration, Article 1). In particular, the Charter bans avoidable animal suffering. The Charter is also more prescriptive in terms of human welfare: *being* more matters more than *having* more. The *Earth Charter* is more timid than the Rio Declaration (Article 8.2) on states' demographic responsibilities; the Charter is more individualistic on this issue than the Declaration, though the former emphasizes the need to strengthen family and education. The Charter is mute on the principle of common, but differentiated-responsibility biased against developed countries (Article 7. 2 of the Rio Declaration already present in the Vienna 1985 Convention on the Protection of the Ozone Layer) because of their larger responsibility for environmental degradation and their larger financial capacities.

The Charter is also mute on the Polluter Pays Principle (Article 16, Rio Declaration) while being softer on the priority responsibility to be assigned to developing countries (Article 6.1, Rio Declaration), and on the need to cooperate to eradicate poverty (Article 5, Rio Declaration). Were these principles simply overlooked, or were they deliberately ignored for the benefit of a consensus? On the other hand, the Charter goes much further with concern for the peace requirement for sustainability, on promoting the equitable distribution of wealth within nations and among nations, and on discrimination against women than what the Rio Declaration does. The latter protects women as rural production agents in less developed countries (Article 20-22). The Charter underlines the need to keep certain vital information in the public domain, while the Rio Declaration does not address this issue. The Charter contains the principle of subsidiarity and the burden of proof on developers (a consequence of the Precautionary Principle), which are absent in the Declaration; it also recognizes a series of human (e.g., food security) and environmental rights, the need for a more equitable distribution of wealth, both within and among nations, debt relief, for more transparency on multinationals' operations. The Rio Declaration promotes trade (Article 12.1), environmental assessment (Article 17), prohibits transfers of dangerous substances (Article 14), and national sovereignty (Article 2.1) that the Charter does not promote. Common principles are: integration of development and environment (Article 4), Precautionary Principle (Article 15), elimination of non-sustainable production and consumption modes (Article 8.1), science and technology transfers (Article 9), citizens' participation (Article 10.1), equality for gender, aboriginals, and the young (Article 20-22), incompatibility of war with sustainability (Article 24-26).

Generally speaking, the Rio Declaration is a pragmatic "realistic," soft law document, while the Charter is more an "idealistic," deontological document which satisfies L. K. Caldwell's requirement of some twenty-three years ago:

> Individual self-interest alone will never save the world. Safeguarding the Biosphere requires a social commitment of a moral, quasi-religious character. It requires dedication to an ethic for life and the world that transcends scientific knowledge, although consistent with it and subject to guidance by its findings. The policies of sustainable development thus call for a fusion of realism and idealism in which the individual sees, in the survival of nature and in working with nature on behalf of a sustainable future for the biosphere, values that he identifies with his own existence. (Caldwell, 1984)

The *Earth Charter* reinforces the previous declarations, but goes beyond them in providing precisely the needed global public good identified by Caldwell. The *Earth Charter* regime value is very much enhanced by the number of its adherents.

Pragmatic Ecology

"Ecological Science and Sustainability for a Crowded Planet: 21st Century Vision and Action Plan for the Ecological Society of America" (M. A. Palmer et al., April 2004) emphasizes the need for Ecology to be pragmatic in a natural world dominated by humans, sharing implicitly the value system of the Rio Declaration. As Botkin et al. (2005) have argued, following implicitly the *Earth Charter* value system, one could object that the report has not even questioned whether this domination by humans is appropriate and whether human population has exceeded the carrying capacity of the Earth, however defined. According to the ESA ecovision, our future environment will consist of human-influenced ecosystems, managed to varying degrees, in which natural services will be harder and harder to maintain. One needs to design ecological solutions through conservation and restoration with reference not only to undisturbed ecosystems and to historical ones, but also to artificial ones. One needs to invent new ecological systems (acknowledging humans as components of these ecosystems), combining ecological principles with technology in order to find alternatives to conservation. Stakeholders need to understand the risks associated with the various alternatives. At least, these risks are acknowledged by the ESA ecovision. An opportunity for direct reference to the Precautionary Principle was opened here but, however, was missed.

According to the ESA ecovision, one also needs to develop the science and the measurement of ecosystem services, i.e., the benefits that ecosystems provide to humans, for the three types of ecosystems, with a view to ecological restoration and design. The science of ecosystem services is especially needed for the identification of irreplaceable services, prohibitively expensive ones to restore, or whose substitutes have undesirable consequences, e.g., clean drinking water (desalination is still expensive), soil stabilization by plants to prevent erosion, buffering of vector-transmitted disease outbreaks, pollination, etc. This reference to irreversibility is completely in tune here with the economic concept of Ricardian decreasing returns (i.e., resource quality is constantly declining) and the policy implications of hysteresis, a mathematical form of irreversibility, that economists are familiar with. The policy implication of hysteresis is that in order to restore a degraded environment to a healthier state, one needs to apply far more resources to restoration, if at all possible, than if the initial state had been reversible. (Brock et al., 2002, esp. p. 288-89) This may be characterized as a form of Ricardian decreasing returns since it means that there are nearly always remedies (substitutes) to depletion (whether of a nonrenewable of renewable resource), but these are much more expensive than if depletion had not occurred.

According to the ESA ecovision, one needs to understand better the processes that sustain ecological services, the activities which degrade them, the activities which mitigate degradation—such as new assemblages of native species—and reverse degradation. One should also ensure that existing knowledge is applied, e.g., greenways, protected riverbank zones, storm drainage infrastructure, rooftop gardens. One should also be able to explore the dynamics of ecosystems at scales that match ecosystem properties such as network linkages like food webs.

Incorporating humans in ecosystems requires interdisciplinary frameworks that incorporate multivariate causality, nonlinear feedbacks, and an understanding of human behavior. The science of ecological restoration and design should help restore ecosystems to a past state and, if this is not possible, should help to create well-functioning communities of organisms that optimize ecological services from coupled natural-human ecosystems. It should identify acceptable baselines below which restoration effort is futile. (Palmer, April 2004; May 2004)

Generally, one needs to identify the tensions between human and ecosystem needs. Major questions for study, in order to design solutions, are urbanization mainly in coastal areas, degradation of freshwater, e.g., along waterways, movement of materials, both living and nonliving, ("ecological commerce") between ecosystems, the impacts of changes in their routes and in their rates of material exchange. Their undesirable effects are the spread of infectious diseases—a medical as well as an ecological problem— and of invasive species, the deposition of oxides of nitrogen (NO_x) and sulfur dioxide (SO_2). Floods, annual migrations, and fires have desirable impacts on ecosystems restoration, but undesirable ones on large human communities.

Two important perspectives seem totally absent from this ESA ecovision. The first one is the perspective of the complex ecosystem, a self-organizing path-dependent system moving toward a plurality of attractor states, none of which is preferable for a given landscape. The ESA ecovision is, to a large extent, an engineering, mechanical vision of ecosystems, in which reversibility to past states is possible. The concept of resilience as an objective of ecosystem management, the protection of the self-organizing properties of a fundamentally unpredictable system investigated through a scenario approach, seems totally absent. (Kay, 2000) The second missing related perspective is the preoccupation with the Principle of Ecological Integrity, i.e., that some portion of the planet should be maintained free of human interference as much as possible. (Karr, 1996; Westra, 1994; Crabbé et al., 2000) The Charter's ethical requirement of protection of nature's "vitality" and "integrity" (perhaps at variance with the Principle of Ecological Integrity) underlines the deficiency of the ESA ecovision.

Ecosystems are public goods, both local and global, since they interact among each other in a hierarchical fashion, in a "panarchy." (Gunderson et al., 2002) Their value to humans depends on the goods and services they provide to us, but, because they are natural public goods, they are overused. Ecosystem restoration is endowed with a public good regime, which is under-provided, and the value of some of its services increases with the number of people who "subscribe" to its restoration. Our ignorance of how ecosystems function justifies the adoption of the Precautionary Principle advocated by the

Philippe Crabbé

Earth Charter. The intrinsic value of ecosystems and their components, as well as an ethics of responsibility, command that humans tread lightly on Earth. This does not rule out that engineering and ecological principles may be applied to artificial ecosystems. What is ruled out is the wanton destruction of natural ecosystems to satisfy futile preferences for *having* more goods and services while nature, preserved, is the source of not easily replaceable spiritual experiences for enhanced *being*.

The Copenhagen Consensus

The Copenhagen Consensus consisted of identifying a series of global challenges earmarked by the UN in its various areas, e.g., its Millennium Development Goals. (MDG; see Table 14.1) Thirty initial challenges were reduced to ten on each of which an expert economist wrote a paper that, if the challenge were resolved, its solution would lead to an improvement in welfare as perceived by a group of economic experts (different from the paper authors; see Table 14.2). The reduction to ten was done through a committee of Danish economists, a committee of Danish non-economic experts and journalists, and the panel of distinguished expert economists (which included three Nobel Prize winners), who were free to add challenges of their own. Each paper had to identify up to five opportunities (specific policies) related to an issue.

Each paper was met with two short rebuttals/reviews. The question asked to the experts was: "What would be the best ways of advancing global welfare, and particularly the welfare of developing countries, supposing that an additional $50 billion of resources were at governments' disposal?" The criterion for ranking the issues was the selection of the median ranking of individual ranking of opportunities (see Table 14.3). The panel's selection criterion was benefit-cost analysis mainly, but not exclusively. (Lomborg, 2004)

Table 14.1: Millennium Development Goals

1. Eradicate extreme poverty and hunger.

2. Achieve universal primary education.

3. Promote gender equality and empower women.

4. Reduce child mortality.

5. Improve maternal health.

6. Combat HIV/AIDS, malaria and other diseases.

7. Ensure environmental sustainability.

8. Develop a global partnership for development.

Table 14.2: Copenhagen Consensus Initial List of Issues

GROSS LIST OF ISSUES
Economy, Environment, Governance, Health, and Population

ECONOMY
- Digital Divide
- **Financial Instability**
- Lack of Intellectual Property Rights
- Money Laundering
- **Subsidies and Trade Barriers**
- Transport and Infrastructure

ENVIRONMENT
- Air Pollution
- Chemical Pollution and Hazardous Waste
- **Climate Change**
- Deforestation
- Depletion of Ozone Layer
- Depletion of Water Resources
- Lack of Energy
- Land Degradation
- Loss of Biodiversity
- Vulnerability to Natural Disasters

GOVERNANCE
- Arms Proliferation
- **Conflicts (civil war)**
- **Corruption**
- **Lack of Education**
- Terrorism

HEALTH AND POPULATION
- Drugs
- **HIV/AIDS**
- **Human Settlements (Population and Migration)**
- Lack of People in Working Age
- **Malaria**
- Living Conditions of Children
- Living Conditions of Women
- Noncommunicable Diseases
- **Undernutrition/Hunger**
- **Unsafe Water and Sanitation**
- Vaccine Preventable Diseases

Table 14.3: Panel Ranking of the Opportunities

PROJECT	RATING	CHALLENGE	OPPORTUNITY
1		Diseases	Control of HIV/AIDS
2		Malnutrition	Providing micronutrients
3		Subsidies and Trade	Trade liberalization
	Very Good		
4		Diseases	Control of malaria
5		Malnutrition	Development of new agricultural technologies
6		Sanitation and Water	Small-scale water technology for livelihoods
7		Sanitation and Water	Community-managed water supply and sanitation
8		Sanitation and Water	Research on water productivity in food production
	Good		
9		Government	Lowering the cost of starting a new business
10		Migration	Lowering barriers to migration for skilled workers
11		Malnutrition	Improving infant and child nutrition
12		Malnutrition	Reducing the prevalence of low birth weights
	Fair		
13		Diseases	Scaled-up basic health services
14		Migration	Guest worker programs for the unskilled
15		Climate	Optimal carbon tax
16		Climate	The Kyoto Protocol
	Bad		
17		Climate	Value-at-risk carbon tax

Would another group of experts, subscribing to the *Earth Charter* ethics, rather than to the professional utilitarian ethics of the expert economists, have arrived at a substantially different ranking than the one indicated in Table 14.3? I do not think so. Scaled-up health services and the carbon tax probably would have ranked higher. Health services play an important role in disease prevention, hygiene education, and malnutrition, but also in reproductive health, and responsible reproduction with its demographic implications. The optimal (progressively growing) carbon tax, as an optimal climate policy, would go a long way toward protecting ecosystems against environmental harm, but it is unacceptable politically.

Of course, issues are not completely separable; they have systemic properties. Health services are also a governance issue. Trade and subsidies may contribute resources needed by all the other opportunities. The solutions for many of these issues see their benefits increase with the number of adherents. The fact that an alternative ethics would not have altered rankings very much is probably because strict benefit-cost analysis was not applied. This was, no doubt, through the lack of data, but also because all issues tend to be global public goods, which are under-provided, even though some issues are more divisible than others (see Table 14.2).

Sachs (2004) has argued that the statement of the policy problem presented to the expert group, i.e., a hypothetical US$50 billion budget constraint of additional financial resources, biased the ranking toward the cheaper opportunities because the amount of money is simply too low. In other words, he argues that the opportunities are not truly divisible. Moreover, the Copenhagen Consensus does not take into account financial commitments already made. The US$50 billion is totally out of proportion (0.03 percent) with the Gross World Product that he estimates to be about US$40 trillion, with $30 trillion directly from the high-income countries.

The Monterrey International Financing Conference on Development reaffirmed the target aid of 0.7 percent of rich countries' GDP, which would amount to US$210 billion. The current level of development aid, US$0.69 billion, amounts to about 0.25 percent of donors' GNP. He also complains that the issues, by their importance, truly required a multidisciplinary approach—especially building bridges between the scientific and the policy community—and that, leaving them only to economists to rank, left them to reductionist economic science. Indeed, benefit-cost analysis was supposed to be the criterion for ranking the opportunities, but several of these were not supported by sufficient data to make the implementation of the criterion feasible. Data on global public goods would be necessarily hard to gather since many of the benefits are externalities, notoriously hard to measure, and are intangible as well.

Then, the panel was left with using its judgment on several opportunities, but "the panel is mostly known for its expertise outside the areas under discussion." (p. 726) Finally, Sachs observed that insufficient time was left to the panel to consider the evidence thoroughly, to consult with external experts, and come to consensus. This led to the panel coming up with decisions, which were not supported by the evidence forwarded in the background papers, and the rationale of which remained unexplained. Initial assessment by the expert group should have been widely circulated for comment before the final report was issued.

Sachs takes the example of climate change as an illustration. The opportunity was found to have a positive net benefit according to the background paper, but disagreement with the paper reviewers about the speed of intervention led the issue to be ranked lowest. Perhaps, Sachs' most devastating criticism is that "It [the process] failed to mobilize an expert group that could credibly identify and communicate a true consensus of expert knowledge on the range of issues under consideration." (p. 726)

Were the opportunities truly indivisible? In other words, could one begin to make a dent in the challenge, given that only a portion of the budget needed would be apportioned? Opportunities related to communicable diseases and climate change probably are indivisible. Other opportunities almost certainly are divisible, such as malnutrition, trade, and water issues. Despite the fact that the selection of the opportunities corresponding to such ominous challenges should not be based on criteria provided by one discipline only, the information provided by benefit-cost analysis remains useful.

Though benefit-cost analysis is a very useful tool for allocative efficiency for private goods and services, it must give way to higher principles when efficiency is not the overriding concern. Page (1994) and others (e.g., Sagoff, 1988) have argued that policy is subject to a two-tier value system: a higher tier which deals with major constitutional issues and moral obligation questions, and a lower one which deals with economic efficiency. Actually, this is probably how the international community selected these issues in the first place (MDGs; see Table 14.1).

Benefit-cost analysis does not work well when there are: (1) concerns about human rights and, generally, about moral obligation, e.g., respect for nature, when these aspects are major considerations; (2) gross inequity concerns for the people affected by the adoption of an opportunity; (3) disjunction between preference satisfaction and welfare enhancement resulting from ignorance about available information. (Adler et al., 1999) The first two situations are certainly at play with the global public goods issues that were ranked by the Copenhagen Consensus. Provision of the global public good does not mean automatic access by all. (Kaul et al., 1999) The third situation applies to ecosystem services, the situation that the ESA ecovision report wanted to remedy. (Palmer, April 2004)

The fact that the climate change opportunities were ranked so low is due, in our opinion, to two factors: (1) disagreement within the economics profession about the current level of needed abatement, reflected in the position paper by an advocate of aggressive abatement, and in the rebuttals by advocates of more lenient abatement (Barrett, 1999); (2) there was only one expert (T. C. Schelling) on the climate change issue on the panel to whose opinion other panelists likely deferred; his long-held position is that, for developed countries at least, climate change is not an economically significant issue and, for developing countries, any abatement by developed countries is tantamount to aid to their future generations at the expense of aid to their current generations. (Schelling, 1997; 1992) Despite the disagreements, all economists involved agreed that at least minimal action—under the guise of Research and Development of climate-friendly technologies—was required.

Conclusions

Because of the policy interface, the *Earth Charter* principles may work hand in hand with the economics discipline, which offers the ancillary service of cost-effectiveness. Ecological Integrity should not focus on natural ecosystems exclusively, but also on human-made ecosystems, for which integrity may still be a systemic emergent property.

Tinkering with natural ecosystems should, of course, remain subject to the Precautionary Principle, a proviso absent from the ESA ecovision report. As a corollary, environmental engineers should be invited to join with the Global Ecological Integrity Group.

The Copenhagen Consensus constituted an interesting exercise, even if it was somewhat flawed. Applying benefit-cost analysis to global public goods has strong limitations, even if some are somewhat divisible (related policies may be incremental). Insufficient data, major issues of equity, rights and moral obligations pertinent to global public goods will always mar a benefit-cost-based process.

In terms of ranking the opportunities, the adoption of an anthropocentric utilitarian ethic or, instead, an ecocentric one does not seem to make much practical difference. The poor ranking of the climate-related opportunities resulted more from disagreements within the economics profession about costs and the current level and type of needed action, than about the necessity to act.

By their global public good nature, the *Earth Charter*, Ecological Integrity, and Economics are, therefore, more complementary than at odds with one other.

Notes

1. The example of the grid is not perfect as electricity subscribers may be denied access to the grid if they decline to pay for the cost of the grid. For this reason, the grid is an impure public good (or club good) while, for example, biodiversity is a pure public good since its provision does not depend on subscription.

2. This may be especially vivid in Canada since, on several occasions, the grid has collapsed locally, not because of crowding, but because of the 1998 ice storm and the 2002 Toronto blackout.

References

Adler, Matthew D., and Eric A. Posner. "Rethinking Cost-Benefit Analysis." *Yale Law Journal* 109 (1999): 167–247.

Barrett, Scott. "Montreal versus Kyoto, International Cooperation and the Global Environment." Pp. 192–219 in *Global Public Goods*, edited by I. Kaul, I. Grunberg, and M.A. Stern. Oxford University Press, 1999.

Botkin, Daniel B., and Kenneth M. Collins. "Clouds among the Ecological Visions." *BioScience* 55 (Jan. 2005): 7–9.

Brock, William A., Karl-Göran Mäler, and Charles Perrings. "Resilience and Sustainability: The Economic Analysis of Nonlinear Dynamic Systems." Ch. 10, pp. 261–89 in *Panarchy*, edited by L. H. Gunderson and C. S. Holling. Washington, DC: Island Press, 2002.

Caldwell, Lynton K. "Political Aspects of Ecologically Sustainable Development." *Environmental Conservation* 11 (1984): 299–308.

Crabbé, Philippe. "Éthique, la Déclaration de Rio et l'Ordre du Jour 21: quelques considérations d'un économiste." *Institute for Research on the Environment and Economy.* University of Ottawa, 1992.

Crabbé, Philippe, Lech Ryszkowski, and Laura Westra. "Introduction." Pp. 1–19 in *Implementing Ecological Integrity*, edited by Philippe Crabbé, A. Holland, L. Ryszkowski, and L. Westra. Dordrecht, Netherlands: Kluwer Academic Publishers, 2000.

Daly, Herman E., and John B. Cobb. *For the Common Good.* Boston: Beacon Press, 1989.

Declaration of the United Nations on the Human Environment. 1972. http://www.unep.org/Documents.multilingual/Default.asp?DocumentID=97&ArticleID=1503 (22 May 2006).

Dessai, Suraje, W. Neil Adger, Mike Hulme, John Turnpenny, Jonathan Kohler, and Rachel Warren. "Defining and Experiencing Dangerous Climate Change." *Climatic Change* 64 (2004): 11–25.

Douglas, Mary, Des Gasper, Steven Ney, and Michael Thompson. "Human Needs and Wants." Pp. 89–194 in *Human Choice and Climate Change,* vol. 1, ch. 2, edited by S. Rayner and E. L. Malone. Columbus, OH: Battelle Press, 1998.

The *Earth Charter.* http://www.earthcharter.org/files/charter/charter.pdf (22 May 2007).

Gare, A. E. *Postmodernism and the Environmental Crisis.* London: Routledge, 1995.

Hassan, Parwez. *A Recollection by Dr. Parwez Hassan.* http://www.iucn.org/themes/law/cel07.html (22 May 2007).

Karr, James R. "Ecological Integrity and Ecological Health Are Not the Same." Pp. 97–106 in *Engineering with Ecological Constraints*, edited by P. Shultze. Washington, DC: National Academy Press, 1996.

Kay, James J. "Uncertainty, Complexity, and Ecological Integrity." Ch. 8, Pp. 121–56 in *Implementing Ecological Integrity*, edited by P. Crabbé, A. Holland, L. Ryszkowski, and L. Westra. Dordrecht, Netherlands: Kluwer Academic Publishers, 2000.

Kaul, Inge, Pedro Conceção, Katell Le Gouven, and Ronald U. Mendoz. *Providing Global Public Goods.* New York: Oxford University Press, 2003.

Kaul, Inge, Isabelle Grunberg, and Marc A. Stern. *Global Public Goods.* New York: Oxford University Press, 1999.

Lee, Kai. *Compass and Gyroscope.* Washington, DC: Island Press, 1992.

Lomborg, Bjørn, ed. *Global Crises, Global Solutions.* Cambridge: Cambridge University Press, 2004.

Page, T. The Discount Rate Problem, unpubl. 1994.

Palmer, Margaret A., Emily Bernhardt, Elizabeth Chornesky, Scott Collins, Andrew Dobson, et al. "Ecological Science and Sustainability for a Crowded Planet: 21st Century Vision and Action Plan for the Ecological Society of America." April 2004 and May 2004. http://esa.org/ecovisions/ppfiles/EcologicalVisionsReport.pdf (29 May 2007).

———. "Ecology for a Crowded Planet." *Science* 304 (28 May 2004): 1251–2.

———. "Supporting Online Material, Ecology for a Crowded Planet." Pp. 1–3, www.sciencemag.org (29 May 2007).

Parson, E. A., and H. Ward. "Games and Simulation." Ch. 2, pp. 105–40 in *Human Choice and Climate Change*, vol. 3, edited by S. Rayner and E. Malone. Columbus, OH: Battelle Press, 1998.

Rip, Arie, and Rene Kemp. "Technological change." Ch. 6, pp. 327–400 in *Human Choice and Climate Change*, vol. 2, edited by S. Rayner and E. Malone. Columbus, OH: Battelle Press, 1998.

Rockefeller, Steven C. "Summary and Survey Prepared for the Earth Charter Project of United Nations." General Principles (Part I) of the World Charter for Nature (1982). *Earth Council.* 1996. http://www.iisd.org/sd/principle.asp ?pid=60&display=1 (22 May 2007).

Sachs, Jeffrey D. "Seeking a Global Solution." *Nature* 450 (12 Aug. 2004): 725–26.

Sagoff, Mark. *The Economy of the Earth.* New York: Cambridge University Press, 1988.

Schelling, Thomas C. "Some Economics of Global Warming." *American Economic Review* 82, no. 1 (1992): 1–14.

———. "The Cost of Combating Global Warming." *Foreign Affairs* 76 (1997): 8–14. Repr. in R. N. Stavins. *Readings in Economics of the Environment.* Norton, 2005.

The UN World Charter for Nature. http://www.un.org/documents/ga/res/37/a37r007.htm (22 May 2007).

Westra, Laura. *An Environmental Proposal for Ethics: The Principle of Integrity.* Lanham, MD: Rowman & Littlefield, 1994.

Chapter 15

Intergenerational Sustainability and Traditional Knowledge in Africa: The Natural Resource Management Perspective

Yemi Oke, Ph.D. (Law)
Lead Counsel/Consultant-in-Chief
MJS Partners, Lagos, Nigeria
MJS Consulting, Toronto, Canada
Contact Information: *8/411 Assiniboine Road, Toronto, Ont. M3J 1L4 CANADA*
Phone: +1 416 650 4481; Email: yemioke@justice.com

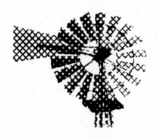

Summary

The challenge of sustainable natural resource management in the African region is unraveled.

In this chapter, we situate the interplay of socioeconomic, cultural, spiritual, magical, epistemological, and other overarching issues involved in the usage, ownership, and management of both renewable and nonrenewable resources. What is termed "traditional knowledge" in the modern regimes of sustainable development and natural resource management at the various levels is, in essence, "customary norms and practices" of natural resource management and utilization.

We illustrate this approach with examples to show that indigenous communities in Africa are repositories of deeply ingrained, well-documented (customary) norms of natural resource management. These norms have existed and been applied over several decades prior to the advent of *Eurocentric* conceptions of sustainability and contemporary paradigms of natural resource management.

A hybrid approach to sustainability, which is *community-based, intergenerational-oriented* and *sustainability-focused,* is advocated. This approach strategically harmonizes both customary and contemporary regimes into one practical model suitable to the African context. It is deemed optimal for attaining the objective of intergenerational sustainability of natural resource management in the region.

The present generations have the responsibility to bequeath to future generations an Earth which will not one day be irreversibly damaged by human activity. Each generation inheriting the Earth temporarily shall take care to use natural resources reasonably and ensure that life is not prejudiced by harmful modifications of the ecosystems and that scientific and technological progress in all fields does not harm life on Earth.[1]

Introduction

The underlying objective of the *Earth Charter* (see the Appendix) is to foster a sustainable[2] global society founded on respect for nature, universal human rights, economic justice, and a culture of peace. It opens up a new vista for instilling the environmental and resource management values needed for bringing about a just, sustainable, and peaceful world. This requires prudent use of Earth's resources for and in the interest of both present and future generations, at risk of increasing threats from classical examples of Hardin's "Tragedy of the Commons."[3] Subsequent activities of the *Earth Charter Community Summits* have further advanced the clamor for ecological integrity, drawing attention to the increasing evidence that our world is becoming increasingly interdependent and fragile. To move forward, according to the Summits, "we must recognize that in the midst of a magnificent diversity of cultures and life forms we are one human family and one Earth community with a common destiny."[4]

In this chapter, we engage with the challenges of intergenerational sustainability and natural resource management along their legal and sociopolitical dimensions. The arguments and analyses of this paper contextualize the peculiar challenges of natural resource management in Africa by situating the interplay of socioeconomic, cultural, spiritual, magical, epistemological, and other overarching issues involved in the usage, ownership, and management of regional, renewable, and nonrenewable resources.

Customary Approaches to Sustainability and the Contemporary Principle of Sustainable Development

Sustainable management of natural resources remains a major challenge to several countries in the African region. Illegal mining continues unabated, for example, in Congo, Ghana, and Sierra Leone. In Cameroon, Liberia, and many others, illicit logging is the issue. In Côte d'Ivoire, poaching for elephant ivory, bush-meat, and related issues still persist, while Nigeria is still living in the nightmare of oil bunkering and resource-induced violence. All these have added to the gloomy picture of Africa in the Western world. The image of Africa is one of epidemic disease, HIV/AIDS, mountainous debt, corruption, abuse of human rights, maladministration, mismanagement of natural resources, political irredentism (i.e., ethnic territorial conflict), as well as broader civil/ethnic unrest. The richness of African countries in terms of natural resources is a manifestation of what scholars generally refer to as the "resource curse."[5] Many observers and scholars tend to wonder whether there is anything positive about Africa aside from the typical images of perpetual epidemics and colossal failures of government and institutions. Often forgotten is the continent's colonial exploitative past, during which period the continent had been depleted of much of its human and resource wealth.

There are many positive things about this region presently unacknowledged. However, apathy to African traditional knowledge and indigenous (customary) practices of natural resource management is the most puzzling of all the positive attributes of Africa that have remained downplayed. What is termed "traditional knowledge" in the modern regimes of environmentally sustainable development and natural resource management at the various levels is in essence "customary norms and practices" of natural resource management. The word "customary" appears to be strategically avoided in the natural resource management literature. Though mindful of the existence of indigenous cultures of the developing countries, the literature tends to ignore the existence of customary approaches to sustainability in natural resource and environmental management in Africa. Sustainability is often conceived as a principle, alien to the developing countries, especially countries in the African region.

Unknown to many, the indigenous communities in Africa are repositories of deeply ingrained, well-documented customary norms of natural resource management which have been in existence for several decades before the advent of *Eurocentric* conceptions of intergenerational sustainability and the contemporary paradigm of natural resource management. The former Deputy President of the International Court of Justice (ICJ), Judge Weeramantry, underscores the importance of African traditional knowledge, and indigenous values and practices, for purposes of managing natural resources and the environment. According to the Jurist, recent books of African philosophical thought are making the wisdom and humanistic bases of African philosophy more accessible to the Western reader. If some of that wisdom had been incorporated into our environmental work, we may not have had some of the major environmental problems we face today.[6]

The sustainability discourses have pervaded the debates around environmentalism since the emergence of the principle of sustainable development in the early 1970s. However, the discourses have been polarized by the so-called civilized standards of the developed countries, and by other Eurocentric perceptions and philosophies of "rights," "duties," "obligations"—of the present generation to future generations.[7] Scholarly attempts in these areas have neither adequately reflected on the perceptions of the concept by local communities in Africa, nor have they sufficiently acknowledged the important roles of customary ways of managing natural resources before the advent of modern regimes of sustainability.

"Sustainability" and "intergenerationality" are not strange concepts to indigenous African communities. Most African communities boast of ingrained, indigenous customary sustainability practices that are encapsulated in the rubrics of intergenerationality. Before the advent of modern sustainability, traditional norms and culture existed among the local communities to manage and conserve natural resources in the interests of both present and future generations within the diverse perceptions and understandings of the term "sustainability" among the local people.[8] The analysis of Mabogunje also corroborates the existence of customary sustainability in Africa.[9] According to Mabogunje:

> In the African context, therefore, sustainability represents, as it were, a modern version of a traditional concept of "usufruct" whereby every generation is seen as no more than a trustee with rights of beneficial use (or usufruct) of the capital stock which it inherited from its ancestors and has responsibility to pass it to posterity as much as possible unimpaired by mismanagement. What is modern or different in this new formulation is the need to see "income flow" as representing overall living standards and the sum total capitals as the productive capacity of a particular society.[10]

Africa and the Task of Achieving Intergenerational Sustainability in Natural Resource Management

The task of effective natural resource management in Africa for purposes of intergenerational sustainability is only realizable where resource exploitation, utilization, or management takes into consideration the social, political, religious, traditional, spiritual, and cultural orientation of the local people.[11] Though relevance of indigenous communities and their traditional knowledge in resource management is being gradually embraced as part of the international regime of sustainability,[12] this remains largely in the realm of theoretical supposition and presently devoid of meaningful application under the local regimes of the state parties in Africa.

Aside from the global-local disconnect in the application of traditional knowledge and customary practices in natural resource management, there is a wide gap in the declared objectives for incorporating these provisions and concrete steps already taken toward their realization. To this extent, Eurocentric models of sustainability adapted by African countries have not achieved the desired results.

Attempts to force alien environmental values and cultures upon the local communities have resulted in environmental dislocation and alterations of the attitude and consciousness of the people in resource management. Some scholars have argued that to demystify the myth of environmental perils and resource mismanagement in developing countries (like Africa) would require a shift in approach toward community-focused sustainability.[13] As argued by Goodland, community concerns and participation are essential ingredients for any resource-based project that aims to promote sustainable development.[14]

It needs to be acknowledged that some African countries have attempted to domesticate the sustainability principle in their natural resource regimes as suggested by Goodland, doing so in harmony with their historical, cultural, and traditional antecedents. For example, an *unborn child* may have no right or be legally expunged in certain *Eurocentric* jurisprudence. On the other hand, developing nations of Africa with established customs and traditions of giving due regard to the *rights and dignity* of the inanimate, rivers, mountains, water, trees, and animals, would not only recognize the right of the human fetus; they would also find justification for mainstreaming related concepts into law and policy. Judge Weeramantry of the International Court of Justice (ICJ) has pointed out that the concept of intergenerationality would subsequently receive overwhelming embracement in Africa and Asia "due to the broader perception of equity under their traditional legal system which contained a deeply ingrained respect for the earth, the atmosphere, the lakes and sea."[15]

However, some fundamental absurdities are noticeable in attempts to give effect to the present regime of sustainability by African countries, when viewed from the perspectives and peculiarities of the people of the region. Though modern environmental instruments tend to advocate usage of traditional knowledge in resource conservation,[16] little regard seems to be given to the preexiting customary norms in domesticating such principles by African countries. A quick look at the regimes of notable countries in the region shows that well-cherished and practically-compatible local customs of achieving sustainability that could well have been identified and harmonized into the modern regime have not received sufficient (or any) attention.

Before the advent of the modern sustainability concept, evidence abounded of the serious commitments of the local peoples and their judicial systems to the principle of environmentally sustainable utilization of resources. These incorporated protection, preservation, and conservation of natural resources for both present and future generations. For instance, in the case of *Busari Aderibigbe v. Abati*, the native court applied local customs and traditions and found the defendant liable of bush burning.[17] Similarly, in *Egba Native Authority v. Aliat*, a court of coordinate jurisdiction also applied local customs in convicting an accused for cutting down an iroko tree without permission.[18] The fine imposed in the latter case was even considered excessive considering the time of commission and offence committed. The court's attitude was to impose stiffer penalties as a way of giving effects to the traditional norms of ensuring sustainability in natural resources utilization, and to deter potential violators.[19]

Among the Tiv of central Nigeria, sustainability consciousness is evident in the rearing and keeping of bees—which is considered a dangerous adventure—in order to replenish the commercially valuable insects. Preservation of particular species of bird *Gbargbar* is also tailored toward the same purpose.[20] Aside from economic reasons, customs often form the basis of preservation as in the case of the Venda and Sutho-Tswana in South Africa, where many wild animals, reptiles, birds, and fish are venerated, and any violation of these taboos attract supernatural sanctions.[21] These and numerous other examples lend credence to the fact that African perceptions and sustainability consciousness vis-à-vis the environment and natural resource management are both strong and popular.[22]

The current "politics of disinterestedness" in traditional, customary approaches to achieving sustainability has been a gradual process, not divestible from the colonial experience and its Eurocentric notions of resource conservation.[23] The traditional systems of resource management, like other pre-colonial values, became jettisoned due to their perceived "unsustainability" in a colonization context, giving way to modern resource conservation, packaged by the colonialists as adequate and sustainable. [24]

Harmonizing the Customary Regime and Modern Approaches to Intergenerational Sustainability

The reality of our world is such that a "standalone" paradigmatic approach to ecological sustainability either in resource management, environmental advocacy and/or in the various spectrums of sustainability, would appear unrealistic. The rate of environmental depletion and resource/ecological degradation makes it indispensable for a shift in the paradigm of natural resource management to embrace a more practical model which is *community-based, intergenerational-oriented* and *sustainability-focused.*

Despite the present inadequacies of the resource management regimes of the African countries, relevance of their customary practice and indigenous philosophies of natural resource management cannot be lightly denied.[25] Given these realities, the panacea for curtailing the level of resource mismanagement in Africa is not in the Western or Eurocentric models. The solution lies in the extent to which valuable customary practices and indigenous cultures are integrated into the design, implementation, or application of natural resource management rules, policies, laws, and directives of countries in the region in a more specific term, as against present ambivalent, awkward domestication.

The notion of Eurocentric "sustainability" indeed provides a means for the spread of Western ideology to other nations which may not share Western ideas. The basis of this critique is that the principle is built on a Western ideology of nature, leading to the marginalization or concealment of alternative views of nature and conceptual notions of sustainability, different from the Western notion of nature and sustainability.[26]

The concealment of alternative views of African indigenous sustainability norms extends to the virtual denial of the existence of local customs or institutions of sustainability and natural resource management. The same seemingly erroneous notion pervades the Eurocentric view of other African values and customs, some of which have now become global practices. For example, "hair-braids" and "tattoos" depict an African sense of beauty, and were once used as yardsticks for labeling Africans "barbaric" for inscribing "stuffs" on their bodies and faces. However, these have become global fashions and expressions of beauty irrespective of the antecedences of misconceptions about the practices in ancient African communities.[27] This indicates that even if such customary practices of natural resource management are not very popular now, they might become the global sustainability norms of the future. According to Richardson, "even where particular communities can rationally deal with environmental issues at the local level, they may have little control over externally generated, complex problems like pollution, climate change, and global warming."[28]

Though application of traditional knowledge might be impracticable in the oil and gas sector, it is nonetheless useful in handling some of the environmental crises and resource-fueled conflicts bedeviling most African countries. The application of traditional wisdom has been suggested as the solution to resource-fueled violence in certain parts of Africa. For instance, customary norms of conflict resolution of the indigenous Tiv community of central Nigeria has been recommended as a model principle of conflict resolution.[29]

Similarly, it could be argued that application of customary practices and systems cannot be totally isolated in all extractive sector operations. Mining, as an extractive sector, is often said to be a traditional sector in certain parts of Africa. Resource laws of certain countries in the region also recognize traditional usage of and practices related to mineral resources. For instance, the galamsey (i.e., artisan miners in Ghana) assert the indigenousness of local mining as the basis for their unwillingness to give up the practice, which contemporary resource managers often perceive as "illegal mining."[30]

The Nigerian mineral law also gives statutory recognition to traditional usage of mineral resources.[31] It is a customary practice of the local people in "winning" minerals, such as salt, soda, potash, or galena, provided that the custom is well established in the community, and the prospective winner of such resources belongs to the community.[32]

Given the above illustrations, the present paradigm of natural resource management needs to be rethought to embrace a more practical model, based on African customary norms of sustainability. This would be better suited to the African situation, and for solving resource management problems in the region. In the arguments below, references are made to specific examples of customary approaches to sustainability in the African communities, and we recommend their adoption.

Illustrations of African Indigenous Sustainability Practices

African communities are replete with various indigenous practices of sustainability and resource management. For instance, the sustainability aspect of the *New yam* festival among the Igbos of Southeastern Nigeria lies in reserving vital parts of the yam harvested in the previous season for consecration unto the gods for a bountiful harvest in the coming season.[33] This could be likened to tithing in the Bible.[34] This cultural practice ensures continuity of production in a most traditionally compatible way, while also ensuring non-degradation of *god-given* natural resources for future use by subsequent generations. Like *New yam* festival, the Argungu fish festival[35] is a celebration of culture and tradition, which also exists in Northern Nigeria for fishermen whose activities are mainly in the river areas. The magnitude of fish display and cultural implications of the festival leave no one in doubt as to the existence of ingrained traditional practices of managing and preserving fish.

The Osun Oshogbo festival is also an internationally acclaimed traditional festival in Osun State, Southwest Nigeria, designed to worship and celebrate ancestral gods for their benevolence including, but not limited to, natural resources of the forest, rivers, and others.[36] This traditional ceremony also has its significance in the preservation of freshwater, marine, and general environment and resources. The Olumo Rock in Abeokuta (Southwest Nigeria) is an example of traditional culture relating to mountains, rock-mining and quarrying. The Olumo Rock[37] is of religious, historical, cultural, and other significance to the Egbas of Southwest Nigeria. According to Egba history, the Rock shielded the Egba people and their warriors from the onslaughts of the Oyo people in the war between the two communities.[38] Though the Olumo Rock has since assumed its own prominence in tourism in Nigeria and Ogun State in particular, it is taboo to allow or conceive any form of rock mining and quarrying of the Rock despite its mining potential.

Generally, in Southern Nigeria, the customary land tenure system and resources beneath the surface are regulated by customary norms. Indigenous conceptions of land are embedded in intergenerational sustainability. Traditionally, land has economic, social, political, and religious significance in Nigeria.[39] Land and resources beneath the surface are conceived as a sacred gift by God for the sustenance of all members of the community; and, by implication, belong to the dead, the living, and the unborn, and to be held and managed as a kind of "ancestral trust" by the living generation. The traditional conceptions of land and ownership of resources beneath the land in Yoruba communities establish a strong case of communality and intergenerationality. Testifying before the West African Lands Commission in 1908, a traditional ruler, Chief Elesi of Odogbolu, (now under Ogun State, Southwest Nigeria) expounded the traditional conception of land in Yorubaland thus: "I conceive that land belongs to a vast family of which many are dead, few are living and countless members are still unborn."[40]

In other parts of Africa like Ghana, ownership of lands is vested in the various communities and held in trust by the communal leaders such as the "stool," the "skin," or the "family"[41] subject to the provisions of the Constitution.[42] In other parts of Ghana, interests in land may be divided broadly into the allodial interest, the customary freehold interest, and other limited rights of tenancy. The allodial interest (i.e., free and full ownership) is the indivisible right of the community to all the land occupied or held in trust for members' future needs.[43]

Traditionally, in several local communities in the districts of Ghana, land is held under the common property regime in trust for the people by chiefs, clans, and family heads, as custodians. As such, access to land and control are governed largely by customary tenancy rules, which spell out the various rules and conditions under which land should be allocated in the community.[44]

Uganda also offers another good example of communities where customary approaches to resource and environmental management have held sway. Before the colonial intervention in Uganda, rural communities had evolved various customary rules, which governed the use of natural resources like forests and wetlands. However, though these traditional management systems survive, customary rules remain inadequately recognized by the national government of Uganda.[45] Notwithstanding, the relevance of customary norms of engaging natural resources is recognized as vital in the country. In a recent study titled "Local Paths for World Development,"[46] the World Bank acknowledged that indigenous knowledge is a major asset for developing countries, whether for natural resource management or healing through plants, the fight against AIDS, or even the prevention of conflict. The study shows one successful example of the association of indigenous and modern knowledge in the district of Iganga in Uganda. In this community, maternal mortality was reduced by almost half in three years because of a combination of local knowledge and modern communications in health deliveries.

In the face of persisting resource-induced violence in certain areas of Africa, the study also shows that conflict resolution mediation could draw inspiration from indigenous values and principles. For example, the study referred to the Tiv community of central Nigeria where the local custom dictates:

[A] good judge is not one who imposes a decision on opposing parties, but one who leads the opposing camps to accept and recognize the legitimacy of the verdict." [The study recognizes that] implications of this principle for the negotiations of contemporary peace agreements in the area are enormous."

Traditional communities in Kenya also have established customs and practices of managing the environment and natural resources for and in the interests of both present and future generations of Kenyans. The nature of indigenous practices for resource management in Kenya led to the conclusion reached by Brokensha and Riley relating to the traditional knowledge of the Mbere communities. Traditional resource management practices were the only popular means of resource and environmental management in pre-colonial Kenya. During colonization, the imperial administration was not able to maintain natural resources. This inability was identified as one of the likely effects of the colonialists' land policy and consequential destruction of the traditional institutions that were once used to sustain resource utilization. According to the duo, "now that people have their own individual pieces of land, there are signs that owners are taking better care of the land, by preserving and planting valuable tress, and by following some basic soil conservation rules."

Conclusions

There exists a regime of sustainability other than the popular Eurocentric model. It is suggested that both customary and Eurocentric sustainability regimes might be pluralized, with each flourishing independently of the other under a clearly defined, harmonized legal and policy framework in the resource sectors of countries in Africa.

Attaining intergenerational sustainability in natural resource management in Africa is inextricably linked to the level of sincere readiness demonstrated in integrating specific, customary approaches and norms of sustainability into present models of natural resource management in the region.

The challenge of attaining sustainability and ecological integrity in the present and future generations in Africa demands across-the-board integrative, community-based approaches that already exist under the indigenous, social, and institutional arrangements in the local communities in the region. Harmonizing compatible customary approaches to natural resource management in achieving the ultimate aim of intergenerational sustainability would not only enhance the effective utilization of natural resources in Africa, it would also create a win-win situation among the various stakeholders in the sector.

On the basis of the observations and arguments in this chapter, we conclude that sustainability and the effective utilization of environmental and natural resources in Africa depend on the integration of relevant traditional practices and customary norms. "Environmental management," "resource utilization," "intergenerationality" and "sustainability" are not alien concepts in Africa. What is alien, however, is the Eurocentric model of "sustainability" which attempts to instill environmental and resource management culture without taking benefit from the ingrained sustainability consciousness and practices of the indigenous African communities.

To achieve intergenerational sustainability and effective natural resource and environmental management in Africa, steps must be taken to identify suitable practices and/or customary approaches to natural resource and environmental management in the region. After carefully identifying these local practices, attempts should then be made to integrate them into the mainstream of the modern regimes of resource and environmental management by countries in Africa.

We believe this to be a more suitable, practical approach to achieving sustainability in the region, and for solving seemingly elusive environmental and resource management problems for and in the interests of both present and future generations of Africans.

The noble objectives of the *Earth Charter* would thereby be more easily achieved in Africa. Given the present ecologically perilous state of countries in the region, bringing about ecological integrity is essential.

Notes

1. Article 4, *UNESCO Declaration on the Responsibilities of Present Generations Towards Future Generations* adopted on 12 Nov. 1997. See Report by the Director-General on the Draft Declaration on the Safeguarding of Future Generations: http://home.um.edu.mt/fgp/Declaration.html (1 Jun. 2007).

2. World Commission on Environment and Development, *Our Common Future* (London: Oxford University Press, 1987), 30.

3. Garrett Hardin, "The Tragedy of the Commons," *Science* 162 (1968): 1243–48.

4. Earth Charter Community Summit, http://www.earthcharter.org (1 Jun. 2007).

5. Richard Auty, *Sustaining Development in Mineral Economies: The Resource Curse Thesis* (London: Routledge, 1993). See also Michael Ross, "The Political Economy of The Resource Curse," *World Politics* 51 (1999), 297–98.

6. Justice Christopher Weeramantry, "International Law and the Developing World: A Millennial Analysis," *Harvard International Law Journal* 41 (2000): 283.

7. Brown Weiss, *In Fairness To Future Generations: International Law, Common Patrimony, and Intergenerational Equity*, (UN University and Transnational Publishers, 1989), 5–12. See also Weiss, "Finance, and the Development Process," *American University Journal of International Law and Policy* 8 (1992): 19 at 24.

8. For example, sustainability means different things to different communities. The attitude of the people to the concept is determined by their respective traditions, taboos, religious, and cultural beliefs.

9. Akin Mabogunje, "Framing the Fundamental of Sustainable Development in Sub-Saharan Africa," CID Workshop Paper No. 104 (Cambridge, MA: Sustainable Development Program, Centre for International Development, Harvard University, 2004), 5.

10. Mabogunje, "Framing the Fundamental," at 5.

11. Yemi Oke, *Sustainable Utilization of Mineral Resources in Sub-Saharan Africa: A Comparative Appraisal of the Mining Regime in Nigeria*, Unpublished LL.M. Thesis on file with author (Osgoode Hall, York University, Canada, 2004), 218.

12. Article 8 (j) *Convention on Biological Diversity*, 31 I.L.M 818 (1992). See also the Preamble and Articles 17, 18 (2) and 19 of *United Nations Convention to Combat Desertification in Those Countries Experiencing Draught and/or Desertification, Particularly in Africa* (Paris), 33 ILM 1328 (1994); the UNCED non-binding, but authoritative statement of Principles *for a Global Consensus on the Management, Conservation and Sustainable Development of All Types of Forests*, UN Document A/CONF.151/6/Rev.1 of 13 Jun. 1992 and Principle 22 of the Rio Declaration, A/CONF.151/26 Vol. I, 8:31 I.L.M 874 (1992).

13. Robert Goodland, "Sourcebook: Policy Options for the World Bank Group in Extractive Industries; How to Achieve Poverty Reduction and Sustainable Development," *Independent Extractive Review for International Finance Corporation and the World Bank Group* (26 Jul. 2004), 9.

14. Goodland, "Sourcebook". See also Weiss, *In Fairness*.

15. Judge Christopher Weeramantry, *The Maritime Boundary Delimitation case of Denmark v. Norway* (1993) ICJ 38.

16. See for example Principle 22 of the Rio Declaration (end of note 12). It provides: "Indigenous people and their communities, and other local communities, have a vital role in environmental management and development because of their knowledge and traditional practices. States should recognize and duly support their identity, culture

and interests and enable their effective participation in the achievement of sustainable development."

17. See *Busari Aderibigbe v. Abati* (reported in A. O. Obilade, *Nigerian Legal System* (London: Sweet & Maxwell, 1979), 83.

18. See the decision of Customary Court Ake, Abeokuta, Ogun State, Southwest Nigeria-Ake, Grade "A" Native Court 50/1934.

19. Decision of Customary Court.

20. Kola Lawal, "Ecology and Culture: Reflections on Environmental Law and Policy in Sub-Saharan Africa," *Environmental Law and Policy,* ed. Simpson and Fagbohun (Lagos: Law Centre, 1998), 31.

21. Wyle J. M. T. Labuschagne, and Chris Boonzaaier, "African Perception and Legal Rules Concerning Nature," *South African Journal of Environmental Law and Policy* 5 (1998): 58.

22. According to Mbiti (James Mbiti, *African Religion and Philosophy*, 1969, at 15–16) Africans have their own ontology which is an extremely anthropocentric ontology in the sense that everything is seen in terms of its relation to man, animals, plants, and natural phenomena, and objects constitute the environment in which man lives, provide a means of existence. Mbiti, at 60.

23. See for example, the *1900 Convention for the Preservation of Wild Animals and Fish in Africa*, 94 B.F.S.P. 715, and *Convention on Fishing and Conservation of the Living Resources of the High Seas 559 U.N.T.S. 285*, (1958), entered into force when most African nations were under the colonial yokes of their imperial masters. These marked the beginning of the now orchestrated modern approach to conservation of nature and natural resources to ensure sustainability.

24. Attwell and Cotterill, "Postmodernism and African Conservation Science," *Biodiversity and Conservation,* (2000), 9 at 559–77.

25. Vincent Tucher, "The Myth of Development: A Critique of a Eurocentric Discourse," *Critical Development Theory: Contributions to a New Paradigm,* ed. R. Munch and D. O'Hearn (New York: Zed Books, 1999), 1–2.

26. Alex Geisinger, "Sustainable Development and the Domination of Nature: Spreading the Seed of the Western Ideology of Nature," *Boston College Environmental Affairs Law Review* (1999): 27 at 68.

27. Rekha Menon, "Transgressions: Redressing Tradition," *Ijele: Art e-journal of the African World* (2002): 4 at 2.

28. Benjamin Richardson, "Environmental Law in Postcolonial Societies: Straddling the Local-Global Spectrum," *Colorado Journal of International Environmental Law and Policy* (2000): 11:1 at 82.

29. The model suggests: "[A] good judge is not one who imposes a decision on opposing parties, but one who leads the opposing camps to accept and recognize the legitimacy of the verdict. [The study recognizes that] implications of this principle for the negotiations of contemporary peace agreements in the area are enormous." Banco Mundial, "World Bank Calls for Indigenous Knowledge to Foster Development", online at: http://www.noticias.info/Archivo/2004/200411/20041116/20041116_40063.shtm (1 Jun. 2007), at 2 [emphasis supplied].

30. Karen Palmer, "Illegal Mining a Threat in Ghana," *Toronto Star,* Sunday 10 Oct. 2004, at F5.

31. *Nigerian Minerals and Mining Act*, 1999.

32. *Nigerian Minerals and Mining Act*, s. 7 (1).

33. This cultural practice is well illustrated in one of the books of Chinua Achebe, (the author of popular *Things Fall Apart*). See Chinua Achebe, *Arrow of God* (London: Heinemann, 1974).

34. *Holy Bible* (New International Version), Malachi ch. 3, verses 10–11.

35. Argungu community is historically known as fishing communities. Argungu, in Northern Nigeria, hosts an internationally-acclaimed fishing contest to mark the end of the growing season and the harvest.   Online   at   http://www.whatsonwhen.com/sisp/index.htm?fx=event&event_id=74481 (1 Jun. 2007).

36. The Osun Oshogbo festival is a week-or-more-long festival in Osun State, Southwest   Nigeria,   mainly   in   honor   of   the   ancient   gods.   See   http://www.motherlandnigeria.com/tourist.html (1 Jun. 2007).

37. See   Olumo   Rock,   Sow   Caves,   http://www.showcaves.com/english/misc/caves/Olumo.html (1 Jun. 2007).

38. Yemi Oke, "Alake of Egbaland Dies, Who's Next? (Alake W'aja, Tani Oba Kan?)," http://nigeriaworld.com/articles/2005/feb/071.html (1 Jun. 2007).

39. Ehi Oshio, "Indigenous Land Tenure and Nationalization of Land in Nigeria," *Boston College Third World Law Journal* 43 (1990): 43.

40. See West African Lands Commission Report (1908) 183 para. 1048.

41. See Kraig Grubaugh, "Profile of Ghana's Mining Industry," Technical Papers, SME Publications Department, Feb. 2002, at 3. In Ghana, the local or traditional governments are known as "stool" or "skin." Stool is the term used in the south while skin is used in the north.

42. Section 36 (8), *Constitution of the Republic of Ghana,* 1992.

43. See further Nii Amaa Ollennu and Gordon Woodman, *Ollennu's Principles of Customary Land Law in Ghana* (University of Birmingham, 1985), at 184.

44. *Ollennu's Principles.* See also Kraig Grubaugh, "Profile," and section 36 (8), *Constitution of the Republic of Ghana* (1992).

45. Benjamin Richardson, "Environmental Management in Uganda: The Importance of Property Law and Local Government in Wetlands Conservation," *Journal of African Law* (1993): 37:2 at 122.

46. Banco Mundial, "World Bank Calls", at 2.

Part V:
Focus (a): Governance amid Ideological Influences in a Globalizing World

To implement the shifts needed to achieve sustainability, the explicit ethical examination of what sustainability means and entails is necessary. The policy debate would thereby become transparent, making clear the values underlying policy alternatives.

In this, the first of four focus areas as part five of the book, policy decisions are shown to be determined by ideological influences. These influences in the United States of America are in the form of powerful think tanks supported by right-wing interests. Hence, there is a push there, and around the world, to maintain the business-as-usual approach, for instance, in our fossil-fuel based, energy intensive infrastructure.

Two examples are discussed that provide insight into how ideologies can be challenged when considering governance.

While the Russian ratification of the Kyoto Protocol relating to climate change provides a successful step toward achieving the Protocol's targets in Europe, many European countries remain behind in their adoption of new technologies. Through ethical analysis of policies and economic measures that have served as barriers to the Protocol's implementation, greater community support for implementation is likely.

In the case of Genetically Modified Organisms (GMOs), new forms of ecologically-based governance are required. The absence of local community understanding of the individual risks and benefits from GMOs could be overcome if new forms of ecological governance were adopted. New forms of governance involve the sharing of competence between national and local government, empowering local jurisdictions to control or prohibit GMO release.

The explicit ethical examination of issues around sustainability is necessary to counter ideological biases when deciding policy directions.

Chapter 16

The Ominous Rise of Ideological Think Tanks in Environmental Policy-Making

Donald A. Brown, J.D. (Juris Doctor), M.A. (Liberal Studies), B.S. (Commerce and Engineering Sciences)

Director, Pennsylvania Consortium for
Interdisciplinary Environmental Policy
Senior Counsel for Sustainable Development,
Pennsylvania Department of Environmental Protection
Harrisburg, PA, U.S.A.

*Contact Information: Science, Technology, Society Program, Penn State University
201A Old Botany Building, University Park, PA 16802 U.S.A.
Phone: +1 814 865 3371; Fax:+1 814 865 3047; Email: climateethics@comcast.net*

Summary

In this chapter, we examine the rise of ideological think tanks that have played a growing role in environmental policy-making in the last few decades in the United States of America.

This examination was undertaken to explore how scientific-like information relating to environmental problems that is ideologically biased, has sometimes been injected into public policy-making. We also determine what effect this information could have had on the policy.

Some of the think tanks are shown to frequently generate science-like analyses of important policy questions that distort the unbiased consideration of issues that need to be considered in policy formation. These think tanks are only one element in the growing anti-regulatory forces in the United States that have been funded by those with economic interests or ideological biases against regulation.

We begin with a brief description of strategies, in addition to think tanks, that have been employed by those opposed to environmental regulation. Next, we sketch the rise of these think tanks in the United States. We then describe how these institutions generate research that advances the interests of the sponsors of research rather than producing unbiased scientific analyses. Finally, we conclude with recommendations for dealing with ideologically-biased arguments on environmental policy.

The Reaction from the Right to the
Birth of the Modern Environmental Movement

How is it possible for civilizations to be blind toward the grave approaching threats to their security even when available evidence is accumulating about these threats? This is the focus of the recent book *Collapse* by Jared Diamond. (Diamond, 2005) This chapter looks at how the rise of think tanks (i.e., interest-group-sponsored organizations designed to undertake research to further the interests of their sponsors) in the United States may contribute to disinformation that can prevent citizens from seeing mounting evidence of serious threats to the environment and, by inference, to human health.

The rise of think tanks over the last thirty years is consistent with other re-actions to the modern environmental movement. Although the beginning of any movement cannot be pegged to one date or event, commentators often point to the first Earth Day on April 22, 1970, as the birth of the modern environmental movement in the United States.

During the next decade, there were many major new environmental laws passed at the federal and state level on air and water pollution, drinking water quality, waste disposal, environmental impact analysis, wetland and species protection, and hazardous sites contamination clean-up. (Hays, 1998)

To ensure that these new environmental laws were minimally economically disruptive, the laws usually contained very detailed provisions specifying how the government must consider economic impacts of regulation in relation to the environmental goals prescribed by the law in the writing of the implementation regulations. As a result, the enacting legislation was often long and complex with statutes frequently exceeding a hundred pages in length. Each of these statutes required hundreds of additional pages of regulations to fill out the regu-latory scheme created by the law.

In less than a decade after the adoption of these laws, by the early 1980s, forces opposing environmental regulation had gathered strength. For the next twenty years, these forces worked to weaken the environmental regime enacted earlier and create roadblocks to expanding the regulatory scheme put in place in the 1970s and early 1980s. (Hays, 1998) These roadblocks were often very tech-nical in nature and not well understood by civil society. They included new rules requiring that regulations pass cost-benefit analysis before their enactment or that regulations could be considered only if the government could base regula-tory requirements on absolute scientific proof of harm.

The justification for these roadblocks was often couched in scientific and economic arguments that initially seemed to be reasonable on their face. Yet, cumulatively, they were deadly to a regulatory agenda that might be necessary to protect the environment and human health for a variety of reasons. Among the reasons is the fact that environmental decisions must be made in the face of uncertainty because ecological systems are too complex to achieve high levels of certainty about the ecosystem-wide impacts of human activities. If the government can regulate only when harms are demonstrated with high levels of proof, then for many serious environmental problems this approach is tantamount to preventing protective action.

With a few exceptions, these cumulative roadblocks would undermine the ability of government to take additional action to protect environmental and human health beyond the authority granted to government in the early fertile regulatory period twenty years earlier. The government regulatory regime that remains today is largely the system of laws and regulations that had been enacted decades ago, although new impediments to the full implementation of these earlier laws have been created.

The existing environmental regulatory regime in the United States has been very effective in ameliorating some environmental problems. For instance, existing United States environmental law has successfully reduced some threats to environmental and human health from point sources of air and water pollution, significantly reduced devastation to land and water from coal mining, protected ground water quality from irresponsible disposing of municipal and hazardous wastes, and protected many endangered species.

Yet, the existing environmental law regime has failed to deal with many emerging environmental problems, including:

- Climate change

- Loss of biodiversity

- Air and water pollution from non-point sources

- Soil loss from erosion

- Alien species invasion of ecosystems

- Over-pumping of ground water resources

- Human exposures to some toxic substances

- Over-exploitation of fisheries.

The ability of government to deal with these problems has been greatly weakened because of right-wing (i.e., conservative government) programs, initiatives, and strategies financed by conservative foundations and corporate money. The programs include executive orders limiting the ability of government to regulate, sophisticated use of public relations firms to have the views of free-market ideology accepted, well-financed use of the media including conservative radio talk shows, increased numbers of lobbyists working on the legislative agenda at federal and state levels, and the creation of think tanks to create what on the surface appears to be scientifically unbiased policy analysis. We examine only one of these elements in the right-wing policy toolbox—namely, the rise of think tanks.

The Rise of Think Tanks

Since the 1970s, there has been an explosion in the number of think tanks that attempt to influence government policy. A think tank is generally understood to be a research organization that performs policy analysis about which it often makes public policy recommendations. Unlike many other organizations that try to shape public policy, think tanks usually perform policy analyses that appear to rest on sound scientific or economic examinations of public policy issues. These analyses purport to be value-neutral and objective. Although not all think tanks are ideological, and among think tanks there are right-, left-, and centrist-leaning institutions, the steep rise in the number of think tanks is often attributed to a 1970 memo by Supreme Justice Powell to the United States Chamber of Commerce. (Powell, 2003) This memo advocated establishing institutes on and off academic campuses where intellectuals would write books and promote the scientific basis for policy from a conservative business perspective. (Powell, 2003)

Since the 1970s, the rise in the number of think tanks has resulted from funding from a number of foundations that have ideological agendas, mostly right-wing libertarian views, and corporations. Although there are left- and center-left think tanks, currently there are now twice as many conservative think tanks as liberal ones, largely because of funding from right-leaning philanthropic organizations and corporations. (Powell, 2003) In addition, the right-wing think tanks tend to be much better funded than the left-leaning think tanks. (Rich, 2007)

On environmental matters, the right-wing think tanks sometimes argue that they constitute a necessary balance to numerous environmental organizations that exist in the United States. Yet in the case of information produced by the environmental organizations, the interests represented by their advocacy are apparent by the very name of the organizations while the financial interests that support the work of the think tanks are much more difficult to discern.

Support of the right-wing think tanks has come largely from a group of twelve mostly conservative foundations. They are:

The Lynde and Harry Bradley Foundation, the Carthage Foundation, the Earhart Foundation, the Charles G. Koch, David H. Koch, and Claude R. Lambe charitable foundations, the Phillip M. McKenna Foundation, the JM Foundation, the John M. Olin Foundation, the Henry Salvatori Foundation, the Sarah Scaife Foundation, and the Smith Richardson Foundation. (Covington, 2007)

Over several decades, these foundations have channeled some $80 million to right-wing policy institutions actively promoting an anti-government, unregulated markets (i.e., free-markets) agenda. (Covington, 2007) These foundations also support the training of the next generation of right-wing leaders in conservative legal principles, free-market economics, political journalism, and policy analysis. (Covington, 2007)

The number of think tanks in the United States between 1970 and 1996 grew from fewer than 60, to well over 300. (Rich, 2007) Although the think tanks that first appeared in the United States in the 1950s were initially non-ideological, the last thirty years have seen enormous growth in think tanks with a clear ideological mission. (Rich, 2007)

Of the four largest think tanks, three are right-wing focused, namely: American Enterprise Institute (AEI), the Heritage Foundation (Heritage), and the Cato Institute (Cato). One of the top four is a centrist-left think tank, i.e., the Brookings Institute (Brookings).

The AEI's budget in 2002 was 8.2 million with 148 employees (55 research, 93 administrative/support). (NIRA, 2007b) AEI's stated mission includes "preserving and strengthening the foundations of freedom-limited government, private enterprise, vital cultural and political institutions, and a strong foreign policy and national defense through scholarly research, open debate, and a variety of publications." (NIRA, 2007b)

According to a Center for Media and Democracy project called Source Watch, between 1985 and 2001, AEI received $29,653,933 from the following funding sources: (a) Carthage Foundation, (b) Castle Rock Foundation, (c) Earhart Foundation, (d) John M. Olin Foundation, Inc., (e) Lynde and Harry Bradley Foundation, (e) Philip M. McKenna Foundation, Inc., (f) Scaife Foundations (Scaife Family, Sarah Mellon Scaife, Carthage), and (g) Smith Richardson Foundation. (Center for Media and Democracy, 2007a)

AEI funding has also come from many corporate sources, such as Amoco, the Kraft Foundation, and the Procter & Gamble Fund. (Source Watch, 2007a) AEI also received over $260,000 from ExxonMobil in 2002. (ExxonMobil, 2007) Although corporate donations to AEI are not public, it is known that during 1997, Philip Morris also contributed $100,000 to the Institute. (University of California, 2007)

The Heritage Foundation had a budget of $34 million and employed 195 (61 research administrative/support) in 2002. (NIRA, 2002d) Heritage's mission is to "formulate and promote conservative public policies based on the principles of free enterprise, limited government, individual freedom, traditional American values, and a strong national defense." (NIRA, 2007d)

According to Source Watch, between 1985 and 2003, the following funders provided $57,497,537 (unadjusted for inflation) to the Heritage Foundation: (a) Lynde and Harry Bradley Foundation, (b) Scaife Foundations (Sarah Mellon Scaife, Scaife Family, Carthage), (c) John M. Olin Foundation, Inc., (d) Castle Rock Foundation, (e) JM Foundation, (f) Claude R. Lambe Charitable Foundation, (g) Philip M. McKenna Foundation, Inc., (h) Charles G. Koch Charitable Foundation, (i) Roe Foundation, (j) Rodney Fund, (k) Ruth and Lovett Peters Foundation, (l) Orville D. and Ruth A. Merillat Foundation, (m) Bill and Berniece Grewcock Foundation, (n) Samuel Roberts Noble Foundation, (o) William H. Donner Foundation, (p) Walton Family Foundation, (q) Armstrong

Foundation, (r) John Templeton Foundation, and, (s) William E. Simon Foundation. (Center for Media and Democracy, 2007b)

Heritage received $1.90 million in funding from corporate funding in 2004, a long and steady flow of support from nearly one hundred major corporations. (Center for Media and Democracy, 2007 b) Cato had a budget of $14 million and employed 98 in 2002 (NIRA, 2007c) Cato's mission is to "broaden public debate to increase consideration of the traditional American principles of limited government, individual liberty, free markets, and peace." (NIRA, 2007c)

Between 1985 and 2001, Cato received $15,633,540 in 108 separate grants from only nine different foundations: (a) Castle Rock Foundation, (b) Charles G. Koch Charitable Foundation, (c) Earhart Foundation, (d) JM Foundation, (e) John M. Olin Foundation, Inc., (f) Claude R. Lambe Charitable Foundation, (g) Lynde and Harry Bradley Foundation, (h) Scaife Foundations (Sarah Mellon Scaife and Carthage Foundation). (Center for Media and Democracy, 2007c) Cato is also funded by corporations including ExxonMobil. (Center for Media and Democracy, 2007c)

Brookings had a budget of $33 million and employed 277 people (117 research, 160 administrative/support) in 2003. (NIRA, 2007a) Brookings's mission is to "improve the performance of American institutions and the quality of public policy by using social science to analyze emerging issues and offer practical approaches to those issues in a language aimed at the general public."

Source Watch lists the Brookings Institution as having received seventy-eight grants totaling $5,711,782 between 1986 and 2003 from the following foundations: (a) John M. Olin Foundation, (b) F.M. Kirby Foundation, (c) Walton Family Foundation, and (d) Smith Richardson Foundation. (Center for Media and Democracy, 2007d)

The Threat of the Think Tanks:
Example from Climate Change

It is clear from the mission statement of many of the right-wing think tanks that they are not likely to produce research leading to conclusions that human activities threatening environmental and human health should be regulated. It is also clear from examining their sources of funding that their very existence may depend upon funding from organizations that are hostile to environmental regulation. Yet, the research and analyses produced by these think tanks are often treated by the media as if they were value-free, objective analyses of policy options. Although they are producers of research and policy analyses, think tanks do not usually subject their work to peer review or diversity of thought—checks that are the norm in academically produced research. Yet, these think tanks implicitly or explicitly claim that their policy analyses are scientifically sound and unbiased. However, it is clear that the ideological think tanks generate analyses that promote the interests of their financial sponsors; that is, right-wing philanthropic organizations or corporations.

Although left-leaning think tanks also do not usually comply with rigorous peer review procedures of normal science either, the right-wing think tanks have been more successful in delivering their messages to the public. By 1994, the media were citing more conservative think tanks in the United States than liberal institutions. (Dolny, 2007) In 1997, the central-leaning Brookings was the most cited by the media, while the next three were the Heritage, AEI, and Cato, all right-wing or libertarian-focused organizations. (Dolny, 2007) In 1997, right-wing think tanks provided more than half of major media's think tank citations, while progressive or left-leaning think tanks received just 16 percent of total citations. (Dolny, 2007)

When these think tanks release reports on policy that are reported on by the press, the ideological focus of these institutions is rarely identified. (Dolny, 1998) For instance, in 1997, only 14 percent of the 132 stories sampled in which the AEI was mentioned, was it identified as conservative. (Dolny, 2007) Cato was similarly not labeled in 68 percent of the 130 stories sampled. It was identified as "libertarian" 13 percent of the time, "conservative" 6 percent of the time, and twice was referred to as both "libertarian" and "conservative." One reference called the institution "free-market oriented." (Dolny, 2007)

When neither the ideological label nor the financial base of the think tanks is identified, the public is deprived of the context for evaluating the opinions offered, implying that the think tank "experts" are neutral sources without any ideological predispositions.

The right-wing think tanks' attack on environmental regulation appears to be premised on a belief that environmental regulations are not necessary to protect environmental and human health and, therefore, environmental regulations create unnecessary burdensome costs on businesses.

The progressive left-approach to regulation assumes that human activities often create real harm to environmental and human health and, therefore, government must act to protect plants, animals, and people from these human activities that threaten the environment.

Climate change is a problem that dramatically demonstrates the harm to society that can come from ideological strategies to prevent regulatory action on environmental issues. Climate change, therefore, is an example of one societal problem that makes obvious the danger of injecting science-based arguments into the public discourse about that problem without identifying the ideological bases for the scientific conclusions in the arguments.

Some conservative think tanks have been engaged in projects for over twenty years to convince governments and private citizens that government action to reduce the threat of climate change is not necessary because there is little evidence that climate change is a real problem. However, by the late 1980s, there was enough scientific evidence to convince many nations in the world that the international community needed to set national targets to reduce greenhouse gas emissions despite some uncertainty about timing and magnitude of climate change impacts. (Brown, 2002)

International climate change negotiations began in the late 1980s with many nations arguing that the world urgently needed to set greenhouse gas emissions targets. (Brown, 2002) During the twenty-year period since international negotiations began, scientific knowledge about the enormous threat from climate change to human health and the environment has grown progressively stronger. (Brown, 2002) In the last few years, every mainstream scientific organization in the United States that has expertise in the field of climate change has now taken a position on climate change and concluded that humans are changing the climate in ways that will adversely effect environmental and human health. (Oreskes, 2004) These institutions include the Intergovernmental Panel on Climate Change (UNIPCC), the United States Academy of Science, the United States Geophysical Union, and the American Association for the Advancement of Science. (Oreskes, 2004) Despite this strong scientific consensus, many of the right-wing think tanks have continued to argue against government actions to reduce the threat of climate change. The right-wing think tanks in the United States have been leading campaigns to prevent the country from making commitments to reduce greenhouse gas emissions.

A few fossil fuel companies have used right-wing think tanks as tools to prevent regulation of their products. According to Mother Jones magazine, ExxonMobil has funded forty think tanks and media outlets to preach skepticism about whether climate change will create serious problems. (Mooney, 2007) These think tanks have made arguments such as:

- The science of climate change has been debunked;
- Global warming can actually save lives;
- Not only is the scientific basis of global warming increasingly uncertain, but Kyoto will also ultimately prove to be an economic disaster for Europe—and the developing world;
- The science behind global warming is inconclusive, and to teach otherwise is fear-mongering;
- Recent evidence shows that global warming may not be happening;
- The scientific hypothesis for global warming is scientifically weak;
- No one seriously claims to know whether the past warming was caused by human activities; whether further warming will occur and, if it does, whether it will result from human activities, and whether such warming in some general sense would be a bad thing; and
- The costs to the United States' economy of dealing with climate change were too great to justify action. (Mooney, 2007)

The think tanks funded by ExxonMobil include the larger think tanks discussed above as well many smaller think tanks that appear to have been created for the express purpose of influencing climate change policy.

The magnitude of the incongruence between the scientific consensus position on climate change held by most climate scientists and the above arguments made by the think tanks is staggering. Although scientific uncertainty about the timing and magnitude of climate-change impacts remains, it is a gross misstatement of the scientific facts to assert, as representatives of the right-wing think tanks have often done, that there is no evidence that humans are changing the global climate system, that if current trends continue Earth may experience catastrophic warming, and that the poorest people on the planet are the most vulnerable to these changes. Yet, the think tanks have been successful in convincing many in the United States that climate change may not be a threat at all and that there is no penalty for waiting until all uncertainties are resolved. All this despite the growing realization in the scientific community of the enormity of the threat to environmental and human health from rising seas, increases in storm damage, vector-borne diseases, droughts and floods, loss of biodiversity, heat-related deaths, and increased water scarcities. In addition, those who will most likely be harmed by climate change are some of the poorest people around the world and particularly the millions of people vulnerable to rising seas, droughts, and floods.

The remaining scientific uncertainties about climate change are, in fact, about the timing and magnitude of impacts, not whether climate change poses a serious threat. Yet, the arguments posed by the think tanks or their representatives try to convince people that there may be no threat at all from climate change. Even if one were to conclude that there is no absolute proof that the serious impacts from climate change will happen, there is no basis for saying that climate change does not pose an enormous threat to human health and the environment—and yet, this is the message put out by some of the think tanks.

As we have seen, most of these think tanks that have been working on climate change are funded largely by organizations having economic interests that might be harmed if governments act to require reductions in greenhouse gas emissions. For instance much of the funding for think tanks comes from fossil fuel interests. Still, these biases are not disclosed when climate change policy analyses are produced by these think tanks.

The role played by the think tanks on climate change has created serious problems for society. Not only is climate change likely to seriously harm human health and the environment in proportion to how long it takes to stabilize greenhouse gas emissions in the atmosphere at safe levels, but also the bogus science produced by the think tanks confuses those who need to act to eliminate the global warming threat.

Serious Harm to Environmental and Human Health

Climate change has already caused damage to some people in some places in the form of more intense and frequent storms, increased droughts and floods, rising seas, and increases in vector-borne disease. Deaths from heat stress are already being experienced by many around the world. The amount of these harms and damages is predicted to increase as the planet heats up in the years ahead. It is already too late to prevent additional warming caused by human activities because of thermal lags in the climate system and the long lead time needed to replace fossil fuel electricity and transportation systems that are pouring greenhouse gases into the atmosphere.

Additional warming will increase the suffering already being experienced because it is probably too late to prevent at least another 2 °C of warming even if a strong international plan to reduce the threat of global warming is implemented in the next few years. For this reason, the think tank projects have contributed to harm and damages from human-induced climate change and these are predicted to accelerate in the years ahead. Therefore, ideologically-based scientific arguments of the type produced by the think tanks are potent examples of how societies can be blinded to impending disasters despite accumulating evidence of the approaching threats.

Substantive and Procedural Injustice

The think tanks have usually insisted on very high levels of proof before action on climate change should be taken, despite strong evidence that climate change poses enormous risks to many around the world. Because the think tanks were often representing the interests of polluters and ignoring the interests of the potential victims of climate change, the think tank arguments have successfully shifted the burden of proof to victims of climate change without their consent. For this reason, the arguments being made by the think tanks raise serious problems of procedural justice. The think tanks have often focused their arguments on U.S. policy, but the harms from delay will be experienced by those outside the United States.

Problems with Cost-Benefit Analysis

Some of the think tank arguments against action on climate change have taken the form of cost-benefit analyses that have concluded that regulatory action to reduce greenhouse gas emissions would be too costly to the American economy. Yet, the use of cost-benefit analysis for this purpose ignores the following problems with cost-benefit analysis in this context:

The Failure to Deal with Distributive Effects of Climate Change

Normally, cost-benefit analyses do not consider how harm and benefits are distributed, that is, that some people will be greatly harmed and others may benefit. Many cost-benefit analyses aggregate harm and benefits even in cases where those causing the harm will enjoy benefits from non-action, and those who did nothing to create the harm will experience the greatest harms. This is so for climate change. The poor are experiencing the harms of not reducing the impact of climate change, while the costs that are expected to be borne to reduce greenhouse gases fall on those who have caused the problem. For this reason, the cost-benefit analyses used by some think tanks hide serious problems of distributive justice.

Problems with Discounting Future Benefits

Normally, cost-benefit analysis calculations are conducted by discounting benefits that will not be experienced until sometime in the future using prevailing discount rates. Under climate change, this approach has had the effect of making benefits from climate change policies that will be experienced, say, twenty years hence, virtually worthless at the time the analysis is performed. In this way, cost-benefit analysis ignores the rights of future generations not to be harmed. The arguments employed by the think tanks therefore not only fail to deal adequately with distributive justice issues among existing people around the world, but also for future generations.

Problems with Valuation of Environmental Entities

Cost-benefit analysis also usually transforms all values that people have about the natural world into dollar amounts, a process that transforms all things into commodities. Many believe that certain entities and places have values that cannot be measured in dollar amounts and, therefore, will be devalued by assigning market values to them in cost-benefit analyses. Because cost-benefit analysis assumes that environmental entities only have values assigned to them by the market, the use of cost-benefit can devalue the values some people hold about environmental entities. The reliance on cost-benefit analysis by the think tanks therefore understates the values that some people would place on entities that will be harmed by climate change. A good example of this is the value of human life because cost-benefit analyses often calculate the value of human life on the earning potential of an individual, which can lead to the perverse result that the lives of poor people are less valuable than those of the affluent.

Failure to Deal with Uncertainty of Costly-High Impacts

Cost-benefit analysis rarely deals adequately with impacts of human action that are highly uncertain. In the case of climate change, cost-benefit analysis has been used to argue against government action to reduce greenhouse gas emissions while ignoring more catastrophic impacts of climate change that were deemed plausible, although less certain. For instance, if the Greenland and Antarctic ice sheets melt—plausible, yet uncertain outcomes—then catastrophic harms could be experienced due to sea level rise of many meters. Yet, the cost-benefit analyses prepared for climate change have often ignored these kinds of uncertain impacts. For this reason, the value of the harms identified in cost-benefit analyses that have been relied upon by some of the think tanks greatly understates the magnitude of the harms that could result from continued release of greenhouse gas emissions.

Undermining Democratic Institutions

Some arguments made by some of the think tanks about climate change have so distorted mainstream scientific consensus views about climate change that they need to be seen as directly undermining democratic institutions. This is so because democratic governments are vulnerable to uninformed citizens on vital issues.

In addition, some of the arguments made by some think tanks have conflated uncertainty about impacts of climate change with uncertainty about whether there is any threat at all from global warming. Although scientific uncertainties about the impacts of climate change have existed and some remain, it is simply not true to say there is no evidence that climate change creates a significant threat to environmental and human health, or that human activities are responsible for at least some of the warming that Earth is experiencing.

For this reason, the think tanks' approach to climate change is a blatant example of how democratic institutions can be undermined by misinformation about approaching problems. Time and time again, associates of think tanks have appeared as witnesses in the U.S. Congress and given testimony that has left the impression there is no evidence that climate change is an enormous threat. For instance, Myron Ebell, director of energy and global warming policy at the Competitive Enterprise Institute, has testified before six Senate and House committees arguing that there was no scientific support for the conclusion that climate change is a crisis. (Competitive Enterprise Institute, 2007)

Recommended Solutions

To counteract the destructive effects of misinformation generated by ideologically biased think tanks, the following steps should be taken.

Establish New Norms about the Rhetoric of Scientific Uncertainty

Since much of the ideological misinformation about environmental threats is created because of the ease of injecting uncertainty about impacts into valid scientific information, scientific institutions need to create new norms about the use of arguments based upon scientific uncertainty. For instance, it should be established that it is ethically problematic to assert there is no evidence of harm from human activities on the basis that the harm has not been proven with high levels of statistical support when, in reality, credible evidence of threats exists.

Society needs to demand great clarity about the use of science-based arguments for public policy options, particularly in regard to questions about the adequacy of proof and with whom the burden of proof lies. To entrench such new norms for using science-based arguments, scientific organizations should encourage the integration of ethical considerations into science-based policy arguments.

Require Disclosure of Hidden Normative Assumptions in Policy Arguments

Scientific and economic arguments about public policy often are based upon controversial normative positions that are not disclosed. For instance, science-based arguments often rest on unstated assumptions about who should bear the burden of proof for proving harm, and what constitutes adequate proof to support government regulatory action. In a similar way, as noted above, economic arguments often contain hidden assumptions. These assumptions need to be identified by proponents of policy arguments so that they may be evaluated by policy-makers and the general public.

Economic Interests in Policy Research Need to Be Disclosed

Every time policy arguments are funded by organizations that either will financially benefit from certain approaches to environmental policy, or that are known to be opposed to regulatory action on ideological grounds, the nature of the interests should be revealed. This disclosure will inform those who may use this information by providing a context for determining whether the information is biased toward certain outcomes, or is designed to protect certain economic interests.

References

American Enterprise Institute (AEI) for Public Policy Research. http://www.aei.org/ default.asp?filter=all (3May 2007).

Brown, Donald. *American Heat: Ethical Problems with the United States Response to Global Warming.* Lanham MD: Rowman & Littlefield, 2002.

Center for Media and Democracy. "American Enterprise Institute." *Source Watch.* (2007a) http:// www.sourcewatch.org/index.php?title=American_Enterprise_Institute# Funding (3 May 2007).

———. "Brookings Institute." *Source Watch.* (2007c) http://www.sourcewatch.org/ index.php?title=Brookings_Institution#Funding (3 May 2007).

———. "Cato Institute." *Source Watch.* (2007c) http://www.sourcewatch.org/ index.php?title=Cato_Institute#Funding (3 May 2007).

———. "Heritage Foundation." *Source Watch.* (2007b) http://www.sourcewatch.org/ index.php?title=Heritage_Foundation#2004_Budget (3 May 2007).

———. "Think Tanks." *Source Watch.* (2007) http://www.sourcewatch.org/index.php? title= Think_tank (3 May 2007).

Competitive Enterprise Institute. "Myron Ebell." http://www.cei.org/dyn/ view_Expert.cfm?Expert=125 (11 Jun. 2007).

Covington, Sally. "How Conservative Philanthropies and Think Tanks Transform US Policy." *Covert Action Quarterly* (2007). http://mediafilter.org/CAQ/caq63/caq63thinktank.html (11 Jun. 2007).

Diamond, Jared. *Collapse, How Societies Choose To Fail or Succeed*. New York: Penguin Group, 2005.

Dolny, Michael. "The Think Tank Spectrum: For the Media, Some Thinkers Are More Equal Than Others." *FAIR (Fairness and Accuracy in Reporting)*. 2007. http://www.fair.org/index.php?page=1357 (11 June 2007).

———. "What's in a Label?: Right-Wing Think Tanks Are Often Quoted, Rarely Labeled." *FAIR (Fairness and Accuracy in Reporting)*. 2007. http://www.fair.org/index.php?page=1425 (11 Jun. 2007).

ExxonMobil. "Public Information and Policy Research." *ExxonMobil Annual Report*. http://www2.exxonmobil.com/files/corporate/public_policy1.pdf (3 May 2007).

Hays, Samuel P. *Explorations in Environmental History*. Pittsburgh: University of Pittsburgh Press, 1998.

Mooney, Chris. "Some Like it Hot: As the World Burns." *Mother Jones*. 2005. http://www.motherjones.com/news/feature/2005/05/some_like_it_hot.htm. (3 May 2007).

National Institute for Research Advancement (NIRA). "American Enterprise Institute." (2007b) *World Directory of Think Tanks*. http://www.nira.go.jp/ice/ nwdtt/2005/DAT/1355.html (3 May 2007).

———. "Brookings Institute." (2007a) *World Directory of Think Tanks*. http://www.nira.go.jp/ice/ nwdtt/2005/DAT/1364.html (3 May 2007).

———. "Cato Institute." (2007d) *World Directory of Think Tanks*. http://www.nira.go.jp/ice/nwdtt/2005/DAT/1370.html. (3 May 2007).

———. "Heritage Foundation." (2007c) *World Directory of Think Tanks*. http://www.nira.go.jp/ice/nwdtt/ 2005/DAT/1395.html (3 May 2007).

———. *NIRA's World Directory of Think Tanks*. http://www.nira.go.jp/ice/nwdtt/2005/index.html (11 Jun. 2007).

Oreskes, Naiomi. "The Scientific Consensus on Climate Change." *Science* 306, 5 Dec. 2004. http://www.sciencemag.org/cgi/reprint/306/5702/1686.pdf (3 May 2007).

Powell, Bonnie Azib. "Framing The Issues: UC Berkeley Professor George Lakoff Tells How Conservatives Use Language to Dominate Politics." *UC Berkeley News*. 2003. http://www.berkeley.edu/news/media/releases/2003/10/27_lakoff.shtml (11 Jun. 2007).

Rich, Andrew. "U.S. Think Tanks and the Intersection of Ideology, Advocacy, and Influence." *NIRA Review*. Winter: 54–59. http://www.nira.go.jp/publ/review/ 2001winter/rich.pdf (3 May 2007).

University of California, *Legacy Tobacco Library*. 1997. http://legacy.library.ucsf.edu (11 Jun. 2007).

Chapter 17

Cutting CO_2 Emissions in the Atmosphere: A Realistic Goal or a Mere Utopian Ideal?

Giulio De Leo, Ph.D. (Ecology)
Dept. of Environmental Science, University of Parma, Parma, Italy

Contact Information: Dipartimento di Scienze Ambientali
Università degli Studi di Parma,Viale Usberti 11/A, 43100 Parma ITALY
Phone: +39 0521 905 619; Fax: +39 0521 905 402; Email: giulio.deleo@unipr.it

Marino Gatto, Professor (Ecology)
Dept. of Electronic Engineering and Information Technology
Politecnico di Milano, Milan, Italy

Contact Information: Dipartimento di Elettronica e Informazione
Via Ponzio 34/5, 20131 Milano ITALY
Phone: +39 02 2399 3536; Fax: +39 02 2399 3412; Email: gatto@elet.polimi.it

Summary

The Russian ratification of the Kyoto Protocol in 2005 established a necessary step toward successful negotiations on greenhouse gas emissions and Global Climate Change (GCC). Yet, most industrialized countries are far behind in their Kyoto schedules and some have actually increased, rather than reduced, their carbon dioxide emissions in the 1997-2004 period.

With the increasing dependence of transportation and other sectors on fossil fuels in both industrialized and developing countries, and the impressive growth of population and consumption in China and India, stabilization of atmospheric CO_2 concentrations in the next fifty years seems utopian.

In this chapter, we discuss obstacles and barriers that still need to be overcome to reverse this pattern. We argue that the lack of effective policies to cope with climate change is strongly connected with the poor understanding of the direct and indirect impacts of GCC at the *local level*.

Local governments and people still do not feel the sense of urgency that drove the success of the Montreal Protocol for the elimination of chlorofluorocarbons (CFCs). As a consequence, there is a need to better identify and evaluate, in a risk assessment framework, the local environmental and socioeconomic effects of GCC, both in physical units of damage (including morbidity and mortality) and, whenever possible and meaningful, in monetary terms.

It is only by identifying and quantifying the hazards and risks that people and markets will actually experience at the local level that we will create the momentum to foster significant changes in consumption and production patterns.

257

The Pathway to Kyoto

The extended effort that brought the Kyoto Protocol into force in February 2005 started more than twenty years earlier, in 1979, when the World Climate Conference in Geneva put climate change at the center of the scientific agenda. In 1988, the World Meteorological Organization (WMO) and the United Nations Environment Programme (UNEP) established the Intergovernmental Panel on Climate Change (IPCC) to periodically review the work of thousands of independent climatologists and other scientists all over the world, to sketch scenarios of future emissions, to assess the potential consequences, and to evaluate the costs of adaptation and mitigation.

The United Nations Framework Convention on Climate Change (UNFCCC)—signed in Rio de Janeiro in 1992 by 172 countries including the United States, China, and India—has been in force since 1994, with the aim of stabilizing "greenhouse gas concentrations in the atmosphere at a level that would prevent dangerous anthropogenic interference with the climate system." Signing Parties agreed with the principle of sharing common, but flexible and differentiated responsibilities for CO_2 abatement. No quantitative goals or measurable commitments were included in the UNFCCC, but the Kyoto Protocol, signed in 1997, set mandatory goals for 2008-2012 of a 5 percent reduction of global greenhouse gas (GHG) emissions relative to 1990.

The Protocol would have entered into force ninety days after ratification by at least 55 Parties of the Framework Convention accounting for no less than 55 percent of the total 1990 carbon dioxide emissions of the Annex I Parties. While more than a hundred countries had already ratified Kyoto by the beginning of the new millennium, the 55-percent-emission threshold was hard to reach because the United States and Russia rejected the Protocol. Several Conferences of the Parties (COP) attempted to convince the United States—which accounts for 37 percent of global emissions with 5 percent of the world population—to sign the Protocol. Flexible mechanisms—namely, Emission Trading, Joint Implementation, and Clean Development Mechanisms—were developed to minimize the cost of GHG reductions. Even though the United States continues to resist Kyoto, Russia ratified the Protocol in November 2004, thanks to indefatigable European diplomacy. The treaty finally came into force as international law on February 16, 2005.

Meanwhile, in 2003, the European Union unilaterally promulgated EU Directive 87/2003 which implemented the CO_2 Emission Trade Market effective January 1, 2005. The goal of the EU directive is to achieve the EU's targeted 8 percent reduction of carbon dioxide emissions by steering the bulk of abatement activities toward those economic sectors where the marginal costs are lower. In March 2007, the European Commission decided to fully endorse the policy on climate change and to take the lead in the climate change global challenge. (European Commission, 2007) The carbon finance, inaugurated in 2000 by the World Bank with the Prototype Carbon Fund, is now very active, and offers several international and regional products and services. An increasing number of local administrations have launched programs to reduce their net contribution to CO_2 emissions. A new era in the battle to reduce GHGs in the atmosphere has begun.

The Other Side of the Coin: Going the Wrong Way

Despite the remarkable effort put into the Kyoto Protocol and the overwhelming scientific evidence of ongoing climate changes, the statistics on GHG global emissions are not encouraging. A substantial amount of carbon stored in fossil fuel over geological time has already been re-injected into the atmosphere in less than two centuries through combustion and land-use change, and this process is accelerating. The rate of increase has risen from 0.7 ppm/year in the middle of the past century, to about 1.4 ppm/year today. Carbon dioxide emissions have consequently more than doubled in the last forty years, and atmospheric concentrations have increased from a pre-industrial 280 ppm, to 380 ppm today, a level unprecedented in the last 450,000 years.

The majority of industrialized countries, those mainly responsible for historical anthropogenic emissions of GHGs, keep increasing their annual emissions despite their Kyoto commitments. The transportation sector is out of control, with a six-fold increase of CO_2 emissions in the last forty years. With no sign of slowing down, it is becoming the most important source of global emissions. Electricity consumption is also steadily rising and summer-peak demand will soon exceed winter peaks in most temperate-zone industrial countries because of the growing popularity of air conditioning.

Were this not enough, developing countries such as China, India, and Brazil are also now consuming impressive quantities of fossil fuel to support their growing economies. The potential magnitude of this phenomenon is dramatic. Consider only China as a representative transitional economy. First, the Chinese population, which is now around 1.2 billion, will reach its peak at more than 1.5 billion in thirty-five to forty years. To provide three hundred million more people with a basic energy supply of 0.81 Ton Oil Equivalents/*capita*/year, seven hundred million tons of additional CO_2 emissions will be released annually (over the present global emissions of about seven billion tons). Second, a large fraction of the Chinese population is expected to move from the countryside to urbanized areas in search of higher living standards and to provide labor for the growing economy. In 1998, rural domestic energy use was about 0.74 TOE/*capita*; forty to fifty years later, seven hundred million more urbanites will need about four times more energy to only reach the 1998 national average per capita energy consumption rate. Third, the anticipated increase in China's per capita income will result in a corresponding increase in per capita energy consumption, as increasing living standards inevitably translate into growing energy demand. Mean energy consumption in China, about 0.84 TOE/*capita* in 1998 (compared to the world average of 1.7 TOE/capita), is thus expected to increase in coming decades toward the 4.6 TOE/capita of OECD countries, and ultimately, the 8.1 TOE/capita of the United States of America.

As a consequence, while China's present per capita CO_2 emission level is only 2.3 tons—that is, 60 percent of the world average, and about 1/5 of OECD and 1/8 of ASA levels respectively—future total CO_2 emissions for 1.5 billion people are expected to catapult China toward the top of emitting countries. India and Brazil will likely follow a similar pattern.

In summary, if present trends hold, GHG emissions from industrialized and from developing countries are slated to continuously increase over the next fifty years. Even under a more optimistic scenario, it is hard to imagine that CO_2 concentrations in the atmosphere will not double before the end of this century.

Fast and Furious: Signs of a Changing Climate

While countries such as the United States are still debating whether to adopt mandatory reduction goals without embracing China and other transitional economies in the Kyoto Protocol, the world climate is showing the first clear signs of change driven by anthropogenic GHG emissions (for updates see the IPCC Working Group I Report "The Physical Science Basis" released in February, 2007).

Over the past one hundred years, the global average temperature has increased by approximately 0.7°C and is projected to rise rapidly to levels not experienced in the last two thousand years. In 2005, the world experienced its warmest known average temperature. The previous eight warmest years in the instrumental record (which dates from about 1860) have all occurred in the last fourteen years. A 0.7°C increase in average world temperature can imply much higher regional increases in maximum daily or monthly temperatures. During the summer of 2003, a record heat wave seared Europe, producing more than thirty thousand deaths, mostly among the elderly.

But, heat waves are not the only effect of a warmer world. Most of the qualitative conjectures made in the 1990s on the effects of increasing GHG concentrations are turning out to be true. For example, on a warmer planet, physical (meteo-climatic) processes are expected to occur more rapidly and more intensively than in the past. Thus, Milly et al. (2002) observed an increasing frequency of great floods in the last hundred years. Tropical sea surface temperature is also abnormally, and alarmingly, high—Kerry (2005) showed that sea surface temperature is correlated with the strength of tropical hurricanes. Almost unnoticed initially except by specialists, Kerry's paper gained prominence three weeks later when Katrina hit New Orleans with unprecedented force. And barely a week after Katrina, Webster et al. (2005) showed that the frequency of devastating hurricanes has significantly increased in the last three decades.

Evidence of climate change has also been recorded in temperate regions. The mean temperature of Southern Europe has significantly increased in the last fifty years; mean annual rainfall has decreased, while the frequency of short, intense rainfall events has gone up—it rains less, but more intensively. (Brunetti et al., 2006) The average cloud cover is also in decline, a sign of climate tropicalization. A negative balance between precipitation and snowmelt over the last twenty to fifty years is causing a dramatic shrinkage of glaciers in the Alps.

Effects on ecosystems of climate change have been also observed. Bayfield et al. (2005) reported an upward shift of European mountain vegetation of about 3-4 meters/decade as an adaptation to rising temperatures; Walther et al. (2002) observed a shift from indigenous-deciduous to exotic-evergreen broad-leaved vegetation in Southern Switzerland with a decrease of frost days during winter in the past century. In a meta-analysis of 143 studies covering 1,468 species from all over the world (ranging from mollusks to mammals and from grasses to trees), Root et al. (2003) found that "more than 80 percent of the species that show changes are shifting in the direction expected on the basis of known physiological constraints of species [to the adaptation to climate change]." They concluded that "the balance of evidence from these studies strongly suggests that a significant impact of global warming is already discernible in animal and plant populations."

Not Only Sea Level Rise: The Direct and Secondary Impacts of Climate Change

The effects of climate change may be classified into two categories: macroscopic direct impacts, and secondary, sometimes indirect—but no less remarkable—impacts. The first category includes sea level rise, heat waves, droughts, tropical hurricanes, and floods—all events that can have devastating effects, especially in developing countries. The second category is fuzzier and, until recently, had not attracted the attention of decision-makers and stakeholders, even though large sectors of civil society and the economies of industrialized countries will be affected (see Epstein and Mills, 2005).

We have analyzed potential local impacts of global climate change in Northern Italy in an integrated project supported by the regional government of Lombardy (Italy). Preliminary results show that heat waves—such as the heat wave in the summer of 2003 that caused more than seven thousand premature deaths among vulnerable groups in Italy alone—are likely to produce even more severe impacts in the future abetted by the progressive aging of the population.

Shorter winters in temperate areas can shorten the vegetative phase of allergenic grasses and plants, inducing early flowering and increasing the incidence of pollen allergies. Increasing CO$_2$ concentrations and rising temperatures may create favorable conditions for the growth and spread of potentially harmful moulds and fungi. For example, under heat stress, some soil microorganisms, such as *Aspergillus flavus* and *Aspergillus parasiticus*, produce carcinogenic mycotoxins that can enter the food chain and eventually affect human health. The high concentration of aflatoxins in grain and dairy products observed in the spring of 2004 in Italy was a consequence of a heat wave that struck the north of the country the previous summer.

The loss of precipitation associated with long periods of drought will reduce air quality in urban areas (such as the large Padana area in Northern Italy where more than fifteen million people live). Rain plays a crucial role in washing away the fine particulate matter (PM_{10} and $PM_{2.5}$) whose concentrations already often exceed the legal limits imposed by the European Union. Moreover, reduced cloud cover will accelerate the photochemical reactions that generate pollutants such as secondary PM_{10} and $PM_{2.5}$ and tropospheric ozone. The latter is a powerful oxidant that can produce respiratory diseases such asthma and bronchitis. The spread of diseases such as malaria and cholera, as a consequence of climate change, is still considered fairly unlikely in most European countries. However, the diffusion of vector-borne diseases, such as Lyme disease and some vector-borne forms of encephalitis, is already occurring in Italy, Switzerland, and Austria, partially because of more favorable environmental conditions for the propagation of animal hosts and their ticks. Similarly, increasing water temperatures in rivers and lakes will create environmental conditions more suitable for the growth and persistence of microorganisms, such as Salmonella and fecal coliforms, harmful to human health.

Climate change will affect many other sectors of civil society and markets in industrialized countries. Increasingly frequent droughts and heat waves will negatively affect agriculture, a particularly vulnerable sector that already requires intensive support by the European Union. Changing climate may foster the spread of agricultural pests. Harmful insects and plant diseases can usually be controlled by pesticides, but this damages soil and water quality, and has important secondary impacts on ecosystems and human health.

Drought will also increase the competition for water among the civil, industrial, and agricultural sectors—especially in late spring and early summer, when water demand in agriculture is greatest. Decreased flows in rivers and lower water levels in lakes will affect navigation. Moreover, water shortages may impair the cooling systems of thermal power plants, as Italy has already experienced during its hot summer of 2003. Lower mean rainfall and snow cover, that has plagued the alpine region in the past twenty years, not only drains the economy of winter tourism, but also reduces the generating capacity of the hydropower industry (which, in Northern Italy and Switzerland, supplies a large fraction of energy demand). New reservoirs to compensate for this loss are unlikely because of the paucity of suitable sites and the need to maintain minimum water flows in rivers and streams as stipulated by the EU Water Framework Directive (2000/60/EC).

Heat waves will exacerbate an ongoing problem—the rising summer energy demand for air conditioning. The heat wave that struck Italy in 2003-2004, generated a one-year 43 percent increase in the sale of domestic air conditioning systems. In order to avoid power failures resulting from systems overload—as experienced in Italy in June 2003, resulting in €400 million's worth of damage to the power generating systems—it will be necessary to increase energy production capacity. If we do not invest in renewable energy and in energy efficiency, the only way to meet anticipated demand will be by using fossil fuels. Regrettably, even the most efficient combined-cycle, gas-turbine power plants, and the more carbon-intensive coal power plants will increase CO_2 emissions, flying in the face of Kyoto goals.[1]

An increase in extreme rainfall events will result in larger floods, such as the one that struck central Europe in 2002, causing €13 billion in damage. Melting permafrost in the mountain regions of central Europe will increase the risk of landslides. More severe droughts will increase the risk of fires in woodland areas. The increase in such catastrophic events will clearly affect the insurance sector and impose extra costs on businesses, directly or indirectly affected by weather conditions and climate change.

But Why Don't We Do More?

Given this potentially tragic picture, it is imperative to ask why industrialized countries do not do more to reduce CO_2 emissions. The reasons are manifold and we cannot review them all here. There is one case in which the international community has proved to be very effective in solving a global problem—the banning of ozone depleting substances (ODSs), particularly CFCs, under the 1987 Montreal Protocol. Of course, the "ozone hole" problem was easier to resolve than climate change: there was a near monopoly in CFC production and, in most applications, end users did not manipulate the substances themselves. Indeed, in many cases, such as refrigeration, consumers did not even know which kind of ODSs were used in their appliances. These factors made the transition toward relatively non-depleting substances much easier. Most importantly, the connection between the use of CFCs and their ultimate effects (e.g., increased skin cancers through ozone depletion) were becoming well known, regardless of people's education or social status. The message was clear: "the use of ODSs is harmful to your health as it can cause skin cancer." Thus, supported by strong public pressure, the development of alternative technologies and good practices evolved more quickly than expected. Consumer behavior changed rapidly, international cooperation was effective, national governments endorsed investments in research and development of alternatives, and financial incentives at the international, regional, and local levels were developed to accelerate the rapid reduction of ODSs.

Such a powerful combination of motivating factors is lacking in the battle against climate change and helps to explain the apparent incapacity of governments to promote the transition to a carbon-free society. This is particularly regrettable because alternative energy strategies and technologies are already available on both the production and demand sides. (Pacala and Soclow, 2004) Missing are a general commitment by industry, government, and consumers, and the policies necessary to overcome the conceptual, technological, and financial barriers that prevent their market penetration.

In the last twenty years, we have faced four problems that have combined to prevent significant mitigating action toward climate change. First, the high level of uncertainty that characterizes climate science and the confusing complexity of positive and negative feedbacks that help to (self-) regulate the biosphere have often been invoked as an excuse for postponing action. Until recently, the public—confused by fuzzy and sometimes purposefully deceptive information disseminated through the media and by oil and gas lobbies (UCS, 2007)—believed that even the scientific community was uncertain about the existence of the problem, to say nothing of its magnitude.

Second, many people believed that the effects of climate change (if any) would become evident only after centuries, because it was proving difficult to identify clear trends in the considerable natural variability (noise) of global climate patterns. Consequently, even with current, relatively low discount rates, observers have perceived the value of future costs of climate change and future benefits of greener scenarios to be relatively low. This favored "business-as-usual" policies—the priority was (and still is) on other, seemingly more pressing economic and social issues (labor costs, market globalization, unemployment, and the like).

Third, when significant signs of climate change actually became apparent, characterizing the problem mainly as "global warming" (the increase in mean global temperature) tended to mask its true nature and magnitude. While scientifically significant, the 0.7°C increase in mean global temperature observed over the past one hundred years means nothing to the average observer: people, including decision-makers, experience much wilder temperature variations—often in the tens of degrees—on a seasonal, monthly, weekly and, sometimes, daily basis. In short, ordinary citizens and politicians alike have been slow to perceive the relatively smooth increase in annual temperature in recent decades as a problem, and the multiple other dimensions of climate change have largely been ignored.

Last, but not least, even as the focus of concern has expanded, it has concentrated mainly on such direct, macroscopic impacts of climate change as sea-level rise, tropical hurricanes, and extended droughts. Unfortunately, these problems are still considered mainly, if not exclusively, to affect developing countries. Moreover, many analysts believe that, unlike the Developing World, the industrialized countries have the scientific knowledge, technological expertise, and economic resources to effectively adapt to climate change. Thus, until recently, the inhabitants of high-income countries have tended to perceive climate change as a problem mainly for Africa (because of drought), for the Caribbean islands (because of hurricanes), and for developing countries such as Bangladesh (because of floods attributable to sea-level rise).

For all these reasons, global climate change has generally remained a low political priority in the industrialized world.

Facing the Challenge: Adaptation vs. Mitigation

Even without reference to the ethical implications of ignoring the consequences of climate change in developing countries, we assert that to rely exclusively on adaptive measures is a failing strategy for industrialized countries. Consider the following reasons: first, climate change may trigger social instability in developing countries, resulting in mass migrations that will inevitably affect industrialized countries (see Norman Myers' 1993 visionary paper "Environmental Refugees in a Globally Warmed World"). Second, hurricane Katrina made it clear that even America is not invulnerable to extreme events. The material damage caused by the storm was extensive—US$10 billion were spent during the first days of the emergency, and Congress subsequently allocated $50 billion more for the reconstruction of the city; businesses were closed for months or years, and there were more than a thousand deaths. It goes without saying that both the financial and social costs weighed most heavily on the poorest and most vulnerable of the city's population. Third, a global-warming induced interruption of the North Atlantic Gulf Stream—while likely decades into the future—would (ironically) expose Northern Europe to winters several degrees Celsius cooler than at present, and possibly as cold as those experienced at similar latitudes in Canada. (Huybrechts and De Wolde, 1999) There would simply be no technological alternative to the warming effect provided by the Gulf Stream, should this disaster scenario come to pass. In short, adaptation alone can no longer be considered a viable option—adaptation may be a necessity, but it is not a sufficient strategy.

There are additional reasons to make mitigation of GHG emissions a higher priority.

First, the direct effects of extreme events are only one side of the problem. As implied above, the secondary impacts of climate change will affect large sectors of the economy, as well as of civil society in industrialized countries. Only rapid action to reduce GHG emissions can avert the worst of these potentially destabilizing effects.

Second, renewable-energy technologies will not only lower GHG emissions, but also significantly reduce local pollution, and therefore provide significant human health benefits. We have demonstrated elsewhere that the health benefits to Italy of respecting the Kyoto Protocol more than compensate the small increase in the cost of electrical energy production. (De Leo et al., 2001) Indeed, the local environmental externalities of air pollution are so great that a greener energy system would be beneficial even in the absence of global change.

Last, but not least, there are many energy conservation strategies and ways to promote energy efficiency that have negligible marginal costs and offer greater savings. Consequently, they guarantee a net economic gain, with reasonable payback times, so that the benefits not only improve the environment, but also enhance the purchasing power of families.

Risk Perception: Closing the Gap between Knowledge and Action

We must all face the challenge of drastically reducing GHG emissions. In order to change consumers' habits, we need to connect individual choices at the local level with their global climate consequences, and the impact of these changes back at the local level.

At the same time, we must advocate for more effective and daring policies from state governments and local administrations. When people and decision-makers finally understand that climate change is costly and will negatively affect their own lives, when they acquire the same sense of urgency that led to the success of the Montreal Protocol, then society will find the economic and intellectual resources to significantly reduce GHG emissions.

In some cases, regional and local authorities are acting despite the resistance or indolence of central governments. For instance, in the United States, at least ten States—including California and ten major cities from San Francisco to Salt Lake City, in addition to hundreds of other towns—have already committed to strict GHG emissions abatement goals. In 2005 in Montreal, at the eleventh session of the Conference of the Parties, India, China, and Brazil agreed to join a working group to discuss reduction goals and mitigation policies for post-Kyoto, 2012-2020. While encouraging, this is not enough. The future outlook is still very grim.

We now depend on the work of thousands of independent climate scientists and on the tireless efforts of NGOs to make people and decision-makers aware of the problem, and of the consequences of inaction. It is only through their work and the positive examples of a growing number of far-sighted local administrations that we still have a chance of mitigating serious climate change.

Acknowledgments

The authors address their many thanks to Mita Lapi for her valuable suggestions on a first draft of the paper, and to *Regione Lombardia*, *ARPA Lombardia* and *Fondazione lombardia per l'Ambiente* for partially supporting our research under the Project "KyotoLombardia." The present work has been partially developed within the Interlink project #II04CE49G8 supported by the Italian Minister of Research.

Note

1.   At present, nuclear power generation is not considered a viable carbon-free option in the European Union, because of well-known (and mostly unresolved) problems of social acceptability, terrorism and sabotage risks, unconventional weapons proliferation, decommissioning costs, nuclear waste disposal, long-term availability of uranium, and risk of large-scale, long-lasting damage in the case of environmental contamination. Measures to safely cope with these problems increase dramatically the costs of nuclear energy production, well above those of other alternative sources of energy production.

References

Bayfield, Neil G., Rob Brooker, and Linda Turner. "Some Lessons from the ECN, GLORIA and SCANNET Networks for International Environmental Monitoring." Pp. 213–22 in *Mountains of Northern Europe: Conservation, Management, People and Nature*, edited by Des B. A. Thompson, Martin F. Price, and Colin A. Galbraith. Edinburgh: The Stationery Office, 2005.

Brunetti, Michele, Maurizio Maugeri, Fabio Monti, and Teresa Nanni. "Temperature and Precipitation Variability in Italy in the Last Two Centuries from Homogenised Instrumental Time Series." *Int. J. Climatol.* 26 (2006): 345–81.

De Leo, Giulio A., Luca Rizzi, Andrea Caizzi, and Marino Gatto. "The Economic Benefit of Kyoto Protocol." *Nature* 413 (2001): 478–79.

Epstein, Paul R., and Evan Mills. "Climate Change Futures: Health, Ecological and Economic Dimensions." *The Center for Help and Global Environment.* Harvard Medical School, November 2005.

European Commission. "Limiting Global Climate Change to 2 degrees Celsius: The way ahead for 2020 and beyond." Communication from the Commission to the Council, the European Parliament, the European Economic and Social Committee and the Committee of the Regions. 2007. http://europa.eu/press_room/presspacks/energy/comm2007_02_en.pdf (4 Jun. 2007).

Huybrechts, Philippe I., and Jan R. De Wolde. "The Dynamic Response of the Greenland and Antartic Ice Sheets to Multiple-Century Climate Warming." *Journal of Climate* 12 (1999): 2169–88.

IPCC. "Climate Change 2007: The Physical Science Basis." Contribution of Working Group I to the Fourth Assessment Report of the Intergovernmental Panel on Climate Change. Cambridge: Cambridge University Press, 2007. Also available at: http://www.ipcc.ch/SPM2feb07.pdf (4 Jun. 2007).

Kerry, Emanuel. "Increasing Destructiveness of Tropical Cyclones over the Past 30 Years." *Nature* 436 (4 Aug. 2005): 686–88.

Milly, P. Christopher D., Richard T. Wetherald, K. A. Dunne, and Thomas L. Delworth. "Increasing Risk of Great Floods in a Changing Climate." *Nature* 415 (2002): 514–17.

Myers, Norman. "Environmental Refugees in a Globally Warmed World." *Bioscience* 43 (1993): 752–61.

Pacala, Steve, and Robert Soclow. "Stabilization Wedges: Solving the Climate Problem for the Next 50 Years with Current Technologies." *Science* 305 (2004): 968–72.

Root, Terry L., Jeff T. Price, Kimberly R. Hall, Stephen H. Schneider, Cynthia Rosenzweig, and J. Alan Pounds. "Fingerprints of Global Warming on Wild Animal and Plants." *Nature* 421 (2003): 57–60.

UCS. "Smoke, Mirrors & Hot Air." Union of Concerned Scientists. 2007. http://www.ucsusa.org/assets/documents/global_warming/exxon_report.pdf (23 May 2007).

Webster, Peter J., Greg J. Holland, Judith. A. Curry, and H.-R. Chang. "Changes in Tropical Cyclone Number, Duration, and Intensity in a Warming Environment." *Science* 309 (Sept. 2005): 1844–46, 16.

Chapter 18

Ecological Governance at Work: A Community Challenge to Genetically Modified Organisms

Prue E. Taylor, Master of Laws (Environmental and Energy Law)

School of Architecture and Planning,
University of Auckland
Deputy Director, New Zealand Centre for
Environmental Law, Auckland, New Zealand

Contact Information: *Building 421, 26 Symonds Street, Auckland NEW ZEALAND*
Phone: +64 9 373 7599; Fax: +64 9 373 7652; Email: prue.taylor@auckland.ac.nz

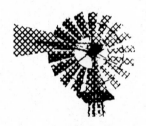

Summary

Around the world, nation-states are putting in place legal procedures in response to the perceived risks and benefits of commercially released genetically modified organisms (GMOs). In many instances, these formal procedures are devised and implemented with limited input or support from the local communities that stand to be most affected by them.

In this chapter, we examine how new forms of ecological governance can empower local communities to seriously challenge the established policies of central government in the interests of protecting the local environment and public health.

The particular example, chosen as the focus of this chapter, is the challenge mounted by a community in the Northland region of New Zealand. This community is using new legislation that gives local government the primary role of promoting sustainable development to confront and test the pro-biotechnology policies and national regulatory procedures of the New Zealand Government.

Ecological governance developments in New Zealand are consistent with international trends. The growing role and competence of localities and regions to implement sustainable development is beginning to test traditional understandings of the role and democratic mandate of the state through its central (i.e., federal or national) governments.

Introduction

The New Zealand Government has claimed exclusive authority to regulate the release of genetically modified organisms (GMOs) since 1996.[1] However, a group of local government authorities in New Zealand has recently begun to challenge this exercise of authority, within its own jurisdiction. The particular focus of this chapter is on the emerging governance role of subnational (or, local government) authorities, and the communities they represent, in responding to a key sustainability issues: the commercial release of GMOs.

While such community-lead governance responses are consistent with theories of strong local democracy and public participation in the path toward sustainable development, as will be demonstrated, the strengthening governance role of subnational government potentially challenges traditional central state authority.

This calls into question how the central government will respond. Will it adjust its understanding of governance to take into account and accommodate local views and interests, or will its formulation of national interests continue to dominate?

This chapter demonstrates that, by virtue of a convergence of factors (scientific, legal, and ethical awareness), local communities in New Zealand (NZ) are beginning to exercise a set of legal competencies to assert their view of what does and does not constitute sustainable land use. In doing so, these communities are acting consistently with evolving theories of ecological governance, which argue that the challenges of sustainable development are best met by moving from traditional top-down policy and decision-making processes, to also incorporate bottom-up processes.

This reflects the view that the people most affected by the outcome of decisions are best placed to make them by virtue of their proximity and understanding of the local environment, culture, economy, and society. (Agenda 21, Ch. 28)

In NZ, a policy of devolution of authority to the subnational level has supported this theory. However, the ultimate test for these new processes of decision-making is what happens if the exercise of local decision-making (in the form of lawful regulation) is directly contrary to the expressed views of the central (or, national) government.

New Zealand local government authorities are not alone in their efforts to regulate GMOs, independently of central government entities. Similar efforts are being made, around the world, but within different jurisdictional structures. In Australia, the United States of America, and within the European Union, there are growing signs of tensions between supranational, national, and subnational levels of government.

While these tensions may or may not be difficult to resolve, depending, in part, on the constitutional position of subnational government, coordination between different levels of government will become critical.

An Overview: Where Do Things Currently Stand?

The New Zealand Government (central government) claims exclusive authority to regulate the release of GMOs. It does so via the Environmental Risk Management Authority (ERMA) and the Hazardous Substances and New Organisms Act (HASNO).[2] This regime was established in 1996, and it requires an applicant to secure the prior approval of ERMA for the importation, development, field testing, and release of GMOs. The methods and criteria to be applied are detailed and complex; in essence, ERMA must evaluate the risks, costs, and benefits. The overriding purpose of this regime is to protect the environment, health and safety of people and communities by preventing or managing the adverse effects of GMOs (sections 4-6).

Central government views the HASNO regime as being consistent with its overall policy approach; to "proceed with caution." This presumes that conventional and GMO crops (for example) can coexist without damaging the nation's "clean green" image. Not all would agree that this is possible. However, local government is not directly challenging this policy, but rather its particular application within their own jurisdictions.

Central government draws political legitimacy for its approach from the outcomes of a Royal Commission of Inquiry (the Commission), which undertook nation-wide consultation to determine the views of New Zealanders on genetic modification. Its report concluded that there were grave risks associated with GMOs, but that the nation's economic future may very well depend upon agricultural innovation offered by biotechnology. (Commission Report, 2001: 2-3)[3] Once some of the recommendations of the Commission where in place, central government lifted the moratorium on GMOs that had been in place between 2001 to 2003.[4]

Central government is proud of its regime. It sees it as robust (providing adequate protection) and politically legitimate, while at the same time being sufficiently welcoming to investment from the biotechnology industry. This investment is considered vital for NZ's agricultural sector to remain internationally competitive.

A cornerstone of central government's policy approach, both domestically and internationally, is the rejection of a comprehensive liability regime. There is no liability under HASNO for damage arising as a result of an activity carried out in accordance with an ERMA approval (section 124 G). Consequently, innocent parties must bear the cost of losses arising from unexpected events or ineffective regulation. Internationally, NZ officials have been actively blocking progress toward adoption of a liability regime under the Cartagena Protocol. (Sustainability Council, 2006) In support of its policy and law, central government has developed extensive financial investment strategies. It is the nation's largest investor in outdoor GMO research. (Terry, 2005: ii)

Despite all this enthusiasm, there remains much political and public sensitivity about the release of GMOs. Notably, ERMA has authorized a number of field-trials, but has not yet received an application for release out of containment. This may indicate that GMO proponents sense that the time is not yet ripe for an application.

It is against this background that local government authorities have taken various initiatives. Several authorities have declared a "GE Free" status for their territories. These are largely symbolic and of no legal force. However, these declarations must be seen in light of New Zealand's history of attaining Nuclear Free status in the 1980s. Local authorities have also, via their national association—Local Government New Zealand (LGNZ), [5] made various submissions for amendments to HASNO that would clarify the potential liability and the role of local government, and strengthen their rights of participation in decision-making. (LGNZ Submission, 2003: 8) With the exception of a small amendment to strengthen notification requirements under HASNO, central government has remained unresponsive to the concerns of local government (section 53[4]).

The most interesting initiative, however, is being undertaken by a group of six local government authorities from the northern region of NZ.[6] It is one of the poorest regions of the nation, but one with an active agricultural (including horticulture) economy. It is also geographically distinct, comprising all the land north of NZ's largest urban centre, Auckland. For financial reasons, and also in the interests of achieving more effective regulation, the Northland local authorities have been proceeding on a coordinated regional basis to pursue what has been termed "community management of GMOs." (Grundy, 2005)

"Community management of GMOs" involves using legal competencies, contained in legislation designed to devolve power down to local government, to implement their own regulatory regime for GMOs. This would, for example, sanction land-use controls that *prohibit, or impose further controls upon,* a GMO release that already has the prior approval of ERMA. This possibility puts them on a direct collision course with central government. The official central government view is that HASNO is a national regime that gives ERMA exclusive decision-making authority, backed by all the necessary skills and resources. Local authorities therefore have no authority and no need to pursue their own regulation. Furthermore, it is said that a "dual" permitting regime (operating at national and subnational levels) would be a retrograde step imposing additional compliance and enforcement costs for all parties.[7]

The development of an independent permitting regime is the primary focus of the Northland local authorities. However, they have also considered an alternative proposal that would see the introduction of a "joint" or "integrated" permitting regime. This would require substantial amendment of HASNO, and, thus far, central government has refused to consider any substantial sharing of authority. (Terry, 2004: 33-36) For this reason, the primary focus is now upon an independent regulatory regime. (Terry, 2005: 34-40)

As noted earlier, investigation of options to achieve "community management of GMOs" is currently being spearheaded by six Northern local government authorities. The law requires extensive community consultation and policy evaluation before they can amend their various planning instruments to give effect to any new regulations. (Resource Management Act 1991, section 32 and Schedule 1) They are about to embark on both of these processes. (Grundy, 2005) In the interim, other local authorities in the country have expressed interest and are watching to see how the communities in the North progress.

Local government has been signaling discontent with the lack of authority to allow or disallow GMO land uses in their territories since 2003. So far, central government has not acted to either preempt or to accommodate local authorities. The initial response was one of skepticism that local authorities had the legal authority they claimed. This gave way to reluctant acknowledgment that they might have legal authority, but that they ought not to exercise it because of difficulties inherent in justifying regulation; and then, implementing it would expose authorities to unnecessary legal liability and significant compliance and enforcement costs. However, the most unfortunate public comment came from the Minister for the Environment in 2004, suggesting that separate regulation would expose local government to expensive legal battles. This was interpreted as a "threat" made by central government, an intent that was later denied by the Minister.[8]

Why Now? The Convergence of Catalysts for Change

NZ has had its national GMO regime in place since 1996. In this section, we consider the convergence of three interrelated and simultaneous factors that, it is contended, are the source of local government motivation to begin to exercise ecological governance since 2003. For the purposes of this chapter, ecological governance is defined as including the following four features:

- Reflects a local community mandate (exercised via democratic structures; e.g., elected local government officials);
- Is regulatory in nature;
- Reflects a local response to a national sustainability issue; and
- Reflects a variety of values.

Power of Pending Doom

There is nothing like urgency to focus the mind and energy. This urgent need has arisen from a number of events.

First, even though HASNO was enacted in 1996, the GMO issue did not begin to gain significant public and political attention until 1999. Central government responded to public calls for debate by appointing a Royal Commission of Inquiry and agreeing to a moratorium, until the inquiry was complete. This Commission consulted nationwide. It identified considerable public concern, in response to a variety of significant risks posed by genetic engineering. It did not, however, recommend continuing the moratorium. Rather, it took a more accommodating approach and recommended that the moratorium be lifted only once a number of improvements to the preexisting law, and its administration, were made. The moratorium was finally lifted in 2003, removing a significant impediment to the commercial release of GMOs. (Commission Report, 2001)

Second, while a number of improvements were made to ERMA and HASNO as a result of the Commission's recommendations, a significant amount of disquiet remained on key issues such as liability for harm. As previously noted, HASNO has a very limited liability regime. This leaves those suffering harm, including economic loss, at the mercy of the considerable weaknesses of common law remedies. Many, including the Commission and the NZ Law Commission, have noted that common law remedies are inadequate to handle the complexities of harm caused by GMO contamination. (Commission Report, 2001: Ch. 12:311-329 and Law Commission, 2002: 16-24) This has led to calls, from local government representatives (and others), for a strict liability regime. (LGNZ Submission, 2003) Compounding this situation is the general state of uncertainty over the potential financial liability of local government for contamination that might occur within their jurisdictions. They are particularly concerned about liability for environmental cleanup costs, and have received no assurances from central government that these costs would not be imposed upon their communities. (Terry, 2005: 34-40)

Third, there have been a growing number of scandals involving the illegal and/or accidental release of GMOs into the environment. At least one such release occurred in the Northland region, during which there was secrecy and little communication between the central government ministry conducting the cleanup and the Northland local authorities.[9] This exacerbated preexisting concerns. In addition, in 2002, a major national political scandal, termed "corngate" erupted during national elections. Again, concerns about a central government coverup of contamination served to feed public concern. (Hager, 2002) More generally, there is growing media coverage, and, therefore, public awareness, of the economic risks associated with GMOs, particularly in light of European and Japanese consumer rejection of GMO food products. Both are important NZ markets. Adding to this assessment of risks has been emerging evidence of human health risks associated with GMO products and growing suspicion concerning the possible irreversible environmental risks. (Terry, 2005)

Emerging Ecological Awareness

Communities are developing a much more sophisticated and well articulated awareness of the multitude of risks associated with GMOs. Reports written for the Northern local authorities, as part of investigation into regulatory options, identified three broad areas of community concern. (Terry, 2004 and 2005) The interesting feature of these concerns is that they demonstrate a range of values, both anthropocentric and ecocentric in nature. Furthermore, thus far the concerns have not been prioritized in any way, demonstrating that they are all of equal importance. This can be attributed to the fact that NZ's environmental legislation specifically encourages and legitimizes a wide array of community values in respect of the environment; socioeconomic, cultural and spiritual, health and safety. Humans are also treated as an integral part of ecosystems. (Resource Management Act 1991, Part II and Nolan, 2005) The three areas of community concern are summarized as follows:

Economic Risk

One of the main concerns is that the cultivation of GM crops will cause trace contamination of non-GM crops. There is considerable uncertainty about how the crops can be successfully kept apart. Harvesting, transport, and processing have also been demonstrated to pose contamination problems. Economic damage can arise from market rejection of a crop from trace GM contamination, or concern about the inability to separate GM and non-GM crops. Markets may also reject a whole range of agricultural products from a GE producing region owing to a perception that a GM crop has caused general contamination.

Environmental Risk

Scientific research into the environmental effects of GM crops is still at an early stage, as these studies require relatively long timeframes. At the basis of environmental risk is the fact that GMOs are living organisms, once released into the environment they can reproduce, change, and spread in ways that cannot be anticipated. Some of the main types of environmental risk include: effects on non-target species, increased persistence, invasiveness and competitiveness with existing native or exotic plants (biodiversity concerns), and impacts on soil ecosystems.

Social and Cultural Risks

GMOs are the result of technology that allows humanity to manipulate nature for its own benefit and according to its own whim. For many New Zealanders, this is deeply inappropriate, unethical, and a spiritually offensive behavior. While other societies may share similar ethical views, these views are particularly strongly articulated in NZ, and have a history of political and legal recognition, despite the secular nature of NZ society.

The Commission was influential in acknowledging and legitimating the importance of social and cultural risks associated with GMOs in NZ. As a consequence, it recommended the establishment of a Bioethics Council (Toi Te Taiao) to ensure that cultural, spiritual, and ethical considerations are not overlooked in making decisions on all new forms of biotechnology. This Council was established in 2002, with the stated goal of "enhancing New Zealand's understanding of the cultural, ethical and spiritual aspects of biotechnology and to ensure that the use of biotechnology has regard for the values held by New Zealanders." (Terms of Reference, 2002)

While the existence of the Bioethics Council is important, of much greater importance is the influence of, and respect for, the Maori (indigenous) culture. The cultural effects of GMOs on Maori are of particular concern. For example, according to the Maori worldview, genetic modification risks interfering with the sanctity of life and the spirit of all living things, of which humanity is an integral part. Maori are responsible for protecting the integrity of nature (as guardians), and a failure to do so could result in harm. Further, Maori place great emphasis on the need for community participation in respect of decisions that have a potential impact upon communities. In the Northland region of NZ, around 47 percent of the population is Maori. (Terry, 2005: 27-30)

The above paragraphs summarize the primary concerns that the Northland communities have about the release of GMOs in their jurisdictions. In the next section of this chapter, we demonstrate how new and preexisting legislative frameworks for ecological governance have been instrumental in giving legal recognition to diverse values, and continuing community concern.

Legal Structures for Ecological Governance

Until recently, discussions about governance, in relation to the powers of central and local government, have been fairly mundane. NZ is not a federal state and has a long history of "centralization." As a result, local governments have been treated as subservient to central government; responsible for "rates, roads, and rats." This very hierarchical relationship has been undergoing change since the 1990s, when local government was given primary responsibility for implementing resource management law. However, the most important change occurred in 2002, with the introduction of the Local Government Act 2002 (LGA). It gave local government significant new powers and purposes.

Under the LGA, the new purpose of local government is to promote sustainable development. This is described as "the social, economic, environmental, and cultural well-being of communities, in the present and for the future." (Section 10) There are, we know, many differing interpretations of sustainable development. However, irrespective of whether one chooses a "strong" or "weak" definition, fundamental value judgments are involved concerning the relationship between humanity and nature. (Bosselmann, 2002) The broad language of Section 10 enables local authorities and their communities to make value judgments about what will, or will not, promote the sustainable development of land (public and private) within their jurisdictions.

One of the most important processes for identifying and implementing the "value choices" of the community is via the transparent and broadly participatory task of creating long-term planning documents (called Long-Term Council Community Plans). Specifically, communities are to use these plans to identify the issues and outcomes they see as important to the "current or future social, economic, environmental or cultural well-being of the community." (Sections 91 and 93) Briefly, these plans are important statements of what sustainable development means in specific communities, and they bind their local government authorities by the requirement that they act consistently with plan content. (Sections 92 and 97)

Communities in the Northland region have been active in using the LGA planning process to articulate their views. As a result, a number contain statements, of which the following is representative: "Council will adopt a precautionary approach to the management of biotechnology in general and to GMO land-uses in particular. It will continue to investigate ways to maintain the district's environment free of GMOs until outstanding issues such as liability, economic costs and benefits, environmental risks, and cultural effects are resolved." (Whangarei District Council, 2004) In short, the LGA makes local authorities a strong (and democratically elected) voice for the will of communities, and the central public entity for giving effect to this will.

The other piece of relevant legislation is the Resource Management Act 1991 (RMA). Under this Act, local government has the responsibility to promote the "sustainable management of natural and physical resources," which includes the control of land use. "Sustainable management" is defined as providing for social, economic, and cultural well-being, in addition to health and safety, while safeguarding ecosystems for future generations. (Section 5[2]) Under this legislation the people of a district may decide that to:

> sustain the principle uses of rural land in the district depends on avoiding or managing environmental risks associated with GMO activities. This may be considered in order to promote a number of values within the purpose provisions of the statute, ranging from social-economic, cultural, health and safety values to concerns about the biophysical environment, for example, biodiversity. (Somerville, 2004: 10)

The legal argument is that the RMA gives local authorities (via submissions from their communities) the legal competence to create exclusion or control zones for GMOs, through district and regional plans. (Somerville, 2004) Some authorities have already received public submissions to this effect.

The combined affect of the LGA and RMA is to give communities, via their local government authorities, the legal means to decide that commercial release of GMOs is inconsistent with their view of sustainable development, and to create the necessary legal regulation to give effect to this decision.

The fundamental problem is that this legal expression of community governance is not recognized by central government. HASNO provides no legal obligation for ERMA to take them into account. ERMA has a wide discretion over the matters it should consider or take into account. It should notify local authorities of applications that it considers might be of interest, but it is under no legal duty to treat local government submissions any differently from other public submissions.[10] Therefore:

> [t]he absence of provisions that compel ERMA to accommodate the positions

of communities thus leaves local government unable to give surety to their communities that HASNO decisions will not override outcomes they have determined they wish to see [in their districts]. (Terry, 2004: 14)

Resolution? Accommodating Community Expression of Values

The preceding sections demonstrate that central government has encouraged bottom-up expressions of ecological governance, via the LGA and RMA. However, there is obviously a limit to which district and regional differences will be tolerated. They may not, it seems, conflict with central government's evaluation of what is in the national interest. Without a doubt, central government is demonstrating a wish to maintain control over this economically significant issue. (Ministry for the Environment, 2003)

What to do? As previously noted, the response of central government has, thus far, been mixed, ranging from threatening tactics, to a refusal to adopt more collaborative decision-making processes. Despite these setbacks, local government is steadily working toward putting in place a regulatory framework that would prohibit, or significantly control, the release of GMOs in their territories. No one is benefiting from this situation, least of all local communities who are currently financing (from local taxes) the considerable costs associated with public consultation and expert opinions. If land use plans are amended to create GMO regimes, further costs will be incurred to implement, monitor, and enforce them. From the perspective of the biotechnology industry, remaining doubt about the extent of regulation in NZ may be inhibiting applications for release.

The current positions of national and subnational governments need not remain on a collision course. Rather it is suggested that an important opportunity now exists for the relationship between national and subnational governments to mature, in the interests of achieving sustainable development. In particular, the present situation offers an opportunity for central government to go beyond its standard rhetoric of "partnership" with local government. (Programme of Action, 2003) As sustainable development issues become more complex, involving both local and national interests, bottom-up and top-down decision-making processes will have to become better coordinated and integrated. To achieve this, central government will need to show a genuine respect for and willingness to engage and empower local government, in a way that does not separate, but rather seeks to "share" legal competencies.

One way of achieving this is to create a "joint" or "integrated" regulatory regime. As previously noted, central government has shown little enthusiasm for this kind of initiative. It would require significant (and therefore expensive) amendment of HASNO. A more simple option would be amendment of HASNO to clarify the relationship between ERMA approvals and community regulation. This could be achieved by making ERMA approvals a minimum standard, enabling community regulation (where it exists) to impose higher standards. There is already precedent for this kind of approach in the context of national and regional environmental standards for issues such as water and air quality. (RMA, section 43B) This approach would enable districts and regions to decide for themselves whether or not they would wish to deviate from central government's view of the national interest.

This solution is consistent with central government policy, which presumes that conventional and GE crops can coexist. That is, GMOs can be freely grown and risks of contamination can be fully managed. Not all would agree that this is possible, or that the nation's "clean green image" would not be damaged by this approach. However, the only way to reverse this policy is for GMO-free status to become a national election issue, in the way that "nuclear-free" status did in the 1980s.

Ultimately, the success of the minimum national standard approach to accommodate community management will also require significant (and perhaps difficult) adjustments in NZ's foreign policy. New Zealand is, at present, adamant in its opposition to a strict liability regime under the Cartagena Protocol, as it is of a labeling regime for living modified organisms. Its position on both of these issues would have to be modified. Similarly, central government would have to be prepared to protect local government from potential claims of WTO violation. These changes will not be easy to achieve. Central government considers determination of foreign policy its exclusive mandate. This attitude is increasingly outdated. Devolution of power to local governments, to determine sustainable development agendas, begins to call into question central government's claimed "exclusive" democratic mandate.

Conclusion

At the outset, we noted that, in Australia, the United States, and the EU, similar efforts to adopt subnational regulation of GMOs were occurring, albeit within very different jurisdictional contexts.[11] The NZ developments, outlined here, are broadly consistent. They are also consistent with more generally observed trends in international governance. As James Rosenau and others have observed, there exist:

> simultaneous tendencies toward globalization and localization, toward more extensive integration across national boundaries and more pervasive fragmentation within national boundaries, toward relocation of authority "upward" to transnational entities and "downward" to subnational groups. (Rosenau, 1995: 272)

Thus, as states accept shifts of authority to transnational entities, and the legal personality of other players develops, the range of issues over which states can claim exclusive competence narrows. Similarly, at the national level, the demands of non-state political entities (and others) for more autonomy over local social, economic, and environmental development, as well as the emergence of stronger local democracy, also begin to narrow the range of issues over which states can claim exclusive authority, and the loyalty of citizens becomes questionable. Combined, the dynamics of globalization and localization create interactive internal and external challenges to the sovereignty of states. This leads to fundamental questions such as, what is the "state" (or, where do we locate it?), and what is the role of this "state?"

With this bigger context in mind, central government in NZ would be mistaken if it dismisses efforts for community management of GMOs as insignificant. Rather, such efforts should be seen as consistent with an international trend toward a strengthening of the authority of local government and (perhaps) a concomitant weakening of the powers of central government. It is hoped that NZ central government will seize the opportunity that exists here to work constructively with local communities. In doing so, it will demonstrate that it is a reflective and responsive government, responsible to accommodate local interests within the bigger picture of national and international sustainability agendas.

Notes

1.   A "genetically modified organism" is defined as: "any organism in which any of the genes or other genetic material—(a) have been modified by *in vitro* techniques; or (b) are inherited or otherwise derived, through any number of replications, from any genes or genetic material which has been modified by *in vitro* techniques." (emphasis original), Hazardous Substances and New Organisms Act 1996, s.2 This Act includes definitions of "organism" and "new organism," but does not cover processed foods.

2   The Education and Science Committee commentary, to the New Organisms and Other Matters Bill (as reported back to Parliament), states the central government view that it has (via ERMA) exclusive authority to regulate GMOs (page 5). ERMA holds delegated authority from central government to regulate GMOs. Central government can also become directly involved in decisions (Hazardous Substances and New Organisms Amendment Act 2003, Section 39, [commenced October 2003]).

3.   NZ should preserve its opportunities by allowing the development of genetic modification whilst minimising and managing the risks involved. (Commission Report, 2001: 2)

4.   The recommendations included legislative changes, some of which were implemented by the Hazardous Substances and New Organisms Amendment Act 2003.

5.   LGNZ represents seventy-four territorial authorities and twelve regional councils.

6.   This group comprises: Whangarei, Far North, Kaipara, and Rodney District Councils, Northland Regional Council and Waitakere City Council. Together they are referred to here as the "Northland local authorities" or "Northland local government authorities." Working together this group refers to itself as the "joint inter-council working group."

7.   Ministry for the Environment letter of August 26, 2003, to the Education and Science Committee considering the Hazardous Substances and Other Matters Bill 2003,

cited in P. F. Fuiava, "Can Local Government Control Land Use Involving Genetically Modified Organisms" (2004) 8 NZJEL 295, at note 56.

8. March 24, 2004, answer to oral questions in the NZ House of Representatives.

9. "Northland GM Maize Sites Remain a Secret," *The Bay Chronicle*, June 11, 2004; and "Response Welcome but Brush Off Irks," *Rural Advocate*, September 15, 2005.

10. Hazardous Substances and New Organisms Amendment Act 2003, s.32 (5) (ii). In contrast, LGNZ's submission called for an explicit opportunity for the interests and views of communities to be taken into account in decision-making, including a requirement that the applicant and decision-maker be required to assess the effect of a GMO release on communities and engage them in dialogue: LGNZ Submission, 2003: 10.

11. In Australia, Federal government assesses applications for GMO release in terms of effects on human health and environment. However, states can decline release in their own territories on the basis of "economic considerations" (Section 21, Australian Gene Technology Act 2000). Thus far, five out of eight states have prevented commercial release in their territories. Federal government has not challenged use of this exemption. In November 2003, ten regions of Europe declared themselves GMO free regions by a document signed by regional agriculture ministers. In California, Marin County is attempting to ban GMO crops, but the State of California is attempting to pre-empt this local jurisdiction ("Biotech Crop Bans Face Hijack Threat," *Marin Independent Journal*, July 6, 2005).

References

Agenda 21 (1992).

Bosselmann, Klaus. "The Concept of Sustainable Development." Pp. 81–96 in *Environmental Law for a Sustainable Society*, edited by Klaus Bosselmann and David Grinlinton. New Zealand Centre for Environmental Law, Monograph Series: Vol 1, 2002.

Cartegena Protocol (Protocol on Biosafety 2000) (Cartegena). *International Legal Materials* 39 (2000): 1027.

Department of the Prime Minister and Cabinet. "Sustainable Development of New Zealand: Programme of Action." Wellington, NZ: 2003. http://www.mfe.govt.nz/publications/sus-dev/ (8 May 2007).

Education and Science Committee. "Commentary to the New Organisms and Other Matters Bill (as reported back to Parliament)." 2003. http://www.parliament.nz/en-NZ/SC/Reports (8 May 2007).

Grundy, Kerry J. "Briefing Paper on GE Initiative." (2005). http://www.wdc.govt.nz/customerservice/?lc=reader&m=tssd&l=3433 (8 May 2007).

Hager, Nicky. *Seeds of Distrust*. Nelson, NZ: Craig Potton Pub, 2002.

Hazardous Substances and New Organisms Act 1996.

Hazardous Substances and New Organisms Amendment Act 2003.

Local Government Act 2002.

Local Government New Zealand. "Submission to the Education and Science Committee in the Matter of the New Organisms and Other Matters Bill 2003" (June 2003). Subsequently renamed the Hazardous Substances and New Organisms Amendment Act 2003.

Ministry for the Environment. "Economic Risks and Opportunities from the Release of Genetically Modified Organisms in New Zealand." Wellington, NZ: 2003. http//:www.mfe.govt.nz/publications/organisms/ (8 May 2007).

New Zealand Law Commission. "Liability for Loss Resulting from the Development, Supply, or Use of Genetically Modified Organisms." *NZLC Special Report* 14. Wellington, NZ: 2002.

Nolan, Derek. *Environmental and Resource Management Law.* Wellington, NZ: LexisNexis, 2005.

Resource Management Act 1991.

Rosenau, James. "Changing States in a Changing World." P. 265 in Commission of Global Governance *Issues in Global Governance.* 1995.

Royal Commission on Genetic Modification. "Community Management of GMOs II: Risks and Options." Wellington, NZ: May 2005. http://www.wdc.govt.nz/customerservice/?lc=reader&m=tssd&I=3433 (8 May 2007).

———. *Report of the Royal Commission on Genetic Modification.* Wellington, NZ: 2001. www.mfe.govt.nz/publications/organisms/royal-commission-gm/index.html (8 May 2007).

Simon Terry Associates Ltd. "Community Management of GMOs: Issues, Options and Partnership with Government." Wellington, NZ: March 2004. http://www.sustainabilitynz.org/community_management_report.asp (8 May 2007).

Somerville, Royden J. "Interim Opinion on Land Use Controls and GMOs." (February 2004). Appears as Appendix 1 to Simon Terry Associates Ltd. "Community Management of GMOs: Issues, Options and Partnership with Government." Wellington, NZ: March 2004. http://www.sustainabilitynz.org/community_management_report.asp (8 May 2007).

Sustainability Council of New Zealand. "Brave New Biosecurity" Wellington, NZ: February 2006. See www.sustainabilitynz.org/docs/BraveNewBiosecurity.pdf (8 May 2007).

Terms of Reference for the Bioethics Council (2002). http://www.bioethics.govt.nz/about-us/terms-of-ref-english.html (8 May 2007).

Whangarei District Council. "Long Term Council Community Plan 2004-2014." www.wdc.govt.nz/customerservice/?lc=links&id=305&LTL=11 (8 May 2007).

Part V:
Focus (b): Rights to
Food and Water

Examples of food security, and of water quality and availability, help to reveal models for future actions to better ensure sustainability.

In this, the second of four focus areas as part five of the book, alarming statistics reveal that world population will double in the next approximately fifty years. Existing suffering through the lack of access to nutritional foods can only worsen as demand and inaccessibility increase. The interrelated availability and functioning of cropland, freshwater, energy, and biodiversity resources is critical. Population growth, through appropriate incentives, must be slowed, and basic resources conserved for our future food security.

Since 1996, the International Law Association has undertaken to reformulate the Helsinki Rules to incorporate international environmental law and international human rights law, resulting, in 2004, in the Berlin Rules on Water Resources. These rules provide a new holistic approach for addressing international water law.

The United Nations Committee on Economic, Social and Cultural Rights issued General Comment No. 15 of 2002. In this General Comment, the constraints on States from limited resources were recognized, declaring inappropriate resource allocation and unaffordable pricing to be forms of discrimination. Sri Lanka, where this General Comment has be cited in the Supreme Court, provides a rich example of how traditional concepts relating to water have blended with modern human rights jurisprudence.

Concerning marine fisheries, another rich example examines the need for cooperation in promoting integrity and socioeconomic justice in marine fisheries. Guided by the *Earth Charter* principles (see the Appendix), the European Union's new fisheries partnership approach could facilitate the needed transition; from serving the socioeconomic self-interests of the parties involved, to progressively promoting ecological integrity and socioeconomic justice toward sustainable fisheries management.

Chapter 19

The Future: World Population and Food Security[1]

David Pimentel, Ph.D.
(Ecology and Agricultural Science)
Dept. of Entomology and Dept. of Ecology and Evolutionary Biology
Cornell University, Ithaca, NY, U.S.A.
Contact Information: 5126 Comstock Hall, Ithaca, NY 14853 U.S.A.
Phone: +1 607 255 2212; Fax: +1 607 255 0939; Email: dp18@cornell.edu

Marcia Pimentel, M.S.
(Nutritional Science)
Division of Nutritional Sciences, Cornell University, Ithaca, NY
Contact Information: same as above

Summary

The current world population is projected to double in the next fifty-eight years to reach thirteen billion, based on its current annual growth rate of 1.2 percent.

The World Health Organization (WHO) finds that 3.7 billion, or over half of the world's people, already suffer from deficiencies of calories, protein, or critical nutrients such as iron, iodine, and vitamins. The Food and Agriculture Organization (FAO) of the United Nations confirms that worldwide food per capita has been declining for the last two decades, based on the availability of cereal grains that provide 80 percent of the world's food supply.

This rapid population growth has been supported by agriculture, fueled by abundant and readily available fossil energy supplies. However, fossil fuels are now depleted, as well as other vital resources such as cropland, freshwater, and biodiversity.

Cropland is reduced by urbanization, soil erosion by wind and rain, and salinization resulting from irrigation. Worldwide, 70 percent of freshwater is used for irrigation of cropland while aquifers and groundwater levels drop. Freshwater is also threatened by pollution from agricultural and industrial sources, and where population growth overwhelms infrastructure of wastewater treatment systems, or where such systems are totally lacking.

If we expect agricultural systems to provide sustenance for the world's ever-increasing population, the interrelated availability and functioning of cropland, freshwater, energy, and biodiversity resources are critical.

Population growth must be slowed, and basic resources conserved for our future food security.

285

Background

In the coming decades, the survival of humans and security of those environmental resources that support them are being threatened by rapid population growth.

Entering the new millennium, stark contrasts are already apparent between the availability of these natural resources and the billions of humans who require them to sustain their lives. (Pimentel and Pimentel, 2003) Daily, about a quarter million people are added to the billions who already live on Earth. (PRB, 2005) Daily, the supply of essential natural resources must be shared by more and more people. These basic resources, essential for life, include ample fertile land and pure water, along with many forms of energy.

Biodiversity of plants, animals, and microbes, often unnoticed, also contribute in vital ways to the quality of all human life. Yet, throughout the world, pollution, degradation, and the overuse of the essential natural resources are depleting them. Some of these resources are finite, nonrenewable, and irreplaceable.

World Population Growth

The current world population of more than 6.5 billion doubled during the last fifty years. Based on its present growth rate of 1.2 percent each year, the world population is projected to double again within a mere fifty-eight years. (PRB, 2005)

Many countries and world regions are experiencing rapid expansions of their population. For example, China's present population of 1.4 billion, despite the governmental policy of permitting only one child per couple, is still growing at an annual rate of 0.6 percent. (PRB World Population Data Sheet, 2005) China, recognizing its serious overpopulation problem, has recently passed legislation that strengthens its one child per couple policy. (China, 2002) Yet, because of its young age structure, the Chinese population is projected to continue to increase for another fifty years. India, with nearly 1.1 billion people and living on approximately one-third the land either of the United States of America (U.S.A.) or China, is experiencing a population growth rate of 1.7 percent. This translates to a doubling time of forty-one years. (PRB, 2005) At present, the populations of China and India constitute more than one-third of the total world population. (PRB, 2005)

Despite the tragedy of the AIDS epidemics, the populations of most African countries continue to expand. For example, Chad and Ethiopia populations have high rates of increase and are projected to double in twenty-one and twenty-three years, respectively. (PRB, 2005)

The United States population also is growing rapidly and currently stands at 330 million, having doubled over the past sixty years. Based on its current growth rate of about 1.1 percent, it is projected to double again to 600 million in less than seventy years. (USBC, 2004-2005) Note that the U.S. population is growing at a per capita rate that is nearly twice that of China.

Worldwide, a major obstacle to limiting population growth is the relatively young age structure that ranges from fifteen to forty years, and has high reproductive rates. (PRB, 2005) Even if all the people in the world adopted a policy of only two children per couple, it would take approximately seventy years before the world population would finally stabilize at approximately 13 billion. This would be twice its current level. (Population Action International, 1993)

As world populations continue to expand, all global resources will have to be divided among increasing numbers of people, and thus, per capita availability will decline to ever-lower levels. As this kind of pressure increases, maintaining personal health, prosperity, a suitable quality of life, and personal freedom will be imperiled.

Malnourishment in the World

The present reports of serious world hunger and shortages of major nutrients needed by humans should alert us to the present and future serious problems concerning the continuing inadequacy of the world food supply. According to the World Health Organization (WHO), more than 3.7 billion people are malnourished. (WHO, 2004) This is the largest number and proportion of malnourished people ever reported! The WHO, in assessing malnutrition, identifies the deficiencies of calories, protein, iron, iodine, and vitamins A, B, C, and D shortages. (Sommer and West, 1996; Tomashek et al., 2001)

The Food and Agricultural Organization (FAO) of the United Nations confirms that food per capita has been declining since 1984, based on available cereal grains. (FAO, 1961-2002) This is especially alarming because cereal grains have long made up about 80 percent of the world's food supply. (Pimentel and Pimentel, 1996) Although grain yields per hectare in both developed and developing countries are still increasing, their rate of increase is slowing, while the world population and its food needs escalate. (FAO, 1961-2002; PRB, 2005) Specifically, from 1950 to 1980, the United States' grain yields increased at about 3 percent per year. Since 1980, the annual rate of increase for grains is only about 1 percent. (USDA, 1980-2004)

World Cropland Resources

More than 99 percent of human food comes from the terrestrial environment, while less than 1 percent comes from the oceans and other aquatic ecosystems. (FAO, 2002) Worldwide, there are a total of 13 billion hectares of land area on Earth. The percentages in use are: cropland, 11 percent; pastureland, 27 percent; forestland, 32 percent; urban, 9 percent; and other 21 percent. (Pimentel and

Pimentel, 2003) Most of the remaining land area (21 percent) is considered unsuitable for crops, pasture, and/or forests. This is because the soil is too infertile or shallow to support plant growth, or the climate of the region is too cold, dry, steep, stony, or wet for use. (FAOSTAT, 2002)

Per Capita Cropland

In 1960, when the world population numbered only 3 billion, approximately 0.5 ha of cropland per capita was available for food production. This area is considered optimum for the production of a diverse, healthy, nutritious diet of plant and animal products—similar to the typical diet of people living in the U.S.A. and Europe. (Pimentel and Pimentel, 2006)

Since then, the human population has continued to increase and expand its diverse activities, including industry and transport systems, plus urbanization. In this way, vital cropland has been covered and/or lost from agricultural production. Consider that each American utilizes 0.4 ha (1 acre) of land for urbanization and highways alone.

China is an example of how rapid population growth is followed by major reductions in the availability of per capita cropland. Now, the amount of available cropland is only 0.08 ha per capita. (Pimentel and Wen, 2004) This relatively small amount of cropland provides the Chinese people with primarily a vegetarian diet.

Chinese cropland is reported to be rapidly declining owing not only to continued population growth, but also because of extreme soil erosion and land degradation. (Pimentel and Wen, 2004)

Worldwide, as a result of population growth, the average available cropland per capita has diminished from 0.5 ha to less than 0.23 ha. (Pimentel and Wen, 2004) This is less than half the amount needed to provide diverse food supplies similar to those enjoyed in the U.S.A. and Europe. In the U.S.A., the average cropland per capita is now down to 0.5 ha, the critical land area essential for food production. (USCB, 2004-2005)

The availability of cropland influences the kinds and amounts of foods produced. For example, about 1,481 kg/yr per capita of agricultural products is produced to feed each American, while the Chinese food supply averages only 785 kg/yr per capita. (Pimentel and Pimentel, 2003) By all available measurements, the Chinese have reached or are exceeding the limits of their agricultural system. (Pimentel and Wen, 2004)

Already, China imports large amounts of grain from the U.S.A. and from other nations, and is expected to increase imports of grains in the near future. (Pimentel and Wen, 2004) Furthermore, the Chinese reliance on large inputs of fossil-fuel-based fertilizers to compensate for shortages of arable land, their severely eroded soils, and their limited freshwater supply, all suggest severe agricultural problems looming in the near future. (Pimentel and Wen, 2004)

Loss of Cropland

Fertile topsoil is a precious agricultural resource. Once lost, topsoil renewal is extremely slow. In fact, it takes approximately five hundred years for 2.5 cm (1 inch) of topsoil to re-form under agricultural conditions. (Troeh et al., 2004; Pimentel et al., 1995)

Along with the intrusion of humans and their activities throughout Earth's land area, degradation of soil has emerged as a major global agricultural problem. (Pimentel and Kounang, 1998)

Throughout the world, current erosion rates are greater than ever before. Improper land management leads to overuse and to the removal of biomass cover that exposes soil to erosion by wind and rainfall, contributing to the loss of fertile soil. (Pimentel et al., 1995)

Under some arid conditions in India and with relatively strong winds, as much as 5,600 tons per hectare per year (t/ha/yr) of soil has been reported lost. (Gupta and Raina, 1996)

During the summer of 2001, the National Aeronautical and Space Administration (2001) photographed an enormous cloud of soil being blown from the African continent toward the South and North American continents (see Figure 19.1).

Every year, soil erosion causes an estimated 10 million ha of world cropland to be abandoned and lost to production. (World Congress, 2001) In arid regions, where irrigation is necessary, another 10 million ha/yr are critically damaged from salinization, in large part as a result of poor irrigation and/or improper drainage methods. (Doorman, 2001)

Furthermore, people, especially in developing countries, have turned to burning crop residues for cooking and heating, and this exposes the soil to wind and rainfall energy that intensifies soil erosion as much as ten-fold.

Soil erosion on cropland ranges from about 10 t/ha/yr in the U.S.A. to 40 t/ha/yr in China. (USDA, 1994; Pimentel and Wen, 2004) During the past thirty years, the rate of soil erosion throughout Africa has increased twenty-fold. (Vaje and Vagen, 2005)

Most of the additional land needed yearly to replace lost cropland is being taken from the world's forest areas. (Houghton, 1994; WRI, 1996) The urgent need to increase crop production accounts for more than 60 percent of the massive deforestation now occurring worldwide. (Myers, 1990)

Brazil is a classic example of massive deforestation caused by a desire for land to grow sugarcane for the growing ethanol program. (Pimentel et al., 2006) In doing so, vast areas of rain forest have been removed. Along with the expansion of sugarcane production intended for conversion to biofuel on farmland formerly used for food production, has been the displacement of peasant farmers and increases in food costs for the people of Brazil.

Granted, some crops can be grown under artificial conditions using hydroponic techniques. However, the cost in terms of energy expenditure and dollars is approximately ten times that of conventional agriculture. (Schwarz, 1995) Such systems are neither affordable nor energy sustainable for the future.

Water Resources

Throughout the world, serious water deficits are emerging. (Brown, 2006) Irrigation demand for crops is one of the prime causes of heavy water demand worldwide. In the U.S.A., 80 percent of the water used is for irrigation. Worldwide, it is 70 percent. (Pimentel et al., 2004a)

All living organisms require significant amounts of freshwater to sustain themselves. At present, the *total* amount of water made available by the world hydrologic cycle is sufficient to provide the current world population with adequate freshwater. Yet, world water supplies are concentrated in some areas, while others experience severe shortages or are outright arid.

Sources of Water

Surface Water

Rainfall provides all the water found in streams, rivers, lakes, and oceans, and it is a vital part of the hydrologic cycle. (Gleick, 1993) When surface water is not managed effectively, the results are water shortages and pollution, both of which threaten humans and the aquatic biota that depend on freshwater.

Disputes concerning freshwater distribution are increasing between states, and between regions within states. (Pimentel et al., 2004a) The Colorado River, for example, is used so heavily by Colorado, California, Arizona, and other adjoining states, that by the time it reaches Mexico, it is usually no more than a trickle running into the Gulf of California.

Ground Water

In addition to rivers and lakes, rainfall is also stored in enormous underground aquifers. Their slow recharge rate from rainfall is usually only between 0.1 percent and 0.3 percent per year. (UNEP, 1991; Covich, 1993) At this slow recharge rate, groundwater resources must be carefully managed to prevent overuse and depletion, but frequently this is not the case. For example, in Tamil Nadu, India, groundwater levels declined 25 to 30 meters during the 1970s because the pumping of irrigation water was excessive. (UNEP, 2003) Similarly, in Beijing, China, the groundwater level is falling at a rate of about 1 m/yr; while in Tianjin, China, it drops 4.4 m/yr. (Postel, 1997)

In the U.S.A., the great Ogallala aquifer located under Nebraska, Texas, and several other states, is being pumped three times faster than its recharge rate. (Pimentel et al., 2004a) In general, in the U.S.A., ground water overdraft is high, averaging 25 percent greater than replacement rates. (Gleick, 2000) An extreme case is now occurring in Arizona, where several aquifers are being pumped out ten times faster than the recharge rate of the aquifers. (Pimentel et al., 2004a)

Rapid population growth and increased total water consumption combine to rapidly deplete water resources. The present and future availability of adequate supplies of freshwater for human and agricultural needs is already critical in many regions of the world. This is especially true in the Middle East and parts of North Africa, where low rainfall is endemic. (Gleick, 1993; 2000)

Water for Food Production

All vegetation requires enormous quantities of water during the crop growing season. For example, in the U.S.A., an average corn crop that produces about 9,000 kg/ha of grain uses more than 6 million liters/ha of water during its growing season. (Pimentel et al., 2004a) To supply this much water to the crop, approximately 1,000 mm of rainfall per hectare must reach the plants. If irrigation is necessary, about 10 million liters (more than 1 million gallons) of irrigation water is required during the growing season. (Pimentel et al., 2004a)

Irrigation supports crop production in arid regions, provided there is an adequate source of freshwater, plus fossil energy to pump and apply the water. Currently, approximately 70 percent of the water removed from all sources worldwide is used solely for irrigated crop production. (Postel, 1997; White, 2001)

Of this amount, about two-thirds is consumed by growing plant-life and is nonrecoverable. (Postel, 1997) For example, an irrigated corn crop requires about 10 million liters per ha of water and uses about three times more energy to produce the same yield as rainfed corn. (Pimentel et al., 1997; Pimentel et al., 2004a)

The limitation of surface and ground water resources for irrigation and its high economic costs, including large energy inputs, will tend to limit future agricultural irrigation. This will be especially true in developing nations where economics cannot support major expenditures for water and energy.

Water Pollution

A major threat to maintaining ample freshwater resources for all human needs is pollution. Although considerable water pollution has been documented in the U.S.A. (USCB, 2004-2005), this problem is of greatest concern in countries where water regulations are not rigorously enforced or do not exist. This is common in the many developing countries that discharge approximately 95 percent of their untreated urban sewage directly into surface waters. (WHO, 1993)

For instance, of India's 3,119 towns and cities, only 209 have partial sewage treatment facilities, and a mere 8 possess full waste-water treatment facilities. (WHO, 1992) Downstream, the polluted water is used for drinking, bathing, and washing.

Energy Resources

For centuries, humans have relied on various sources of power, with solar energy providing the most reliable source. Indeed, solar energy is vital to the survival of all organisms in natural ecosystems on Earth. Although about 50 percent of all solar energy captured worldwide is used by humans, it is still inadequate to meet all human needs. This solar energy gathering and utilization includes food production, forest products, and other biomass needs. (Pimentel, 2001) In addition to solar, energy sources have ranged from human, animal, wind, tides, and water energy, to wood, coal, gas, oil, and nuclear sources for fuel and power.

Fossil Energy

Since about 1700, abundant fossil fuel energy supplies have supported agricultural production that has been needed to feed an increasing number of humans, as well as to improve the general quality of human life. In agriculture, fossil energy is used in production for the powering of farm machinery that reduces the need for human power, and also to make fertilizers and pesticides that help increase crop yields. Also, ample and affordable fossil energy has made it possible to purify and transport water, as well as to support industry and an extensive transport system. All these energy-based improvements have enhanced human health and the quality of life.

Worldwide, about 350 quads (1 quad = 1 x 10^{15} BTU) of fossil energy, mainly oil, gas, and coal, are utilized each year for all activities. (International Energy Annual, 2001) Of this, 103 quads are utilized in the U.S.A. (USCB, 2004-2005) Taken together, developed nations annually consume about 70 percent of the fossil energy worldwide, while the developing nations, which have about 75 percent of the world population, use only 30 percent. (International Energy Annual, 2001) The U.S.A., with only 4.5 percent of the world's population, consumes about 25 percent of the world's fossil energy output. (USCB, 2004-2005)

Per capita use of fossil energy in the U.S.A. is about 10,000 liters of oil equivalents per year, more than twelve times the per capita use in China. (Pimentel and Wen, 2004) Industry, transportation, home heating, and food production account for most of the fossil energy consumed in the U.S.A. (USCB, 2004-2005)

In essence, ample energy supplies, especially fossil energy, have been supporting agricultural production and thus, rapid population growth. In fact, the rate of energy use from all sources has been growing even faster than world population growth. From 1970 to 1995, energy use increased at a rate of 2.5 percent per year (doubling every thirty years) compared with the worldwide population growth of 1.7 percent per year (doubling every forty years approximately). (Pimentel et al., 2004b) During the next twenty years, energy use is projected to increase at a rate of 4.5 percent per year (doubling every sixteen years) compared with a population growth rate of 1.2 percent per year (doubling every fifty-eight years). (USCB, 2004-2005)

Some nations, like China, and others that have high rates of population growth, are increasing fossil fuel use to augment their agricultural production of food and fiber. For example, in China, since 1955, there has been a one-hundred-fold increase in fossil energy use in agriculture for fertilizers, pesticides, and irrigation. (Pimentel and Wen, 2004)

However, in general, world fertilizer use per capita has declined by more than 17 percent since 1989. This is especially true in the developing countries because of fossil fuel shortages and high prices. (Vital Signs, 2001) This has had a negative effect on food production and the availability of food.

Future Fossil Energy Supplies

All fossil fuels must be considered finite energy resources. The world supply of oil is projected to last approximately forty to fifty years at current production rates. (BP, 2003) Worldwide, the natural gas supply is considered adequate for forty to fifty years, and coal for fifty to one hundred years. (BP, 2003)

Furthermore, current oil and gas exploration drilling data have not borne out the earlier optimistic estimates for the amount of these resources yet to be found in the U.S.A. (Youngquist, 1997) Both the production rate and proven fossil fuel reserves have continued to decline. The United States' domestic oil and natural gas production have been declining for more than thirty years and are projected to continue to decline. (USCB, 2004-2005) Approximately 90 percent of the United States' oil resources already have been mined. (Youngquist, 2002; Pimentel et al., 2004b) Natural gas supplies already are in short supply in the U.S.A. and it is projected that the country will deplete its natural gas resources in about twenty years. (Youngquist and Duncan, 2003)

At present, the U.S.A. is importing about 63 percent of its oil. (USCB, 2004-2005) This dependency puts the American economy at risk from fluctuating oil prices and difficult political situations, such as the 1973 oil crisis, and the 1991 Gulf War.

Renewable Energy Sources

Along with population growth, energy use of all sources will escalate. The U.S.A. is now using more than 103 quads of energy. (USCB, 2004-2005)

Attention is turning to possible sources of energy that will be renewable for use in agriculture, industry, and transportation. The most reliable renewable sources are solar-based, like wind, biomass, photovoltaics, hydropower, and solar thermal. (Pimentel et al., 2002) The efficiency of each depends on their geographic location. All require inputs of fossil fuel and large amounts of land.

In general, these renewable sources would need to occupy about 17 percent of total U.S. land in order to collect sufficient solar energy. No cropland would be used, but some of the land use would compete with forest and pasture land use.

The conversion of biomass, whether corn or sugarcane, for ethanol production, is not sustainable. Using corn and sugarcane biomass requires large acreages of land, enormous quantities of water, plus large quantities of fossil energy for fertilizers and the numerous other inputs necessary to produce and process the corn and sugarcane (Pimentel, 2001).

Even if all these technologies could be perfected and constructed, and be operating, they would provide less than 50 percent of current U.S. energy use. (Pimentel et al., 2002)

Population Growth and Natural Resources

No one can predict for exactly how long the world population can continue to expand before life-supporting resources are exhausted. Wisdom would suggest that population expansion must be slowed and major efforts made to conserve basic resources.

Such major shifts that are needed are not apparent as yet in the world. Rapid population growth is the potential breeding ground for terrorism and global unrest. (UN, 2003) Current evidence concerning hunger and malnutrition suggests that food security is declining. The poor and destitute become environmental refugees, as food, water, energy, and biodiversity decrease and global insecurity increases.

Biodiversity

Population growth, including the spread of humans into the natural habitats, causes the loss of biodiversity. Many organisms provide essential services for agriculture and other aspects of human life. For example, if bees were lost and the pollination of plants consequently greatly reduced, approximately 33 percent of all world food would be lost. Also, the organisms in soil play a vital role in recycling waste organic matter and contribute to soil formation. The earthworms and fungi in soil can weigh more than 3,000 kg per hectare. The average weight of humans per hectare in the U.S.A. is only 68 kg.

Climate

The burning of fossil fuels, removal of forests, and soil erosion are all contributing to the increase of carbon dioxide in the atmosphere. That these are all contributing to the global warming problem is already in evidence with the spread of birds and insects northward and the loss of some alpine plants.

Charting the Future

The imbalance between human numbers and the reservoir of Earth's resources that protect and enhance human survival seems to be accelerating.

Many changes already are occurring throughout the world. Food security is threatened by loss of cropland, forestland, and vital freshwater. Pollution of water and land resources, as well as global warming, adds to the complexity of the situation. Along with all this, the loss of fossil fuels, especially oil and natural gas, is a major threat to food and other basic needs.

Plans for survival will depend not only on government programs, but also on the participation of individuals. The first step is to control population growth. Then, conserving soil, water, and energy resources is vital. At the same time, research is needed on the development and implementation of renewable energy technologies.

The situation is critical, with 3.7 billion humans already malnourished on Earth, and grain production per capita continuously on the decline for more than two decades.

The African Dust Cloud of 2001

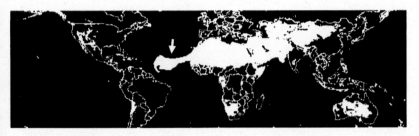

Figure 19.1. NASA's Total Ozone Mapping Spectrometer primarily measures atmospheric ozone, but can also detect particulates in the air. The African dust cloud of 2001 is clearly visible in this Aerosol Index animation screen shot (with contrast enhanced). (Source: http://science.nasa.gov/headlines/y2001/ast26jun%5F1.htm, reproduced with permission. Site accessed 31 May 2007.)

Notes

1.   David Pimentel and Marcia Pimentel. *Food, Energy, and Society*, 3rd Edition (Boca Raton, FL: Taylor and Francis. In Press. Expected in October, 2007).

References

BP. *British Petroleum Statistical Review of World Energy*. London: British Petroleum Corporate Communications Services, 2003.
Brown, Lester R. *Plan B 2.0. Rescuing a Planet under Stress and a Civilization in Trouble*. New York: W. W. Norton Co., 2006.
China. One-child Per Couple Legislation. 2002.

Covich, Alan P. "Water and Ecosystems." Pp. 40–55 in *Water in Crisis*, edited by P. H. Gleick. New York: Oxford University, 1993.

Doorman, Frans. "Global Land and Water Management: Planning and Implementation." *The World Development Federation*. 2001. http://www.wdf.org/gspc/virtual2001/session4.htm (5 May 2007).

FAO. "Food Balance Sheets." Rome: Food and Agriculture Organization of the United Nations, 2002.

———. "World Grain Production." *United Nations Food and Agriculture Organization*. 1961–2002.

FAOSTAT. "Statistical database." Food and Agricultural Organization of the United Nations, 2002.

Gleick, Peter H. *Water in Crisis*. New York: Oxford University Press, 1993.

———. *The World's Water*. Washington, DC: Island Press, 2000.

Gupta, J. P., and P. Raina. "Wind Erosion and Its Control in Hot Arid Areas of Rajasthan." Pp. 209–18 in *Wind Erosion in West Africa: The Problem and its Control*, edited by B. Buerkert, B. E. Allison, and M. von Oppen. Berlin: Margraf Verlag, 1996.

Houghton, Richard A. "The Worldwide Extent of Land-Use Change." *BioScience* 44, no. 5 (1994): 305–13.

International Energy Annual. DOE/EIA. Washington, DC: U.S. Department of Energy, 2001.

Myers, Norman. *The Non-Timber Values of Tropical Forests*. Forestry for Sustainable Development Program, University of Minnesota, Nov. 1990. Report 10.

Pimentel, David. "The Limitations of Biomass Energy." Pp. 159–71 in *Encyclopedia on Physical Science and Technology*, 3rd ed., vol. 2. San Diego, CA: Academic Press, 2001.

Pimentel, David, Bonnie Berger, David Filberto, Michelle Newton, Benjamin Wolfe, et al. "Water Resources: Current and Future Issues." *BioScience* 54 (2004a): 909–18.

Pimentel, David, Celia Harvey, Pradnja Resosudarmo, K. Sinclair, D. Kurtz, et al. "Environmental and Economic Costs of Soil Erosion and Conservation Benefits." *Science* 267 (1995): 1117–23.

Pimentel, David, Megan Herz, Michele Whitecraft, Matthew Zimmerman, Richard Allen, et al. "Renewable Energy: Current and Potential Issues." *BioScience* 52, no. 12 (2002): 1111–20.

Pimentel, David, James Houser, Erika Preiss, Omar White, Hope Fang, et al. "Water Resources: Agriculture, the Environment, and Society." *BioScience* 47, no. 2 (1997): 97–106.

Pimentel, David, and Nadia Kounang. "Ecology of Soil Erosion in Ecosystems." *Ecosystems* 1 (1998): 416–26.

Pimentel, David, Tsveta Petrova, Marybeth Riley, Jennifer Jacquet, Vanessa Ng, et al. "Conservation of Biological Diversity in Agricultural, Forestry, and Marine Systems." *Focus on Ecology Research*. Hauppauge, NY: Nova Science, (2006) In press.

Pimentel, David, and Marcia Pimentel. *Food, Energy and Society*. Boulder, CO: Colorado University Press, 1996.

———. "World Population, Food, Natural Resources, and Survival." *World Futures* 59 (2003): 145–67.

———. "World Population, Food, Natural Resources, and Survival." Pp. 27–55 in *Global Survival*, edited by Ervin Laszilo and Peter Seidel. New York: SelectBooks, Inc., 2006.

Pimentel, David, Andrew Pleasant, Jason Barron, Jennifer Gaudioso, Nathan Pollock, et al. "U.S. Energy Conservation and Efficiency: Benefits and Costs." *Environment Development and Sustainability* 6 (2004b): 279–305.

Pimentel, David, and Dazhong Wen. "China and the World: Population, Food and Resource Scarcity." Pp. 103–16 in *Dare to Dream: Vision of 2050 Agriculture in China*, edited by T. C. Tso and He Kang. Beijing: China Agricultural University Press, 2004.

Population Action International. *Challenging the Planet: Connections between Population and Environment.* Washington, DC: Population Action International, 1993.

Postel, Sandra. *Last Oasis: Facing Water Scarcity.* New York: W. W. Norton and Co., 1997.

PRB. *World Population Data Sheet.* Washington, DC: Population Reference Bureau, 2005.

Schwarz, Meier. *Soilless Culture Management.* New York: Springer-Verlag Publisher, 1995.

Sommer, Alfred, and Keith P. West. *Vitamin Deficiency: Health Survival and Vision.* New York: Oxford University Press, 1996.

Tomashek, Kay M., Bradley A. Woodruff, Carol A. Gotway, Peter Bloand, and Godfrey Mbaruku. "Randomized Intervention Study Comparing Several Regimens for the Treatment of Moderate Anemia in Refugee Children in Kigoma Region, Tanzania." *American Journal of Tropical Medicine and Hygiene* 64, no. 3–4 (2001): 164–71.

Troeh, Frederick, R., J. Arthur Hobbs, and Roy L. Donahue. *Soil and Water Conservation,* 3rd ed. Englewood Cliffs, NJ: Prentice Hall, 2004.

UN. 2003. "Menace of Terrorism Requires Global Response, Says Secretary-General, Stressing Importance of Increased United Nations Role." http://www.un.org/News/Press/docs/2003/sgsm8583.doc.htm (5 May 2007).

UNEP. *Freshwater Pollution. Global Environment Monitoring System.* Nairobi, Kenya: United Nations Environment Programme, 1991.

———. *Global Environment Outlook 3: Past, Present and Future Perspectives.* London: Earthscan Publications, 2003.

USCB. *Statistical Abstract of the United States.* Washington, DC: U.S. Bureau of the Census, U.S. Government Printing Office, 2004–2005.

USDA. *Agricultural Statistics.* Washington, DC: USDA, 1980–2004.

———. *Agricultural Statistics.* Washington, DC: USDA, 1980–2003.

———. *Summary Report 1992 National Resources Inventory.* Washington, DC: Soil Conservation Service, USDA, 1994.

Våje, Per Ivar, and Tor-Gunnar Vågen, 2005. "The Impact of Soil Erosion on the Environment and on Agricultural Production." http://gammel.jordforsk.no/jfnytt/engelsk/theimpac.htm (31 May 2007).

Vital Signs. *Vital Signs 2001.* Washington, DC: The Worldwatch Institute, 2001.

White, Rodney. *Evacuation of Sediments from Reservoirs.* Bristol, UK: Thomas Telford Limited, 2001.

WHO. "Global Health Situation." *Weekly Epidemiological Record. World Health Organization* 68 (12 Feb. 1993): 43–44.

———. *Our Planet, our Health: Report of the WHO Commission on Health and Environment.* Geneva: World Health Organization, 1992.

———. Women of South East Asia: A Health Profile. 2004. http://www.searo.who.int/EN/Section13/Section390/Section1376.htm (5 May 2007).

———. *World Hunger Facts 2004.* World Hunger Education Service. Geneva: World Health Organization of the United Nations, 2004.

World Congress. "First World Congress on Conservation Agriculture: A World-Wide Challenge." 2001. http://www.ecaf.org/documents/Madrid_Report.pdf (31 May 2007).

WRI. *World Resources 1996–97*. Washington, DC: World Resources Institute, 1996.

Youngquist, Walter. Personal communication with Walter Youngquist, petroleum geologist, Eugene, Oregon. 2002.

———. *GeoDestinies: The Inevitable Control of Earth Resources over Nations and Individuals*. Portland, OR: National Book Company, 1997.

Youngquist, Walter, and Richard C. Duncan. "North American Natural Gas: Data Show Supply Problems." *Natural Resources Research* 12, no. 4 (2003): 229–40.

Chapter 20

Refining International Water Law

Joseph W. Dellapenna, J.D. (Juris Doctor)
Professor of Law, Villanova University
Villanova, PA, U.S.A.

Contact Information: 299 North Spring Mill Road, Villanova, PA 19085-1682 U.S.A.
Phone: +1 610 519 7075; Email: dellapen@law.villanova.edu

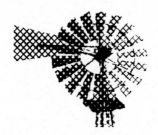

Summary

Over the past century, nations have constructed, for freshwaters that flow across international boundaries, a body of customary international law built around the principle of fair access (i.e., equitable utilization). The earliest complete formulation of this body of law was the Helsinki Rules on the Uses of International Rivers, approved by the International Law Association in 1966.

Like all customary law, this body of law achieves flexibility through vagueness and contemplates only relatively primitive enforcement mechanisms.

The United Nations (UN) subsequently drafted a convention to codify the customary law of international waters. Even before the UN Convention enters into force, it has been taken as a cogent summary of the relevant customary international law.

The UN Convention, however, fails to integrate into the older body of international water law, environmental or ecological concerns, and relevant human rights. These missed considerations have crystallized as international law over the past forty years.

In 1996, the International Law Association undertook a revision of the Helsinki Rules, to incorporate international environmental law and international human rights law. The project concluded in August 2004, with the Association's approval of the Berlin Rules on Water Resources.

The Berlin Rules present a new approach for addressing international water law, introducing a focus on ecological integrity, sustainability, public participation, and the minimization of environmental harm for national as well as international waters. These principles are not reflected in the Helsinki Rules, and were developed only in rudimentary form for transboundary waters in the UN Convention. The Berlin Rules thus provide a more modern and holistic water regime.

Background

In 1966, the International Law Association approved the Helsinki Rules on the Uses of International Rivers. (ILA, 1966) The Helsinki Rules quickly were accepted as the authoritative summary of the customary international law on transboundary (internationally shared) waters.

Customary international law consists of the practices of states undertaken out of a sense of legal obligation, out of a sense that the practice is required by law. (Dellapenna, 2001) As with treaties, the customary rule becomes law because states have consented to the rule.

While this will strike some as a strange concept, customary international law actually provides the bulk of international law and works quite satisfactorily in many areas of international life. Examples include the law of diplomatic immunity or a good deal of international commercial law. (Wolfke, 1993)

Although national governments rapidly accepted the Helsinki Rules as the basis of their negotiations and practices relating to internationally shared waters, the UN General Assembly refrained from endorsing the Helsinki Rules in 1970, instead requesting the International Law Commission to prepare draft articles on the "non-navigational" uses of international watercourses modeled on the Helsinki Rules.

The Commission completed its work on this project in 1994. The Commission's Draft Articles in turn were reworked by the Sixth (Legal) Committee of the General Assembly into the United Nations Convention on the Law of Non-Navigational Uses of International Watercourse, approved by the General Assembly by a vote of 103-3 on May 21, 1997. (United Nations, 1997) While ratifications of the UN Convention have proceeded slowly and it has yet to enter into force, it has been recognized as the authoritative summary of the customary international law governing the issues it addresses. Meanwhile, on August 21, 2004, the International Law Association, meeting in Berlin, approved the Berlin Rules on Water Resources as yet another authoritative summary of the customary international law applicable to waters—but this time to all waters, and not only to transboundary or international waters. (ILA, 2004)

The Importance of the International Law Applicable to Water Resources

Given the importance and growing scarcity of water resources in the world today, few areas of international law are of greater significance than that relating to water resources. For individuals, communities, and nations, water problems are magnified by the reality that water moves, and in moving, largely ignores human boundaries.

The 264 largest rivers in the world flow through basins shared by more than one nation—basins that are home to at least 40 percent of the world's population. (Wolf, 1998) The most cooperative of neighboring states find it difficult to achieve mutually acceptable arrangements for governing transboundary surface waters, even in humid regions were freshwater is usually sufficient to satisfy most or all needs. (McCaffrey, 2001)

In arid regions, such conflicts become endemic and intense, despite otherwise friendly relations or even membership in a federal union. No wonder the English derived the word "rival" from the Latin word "rivalis," meaning persons living on opposite banks of a river.

Moreover, problems with transboundary aquifers have hardly begun to be recognized (Symposium, 2003), and some even predict wars over water among neighboring nations or communities.

The outlook is not altogether bleak. Water's movement creates a need for cooperation among the groups who contend over its allocation. Considerable evidence suggests that cooperative solutions to water scarcity problems are more likely than prolonged conflict.

In the twentieth century, water facilities mostly have remained off limits to combat activities, cooperative water arrangements have been negotiated, and preexisting arrangements have been honored even while the bullets are flying—especially when disputes over water have played a central role in the conflict. (Dellapenna, 1997)

India and Pakistan, for example, have engaged in three full-scale wars since 1948, as well as numerous other skirmishes and serious threats of war—for reasons largely unrelated to their shared water resources. They even developed nuclear weapons to threaten each other. During this same period, however, the two nations negotiated and implemented a complex treaty on sharing the waters of the Indus Basin. They did not target water facilities, and further carried through with the cooperative water management arrangements, even during periods of full-scale hostilities.

As Collins observed about the Nile, "Perhaps the weight of history lies too heavy in the silt of the Nile valley, but man will always need water; and in the end this may drive him to drink with his enemies." (Collins, 1996)

The problem is how to structure cooperation in a way that increases trust and eliminates water as a possible reason for war while ensuring efficient and ecologically sustainable water management and use. Customary international law by itself cannot solve this problem, but international law is an essential element of any solution.

Without law, any agreement lacks the stiffening necessary to make non-compliance costly, and, depending on the efficacy of the legal structures created or invoked in the agreement, the possibility of enforcement. This chapter addresses the evolving body of customary international law as a vehicle for addressing water management problems, by specifically focusing on the Berlin Rules of Water Resources. (ILA, 2004)

The Traditional Customary
International Law of Water Resources

The claims and counterclaims among states involved in disputes over surface waters follow a set pattern that diverges sharply according to whether the state making the claim is an upper or a lower riparian (a riparian state is one that is contiguous to a river or other body of water). (Dellapenna, 1997; McCaffrey, 2001)

Upper riparian states initially claimed "absolute territorial sovereignty," claiming the right to do whatever they choose with water within their borders regardless of its effect on other states. Downstream states initially claimed a right to the "absolute integrity of the watercourse," claiming that upstream states can do nothing that affects the quantity or quality of water that flows down to the lower state.

These utterly incompatible claims could not both prevail, yet the claims offered no solution for the conflicting interests of the upper and lower riparians. Eventually, through a process often requiring decades, states found solutions through the principle of "equitable utilization," which recognizes the right of all riparian states to use water from a common source so long as the uses do not interfere unreasonably with uses in another riparian state. Today, nearly all states agree on the rule of customary international law that each state's sovereignty over its water resources is restricted by the obligation not to inflict unreasonable injury on another state. (ILA, 1966; ILA, 2004; United Nations, 1997) The German *Reichsgerichtshof* expressed the point in these words:

> The exercise of sovereign rights by every State in regard to international rivers traversing its territory is limited by the duty not to injure the interest of other members of the international community. Due consideration must be given to one another by the States through whose territories there flows an international river. No State may substantially impair the natural use of the flow of such a river by its neighbors. (Donauversinkung Case, 1927)

The consensus of all relevant sources on the customary international law of transboundary waters on the rule of equitable utilization was crystallized and codified in the Helsinki Rules and the UN Convention. (ILA, 1966; UN, 1997) These documents, however, raise a possibility that other customary international legal law applies to the waters of the world, in addition to the rule of equitable utilization.

The Helsinki Rules on the Uses of International Rivers

Every group of international legal experts to consider the customary international law of internationally shared waters embraced the rule of equitable utilization. These groups have no official standing, but their opinions carry special weight because of the stature of the members who worked on these projects. Foremost among these groups is the International Law Association, a highly regarded nongovernmental organization of legal experts founded in 1873. The International Law Association completed the best-known study of the customary international law of transboundary waters in 1966—the Helsinki Rules on the Uses of International Rivers. (ILA, 1966) The Helsinki Rules heavily influenced state practice as well as the efforts of other groups studying the law of internationally shared freshwaters.

The Helsinki Rules treat international drainage basins (watersheds extending over two or more states) as indivisible hydrologic units to be managed jointly to ensure the "maximum utilization and development of any portion of its waters." (Article II) This rule explicitly includes all tributaries (including tributary groundwater) within the concept of "drainage basin," extending the reach of the rules beyond the primary international watercourse itself.

The Helsinki Rules first formulated the phrase "equitable utilization" to express the rule of restricted sovereignty applicable to freshwaters: "Each basin State is entitled, within its territory, to a reasonable and equitable share in the beneficial uses of the waters of an international drainage basin." (Article IV) The Helsinki Rules also addressed pollution, navigation, timber floating, and procedures for preventing and settling disputes.

The International Law Association later drafted rules on water-centered activities addressed indirectly or inadequately by the Helsinki rules, including flood control (1972), pollution (1972, 1982), navigability (1974), protection of water installations during armed conflicts (1976), joint or cooperative administration (1976, 1986), flowage regulation (1980), general environmental management concerns (1980), groundwater (1986), cross-media pollution (1996), and remedies for private persons injured through water management projects or decisions in other states (1996). Some of these supplemental rules developed a second basic principle governing internationally shared waters, namely that states not cause "substantial damage" to waters beyond the limits of the nation's jurisdiction. In general, however, the International Law Association remained focused on the rule of equitable utilization as the only significant rule in the customary international law of water resources.

The UN Convention on the Law of Non-Navigational Uses of International Watercourses

The UN General Assembly approved the United Nations (UN) Convention on the Law of Non-Navigational Uses of International Watercourses (United Nations, 1997), which is closely modeled on the Helsinki Rules. The central debate in the drafting of the UN Convention was over the relation of the rule of equitable utilization and the so-called no-harm rule. (Dellapenna, 2001) The two rules, as finally approved by the General Assembly, are set forth in articles 5 and 7:

Article 5
Equitable and reasonable utilization and participation

Watercourse States shall in their respective territories utilize an international watercourse in an equitable and reasonable manner. In particular, an international watercourse shall be used and developed by watercourse States with a view to attaining optimal and sustainable utilization thereof and benefits therefrom, taking into account the interests of the watercourse States concerned, consistent with adequate protection in the watercourse.

Watercourse States shall participate in the use, development and protection of an international watercourse in an equitable and reasonable manner. Such participation includes both the right to utilize the watercourse and the duty to cooperate in the protection and development thereof, as provided in the present articles.

Article 7
Obligation not to cause appreciable harm

Watercourse States shall, in utilizing an international watercourse in their territories, take all appropriate measures to prevent the causing of significant harm to other watercourse States.

Where significant harm nevertheless is caused to another watercourse State, the States whose use causes such harm shall, in the absence of agreement to such use, take all appropriate measures, having due regard for the provisions of articles 5 and 6, in consultation with the affected State, to eliminate or mitigate such harm and, where appropriate, to discuss the question of compensation.

While there is room for debate, Article 7 appears to be subordinated to the rule of equitable utilization in Article 5. The reality is that each state's actions, if undertaken without regard for the interests of the other state, would inflict harm on the other. In such circumstances, a simple injunction to each state not to harm the other must fail: Even complete non-action could result in harm to or in another state. As a result, one must inevitably fall back on the principle of equitable utilization or equitable sharing to resolve any dispute, with the no-harm rule providing at best a command to avoid harm when reasonably possible. (Dellapenna, 1996)

The UN Convention contains thirty-seven articles dealing with the obligations of riparian states to share common water resources, to consult each other, to protect the environment, and to resolve disputes. The articles on international consultations, environmental protection, and on dispute resolution go well beyond the comparable provisions of the Helsinki Rules. The drafters' intent was to codify customary international law rather than to "progressively develop" it as shown by their generally cautious approach—limiting their work to transboundary water issues and even refusing to include groundwater within the scope of the convention unless directly connected to a surface international watercourse. This is important because ratifications of the UN Convention have proceeded slowly, raising doubt whether or when it would enter into effect. Eight years after the General Assembly approved the UN Convention, only fifteen states had ratified it, a full decade after the UN General Assembly approved the Convention.

Yet, simply because the Convention is not being ratified, does not mean that it has no effect. In the year that the General Assembly approved the Convention, the International Court of Justice referred to the Convention as expressing the customary international law of transboundary waters—specifically, the new rules on environmental protection. (Gabcíkovo-Nagymoros Case, 1997) Whether other new rules similarly reflect customary international law remains unclear.

Groundwater

Groundwater makes up about 97 percent of the world's freshwater. Yet, in contrast to the considerable state practice toward surface water sources, little state practice has been directed as shared underground water sources. Newer technologies and exponential growth in demand for water in the second half of the twentieth century have made groundwater a critical transnational resource that is increasingly the focus of disputes between nations.

To date, no consistent body of state practice has, however, emerged. For example, the United States of America and Mexico have several treaties governing the waters of the border regions, yet their water treaties are silent on groundwater. (Aparicio and Hidalgo, 2004; Symposium, 2000) As a result, the International Boundary and Water Commission that the two nations created to attend to transboundary water concerns have hardly begun to address the increasing stresses on their shared groundwater. (Mumme, 2002) Yet, all commentators have concluded that groundwater must be subjected to the same rules as surface waters—if only because groundwater and surface water is the same thing in differing stages of the hydrologic cycle.

The UN Convention, however, adopted an extremely restrictive approach, including only groundwater that drains to a "common terminus" within the definition of surface waters. (United Nations, 1997, Article 1) This definition ignores the fact that groundwater might be interdependent with surface water sources and yet follow other paths to its "terminus."

The Berlin Rules on Water Resources

In January 1996, the Water Resources Law Committee of the International Law Association voted to compile and review the entire body of its and preceding committees' work from the Helsinki Rules and various supplementary rules approved by the Association from 1966 to 1996. The Committee and the Association confirmed this decision at the biennial conference of the Association in August 1996. This effort concluded in 2004 with the International Law Association's approval of the Berlin Rules on Water Resources. (ILA, 2004) What follows is a brief survey of these Rules.

The Berlin Rules set forth a clear, cogent, and coherent summary of the relevant customary international law, incorporating the development of important bodies of international environmental law, international human rights law, and humanitarian law relating to war and armed conflict, as well as the adoption by the General Assembly of the UN Convention.

The Berlin Rules include within their scope both national and international waters to the extent that customary international law speaks to those waters. Indeed, some of the rules go beyond speaking strictly about waters by also addressing the surrounding environment of the waters (the "aquatic environment"). The major changes in the Berlin Rules relate to the rules of customary international law applicable to all waters—national as well as international, although there are certain refinements in the rules relating strictly to international waters. By including all of these matters within a single set of rules, a lawyer, a jurist, a water manager, a water policy-maker, or anyone else concerned with the rules of customary international law pertaining to water will, for the first time, find all the relevant rules in one instrument, with attention to the interrelationships of the rules, as well as to their clear statement.

After an initial chapter setting forth the scope and key definitions, chapter 2 describes the general principles applicable to all waters: the right of public participation, the obligation to use best efforts to achieve both conjunctive and integrated management of waters, and duties to achieve sustainability and the minimization of environmental harm.

Chapter 3 sets forth the basic principles applicable solely to international waters. The remaining chapters develop these basic principles in detail. The refinements in the rules which are solely applicable to international waters (principally found in chapters 3, 9, 11), pertain mostly to recognizing the importance of the obligations regarding environmental protection and public participation.

The International Law Association has, once again, revisited the recurring debate about the relation of the rule of equitable utilization and the rule requiring the avoidance of significant harm, with a new formulation of that relationship that will no doubt attract yet more debate. (Articles 12 and 16) Certain other chapters relating to armed conflict (chapter 10), state responsibility (chapter 12), private legal remedies (chapter 13), and international disputes (chapter 14) also contain certain refinements without making any substantial departure from the Helsinki Rules and the UN Convention.

Much or most of the chapters dealing with both national and international waters are either new, or they significantly differ from the content of the Helsinki Rules and the UN Convention, both of which initially restricted their application solely to international waters.

Chapter 4 deals with the rights of persons (including, in Articles 20 and 21, the rights of persons organized as communities). Chapter 5 deals in considerable detail with environmental protection, including the obligation to protect the ecological integrity of the aquatic environment (including, but not limited to, the duty to protect ecological flows and the prevention of the introduction of alien species); the obligation to apply the precautionary approach; and the duty to prevent, eliminate, reduce, or control pollution as appropriate (including a special rule on hazardous substances). Chapter 6 addresses the obligation to undertake the assessment of environmental impacts of programs, projects, or activities relating to all waters—national and international. Chapter 7 sets forth obligations for cooperative and separate responses to extreme situations, including highly polluting accidents, floods, and droughts.

What are perhaps the most significant innovations in the Berlin Rules can be found in Chapter 8 dealing with groundwater. The Seoul Rules, approved by the International Law Association in 1986 as a supplement to the Helsinki Rules (ILA, 1986), only stipulated that the same rules applied to groundwater as those that applied to surface waters. The UN Convention provided even less for groundwater. While it is true that, in principle, the same rules apply to groundwater (the obligation of conjunctive management implies as much), the characteristics of groundwater are so different from surface water sources that the Berlin Rules set about to spell out in some detail how the general principles and rules apply specifically to the management of aquifers. Most of the rules in chapter 8 apply to all aquifers (national and international), although one rule speaks specifically to legal issues relating to transboundary aquifers. (Article 42) The chapter also makes explicit provision that its rules apply to all aquifers, regardless of whether the aquifer is connected to surface waters or whether it receives any significant contemporary recharge. (Article 36)

The Berlin Rules incorporate the experience of some four decades since the Helsinki Rules were adopted, by considering the development of important bodies of international environmental law, international human rights law, and the humanitarian law relating to war and armed conflict, as well as the adoption of the UN Convention. The Berlin Rules represent a bold departure in the formulation of the customary international law relating to water resources, especially when compared to the Helsinki Rules. Yet, compared to international environmental law and the international law of human rights, the Berlin Rules are not bold at all.

The New Paradigm of International Water Law

Time will tell whether governments, courts, and international lawyers will accept the Berlin Rules as unconditionally and rapidly as what they have accepted the Helsinki Rules. Although there are some refinements in certain of these rules, there certainly are few changes in the rules applicable solely to international waters (chapters 3, 9, 11). Certain other chapters relating to armed conflict (chapter 10), state responsibility (chapter 12), private legal remedies (chapter 13), and international dispute settlement (chapter 14) have also been refined without substantially departing from the Helsinki Rules and the UN Convention.

The Helsinki Rules and their supplementary rules largely limited their approach to the rule of equitable utilization and the prevention of transboundary harm. The UN Convention, while giving more attention to the prevention of various kinds of harm, also limits its rules to transboundary contexts. The nature of customary international law being as it is, there is always room for debate whether particular practices of states have reached the status of binding international law, as well as about the precise content of these customary law rules. Some of the new articles are firmly grounded in international human rights law, and are well beyond question. Other articles are supported strongly by international environmental agreements that have entered into force and are widely endorsed, even by nations that have not ratified them.

The International Law Association concluded that these rules do, indeed, correctly summarize the current state of customary international law as it relates to water resources. In doing so, the Association approved a new paradigm for synthesizing the somewhat disparate rules into a coherent whole based on a recognized set of legal principles. However, some of the new articles indicate only that states are to use "best efforts" or "take all appropriate measures" or the like, rather than proclaiming absolute standards. This may, to some extent, reflect the uncertain reach of some of the new rules.

The new paradigm found in the Berlin Rules has gained acceptance in customary international law over the last thirty years without being fully identified or articulated before. This paradigm includes five general principles that apply to states in the management of all waters, both national or domestic waters, as well as internationally shared waters: participatory water management (Articles 4, 17-21, 30, 69-71); conjunctive management (Articles 5, 37); integrated management (Articles 6, 22-24, 37-41); sustainability (Articles 7, 10[1], 12[2], 13[2][h], 22, 23[1], 29, 35[2][c], 38, 40, 54[1], 58[3], 62, 64[1]); and minimization of environmental harm (Articles 8, 13[2][i], 22-35, 38-41). Additionally, the Berlin Rules posit three further rules relating to water in a strictly international or transboundary context. These include: cooperation (Articles 9[2], 10, 11, 32-35, 42, 56-67); equitable utilization (Articles 12-15, 42); and avoidance of transboundary harm (Articles 16, 42).

Conclusion

The Berlin Rules present a new synthesis of the customary international law pertaining to water resources. In addition to the traditional focus on the equitable sharing of transboundary waters or their benefits that characterized the old synthesis as found in the Helsinki Rules and the UN Convention, the Berlin Rules introduce a focus on cooperative management, ecological integrity, sustainability, public participation, and the minimization of environmental harm for national as well as international waters. These principles are not reflected in the Helsinki Rules, and were developed only in rudimentary form for transboundary waters in the UN Convention. The Berlin Rules thus provide a more holistic water regime, a new paradigm that should serve lawyers, water managers, and other decision-makers well.

Acknowledgments

The author served as Rapporteur, from 1996 to 2004, for the International Law Association's revision of the Helsinki Rules resulting in the Berlin Rules on Water Resources.

References

Aparicio, Javier, and Jorge Hidalgo. "Water Resources Management at the Mexican Borders." *Water International* 29, no. 3 (2004): 362–74.

Collins, Robert. *The Waters of the Nile: Hydropolitics and the Jonglei Canal, 1900–1988.* Princeton, NJ: Markus Wiener Publishers, 1996.

Dellapenna, Joseph W. "The Customary International Law of Transboundary Fresh Waters." *International Journal of Global Environmental Issues* 1, no. 3/4 (2001): 264–305.

———. "Population and Water in the Middle East: The Challenge and Opportunity for Law." *International Journal of the Environment and Pollution* 7, no. 1 (1997): 72–110.

———. "The Two Rivers and the Land between: Mesopotamia and the International Law of Transboundary Waters." *BYU Journal of Public Law* 10, no. 2 (1996): 213–61.

Donauversinkung Case (*Württemberg and Prussia v. Baden*). *Entsheidungen des Reichsgerichts in Zivilsachen* 116:1 (Germany *Staatsgerichtshof* 1927), reprinted in *Annual Digest of Public International Law* 4: 128–33. (H. Lauterpacht ed. 1931).

Gabcíkovo-Nagymoros Case (*Hungary v. Slovakia*). ICJ, no. 92 (1997).

International Law Association. (ILA, 2004). "The Berlin Rules on Water Resources." Report of the Seventy-First Conference (Berlin). London: International Law Association, 2004.

———. (ILA, 1966). "The Helsinki Rules on the Uses of the Waters of International Rivers." Report of the Fifty-Second Conference (Helsinki). London: International Law Association, 1966.

———. "International Rules on Groundwater." Report of the Sixty-Second Conference (Seoul 1986). London: International Law Association, 1986.

McCaffrey, Stephen C. *The Law of International Watercourses: Non-Navigational Uses.* Oxford, UK: Oxford University Press, 2001.

Mumme, Stephen P. "The Case for Adding an Ecology Minute to the 1944 United States-Mexico Water Treaty." *Tulane Environmental Law Journal* 15, no. 2 (2002): 239–56.

Symposium. "Transboundary Aquifers." *Water International* 28, no. 2 (2003): 143–200.

———. "Transboundary Groundwater Management on the U.S.-Mexico Border." *Natural Resources Journal* 40, no. 2 (2000): 185–473.

United Nations. "UN Convention on the Law of Non-Navigational Uses of International Watercourses." UN Doc. No. A/51/869, 1997.

Wolf, Aaron T. "Conflict and Cooperation along International Waterways." *Water Policy* 1, no. 2 (1998): 251–66.

Wolfke, Karol. *Custom in Present International Law*, 2nd ed. Dordrecht, Netherlands: Martinus Niehoff Publishers, 1993.

Chapter 21

Water as a Human Right: The Sri Lankan Experience

Ruana Rajepakse, LL.B.
Barrister of the Inner Temple, London
Attorney-at-Law of the Supreme Court of Sri Lanka
Contact Information: No. 56, 6th Lane, Nawala Road, Rajagiriya SRI LANKA
Phone and Fax: +94 11 4403337; Email: iromiruana@yahoo.com

Summary

On November 26, 2002, the Economic and Social Council of the United Nations (UN) adopted and issued General Comment No. 15 of 2002, entitled "The Right to Water" by which it declared that "Water is a limited natural resource and a public good fundamental for life and health. The human right to water is indispensable for leading a life in human dignity. It is a prerequisite for the realization of other human rights."

This General Comment, like the many others that have preceded it, was drafted by the Committee on Economic, Social and Cultural Rights established by the UN Economic and Social Council in 1985. The legal status of such General Comments is often unclear and not universally accepted. Indeed, the third World Water Summit held in March 2003 in Kyoto, Japan, omitted any mention of General Comment No. 15 in its concluding statement. Despite this, such documents do indicate how a panel of international legal experts both define the content of the various rights set out in the International Covenant on Economic, Social and Cultural Rights (ICESCR), and recommend measures necessary for their progressive realization.

General Comment No. 15 was not the first UN document to have mentioned water in the context of human rights. It was issued at a time when looming water scarcity had become a major concern of international development agencies as well as affected countries (or, states). Among the latter are some countries that give express recognition to water rights in their national constitutions, and a great many that do not.

Yet, disputes involving water are forcing courts in many countries to make rights-based judgments on water issues. In this chapter, we examine one country—Sri Lanka—where human rights issues involving water have gone to the Supreme Court. We consider how the various elements of the right to water as set out in the General Comment may be given effect in legal systems that do not specifically recognize water in human rights terms.

Reasoning behind the Declaration of Water as a Human Right

Prior to the issue of General Comment No. 15, the following United Nations (UN) documents had already implicitly recognized a right to water:

- The Geneva Conventions of 12 August 1949 and the Additional Protocol relating to the Protection of Victims of Non-International Armed Conflicts require the protection of objects indispensable to the survival of the civilian population including drinking water installations and supplies and irrigation works.
- The Convention on the Elimination of All Forms of Discrimination Against Women (CEDAW), 1979 (Article 14) requires States Parties to take all appropriate measures to eliminate discrimination against women in rural areas in order to ensure, inter alia, that they enjoy adequate living conditions, particularly in relation to housing, sanitation, electricity, and water supply.
- The Convention on the Rights of the Child (CRC), 1989 (Article 24) requires States Parties, inter alia, to take appropriate measures to ensure to children clean drinking water.

In 1988, the UN Committee on Economic, Social and Cultural Rights decided to begin preparing "general comments" on the rights and provisions contained in the International Covenant on Economic, Social and Cultural Rights (ICESCR) with a view to assisting States Parties to fulfill their reporting obligations, and to provide greater interpretative clarity as to the intent, meaning and content of the ICESCR. According to the Office of the UN High Commissioner for Human Rights, the Committee viewed the adoption of such General Comments as a means of promoting the implementation of the Covenant, by drawing the attention of States Parties to insufficiencies disclosed by a large number of States Parties' reports, and by inducing renewed attention to particular provisions of the Covenant on the part of States Parties, UN agencies, and others.[1]

Acknowledging the fact that water is not expressly mentioned in the ICESCR, the Committee on Economic, Social and Cultural Rights[2] based its stand on the provisions of Articles 11 and 12 of the ICESCR. Noting that Article 11(1) of ICESCR specifies a number of rights emanating from, and indispensable for, the realization of the right to an adequate standard of living "including adequate food, clothing and housing," the Committee held that the use of the word "including" indicated that this catalogue of rights was not intended to be exhaustive. It went on to state that the right to water clearly fell within the category of guarantees essential for securing an adequate standard of living.

In terms of General Comment No. 15, the principal elements of the right to water are *availability*, *quality* and *accessibility*. On the face of it, this would seem to distinguish the UN Committee's thinking from that of the constitution framers of many countries, where the relevant human right is defined as "access to water." Yet a closer study of the text of this General Comment reveals that the words "availability" and "quality" are actually amplifications of the basic idea of "access." This is underscored by the fact that accessibility is divided into the physical and the economic. Physical accessibility requires that adequate water supply be within safe reach for all sections of the population, including households, educational institutions, and workplaces. Economic accessibility means that water and water services should be affordable to all, inclusive of direct and indirect costs. Access should also be nondiscriminatory, with special care for vulnerable and marginalized groups. Recognizing that the ICESCR prohibits communities from being deprived of their means of subsistence, the General Comment also recognizes the water needs of subsistence farmers and indigenous peoples. Access to water-related information is also included under the heading of accessibility.

At this point, it should be noted that General Comment No. 15, being issued in the context of international human rights, is essentially anthropocentric in its content. Although para. 28 of the General Comment makes reference to the need to assess the impacts of actions that may impinge on natural ecosystem watersheds, this is set firmly in the context of ensuring sufficient water for present and future generations of human beings.

Obligations of States Parties to the Covenant

While recognizing that the ICESCR provides for the progressive realization of the rights mentioned therein,[3] the General Comment notes that States are nevertheless required to take "deliberate, concrete and targeted" steps toward the full realization of such rights. It also notes that certain requirements, such as nondiscrimination and equitable access, are mandatory.[4] Inappropriate resource allocation is considered a form of covert discrimination. This is clear from the provision that: "Investments should not disproportionately favor expensive water supply services and facilities that are often accessible only to a small fraction of the population, rather than investing in services and facilities that benefit a far larger part of the population."[5]

In terms of the General Comment, the obligations of States in relation to the right to water are both passive and active, which is consonant with the fact that socioeconomic rights under the ICESCR are subject to progressive realization. The authors of the General Comment define this as a threefold obligation to *respect, protect,* and *fulfill* water rights.

Respect requires a State to refrain from arbitrary interference in the enjoyment of water rights, including traditional systems of water allocation. It also includes refraining from causing water pollution, and from destroying civilian water facilities during armed conflict.

The obligation to *protect* includes preventing third parties, whether individuals, groups, or corporations, from denying access to, or polluting, or inequitably extracting from water resources. The General Comment does not rule out the control of water services or even access to water sources by private parties but requires the State, in such event, to have an effective regulatory system to prevent abuse and ensure that water that is safe and of an acceptable quality is made available to all at an affordable price.

The obligation to *fulfill* the right to water requires that legal recognition be given to the right to water within the national legal system. Each State is also expected to adopt a national strategy and plan of action for ensuring that water is physically accessible and affordable to everyone.[6] In addition, the State is also required to ensure that persons denied their right to water, do have access to effective remedies. Institutions such as ombudsmen and human rights commissions are listed among those that should be permitted to address water rights issues.

International Obligations of States, and Obligations of Multilateral Agencies

General Comment No. 15 calls for international cooperation and assistance to achieve the full realization of the right to water. Action taken within a State's area of jurisdiction should not deprive another country of the ability to realize the right to water of its people. This is clear from the provision that: "Water should never be used as an instrument of political and economic pressure"[7] even though this is more often than not the case in reality.

Steps should be taken by States Parties to prevent their own citizens and companies from violating the right to water of individuals and communities in other countries. International assistance should be provided in a manner that is consistent with the Covenant and other human rights standards, and such assistance should be "sustainable and culturally appropriate." "Agreements concerning trade liberalization should not curtail or inhibit a country's capacity to ensure the full realization of the right to water."[8]

Sri Lanka's Water-Related Cases

The "fundamental rights" chapter of Sri Lanka's current (1978) Constitution includes mostly civil and political rights.[9] There is no reference to the right to water or any of the rights in the ICESCR from which the right to water is said to be derived, such as the right to adequate food or the highest attainable standard of health.

Nevertheless the concept of equitable water management, to which water rights are necessarily linked, has been accepted since ancient times and codified in the Irrigation Ordinance,[10] which was enacted under British colonial administration and adopted and amended several times by Sri Lanka's post-independence governments.

In two separate cases decided before the publication of General Comment No. 15 of 2002, the right to equitable access to water resources, and the right not to have one's water resources polluted for the profit of another, were accepted by Sri Lanka's Supreme Court as falling within the ambit of fundamental rights. Both cases involved the application of Article 12(1) of Sri Lanka's Constitution which declares that: "All persons are equal before the law and are entitled to the equal protection of the law" read together with Article 14(1)(g), which declares that: "Every citizen is entitled to the freedom to engage, by himself or in association with others, in any lawful occupation, profession, trade, business or enterprise."

The latter article was relevant because in both cases the petitioners were farmers whose water resources were in danger of being interfered with.

The first of the cases referred to above was that of *Bulankulama and others v. Secretary, Ministry for Industrial Development and others* (popularly known as the "Eppawela" case) decided in 2000.[11] This case concerned the proposed commercial exploitation of a phosphate deposit at Eppawela in Sri Lanka's agriculturally rich North Central Province which contains some of the country's most important modern and traditional irrigation systems. Therefore any large-scale pollution of this area would have had a serious impact on the country's water resources and food security.

Phosphate from this deposit was already being exploited at the rate of about 40,000 metric tonnes (MT) per year, and Sri Lankan scientists were of the view that the country could sustain an increase to about 150,000 MT per year. Sustainability was considered important because phosphate is a nonrenewable resource with worldwide stocks dwindling. However, the Government of Sri Lanka was about to enter into an agreement with two multinational corporations to carry out a high intensity mining project with related chemical processing operations. These activities would have been an economic and environmental disaster, exhausting the country's known phosphate reserves in a single generation, and causing massive environmental pollution in the process.[12]

The petitioners before the Supreme Court were persons whose land and livelihoods, including water sources to irrigate their lands, were in danger of being expropriated for this project. They accordingly claimed an imminent infringement of their fundamental rights under Articles 14(1)(g) and 14(1)(h) of the Constitution (i.e., the right to choose one's occupation, and the right to choose one's place of residence).

While land may be lawfully acquired for a public purpose with payment of compensation, these petitioners argued that this project was so damaging that any such acquisition could not reasonably be considered to be for a "public purpose." They also claimed a violation of Article 12(1) because no environmental impact assessment, as required by Sri Lanka's National Environmental Act No. 47 of 1980 as amended, was to be conducted in respect of this project, thereby denying them a safeguard given to persons affected by other projects of such magnitude.[13] The Supreme Court upheld their claims in all these respects.

In the course of its judgment, the Court referred to diverse sources from traditional principles recorded in ancient historical chronicles, to Sri Lanka's modern Constitution and recent international instruments. The Court drew a distinction between the public ownership of natural resources and the role of the State as guardian of such resources:

> The organs of the State are guardians to whom the people have committed the care and preservation of the resources of the people. This accords not only with the scheme of government set out in the Constitution but also with the high and enlightened conceptions of the duties of our rulers in the efficient management of resources in the process of development which the Mahavamsa [historical chronicle] sets forth.[14]

The historical source referred to by Amerasinghe J. was the reported words of a medieval king who commanded that "let not even a small quantity of water obtained by rain go to the sea, without benefiting man."[15]

In the course of its judgment, the Court also cited the definition of sustainable development in the UNCED Report of 1987,[16] namely: "Development that meets the needs of the present without compromising the ability of future generations to meet their own needs."

By this definition, the Court found the proposed project to be contrary to the needs of future generations because it would have altered the ongoing activities at Eppawala from a quarrying operation yielding about 40,000 MT of phosphate annually to a high-intensity mining operation yielding about 26 million MT per annum which would, in all probability, have exhausted known reserves in about thirty years.

The Court further emphasized that the principle of intergenerational equity is recognized in Sri Lanka's National Environmental Act which states that: "The [Central Environmental] Authority in consultation with the [Environmental] Council shall recommend to the Minister the basic policy on the management and conservation of the country's natural resources in order to obtain the optimum benefits therefrom and to preserve the same for future generations."[17]

With particular regard to water resources, the Court described the preservation of the ancient but technically sophisticated irrigation network of the area as being a matter of "grave and immediate personal concern" to the petitioners "for the pursuit of their occupations and indeed for sustaining their very lives."[18]

The next occasion when Article 12(1) of the Constitution was invoked in relation to water, involved an attempted intersectoral transfer of water from rural to urban use in the case of *H. B. Dissanayake and others v. Gamini Jayawickrema Perera and others*, popularly known as the "Thuruwila case."[19] The petitioners were rice farmers who had traditionally cultivated their lands with water from the Thuruwila Tank, a self-contained rainfed tank in Sri Lanka's agriculturally rich Anuradhapura District in the North Central Province. An Asian Development Bank-sponsored water supply scheme for the nearby Anuradhapura New Town, proposed to convert this self-contained tank into a storage basin to accumulate water from the Mahaweli River system (Sri Lanka's longest and most important river system, administered by the "Mahaweli Authority") in order to serve the water needs of the new town. The capacity of the Tank was to be increased so that 21,000 m³ of water per day could be drawn from it until 2020, increasing to 36,500 m³ thereafter. No mention was made as to how the water needs of the Thuruwila farmers were to be met.

The farmers petitioned the Supreme Court on the basis of an imminent infringement of their fundamental rights under Articles 12(1) and 14(1)(g), as in the Eppawela case discussed above. The Court, conscious of the water needs of both the farmers and the town folk, encouraged the parties to formulate a scheme that would satisfy the interests of both. Terms of settlement were accordingly entered with the consent of both sides, which included the following:

- The Mahaweli Authority would as far as practicable ensure a daily input of 27,000 m³ of water into the Tank;
- Maximum daily extraction from the Tank would not exceed 21,000 m³; in any event, the daily extraction would not exceed the input;
- Daily input and extraction would be monitored by instruments and a record will be kept, which would be accessible to the petitioners and other members of the public;
- Two million Sri Lankan rupees was to be made available to compensate the petitioners for any losses suffered as a result of the project;
- In the event of damage being caused to the tank bund, in the execution of the project, the petitioners would be entitled to pursue additional claims for compensation from the relevant authorities.

This case confirmed that the equitable allocation of water resources was a matter firmly within the ambit of Article 12(1) of the Constitution, but the fact that the Supreme Court had virtually to perform the role of a water management body when there was already a "Mahaweli Authority" for that task, indicates that a rights-based approach to water management has yet to take root in the minds of administrators.

Reference to General Comment No. 15 in Sri Lankan Jurisprudence

The only water-related case in Sri Lanka in which the UN General Comment No. 15 was cited was the determination by the Supreme Court on the constitutionality of a proposed Water Services Reform Bill that was put forward by the Government in 2003. Under Sri Lanka's Constitution, any citizen can challenge a Bill (i.e., a proposed Act of Parliament) within one week of it being laid on the order paper of Parliament, on the grounds of inconsistency with any provision of the Constitution. The Water Services Reform Bill was principally designed to transfer the control of water services from the public to the private sector.

This Bill was challenged in the Supreme Court on three grounds.

- First, that within five years, the powers of public bodies, including local authorities to handle water services, would be phased out in favor of the private sector, with a newly created "Public Utilities Commission" to license such services. It was argued that this was unconstitutional because local councils were empowered by law to provide water services and, under a 1987 amendment to the Constitution, the powers of local authorities could only be added to, and not be diminished.[20]
- Second, that the Bill violated the equal protection of the law guaranteed by Article 12(1), by being heavily weighted in favor of the commercial water service providers as against the consumer.
- Third, that in terms of General Comment No. 15, the right to water forms part of the rights guaranteed by Articles 11 and 12 of the ICESCR to which Sri Lanka is a signatory, and that the provisions of Sri Lankan law, including the fundamental rights chapter, should be interpreted in light of its obligations under the Covenant. Because these fundamental rights are declared to form part of the "sovereignty of the people" under Articles 3 and 4 of the Constitution, it was further argued that the removal of the function of providing water from public bodies and vesting that function solely in the private sector was a violation of the sovereign rights of the people under the Constitution.

While all three arguments were set out in the judgment of the Supreme Court,[21] it was the first of these grounds that gave rise to the *ratio decidendi* of the case. This was because, under the 1987 amendment to the Constitution referred to above, the functions of local authorities are included in the "Provincial List" of subjects requiring that the Government not pass legislation without first referring such legislation to the Provincial Councils.[22] As such reference had to take place *before* the Bill was laid before Parliament, and this requirement had not been complied with, the Court ruled that the Bill could not become law on this procedural ground and it was unnecessary to make a determination on the other matters raised by the petitioners at that stage. Neither the Government of the day nor its successor has thus far made any attempt to revive the Bill.

Conclusions

Water related rights have been recognized in Sri Lanka's predominantly agrarian society since time immemorial. The subsequent growth of the urban population has put pressure on ancient rights and usages, as illustrated by the "Thuruwila" case,[23] while industrial greed poses a threat in terms of the pollution of water sources, as illustrated by the "Eppawela" case.[24]

The overarching provisions of the fundamental rights chapter of the Constitution have proved to be a useful tool to counter inequities in any sector, or between sectors, while specific issues (such as pollution of the natural environment by industrial activities), are to be dealt with under environment-specific laws such as the National Environmental Act.[25]

What then is the role of General Comment No. 15 against this background? With regard to the adoption of international law, Sri Lanka follows a "dualist" system in terms of which the provisions of an international treaty or covenant do not become directly enforceable in Sri Lankan courts unless Parliament has passed enabling legislation to that effect. The Sri Lankan Parliament has not done so in respect of any of the rights set out in Articles 11 and 12 of the ICESCR, let alone the right to water which is not expressly mentioned therein. Hence, the argument of the petitioners in the Water Services Reform Bill case, that Sri Lanka's fundamental rights chapter be interpreted in the light of that country's obligations under the ICESCR, was somewhat tenuous. While the Supreme Court made no pronouncement on this argument, having decided to reject the Bill on a different ground as set out above, it emphatically reaffirmed Sri Lanka's "dualist" system in a subsequent case involving the International Covenant on Civil and Political Rights.[26]

It could therefore be said that the unique features of the General Comments, including Comment No. 15, is the manner in which they provide a practical guide to the progressive realization of ICESCR rights. They serve to transform socioeconomic rights from being mere statements of good intention to becoming mechanisms for improving lives and livelihoods. They are, in a sense, an administrator's handbook on how the right to water should be given effect at the operational level. This is in harmony with the purpose of the UN Committee on Economic, Social and Cultural Rights in issuing General Comments, as set out at the beginning of this chapter.

It is also interesting that the one obligation in relation to such rights that is said to be immediate and non-derogable is that of nondiscrimination. It is this obligation, tied up with the right to equality before the law, and equal protection of the law, that has proved to be most fruitful in Sri Lanka's legal system that does not, as yet, expressly recognize a right to water. Since much of General Comment No. 15 is about equitable access, equitable (not necessarily equal) pricing, and equitable resource allocation, there is little doubt that the courts would give effect to such principles in cases that come up for adjudication. However, there is little doubt that legislation in the form of a Water Act, giving express recognition to the relevant principles, would encourage administrators and others to respect, protect, and fulfill water rights before the need for litigation arises.

Notes

1. Fact Sheet No. 16 (Rev. 1), Committee on Economic, Social and Cultural Rights, issued by Office of High Commissioner for Human Rights, Geneva, Switzerland, http://www.unhchr.ch/html/menu6/2/fs16.htm#6 (23 May 2007).
2. The Committee comprises of eighteen members who are experts with recognized competence in the field of human rights. Members of the Committee are independent and serve in their personal capacity, not as representatives of Governments.

3. ICESCR Article 1.

4. ICESCR Article 2.

5. General Comment No. 15, para.14.

6. In order to ensure that water is affordable to all the State is required to adopt "necessary measures" which may include "appropriate" pricing policies. (General Comment No. 15, para. 27).

7. General Comment No. 15, para. 32.

8. General Comment No. 15, para. 35.

9. The very few socioeconomic rights that are included such as the right to form or join a trade union are of no application to the topic under discussion.

10. Legislative Enactments, Ch. 285.

11. *Bulankulama and others v. Secretary, Ministry for Industrial Development and others*, [2000] 3 Sri Lanka Reports 243.

12. *"The Government's Proposed Eppawela Phosphate Project"* (1998) pub. National Academy of Sciences of Sri Lanka, an independent body incorporated by statute, and *"A Report for Optimal Use of Eppawela Rock Phosphate in Sri Lankan Agriculture"* (1999) pub. National Science Foundation, a semi-governmental foundation under the Ministry of Science and Technology both reached similar conclusions. These reports were filed in court by the Petitioners and were referred to in the judgment.

13. The agreement that was to be entered into provided instead for an international environmental expert of the project proponent's choice to do an EIA. Such a process would not have allowed for public participation as was compulsory under Sri Lankan law.

14. *Bulankulama*, Amerasinghe J., p. 253–54.

15. Mahavamsa 68, 8–13, translated by Mudaliyar L. De Zoysa, *Journal of the Royal Asiatic Society* III (C. B.), No. IX.

16. United Nations Commission on Environment and Development, chaired by Gro Harlem Bruntland.

17. National Environmental Act No. 47 of 1980.

18. *Bulankulama*, Amerasinghe J., 293.

19. *H. B. Dissanayake and others v. Gamini Jayawickrema Perera and others*, S.C.F.R.329/2002, S. C. Minutes of 30.09.2002.

20. Thirteenth Amendment to the Constitution, Ninth Schedule.

21. S. C. Special Determinations Nos. 24 and 25 of 2003. Reported in 8 S.C.S.D. 35.

22. Article 154G of the Constitution.

23. *H. B. Dissanayake v. Gamini Jayawickrema Perera.*

24. *Bulankulama.*

25. *National Environmental Act.*

26. *Nallaratnam Singarasa v. Attorney-General*, S. C. Special Leave Application 182/99, S. C. Minutes of 15.09.2006. Under the "monist" theory international law and national law constitute one legal system while under the "dualist" theory they are two different systems, the one regulating relations between States and the other, derived from a country's national constitution, governing the rights and duties of persons within each State.

Chapter 22

Cooperation in Promoting Ecological Integrity and Socioeconomic Justice in Marine Fisheries: European Community–West African Relations

Emma Witbooi, Ph.D. (Law)

University College London, London, formerly of the
University of Cape Town, South Africa

Contact Information:
Email: emmavdingle@yahoo.com

Summary

There is a crisis in marine fisheries, with many species over-exploited and on the brink of collapse. Failure to pursue sustainable fishing is a major contributor to this dire scenario; change away from this decline is desperately needed.

In the marine fisheries context, realization of the *Earth Charter* principles entails ensuring the sustainable use of fisheries, including protection of the rights of coastal inhabitants to food security and secure livelihoods. International law echoes these aspirations, but its realization is deficient.

Achieving these goals is particularly important in developing coastal African states, but various factors obstruct their attainment, including competition for fisheries resources—especially in West Africa, where foreign fleets like the European Community (EC) vie for access in terms of bilateral fisheries agreements. The EC's fisheries policy requires the EC to practice sustainable fishing in external waters, but the extent to which this has occurred, in particular in West African waters, is debatable.

In this chapter, we highlight the need to harness the potential of international law via increased inter-state cooperation to promote The *Earth Charter* goals of ecological integrity and socioeconomic justice toward sustainable fisheries management, particularly along the West African coast. The effect of the most recent EC-Senegalese bilateral fisheries agreement is examined as an illustrative case study.

Failure to take this route will instead likely see any such future agreements continue to serve the socioeconomic self-interests of the parties involved. The EC's new fisheries partnership approach, if guided by the *Earth Charter* principles, offers a potential means to facilitate the necessary transition. It remains to be seen whether it will rise to the occasion.

Background

The sustainable management of global marine fisheries has proved elusive. While the law attempts to guide parties toward this objective, it has to date not succeeded. Arguably, its efforts must be bolstered. The *Earth Charter* (see the Appendix), an international policy instrument dedicated to the pursuit of sustainability, promotes two core principles: ecological integrity and socioeconomic justice. Their implementation in the marine fisheries context would foster sustainable fishing and protect the sustainable livelihoods of coastal communities.

International law endorses these goals, promoting sustainable fishing and cooperation to eradicate poverty and realize the right to adequate food. These are particularly important objectives in developing coastal African states where fish, supplied by small-scale, traditional ("artisanal") fishers, constitutes a vital protein component of the local diet. But the law is not being effectively translated into practice, hampered by various factors, including the activities of distant-water fleets harvesting in the region. This is particularly evident in West Africa, where coastal states have entered into numerous bilateral fisheries agreements with, in particular, the EC.

The EC subscribes to key international environmental law principles, including those embraced by the *Earth Charter*. Yet, while its legal regime supports fostering sustainable fisheries development in third countries and enjoins the EC fleet to engage in sustainable harvesting in their waters, it is arguable that, to date, EC bilateral fisheries agreements with various West African coastal states have inadequately promoted these goals, with insignificant attention being paid to sustainable local artisanal fisheries development. "Third countries" is a term used in the Treaty of Rome and in Community documents. It is not legally defined; it refers to countries that are not member states of the European Union.

This reflects the international regime's tolerance of dependent (and in some cases, outright exploitative) inter-state fishing relations. The EC's new cooperative partnership approach to bilateral fishing relations with developing third countries seeks to address these deficiencies. The EC has begun the incremental implementation of this approach. The most recent bilateral fisheries agreement with Senegal served as a transition between the old and new policy. But, much work remains to promote genuine, constructive cooperation between the parties in negotiating and implementing agreements in pursuit of sustainable fishing. This reflects the broader need, at the international level, for increased cooperation to promote the principles of ecological integrity and socioeconomic development in marine fisheries.

Objectives

In support of the goal of sustainable fishing, we argue for enhanced inter-state cooperation in harnessing the law to realize the *Earth Charter* principles of ecological integrity and socioeconomic justice in marine fisheries. This is particularly necessary in EC–West African fisheries interactions, as illustrated by reference to the EC-Senegalese example.

The *Earth Charter* Principles

The *Earth Charter*'s principle of ecological integrity enjoins parties to "protect and restore the integrity of the Earth's ecological systems, with special concern for biological diversity and the natural processes that sustain life." Specifically, parties must "manage the use of renewable resources such as . . . marine life in ways that do not exceed rates of regeneration and that protect the health of ecosystems." This echoes the current global emphasis on the sustainable use of living marine resources; "sustainability" referring to the restraint on human activities to protect natural resources while maximizing economic benefits and preserving social systems. (Bowers, 1997, p. 192)

The *Earth Charter* also promotes the goal of social and economic justice, aimed at "eradicat[ing] poverty as an ethical, social and environmental imperative." The right to food is foundational to this goal, as is the empowerment of all persons to secure a sustainable livelihood. Promoting these goals in marine fisheries necessitates ensuring that all fishing activities contribute toward food security in developing coastal states and foster domestic socioeconomic development. These objectives are reflected in numerous legal instruments.

Earth Charter Principles Reflected in International Law

We now examine the extent to which the international legal framework reflects the two relevant and foundational principles from the *Earth Charter*.

Ecological Integrity: Promoting Sustainable Fisheries

The goal of sustainable fishing is most strongly promoted by the United Nations Convention on the Law of the Sea (UNCLOS). It clarifies the existence and extent of maritime zones, entitling all coastal states to claim a 200-nautical-mile exclusive economic zone (EEZ) in which they can exercise legal control over fisheries. Coastal states must ensure the conservation and optimal utilization of fisheries resources in this zone and must determine their total allowable catch (TAC).

As fish are migratory by nature, however, it is impossible for any single state to exercise exclusive control over a species throughout its entire life cycle. (Appleton, 2002, p. 1) Straddling stocks and highly migratory species are particularly difficult to manage. (Kaitala and Munro, 1995) To ensure that fish are sustainably harvested, states must thus practice sustainable fisheries management in their own waters and cooperate at regional and international levels to this end. UNCLOS obliges parties to conserve and manage high seas marine resources and straddling stocks through cooperative arrangements, as does the 1995 United Nations Agreement on Management of Straddling Stocks and Highly Migratory Species.

Also relevant is the Food and Agriculture Organization Code of Conduct for Responsible Fisheries (FAO Code of Conduct), which encourages parties to implement voluntary principles and standards toward sustainable fishing and to assist developing nations to this end through financial and technical means. Within the framework of the Code, the International Plan of Action to Prevent and Eliminate Illegal, Unreported and Unregulated Fishing was developed in 2001. It suggests means to reduce illegal, unreported, and unregulated (IUU) fishing, and urges parties to cooperate in this regard.

Social and Economic Justice: The Rights to Food Security and Sustainable Livelihoods

The right to food is protected by international human rights-based instruments, most importantly the International Covenant on Economic, Social and Cultural Rights (ICESCR), which recognizes the right of all persons to adequate food and enjoins parties to realize this right. The 1989 United Nations Convention on the Rights of the Child echoes the right in relation to children, obliging parties to take measures to combat disease and malnutrition, including providing adequate nutritious foods. The World Food Summit Plan of Action (WFSPA) of 1996 promotes the operationalization of the right of all persons to access safe, nutritious food. It emphasizes the importance of international cooperation to realize this right, as does ICESCR.

In the context of marine fisheries, UNCLOS does not expressly promote the right to food, but it recognizes the socioeconomic importance of fisheries in developing coastal states and the potential of bilateral fisheries agreements to foster development in these countries. (Kwiatkowska, 1989, pp. 64-65) Article 62[2] obliges coastal parties lacking the capacity to fully harvest their TACs to grant other states reasonable access to the surplus on the basis of agreement.

"All relevant factors" must be considered in determining conditions of access, including the significance of fisheries to the coastal state's economy. Unfortunately, some developing coastal states (driven by the need for foreign currency) over-estimate their surplus, resulting in bilateral fisheries agreements that are contrary to the long-term socioeconomic well-being of their populations. Because UNCLOS does not subject the validity of declared surpluses to question, it implicitly tolerates these agreements, which in many instances perpetuates dependent North-South fisheries relations.

The FAO Code of Conduct emphasizes the right of artisanal fishers to a secure livelihood and preferential access to traditional fishing grounds, requiring state parties to consider artisanal fishers' interests when devising fisheries management measures and to set aside coastal zones for their use. Protecting artisanal fishers is particularly important in West Africa where they play a vital socioeconomic role.

The Significance of the *Earth Charter* Principles in Coastal West African States

In developing West African coastal states, fish is an important protein component of the local diet. (FAO, 2002, and Commission 2000a, para. 1) It is supplied by domestic artisanal fishers who contribute toward food security and provide local employment opportunities. Their activities are often frustrated by domestic and foreign industrial fishers who compete for fishing grounds and stocks; the by-catch of foreign fleets (such as the EC) frequently includes species targeted by the artisanals for local consumption. (FAO, 2002, p. 2) Bilateral fisheries agreements between coastal West African states and the EC should therefore include adequate by-catch limitations and sufficient measures to protect the artisanal fishers, including defined fishing zones for their use and suitable gear restrictions for the EC fleet.

EC vessels fish largely off-shore, while artisanal fishers traditionally favor in-shore coastal waters; their fishing grounds thus theoretically do not coincide. The EC, however, sometimes fishes in-shore, contrary to local fishing laws. (Deere, 2000, p. 41) At the same time, technological advances (largely motorization) have increasingly enabled artisanal fishers to harvest further from the coast for higher value demersals (i.e., species located near the bottom of the ocean within fairly confined areas) that are also targeted by the EC. (UNEP, 2002, para. 3.2.1) This increases the potential for contentious interaction.

The EC's off-shore harvesting arguably also impacts the in-shore species targeted by artisanal fishers. Cumulatively, these factors necessitate effective regulatory measures in bilateral fisheries agreements. This is particularly so with regard to Senegal, where overlapping sectoral and domestic-foreign fishing interests have resulted in the over-exploitation of various coastal demersal stocks and confrontational encounters between fishers. (DPM, 2006)

The EC's Fishing Relations with Particular West African Coastal States

The EC's relations with Africa have traditionally focused on development cooperation, policy dialogue, and trade. Current trade and cooperation relations are regulated by the 2000 Cotonou Agreement, which aims to merge these areas into a single policy framework to pursue the objectives of poverty-reduction, sustainable development, and the progressive integration of the ACP countries into the world economy. (Commission, 2000b, para. 4.3)

EC fishing relations with West African states are largely conducted bilaterally, formalized by bilateral fisheries agreements. Over half of the EC's current twenty-odd bilateral fisheries agreements are with African states, primarily on the west coast. Cotonou provides the broad framework for EC-ACP relations, but also specifically refers to ACP fisheries, requiring cooperation toward their sustainable use and management, and policy coherence; specifically, the EC and ACP states must "pay due consideration to consistency with the development strategies in the ACP area" in negotiating bilateral fisheries agreements. This is particularly important, given the potential for these agreements to foster development in ACP states.

Fisheries in West Africa provide a prospective source of foreign income, economic growth and employment, and contribute to local rural livelihoods, food supply, and nutrition. (IDDRA, 2004, para. 6.5.1 and ADE-PWC-EPU, 2002) The EC acknowledges the potential of its bilateral fisheries agreements to contribute to sustainable development and poverty alleviation in these countries (Commission 2002a, para. 2.2 and Committee on Fisheries, 1997, p. 10), and the importance of policy coherence in realizing this role. In 2002, it suggested a new partnership approach to such agreements to realize these goals (discussed below). (Commission 2002b, para. 5.3)

European Community Law Governing Bilateral Fisheries Agreements

Introduction to the Common Fisheries Policy (CFP)

The EC's Common Fisheries Policy (CFP) promotes the "sustainable exploitation of living aquatic resources . . . in the context of sustainable development, taking into account the environmental, economic and social aspects in a balanced manner." (Council, 2002) Sustainability was not an original feature of the CFP, but was gradually incorporated into the policy in response to international law developments, mirroring its increasing emphasis in the EC Treaty and other policies. The goal of "sustainable" Community fishing was first introduced in 1992, and was strengthened by the introduction of Regulation 2371/2002. "Sustainable exploitation" of fisheries is defined as "the exploitation of a stock in such a way that the future exploitation of the stock will not be prejudiced and that it does not have a negative impact on the marine eco-system" (Council, 2002), emphasizing both biological sustainability and intergenerational equity. The EC is obliged to promote "sustainable and responsible fisheries outside

Community waters with the same commitment as in its own waters." (Commission, 2002b, para. 5)

The EC's External Fishing Activities

Introduction

The EC's external fishing relations comprise bilateral fisheries agreements, involvement in international fisheries instruments, and participation in regional fisheries organizations (RFOs). Its bilateral fishing interactions are primarily shaped by CFP rules, but are also guided by its other policies, such as the environmental and development cooperation policies; the international fisheries regime provides the broad legal framework. Together, these influences prompted the EC to expressly incorporate sustainability into its bilateral fisheries agreements with developing third countries.

Bilateral Fishing Relations and Bilateral Fisheries Agreements

Bilateral fisheries agreements are important to the EC because many of its vessels fish in third country waters. The initial impetus to conclude such agreements was the claims by various states in the 1970s to sovereign fishing zones off their coasts. The subsequent legal recognition of 200-nautical-mile EEZs in 1982, rendered vast areas of the EC's former high seas fishing grounds subject to national jurisdictions. (Johnstone, 1996, p. 1 and Acheampong, 1997) The first bilateral fisheries agreement was signed with the United States of America in 1977, and in 1980, the EC concluded its first such agreement with an African state: Senegal. (Council, 1980)

The EC is motivated to conclude bilateral fisheries agreements by its socioeconomic interests, namely ensuring continued access to fisheries resources and securing employment for its citizens. (Kaczynski and Fluharty, 2002, p. 77 and Commission, 2000a, para. 2) The agreements also help to reduce the overcapacity of the EC fleet, and diminish fishing pressure in EC waters while meeting the European market's demand for fish. (Foders, 1994, p. 23; Kaczynski and Fluharty, 2002, pp. 76, 77; ADE-PWC-EPU, 2002, p. 35)

Third countries enter into bilateral fisheries agreements primarily for the financial benefits: the most common types of fisheries agreements are "first generation" agreements, concluded primarily with developing countries, granting access in exchange for generous EC financial compensation. (Johnstone, 1996, p. 1 and Lequesne, 2000, pp. 366-367) The Community subsidizes up to 80 percent of access costs, with European ship-owners paying the remainder (comprising license fees). (IFREMER, 1999 at para. 3.7 and Kaczynski and Fluharty, 2002, pp. 79, 90) Compensation is divided between non-targeted and targeted contributions. The former (and significantly larger) component comprises an annual cash payment by the EC to the coastal state in exchange for access rights, while targeted payments (which were introduced a little later) fund various local fisheries development activities. All bilateral fisheries agreements with West

African states are "first generation" agreements. (IFREMER, 1999 at para. 1.1 and ADE-PWC-EPU, 2002, p. 36)

Controversial Aspects of Bilateral Fisheries Agreements

There are various criticisms of the EC's bilateral fisheries agreements with developing third countries. Below, we briefly discuss two.

First, fishing opportunities: a significant portion of the CFP budget is allocated to bilateral fisheries agreements, but it is debatable whether the value of the EC catch justifies the ever-increasing cost of the agreements. (Committee on Fisheries, 1997 and ADE-PWC-EPU, 2002, p. 36) Third countries' demands for greater compensation attract EC requests for increased fishing opportunities, but as the stocks of many third countries are fully exploited, this runs counter to the goal of sustainable fishing. The difficulty in reaching a compromise was illustrated by the negotiations of the most recent EC-Senegalese fisheries agreement, which deadlocked on numerous occasions in 2002. To prevent this becoming a future trend, sustainability must guide future fisheries agreement negotiations, dictating reduced fishing opportunities in return for necessarily decreased financial compensation.

A second criticism concerns stock evaluation. In terms of UNCLOS Article 62(2), bilateral fisheries agreements may grant access only to coastal states' *surplus* fisheries stocks. The EC recently re-committed itself to this principle, (Commission 2001, para. 5.8 and 2002b, para. 5), but has been criticized for continuing to enter fisheries agreements with developing coastal countries that are fully able to exploit their own stocks, like Senegal. (UNEP, 2002, para. 5.4) The conclusion of these agreements despite the nonexistence of surplus reflects the third countries' inability to conduct accurate stock assessments, its unwillingness to do so, or a combination of these factors.

Legally, the EC has no obligation to conduct or verify the accuracy of third country stock assessments prior to concluding fisheries agreements with them or during the operation of these agreements; the obligation lies with the third country in question to conduct these assessments. This is arguably a significant failing of international law in the context of developing coastal states. It has thus been suggested that the EC should assist such states in developing their stock assessment capacity and, where necessary, should help conduct the assessments. (Commission, 2003, para. 3.4.2 and ADE-PWC-EPU, 2002, p. 42, 43)

Furthermore, in 2002, the Commission recommended that the EC should conduct "sustainability impact assessments" (SIAs) prior to concluding bilateral fisheries agreements (Commission 2002a, paras. 3.1 and 4 and Commission 2002b, para. 5.3); it has recently begun to do this in relation to various West African coastal states. (EC DG Fisheries, 2006)

There was also a noticeable trend in the most recent EC-Senegalese fisheries agreement to foster improved stock assessment—compensation was earmarked to support local stock evaluation and monitoring, and the parties were expressly committed to conducting joint stock evaluations throughout the operation of the agreement. Unfortunately, however, these provisions were not particularly successful. (DPM, 2006)

Legal Obligations in Third Country Waters

The EC must promote sustainable fishing in third country waters consistent with international law and the CFP; its bilateral fisheries agreements must reflect this. They must also accord with Treaty obligations concerning policy coherence and environmental protection. Community efforts to ensure fisheries agreements' compliance with these obligations have evolved over time from an *ad hoc*, case-by-case method to a new "partnership" approach, which seeks to remedy past failures to promote sustainability and to foster coherence with third countries' development policies. (Kaczynski and Fluharty, 2002, p. 76; Johnstone, 1996, p. 73; UNEP, 2002, para. 5; Commission, 2001, para. 5.8.2)

The New Fisheries Partnership Approach

Introduction

The EC's new distant water fishing strategy, released in 2002, comprises four action plans aimed respectively at achieving the eradication of IUU fishing, improving the evaluation of accessible distant water stocks, building new alliances with developing coastal states, and developing an integrated framework for future fisheries partnerships. (Commission 2002b, para. 5) We focus here on only the last.

Fisheries Partnership Agreements (FPAs)

In 2001, the EC sought to reshape its bilateral fisheries agreements to foster sustainable fisheries management in developing third countries, suggesting that they could operate as "development vectors." (Commission, 2001, para. 5.8) It proposed remolding such agreements into cooperative fisheries partnership agreements (FPAs) to this end as part of an enhanced policy dialogue between the EC and the developing third country in question. (Commission, 2002a, para. 3.2 and Commission, 2002b, para. 5) The guiding principle of FPAs would be mutual cooperation toward promoting the two-fold goal of fostering sustainable fisheries management in third countries' waters, and facilitating the EC's continued access to their surplus stocks. (Commission, 2001, para. 5.8.2) Financial compensation would be structured differently from past bilateral fisheries agreements, distinguishing clearly between compensation for access rights and payments for specific "partnership activities." The latter (new) type of payment would be an "investment" toward sustainable fisheries in the third country for the mutual benefit of both parties, allocated to specific projects to this end, such as the development of a sound domestic fishing policy, conducting scientific stock assessments, and improving fisheries control and monitoring. (Commission 2002a, para. 2.2)

The EC has been criticized for heavily subsidizing its distant water fleet, "exporting" excess capacity to third countries and encouraging over-fishing in their waters. (Kaczynski and Fluharty, 2002, p. 77) FPAs support reducing subsidization, promoting a shift from emphasis on non-targeted compensation to targeted partnership activities, and requiring vessel owners to increasingly bear the costs of fishing licenses. The "permanent transfer" of vessels to third countries through "joint enterprises" nevertheless remains an official method of reducing EC capacity, with FPAs cited as appropriate instruments to facilitate their operation. (Council, 2002a) While joint enterprises may be concluded only if "appropriate guarantees" are given that international marine management law is "not likely" to be infringed, nor CFP objectives, arguably, this vague regulatory wording lends itself to potential abuse.

Transition between the Old and the New Approach: The Most Recent EC-Senegalese Agreement

Introduction

The new FPA approach was due to be progressively implemented from 2003. To what extent has this new sustainability-driven approach been operationalized? To begin answering this question, we examine the most recent EC-Senegalese bilateral fisheries agreement: in force from July 1, 2002, until June 30, 2006, the agreement was signed on the cusp of the publication of the new strategy and thus provides an ideal illustrative case study of early efforts to begin the transition from the old to the new approach.

Fisheries in Senegal

The Senegalese fishing industry has great socioeconomic importance, contributing to the growth of the national economy and to local food security, and generating employment. (UNEP, 2002, para. 1 and Ndiaye, 2003) Senegal has re-negotiated numerous bilateral fisheries agreements with the EC since 1980. They have generated various positive outcomes, but have also had severe adverse domestic effects, including contributing toward the over-fishing of certain species, disrupting artisanal fisheries, and threatening local food security. Combined with internal factors, such as export support mechanisms, currency devaluation, and artisanal fisheries support policies, these impacts have resulted in a disequilibrium in resource exploitation and market supply in Senegalese fisheries. Despite the over-exploitation of certain coastal demersal species, many artisanal fishers continue to target them for export rather than supplying the local market with small pelagics (migratory species, such as mackerel, herring and sardines with low commercial value) leading to a shortage of fish for local consumption and a rise in domestic fish prices. (Ndiaye, 2003, paras. 2.3, 4 and UNEP, 2002, paras. 3.1, 3.2 and 4) At the same time, EC fishing opportunities were continually granted to these demersal species under past agreements, giving rise to a situation that was clearly unsustainable.

The Most Recent EC-Senegalese Bilateral Fisheries Agreement

The most recent EC-Senegalese fisheries agreement was not by definition an FPA (DPM, 2006), but it is clear from its text that it attempted to incorporate certain aspects of the new approach, serving as a transition between old- and new-style fisheries agreements. First, to promote sustainable fishing, the EC's fishing opportunities were decreased: demersal possibilities were reduced for coastal and deep sea species, and there was no access to pelagics. In addition, operational and technical measures aimed to foster sustainable fisheries development were included, such as a reduction of the EC's fishing zones, an increase in the number of locals to be employed on EC vessels, heightened catch-landing requirements, provision for the declaration of compulsory biological rest periods, and stricter by-catch limitations.

Three million euros was allocated annually for "partnership" activities to "ensure the development of sustainable and responsible fishing" in Senegal, including improved monitoring and stock evaluation, the development of institutional structures to support sustainable fisheries management, and skills training for local fishers. Detail was lacking, however, on what exactly these activities comprised and how they might be realized. Some form of execution was guaranteed because continual annual payments were conditional on "actual implementation" of the measures, but the yardstick for meeting this test was not identified. This fueled allegations that the EC was not genuinely committed to promoting development through such agreements (Kaczynski and Fluharty, 2002, p. 77, 91 and Acheampong, 1997) and severely frustrated the successful implementation of these provisions.

Improved stock-monitoring measures were also included, obliging parties to "make every effort" to jointly monitor the state of fish stocks during the agreement. A joint annual scientific meeting was required to be held, following which the parties could agree to institute sustainable management measures for certain species. If this necessitated a decrease in EC fishing opportunities, however, a proportional adjustment in the EC financial compensation would follow—arguably a disincentive for the Senegalese to agree to such measures. Targeted financial provisions were included to improve monitoring and control, and EC vessel owners were obliged to take Senegalese observers on board, to notify local authorities on entering and exiting Senegalese waters, and to comply with trans-shipment reporting requirements.

In sum, the EC-Senegal agreement went some way (at least on paper) toward promoting sustainable fisheries. But research suggests that these efforts were inadequate; in particular, many of the innovative sustainability-driven provisions were not successfully operationalized—perhaps a case of too little too late.

The agreement was not renewed post-June 2006. Should the parties later decide to renew negotiations, the way forward lies in genuine cooperation and commitment to make sustainability the key to future fisheries interactions. At an inter-state level, this will involve significant compromise by both parties; at an international level, a new interpretative approach to article 62(2) of UNCLOS is required.

Conclusions

The EC's newly proposed cooperative partnership approach to bilateral fishing relations with developing third countries highlights the need to actively promote sustainable fishing and to enhance policy coherence with development goals, including those of food security and the protection of sustainable livelihoods. Cooperation is a key component, particularly in the negotiation of FPAs and in the determination and realization of "partnership" activities. The EC's incremental operationalization of its new methods illustrated by the negotiation and contents of its most recent bilateral fisheries agreement with Senegal, demonstrates this.

Significant progress in this regard is clearly still required, however. The success of the EC's fisheries partnership approach depends largely on enhanced, genuine cooperation between itself and its partner third countries to actively promote sustainable fishing. This mirrors a similar, urgent need at an international level: the necessary legal framework is in place, but its interpretation and implementation must be guided by the *Earth Charter* principles of ecological integrity and socioeconomic development toward the goal of enhanced worldwide sustainable fisheries management.

Acknowledgments

This chapter draws on the author, Emma Witbooi's, Ph.D. research. She acknowledges the Commonwealth Scholarship Commission and the British Council for generously funding her Ph.D. studies. Dr. Jane Holder, Ph.D. Supervisor, is gratefully acknowledged for her constant guidance and support. The University College London Graduate School is thanked for sponsoring her participation in the 2005 Global Ecological Integrity Group Conference in Venice, Italy, at which an earlier version of this work was presented.

References

Acheampong, Anthony. "Coherence between EU Fisheries Agreements and EU Development Cooperation: The Case of West Africa." ECDPM Working Paper No. 52, 1997.

ADE-PWC-EPU. "Evaluation of the Relationship between Country Programmes and Fisheries Agreements Final Report to the European Commission." 21 Nov. 2002.

Appleton, Barry. "Fisheries: Managing International Common Resources." Paper presented at the Ditchley Conference, 2002. Document No. D00/02.

Bowers, John. *Sustainability and Environmental Economics: An Alternative Text.* Harlow, UK: Addison Wesley Longman, 1997.

Commission of the European Communities. *Communication from the Commission Improving Scientific and Technical Advice for Community Fisheries Management* OJ (2003) C 47/5.

———. *Communication from the Commission on an Integrated Framework for Fisheries Partnership Agreements with Third Countries* COM (2002) 637 final. Luxembourg: European Communities Office for Official Publications of the European Communities, 2002a.

———. *Communication from the Commission on the Reform of the Common Fisheries Policy: Roadmap.* Luxembourg: European Communities Office for Official Publications of the European Communities, 2002b.

———. *Communication from the Commission to the Council and the European Parliament: Fisheries and Poverty Reduction.* COM (2000) 724 final. Luxembourg: European Communities Office for Official Publications of the European Communities, 2000a.

———. *Communication from the Commission to the Council and the European Parliament: The European Community's Development Policy* (2000) COM (2000) 212 final. Luxembourg: European Communities Office for Official Publications of the European Communities, 2000b.

———. *Green Paper on The future of the Common Fisheries Policy* (2001) COM (2001) 135 final. Luxembourg: European Communities Office for Official Publications of the European Communities, 2001.

Committee on Fisheries (European Parliament) *Report on International Fisheries Agreements* (1997) A4-0149/07 of 22 Apr. 1997.

Deere, Carolyn. *Net gains: Linking Fisheries Management, International Trade and Sustainable Development.* Washington, DC: IUCN, 2000.

DPM (Direction des Pêches Maritimes). Dakar, Senegal. Personal communications with officials. Feb. 2006.

EC DG Fisheries (European Commission—Directorate General for Fisheries and Maritime Affairs). Personal communication with officials, 2006.

Foders, Federico. "Reforming the European Union's Common Fisheries Policy: Issues in Conservation and Policy Options." London: European Policy Forum Ltd, 1994.

Food and Agriculture Organization (FAO) "Report of the Sustainable Fisheries Livelihood Programme (GCP/INT/735/UK) and FAO Advisory Committee on Fisheries Research Joint Working Party on Poverty in Small-Scale Fisheries: Promoting the Contribution of the Sustainable Livelihoods Approach and the Code of Conduct for Responsible Fisheries in Poverty Alleviation (2002)." FAO Fisheries Report No. 678.

Hanna, Susan, and Mohan Munasinghe, eds. *Property Rights and the Environment: Social and Ecological Issues.* Washington, DC: World Bank, 1995.

IDDRA (Institut du développement durable et des ressources aquatiques). "Policy Coherence in Fisheries: A Scoping Study. A report for the Organisation for Economic Co-operation and Development (OECD)." Apr. 2004.

IFREMER Institut français de recherche pour l'exploitation de la mer). "Study: Evaluation of the Fisheries Agreements concluded by the European Community." Summary Report, Community Contract No 97/S 240-152919 of 10 Dec. 1997, 1999.

Johnstone, Nick. "Economics of Fisheries Access Agreements: Perspectives on the EU-Senegal Case." Discussion Paper DP 96-02. International Institute for Environment and Development, Environmental Economics Programme. London: International Institute for Environment and Development, 1996.

Kaczynski, Vladimir. M., and David L. Fluharty. "European Policies in West Africa: Who Benefits from Fisheries Agreements?" *Marine Policy* 26 (2002): 75–93.

Kaitala, Veijo. T., and Gordon R. Munro. "The Management of Transboundary Resources and Property Rights Systems: The Case of Fisheries." Pp. 69–83 in *Property Rights and the Environment: Social and Ecological* Issues, edited by Susan Hanna and Mohan Munasinghe. Washington, DC: World Bank, 1995.

Kwiatkowska, Barbara. *The 200 Mile Exclusive Economic Zone in the New Law of the Sea.* Dordrecht, Netherlands: Martinus Nijhoff Publishers, 1989.

Lequesne, Christian. "The Common Fisheries Policy: Letting the Little Ones Go?" Pp. 346–71 in *Policy-making In the European Union*, edited by H. Wallace and W. Wallace. Oxford: Oxford University Press, 2000.

Ndiaye, Ousmane. "International Fish Trade and Food Security—Case of Senegal." Report of the Expert Consultation on International Fish Trade and Food Security, Casablanca Morocco, 27–30 Jan. 2003, FAO Fisheries Report No. 708. Rome: FAO, 2003.

United Nations 1995 Agreement for the Implementation of the Provisions of the United Nations Convention on the Law of the Sea of 10 December 1982 Relating to the Conservation and Management of Straddling Fish Stocks and Highly Migratory Fish Stocks, in force from 11 Dec. 2001.

United Nations Convention on the Law of the Sea (UNCLOS) (1982) UN Doc. A/CONF. 62/122, art. 57, 21 ILM 1261.

United Nations Environment Programme (UNEP). "Integrated Assessment of Trade Liberalisation and Trade-Related Policies: A Country Study on the Fisheries Sector in Senegal." New York and Geneva: United Nations, 2002.

United Nations Food and Agriculture Organization (FAO). *Code of Conduct for Responsible Fisheries.* 1995.

———. *International Plan of Action to Prevent and Eliminate Illegal, Unreported and Unregulated Fishing* (2001).

United Nations General Assembly Resolution 2200A (XXI), Annex, of 16 Dec. 1966.

United Nations General Assembly Resolution 44/25, Annex, of 20 Nov. 1989.

World Food Summit Plan of Action adopted by the World Food Summit, Rome, 13–17 Nov. 1996, FAO, Report of the World Food Summit, Part One, Rome.

Community Law and Bilateral Fisheries Agreements

Consolidated Version of the Treaty Establishing the European Community (EC Treaty) [2002] OJ C325/01. Partnership Agreement between the Members of the African,

Caribbean and Pacific Group of States (ACP) of the one part, and the European Community and its Member States, of the other part, signed in Cotonou on 23 June 2000. OJ (2000) L 317/3.

Council Regulation (EEC) No. 2212/80 of 27 Jun. 1980 on the Conclusion of the Agreement between the government of the Republic of Senegal and the European Economic Community on fishing off the coast of Senegal, OJ (1980) L 226/16.

Council Regulation (EC) No 2323/2002 of 16 Dec. 2002 on the conclusion of the Protocol setting out the fishing opportunities and the financial contribution provided for by the Agreement between the European Economic Community and the Government of the Republic of Senegal on fishing off the coast of Senegal for the period from 1 July 2002 to 30 June 2006, OJ (2002) L 349/4.

Council Regulation (EC) No 2369/2002 of 20 Dec. 2002 amending Regulation (EC) No. 2792/1999 laying down the detailed rules and arrangements regarding Community structural assistance in the fisheries sector, OJ L 358 , 31 Dec. 2002a.

Council Regulation (EC) No. 2371/2002 O.J 358, 31 Dec. 2002b, p. 59.

Council Resolution of 3 Nov. 1976 (O. J. C 105, 7.5. 1981).

Protocol setting out the fishing opportunities and the financial contribution provided for in the Agreement between the European Economic Community and the Government of the Republic of Senegal on fishing off the coast of Senegal for the period from 1 July 2002 to 30 June 2006, OJ (2002) L 349/46.

Treaty Establishing the European Economic Community (Treaty of Rome), 25 Mar. 1957, reprinted in 298 U.N.T.S.11.

Part V:
Focus (c): Social Forces at Play in Environmental and Human Catastrophes

Social forces that are reflected in public policy have a powerful influence on the occurrence of both environmental and human catastrophes. The use of science in social policy is to provide evidence to aid the process of deliberation intended to make for more rational policy.

This, the third of four focus areas as part five of the book, presents the case to stop using institutionalized violence against communities. The forced removal of communities to make way for such projects as highways, mines, irrigation schemes, and power plants, results in serious harms, both to affected communities and to the individuals that make up these communities. We must require application of the principle of "prior fully informed consent" to prevent harms to affected communities through forced displacement that dislocates cultural and economic integrity, and where indigenous knowledge is lost.

Another area of focus contrasts the experiences of Vietnam and Mexico, demonstrating the effects of trade policy on rural livelihoods. Local communities have no say in policy formulation that dramatically affects their way of life. From the sustainability perspective, local indigenous knowledge is central for guiding us to live within the limits and productive capacities of the ecosystems on which we depend, and of which we are a part.

The specialty of public health cannot ignore the warnings from other sciences that point to declines in ecological systems on which humans depend for their sustenance. The two examples above reflect the kinds of impacts on population health that epidemiologists could help to prevent. Ways of expanding the application of the subspecialty of ecoepidemiology are described that would permit public health scientists to evaluate social and ecological factors in ways that would anticipate health harms to communities. By including the health dimension in policy discussions, greater protections to the health of communities would be realized. To be effective, new epidemiological tools and the application of existing tools need to be brought to bear in this area of public health science, traditionally oriented toward informing policy.

Chapter 23

The Institutionalized Use of Force in Economic Development: With Special Reference to the World Bank

Robert Goodland, Ph.D. (Environmental Sciences)

The World Bank Group's Chief Environmental Advisor,
1978-2001
Washington, DC, U.S.A.

Contact Information: 613 Rivercrest, McLean, VA 22101 U.S.A.
Phone: +1 703 356 2189; Email: rbtgoodland@aol.com

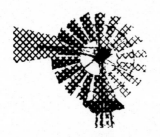

Summary

Many economic development projects depend on the displacement of people from their homes and land to make way for large-scale projects such as highways, mines, land colonization, irrigation schemes, and hydro reservoirs. Such projects often result in trauma to the affected communities.

There are two contrasting types of involuntary displacement: first, urban displacement, and second, rural displacement.

Urban displacement often has less of impact because, while people are forcibly removed from their dwellings, their jobs, their markets, and their support groups, their society and relationships remain relatively intact, and they usually find another dwelling in a nearby street. Traumatic and harmful as urban displacement often is, it is not the focus of this chapter.

Rural displacement, our focus in this chapter, shatters the family from its resource base, confiscates land and farms, smashes informal relationships and support groups, ruptures market links, and precludes the informal gathering of forest products, fish, and aquatic resources, as well as medicinal substances.

Development agencies openly accept the use of force as a normal tool, not merely tolerated, but considered inevitable. However, routine reliance on force has become unacceptable, and should be prohibited in economic development projects. Readily available alternatives, such as "Prior Fully Informed Consent," must become the norm.

339

Introduction

Force, violence, and other human rights abuses are widespread in economic development projects in developing countries. (Westra, 2004) Many projects depend on the local military or mercenaries to protect corporate investments and property. Too often, however, security forces deteriorate into enforcers of illegal policies, such as repression, intimidation, and suppression of dissent.

The major asymmetry of power between the impacted poor and the multinational corporations promoting their project is intensified when development agencies side with corporations against impacted people, such as by banning trade unions, freedom of association, and collective bargaining. This is especially common in extractive industry projects (e.g., oil, gas, and mining).

Currently, the World Bank Group (WBG) is revamping mining codes worldwide in order to become "industry friendly," which intensifies impact on the poor. (EIR, 2003; Colchester et al., 2003) This reduction of normal freedoms stems from the indirect use of force to promote economic development. Two main categories of force are seen in economic development, and they are intensifying.

First, violence has been used to impose the will of developers. Casual beatings and unjustified arrests are the most common types of force used to make people compliant with planned developments. The most thorough source for the documentary evidence of the use of force in general is in the Human Rights Watch's World Report. (HRW, 2007)

Second, violence is used to displace people to make way for development projects. (Goodland, 2007a, 2007b) This is the present chapter's focus because the practice appears to have become institutionalized. Some development officials may consider the use of force as somewhat regrettable, yet necessary. Yet, such agencies are not seeking to end this systematic reliance on force as a tool in economic development. In fact, forced resettlement is likely to increase as population rises in developing countries.

More than ten million people are involuntarily displaced (i.e., are ousted, hence are "oustees") every year to make room for development projects. Their trauma and impoverishment violate human rights. As opencast mining, highways, reservoirs, and agribusiness burgeon, the numbers of humans ousted are expected to soar. (Ali, 2003; Moody, 1992; Slack, 2004; Thakkur, 2004; WCD, 2000; WWF, 2004) The WBG's review of involuntary resettlement in WBG-assisted projects between 1986 and 1993 found that only one project had satisfactorily compensated and rehabilitated affected people. (World Bank, 1996) Yet the policy (OP, 4.30) on Involuntary Resettlement was weakened in 2002. Consequently, the WBG's response to impoverishing some two million people was to lower Bank standards. (McDowell and Van Hear, 2006; Downing, 2002)

Compensation is often withheld or is grossly inadequate. Cernea (2003) details the reasons why compensation has failed. For these reasons, rural, forced displacement usually fails, thus intensifying poverty. The poor are suddenly evicted from their lands and dwellings, and many end up in temporary refugee-type camps, often for years or even permanently. Where there is a resettlement plan, it usually fails to restore pre-move standards of living. It is exceedingly rare for displaced people to regain their previous livelihoods after their relocation. A tiny proportion of ousted people regain previous standards, but only after years at lower standards. This is probably the worst feature of economic development today. Involuntary rural displacement means that the poor subsidize the proponent who externalizes resettlement costs onto the impacted people. Impoverishing displaced people is the most pervasive type of force in economic development.

Text Box 23.1. Four Examples of Violence in Economic Development

1. **Brazil:** In March 2001, three hundred protesters from the Tractebel and International Development Bank (IDB)-financed Cana Brava dam (Tocantins, Goias) were beaten by military police and denied access to drinking water (and food) for three days. Despite this incident, the IDB awarded itself the "Best project team" for "outstanding work with civil society" in October 2001. The reservoir filled in 2002. IDB's official enquiry in 2004 added only twenty-four families for compensation.

2. **Indonesia:** Human Rights Commission (1994) the army around Freeport-McMoran's mine had killed an estimated two thousand people, mostly ethnic minorities. After this, the mining corporation severed all ties with the World Bank and the Overseas Private Investment Corporation of the U.S. Government in order to stifle an official enquiry.

3. **India:** Narmada Hydro and Irrigation program: Human Rights Watch (2007) "Thousands of arbitrary arrests, beatings, illegal detention, and other forms of physical abuse." Hundreds of protesters were beaten and arrested by police in Gujarat, Madhya Pradesh, and Maharastra on several different occasions between 1990 and 1993 when India cancelled the World Bank loan in order to reduce scrutiny.

4. **India:** Orissa: Utkal Bauxite Mine: Many Adivasis (ethnic minorities) shot, intimidated, raped or maimed by police at several massacres in the last few years to make way for the bauxite mine (Goodland, 2007b)

5. **Senegal:** Manantali Irrigation: Human Rights Watch (2007) "indiscriminate killings, detention, rape and beatings by security forces;" six hundred executed or tortured to death, sixty thousand people fled or were deported; tens of thousands were forcibly expelled from Mauritania. (McCully, 1996).

6. **Suriname:** Chinese Logging Corporations logged the forest and destroyed farms belonging to Maroons of the Saramaka Tribal People. The Army supported illegal Chinese Logging Corporations (Goodland, 2007a) (Sources: Human Rights Watch, Amnesty International)

The United Nations and Human Rights

Ironically, creation of the Bretton Woods twins in 1945 (i.e., the International Monetary Fund [IMF] and the World Bank [WB]) was closely connected to the adoption of the Universal Declaration of Human Rights in 1948, but the two have since diverged. During the decade since the 1992 United Nations (UN) Rio Conference on Environment and Development, human rights arguments have been applied and tested to meet sustainable development goals in many national, regional, and multilateral settings.

Since 1997, the UN Secretary General has consistently urged mainstreaming human rights across the UN system. Economic, social, and cultural rights are now on a par with civil and political rights. The UN's 1998 Annual Report concluded that society has an obligation to respond to the inalienable rights of individuals and empower people to demand justice as a right, not as charity. Handl (1991, 2001) makes the case that rights-based development is becoming international customary law.

The Private Sector and Human Rights

Of course, Organisation for Economic Co-operation and Development (OECD) countries would not countenance slavery and child labor at home; nor should they overseas. Corporations should follow the more important UN (e.g., ILO, IPEC, OECD, WBG) and other norms (see Text Box 23.1) all the time, especially in developing countries. Better mining corporations have incorporated the Universal Declaration of Human Rights into their own mandatory corporate codes of conduct. Extractive industry majors (e.g., Chevron-Texaco, Shell, Conoco, BP, RTZ, Freeport McMoran) have joined the Governments of the United States of America, the United Kingdom, and the Netherlands in agreeing to the "Voluntary Principles on Security and Human Rights," which, since 2000, have sought to promote best human rights practices with respect to the use of security and other forces in extractive projects.

The WBG and Human Rights

The WBG's posture on human rights lags behind that of the UN family, and behind industry leaders. Until recently, the WBG emphasized that its articles prohibit the use of non-economic criteria in lending; hence human rights should not be used in lending decisions. This is progressing to cautious engagement in a few specifics.

As long ago as 1981, the WBG adopted the official policy on vulnerable ethnic minorities or indigenous peoples (Goodland, 1981), which is essentially a human rights issue. The WBG's General Counsel, Ibrahim Shihata, called the Bank's policy on ethnic minorities a human rights policy; he started publishing on human rights issues from 1988. He ruled that: "balanced development can only be achieved if the basic human rights are secured for persons affected by development." Shihata came round to the opinion that human rights could be considered in Bank work when they crossed a threshold and became so important that they constituted an economic issue. (Shihata 1991, 1997)

Mention of human rights was practically taboo until recently. However, the 2006 World Development Report at least mentions human rights in passing. (World Bank, 2006) The day he retired, the WB's General Counsel published a legal opinion that human rights can be a legitimate criterion in WB work (Dañino, 2006). More than 190 countries have ratified the six main human rights conventions (HRW, 2007); the WBG has not.

From Participation to Consent

Community participation is part of the trust-building process necessary for developers to earn a social license to operate, and is a standard component of corporate social responsibility. Participation means gaining agreement on precautions, mitigation, and compensation. The distribution of benefits between the developer, local and central government, and affected communities is a central element of participation. The WBG now requires "meaningful" participation. It starts well before permitting and licensing, and it leads to public acceptance and consent.

Free Prior Informed Consent

"Informed Consent" derives from the principle of "Respect for Autonomy" which has been dominant in medical research since after World War II. It is a process that aims to secure from individuals, voluntary, prior, (usually written) informed consent before undergoing a medical procedure, or participating in medical research.

Not unlike it, the principle of "Free Prior Informed Consent" (FPIC) is a process that can be implemented to improve the social situation around economic development projects. While not a perfect process, FPIC is a preferable alternative to the use of force or imposing involuntary conditions on impacted people. FPIC provides potentially impacted communities with information about a proposed development project and encourages their consent. It begins with the provision of details on the nature of a proposed action, including the risks, benefits, and alternatives to the proposed action. FPIC protects community members by providing relevant information to them in order to make informed choices; it can also be used as a tool to help developers achieve a "social license" to operate.

The FPIC process can ensure that potentially affected communities have all the relevant information at their disposal in order to ensure balanced and fair negotiations with project proponents. Balanced negotiation requires the education of all stakeholders (i.e., governments, proponents, affected communities) with regard to their rights and responsibilities. Negotiation between asymmetrical parties usually requires the aid of advocates, facilitators, and technical assistance.

FPIC means affected communities have to agree to a project prior to it being permitted. This belief began to take hold in the early 1980s, when there was the first international acceptance that displacement of people should not go ahead if the potentially affected communities found it unacceptable. Since then, this belief has been gradually strengthening. All displacement should be so attractive that it would be entered into voluntarily; "general acceptance" would be the norm.

When convenient, the WB claims that its work must be based on economic principles. If a project is not economic, the project should not go ahead as designed. The main principle of economics applied in this case is "willing seller/willing buyer." If buyer or seller is unwilling, economics does not apply. In the unwilling case, the project descends into the use of force; economics is suspended. The WB sometimes says that it is prevented from fulfilling a clear desire or standard "because it is not economic," and that its Articles of Agreement prohibit the use of non-economic factors. If the WB wants to comply with its Articles, it has to ensure willing seller/willing buyer. Rejecting FPIC means that the WB is rejecting standard economics and choosing coercion or force instead. This is unacceptable.

If they are willing to be displaced, oustees would become project beneficiaries. Any form of development that would require the use of force, being involuntary in any sense, or one that would increase poverty, would become unacceptable. Development must become consensual and democratic. A project is likely to fail if there is significant broad-based opposition. Development projects that depend on mass involuntary displacement, such as reservoirs in densely populated farmland, should be redesigned. Alternatively, development projects should achieve FPIC by guaranteeing benefits to the impacted communities through insurance, performance bonds, or escrowed trust funds.

In the mid-1990s, the WBG ruled that "meaningful" consultation must be interpreted as the possibility of the impacted community saying no. With this veto power comes the correlative power to negotiate on equal terms with the project proponent. This does not mean that a single obstinate family can cancel a project; eminent domain should remain available for such cases, as long as it is sparingly invoked. On June 4, 2004, the WBG accepted that it "requires a process of free, prior, informed consultation . . . that leads to the affected community's broad acceptance of the project." The WB realizes that the "consent" includes the right of a community to reject a proposed project, hence the weasel word "consultation" instead of "consent;" sadly, their August 2 legal ruling (World Bank, 2004b) fails to distinguish between consent and consultation.

FPIC helps the poor more than the rich, who usually are not forced into accepting potentially harmful actions, in part because the rich have more power. The poor tend to accept riskier jobs and unsafe labor conditions, and may provide consent more readily than the rich because of need. Therefore, FPIC is a necessary, but not sufficient, condition for a development project to be permitted.

Text Box 23.2. Eminent Domain: The Despotic Power

Eminent domain (ED) is designed to create government flexibility in the provision of public services, such as highways and bridges. ED is defined as the right of a government legally to seize, condemn, expropriate or confiscate private property for public use, in exchange for payment of the fair market value of the property, plus relocation expenses and payment for any consequential damages, including to tenants. ED may be invoked only when good faith negotiations have failed. In 1795, the U.S. Supreme Court described ED as the "Despotic power" because ED can be abused. The U.S. Constitution and the U.S. Supreme Court seek to limit such abuse by emphasizing first, that ED may be used strictly for "public use," and not for private use such as offices, housing, casinos, or malls. Neither should ED be used in the case of public/private sector partnerships. And second, that compensation must be just, agreed upon by three independent arbiters, and subject to appeal in the courts. ED still is coercive in that if a household resists through the entire process of negotiations, arbitrations, and appeals, it will eventually be evicted by bailiffs. The limited use of ED with households well versed in using money would be better than today's use of force. Certainly, the ED process would be far better than today's much more common involuntary displacement because the latter has no process of negotiation, arbitration, and appeal. Dealing with individual households in general is less satisfactory than negotiating with the community as a whole as required for FPIC. (Berliner, 2003; Epstein, 2005; Kotoka and Cellies, 2002; Rypinski, 2002; Snyder, 2006).

One of the earliest formal codifications of FPIC was in the Nuremberg Code of 1947, concerning the conditions under which research and experimentation could be carried out on human beings. FPIC is still intensively discussed in the field of medical ethics.

The International Bill of Rights, International Covenant on Economic, Social and Cultural Rights, and International Covenant on Political and Civil Rights all provide clearly for self-determination and free pursuit of people's own development. The OECD and UN system (e.g., ILO, FAO, GEF, UNEP, and WSSD) have been increasingly relying on FPIC. The UN Declaration on the Rights of Indigenous Peoples, and the InterAmerican Declaration on the Rights of Indigenous Peoples, explicitly recognize FPIC. The International Labor Organization (ILO) Convention 169 provides for prior informed consent in case of displacement. The UN Food and Agriculture Organization (FAO) Code of Conduct was amended in 1989 to make FPIC mandatory. The 1989 Basel Convention on Hazardous Wastes, the 2001 Stockholm Convention on Persistent Organic Pollutants, and the 2002 Convention on Biological Diversity, all contain strict FPIC requirements. The Rotterdam Convention on Prior Informed Consent was adopted in 1998. FPIC has long been a requirement for indigenous peoples potentially being impacted by a development project. (Athialy, 2003; Colchester, 2003; Goldzimer, 2000; Goodland, 2004; MacKay, 2004; Callies et al., 2003; FPP, 2004; Bosshard, 2004)

Listening to people who were usually harmed by development is a relatively new process. In the 1950s and 1960s, people about to be harmed by a project might be warned, but rarely helped. "Meaningful consultation" became mandatory in WBG-assisted projects in the late 1980s. Meaningful stakeholder participation became mandatory in 1992. The WBG's Legal Department interpreted the term "meaningful" to mean that the communities being consulted had a right to say "no" to the proposal.

Text Box 23.3. Prior Consent and Australia's Aboriginal Land Rights

The 1976 Act mandates prior consent, including the right to veto exploration on the lands of Australia's Aboriginal population. The governor can override a community's veto in cases of the national interest, but has not yet done so to date. Over the last twenty years, Aboriginal communities have vetoed at least 122 exploration license applications. The Act was weakened in 1987 so that consent for exploration sufficed if the proponent later decided to mine. In 1992, courts ruled that the Aboriginal Land Council could not require further consent, even if the mining corporation agreed to seek a second FPIC for mining, hence further weakened the Act. While the Act provides that state and federal royalties accrue to the Aboriginal Benefit Account, it does not insist on prior provision of adequate information. (Bass et al., 2004)

Consultation and participation ring hollow if the potentially affected communities cannot say anything except "yes." "Meaningful participation" if properly implemented can achieve FPIC. However, "meaningful participation" is open to various interpretations, depending on who is facilitating the participation. FPIC has been clearly operationalized by Mehta and Stankovitch (2000), MacKay 2004, and Bass et al. (2004) provides detailed case studies showing how FPIC has been approached in the case of mining projects.

FPIC is still not always accepted as a requirement for development projects:

a.   In 2000, the World Commission on Dams (WCD) called for FPIC to be applied to indigenous peoples involved in dam projects. WCD amplified adjudication procedures and did not mention veto. WCD's recommendation was rejected by the WBG.

b.   A call for FPIC for non-indigenous peoples to be included in the 2001 revision of the WBG's involuntary resettlement policy was similarly rejected by the WBG.

c.   In February 2003, the WBG announced its "high risk/high reward" policy of resuming financing for big infrastructure projects and a new water strategy paper emphasizing big dams, after a decade-long suspension. Civil Society responded with "Gambling with peoples lives: what the WB's new 'High Risk/High reward' strategy means for the poor and the environment" (Bosshard et al., 2003), urging the WBG to adopt FPIC.

d.   Commendably, FPIC is sought these days in some WBG projects, though it is not yet clearly mandated by WBG policies. (Colchester et al., 2003; Goodland, 2005)

e.   The WBG's June 4, 2004 response to the Extractive Industry review stated that the WBG "requires . . . free prior informed consultation . . . that leads to the affected communities' broad acceptance of the project."

Characteristics of Fully Informed Prior Consent

The main characteristics of fully informed prior consent (FPIC) are that it is: (1) freely given, (2) fully informed, (3) obtained before permission is granted to a proponent to proceed with the project, and (4) consensual.

"Freely-given" means that potentially affected people must freely offer their consent. Consent must be entirely voluntary; they must not be coerced or tricked into consent.

"Fully-informed" means that the affected people know and understand as much about their own rights and the implications of the proposed project as do the proponents in order to ensure balanced negotiation. This means two categories of information sharing. First, the vulnerable and weaker of the two sides must understand what their rights are, including their historic territorial rights, their rights to lands where they have been living for generations, and their rights of access to natural resources on which they depend, such as fish in the nearby river. Indigenous peoples have the right to determine the course and pace of their own development and the right to self-determination. Facilitating the process of FPIC is usually best done by neutral agents. This may preclude the WBG from acting as the facilitator for a FPIC process, because it usually has a vested interest in the positions of governments and corporations as much as in the rights of potentially affected peoples. (Colchester et al. 2003)

The second category of information concerns the nature of the project being contemplated by the proponent. Affected people must understand the potential harm and risks that might accrue if they accept the project. Worst-case scenarios and potential disasters need to be understood. In the experience of many indigenous peoples, it may be beyond their imagination and even beyond their vocabulary for a river to die. However, an industry can easily kill a river.

The possible death of a river, the sterilization of an area of ocean, or the irreversible removal of a tract of forest is not easy for many indigenous peoples to imagine. Even the damage from a rare and devastating forest fire, within living memory, or in oral history, is not irreversible. Regeneration restores many resources after a few decades. Showing a cartoon or video film of a similar project or accident elsewhere cannot be assumed sufficient to bring affected people up to speed for the "fully informed" comprehension criterion.

"Prior" means FPIC has to be obtained before permission is granted to the proponent to proceed with the proposed project that will affect the communities; this means well before a financing agency considers the request to finance the project. FPIC is best achieved as part of the standard Environmental and Social Impact Assessment process. The impacts are predicted together, and their mitigation is also designed together.

"Consent" means harmonious, voluntary agreement with the measures designed to make the proposed project acceptable to the potentially affected communities. Tacit consent is avoided by the "fully informed" criterion: silence is not the consent required for FPIC.

FPIC does not demand absolute consensus: a significant majority suffices. A majority of 51 percent suffices in democratic elections, which may be used as a guide to the definition of a "significant majority." If there is substantial opposition to the proposed project, FPIC becomes less achievable. Although there are no hard and fast rules about the fraction agreeing, the point is usually less important than it at first appears. Most societies discuss important issues together as a community, with leaders or representatives, and often for days on end, until the spirit of consensus is reached.

Text Box 23.4 Canada's First Nations, FPIC, and Extractive Industries

In the early 1970s, Canada wanted to extract hydrocarbons from the Yukon and Mackenzie Valley, territories of Canada's Indigenous People or "First Nations." The 1974-1977 Royal Commission, headed by Supreme Court Judge Thomas R. Berger, sided with the First Nations' rejection of the project because the likely impacts looked too severe, the offered benefits too meager, and the promises aspirational. Since then, political evolution and forceful legislation have improved protection for the First Nations and strengthened their bargaining power, partly by devolving control from Ottawa to the First Nations. The First Nations communities now have some ownership rights over both surface and sub-surface resources. In 2001 oil corporations and First Nations became partners with most of the potentially impacted First Nations negotiating a financial stake in the proposed pipeline. Now it seems as if the First Nations will provide FPIC. Pipeline planning began in earnest in 2003. It seems that the thirty-year delay has been justified. (The EcoLibertarian, 2007)

In summary, FPIC requires that the affected communities must understand that they will benefit from the proposed project, and that these specific benefits will far exceed any worst-case scenario of unforeseen impacts. Affected communities must become convinced, organically and in their own way and time, that:

- prudent mechanisms are in place to guarantee their benefits,
- compensation will be just, and
- rehabilitation will ensure the communities are promptly and clearly better off with the project.

In addition, affected people must be seen to understand that they will be fully involved in legally enforceable monitoring to ensure compliance with whatever they are consenting to.

World Bank's Current Stance on Human Rights

Apart from the 1981 ethnic minority policy, IFC's 1997 adoption of two of ILO's core labor standards (child labor and slavery), and Shihata's publications up to 2000, the WBG fended off human rights. Attention to the relatively new issues of governance and corruption led the Bank to confront human rights from 2005. (Kaufmann, 2005; Dañino, 2006) The topic recently (2006) was added to the Frequently Asked Questions section of its official Web site. A human rights focal point, human rights unit, human rights trust fund, guidance to staff, or even a policy may be forthcoming within the organization.

1.   The WBG now considers labor unions, collective bargaining, and other civil liberties to be "economic," according to WBG's own research (e.g., Isham et al. 1997; Aidt and Tzannatos, 2003).
2.   The International Court of Justice has ruled that the WBG's Articles of Agreement need to be interpreted in the context of contemporary law, in which human rights are of international concern, rather than political matters exclusively the purview of domestic governments.
3.   WBG President Wolfensohn stated in 1999 that no equitable development is possible without protection of human rights.
4.   A Human Rights Policy approach paper was discussed by WBG Executive Directors in 2003, but was rejected. Industrial country representatives were positive, but developing country representatives felt human rights could be misused as a form of trade protectionism.
5.   IFC's Peter Woicke raised the need for a Safeguard Policy on Human Rights at least twice during the 2002-2004 independent Extractive Industries Review (EIR). (Goodland, 2003) In addition, he published his desire for a new, official, Human Rights Safeguard Policy both in the Financial Times, and again on Human Rights Day (December 10, 2003), and again at the March 2004 Human Rights and Development conference in New York.
6.   Almost all WBG member countries have ratified human rights standards in international conventions. But, WBG's policies prohibit it from supporting violations of member countries' commitments to uphold international treaties, including human rights obligations. Shihata (1997; 1991-2000) ruled that obligations under the UN Charter (Article 103) prevail over the WBG's Articles of Agreement.
7.   The WB's "Management Response" to the independent (World Bank, 2004a) rejected EIR's recommendations on FPIC and human rights, and even the two UN ILO Core Labor Standards that IFC had adopted in 1997. President Wolfensohn distanced himself from this response, and ordered a more positive re-think. The final 2004 response of the WBG to the EIR mandated "Prior In-

formed Consultation . . . and broad acceptance of the project by affected communities."

8.   The WB's official legal note on FPIC (World Bank, 2004b) was emitted by: (a) the Senior Vice President and General Counsel of the WB, (b) the General Counsel of IFC, and (c) the Vice President and General Counsel of MIGA. Oddly, it fails to distinguish between "consultation" and "consent;" in practice, as of mid-2007, they are converging.

Conclusions and Recommendations

Several changes are called for in the way that development projects are undertaken:

1.   Economic development should not rely on force. Coercion means people are being excluded and are forced to subsidize the developer.

2.   The Bank should follow its Articles of Agreement and stick to standard economics. If willing seller/willing buyer is not upheld, force is used and economics does not apply.

3.   FPIC should be required for all operations (e.g., displacement) involving indigenous and non-indigenous peoples, and all projects impacting communities.

4.   Policies on displacement, resettlement, compensation, consultation, participation, disclosure, and transparency should require that FPIC is the main criterion to be used as a social license to operate, hence as the main tool in deciding whether to permit a development operation once FPIC has been legitimately obtained.

5.   Because genuine FPIC is difficult and time consuming to obtain, it is best sought by reputable, objective, and independent agents, rather than either by the proponent, the government, or by development agencies.

6.   The conditions under which "Eminent Domain" is permissible need to be clarified, especially in resettlement. Eminent Domain must be used for public use only, not for private or corporate use.

7.   Resettlement policy needs to be revamped as a matter of urgency, such that all people displaced become modestly better off promptly after their resettlement. Performance bonds, insurance, fractions of sales receipts, and escrow accounts should be used to guarantee that no oustee is worse off than before the project was identified.

Acknowledgments

I am most grateful for the useful comments of Professor Ted Scudder. Professor Colin Soskolne deserves more than acknowledgment for his superb editing without which this chapter would not have seen the light of day.

References

Aidt, Toke, and Zafiris Tzannatos. *Unions and Collective Bargaining: Economic Effects in a Global Environment.* Washington, DC: The World Bank, Publ. No. 24730, 2003.

Ali, Salim. H. *Mining, the Environment and Indigenous Development Conflicts.* Tucson: University of Arizona Press, 2003.

Alston, Philip, and Mary Robinson. *Human Rights and Development: Towards Mutual Reinforcement.* New York: Oxford University Press, 2005.

Athialy, John. *Free Prior Informed Consent of Communities in Large Hydroprojects: The Case of the James Bay Projects.* Worcester, MA: Clark University, International Development, Community and Environment, 2003.

Bass, Susan, Pooja Seth Parikh, Roman Czebiniak, and Meg Filbey. *Prior Informed Consent and Mining: Promoting the Sustainable Development of Local Communities.* Washington, DC: Environmental Law Institute, 2004.

Berliner, Dana. *Public Power, Private Gain: a Five-Year, State-by-State Report Examining the Abuse of Eminent Domain.* Arlington, VA: Institute for Justice, 2003. http://CastleCoalition.org (31 May 2007).

Bosshard, Peter. *Free Prior Informed Consent: No Longer a Question of Omelettes and Eggs.* Berkeley, CA: International Rivers Network, 8 March presentation to the Berne Declaration, 2004.

Bosshard, Peter, Janneke Bruil, Korinna Horta, Shannon Lawrence, and Carol Welch. *Gambling with People's Lives: What the "High-Risk/High-Reward" Strategy Means for the Poor and the Environment.* Environment Defense, Friends of the Earth, International Rivers Network, 2003.

Callies, David L., Daniel Curtin, and Julie Tappendorf. *Bargaining for Development: A Handbook on Development Agreements, Annexation Agreements, Land Development Conditions, Vested Rights and the Provision of Public Facilities.* Washington, DC: Environmental Law Institute, 2003.

Cernea, Mikhail. "For a New Economics of Resettlement: a Sociological Critique of the Compensation Principle." *International Social Science Journal* 1, no. 175 (2003): 37–46.

Colchester, Marcus, Ann Loreto Tamayo, Raymundo Rovillos, and Emily Caruso, eds. *Extracting Promises: Indigenous Peoples, Extractive Industries and the World Bank.* Baguio City, Philippines: Tebtebba Foundation, 2003.

Dañino, Roberto. *Legal Opinion on Human Rights and the Work of the World Bank.* IFIwatchnet, 2006. www.ifiwatchnet.org/sites/ifiwatchnet.org/files/DaninoLegalOpinion 0106.pdf (5 Jun. 2007).

Downing, Theodore. "Creating Poverty: The Flawed Economic Logic of the World Bank's Revised Resettlement Policy." *Forced Migration Review* 12 (2002).

EcoLibertarian. http://ecolibertarian.com/2007/04/28/a-decades-delay-for-the-mackenzie-valley-pipeline (17 Jun. 2007).

EIR. *The Independent Extractive Industries Review: Final Report to the World Bank Group (Dr. Emil Salim's Report).* Jakarta and Washington, DC: EIR: 2003.

Epstein, Richard A. *Takings: Private Property and the Power of Eminent Domain.* Cambridge, MA: Harvard University Press, 2005 (reprint edition).

Forest Peoples Program. *Indigenous People's Right to Free, Prior and Informed Consent and the World Bank's Extractive Industry Review.* Moreton-in-the-Marsh, UK: (Fergus MacKay), Forest Peoples Program, 2004.

Goldzimer, Aaron Marc. *Prior Informed Consent of Project-Affected Indigenous Peoples.* Cambridge, MA: John F. Kennedy School of Government, 2000.

Goodland, Robert. *Case of Twelve Saramaka Clans (Case 12.338) v. Suriname: Affidavit.* San José, Costa Rica. Inter-American Court of Human Rights: April 2007a.

———. *Economic Development and Tribal Peoples: Human Ecological Considerations.* Washington, DC: The World Bank, 1981.

———. "Free Prior Informed Consent and the World Bank." *Sustainable Development Law and Policy* 4, no. 2 (2004): 66–74.

———. *India: Utkal Bauxite Project: Human Rights and Environmental Impacts.* Washington, DC: 2007b. (In press).

———. "Strategic Environmental Assessment in the World Bank." *International Journal of Sustainable Development & World Ecology* 12 (2005): 1–11.

———. *Sustainable Development Sourcebook for the World Bank's Independent Extractive Industries Review: Examining the Social and Environmental Impacts of Oil, Gas and Mining.* Washington, DC: Extractive Industries Review [for the] World Bank Group, 2003.

Handl, Günther. "Environmental Security and Global Change: The Challenge to International Law." *Environmental Protection and International Law*, edited by Winfried Lang et al. London: Graham & Trotman/Martinus Nijhoff, 1991.

———. *Multilateral Development Banking: Environmental Principles and Concepts Reflecting General International Law and Public Policy.* The Hague, Netherlands: Kluwer Law International, 2001.

Human Rights Watch. *World Report.* Washington, DC: HRW, 2007.

Isham, Jonathan, Daniel Kaufman, and Lant Pritchett.. "Civil Liberties, Democracy and Performance of Governments." *The World Bank Economic Review* 11, 1997.

Kaufmann, Daniel. "Human Rights and Governance: The Empirical Challenge." *Human Rights and Development: Towards Mutual Reinforcement*, edited by Philip Alston, and Mary Robinson. New York: Oxford University Press, 2005.

Kotaka, Tsuyoshi, and David L. Callies. *Taking Land: Compulsory Purchase and Regulation in Asian-Pacific Countries.* Honolulu: University of Hawai'i Press, 2002.

MacKay, Fergus. "Indigenous Peoples Right to Free, Prior and Informed Consent and the World Bank's Extractive Industry Review." *Sustainable Development Law and Policy* 4, no. 2 (2004): 43–65.

McCully, Patrick. *Silenced Rivers: The Ecology and Politics of Large Dams.* London: Zed Books, 1996.

McDowell, Christopher, and Nicholas Van Hear. *Catching Fire: Containing Forced Migration in a Volatile World.* Lanham, MD: Lexington, 2006.

Mehta, Lyla, and Maria Stankovitch. "Operationalisation of Free Prior Informed Consent." Institute of Development Studies (UK) [and] World Commission on Dams, Contributing Paper, 2000.

Moody, Richard. *The Gulliver File: Mines, People, Land: A Global Battleground.* London: Pluto Press, 1992.

Rypinski, Richard G. *Eminent Domain: A Step-by-Step Guide to the Acquisition of Real Property.* Point Arena, CA: Solano Press, 2002.

Shihata, Ibrahim F. I. *Complementary Reform: Essays on Legal, Judicial, and Other Institutional Reforms Supported by the World Bank.* The Hague, Netherlands: Kluwer Law International, 1997.

———. *The World Bank in a Changing World.* Dordrecht, Netherlands: M. Nijhoff Publishers, 1991–2000.

Slack, Keith. "Sharing the Riches of the Earth: Democratizing Natural Resource-Led Development." *Carnegie Council on Ethics and International Affairs*, 2004.

Snyder, David B. "Debate over What Justifies the Use of the Power of Eminent Domain." *Mortgage Banking* 66, no. 5 (2006): 66–71.

Thakkur, Hemanshu. "Lessons Unlearned? The Case of India's Allain Duhangan Dam and the World Bank." *World Rivers Review* 19, no. 1 (2004): 10–11.

WCD. *Dams and Development: A New Framework for Decision-Making.* London: Earthscan, 2000.

Westra, Laura. *Ecoviolence and the Law: Supranational Normative Foundations of Ecocrime.* Ardsley, NY: Transnational Publishers, 2004.

World Bank. *Equity and Development.* Washington, DC: World Development Report, 2006.

———. *Legal Note on Prior and Informed Consultation.* Washington, DC: The World Bank (2 Aug.), Three General Counsels, 2004b.

———. *Management Response to the Independent Extractive Industry Review.* Washington, DC: (23 Jan.), WBG, 2004a.

———. *Resettlement and Development: The Bankwide Review of Projects Involving Involuntary Resettlement 1986–1993*, 2nd ed. Washington, DC: The World Bank (1994), 1996.

World Wildlife Fund. *Dam Right: WWF's Dams Initiative.* Gland, Switzerland: WWF Working Paper, 2004.

Chapter 24

Globalization and the Degradation of Rural Livelihoods: A Comparative Study of Mexico and Vietnam under Trade Liberalization

Jack P. Manno, Ph.D. (Social Science)

College of Environmental Science and Forestry
State University of New York, Ithaca, NY, U.S.A.

Contact Information: 24 Bray Hall, Syracuse, NY 13210 U.S.A.
Phone: +1 315 470 6816; Email: jpmanno@syr.edu

Thanh Vo, Ph.D. Candidate (Environmental and Natural Resource Policy)

Dept. of Science and Technology of Thua Thien Province, Vietnam

Contact Information: 105 Marshall Hall, Syracuse, NY 13210 U.S.A.
Phone: +1 315 395 0973; Email: tdvo@syr.edu

Summary

How we understand the world is deeply rooted in our primal relationship to a provisioning Earth and in the ways we obtain our food.

Any significant change in food production and distribution transforms social, cultural, and spiritual life. This is why impacts of free trade on agriculture, especially staple foods like rice and corn that have sustained human populations for millennia, are so important. Agricultural skills and knowledge are place-specific and cannot be readily transferred.

Much of value in the relationship between land and people is not reflected in the values of the market. The intensified commoditization of agriculture, which is the intention of free trade agreements, disrupts rural livelihoods.

In this chapter, we analyze the impact of free trade agreements on corn farming in Mexico, and apply the lessons learned to rice cultivation in Vietnam.

With policies to protect the non-market values produced by sustainable rural livelihoods, the benefits of increased productivity and efficiency can be achieved while protecting ecologically unique, locally productive economies. To do this, "modernizing" nations, like Mexico, Vietnam, and many other so-called developing nations, must reconsider what it means to "modernize."

To be truly "modern" in the twenty-first century, one must learn the lessons of the past to shape the future for true sustainability. This will permit us to broadly support a high quality of life for a long time, while living within the limits and productive capacities of the ecosystems on which we depend and of which we are a part.

Background

What we sometimes call "traditional environmental knowledge" is amassed by living in a place for a long time, carefully observing, experimenting, systematizing, and communicating insights and skills for how to survive well in a given place. In every part of the world, indigenous horticulturalists have *created*, so to speak, many varieties of grains suited to the ecology of the place and the nutritional needs of the people who inhabit it. These grains are products of human culture, and human culture is a product of these grains. It is not an overstatement to talk about "maize culture" and "rice culture." Agricultural livelihoods are as much an expression of human intelligence and creativity as are great works of art; they reflect the outcome of active engagement with the raw materials of an environment.

As Mexican economist, David Barkin has written about maize agriculture:

> The technological developments required for maize production demanded an ever increasing knowledge of ecosystems and the lands where it was planted, of the needs of the seeds themselves, of the techniques for cultivating the lands, for assuring its timely flowering and the maturation of the plant. Cultivation required the manufacture of specialized tools for the clearing and preparation of the land and for the care of the crop, for the setting of the seeds and the harvesting and cleaning of the cobs. Infrastructure for storage and sophisticated new technologies were developed to extract the greatest benefit possible from the grain. A large variety of associated crops—a diversity of beans and squash are among the best known—and by-products like huitlacoche were introduced or collected, converting the complex milpa system into an object of admiration and emulation by connoisseurs, for its extraordinary diversity and the mechanisms by which the various elements protect each other and ward off external predators, without the need to resort to poisonous substances that are so necessary in today's specialized single-crop systems. (Barkin, 2002: 76)

To the extent that international and global political institutions, such as those anticipated by the *Earth Charter* (see the Appendix), can create the conditions to support and sustain rice and maize culture and agriculture, the prospects for sustainability and the promotion of ecological integrity will be enhanced.

Objectives

This chapter contributes by carefully analyzing two cases unfolding as we write. First, we explore recent changes in maize agriculture in Mexico to analyze the effects of trade and regional economic integration. Then, we ask what lessons can be drawn, specifically for Vietnam as its rice production systems are similarly and increasingly integrated into the regional and global economy through the Asian Free Trade Agreement (AFTA) and the World Trade Organization

(WTO). Finally, we explore the implications of these changes to agricultural and social policies in both countries, and globally. What we find in Mexico and expect to see in Vietnam is that the effects are very different for different kinds of agriculture. Both countries' agriculturalists can be divided into three groups, depending on size, land quality, and source of water. (Nadal, 2000; Oxfam, 2001; Pandey and Dang, 1998) In Mexico these are:

- *Competitive producers.* Farms larger than 10 ha, typically on soil, drainage, and slope conditions with ready access to credit and skills to apply advanced technologies. They have been able to increase yields to compete economically with imported corn under NAFTA. In some cases they have been able to shift to higher value crops (flowers, fruits, and vegetables) for export to the United States of America (U.S.A.) and Europe.
- *Intermediate producers.* Midsize producers cultivate plots from 2 to 10 ha. These farmers utilize a variety of cultivation techniques. They have been able to maintain stable production, but have been badly affected by lower prices and increased competition under the new market regimes. Some have been able to adjust their production methods, their crops, or they have found alternative livelihoods.
- *Traditional producers.* The majority of farmers in Mexico practice traditional methods of multi-cropping and shifting cultivation known as *milpa* for their own household, and take whatever is surplus to local markets. Their land is almost exclusively rainfed.

Table 24.1 Three Groups of Farmers in Mexico

Categories Characteristics	Competitive	Intermediate	Subsistence
Land area	> 10ha	2-10 ha	<2ha
Financial capital	Capitalized Readily available capital	Difficult to access credit especially bank, and commercial investment	Little or no savings Almost no credit accessibility
Physical, natural capital, and technological capabilities	Applying new technologies Good land/soil conditions/irrigation	Using various cultivation techniques Fairly good land, partly irrigated	Traditional cultivation methods Marginal land, rainfed
Market relationships	Competitive under NAFTA Produce for national and export markets	Difficult to compete under NAFTA	Produce for household consumption, surplus to market Produce multiple non-market values Sensitive to market and monetary flows

Trade liberalization predictably leads to at least temporary growth of large-scale industrial farming, large losses in intermediate family farms, and while subsistence agriculture, perhaps surprisingly, continues—largely because of farmers' commitment to it even when "rational" economists might advise otherwise.

Corn in Mexico

At the center of origin and diversity of maize, Mexican cultivators have created myriad varieties adapted to different climates and altitudes, from 2,700 meters above sea level and down. A typical small-scale Mexican maize grower cultivates *milpa,* an ancestral method handed down from indigenous growers. A *milpa* may include many crops in addition to corn. The corn provides structure on which legumes can climb, beans fertilize the soil by fixing nitrogen from the air, while broad squash leaves shade out competitive weeds. The roots of each of these symbiotic plants take nutrients from different depth and range of soil. Eaten together, we have a nutritionally complete meal; each plant provides essential amino acids missing in the others.

Farmers typically also grow companion crops that provide a range of vitamins, minerals, and vegetable fats such as avocados, melons, tomatoes, chilies, amaranth, jicama, mucuma, and sweet potato. They also farm in ways designed to attract birds and other animals taken as game. In addition to the complex symbiotic cooperation among the crop elements of this farming system, it requires a high level of cooperation among farmers for road building and maintenance, mutual aid during clearing and harvesting, animal control, and water management. Much of this was institutionalized in the *ejidos,* the village and family-based collective ownership of common agricultural lands that grew out of post-revolutionary Mexico's land reform, but which had its roots in indigenous forms of commons management. (Barkin, 2002; Faust, 1998) What is lost if *milperos* abandon their fields is a vast amount of non-market, but culturally and ecologically valuable, traditional knowledge and skills that have provided healthy food and relative, but uneasy food security for hundreds, perhaps thousands of years.

The destruction of traditional *milpa*-based livelihoods was certainly not the purpose for Mexico of the North American Free Trade Agreement (NAFTA), nor is reducing traditional rice cultivation motivating Vietnam in a similar direction. The strategic economic objective when governments "modernize" their agriculture away from "outmoded" practices is efficiency.

We learn about the benefits of trade in economics courses. Here is how the argument goes: trade encourages each nation to employ its natural and human resources producing those goods that its endowments of climate, soil, raw materials, skills, technology, and culture make it most efficient at producing, selling those to others, and thereby earning the money needed to purchase those goods and services the nation may be poorly suited to produce. Free trade encourages specialization and productive innovation. The net result: economic efficiency improves everywhere. Any interference in trade tends to undermine trade's efficiency gains. The purpose of free-trade agreements is to maximize the opportunities to capture the benefits from trade.

In theory, this works. But there are things other than economic efficiency that people value: security, independence, environmental protection, and social cohesion. These might well be undermined by the unintended consequences of free trade. Those who suffer the negative consequences are not always or even often the same people who gain the benefits from trade, thus making the balancing of costs and benefits politically complicated, if not impossible. In general, those who stand to gain by the liberalization of trade in food staples are the urban middle-class consumers for whom the price of food steadily declines. The losers tend to be rural producers whose services are necessary if traditional cultivation is to continue.

Among Mexico's comparative advantages in North American trade are fossil fuels, other natural resources, and cheap labor for industrial farms and the factories where consumer goods are assembled for shipping to the U.S.A., the so-called *maquiladoras*. Between the signing of NAFTA in 1994 and 2005, trade between Mexico, Canada, and the U.S.A. had tripled, and Mexico was annually exporting $187 billion worth of goods and services to the U.S.A. while importing from the U.S.A. $123 billion, for a $64 billion trade surplus with the U.S.A. (CIA, 2006)

By importing corn and therefore lowering food prices, "inefficient" farmers and the women from farm families are encouraged to join the mass of workers available to expanding economic sectors, assembly and tourism, thereby dampening wage pressures in those industries. At the same time, lowering the price of staple food was expected to lower inflation overall. It also was expected to relieve the government treasury of the need to subsidize farm income while supplying government corn at artificially low prices, and ease the environmental pressure resulting from an expanding rural population by clearing more marginal land on which to inefficiently grow corn. (Nadal, 2000) By focusing Mexico's resources on the greatest possible economic productivity, a wide variety of objectives were being achieved.

Mexico, like most "developing" countries and like Vietnam, seems to have little choice but to organize its domestic economy to meet the demands of the global financial system. It is either that, or accepting isolation and less investment at the same time that population growth and rising popular expectations create much greater need for foreign investment. The result is the spread of a pattern of investing public resources in ways to stimulate and improve market-focused productivity; in other words, to give highest priority to the production of those commodities (goods and services for sale in broad markets) that the country is most economically suited to produce. This has the tendency (described in detail in Manno, 2000) of systematically underdeveloping those non-market goods that do not function well in markets. What cannot easily enter markets are those values that are place- and relationship-based, those non-commodities, things like ecological health, community knowledge of the specifics of soil and place, and other goods that are non-commoditizable because their value cannot be alienated from specific relationships and be transferred, sold, or exported.

The systematic loss of the ability and will to support and sustain the production of these non-market goods and services is an outcome of the increasing control of market forces over productive resources (energy, raw materials, human attention, and creativity). Indigenous and organic methods of farming rely heavily on local natural resources, community networks of cooperation, and personal skills that cannot be separated from their local and cultural context and be transferred to a willing buyer. The most important resources required for and produced by *milpa* are non-market but valuable goods and services. Agricultural commoditization operates at the level of inputs and practices, preferentially developing commoditizable inputs (like hybrid seeds, fertilizers, pesticides, equipment) and farming methods that best utilize these inputs. Commoditization also operates on the outputs, favoring standardized crops marketed broadly, and selecting out varieties with characteristics that are locally adapted to unique soil and farming circumstances.

Mexican officials were not unaware that freer trade would threaten important cultural and social values tied to peasant farms and the communities they supported. Because of the importance of domestic corn production, the Mexican government planned a fifteen-year transition during which local corn prices would be expected to equilibrate with global prices. During this time, NAFTA rules allowed, and the Mexican government promised, to maintain quotas and tariffs to keep corn imports below 2.5 million tons per year, while continuing agricultural subsidies to stabilize domestic production. (Nadal, 2002) However, the 1994 financial crisis made it difficult if not impossible for the Mexican government to fund the transition plans. Furthermore, with the argument that lower corn prices were needed to reduce inflationary pressures, the Mexican Government abandoned the tariff and quota provisions as originally planned. Cheap U.S.A. corn flooded the Mexican domestic market. With the increase of cheap imported corn from the U.S.A., prices fell by 48 percent between 1994 and 1996. Local producers had to sell at prices below their costs of production.

Mexico's strategy was to shift farm labor from maize to higher-market value, labor-intensive crops like tropical fruit and vegetables, flowers, and decorative plants for export to the U.S.A. and Canada, particularly during the North American winter. The NAFTA parties' official economic analysis by Levy and Van (1992) predicted that there would be substantial change in production away from maize, and a large increase in farm wage labor. However, according to De Janvry and Sadoulet (1995) and Nadal (2000; 2002) the shift in labor allocation from corn to other crops was much more complicated. The demands of meeting the shelf-life and visual quality control standards of North American consumers make cultivation for fruit and vegetable export not only labor, but also highly energy-, chemical-, and technology-intensive. Without financial and technical support from the government on the scale needed and that it was in no position to provide, NAFTA would not transform corn farmers to fruit and vegetable farmers.

Moreover, government officials appeared to misjudge how corn producers would change their livelihood strategies in reaction to lower prices. Maize farmers' livelihood decisions result from many factors among which market price of corn and realistic alternative crops are important, but not necessarily determining. Other factors include the cost of labor, alternative employment opportunities, interest rates and availability of credit, and a variety of family, social, and cultural commitments and preferences. Perhaps what was least understood was the persistence and determination of Mexican farmers to continue to grow corn.

Owing to the lack of understanding of producers' motives, the government largely failed to implement transitional support programs. As a result, Mexican corn growers continued to farm while having to absorb the shock of rapidly declining terms of trade for their products. This took place in an atmosphere of trade liberalization and accompanying dramatic changes in the Mexican retail market where giant international corporations, including Wal-Mart and Price-Costco, merged with large domestic retailers. Since the early 1990s, supermarkets and chains of convenience stores have dominated over half of the retail market, crowding out the traditional producers' markets, making transport, refrigeration, and packaging demands, reducing dramatically the farmer's share of the food dollar, and further undermining the peasant economy. (Schwetsius and Gomez, 2002)

Perhaps the most remarkable part of this story is the fact that, in the face of devastating changes in the rural economy, peasants have not stopped or even significantly reduced their production of native maize for their own consumption and their community.

Table 24.2. Corn Production in Mexico from 1988–1998

	'88	'89	'90	'91	'92	'93	'94	'95	'96	'97	'98	'99	'00	'01	'02
Total (Millions of tonnes)	10.6	10.9	14.6	14.2	16.9	18.1	18.2	18.3	18.0	17.7	18.5	17.7	17.5	20.1	19.3
I (percent.)	25	25	23	30	32	43	47	34	32	39	33	28	29	NA	NA
R (percent.)	75	75	77	70	68	57	53	66	68	61	67	72	71	NA	NA
Harvested Area (Millions of Hectares)	6.5	6.5	7.3	6.9	7.2	7.4	8.2	8.0	8.0	7.4	7.9	7.2	7.0	7.8	7.1

I: irrigation; R: rainfed; Percentages refer to share of total production
Surface: million hectares; Corn: millions of tonnes (metric)
Sources: Centro de estadistica agropecuaria (SAGAR) quoted in Nadal, 2000; SAGAR and others; in Barkin, 2002; and FAO Statistics. NA: nonapplicable

While corn imports rose by a factor of five between 1970 and 1998, domestic production more than doubled while land under cultivation mostly remained the same. During the period of most dramatic change, 1992-1994, production largely shifted to irrigated, competitive farms, and by the end of the century, the distribution of production between rainfed and irrigated land had returned to levels of the early 1980s.

Both intermediate and subsistence producers have increased corn planting. Their ability to continue to cultivate corn has been subsidized by income generated by family members who have left their communities for work in Mexico's cities and abroad. In addition, new markets for traditional varieties of corn have developed among Mexico's urban consumers, creating specialty outlets where foods understood as more authentic or healthier and prepared in traditional ways, command a higher price.

Although rural Mexicans have creatively responded to the economic changes of regional economic integration by diversifying their productive activities, the toll is high on rural communities. Many villages have been depopulated especially by migration of young adults, devastating the social structures that play a key role in natural resource management in the rural areas of Mexico. The environmental effects for Mexico have been considerable, including water pollution, water depletion, the spread of genetically modified corn, soil erosion, and biodiversity loss. (Ackerman et al., 2003)

This suggests significant ways that economic integration affects the natural environment, with all of its implications for ecological integrity. Trade liberalization policies have diverse and complex affects on dynamic rural systems. The economic changes of NAFTA shift local livelihood strategies and therefore alter the traditional incentives to conserve and protect local environments.

These livelihood changes have led to the declining collective labor action for natural conservation and the erosion of indigenous knowledge and skills for *in situ* conservation of genetic resource of corn in Mexico. (Nadal, 2000; CEC, 2002) The loss of local varieties of corn threatens not only food security and the life of many subsistence farmers in mountainous and remote areas, but national food security as well. According to the study by the tri-national environmental commission created by NAFTA, the Commission on Environmental Cooperation (CEC, 2002), changes in production processes, technology, social organizations, and environmental impacts are all highly related and interdependent.

In considering the environmental impacts of trade policies, we borrow the conceptual framework (Figure 24.1) proposed by Slootweg, Vanclay, and van Schooten cited in Vanclay (2002). According to this framework, as policies create incentives and disincentives that stimulate changes in people's patterns of productive activities, their impacts on the environment change as well. It is an iterative, coevolutionary process in which the social and biophysical are entwined.

Trade Policy and Environmental Impacts

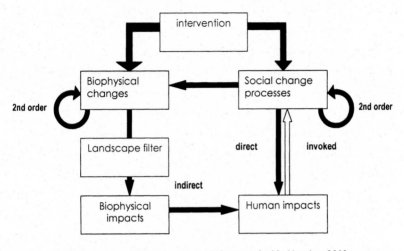

Sources: Slootweg, Vanclay, and van Schooten, cited in Vanclay, 2002.

Figure 24.1. Relationship between Trade Policy and Environmental Impacts

Rice in Vietnam

Rice provides the majority of calories for half the people in the world. Even today, most rice is either produced by and for the household, or obtained from small-scale farmers through local markets. Rice farmers produce more than rice. Traditional rice production systems include several plants and animals that contribute to rural diets and incomes. Rice is the main staple crop in Vietnam and is cultivated throughout the country.

Vietnam is known as one of the original centers of rice cultivation. Water-rice production has played an important role in shaping Vietnamese culture and landscapes. (UNEP, 2003; Oxfam, 2001; CEMMA, 2002)

The following numbers demonstrate how important rice is to Vietnam:

- Rice accounts for 75 percent of Vietnam's food calories.
- Ninety-five percent of rural households, representing 80 percent of the total population, grow rice. Almost half of them produce a surplus for sale.
- Rice production is the main source of income for rural households, contributing from 44 percent to 51 percent of rural household's annual revenue.
- In the year 2005, there were 7.4 million hectares of land under rice cultivation, yielding 40 million tons, and exporting 5.2 million tons of rice, making it the second-largest exporter of rice in the world. (MARD, 2006)

World trade in rice continues to grow, as does the international system of production and distribution. During the "Doi moi" (renovation) period of the late 1980s, socialist Vietnam liberalized its economy and began to cooperate in the regional integration of Southeast Asia.

Now a state-member of the Association of South East Asia Nations (ASEAN), Vietnam fully joined the ASEAN Free Trade Agreement (AFTA) in 2006. It has been officially a member of the WTO since January 2007 and is also in the process of joining the WTO. This will result in the gradual reduction and eventual elimination of tariffs and quotas on imported goods. (MARD, 2002a, 2002b)

As we saw in Mexico, one of the great tensions created by trade liberalization with its general tendency to favor overall productivity and efficiency is its effects on crop diversity.

Vietnam can be divided into seven distinct ecological zones where topography, soil conditions, and climate vary. The great proliferation of rice varieties and growing methods over time and across geography results from the work of farmers who have created or adopted crop varieties and farming methods that are best fit for specific ecological conditions.

This leads to very different levels of output depending on conditions. In 1995, in the northern mountainous highlands and midlands, the northern central coast, the central highlands, and the south eastern region, per capita food crop output was below 250 kilograms, while production in the Mekong Delta was 775 kilograms. (Luu, 2003)

Again like Mexico, the pattern of rice cultivation differs from region to region, with two main cultivation systems: irrigated and rainfed. The largest yields and the greatest concentration of production are in the irrigated lowlands of Vietnam's two main deltas: Red River in the North and Mekong in the South. With increasing population and expansion of export agriculture, more and more pressure is placed on water management systems, while at the same time, the increasing use of fertilizers and pesticides threatens water quality.

More than fifty distinct ethnic groups live in the humid forest zones of the Vietnamese highlands and rely on rainfed rice. Most upland rice cultivation involves shifting cultivation of the slash and burn variety. (Xuan and Arraudeau, 1995, cited in Luu, 2003) Owing to the climatic, soil, and topographical conditions, yields tend to be comparatively low.

In general, upland farmers do not use chemical fertilizers or pesticides when planting traditional varieties; instead, they use organic fertilizer from the burned left-over leaves after harvesting. (Luu, 2003) Use of traditional varieties throughout Vietnam is still considerably high, though it is much lower than that of modern varieties. The total area planted with traditional varieties accounts for 3.6 percent to 21.4 percent of the total area under rice production, depending on the region.

Attempts to introduce new high-yielding rice varieties in the uplands have usually failed because of the climatic and topographical conditions of these regions, which limit both the development of irrigation systems and the ecological viability of modern varieties. (EWC and CRES, 2001; CEMMA, 2002) The continued use of "lower yield" local varieties is thus necessary for local food security and the livelihoods of highland communities.

To draw inferences for Vietnam from Mexico, we need to consider some of the differences and similarities between the two experiences.

While both crops are important to the rural and national economies of the each country, there is a significant difference in the direction and terms of agricultural trade. Mexico expected to, and did become, a major importer of corn from the Corn Belt of the fertile plains of the U.S.A., its primary trading partner, while Vietnam has become a major exporter of rice.

Surprisingly though, whether one is a net exporter or an importer, the impacts on rural livelihoods and the environment are, largely, that the increasing commoditization of agriculture means that emphasis is placed on farms and practices that produce the most market value.

Both Mexican and Vietnamese agriculture have been highly heterogeneous. In each country, there are significant differences in methods used and crop yields between regions. In both countries, small-scale and subsistence farmers have traditionally played major roles in providing food for communities where there are marginally productive ecological conditions. In both countries, village-level producer associations and larger farm support institutions have long organized production and marketed products.

With privatization, access to credit becomes increasingly important. Just as in Mexico before NAFTA, poor farmers in Vietnam have little access to credit. (MARD and UNDP, 2003)

The history of land reform, land ownership, and market liberalization has also been similar in the two countries.

In Mexico, the shift away from village-based land collectives, known as *ejidos*, has led to concentration into large-scale farms, and created the conditions for many small and medium farmers to leave their lands and shift their livelihood strategies.

Though it is recent, land reform in Vietnam has already led to the emergence of many new large-scale farms, and evidence of an emerging class of landless farmers.

Similar to the migration and off-farm-labor trend in Mexican rural communities before NAFTA, migration and off-farm labor have increased in rural communities in Vietnam, leading to rapid increases in urban population. (Martin, 2001; Nadal, 2000; Akram-Lodhi, 2005; Haroon Akram-Lodhi, 2005)

NAFTA and AFTA are both regional trade agreements that adopt similar trade measures such as lifting tariffs and quotas, reducing government intervention in markets, and promoting goods and production strategies based on theory of comparative advantage.

The comparative conditions of rice production systems in Vietnam and corn production in Mexico can be summarized in the following table.

Table 24.3. **Comparative Conditions of Rice Production Systems in Vietnam and Corn Production in Mexico**

Issues	Mexican Corn	Vietnamese Rice
Market Conditions	Local and domestic market prices	Local and domestic market prices
Institutions	CONASUPO, and *Ejidos*	SOC and collectives
	Technical support, financial support, and credit from government	Technical support but still not very effective (information and transferring into other crops)
	PRONASOL focus small producers	Lack of credits and financial supports)
	Lack of family saving	Lack of mechanism for family saving
Other Incentives	Maintenance genetic resources for subsistence and medium farmers	Local varieties for local conditions
	Food security	Food security
	Not many options to shift to other crops in difficult conditions	Difficult to shift to other crops
	Social capital in corn production and natural conservation	Similar
	Tradition and capacity to use traditional methods	Similar

Conclusions

The lessons from Mexico's experiences under NAFTA suggest the need to reverse the familiar injunction to "Think globally and act locally" by making certain that trade and other officials in Vietnam and elsewhere think locally when they are acting globally. As the spirit of the *Earth Charter* promotes, there is no alternative to acting globally because our fates are now forever intertwined. And clearly there are many reasons to cooperate economically and make the wisest and most efficient use of Earth's precious and limited resources.

The key is remembering and acting on what we all know: i.e., that not all goods are market goods and that our trade agreements must be designed to protect what we can ill afford to lose—chief among these goods are the skills, knowledge, cultural, and social infrastructure needed to sustain ecologically diverse, place-based cultivation of the world's important food grains. The fact that Mexican peasants have, against all odds, continued to practice and improve traditional maize cultivation, suggests that such an approach can succeed. Signs that Mexican consumers are willing to pay for the health and cultural benefits of traditional tortillas is another positive sign. Policies are needed to protect and sustain rural livelihoods within the Asian Free Trade Agreement and during the implementation of WTO agreement, that respect the heterogeneity of production systems, and that develop support mechanisms for the development of all three types of rice farmers.

It is clear that trade economists need to expand their understanding of how people make livelihood choices. Unless the importance of the relationships between people and place, communities and ecosystems, individuals and families are taken into account when designing economic development strategies, economic strategies will fail.

During any transition into larger, more competitive trade regions, diverse farmers will need diverse supports, including access to affordable credit, investment in marketing infrastructure, and technical skills. Most of all, we need national and global commitments that understand and respect the enormous value that traditional farmers have given and, indeed, continue to provide through their profound understanding of their environment. Their careful and patiently coaxed food from nature has so far meant the flourishing of our species.

References

Ackerman, Frank, Timothy A. Wise, Kevin Gallagher, Luke Ney, and Regina Flores. "Free Trade, Corn, and the Environment: Environmental Impacts of U.S.-Mexico Corn Trade under NAFTA, Global Development and Environment." Medford, MA: Tufts University Working Paper No. 03–06, Jun. 2003.

Akram-Lodhi, A. Haroon. "Vietnam's Agriculture: Processes of Rich Peasant Accumulation and Mechanisms of Social Differentiation." *Journal of Agrarian Change*, 5 (Jan. 2005): 73–116.

Barkin, David. "The Reconstruction of a Modern Mexican Peasantry," *Journal of Peasant Studies* 30, no. 1 (Oct. 2002): 73–90.

CIA (U.S. Central Intelligence Agency). https://www.cia.gov/library/publications/the-world-factbook/index.html (26 May 2006).

Commission for Environmental Cooperation (CEC). Issue Study 1. Maize in Mexico: Some Environmental Implications of the North American Free Trade Agreement (NAFTA). 2002. http://www.cec.org/files/PDF/ECONOMY/engmaize_EN.pdf (26 May 2007).

Committee Ethnic Minority and Mountainous Affair (CEMMA). *Vietnamese Mountainous Area Progresses and Development in Renovation Time.* Hanoi: Agriculture Printing House, 2002.

De Janvry, Alain, Elisabeth Sadoulet, and Gordillo De Anda. "NAFTA and Mexico's Maize Producers." *World Development* 23, no. 8 (Aug. 1995): 1349–62.

East West Center and Center for Resources and Environmental (CRES) Study. *Northern Mountainous Areas of Vietnam's Environmental and Socio-Economic Problems.* Hanoi: National Political Printing House, 2001.

FAO Statistical Databases (Food and Agriculture Organization of United Nations). http://faostat.fao.org/default.aspx?alias=faostat&lang=en (26 May 2007).

Faust, Betty B. *Mexican Rural Development and the Plumed Serpent.* Westport, CT: Bergin & Garvey, 1998.

Levy, Santiago, and Sweder van Wijinbergen. "Technical Paper No. 63. Mexican Agriculture in the Free Trade Agreement: Transition Problems in Economic Reform." *OECD Development Centre.* May 1992.

Luu, T. D. Hai. "The Organization of the Liberalized rice Market in Vietnam." Doctoral Dissertation of Rijksuniversiteit Groningen University, 2003.

Manno, Jack P. *Privileged Goods Commoditization and Its impact on Environment and Society.* FL: Lewis Publishers, 2000.

Martin, Philip. "Mexico-U.S. Migration." Institute for International Economics. 2001. http://www.iie.com/publications/chapters_preview/332/08iie3349.pdf (26 May 2007).

Ministry of Agriculture and Rural Development of Vietnam (MARD). "Evaluation of Potential Impacts on Vietnam's Agriculture during Implementing Common Effective Preferential Tariff Program (CEPT) under Agreement on ASEAN Free Trade Area (AFTA)." 2002a. http://www.isgmard.org.vn/Information%20Service/Report/Agriculture/KHQH-ASEAN-e.pdf (26 May 2007).

———. "General Report on Analysis of Vietnam Agriculture Policy under Context of WTO." Hanoi. 2001. http://www.isgmard.org.vn/Information%20Service/Report/Agriculture/General%20report-WTO-e.pdf. (26 May 2007).

———. "Planting Seeds for Future Growth." Online. 2006. http://english.vietnamnet.vn/biz/2006/01/537596/ (26 May 2007).

———. "Vietnam's Agriculture: A Strategy toward WTO." Hanoi. 2002b. http://www.isgmard.org.vn/Information%20Service/Report/Report.asp. (26 May 2007).

Ministry of Agriculture and Rural Development of Vietnam and United Nations Development Programme. *Farm Need Study.* Hanoi: Statistical Publishing House, 2003.

Nadal, Alejandro. "The Environmental and Social Impacts of Economic Liberalization on Corn Production in Mexico." Study Commissioned by Oxfam GB and WWF International. 2000. http://assets.panda.org/downloads/cornstudymexico.pdf (26 May 2007).

Nadal, Alejandro, and Zea Mays. "Effects of Trade Liberation of Mexico's Corn." *Greening the Americas. NAFTA's Lessons for Hemispheric Trade,* edited by Carolyn L. Deere and Daniel C. Esty. Cambridge, MA: MIT Press, 2002.

Oxfam. "Rice for the Poor and Trade Liberalization in Vietnam." 2001. http://www.maketradefair.com/en/assets/english/VietnamRiceResearch2001Final.pdf (26 May 2007).

Pandey, Sushil, and Dang Van Minh. "A Socio-Economic Analysis of Rice Production Systems in the Uplands of Northern Vietnam." *Agriculture, Ecosystems & Environment* 70, no. 29 (Oct. 1998): 249–58.

Schwentesius, Rita, and Manuel A. Gomez. "Supermarkets in Mexico: Impacts on Horticulture Systems." *Development Policy Review* 20, no. 4 (Sept. 2002): 487–502.

United Nations. "Environment Program. Final report on Integrated Assessment of Trade Liberalization in the Rice Sector of Vietnam." 2003. http://www.unep.ch/etu/review%20meeting/final%20vietam%20report.pdf (26 May 2007).

Vanclay, Frank. "Conceptualizing Social Impacts." *Environmental Impact Assessment Review* 22, no. 3 (May 2002): 183–211.

Chapter 25

A Toolkit for Ecoepidemiological Enquiry under Global Ecological Change

Brian D. Ladd, M.Sc. (Epidemiology)

Dept. of Public Health Sciences, School of Public Health
University of Alberta, Edmonton, Alberta

Contact Information: 13-103 Clinical Sciences Building
Edmonton, Alb. T6G 2G3 CANADA
Phone: +1 780 452 7239; Fax: +1 780 492 0364; Email: bladd@ualberta.ca

Colin L. Soskolne, Ph.D. (Epidemiology)

Dept. of Public Health Sciences, School of Public Health
University of Alberta, Edmonton, Alberta

Contact Information: 13-103 Clinical Sciences Building
Edmonton, Alb. T6G 2G3 CANADA
Phone: +1 780 492 6013; Fax: +1 780 492 0364; Email: colin.soskolne@ualberta.ca

Summary

Epidemiologists need new conceptual and analytical tools if they are to contribute to reducing negative health consequences from global ecological change. Appropriate tools that can help focus research on the key features of complex systems are needed to improve our understanding of more upstream, systemic drivers, and facilitate a more complete characterization of downstream exposures and their effects. A systems-based approach is what, in fact, characterizes the emerging field of ecoepidemiology.

In this chapter, we review several conceptual and analytical tools. We argue that these tools can support more systemic approaches to emerging ecology-health problems, and also serve as departure points for transdisciplinarity.

The Ecological Footprint is considered for its value in prompting questions about the health implications of living beyond our ecological means. The disaggregated Footprint is discussed as a means of establishing links between consumption in one location and ecologically-mediated health risks in other locations. The DPSEEA framework is emphasized for its value in resolving systemic features of economically-driven, ecology-human health relationships. Product Life-Cycle Analysis is viewed mainly as a tool for guiding the Ecological Footprint disaggregation process. The I=PAT model is discussed for its value in affirming that major drivers of human impact on the biosphere cannot be treated in isolation. Finally, Environmental Kuznets Curves are promoted to generate hypotheses and focus research questions.

These tools need to be employed and evaluated. They may be most effective for the improved modeling of human health and global ecological change.

369

Introduction

Epidemiologists study where diseases and ill-health occur, how these conditions are distributed in communities, what trajectories they follow, and what causes them. Throughout its history, epidemiology, as a science, has undergone numerous methodological and conceptual developments. (March and Susser, 2006) It also has been characterized in terms of its eras, such as the infectious disease era and the "risk factor" era. (Susser and Morabia, 2006) Developments in the field of epidemiology have paralleled changes in understandings of disease causation and have been shaped by society's needs both to effectively treat illnesses and to prevent disease.

Linear, reductionist approaches to research questions, focusing on closely-related cause-effect relationships, have characterized much of what epidemiology has contributed to public health. Only recently did ecoepidemiologists begin to grapple with the population health implications of the total ecological impress of human activity. Confronting human health risks from processes on as grand a scale as regional or even global ecological change inevitably draws us into the study of complex systems.

Epidemiology's methods and its breadth of concern have been challenged by this unprecedented scale of change in ecosystems whose ongoing functions in supporting life had, until recently, been taken for granted (e.g., predictable ranges of seasonal temperature variation, and the perceived infinite capacity of natural sinks to assimilate wastes). (McMichael et al., 2003) Changes now recognized by the public and broader scientific community alike, such as those to the global climate system, have been occurring in concert with social changes. These changes include: increased forced and voluntary movements of people internationally, urbanization and the expansion of consumption-intensive lifestyles, global trade, growing gaps between rich and poor within and among countries and regions, catastrophic failures of technology and management such as the Chernobyl nuclear disaster and the massive chemical release at Bhopal, the resurgence of known infectious diseases such as tuberculosis, and threats posed by new-found pathogens such as the human immunodeficiency virus (HIV) and avian influenza. Alone, traditional epidemiological methods are inadequate for dealing effectively with these processes and events.

Recognizing these challenges, the term "ecoepidemiology" has been used to describe epidemiological research that embraces:

- the multilevel causation of disease,
- the importance of gene-environment interactions,
- the need to consider exposures over the life course and even over multiple generations,
- the utility of methodological cross-fertilization between communicable- and chronic-disease-focused epidemiology, and

- the importance of broad contextual factors in the determination of population health states. (Susser, 2004)

In an intentional exploitation of the dual meaning of "ecological," Soskolne and Broemling (2002) further distinguished ecoepidemiology by discussing it in terms of its focus of inquiry: relationships between ecosystem disintegrity and risks to human health. Still, even as the term "ecoepidemiology" was beginning to take on meaning and find parlance, Soskolne and Bertollini (1999) were urging epidemiologists, as well as scientists and practitioners in other disciplines, to stretch their conventional conceptual and methodological boundaries so that important questions of sustainability and health at multiple scales might be addressed holistically, or systemically.

Many tools and models are available to help with this conceptual and methodological stretching. In this chapter, we discuss a selection of potentially useful analytical and conceptual tools for ecoepidemiological research into the health implications of global change: conventional and disaggregated Ecological Footprint (EF) analysis, the DPSEEA framework, Product Life-Cycle Analysis (PCLA), the I=PAT model, and Environmental Kuznets Curves. These tools are windows through which, among other factors, our often unexamined consumption and production patterns can be viewed as ecologically and epidemiologically relevant dynamics.

Pioneering work by Sieswerda et al. (2001), and subsequent confirming and enhancing work by Huynen et al. (2004), revealed important obstacles in the search for a clear relationship between indicators of ecological disintegrity and human health at the country level. These included the complicating factor of international trade, where raw and processed products and wastes cross international boundaries; the need to use multiple proxy measures to approximate the meaning of ecological disintegrity; and the questionable utility in these kinds of investigations of conventional multivariate regression techniques, which require that other factors must be held or assumed constant as relationships between pairs of variables are estimated.

Rainham and McDowell (2005) did find that life expectancy was correlated strongly with the size of a country's Ecological Footprint, with some notable exceptions (see chapter by Rainham et al. in this volume); however, since EF and monetary wealth (GDP) are strongly linked, this finding is not remarkable. It does remind us, nonetheless, that increases in wealth and improvements in life expectancy within countries have paralleled large and apparently unsustainable demands on the ecological foundations of the planet. In cases where the EF of a nation is greater than its geographical area, these kinds of societal gains are connected to, or even "founded" upon ecosystems outside of the benefiting country's political boundaries. Some groups in countries from which ecological capital has been extracted and processed for export, or into which wastes from other countries have been dumped, have benefited financially from these transactions; however, this has often enhanced intranational wealth disparities. (Firebaugh, 2006)

The tools discussed here cannot by themselves deal with the problem of complex systems where multiple factors vary simultaneously—an appropriate causal modeling approach is needed for that. However, these tools may help us better understand and frame our investigations of the upstream drivers of multi-scale ecosystem impacts—notably, the forces that fuel modern industrial enterprises and their markets—and the downstream implications for human health.

Conventional and Disaggregated Ecological Footprint Analysis

Ecological Footprint Analysis (EFA), developed in the 1990s by Dr. William Rees at the University of British Columbia and his then Ph.D. student Mathis Wackernagel, has experienced wide popular uptake and appreciation. EFA has been applied to consuming entities or units at various scales, such as the individual, household, institutional, city, and national scales, and has been utilized in governmental policy and planning (e.g., Germain, 2001; Lenzen and Murray, 2001; Tyedmers, 2000; Bicknell et al., 1998; and Wackernagel and Rees, 1996).

EFA requires first scoping and taking inventory of the analyzed entity's consumption. In a nation, for example, this would involve accounting for the tons of wheat, steel, and timber used by its citizens on an annual basis. Mineral resource use is not counted, and is assumed inherently unsustainable, but energy derived from carbon-based fuels is tracked and boiled down into tonnes of carbon emitted. Once all the consumable goods are identified, the bioproductive land or water area required to support the annual provision of each consumable good is assigned, based on the world-average productivity of the specific ecosystems supplying these goods.

For example, a country's annual wheat consumption would be translated into the number of hectares of cropland required to provide this amount of wheat in a year—again, based not on the productivity of the actual cropland supplying the good, but rather on the average productivity of this type of land use. For carbon emissions from energy consumed, hectares of "energy land" are added. The assumption here is that any emissions of carbon into the atmosphere are unsustainable if they are not offset at least equivalently by land-based sequestration. Once all of the average land and water areas are defined, they can be summed to arrive at the total Ecological Footprint (EF) for the analyzed entity. The EF is expressed in terms of global hectares, and thus provides a measure of the total bioproductive space demanded by the analyzed entity, regardless of where on Earth that space is located.

Specific criticisms of, and adaptations made to EFA are not discussed at length here, and can be found elsewhere (e.g., Lenzen and Murray, 2003 and 2001; van den Bergh and Verbruggen, 1999; and Levett, 1998), but it is useful to note that these issues can be grouped into three main areas:

- criticisms of sustainability assumptions, such as the implied assumption that atmospheric carbon dioxide concentration above that present at the time of analysis is unsustainable;
- concerns with the calculation of world-average productivities of the different ecosystem types employed in EFA; and
- questions about the meaning and usefulness of the aggregate EF itself.

On the latter point, for example, what does it mean for human beings or other life forms if our collective EF is greater than the amount of bioproductive land and water area available on Earth? And what does it mean in tangible ecological and population health terms for a single country, like Canada, to have an EF of about 150 million global hectares?

Epidemiologists stand to gain insight into macro-level ecological correlates and determinants of population health problems by answers to these questions, but the identification of real ecosystem impacts in real locations on the planet is perhaps more germane. The process of identifying the actual ecosystems from which resources are being drawn to support the consumption patterns in a specified entity (such as a country) entails a disaggregation of the Ecological Footprint. Once an EF of a particular size has been identified, the various particular ecosystems from which the analyzed entity is drawing resources can be located. This may be relatively straightforward for basic agricultural products such as wheat, and considerably more difficult for multi-material manufactured goods with an international pedigree.

Ideally, insults to the integrity of the source ecosystems would be measured in terms demonstrably linked to population health—which at some scales remains a critical challenge, as noted earlier. Once these population health risks and benefits are identified, consumption behaviors on the front end can be seen more clearly as determinants of health worthy of investigation and consideration as points for intervention. Those consumption behaviors are tied to the output of particular industries. Because of this, the question of sustainability becomes also a question of social values and social pressures, popular images of the good life, and the means by which it is obtained, including the organization, control, and expansion of the specific means of production in specific societies. Transdisciplinary investigations of these dynamics could open up new dimensions of debate and practice in the fields of epidemiology, global health, and public health ethics, as well as informing scale-appropriate policy change for ecological and social sustainability.

The DPSEEA Framework

In the late 1990s, in connection with the HEADLAMP environment-health linkages project, the World Health Organization (WHO) began using the DPSEEA (Driving forces—Pressures—States—Exposures—Effects—Actions) framework for understanding complex systems that affect human population health. (See

Corvalán et al., 1996, for a thorough description of the early formulation.) Closely related and foundational to the DPSEEA framework is the earlier Pressure-State-Response (PSR) framework, often attributed to the Organisation for Economic Co-operation and Development, or OECD. (Spangenberg and Bonnioto, 1998) Seen through the lens of PSR, the (conventional) EFA approach discussed immediately above is basically a "PS" approach, since it aims to identify the human load (Pressure) on Earth's ecological capacity, and to determine if that load creates an unsustainable (S)tate such as an eroding biological resource base stemming from planetary ecological overshoot. The DPSEEA framework, in comparison, directs the researcher to look further upstream (to Driving Forces) and further downstream (to Exposures, Effects, and Actions).

Almost any human activity can be viewed through the DPSEEA framework. For example, Kjellström and Hill (2002) applied the DPSEEA framework to the analysis of transport-related health impacts in New Zealand. They noted:

- Driving forces such as population growth and an increased demand for transport from a growing economy;
- Pressures such as more cars and trucks on the road, more noise, and more toxic emissions;
- States such as diminished air quality and more congested roads;
- Exposures such as air pollutants and physical traffic risks;
- Effects such as respiratory problems, injuries, and fatalities from traffic accidents; and
- Actions for health promotion and protection, including educational initiatives and changes in legislation.

Theoretically, any of the elements in the DPSEEA framework can be the point of entry for investigation; a researcher might be aware of (E)ffects, and then look both retrospectively to determine (E)xposures, (S)tates, (P)ressures, and (D)rivers, and prospectively toward effective (A)ctions.

However, the elements of the DPSEEA framework are connected by positive and negative feedback loops, and are not necessarily connected in a linear fashion. Thus, for example, an Effect may change the States or Pressures in other parts of the framework. Because the DPSEEA framework is understood mainly as an environmental health framework, the WHO (1999) does caution that it is less useful (or, at least, must be carefully adapted) in situations involving physical risks where "Pressure" is difficult to quantify and interpret. These include risks posed by natural hazards and technology (e.g., automobiles, as in the Kjellström and Hill study), and risks such as those posed by the products of nanotechnology or the synergistic action of multiple chemical exposures.

The DPSEEA framework is oriented toward public health (A)ction, as informed by improved understanding of the underlying forces that perpetuate or amplify certain health conditions. It is a tool for thinking systemically about the relationships among exposures, outcomes, and their causal antecedents. The DPSEEA framework is also useful for structuring a broadly causal description, or even the outline of a testable causal model, of a particular economic enterprise and its ecologically-mediated health impacts, since it invites looking at spatially and temporally proximal and more distant factors that affect present and future exposure contexts. In addition, it helps locate the industry within an environment of positive and negative feedback loops.

Recent trends in the use of traditional food and feed crops, such as corn for biofuel synthesis, and the global, rapidly-growing palm oil industry, are two modern examples of where the DPSEEA framework could usefully direct ecoepidemiological research. Ecoepidemiologists might inquire into what health-relevant (E)xposures are associated with (S)tates—such as a higher-priced food supply in producing countries or their markets—and also into the (P)ressures and the (D)riving forces—such as increased demand for low-cost automotive fuel—that are responsible for those food price increases.

The DPSEEA framework does not endorse or describe particular methods for analyzing and interpreting the relationships that it describes, but it can suggest critical areas for research attention, help identify the parameters of testable models, and help identify potential points of intervention. The DPSEEA framework also fosters recognition of the interplay between micro-, meso-, and macro-level determinants of health risks and impacts within particular sociopolitical and economic systems. More specifically, the DPSEEA framework can be applied to specific industries which have expanded to take advantage of new markets in other countries.

Product Life-Cycle Analysis

In our world, where growing global markets drive the mass production and movement of goods over long distances, Product Life-Cycle Analysis techniques may be especially useful for identifying the ecological impacts and associated human health impacts of global industries, and thus be valuable for framing ecoepidemiological studies of these enterprises. Product Life-Cycle Analysis (PLCA) grew out of the field of global energy audits in the 1960s and 1970s as a means of improving process efficiency in production, reducing costs and wastes, and minimizing certain types of environmental impact. (Ciambrone, 1997)

PLCA may be used as a tool for determining a product's impact in terms of gross material flows, pollutants and emissions, or even gross ecological space demands, akin to the Ecological Footprint. PLCA is also useful for identifying points in a product's life cycle where interventions can be made to improve the relative material or energy efficiency of these stages. PLCA generally does not go as far as EFA in that it focuses on emissions or gross material and energetic demands throughout a product's life cycle—and not on the translation of these demands into measures of appropriated biocapacity, such as the standardized global hectares of EFA. For example, a sample PLCA data collection sheet from the International Standards Organization (ISO, 1998) recommends quantifying emissions to air, water, and land, among other "impacts." PLCA as currently structured can help in the identification of a more complete collection of relevant (D)rivers and (P)ressures, and perhaps (S)tates (see description of the DPSEEA framework), but typically not (E)xposures or (E)ffects, since clarification of these elements requires reliable contextual information on the human interface with product manufacture, use, and deposition after use. PLCA also may prove useful for the task of disaggregating the EF of specific global industries and pinpointing their health-relevant ecological impacts.

The I=PAT Model

The I=PAT model specifies that environmental Impacts (I) are functionally related to the product of Population (P), Affluence (A = per capita consumption or production, often expressed in monetary terms), and Technology (T = impact per unit of consumption or production). (York et al., 2003) Since its original proposition, often attributed to Ehrlich and Holdren (1971), the I=PAT model has served as a focus for dialogue about the relationship between key population-level factors contributing to the aggregate impacts on the planet of modern human life. As a theoretical equation, each of the terms is open to multiple operational definitions, and the relationships between them are fuel for ongoing debate.

Fischer-Kowalski and Amann (2001) note that the debate has been somewhat cyclical, shifting back and forth over the years from individual factors and types of impacts to systemic features. Waggoner and Ausubel (2002) stress that determining and using correct dimensions in the I=PAT model can generate information on the drivers of environmental impacts and thereby effectively predict the result of interventions.

The "I" side of the formulation often has been identified with impacts on local or regional air or water quality by particular pollutants, and not usually conceived as the sum of all measurable types of environmental impact, nor as a measure of global ecological integrity or carrying capacity—as proposed by Sieswerda et al., 2001. The I=PAT model does not suggest what kind or amount of "I" is desirable for a region, country, or planet. It also provides no indication as to how much "I" Earth can sustain without fundamental damage to the bioproductivity of its ecosystems, nor (without much clearer definitions of the factors and better empirical data) how (P)opulation, (A)ffluence, and (T)echnology are actually related at community, region, country, ecoregional, global North versus global South, or whole-planet scales. As such, the I=PAT model, simply stated, has limited value as a tool for informing environmental policy.

In order for the I = PAT model to be useful for ecoepidemiological investigations involving the material relationships between nations, the factor definitions in the equation, and the manipulation of them, would have to incorporate the recognition that the prevalence of international trade—understood in material/energetic and not monetary terms—effectively "splits" the factors spatially and complicates interpretation. For example, a measure of regional biodiversity loss from export-oriented banana cultivation in a tropical country—the (I)mpact—might follow from the application of a range of (T)echnologies that include heavy chemical pesticide, herbicide, and fertilizer use and mono-cropping. However, if consumption is entirely international, then the (P)opulation and per capita level of banana consumption, or (A)ffluence, within the consuming countries will be powerfully determinative of the (I)mpact, as-suming that the amount of (T)echnology is tied closely to international demand. The context-dependence of both the relative magnitude of the input factors and the nature of the relationships between them, as well as the extent of interna-tional trade, suggests that the simple form of the I=PAT model has utility mainly as a springboard for further debate and research.

Even so, constructive criticism of the shortcomings of the I=PAT model has attempted to remedy the problem of defining "I" (and the contributing factors) simply by whatever results in an equality. For example, I=PAT has been refor-mulated as a probabilistic model. Rosa and Dietz (1998) call this revised version "STIRPAT" (Stochastic Impacts by Regression on Population, Affluence, and Technology).

The reformulated version of the I=PAT model allows some hypothesis test-ing and regression analyses, since it takes the form of a multiplicative regression equation that includes (T)echnology as the error term. This error term is likely to include many factors other than strictly technological ones—indeed, any social, economic, ecological, or other factors not subsumed in the (P) and (A) terms. In such a model, population health terms could be employed as outcome variables (I's), which, given clearly defined (P) and (A) terms, could help focus research on the relationship between (P) and (A) in all the contexts noted earlier, as well as on the content and relative explanatory power of the error term. Great care would still need to be applied in interpreting models or statistical tests where (I)mpacts are the result of (T)echnologies applied in one location but determined in large part by the (P)opulation and (A)ffluence of a distant consumer base. Also, treating the I=PAT model as a regression equation may depart substan-tially from the original intent of the formulation, which was primarily to provide a concise statement of the formulators' general beliefs about the interplay of societal forces as they relate to environmental impacts.

In short, the greatest value of the I=PAT model to the field of public health, and to ecoepidemiological research, may lie in its revelation of the contextually-modified interdependence of variables historically viewed as "independent" fac-tors in academic and advocacy circles. Population growth, materially-intensive consumption and/or the accumulation of monetary wealth through materially-intensive production in distant regions, and the expansion of high impact tech-nologies may be relatively more or less important as risk factors for specific population health problems; for example, population alone increases certain risks if population density becomes extremely high.

However, treating these factors independently for the purpose of simplifying foreign and domestic policy initiatives misses the point. That point is that the questions of *which* population *where*, *what* levels and types of consumption or monetary wealth accumulation and distribution, and *which* types of technology are being used, all implying the importance of context, are also critically interdependent concerns. The I=PAT model and the ongoing clarification of its components may be useful for framing discussions about, and initiatives to slow global ecological decline because it reminds us of the impropriety of singling out any one factor for attention over any other factor.

Environmental Kuznets Curves

Environmental Kuznets Curves (EKCs), named for economist Simon Kuznets (see Kuznets, 1955), have been used to help develop research hypotheses about the relationship between income growth and changes in industrial output and technology, public pressure for pollution reduction, and public policy on numerous indicators of environmental quality. (Cole et al., 1997; Panayotou, 1997) For epidemiologists concerned with the economic drivers of ecological changes, and with the impacts of those changes on human health, the construction of EKCs can be useful. EKCs can help in generating hypotheses, challenging beliefs about the relationship between aggregate income and indicators of environmental quality, and resolving relationships that may present differently at local, regional, national, and global levels.

Kuznets (1955) was interested in the relationship between national income and income inequality as countries become more industrialized and urban. Only later was the inverted "U"-shaped curve (which Kuznets hypothesized for the relationship between national income and income inequality in developed nations) used as a graphical description of how specific industrial pollutants would parallel rising national income until sufficient income was generated to implement pollution control measures. In the concluding section of his original article, Kuznets tempered his arguments by saying that "the paper is perhaps 5 percent empirical information, and 95 percent speculation, some of it possibly tainted by wishful thinking." (Kuznets, 1955)

EKCs should likewise be treated with caution, and employed mainly to clarify implicit beliefs and generate hypotheses about how, and by which forces (e.g., market signals or government regulation), ecologically damaging activities (e.g., the emission of toxic gases) are reduced or halted. Improved understanding of these dynamics is valuable for addressing questions about the relationship between ecological integrity, human health, and confounding or modifying wealth variables.

For example, Harbaugh et al. (2002) concluded that the evidence was unconvincing that ambient levels of sulfur dioxide, total suspended particulates (TSP), and smoke declined (i.e., followed the classic inverted "U" pattern) as income rose well beyond the expected per capita income "turning point" identified by Grossman and Krueger (1995). Could it be that the slow pace at which the often externalized health costs of these environmental challenges are internalized hinders the adoption of control measures? If so, this is relevant information for ecoepidemiology. To use DPSEEA language, it helps place, within the realm of (D)riving forces, elements such as private or public sector accounting practices and specific types of market failures. These factors are recognized occasionally for their contribution to ecological data gaps (e.g., Anielski and Wilson, 2007), but less so for their contribution to downstream population health impacts.

Hypothetical EKCs force investigators to clearly define the scale of analysis and the ways in which terms are operationalized—critical tasks in research dealing with potentially ambiguous concepts such as "ecological integrity" and "sustainability." Some research, for example, suggests that while the classic EKC inverted-"U" shape may hold for some environmental pollutants at the local or regional level, a quite different relationship may characterize compounds such as CO_2. Carbon dioxide is emitted at multiple discrete points, but has impacts on ecological conditions (and human health) through its effects on the total global climate system—effects which may result in local or regional ecological impacts at great distance from the original generators. Possibly because of the lack of, or greatly lagged evidence of any kind of "problem" at local or even national scales, CO_2 emissions appear to rise monotonically with income. (Arrow et al., 1995) Finally, as relationships between economic and political systems and ecological health are explored (e.g., Rainham et al., this volume; Franco et al., 2004), EKCs may help generate hypotheses about how specific practical features of these different systems (in contrast to broad ideological categories) affect the production of specific ecosystem-affecting agents (such as CO_2 or mercury) over time.

Conclusions

The conventional and disaggregated Ecological Footprints, the DPSEEA framework, Product Life-Cycle Analysis, the I=PAT model, and Environmental Kuznets Curves all offer something to the growing field of ecoepidemiology as applied to global ecological change.

Conventional Ecological Footprint Analysis prompts macro-level sustainability and associated population health questions. But disaggregating the Ecological Footprints of consuming units such as households, corporations, or countries, enables more focused investigation of the human health implications of specific ecosystem impacts.

Product Life-Cycle Analysis can assist in the disaggregation of the Ecological Footprint and ensure that ecological impacts associated with post-consumer deposition (e.g., landfilling, incineration, recycling) are not neglected.

The I=PAT model provides an important reminder to be context-sensitive and systems-oriented, and to be clear about definitions and dimensions when researching and interpreting relationships among human drivers of ecologically-mediated human health impacts.

Environmental Kuznets Curves can point to testable hypotheses about wealth, ecology, and health relationships, and serve as prompts for questions about the scale of analysis, the function of different chemical actors in the environment and in the economy, and the effects of policy interventions at different levels, and among different types of governance.

The tools discussed in this chapter provide a sample of those available and conceivable. As tools, they need testing and refinement in actual eco-epidemiological investigations. Moreover, to avoid further fragmentation of knowledge relevant to social/ecological sustainability, these tools need application within a larger analytical structure that includes modeling methods better suited than multivariate regression for dealing with complex relationships. (See Greenland and Brumback, 2002, for a discussion of four such approaches, including causal and structural equation modeling.) The tools discussed here also could be tested further in problem-oriented transdisciplinary research that encourages the adaptation and adoption of formerly discipline-specific methods into other disciplines, and the development of new conceptual frames.

Acknowledgments

The authors acknowledge financial support from Social Sciences and Humanities Research Council (SSHRC) Grant #410-2004-0786: "Controlling Eco-Violence: Linking Consumption and the Loss of Ecological Integrity to Population Health, Eco-Justice and International Law" (Dr. William E. Rees, University of British Columbia, Principal Investigator), and also the valuable conceptual and editorial input of Dr. Duncan Saunders (University of Alberta) and Mr. Mark Anielski (University of Alberta).

References

Anielski, Mark, and Sara Wilson. *The Real Wealth of the Mackenzie Region: Assessing the Natural Capital Values of a Northern Boreal Ecosystem*. Ottawa: Canadian Boreal Initiative, 2007.

Arrow, Kenneth, Bert Bolin, Robert Costanza, Partha Dasgupta, Carl Folke, et al. "Economic Growth, Carrying Capacity and the Environment." *Ecological Economics* 15, no. 2 (1995): 91–95.

Bicknell, Kathryn B., Richard J. Ball, Rowena Cullen, and Hugh R. Bigsby. "New Methodology for the Ecological Footprint with an Application to the New Zealand Economy." *Ecological Economics* 27 (1998): 149–60.

Ciambrone, David F. *Environmental Life Cycle Analysis*. Boca Raton, FL: CRC Press, 1997.

Cole, Matthew A., Anthony J. Rayner and John M. Bates. "The Environmental Kuznets Curve: An Empirical Analysis." *Environment and Development Economics* 2 (1997): 401–16.

Corvalán, Carlos, David Briggs, and Tord Kjellström. "Development of Environmental Health Indicators." *Linkage Methods for Environmental and Health Analysis: General Guidelines*, edited by D. Briggs, C. Corvalán, and M. Nurminen. Geneva: World Health Organization, 1996.

Ehrlich, Paul R., and John P. Holdren. "Impact of Population Growth." *Science* 171 (1971): 1212–17.

Firebaugh, Glenn. *The New Geography of Global Income Inequality*. Cambridge, MA: Harvard University Press, 2006.

Fischer-Kowalski, Marina, and Christof Amann. "Beyond IPAT and Kuznets Curves: Globalization as a Vital Factor in Analysing the Environmental Impact of Socioeconomic Metabolism." *Population and Environment* 23, no. 1 (2001): 7–47.

Franco, Álvaro, Carlos Álvarez-Dardet, and Maria Teresa Ruiz. "Effect of Democracy on Health: Ecological Study." *British Medical Journal* 329 (2004): 1421–24.

Germain, Susan. "The Ecological Footprint of Lions Gate Hospital." *Hospital Quarterly* 5, no. 2 (2001–2002): 62–63.

Greenland, Sander, and Babette Brumback. "An Overview of Relations among Causal Modeling Methods." *International Journal of Epidemiology* 31 (2002): 1030–37.

Grossman, Gene M., and Alan B. Krueger. "Economic Growth and the Environment." *Quarterly Journal of Economics* 110 (1995): 353–77.

Harbaugh, William T., Arik Levinson, and David M. Wilson. "Re-examining the Empirical Evidence for an Environmental Kuznets Curve." *The Review of Economics and Statistics* 84, no. 3 (2002): 541–51.

Huynen, Maud M. T. E., Pim Martens, and R. Dolf S. De Groot. "Linkages between Biodiversity Loss and Human Health: A Global Indicator Analysis." *International Journal of Environmental Health Research* 14, no. 1 (2004): 13–30.

International Standards Organization (ISO). "Environmental Management—Life Cycle Assessment—Goal and Scope Definition and Inventory Analysis." Geneva: International Organization for Standardization, 1998.

Kjellström, Tord, and Sarah Hill. "New Zealand Evidence for Health Impacts of Transport." A background paper prepared for the Public Health Advisory Committee. Wellington, New Zealand: National Health Committee, 2002.

Kuznets, Simon. "Economic Growth and Income Inequality." *American Economic Review* 45, no. 1 (1955): 1–28.

Lenzen, Manfred, and Shauna A. Murray. "The Ecological Footprint—Issues and Trends." *ISA Research Paper 01-03*. Sydney: University of Sydney, 2003.

———. "A Modified Ecological Footprint Method and Its application to Australia." *Ecological Economics* 37 (2001): 229–55.

Levett, Roger. "Footprinting: A Great Step Forward, but Tread Carefully—A Response to Mathis Wackernagel." *Local Environment* 3 (1998): 67–74.

March, Dana, and Ezra Susser. "The Eco- in Eco-epidemiology." *International Journal of Epidemiology* 35 (2006): 1379–83.

McMichael, Anthony J., Colin D. Butler, and Carl Folke. "New Visions for Addressing Sustainability (Viewpoint)." *Science* 302 (2003): 1919–20.

Panayotou, Theodore. "Demystifying the Environmental Kuznets Curve: Turning a Black Box into a Policy Tool." *Environment and Development Economics* 2 (1997): 465–84.

Rainham, Daniel G. C., and Ian McDowell. "The Sustainability of Population Health." *Population and Environment* 26, no. 4 (2005): 303–24.

Rosa, Eugene, and Thomas Dietz. "Climate Change and Society: Speculation, Construction, and Scientific Investigation." *International Sociology* 13, no. 4 (1998): 421–55.

Sieswerda, Lee E., Colin L. Soskolne, Stephen C. Newman, Donald Schopflocher, and Karen E. Smoyer. "Toward Measuring the Impact of Ecological Disintegrity on Human Health." *Epidemiology* 12, no. 1 (2001): 28–32.

Soskolne, Colin L., and Roberto Bertollini. "Global Ecological Integrity and 'Sustainable Development': Cornerstones of Public Health: A Discussion Document." *World Health Organization, European Centre for Environment and Health, Rome Division, Italy.* 1999. http://www.euro.who.int/document/gch/ecorep5.pdf (25 May 2007).

Soskolne, Colin L., and Natasha Broemling. "Eco-epidemiology: On the Need to Measure Health Effects from Global Change." *Global Change & Human Health* 3, no. 1 (2002): 58–66. http://www.springerlink.com/content/v97xv0l42845407u/fulltext.pdf (26 May 2007, access to this paper is restricted or may be purchased).

Spangenberg, Joachim H., and Odile Bonnioto. "Sustainability Indicators: A Compass on the Road Towards Sustainability." *Wuppertal Papers* no. 81, (Feb. 1998). Wuppertal, Germany: Wuppertal Institute.

Susser, Ezra. "Eco-epidemiology: Thinking outside the Black Box (Commentary)." *Epidemiology* 15, no. 5 (2004): 519–20.

Susser, Ezra, and Alfredo Morabia. "The Arc of Epidemiology." *Psychiatric Epidemiology: Searching for the Causes of Mental Disorders*, edited by E. Susser, S. Schwartz, A. Morabia, and E. J. Bromet. New York: Oxford University Press, 2006.

Tyedmers, Peter H. *Salmon and Sustainability: The Biophysical Cost of Producing Salmon through the Commercial Salmon Fishery and Intensive Salmon Culture Industry (Ph.D. thesis).* University of British Columbia (Vancouver, BC), Department of Resource Management and Environmental Studies. Ottawa: National Library of Canada, 2000.

Van den Bergh, Jeroen C. J. M., and Harmen Verbruggen. "Spatial Sustainability, Trade and Indicators: An Evaluation of the 'Ecological Footprint.'" *Ecological Economics* 29 (1999): 61–72.

Wackernagel, Mathis, and Willliam E. Rees. *Our Ecological Footprint: Reducing Human Impact on the Earth.* Gabriola Island, BC: New Society Publishers, 1996.

Waggoner, Paul E., and Jesse H. Ausubel. "A Framework for Sustainability Science: A Renovated IPAT Identity." *Proceedings of the National Academy of Sciences* 99, no. 12 (2002): 7860–65.

World Health Organization (WHO). *Environmental Health Indicators: Framework and Methodologies. Protection of the Human Environment—Occupational and Environmental Health Series.* Geneva: World Health Organization, 1999.

York, Richard, Eugene A. Rosa, and Thomas Dietz. "Footprints on the Earth: The Environmental Consequences of Modernity." *American Sociological Review* 68, no. 2 (2003): 279–300.

Part V:
Focus (d): The Rights of Children: Health and the Culture Environment

In this, the fourth and final of the four focus areas comprising part five of the book, concern about children is our primary focus.

The first concern relates to the cultural environment and the role of the media in influencing behaviors which are formative for future voters. Media programming of violence and consumer-driven value systems are shown to be especially harmful to children, and hence to the democracies into which these children will be socialized. Persistent obstacles are discussed to meaningful change in media programming that is becoming increasingly pervasive and centralized, and is drifting out of democratic reach.

The second concern relates specifically to physical and mental developmental health challenges which face all children, from conception through adulthood, from environmental conditions, such as chemical pollution. These conditions can have long-term consequences for the mental and physical development of the child. Only through national, international, and supranational law will mechanisms for change toward the sustainability of life on Earth be accomplished. Indeed, only if the World Health Organization (WHO) takes a proactive stance will the mechanism for change toward the sustainability of life on Earth by enabling the health and survival of future generations be more assured.

Both concerns address the rights of children to a healthy life. Aggressive marketing of cultural commodities that target children from a very early age in a cut-throat grasp for market share is not only fueling youth violence and materialism as lifestyles, but precipitating serious mental and physical health issues such as attention deficit disorder, hyperactivity, obesity, heart disease, and juvenile diabetes owing to the sedentary nature of electronic entertainment and the promotion of junk food.

Environmental justice must include considerations of both intergenerational and intragenerational rights. This applies regardless of whether we are discussing the cultural, media-saturated environment, or the physical environment involving synthetic chemical pollutants.

Chapter 26

The Culture Environment: Implications for Public Health, Human Rights, and Ecological Sustainability

Rose A. Dyson, Ed.D. (Doctor of Education)
Consultant in Media Education,
External Research Associate,
York University, Toronto, Canada

Contact Information: *167 Glen Road, Toronto, Ont. M4W 2W8* CANADA
Phone: +1 416 961 0853; Fax +1 416 929 2720; Email: rdyson@oise.utoronto.ca

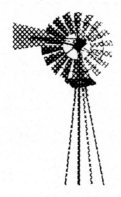

Summary

Countless studies have dealt with the effects of media on human behavior over the past fifty years. Some have focused on the harmful aspects of violent content; others, on sexual explicitness.

Different ways in which communications technology is used for reporting and editorializing the news, advertising, and entertainment have been examined.

Some inquiries demonstrate that media, such as film, television, music lyrics, video, computer games, print, and the Internet, coalesce into a seamless, pervasive, and increasingly centralized, globalized cultural environment that is drifting out of democratic reach.

Despite mounting evidence of trends that detract from good health, community safety, optimal educational opportunities for people of all ages, and of future sustainability, little progress has been made on the implementation of cultural policies consistent with global ecological governance.

In this chapter, we assess the current debate over harmful effects. The focus is on persistent obstacles to meaningful change and how these can be overcome.

Introduction

Much has been said about the disappearing boundaries between various forms of media. Advertising messages now surface regularly as product placements in print media, films, and television programs produced for entertainment purposes. Television news producers consider the entertainment component as well as the facts in how they choose to impart information to viewers. Talk shows often border on the bizarre and mean-spirited in the search for audiences in an ever more competitive market. Converging technologies, as well as content, have fueled the billion dollar pornography and video game industries. These have overtaken the film and television production industries in annual revenues. Meanwhile, violence is increasingly being used as a cheap commercial ingredient because it sells well on a global market and translates easily into any language. (Signorielli et al., 1995)

Much less has been said about how these media impact on our health, community safety, foreign policy, and ecological sustainability. In addition to the exploitative aspects of child pornography, there is a fifteen billion USD per year advertising industry targeting children. There are also the violent, blood drenched thrillers on our movie, television, and computer screens, targeting teens and young adults.

Advocates for any kind of regulation tend to be countered with cries of censorship, accusations of moral intolerance, religious fundamentalism or all of the above. The popular assumption is that media literacy, taught in schools, will help students decode and deconstruct messages, enabling them to read between the lines and navigate their way toward responsible citizenship and self-sufficiency. Vigilance from parents is also expected, with round the clock supervision, if necessary, of media diets for their children.

Media Violence

Consider the issue of media violence, first within a paradigm of spirituality and health care, and then bearing in mind the vulgar, profane, woman-hating, gun-toting, and threatening lyrics of "gangsta" rap in hip-hop music, now such a staple among black urban youth.

We can start with the notion that we are what we eat. The psychological and emotional corollary to this is that we are also what we read, see, and hear in the media. Indeed, there is growing evidence of long-lasting physiological responses to the ingestion of media violence, in addition to the host of better-known harmful effects such as desensitization, aggression, fear and anxiety, among others. New magnetic resonance imaging techniques, employed for medical diagnostic purposes, have yielded evidence that when a video game player participates in simulated violence, his heart rate and blood pressure rise, and brain cells that normally counsel empathy, are shut down. Furthermore, these images are burned into his long-term memory, like post-traumatic stress disorder from real life events. (Atkinson, 2004: F8; Linn, 2004)

Indeed, we are surrounded by evidence of diminishing empathy in the aftermath of extreme violence. Prior to his massacre of thirty people on April 16, 2007, followed by his suicide, Virginia Tech senior, Cho Seung Hui, sent a video to NBC Television News, to ensure the widest possible coverage of his killings. Criticism over NBC's decision to oblige him erupted around the world with its ethical dimensions seriously questioned. Amid the yards of ink and endless repetition of images from this tragic event on television news screens, USA Today made the following observation: "if only we were as good at preventing tragedies as we've become at recording them." (April 18, 2007: D1) Nevertheless, Robert Bianco went on to rate the response of various reporters and news outlets, justifying "wall-to-wall coverage" on the basis that the event was one which "we're all expected to share." Ironically, advertisements for violent entertainment were never pulled from any of the American television stations. It was and still is "business as usual."

Given this evidence, consider the potential impact of a video game such as "Manhunt." Any twelve-year-old can easily assume the persona of James Earl Cash in this game, cast as the ultimate killing machine, with no clear indication of whether he is the "good guy" or the "bad guy." Operant conditioning that takes place when young people play these games in which they are frequently rewarded with points for making heads roll and blood splatter, is leading to what Lieutenant Colonel David Grossman in the United States of America calls Acquired Violence Immune Deficiency Syndrome. So far, we have tended to overlook the powerful, educational impact of such interactive communications technologies.

In 2003, the Canadian Teacher's Federation (CTF) published findings that one of the most popular games for boys in the younger grades was Grand Theft Auto, a series of violent-action video games, involving murder and prostitution. More than half the students among the 5,700 interviewed, said they had seen an aggressive act emanating from television, the movies or computer games carried out on the playground.

World Wrestling Entertainment programs (WWE) exemplify some of the most graphic examples of both sex and violence in media marketed to an audience where 40 percent of the viewers are children under the age of eighteen. These programs are known to encourage bullying and school yard injuries. (CTF, 2003) In the world of WWE, conflicts are resolved by violence, people are rewarded for cruelty, and the arbitrary whims of one powerful person are law. For high school boys, watching wrestling regularly has been linked with, among other deviant behaviors, picking a fight with a date, being a date fight victim, carrying a gun or some other weapon, drug and alcohol abuse, and reckless driving. (Linn, 2004) As children mature, they sometimes confuse this kind of fantasy with reality.

Since the 1990s, the violence-saturated cultural environment in which children are socialized has grown progressively worse. Similarly, movies and television programs for adults have included greater amounts of violence and more graphic ways of depicting it. And, as has been pointed out time and again, once a cultural product is on the market, people of all ages—including children—tend to end up with access to it, regardless of blocking devices, warning symbols, and classification criteria designed to assist parents in their guidance of children's media habits. (Dyson, 2000)

In fact, the Federation found distressing indications that children receive little or no parental restrictions when it comes to what they watch on television, and which video games they can play. With this evidence in mind, is it any surprise that "baby-faced bicycle bandits" in upscale neighborhoods are holding up gas stations using fake rifles and handguns? (Freeze, 2004: A1) Or, that youth gang violence is escalating with gun shootings among poor, urban, black youth who taunt each other with trivial demands for "respect?"

Schools and community centers are now expected to fill the supervisory gaps left in the lives of children as parents work long hours to make ends meet. At home, there is increasing reliance on television, computers, and video games as electronic babysitters. As a society, we have largely abdicated our responsibility to shape the value systems of the young to large, profit-driven, media conglomerates. Yet, we continue to blame the increasingly beleaguered and under-funded public education system for mushrooming problems. Meanwhile, evidence accumulates that violent, action-filled stories in video games and other cultural commodities are causing young boys in particular, to show less and less interest in the gentle narratives stressed in schools. (Fine, 2000: A1)

More trouble is evident in signs of collective desensitization on the part of ice hockey players and their audiences. These are surfacing in both professional arenas and little league rinks where games are sometimes cancelled because of unruly behavior, not on the part of children, but of parents and volunteer coaches. Screaming, shouting, and hitting among adults involved are ruining children's sports, in hockey, soccer, basketball, baseball, and football. (Deacon, 2001: 21) The issue of violence in hockey has been present for over a quarter of a century, but there is little evidence of change for the better. Instead, each year, violence becomes increasingly acceptable, in both professional and little league rinks, with each new generation of professional hockey players idolized by young aspirants. (Naylor, 2004: S1)

Today, computer and video games offer a myriad of interactive forms of engagement for everyone. Internet access provides instant opportunity, not only for worldwide communication for financial, educational, and organizational information-sharing purposes, but for sexual predators who prey on children in chat rooms, fueling the rapidly-growing, illicit, global sex slave trade involving women and children. On the basis of these unsettling trends, the need to stem the tide of unfettered, completely unregulated, profit-driven, Western-styled entertainment, laced with sex, violence, foul, racist, and misogynist language, with some restrictions is becoming increasingly urgent. Can we really justify protection for these billion dollar industries as an inalienable civil right that benefits us all under the guise of freedom of expression and wholesome democracy?

Individual rights must be balanced with collective rights according to our founding principles. But now, we have arguments against government intervention of any kind. On the political right, there is opposition in areas known to have an impact on reducing youth violence, such as gun ownership restrictions. On the left, equally fervent opposition exists against any restrictions on violent or sexually explicit content in popular culture, usually from film and television producers. These people tend to support gun control and sex education in public schools, but oppose any regulation of how medias are marketed. (Ziauddin and Davies, 2002) Such self-serving selectivity on how responsibility and accountability should be practiced, protects the status quo and ensures that the finger of blame remains pointed at the teacher, the parent, and the errant youth. Meanwhile, powerful and dominant economic interests determine what is produced, distributed, and consumed.

Commercial Exploitation of Children

Children are increasingly being targeted by aggressive, profit-driven marketing interests. Selling of lifestyle is now a central construct in the strategies employed by advertising industries. Themes in popular culture commodities often go far beyond the production of a film or television show, itself. The result is a formation of attitudes and values from a very early age, regardless of whether these involve sedentary activity, poor eating habits or an inclination to resort to violence as a form of conflict resolution. Cereals, cookies, T-shirts, bubble bath, lunch boxes, toy guns, army tanks, swords, and laser zappers are examples of spin-offs from popular children's electronic entertainment. In fact, many children's television programs are little more than one-half hour advertisements for these commodities. Such developments are the antithesis of what needs to happen to ensure that children are physically active to offset their growing predilection to obesity and other physical ailments resulting both from the sedentary inactivity encouraged by electronic entertainment as well as the marketing of junk food. (www.healthiergeneration.org, accessed 31 May 2007; Picard, 2004)

Advertising through nagging, as classified by marketing research targeting children for profit, comes in two flavors: "persistence nagging," which involves children repeatedly and incessantly badgering their parents until they give in; and the much more effective "importance nagging," in which children are offered a reason why they must have a particular product—one that is included in the advertisement itself, of course.

Susan Linn, founder of the Campaign For A Commercial-Free Childhood (CCFC), Instructor at the Harvard Medical School and Associate Director of the Judge Baker Children's Center, says: "As corporations vie more and more aggressively for young consumers, popular culture—which traditionally evolves from creative self-expression that captures and informs shared experience—is being smothered by commercial culture relentlessly sold to children by people who value them for their consumption, not their creativity." (Linn, 2004: 7) In her book, *Consuming Kids: The Hostile Takeover of Childhood*, she provides countless examples of how consumerism as a value is marketed to children even in their toys. She also explains how schools themselves are being modeled after corporations, as marketers conclude that all roads eventually lead to the classroom. Advertising in schools, which began to escalate in the 1990s, now includes, among other things, corporate-sponsored newscasts, field trips, classroom materials, vending machines, gymnasiums, walls, and whole buildings.

These trends are undermining the very qualities we rely on to ensure a healthy democratic citizenry. They promote materialism, impulsiveness, entitlement, unexamined brand loyalty, disengagement, and cynicism toward parents and other authority figures. Materialistic values are harmful, not just to individual health and happiness and sustainable democracies, but also to the well-being of our planet. In this context, advocacy for responsible stewardship and care of our cultural environment is every bit as critical to our long-term survival as a species as old-growth forests, clean air, and water.

The Values Debate

It is not uncommon for the principles of child development, pioneered by Piaget, Erikson, and Kohlberg, to be applied to marketing and product development. Industrial psychologists now help the marketing industry to target children by exploiting their developmental vulnerabilities. Ways in which their cognitive, social, emotional, and physical development influence decision-making, their likes, dislikes, activities, and insecurities are carefully examined in the cut-throat competition for market share.

And while the pervasiveness of sexual innuendo in advertisements is not new, what is new is the alarming degree to which the advertising industry has insinuated itself into the value systems of children. Indeed, there is even discussion of them in scholarly journals with titles such as, "Children's Relationship to Brands: 'True Love' or 'One Night Stand?'" and "Brands: The New Religion." (Linn, 2004: 186)

Identity and belonging have always been key issues for human beings. However, what used to be trusted, reliable and consistent sources of support and direction, such as teachers, family, government and religion, are now objects of growing cynicism and rejection. The resulting vacuum has not been lost on the marketing experts. "Could," one speculates, "brands take over the role that religions and philosophical movements used to own?" (Linn, 2004: 187)

Among psychologists themselves, these trends have spawned concern over erosion of their own ethics and governing principles, meant to encourage "contribution of their knowledge for the good of human welfare." (Ruskin, 1999) As a result, the American Psychological Association has called for restrictions on "Children-Oriented Advertising." (Teinowitz, 2004)

Traditionally, in debates within the cultural environment, values have been ceded to political conservatives, in particular the religious right, with most media scholars avoiding the terrain entirely. Unfortunately, we cannot escape values, either our own or those of others. Like the illusion of total objectivity in the world of journalism, we communicate our values as much through silence and inaction as through protest, depending on what we voluntarily choose to do or write about. So far, we have abdicated our children's value systems to corporate media giants and are now faced with, among other problems, trends toward increasing emphasis on aggression, sexual content, alcohol and cigarette consumption in advertisements targeting youth. (McGinley, 2004)

The usual response from the media industries when criticized for such excesses is a promise of self-regulation. But it is clear that self-regulation is not working. According to a report released in April of 2004, North Americans overwhelmingly believe that marketing harms children, and favor restrictions to protect children.

Reasons why industry self-regulation does not and cannot work are provided in the Canadian documentary, *The Corporation*, and Law Professor Joel Bakan's book by the same title. Both explain how the modern corporation is recognized in the law as a person. One perceived right is freedom of expression. Yet, in psychological terms, most corporations tend to behave like psychopathic individuals, incapable of guilt, shame or remorse, and extremely skilled at manipulation and deceit. Nowhere are these behavioral deviancies more prevalent than in the cultural industries. Consequently, it becomes an exercise in futility to rely on business ethics or good corporate citizenship without a little help from government and the rule of law.

Changing the System

What is needed within the research community as a whole, particularly on the subject of media effects, is more attention to how, when, and why studies are done at all. Now, researchers within the different disciplines seldom talk to each other about either their findings or their methods. This has led to calls for more interdisciplinary studies, and some impressive strides have been made. However, findings and recommendations still tend to be marginalized by media news coverage, where it is usually argued that any move beyond vigilance over media diets on the part of parents, imperils our basic civil liberties.

The existing pattern is for substantive studies, initiated by governments or within the health sector of society, to be followed up by release of industry-supported findings, either demonstrating inconclusive evidence of harmful effects, or attacks on the methods used in studies reporting the opposite. This ensures that the pendulum of public debate never goes beyond the issue of conclusive evidence of harmful effects, and then onto policy.

In the past, we have observed these same trends on the issue of tobacco smoking and cancer. The result is a fertile climate for unbridled capitalism, nurtured by assumptions that nothing can be done to restrict ruthless, profit-driven marketing campaigns, which target children, because of dangers posed to freedom of expression for us all. Politicians, paralyzed with fear of being branded as censors or prudish conservatives, tend to avoid the issue entirely.

Similarly, media literacy educators, in order to attract and sustain funding, tend to define their work by emphasizing that they do not involve themselves in advocacy. Perceived limitations to these restricted approaches within both the fields of education and research , have led, in recent decades, to the development of action-oriented, participatory forms of qualitative research, where data collection, education, and advocacy are combined.

One of the first lessons in media education ought to be that better distinctions must be made between individual freedom of expression and corporate freedom of enterprise. Diversity of opinion, a cornerstone of any healthy democracy, involves conflict in the form of competing ideas. But now, in our information-based economy, postmodern society on a global scale, democratic or otherwise, consists of extremely mobile populations. What we tend to end up with, rather than healthy debate on competing ideas, is their fragmentation, with half-truths and propaganda slogans, framed in media spin that seldom leads to meaningful consensus, conclusions, or sound policy.

Despite these obstacles, meaningful change is emerging on the international front. In May of 2004, the World Health Organization (WHO) adopted its first-ever global strategy on diet, physical activity, and health. One year earlier, it approved the first-ever international health treaty, aimed at curbing tobacco consumption, designated as one of the world's leading causes of preventable death. (Picard, 2004: A19) These are blueprints for countries to develop and implement policies to make it easier for people to eat healthier, be more active, avoid violence as a conflict resolution strategy, and engage in economic activity that supports ecological sustainability.

At the national level, these WHO initiatives provide opportunities during federal election campaigns for policy proposals on the perennial issue of escalating health care costs with an emphasis on savings through prevention and health promotion. At the community level, seed money could be provided to organizations advocating health and violence prevention. On the hard issue of tax cuts, a starting point should be to eliminate grants, subsidies, tax credits, and exemptions for hip-hop music, video, film, and television productions with extremely violent and pornographic content.

There is also the urgent need to restrict advertising directed to children on a global scale. Recent consensus around legal approaches to the problem of obesity shows that the food industry is most vulnerable on the issue of marketing to children. Indeed, long before the current epidemic of overweight children evolved, the harmful effects of advertising anything at all to them, but especially violence in popular culture, led to banning of advertising in the province of Quebec to children thirteen years and under, and in several European countries as well. The UK followed suit in January, 2007. (BBC News, November 17, 2006)

A coalition of over sixty psychiatrists, psychologists, and other health professionals have called on the U.S. Congress to adopt similar measures and such proposals are also before the entire European Union. (Linn, 2004; Dyson, 2000) Said the APA: "Given that young children inherently lack the cognitive capability to effectively recognize and defend against television commercial persuasion, we recommend that policymakers pursue efforts to constrain advertising specifically targeting this particular age group." (Teinowitz, 2004)

The Federal Communications Commission in the United States and the Canadian Radio-television and Telecommunications Commission (CRTC) do, on occasion, respond to demands that something be done to reverse the media's race to the bottom when it comes to indecency and pollution on the public airwaves, and they need to be encouraged. U.S. federal law bars radio and noncable television stations from airing references to sexual and excretory functions between 6:00 a.m. and 10:00 p.m. when children may be tuning in. In 2004, the House of Representatives in the United States voted to raise the maximum indecency fines with a cap of three million USD a day. (Kerr, 2004, R3)

In Canada, also in 2004, the CRTC decided not to renew the license for CHOI-FM in Quebec City, citing a pattern of offensive comments by its morning-show hosts, and because it did not clean up its act despite several warnings. (Blackwell, 2004: A1) The trash-talking French Canadian shock jock radio station was aimed at the much coveted eighteen to thirty-four-year-old demographic. Industry reaction and related publicity focused primarily on the "censorship" aspects of the decision, ignoring entirely the broader implications of the Broadcast Act's requirements for broadcasters to provide a "high standard of balanced programming" and to refrain from abusive comments on the basis of an individual's or a group's race, national or ethnic origin, color, religion, sex, sexual orientation, age, or physical or mental disability. (Marotte, 2004: A5) The CRTC needs public support to ensure that these criteria remain relevant and enforceable. (Canada, 1991)

In addition, to their harmful effects, communications technologies also offer us unprecedented opportunities for networking and coalition building. This is especially true of the Internet. Web sites, established by numerous professional and community based groups, provide countless examples of established linkages, information sharing, and action being taken to change the status quo and point us, as a species, toward development of a more wholesome and sustainable cultural environment. (www.C-CAVE.com; www.commercialexploitation.org, both accessed 15 May 2007)

Conclusion

Our new reality, brought on by higher education, mass media exposure, travel, and migration, is making us increasingly interdependent. The perils of modern

life have been heightened both because of and in spite of new technologies enabling rapid mobility and instant communications. Much is being made of the
need to strike a balance between the public right to know and national security.
There is an equally pressing need for similar trade-offs on health care delivery
and crime prevention, protection of children and abuses of corporate media
through tax privileges and credits. Ideological child abuse is now an integral part
of our information-based global economy because of the bizarre synergies inherent in the self-governing incoherence of free-market forces. That needs to
change.

The popular myth that complete freedom for the media means democracy
and freedom for everyone else as well, serves the ever more powerful and fewer
media moguls best. By helping to fuel global media monopolization it ensures
for them, alone, the privilege of deciding what the rest of us see, hear and read.
Global trends toward convergence in communications demonstrate increasing
urgency for the examination of capital flows as well as technology and content
for the development of sound, international, public policy. Only then will we
begin to move toward a more holistic and sustainable approach to spiritual,
physical, and mental well-being. Only then will the young and adults alike be
more open to embracing the *Earth Charter* (see the Appendix).

References

Atkinson, William Illsey. "Video Mind Games." *The Globe and Mail*, 13 Mar. 2004, F8.
Bianco, Robert. "Wall-to-Wall Coverage Reflects Monumental Scale, Sadness." *USA TODAY*. 18 Apr. 2007, D1.
Blackwell, Richard, Tu Thanh Ha, and Simon Tuck. "Radio Crackdown Opens Deep Divide." *The Globe and Mail*. 15 Jul. 2004, A1.
Canada. *Broadcasting Act* (Rev. ed.) Ottawa: Minister of Supply and Services, 1991.
Canadian Teachers Federation. *KIDS' TAKE ON MEDIA What 5,700 Canadian Kids Say about TV, Movies, Video and Computer Games and More*. Ottawa, 2003.
Deacon, James. RINK RAG *Maclean's Canada's Weekly Newsmagazine*. Toronto: Rogers Media, 26 March 2001.
Dyson, Rose. *MIND ABUSE Media Violence In An Information Age*. Montreal, Toronto, New York, London: Black Rose Books, 2000.
Fine, Sean. "Are Schools Failing Boys?" *The Globe and Mail*. 5 Sept. 2000, A9.
Freeze, Colin. *The Globe and Mail*. 25 May 2004, A1.
Kerr C. Jennifer. "CBS Hit by Record FCC Fine for Janet Jackson Flash." *The Globe and Mail*. 23 Sept. 2004, R3.
Linn, Susan. *Consuming Kids: The Hostile Takeover of Childhood*. New York, London: The New Press, 2004.
Marotte, Bertrand. "Boss of Shock-Jock Station 'Straight-Arrow' Accountant." *The Globe and Mail*. 15 Jul. 2004, A5.
McGinley, Laura. Press Release: *Consuming Kids: The Hostile Takeover of Childhood*. New York, The New Press, 2004.
Naylor, David. "Justice Delayed?" *The Globe and Mail*. 18 May 2004, S1.

Picard, Andre. "Canada is Trailing on Health Promotion." *The Globe and Mail.* 27 May 2004, A19.

Ruskin, Gary. Press Release: *Commercial Alert, Psychologists, Psychiatrists Call for Limits on the Use of Psychology to Influence or Exploit Children for Commercial Purposes.* 30 Sept. 1999. www.commercialalert.org/issues/culture/psychology/commercial-alert-psychologists-psychiatrists-call-for-limits-on-the-use-of-psychology-to-influence-or-exploit-children-for-commercial-purposes (27 Aug. 2007).

Signorielli, Nancy, George Gerbner, and Michael Morgan. "Violence on Television: The Cultural Indicators Project." *Journal of Broadcasting & Electronic Media* 39, no. 2 (1995): 278–83.

Teinowitz, Ira. Reports Hits "Commercialization of Childhood." Washington, DC: 24 Feb. 2004. www.AdAge.com (31 May 2007).

Ziauddin, Sarder, and Merryl Wyn Davies. *Why Do People Hate America?* Cambridge, UK: Icon Books, 2002.

Chapter 27

The Child's Rights to Health and the Role of the World Health Organization[1]

Laura Westra, Ph.D. (Law); Ph.D. (Philosophy)
Professor Emeritus, University of Windsor
Windsor, Ontario, Canada
Adjunct Professor of Social Science,
York University, Toronto, Canada
Contact Information: 222 Barrhill Road, Maple, Ont. L6A 1L2 CANADA
Phone: +1 905 303 8181; Fax: +1 905 303 8211; Email: lwestra@interlog.com
GEIG: www.globalecointegrity.net

Summary

Most people would agree with the proposition that newborns have a right to a healthy life. But many would not recognize the cardinal importance of the environmental conditions surrounding both the newborn and its mother for them to achieve a healthy life.

Even the latest *Convention on the Rights of the Child* omits this. That document, like others, tends to view the child as a small adult, rather than as someone with a different biology and physiology, and one far more vulnerable than any adult to environmental insults. One result is that children have become the new "canaries"—abnormal development and diseases in children warn us that unsafe conditions are present in our day-to-day lives.

The negligence of industrial and corporate practices, and the effects on children of our carelessness, can be found in a body of well-supported research of the World Health Organization (WHO). This research emphasizes the harms to both pre-born and infants from our present affluent and technologically advanced lifestyles.

The first generation is already bearing burdens from our practices. While many international treaties and the like support the rights of future generations, the rights of the first generation (i.e., today's children) are not addressed.

To remedy this omission, environmental justice must include considerations of both intergenerational and intragenerational rights. We argue that the WHO, as a United Nations' agency, can and should lend its authority to regulatory planners and governments by insisting that scientific findings be reflected in health regulations, and that the grave effects of ignoring that evidence be shared internationally.

Introduction—Child Protection and Future Generations' Rights: The Road to Ecojustice

This chapter starts with, and is based on, the foundational role played by the environment in childhood development. Evidence for this role amassed by the WHO is the starting point but, as we shall see, that evidence complements the findings of much epidemiological, ecological, and social literature. Indeed, findings from many disciplines support the expansion of human rights for which this chapter argues.

Of course, arguments based on science and moral principles are not enough to ensure that public policy will be consonant with the data. We need to understand the full import of the harms perpetrated against children, who now seem to be viewed as the new "canaries" (analogous to canaries used by miners as sentinels for methane gas emissions), by today's flawed and incomplete laws and regulations. Both the laws that spell out children's rights and the duty to protect children, and those that deal with environmental protection are complicit. These two forms of protection are inseparable, and their interface forms the basis for "ecojustice," justice that is simultaneously intragenerational and intergenerational.[2]

The first of the future generations—today's children—is at grave risk here and now. An understanding of the present situation must be the starting point, the basis for all future-oriented legal instruments. An example of a document that truly embraces all necessary requirements and lays out foundational principles is the *Earth Charter*[3] (see the Appendix).

Environmental protection is insufficient if it does not include the consideration of all life, present and future: scientific uncertainty, and the increasing relevance of the Precautionary Principle, make such an approach mandatory. Child protection, although it includes many important issues beyond the protection of life, health, and normal function, *must* start with these "basic rights." Protection of the child's right to religious freedom, to education, to a responsible and responsive family or substitute to nurture her growth and development, means little if the child is born with serious mental, physical or emotional challenges, caused by pre-birth or other early environmental exposure. Finally, future generations cannot be protected if high-sounding rhetoric incorporated into instruments ostensibly designed for their protection does not generate positive action. Certainly the first of those generations will be negligently and carelessly harmed, often chronically or permanently.

To develop a just developmental ethic, we must seek to implement a form of global governance that includes the preconditions of human rights.[4] From that standpoint, the ecological basis for the developmental rights of infants and children can be equally protected. As we will show, the foundations of children's rights to health must be built and respected long before the child sees light. "*Developmental rights*," when the referents are children, must acquire a meaning analogous to the generally accepted meaning of the rights of all peoples to development.

No people or nation can truly achieve successful development, understood as including satisfactory social and economic conditions and the availability of education and personal freedom, unless each group member's rights, including necessary "pre-conditions," are fully respected *from the start*.[5] The history of the rights of children to health and the environment[6] clearly demonstrates how early these "pre-conditions" must be considered and factored into public policy in the form of binding legal instruments.

The argument proposed herein is not that we ought to have as many children as possible: "responsible reproduction" means ensuring that reproductive choices include serious consideration of the rights of those living now and of future generations in the least developed countries, people who have a strong right to their own resources and livelihoods. It does mean, however, that the presence of a pregnancy imposes an immediate duty of respect for the health and the life of the embryo and the fetus. This responsibility accrues not only to the parents and their lifestyle choices—both national governments and institutions, and multinational corporations, carry a similar responsibility in all their operations. This should be reflected in the regulatory regimes affecting everything from resource extraction and economic production and waste disposal, through consumer advertising, to the so-called free trade practices so prevalent today.

This chapter starts with a consideration of the Convention of the Rights of the Child. It then examines the foundation of child's rights and the duty of institutional protection on the part of governments and individuals. Following that, we consider the presence of an all-pervasive "ecoviolence" against human life before discussing the WHO's research regarding harms to children. This chapter is intended as a survey of present circumstances, based on the WHO's research, and an initial discussion of obstacles and possible remedies for the child's health. We conclude by proposing a stronger role for the WHO, and even the possibility of mandated interventions based on the "international duty to protect."

The Convention on the Rights of the Child
and Its Background

In Geneva, the Fifth Assembly of the League of Nations, adopted the Declaration of the Rights of the Child. (Records of the Fifth Assembly Supplement No. 23, League of Nations Official Journal, 1924) This Declaration proposes five major principles to establish the duty of society regarding children:

- The child must be given the means requisite for its normal development, both materially and spiritually.

- The child that is hungry must be fed; the child that is sick must be nursed; the child that is backward must be helped; the delinquent child must be re-claimed; and the orphan and the waif must be sheltered and succoured.
- The child must be the first to receive relief in times of distress.
- The child must be put in a position to earn a livelihood, and must be pro-tected against every form of exploitation.
- The child must be brought up in the consciousness that its talents must be devoted to the service of its fellow men. (U.N.DOC E/CN.4/1989/29)

Nevertheless, unlike most modern human rights instruments, this document only "invites states . . . to be guided" by these principles. It makes no attempt to place binding obligations upon states.[7]

Notably, the major rights to be recognized at later dates are not specifically mentioned in this document: the right to life, the right to nationality, and hence, to protection. We discuss both of these rights below, as they represent core val-ues and principles that support not only the principles pertaining to the Rights of the Child (1924), and the recommendations of later documents, but also the find-ings of the WHO.[8]

Although the principles of the Geneva Declaration were non-binding, the instrument formed the basis of the "Social Commission of the Economic and Social Council of the United Nations" instruments intended to lead to a *United Nations Charter of the Rights of the Child.* The Charter was eventually adopted by the General Assembly on November 20, 1959.[9] It includes a "Preamble" and ten Articles. Notably, according to Principle 3, a child is entitled to a name and nationality, and principle 4 adds the right to "adequate nutrition, housing, recrea-tion and medical services." Protection (against neglect) is explicitly mentioned in Principle 9. This Charter will not be the main focus here because it has been superseded by the "Convention on the Rights of the Child"[10] (1989). However it is important to note with Van Bueren, that: "by 1959 . . . children are beginning to emerge no longer as passive recipients, but as subjects of international law recognized as being able to enjoy the benefits of specific rights and freedoms."[11]

This emergent reality has a further effect: "the proposition that individuals can be subjects of international rights necessarily involves the corollary that they can be subjects of international duties; the cogency of the claim to the former gains by an admission of the latter."[12]

Thus we must not lose sight of the fact that entrenching the rights to life and to protection in international law does far more that exhort states to ensure gen-eral human rights and perhaps other special duties to children. It obligates both states and individuals (natural and legal) to fulfill these obligations.

As human rights instruments evolved and proliferated, it became increas-ingly clear that children require rights in addition to those enjoyed by adults because of their "special vulnerability and immaturity."[13] Thus, even the same rights that are present in instruments intended for adult individuals require dif-ferent forms of interpretation when the focus is the child. For instance, there is far less controversy internationally on what defines an adult, than on the inception of childhood.[14]

This question is one of the major focuses of this work, given the ample evidence provided by the WHO and others on prenatal environmental violence.[15] For now, it is sufficient to note that, although the general consensus is that states are allowed to establish the point where life begins and thus where the state is required to guarantee protection, the *American Convention on Human Rights* states: "Every person has the right to have his life respected. This right shall be protected by law and in general from the moment of conception."[16]

The *Declaration of the Rights of the Child* of 1959, also provides: "Whereas the child by reason of his physical and mental immaturity needs special safeguards and care, including appropriate protection, before as well as after birth."

But in 1924, no definition of the child was provided, thus leaving this critical issue not discussed: "The issue, however, is critical, because if childhood begins from the moment of conception, then the child's 'inherent right to life' contained in Article 6(1) of the Convention on the Rights of the Child and in other international treaties, applies from the moment of conception."[17]

The *Convention on the Rights of the Child* (CRC) was adopted by the UN General Assembly on November 20, 1989[18] and entered into force on September 2, 1990.

The Definition of the Child and the Positive Duty of Physical Protection from Harm

There is no need to revisit the vast literature available on environmental hazards caused by current business practices, consumption patterns,[19] and climate change.[20] The important issue from our standpoint is whether these hazards produce more significant harms when children are affected, and if so, what follows from this discovery.

The sequence appears to be:

1. A child has nationality from birth;
2. Nationality entails physical protection; therefore
3. The latter is unequivocally due to the child who would have neither the motive nor the means to fail in her or his allegiance to the state.

But a difficulty arises, in that modern science indicates that the child cannot simply be protected from birth, if the duty to protect is taken seriously.[21] If a child at birth or thereafter manifests the effects of exposure to a toxicant *in utero*, that harm to the present child and to the future adult denotes a failure on the part of the government in the duty to protect.

This duty could be discharged by controlling the production and distribution of the toxic substance, by insisting on mandatory disclosure of all possible effects of that substance, or even by disallowing the substance altogether. Such duty, of course, is not theirs alone. Industries and business corporations, including pharmaceutical companies, that may be producing these toxic substances, are also under the duty not to do harm, and to disclose fully what their Research and Development departments are discovering. Above all, they have the duty not to produce and distribute any substance that has not been fully tested.

The Precautionary Principle,[22] rather than economic necessity, should govern the decisions of when to release products that may not have been fully tested, in the absence of precautionary practice. According to the Declaration of Helsinki on Human Testing, neither individuals nor groups can be treated as guinea pigs to test these products. An example of the dangers of untested products is the story of thalidomide: drugs containing thalidomide were clearly not tested enough to ensure that, once in the marketplace, they would not result in the birth of children with flippers instead of arms and legs, as well as other malformations. Such substances do not harm the mothers, but they produce devastating effects on embryos or fetuses and thus, on the children that will be born. Any regulative instrument that limits its reach to postnatal infants misses the many ways fetuses may be affected.[23] Therefore, governments committed to the protection of human rights should extend this protection to unborn persons, even when the resulting principles of justice fly in the face of custom or practice.

Indirect harms, perpetrated through the environment and the ingestion or aspiration of toxicants, must be considered when regulatory bodies enact laws. This need is vital for adults, but is particularly acute for children. For the issue of children's specific needs, the definition of the child in international law is a critical starting point.

Traditionally a child has been defined as a comparative negative: a child is an individual who is not yet an adult.[24]

But the Preamble to the Declaration of the Rights of the Child (1959) is the first legal instrument to focus on the most debated point, that is, the start of the child's life: "Whereas the child by reason of his physical and mental immaturity needs special safeguards and care, including appropriate legal protection, before and after birth."

In addition, Article 4 of the *American Convention on Human Rights* provides that, "He shall be entitled to grow and develop in health; to this end, special care and protection shall be provided to him and his mother, including adequate prenatal and post-natal care."

These documents are clear and correspond to the general popular belief in the mother's right to prenatal care and hence, to the pre-birth rights of the child, even though the full extent to the effect of endocrine disruptors and other toxic substances on fetuses was not known. Only the *American Convention on Human Rights* provides that, "Every person has the right to have his life respected. This right shall be protected by law and in general from the moment of conception." The words "in general" would allow the State to intervene to save a mother's life, or in the case of rape. Similarly, the European Commission rejects guaranteeing an absolute right to life to the fetus although it concedes that, "certain rights are attributable to the conceived but unborn child, in particular the right to inherit."[25]

Yet the right of the unborn not to be injured by violence directed at the mother, or through alcohol or drugs, exists today. For instance, as early as 1987, Thomas Murray compellingly argued that the age of the fetus is not relevant to the harms it may suffer in the womb. If someone attacks a pregnant woman and beats her without killing either her or her fetus, but the child is subsequently born paralyzed or otherwise harmed, the impact on the child is both morally wrong and actionable.[26] Murray concluded that "the timing of the harm is irrelevant," and his position is supported by the U.S. Congress, Office of Technology Assessment's document on "Reproductive Health Hazards in the Workplace."[27]

In 1964, W. L. Prosser[28] argued that after 1946 we witnessed: "the most spectacular abrupt reversal of a well-settled rule in the whole history of the law of torts. The child, provided that he is born alive, is permitted to maintain an action for the consequences of prenatal injuries, and if he dies of such injuries after birth, an action will lie for wrongful death."

All arguments proposing a role for viability in our consideration of fetal harms are unsound, especially after the discovery of the effects of a mother's exposure to endocrine disruptors and other environmental toxicants, including non-ionizing electromagnetic fields, alcohol, tobacco smoke, pesticide residues, and some pharmaceuticals.[29] The effects of these exposures are particularly grave in the earlier stages of embryonic life.

Children's Right to Health: Obstacles, Challenges, and the Role of the WHO

Before turning to the WHO's "state of the art" summary of relevant science on the relationship between an ecologically sound environment and human rights, specifically those of children, we need to define public health and the role of the WHO. What is "public health?" It can be defined as "what we as a society do collectively to ensure the conditions in which people can be healthy."[30]

Thus, we understand public health to be more than disease control; it must involve society as a whole in the activities required both to achieve public health, and to defend it from countervailing forces. The definition emphasizes that it is *collective* responsibility, not exclusively a state responsibility as was argued in Section 2. The goal of Public Health requires consideration under three headings. Fidler explains:

- *Assessment* means collecting and analyzing data in order to identify and understand the major health problems facing a community.
- *Policy Development* establishes goals, sets of priorities, and develops strategies to address health problems.

- *Assurance of Services* involves the design, implementation and evolution of programs to address priority health problems in the community.[31]

The largest and most authoritative body concerned with public health is the WHO and its definition of health (in the "Preamble" of the *Constitution of the World Health Assembly*[32]). It merits serious consideration: "Health is a state of complete physical, mental and social well-being and not merely the absence of disease or infirmity."

In the same "Preamble," the health of Children is mentioned, and its relation to the environment is noted: "Healthy development of the child is of basic importance; the ability to live harmoniously in a changing total environment is essential to such development." (See also Chapter II, Article 2 [1])

As part of the UN, the World Health Organization is an authoritative body, not solely a medical/technical agency. WHO's status was clearly demonstrated when the organization requested an *opinio juris* from the UN General Assembly, after the International Court of Justice in the *Legality of the Use by a State of Nuclear Weapons in Armed Conflict*[33] had determined that the WHO lacked the constitutional authority to ask the question it had posed.[34] The question posed was: "In view of the health and environmental effects, would the use of nuclear weapons by a State in war or other armed conflict be a breach of its obligations under international law including the WHO Constitution?"

The response of the Court was that, although Article 65, Paragraph 1 of the Court's Statute provides that "The Court may give an advisory opinion," in this case, the Court refused because of the Court's lack of jurisdiction in this case, and because the question, as posed, was "vague and abstract." When the question was again posed, this time by the General Assembly, "the Court concluded that it has the authority to deliver an opinion on the question posed by the General assembly, and that there exist no "compelling reasons" which would lead the Court to exercise its discretion not to do so." This historic encounter between the International Court and the WHO ended with a debate and a weak opinion, but an opinion nonetheless. Kindred et al. describe the event:

> The Court held unanimously that there is in neither customary nor conventional international law any specific authorization of the threat or use of nuclear weapons; by eleven votes to three, that there is in neither customary nor conventional international law any comprehensive and universal prohibition of the threat or use of nuclear weapons as such; unanimously, that threat or use of force by means of nuclear weapons that is contrary to Article 2, para. 4, of the U.N. Charter and that fails to meet all the requirements of Article 51, is unlawful.

As consequence, by the President casting his vote to break a seven-to-seven tie, the Court held:

> It follows from the above-mentioned requirements that the threat or use of nuclear weapons would generally be contrary to the rules of international law ap-

plicable in armed conflict, and in particular the principles and rules of humanitarian law; however, in view of the current state of international law, and of the elements of fact at its disposal, the Court cannot conclude definitively whether the threat or use of nuclear weapons would be lawful or unlawful in an extreme circumstance of self-defense, in which the very survival of a State would be at stake.[35]

The importance of this decision, incomplete and tentative though it is, has been emphasized in the work of Falk[36] and many legal scholars, including the author.[37] Nevertheless, whatever its shortcomings, the "Opinion" places the WHO squarely in the realm of international players, with more than simply a research and advisory capacity. Furthermore, by virtue of membership in WHO, member countries have the obligation to respond to its guidance in some measure. We argue here that WHO's capacity needs to be brought out fully once again in the services of humanity, and children in particular. Although its effects are not immediately visible as a mushroom cloud (i.e., a nuclear blast) would be, the insidious effects of nuclear power could kill, harm, and adversely affect many more people than the Hiroshima disaster ever did.

The WHO's organizational ideology includes the formulation of broad goals and principles: "In 1977, the WHO defined the broad goal of the organization as 'health for all by the year 2000.'"[38]

Although (then) Director-General Mahler labored toward this goal, subsequent directors exhibited a less idealistic and more managerial leadership style, including placing more focus on specific issues and goals. With the appointment of Bruntland to the post in 1998, "the WHO's vision and political momentum," which had dissipated during the leadership of Makajima, were partially regained.[39]

Nevertheless, the increasing power of the WTO and the World Bank posed a challenge to the role of the WHO on global public health. Abbassi says that a WHO representative expressed a similar sentiment in arguing that "the World Bank is the new eight-hundred-pound gorilla in world health care."[40]

The *World Development Report 1993* introduced the concept of the "Disability-Adjusted Life Year" (DALY).[41] Thus the World Bank introduced a regime intent on quantifying and rendering more cost effective all health interventions, and WHO Director Bruntland apparently also accepted this pragmatic approach.[42a]

Nevertheless, the traditional approach of WHO sees health as a "fundamental human right" that should be pursued for its own sake.[42b] In order to ensure that this traditional vision prevails once again, the WHO needs to re-integrate its global public health mission into international law,[43] including trade law, environmental law, and human rights law,[44] and, we add, the law concerning the rights of the child, as it did when it scrutinized South African policies in their area of competence, during Apartheid.

Hence it is vitally important to learn all that the WHO 2002 document (Note 14) can offer about children's health, perhaps recognizing in this document also a portent of the return to the vision and the traditional leadership of the WHO. This document, aware of the 1989 CRC, states that, contrary to the commitments made in that instrument and in several other international instruments, the situation for children does not show significant improvement.[45] The WHO concludes that:

> Children are at risk of exposure to more than fifteen thousand synthetic chemicals, nearly all of them developed over the past fifty years and to a variety of physical agents. In addition, developing organisms are more vulnerable to environmental contaminants for several reasons, including greater and longer exposure and particular susceptibility windows. We are witnessing an unprecedented increase in the incidence of asthma; some childhood concerns also show an upward trend; injuries still represent a high burden for children and young adults; and there is increasing concern regarding the neurotoxicity, immunotoxicity and endocrine-disrupting properties of substances that are widely dispersed in the environment.[46]

The magnitude of the problem demonstrates why the WHO should gain (or regain) world leadership and why it must have a significant role in the formulation of laws and the decisions about the appropriate punishment for noncompliance of either states or juridical persons, whose interests and economic transactions give rise to most of the problems listed above. The role of the WHO ought not to be limited to responding to crises or proposing courses of treatment to various diseases. Following upon the 1997 Declaration of the Environmental Leaders of the Eight, the WHO is committed to promote and encourage health measures into areas of emerging concern to children's health on the basis of the Precautionary Principle, and, in general "to develop and implement" preventive measures in all areas of concern to children.[47]

World Health Organization Findings for Policy Guidance

Children are particularly vulnerable to environmental threats. This heightened susceptibility derives primarily from the unique biological features that characterize the various stages of development from conception to adolescence.[48]

There are many examples of this heightened susceptibility. For instance, in the early years of a child's life, the brain and nervous system develop so that cells destroyed by chemicals (e.g., lead or mercury) during this period will not recover, and the resulting impairment will be "permanent and irreversible."[49] Another example is the greater exposure of children "per unit of body weight" to environmental toxins than adults.[50] Because children sometimes eat, drink, and even breathe more deeply than adults, the effect of toxins will be more harmful to them than they might be to adults.[51] In addition, the child's life lies mostly ahead, so it is more likely through the long latent period of so many toxicants that she or he will develop diseases caused by exposure to environmental contaminants.[52] To make matters worse, many chemicals have long-term and even intergenerational effects through bioaccumulation.

Each period of a child's development has specific risks. Even before conception, ionizing radiation may damage the reproductive organs of either parent or may be stored in the mother's body to be reactivated during pregnancy, thus harming the fetus directly. Eggs and sperm can also be damaged by exposure to PCBs or other occupational toxicants.[53]

During embryonic and fetal development, toxicants may reach the fetus directly through the placenta. Ionizing radiation and electromagnetic fields may also cause prenatal damage.[54] Newborns have their own susceptibilities, such as exposure to plastic solvents and industrial pollutants, household chemicals, and other substances through contact with their permeable skin. They also suffer more severely than adults from the effects from airborne pollutants including tobacco smoke.[55] In the early years, not only eating and breathing, but also direct contact with harmful surroundings, from carpets and paints to garden chemicals and soil, can introduce harmful substances to the child. The contacts and any effects may be multiplied during adolescent stages as exposure to the media becomes routine.[56]

These are some of the general findings addressing particular issues at various stages of a child's development. The next topic is a brief summary of some of the worst substances that harm children and some of the most serious diseases and malfunctions that result. Among the environmental "contaminants" that affect children are tobacco smoke;[57] pesticides;[58] ultraviolet radiation;[59] and electromagnetic fields.[60, 61] Health impacts include: (1) asthma and other respiratory problems, generally on the rise in industrial countries;[62] (2) neurodevelopmental disorders from chemical or pesticide exposure;[63] (3) cancers, as "children are likely to be more prone than adults to events related to carcinogenesis," although cancer is still considered to be primarily a disease of adulthood and old age;[64] (4) birth defects, at a rate of about 5 percent of live births; these also represent the "leading cause of infant mortality in the developed world for more than twenty years, with a rate of 173.4 per 100,000 live births in 1994";[65] (5) "waterborne gastrointestinal disease due to biological contamination and acute and chronic poisoning by a variety of chemicals."[66] The weight of evidence is overwhelming, so that policies need to be developed to enforce children's right to protection. The WHO document we have briefly summarized proposes the following:

16.2. Rationale and guiding principles for Protective Policies for Children
- Children cannot be regarded as little adults because their behavior, physiology, metabolism and diet are different.
- Children have different susceptibilities from adults due to their dynamic growth and to their biological systems which are not yet fully developed.
- Children have very different exposure patterns compared to adults.

- For children, the stage in their development when the exposure occurs is as important, if not more important than the type and dose of exposure.
- Children are exposed to different types of toxicants in different combinations throughout their lives.
- Children can have very different health outcomes from adults exposed to the same toxicant; such health outcomes alter normal development and can be permanent.
- Children have more years during which they may be exposed to a variety of toxicants, which can lead to disease in later life.

Summary and Conclusions

The argument in this chapter starts with the established principle that children have a right to nationality and that nationality implies government protection of rights, starting with the right to life, health, and physical integrity. We make the case that effective protection implies "ecological rights"[67] which means that industrial and related economic activity should be assessed routinely, case by case, for any negative environmental impacts that would be hostile to health and normal life function, particularly for children.

Science increasingly demonstrates that "protection" implies special attention to children. Children, as the WHO has shown, are not simply "small adults" (supra, Section 6.a) and their special needs must be codified in the "rights of the child." In essence, since (a) the "preconditions of human agency"[68] are established long before birth and (b) pre-birth and early infancy are the most vulnerable periods of human life because the developing child is the most sensitive to various toxicants, it follows that (c) the rights of the child must start with a healthy environment, capable of supporting and protecting his or her biological integrity, from the start of the child's individuated biological life. (In this latter regard, we should distinguish no difference between different sorts of rights. Some rights based on potentiality are already accepted and entrenched in law while others, although equally future-oriented, are not. This distinction must be abandoned.)

Perhaps the most effective corrective would be to recognize the injustice inherent in the grossly inequitable ecological footprints imposed on the planet by the wealthy, including most residents of the more affluent countries.[69] Although it can be argued that favorable socioeconomic circumstances improve the health of affluent populations, there is no corresponding "trickle down" effect on the health of the impoverished, any more than there is for economics. Moreover, excess consumption and waste production by the already rich now compromise the development potential of the poor.[70] The favorable "pre-conditions" of health, if understood in the sense of improved economic circumstances for some, increasingly entail depriving those in developing countries of essential domestic resources.[71] All other rights—to education, to family life, nondiscrimination, etc.—diminish in importance when compared to the basic, foundational right of health. If the Rights of the Child are to be accepted as more than simply an incomplete, misunderstood extension of present, limited, human rights instruments, it is our collective responsibility to ensure that these rights be fully researched in all their implications, and that the duties they impose, fully embraced.

Notes

1. Laura Westra, *Environmental Justice and the Rights of Unborn and Future Generations—Law, Environmental Harm and the Right to Health* (London: Earthscan, 2006).

2. Westra, *Environmental Justice*, ch. 6.

3. Steven Rockefeller, "Foreword," in *Just Ecological Integrity* (Lanham, MD: Rowman & Littlefield), x–xiv.

4. Prudence Taylor, "From Environmental to Ecological Human Rights: A New Dynamic in International Law?" in *The Georgetown Int'l Environmental Law Review* 10, 309.

5. Alan Gewirth, *Human Rights: Essays on Justification and Applications* (Chicago: University of Chicago Press, 1982).

6. EEA Report no. 29, *Children's Health and the Environment: A Review of the Evidence*, ed. Giorgio Tamburlini, Ondine van Ehrenstein, and Roberto Bertollini, Geneva (henceforth *WHO 2002*).

7. Geraldine Van Bueren, *The International Law on the Rights of the Child* (The Hague: Martinus Nijhoff Publisher, 1995), 7.

8. *WHO 2002*.

9. *United Nations Charter of the Rights of the Child*, GA Res. 1386 XIV.

10. *Convention on the Rights of the Child*, U.N.Doc E/CN.4/1989/29; in force 20 Nov. 1990.

11. Van Bueren, *International Law*, 12.

12. Sir Herch Lauterpacht, *International Law and Human Rights* (New York: Archon Books, 1968).

13. *WHO 2002*.

14. Van Bueren, *International Law*, 32–38; Sharon Detricks, *A Commentary on the United Nations Convention on the Rights of the Child* (The Hague: Kluwer Law International, 1999), 5.

15. *WHO 2002*; see also Colin Soskolne and Roberto Bertollini, "Global Ecological Integrity and 'Sustainable Development': Cornerstones of Public Health. A Discussion Document," 1999, http://www.euro.who.int/document/gch/ecorep5.pdf (3 Jun. 2007); Theo Colborn, Dianne Dumanski, and John Peterson Myers, *Our Stolen Future* (New York: Dutton/Penguin, 1996).

16. *American Convention on Human Rights* (Interamerican Yearbook, 1968), 321.

17. Van Bueren, *International Law*, 33; see Art. 6(1) *International Covenant on Civil and Political Rights*; Art. 2.2 *European Convention on Human Rights*; Art. 4 *American Convention on Human Rights*.

18. (UN DOC.E/CN.4/1989/29/Rev.1), followed the *U.N. Declaration on the Rights of the Child, 20 Nov. 1959.*

19. Laura Westra, *Living in Integrity* (Lanham, MD: Rowman & Littlefield, 1998); William Rees and Laura Westra, "When Consumption Does Violence: Can There Be Sustainability and Environmental Justice in a Resource-Limited World," in *Just Sustainabilities*, ed. J. Agyeman, R. Evans, and R. D. Bullard (London: Earthscan Publications, 2003), 99–124.

20. Anthony McMichael, *Planetary Overload* (Cambridge: Cambridge University Press, 1995); A. J. McMichael, "Global Environment Change in the Coming Century: How Sustainable Are Recent Health Gains?" in *Ecological Integrity: Integrating Environment, Conservation and Health*, ed. D. Pimentel, L. Westra, and R. Noss (Washington, DC: Island Press, 2000), 245; Donald Brown, *American Heat* (Lanham, MD: Rowman & Littlefield, 2002).

21. Colborn et al., *Our Stolen Future; WHO 2002.*

22. Carolyn Raffensperger, and Joel Tickner, *Protecting Public Health and the Environment: Implementing the Precautionary Principle* (Washington, DC: Island Press, 1999).

23. *WHO 2002.*

24. Van Bueren, *International Law*, 33.

25. Van Bueren, *International Law*, 35.

26. Thomas H. Murray, "Moral Obligations to the Not-yet Born: the Fetus as a Patient," in *Biomedical Ethics*, ed. T. H. Mappes and D. De Grazia, 4th ed. (New York: McGraw-Hill, 1996), 464–73.

27. U.S. Government Printing Office (Washington, DC, 1985).

28. William L. Prosser, *Handbook on the Law of Torts*, 3rd ed., (St. Paul, MN: West Publishing Co., 1964).

29. Colborn et al., *Our Stolen Future, WHO 2002*, 104–10.

30. Institute of Medicine 1988, United States; as cited in Fidler, 2000: 3 (see below).

31. David Fidler, *International Law and Public Health* (Ardsley, NY: Transnational Publishers Inc., 2000), 5.

32. EB101.R.2, Jan. 1998.

33. [1996] I.C.J. Rep. 66.

34. Hugh M. Kindred, Karin Mickelson, Rene Provost, Ted L. McDonald, Armand L. C. de Mestral, and Sharon A. Williams, *International Law*, 6th ed. (Ottawa: Edmond Montgomery Publications Ltd, 2000), 1180; see also pp. 363–67.

35. Kindred, *International Law*, 367.

36. Richard Falk, *Law in an Emerging Global Village* (Ardsley, NY: Transnational Publishers Inc., 1998).

37. Laura Westra, *Ecoviolence and the Law (Supranational, Normative Foundations of Ecocrime)* (Ardsley, NY: Transnational Publishers, 2004).

38. Fidler, *International Law*, 100.

39. Fidler, *International Law*, 109; see also Leon Gordenker, "The World Health Organization: Sectoral Leader or Occasional Benefactor?" in *U.S. Policy and The Future of The United Nations,* ed. R. Coate (Century Foundation, 1994), 167–91.

40. Kamran Abbasi, "Changing Sides" *Brit. Med. J.* 318 (1999), 865.

41. The World Bank, *Investing in Health: World Development Report 1993* (Oxford: Oxford University Press, 1993).

42 a–b. Fidler, *International Law*, 112.

43. David Fidler, "The Future of the World Health Organization: What Role for International Law?" *Vanderbilt J. Transnat'l Law* 31 (1998): 1079–126.

44. Fidler, *International Law*, 119.

45. Agenda 21, especially Chapter 6; the *1997 Declaration of the Environmental Leader of the Eight on Children's Environmental Health* (Miami, FL, 5–6 May 1997, http://www.g8.utoronto.ca/environment/1997miami/children.html (4 Jun. 2007); UNICEF, *The State of the World's Children* (New York: Oxford University Press, 1994); the *UNECE Environment and Human Settlement Division*, "Convention on Access to Information, Public Participating in Decision-Making and Access to Justice in Environmental Matters" (Aarhus, Denmark, Jun. 1998).

46. *WHO 2002*, 12.

47. *WHO 2002*, 14.

48. Giorgio Tamburlini, 2002, "Children's Special Vulnerability to Environmental Health Hazards: An Overview," in *WHO 2002*, 18.

49. Deborah Rice and Stanley Barone Jr., "Critical Periods of Vulnerability for the Developing Nervous System: Evidence from Human and Animal Models," *Environmental Health Perspectives* 108, Supp. 3 (2002): 511–33.

50. Tamburlini, *WHO 2002*, 19.

51. Wayne R. Snodgrass, "Physiological and Biochemical Differences between Children and Adults as Determinants of Toxic Exposure to Environmental Pollutants," in *Similarities and Differences between Children and Adults: Implications for Risk Assessment*, ed. Philip S. Guzelian, Carol J. Henry, and Stephen S. Olin (Washington, DC: ILSI Press, 1992), 35–42; Cynthia F. Bearer, "How are Children Different from Adults?" in *Environmental Health Perspectives* 102, Supp. 6 (1995): 7–12.

52. Tamburlini, *WHO 2002*, 19.

53. Joseph L. Jacobson and Sandra W. Jacobson, "Intellectual Impairment in Children Exposed to Polychlorinated Biphenyls in Utero," *N. Engl. J. Med.* 335, 783–9; Bu-Tian Ji, Xiao-Ou Shu, Martha S. Linet, et al., "Paternal Cigarette Smoking and the Risk of Childhood Cancer among Offspring of Non-Smoking Mothers," *J. Natl. Cancer Inst.* 89 (1997): 238–44; David A. Savitz "Effects of Parents Occupational Exposures on Risk of Stillbirth, Preterm Delivery, and Small-for-Gestational-Age Infants," *Am. J. Epidemiol.* 129 (1989): 1201–10.

54. Tamburlini, *WHO 2002*, 20.

55. L. M. Plunkett, D. Turnbull, and J. V. Rodricks, " Differences between Adults and Children Affecting Exposure Assessment," in *Similarities and Differences between Children and Adults: Implications for Risk Assessment*, ed. P. S. Guzelian (Washington, DC: Ilsi Press, 1992), 79–94.

56. Tamburlini, *WHO 2002*, 22; Rose Dyson, *Mind Abuse: Media Violence in an Information Age* (Montreal, Canada: Black Rose Books, 2000).

57. Carol M. Courage, "Environmental Tobacco Smoke," in *WHO 2002*, 142.

58. Cristina Tirado, "Pesticides," in *WHO 2002*, 152.

59. Eva A. Rehfuss and Ondine S. von Ehrenstein, "Ultraviolet Radiation," in *WHO 2002*, 161.

60. Kristie L. Ebi, "Electromagnetic Fields," in *WHO 2002*, 172.

61. Joy Carlson and Giorgio Tamburlini, "Policy Developments," in *WHO 2002*, 207.

62. Ondine S. von Ehrenstein, "Asthma, Allergies and Respiratory Health," in *WHO 2002*, 44.

63. Philippe Grandjean and Roberta White, "Neurodevelopmental Disorders," in *WHO 2002*, 66.

64. Bernedetto Terracini, "Cancer," in *WHO 2002*, 79.

65. Tina Kold Jensen, "Birth Defects," in *WHO 2002*, 99.

66. Kathy Pond, "Waterborne Gastrointestinal Diseases," in *WHO 2002*, 113.

67. Prudence Taylor, "From Environmental to Ecological Human Rights: A New Dynamic in International Law?" *The Georgetown Int'l Environmental Law Review* 10 (1998): 309.

68. Alan Gewirth, *Human Rights: Essays on Justification and Applications* (Chicago: University of Chicago Press, 1982).

69. Rees and Westra, *Just Sustainabilities*.

70. William E. Rees, "Globalization and Sustainability: Conflict or Convergence?," *Bulletin of Science, Technology and Society* 22, no. 4 (2002): 249–68; W. E. Rees, "Ecological Footprints and Bio-Capacity: Essential Elements in Sustainability Assessment," ch. 9 in *Renewables-Based Technology: Sustainability Assessment*, ed. Jo Dewulf and Herman Van Langenhove (Chichester, UK: John Wiley and Sons, 2006), 143–58.

71. Vandana Shiva, *Staying Alive* (London: Zed Books, 1989).

Conclusions

Challenging Our Individual
and Collective Thinking about Sustainability

Colin L. Soskolne, Louis J. Kotzé, Brendan Mackey, and William E. Rees

We conclude with a distillation and synthesis of the diverse array of specialist perspectives on the theme of sustainability presented in this book. We suggest that a coherent case for individual and social policy change, and a development path that is more just, sustainable, and peaceful, can be guided by the *Earth Charter* (see the Appendix). Certainly, the *Earth Charter* prescription is more likely to ensure a habitable Earth than the ominous road that we currently tread. Indeed, we argue that global adoption and implementation of the *Earth Charter* would offer humanity true hope for a promising future.

The Need for Context and Hope

Cassandra foresaw the destruction of Troy. She had warned the Trojans about the treacherous hollow horse (that would soon become the best-known icon of their city), the death of Agamemnon, and her own demise. Yet, Cassandra's premonitions failed to forestall those tragedies. In Greek mythology, Cassandra (Greek: Κασσάνδρα "she who entangles men") was a daughter of King Priam and Queen Hecuba of Troy. Her beauty inspired Apollo to grant her the gift of prophecy. However, when she did not return his love, Apollo placed a curse on her so that no one would ever believe her predictions.

We do not assume to have the power of prophecy. We do, however, hope that the reader will find sufficient coherence in our story to reflect and act on our analysis and warnings.

This book, as others before it, sounds a clarion call for action based on already evident declines in that which sustains us; it forewarns of a looming crisis that threatens much of what we value in nature, culture, and civilization. Why is it that the world community has not responded to previous warnings with effective action? What forces are at play that seem to herd humanity, in all of its diversity, along so precarious a development path?

Changing course is never easy, and the kinds of social, economic, cultural, and technological changes needed for sustainability will not emerge accidentally. Success will require the engagement of many specialists from countries and cultures around the world, and will touch on every aspect of life. Our survival depends on a collective, collaborative approach.

This book brings together insights from the ecological, biological, environmental, agricultural, and social sciences, and from economics, moral philosophy, epidemiology, public health, law, education, and theology. Many nations and

413

cultural viewpoints are represented. The book thereby provides both a broad and deep understanding of global change, and of the implications of human activities for the future of life on Earth. We suggest that only by adopting new international institutions and instruments like the *Earth Charter*, and adopting a morally deliberative stance toward both fellow humans and nonhuman life, can we more assure a satisfying future for ourselves and successive generations.

Are we Tilting at "Windmills?"

Don Quixote has been a hero of Western literature since the Spanish novel of that name by Miguel Cervantes was published in 1605. The senile old Don had read too many stories about medieval knights, and he came to believe that he was one himself. In one of his most famous adventures, he imagines that windmills are giant monsters and he violently attacks them.

Medieval knights fought on horseback, charging at their opponents with long lances. They were said to be "tilting at" their enemies. Today, when a person is said to be "tilting at" windmills, it implies that she or he is fighting something that she or he thinks is an enemy when, in fact, it may be perfectly harmless, irrelevant, or even beneficial. In short, "tilting at windmills" means that a person is misguided in her or his actions.

We attack the current growth-oriented business-as-usual paradigm as a genuine monster in our midst. Our intellectual lance is an integrated and, we hope, objective analysis of many relevant contemporary facts and perspectives on sustainability. Of course, others argue that the current, growth-based, business-as-usual paradigm will actually prove to be beneficial to both humans and nonhumans over the long term. These colleagues may well accuse us of "tilting at windmills." Our only response is "let the evidence and our assessment speak for themselves." We trust that the reader will at least agree from our synthesis that business-as-usual is no mere windmill for self-deluded knights.

We also hope that, after due consideration, readers will see the need for cross-cultural behavioral changes to ensure a sustainable future. These changes must bear upon development plans, policies, laws, and governance mechanisms, including the moral and ethical premises that underpin them.

To begin, the world community must come to agreement on the essential elements of economic, social, and ecological sustainability. By this agreement, present-day economies and governance policies must be acknowledged as being fundamentally unsustainable.

The next step is to identify conceptual approaches and workable mechanisms for a sustainable future. As demonstrated throughout this book, many of the approaches and mechanisms need not be created from scratch, but have already been articulated in detail. For example, the *Earth Charter* provides a comprehensive framework of sustainability principles and objectives, and the various national and international legal mechanisms described herein could also contribute to more sustainable governance strategies. This final chapter provides recommendations for governance practices to sustain life on Earth, distilled from the individual contributed chapters.

The Need for Interdisciplinary Work

To generate this synthesis, we struggled to integrate wide-ranging contributions from an array of specialists from both the physical sciences and the humanities. Interdisciplinarity is difficult because it forces us to think beyond the familiar, but it is also an opportunity for the same reason. In bringing together various disparate perspectives, including culturally and professionally unique ways of evaluating and solving problems, we can engage the sustainability agenda from a fresh perspective.

In particular, we have tried to emphasize that the world is a complex system made up of many interconnected subsystems. As pressures mount on one subsystem, they cannot only force that system to change or collapse, but also can induce negative effects on other subsystems. As populations, demand for energy, waste production, the use of ecologically noxious technologies, the gap between rich and poor, and so on, steadily increase, they generate forces that weaken the very life-supporting functions upon which we all depend for survival. Indeed, many entire ecosystems are degraded and verging on collapse.

Any application of human-built capital or its products may result in the misuse or inappropriate use of technology. Indeed, almost all modern production processes reduce the complexity and diversity of the natural world, and increase the entropy of the larger global system. For example, both essential manufacturing and the production of useless gadgets may involve polluting industrial infrastructure that impedes ecosystem functions, and this, in turn, can endanger human health and well-being. While appropriate technology is part of the solution, we cannot assume that technological "fixes" can substitute for planetary life-supporting functions, or save us from our abuse of critical life-sustaining ecosystems.

To become better stewards of nature, we must recognize our connections with ecosystems, and adopt an interdisciplinary approach framed by systems thinking. Large-scale problems require holistic analysis that is cognizant of the complexity of natural systems and their propensity for counterintuitive nonlinear behavior. Significantly, the *Earth Charter* recognizes that the complexity of natural systems demands a correspondingly holistic approach to environmental governance.

The *Earth Charter* also calls on post-industrial society to rethink its core values, its traditional methods, and its moral stance toward both other peoples and the larger community of life. Conventional approaches to resources management and environmental governance are silo-based and hence limited in perspective and effectiveness. Lawyers alone cannot solve the sustainability conundrum. Neither scientists nor humanists have sufficient tools or insight to face the challenges of unsustainability on their own. Sustainability can be negotiated and achieved only through broadly-based analysis and holistic understanding. We hope that the reader will be inspired by both the transdisciplinary perspective and the moral stance reflected in the *Earth Charter* and work with us to realize its potential contribution to the quest for global sustainability.

Encouraging Signs

The Global Ecological Integrity Group (GEIG) has enjoyed fourteen years of transdisciplinary interaction and engagement focusing on what present-day governments and people of the world are doing to the life-supporting systems upon which we all depend. This has been a difficult challenge, but we have had some tangible signs of success from our endeavors. In 1998, at the World Health Organization's (WHO) European Centre for Environment and Health in Rome, we participated in a formal workshop on the topic of global ecological integrity. The report from that meeting became the most accessed document on the European Web site of the WHO for three successive years. Our WHO report is acknowledged as a fine example of transdisciplinary thinking on interconnected, system-wide problems.

We hope that this book provides further impetus for thinking about system-wide issues from a multi-specialist vantage point. Each discipline not only attracts a certain type of intellect, but it also fashions a certain kind of persona. Specific disciplines tend to socialize their students in ways that make them more or less insensitive to the background and training of those from other disciplines. Readers with strong disciplinary leanings may be similarly hampered.

However, we argue that we must all have the courage to think beyond our disciplinary comfort zones in responding to the (un)sustainability conundrum. How can we choose to sit idly by when all indications are that the path we are on is already leading to systems failure and collapse? We hope that this book provides encouragement for others to venture out and tackle broader system-wide concerns.

The Urgency of Our Times

We have emphasized the impact of global change on population health, examined the role of legal and paralegal instruments in effecting change, and identified the *Earth Charter* as a model covenant to help guide us onto a path of justice, sustainability, and peace. This integrated perspective argues that we need policies and guidelines that are not simply "procedural," but that are ethically framed and morally substantive. We hope that our arguments encourage action for transformative democratic change in the ways that we conduct our individual and collective lives.

Unfortunately, vested interests still argue a case for the *status quo*, and they sometimes mount disinformation campaigns on critical issues. The corporate sector also, in particular, has undue influence over policy-makers. The net result is to distort the public policy debate on vital environmental health issues. This creates doubt about our message in this book, and it makes the work of formulating effective policy all the more difficult.

The role of the tobacco industry in influencing public policy is a classic case. For more than fifty years, scientists had warned about tobacco products as health hazards. Yet, it was only after millions of unnecessary, entirely preventable deaths and disabling illnesses that governments accepted the warnings, revamped tobacco product labeling accordingly, and began to outlaw smoking in public places.

How long has it taken our national governments and energy-intensive industries to accept the reality of climate change and the need for urgent action? For many years, vested interests sought to discredit sound scientific assessments and provide governments with reasons not to take preventive actions. Resultant delays benefited industry, but are a great disservice to the goal of sustainability. Nevertheless, the world is finally coming to recognize that the old maxim, "an ounce of prevention is worth a pound of cure" applies to climate change. Today, even the Security Council of the United Nations formally recognizes climate change as a pressing concern requiring urgent attention. Perhaps it is because of concern about climate change impacts at the local level that mass support for action is growing.

Of course, we need to move beyond political rhetoric to effective environmental governance mechanisms. Generating these will require inputs from all fields of science, public participation, and support from all interested parties. Our choice is to act now to minimize the inevitable harms from the collapse of ecological systems, or to wait for catastrophic environmental upheavals. Since the longer we wait, the more costly the consequences, we can only recommend a proactive, precautionary approach.

Indeed, preventive action is an imperative of international environmental law. When scientific knowledge regarding the negative environmental effects of our activities is uncertain, but there is potential for significant or irreversible harm, we should proceed with the utmost care to avoid or minimize harm. In cases where harm has already been caused and a reactive approach is the only available strategy, citizens should have adequate legal and extralegal mechanisms, institutions, procedures, and remedies to address these harms.

Whether acting proactively or reactively, public servants have an obligation to protect the long-term public interest against incursions from other entities whether the latter are from the industrial/corporate sector, government agencies, labor organizations, or any other privileged group. The *Earth Charter*, for example, suggests that caring for the greater community of life, commensurate with our circumstances, capacities, and access to resources, is a prerequisite for sustainability.

One barrier to exercising caution is that it lacks the heroic cachet associated with rushing forward in reaction to a crisis. Nevertheless, it is clearly better to save lives by building ships that stay afloat than to have to pluck bodies from the water. Global society must embrace prevention and precaution as fundamental principles of sustainability. And the emerging field of ecoepidemiology is positioned to help inform this new course.

On Democracy and the Need for Its Full Application

In striving for eco-integrity, nonviolence, and peace, Principle 13 of the *Earth Charter* points to the need to "strengthen democratic institutions at all levels, and provide transparency and accountability in governance, inclusive participation in decision making and access to justice." Many countries hold democratic elections, people vote, and elected officials take office. But often, even in these countries, the level of participation in democratic processes is very low.

Clearly, concerned citizens must become informed about the sustainability crisis and become more involved in the political process. It is essential that such people register and vote, and that they help nominate candidates with the integrity and wisdom to protect the long-term public interest through their tenure in government.

In any democratic election, there are winners and losers. Majority rule by the winners is a means for organizing government and deciding on priority public issues—it should not be just another road to oppression. Just as no self-appointed group has the right to oppress others, so no majority, even in a democracy, should take away the basic rights and freedoms of any minority group or individual. The principles of majority rule and the protection of individual and minority rights are, in fact, the twin pillars foundational to democratic government.

Nevertheless, the losers of a democratic vote are sometimes excluded from the governance process altogether. And what of disenfranchised groups whose opinions were not even counted in the election process? Elected governments theoretically have responsibilities for, and obligations to, various such minority groups. Indeed, all minorities, whether ethnic, religious, geographic, economic, or simply the losers of elections, enjoy basic human rights that no government or ruling elite should remove.

In present circumstances, basic human rights should be extended to include a universal right to a healthy environment. This means clean air, water, and soil; the right to safe food and to products that will not endanger health and well-being; and the right to the security afforded by stable, predictable climate and dependable life-supporting functions provided by the biophysical systems of the ecosphere.

Increasingly, fundamental rights, especially those relating to children, food, water, housing, health care, and the environment, are formulated as socio-economic rights. These place a positive duty on government not only to safe-guard its citizens from rights infringement, but also, progressively and posi-tively, to realize and fulfill these rights. Among the most pressing are rights relating to fisheries agreements and access to water.

And, whose rights need to be protected more than those of the disenfran-chised youth, children, and infants of the world? What must we do to prepare our children for the future? How can we ensure that their expectations are ade-quately informed? What skills will they need to deal with an uncertain future in a globalizing world? How do we help them to develop the knowledge and values that they will need to deal with emerging problems in both ethically- and cultur-ally-appropriate ways? How do we instill hope and, above all, what examples do we set as role models for them?

Environmental justice must include considerations of both intergenerational and intragenerational rights. This applies regardless of whether we are discuss-ing the cultural, media-saturated environment, or the physical environment in-volving synthetic chemical pollution. Both have profound impacts on values, culture, and the health and well-being of children, with extension into fully actualized and voting adults.

The very poor and those dependent on the land for maintaining a rural live-lihood also deserve special consideration as being most vulnerable, not only to the effects of climate change, but also to the effects of globalization. By protect-ing the rights of the weak and vulnerable in society to a life of quality, we will ensure these rights for all people.

All that said, it is often difficult for citizens to hold governments to account between elections, or to censure them for inappropriate conduct. Highlighting government failings is often left solely to the activism of Non-Governmental Organizations (NGOs). If we are to be responsible stewards of Earth, we must acknowledge how our actions today will impact generations to come. For exam-ple, better stewardship today means less emphasis on wealth accumulation by the few, and more emphasis on mechanisms for income redistribution within, between, and among the nations of the world.

Obviously, this will be a challenge and uphill battle. Our arguments are continuously drowned out by the strong voices of self-interested vested interests with narrow perspectives on the world. Indeed, the odds are against us if only because, for every dollar available to promote the sustainability message, many more dollars are spent on disinformation campaigns to mislead the public. (Re-member, again, the story of tobacco over the past several decades.)

Nevertheless, sustainability educators must ensure that students—perhaps, today, especially those in economics and business administration—develop the capacity to critically evaluate the global situation so that they graduate as ecol-ogically-literate and democratically-engaged citizens. In the absence of clear sustainability policies, confusion and hypocrisy at all levels of society will pre-vail. Dare we hope that, with improved popular understanding, we will soon see a groundswell of public support for government policies and programs in support of sustainability?

On Economics and the Need for Its Proper Application

Why is it that the *Earth Charter* Principle 9: "Eradicate poverty as an ethical, social, and environmental imperative," and the first of the Millennium Development Goals, "Eradicate extreme poverty and hunger" are proving to be such formidable challenges?

One source of the problem is conventional economics. Neo-liberal market economics is defined as the science that deals with the efficient (i.e., maximal) production, allocation, and consumption of wealth. As "science," economic theory eschews moral and ethical considerations. It assumes a mythical "economic man" (*Homo economicus*), a pleasure-seeking autonomous individual, unburdened by thoughts of family or community, who mechanically maximizes her/his personal utility measured strictly in monetary terms.

According to the prevailing paradigm, if the economy is not growing in conventional, narrowly defined terms, then the demand cannot be met for health care, jobs, services, and so on.

Economic policies in support of these objectives place money and the control of money-generating activity above all other values. Thus, if an ecological good or service cannot be measured in monetary terms, it is often deemed to have no tangible value.

This is problematic because most of nature's services are derived free from ecosystems and thus remain unpriced. In the absence of obvious scarcity value (dollar prices), people tend to mistakenly assume that natural resources, including critical waste sinks, are unlimited. This permits perpetual material growth to remain an unquestioned yet unsustainable social expectation at the expense of ecosystems and critical life-supporting functions of greater value.

In effect, then, markets are blind to the harmful ecological consequences of growth. And because the relentless pursuit of economic efficiency and material wealth has no moral or ethical compass either, we continue to erode natural systems whose sustainability demands the consideration of time horizons that extend far beyond year-end shareholder reports and four-yearly election cycles.

We wish to remind the reader that the word "economy" derives from the Greek, meaning "managing the home." By this definition, sustainability demands the cultural morphing of our species into a new cultural subspecies we might call *Homo sapiens* var., *ecologicus*; a thoughtful, ecologically literate human, motivated by a sense of responsibility for the planet.

Such an individual would recognize that economic efficiency is not all that motivates either individual or collective decisions. Several of the preceding chapters suggest that our limited economic perspective is a proximal cause of many of the world's social ills, and explains the ecological uncertainty facing life on Earth.

In addition, *H. sapiens* var. *ecologicus* would realize that a steady-state economy can also produce viable socioeconomic outcomes. Indeed, with the human enterprise in overshoot, it is human health and well-being, and Earth's enabling systems that must be the focal point for public policy. The economy should be a means to that end; not, as it has become, an end in itself.

In summary, the "disconnect" between our scientific understanding of ecological integrity and economic measures of well-being is an impediment to addressing our current crisis. Our focus must shift from how people can be used to serve the economy, to determining how best the economy can be restructured to serve humanity and the ecosphere, now and in the future. A major challenge is to ensure that the economy does not degrade the very ecological integrity upon which geopolitical stability, social order, and the economy itself depend.

Spanning Generations and the Need for Collective Wisdom

How far are we willing to tempt fate by pushing systems to their breaking points? We are playing a hazardous game that no one can win.

In the search for win-win solutions, there is much to learn from ecology and cumulative human experience. Why ignore the lessons of cultures that have survived for millennia? Consider just the "Seventh Generation Principle." Thinking through the consequences for future generations of actions taken today remains the essence of sustainability.

Public pressure for policies and programs to amend our unsustainable ways is growing as witnessed by concern for global warming and carbon emissions in 2007. There is also expanded awareness of the wealth and power disparities among "have," "have less," and "have not" communities within and across countries. Mass support for G8 countries to make poverty history is no longer only a concern of marginal groups.

Some contemporary communities are considerably more vulnerable to phenomena like global warming than others. Concern should therefore be focused not only on seven generations hence, but also on children living today in poorer regions or in low-lying island nations. We all gain by protecting the most vulnerable of all societies, species, and ecosystems.

Toward Justice and Integrity

The current sustainability challenge requires that we incorporate justice (or "fairness") into our decision-making, policy, legislative, and governance processes. Justice is understood differently by different people, but one commonality is that state institutions should deal with people equally. Justice includes the notion of environmental justice where people equally share in ecological benefits, and no one segment of society bears an unfair burden of negative consequences from human-induced or natural disasters. Recognition of environmental justice in our governance mechanisms will contribute to global peace, democracy, political and social stability, and, ultimately, to sustainability.

There is a clear need to reconfigure or reinvent political and economic systems to answer to the obligations and ethical imperatives articulated in, among other places, the *Earth Charter*. The Charter is a covenant that can be used to help design new forms of just and ecologically sustainable governance rooted in the concept of ecological integrity.

With regard to more local rights issues, the use of institutionalized force in the removal of communities is a fact of the past and it continues today. When large-scale economic development projects are planned (such as dams, highways, mines, and irrigation schemes), the need for prior fully informed consent from the affected communities is essential if justice and integrity are to prevail. The imposition of solutions that do not embrace local knowledge serves not only as an injustice to the local people, but also is counter to sustainability.

As we have shown, it is possible to compare the relative integrity of nations. Those with a high integrity score must assist those with a lower score to improve their performance rankings. It is only with a strong concerted effort that we will be able to establish an acceptable global level of integrity that is conducive to addressing sustainability challenges.

The moral power of human rights as a means to address issues of environment, health, and well-being, should not be underestimated. There are various fundamental rights that, either directly or indirectly, link with environmental considerations. These include rights to life, dignity, equality, food, water, social security, health care, and any other entrenched explicit environmental rights.

However, rights are in themselves of little value if they are not formally adopted by the international community and individual nations, observed by citizens, and enforced by vigilant organs of state. We therefore urge that citizens' organizations promote fundamental rights, and that states adopt them in international and national legal and extralegal instruments as a means to achieve a more environmentally just and sustainable society. In this context, the *Earth Charter* can serve as a useful reference set of paralegal principles.

The Need for Enduring Hope

This book comes to completion in a year that is taking debate on national and international environmental policy in a direction that would not have been thought possible even twelve months ago. As the result of public concern for global warming, the stars may be aligning now for concerted action at all levels and in all sectors. Public concern has been catalyzed by many things, including more than twenty years of reports from the Intergovernmental Panel on Climate Change, media uptake, analysis of the economic consequences of inaction by Nicholas Stern, common sense experience that weather patterns are changing, and the popularization of the issue by Al Gore. All point to a change in the way our knowledge is being constructed to reflect the new values of environmental concern.

These are encouraging signs. The better informed now need to help concerned people everywhere to understand the underlying issues and what is at stake in the (un)sustainability crisis. After all, global warming is but a symptom, albeit a serious one, of a deeper systemic malaise. This book provides the broader perspective necessary to better understand the challenges of sustainability.

Governments, the corporate sector, NGOs, and individuals alike must stop tinkering on the periphery with unlikely and illusory solutions. It is time to get serious about sustainability. We need a true paradigm shift to more socially and ecologically adaptive values, beliefs, and assumptions about the place of *H. sapiens* in nature. To begin, we must create policy incentives and disincentives at all levels of government to move the economy—indeed, the entire human enterprise—onto a path of sustainability. As several of our chapters suggest, the *Earth Charter* provides a coherent set of values and one consistent set of directions. Given such lucid blueprints and the current momentum for change, we hope that our readers will emerge with renewed enthusiasm and commitment to work for the great transition. The entire human family yearns for a more just, sustainable, and peaceful world. Collective wisdom and intelligent action are urgently needed. This book paves the way.

Acknowledgments

This concluding chapter is a distillation and synthesis of the twenty-seven preceding chapters from which the ideas and messages expressed here have emerged. The following Web sites were helpful to us in framing this chapter:

On Windmills and Cassandra: www.wikipedia.com (accessed on June 13, 2007); On the **G8 Summit in 2007**: http://en.wikipedia.org/wiki/33rd_G8 _summit (accessed on June 13, 2007); **On Democracy and Majority Rule**: http://usinfo.state.gov/products/pubs/principles/majority.htm (accessed on June 13, 2007), http://www.dwatch.ca/ (accessed on June 13, 2007), http://www.demcoalition.org/pdf/warsaw_english.pdf (accessed on June 13, 2007); **On the WHO's role with the GEIG**: http://www.euro.who.int/ document/gch/ecorep5.pdf (accessed on June 13, 2007).

Brian Ladd provided helpful editorial assistance in finalizing this chapter.

424   Colin L. Soskolne, Louis J. Kotzé, Brendan Mackey, and William E. Rees

In particular, we acknowledge Mark Anielski whose recently published book *The Economics of Happiness: Building Genuine Wealth* (Gabriola Island, BC: New Society Publishers, 2007) has helped us to present some focused messages on economics.

Appendix: The *Earth Charter*

Preamble

We stand at a critical moment in Earth's history, a time when humanity must choose its future. As the world becomes increasingly interdependent and fragile, the future at once holds great peril and great promise. To move forward we must recognize that in the midst of a magnificent diversity of cultures and life forms we are one human family and one Earth community with a common destiny. We must join together to bring forth a sustainable global society founded on respect for nature, universal human rights, economic justice, and a culture of peace. Towards this end, it is imperative that we, the peoples of Earth, declare our responsibility to one another, to the greater community of life, and to future generations.

Earth, Our Home

Humanity is part of a vast evolving universe. Earth, our home, is alive with a unique community of life. The forces of nature make existence a demanding and uncertain adventure, but Earth has provided the conditions essential to life's evolution. The resilience of the community of life and the well-being of humanity depend upon preserving a healthy biosphere with all its ecological systems, a rich variety of plants and animals, fertile soils, pure waters, and clean air. The global environment with its finite resources is a common concern of all peoples. The protection of Earth's vitality, diversity, and beauty is a sacred trust.

The Global Situation

The dominant patterns of production and consumption are causing environmental devastation, the depletion of resources, and a massive extinction of species. Communities are being undermined. The benefits of development are not shared equitably and the gap between rich and poor is widening. Injustice, poverty, ignorance, and violent conflict are widespread and the cause of great suffering. An unprecedented rise in human population has overburdened ecological and social systems. The foundations of global security are threatened. These trends are perilous but not inevitable.

The Challenges Ahead

The choice is ours: form a global partnership to care for Earth and one another or risk the destruction of ourselves and the diversity of life. Fundamental changes are needed in our values, institutions, and ways of living. We must realize that when basic needs have been met, human development is primarily about

425

being more, not having more. We have the knowledge and technology to provide for all and to reduce our impacts on the environment. The emergence of a global civil society is creating new opportunities to build a democratic and humane world. Our environmental, economic, political, social, and spiritual challenges are interconnected, and together we can forge inclusive solutions.

Universal Responsibility

To realize these aspirations, we must decide to live with a sense of universal responsibility, identifying ourselves with the whole Earth community as well as our local communities. We are at once citizens of different nations and of one world in which the local and global are linked. Everyone shares responsibility for the present and future well-being of the human family and the larger living world. The spirit of human solidarity and kinship with all life is strengthened when we live with reverence for the mystery of being, gratitude for the gift of life, and humility regarding the human place in nature.

We urgently need a shared vision of basic values to provide an ethical foundation for the emerging world community. Therefore, together in hope we affirm the following interdependent principles for a sustainable way of life as a common standard by which the conduct of all individuals, organizations, businesses, governments, and trans-national institutions is to be guided and assessed.

Principles

I. RESPECT AND CARE FOR THE COMMUNITY OF LIFE

1. Respect earth and life in all its diversity.
    a.   Recognize that all beings are interdependent and every form of life has value regardless of its worth to human beings.
    b.   Affirm faith in the inherent dignity of all human beings and in the intellectual, artistic, ethical, and spiritual potential of humanity.

2. Care for the community of life with understanding, compassion, and love.
    a.   Accept that with the right to own, manage, and use natural resources comes the duty to prevent environmental harm and to protect the rights of people.
    b.   Affirm that with increased freedom, knowledge, and power comes increased responsibility to promote the common good.

3. Build democratic societies that are just, participatory, sustainable, and peaceful.

a.   Ensure that communities at all levels guarantee human rights and fundamental freedoms and provide everyone an opportunity to realize his or her full potential.
b.   Promote social and economic justice, enabling all to achieve a secure and meaningful livelihood that is ecologically responsible.

4. Secure Earth's bounty and beauty for present and future generations.

a.   Recognize that the freedom of action of each generation is qualified by the needs of future generations.
b.   Transmit to future generations values, traditions, and institutions that support the long-term flourishing of Earth's human and ecological communities.

In order to fulfil these four broad commitments, it is necessary to:

II. ECOLOGICAL INTEGRITY

5. Protect and restore the integrity of Earth's ecological systems, with special concern for biological diversity and the natural processes that sustain life.

a.   Adopt at all levels sustainable development plans and regulations that make environmental conservation and rehabilitation integral to all development initiatives.
b.   Establish and safeguard viable nature and biosphere reserves, including wild lands and marine areas, to protect Earth's life support systems, maintain biodiversity, and preserve our natural heritage.
c.   Promote the recovery of endangered species and ecosystems.
d.   Control and eradicate non-native or genetically modified organisms harmful to native species and the environment, and prevent introduction of such harmful organisms.
e.   Manage the use of renewable resources such as water, soil, forest products, and marine life in ways that do not exceed rates of regeneration and that protect the health of ecosystems.
f.   Manage the extraction and use of non-renewable resources such as minerals and fossil fuels in ways that minimize depletion and cause no serious environmental damage.

6. Prevent harm as the best method of environmental protection and, when knowledge is limited, apply a precautionary approach.

a.   Take action to avoid the possibility of serious or irreversible environmental harm even when scientific knowledge is incomplete or inconclusive.
b.   Place the burden of proof on those who argue that a proposed activity will not cause significant harm, and make the responsible parties liable for environmental harm.
c.   Ensure that decision making addresses the cumulative, long-term, indirect, long distance, and global consequences of human activities.

d.   Prevent pollution of any part of the environment and allow no build-up of radioactive, toxic, or other hazardous substances.

e.   Avoid military activities damaging to the environment.

7. Adopt patterns of production, consumption, and reproduction that safeguard Earth's regenerative capacities, human rights, and community well-being.

a.   Reduce, reuse, and recycle the materials used in production and consumption systems, and ensure that residual waste can be assimilated by ecological systems.

b.   Act with restraint and efficiency when using energy, and rely increasingly on renewable energy sources such as solar and wind.

c.   Promote the development, adoption, and equitable transfer of environmentally sound technologies.

d.   Internalize the full environmental and social costs of goods and services in the selling price, and enable consumers to identify products that meet the highest social and environmental standards.

e.   Ensure universal access to health care that fosters reproductive health and responsible reproduction.

f.   Adopt lifestyles that emphasize the quality of life and material sufficiency in a finite world.

8. Advance the study of ecological sustainability and promote the open exchange and wide application of the knowledge acquired.

a.   Support international scientific and technical cooperation on sustainability, with special attention to the needs of developing nations.

b.   Recognize and preserve the traditional knowledge and spiritual wisdom in all cultures that contribute to environmental protection and human well-being.

c.   Ensure that information of vital importance to human health and environmental protection, including genetic information, remains available in the public domain.

III. SOCIAL AND ECONOMIC JUSTICE

9. Eradicate poverty as an ethical, social, and environmental imperative.

a.   Guarantee the right to potable water, clean air, food security, uncontaminated soil, shelter, and safe sanitation, allocating the national and international resources required.

b.   Empower every human being with the education and resources to secure a sustainable livelihood, and provide social security and safety nets for those who are unable to support themselves.

c.   Recognize the ignored, protect the vulnerable, serve those who suffer, and enable them to develop their capacities and to pursue their aspirations.

10. Ensure that economic activities and institutions at all levels promote human development in an equitable and sustainable manner.

    a.   Promote the equitable distribution of wealth within nations and among nations.

    b.   Enhance the intellectual, financial, technical, and social resources of developing nations, and relieve them of onerous international debt.

    c.   Ensure that all trade supports sustainable resource use, environmental protection, and progressive labor standards.

    d.   Require multinational corporations and international financial organizations to act transparently in the public good, and hold them accountable for the consequences of their activities.

11. Affirm gender equality and equity as prerequisites to sustainable development and ensure universal access to education, health care, and economic opportunity.

    a.   Secure the human rights of women and girls and end all violence against them.

    b.   Promote the active participation of women in all aspects of economic, political, civil, social, and cultural life as full and equal partners, decision makers, leaders, and beneficiaries.

    c.   Strengthen families and ensure the safety and loving nurture of all family members.

12. Uphold the right of all, without discrimination, to a natural and social environment supportive of human dignity, bodily health, and spiritual well-being, with special attention to the rights of indigenous peoples and minorities.

    a.   Eliminate discrimination in all its forms, such as that based on race, color, sex, sexual orientation, religion, language, and national, ethnic or social origin.

    b.   Affirm the right of indigenous peoples to their spirituality, knowledge, lands and resources and to their related practice of sustainable livelihoods.

    c.   Honor and support the young people of our communities, enabling them to fulfil their essential role in creating sustainable societies.

    d.   Protect and restore outstanding places of cultural and spiritual significance.

IV. DEMOCRACY, NONVIOLENCE, AND PEACE

13. Strengthen democratic institutions at all levels, and provide transparency and accountability in governance, inclusive participation in decision making, and access to justice.

    a.   Uphold the right of everyone to receive clear and timely information on environmental matters and all development plans and activities which are likely to affect them or in which they have an interest.

b.   Support local, regional and global civil society, and promote the meaningful participation of all interested individuals and organizations in decision making.

c.   Protect the rights to freedom of opinion, expression, peaceful assembly, association, and dissent.

d.   Institute effective and efficient access to administrative and independent judicial procedures, including remedies and redress for environmental harm and the threat of such harm.

e.   Eliminate corruption in all public and private institutions.

f.   Strengthen local communities, enabling them to care for their environments, and assign environmental responsibilities to the levels of government where they can be carried out most effectively.

14. Integrate into formal education and life-long learning the knowledge, values, and skills needed for a sustainable way of life.

a.   Provide all, especially children and youth, with educational opportunities that empower them to contribute actively to sustainable development.

b.   Promote the contribution of the arts and humanities as well as the sciences in sustainability education.

c.   Enhance the role of the mass media in raising awareness of ecological and social challenges.

d.   Recognize the importance of moral and spiritual education for sustainable living.

15. Treat all living beings with respect and consideration.

a.   Prevent cruelty to animals kept in human societies and protect them from suffering.

b.   Protect wild animals from methods of hunting, trapping, and fishing that cause extreme, prolonged, or avoidable suffering.

c.   Avoid or eliminate to the full extent possible the taking or destruction of non-targeted species.

16. Promote a culture of tolerance, non-violence, and peace.

a.   Encourage and support mutual understanding, solidarity, and cooperation among all peoples and within and among nations.

b.   Implement comprehensive strategies to prevent violent conflict and use collaborative problem solving to manage and resolve environmental conflicts and other disputes.

c.   Demilitarize national security systems to the level of a non-provocative defence posture, and convert military resources to peaceful purposes, including ecological restoration.

d.   Eliminate nuclear, biological, and toxic weapons and other weapons of mass destruction.

e.   Ensure that the use of orbital and outer space supports environmental protection and peace.

f.   Recognize that peace is the wholeness created by right relationships with oneself, other persons, other cultures, other life, Earth, and the larger whole of which all are a part.

The Way Forward

As never before in history, common destiny beckons us to seek a new beginning. Such renewal is the promise of these *Earth Charter* principles. To fulfil this promise, we must commit ourselves to adopt and promote the values and objectives of the Charter.

This requires a change of mind and heart. It requires a new sense of global interdependence and universal responsibility. We must imaginatively develop and apply the vision of a sustainable way of life locally, nationally, regionally, and globally. Our cultural diversity is a precious heritage and different cultures will find their own distinctive ways to realize the vision. We must deepen and expand the global dialogue that generated the *Earth Charter*, for we have much to learn from the ongoing collaborative search for truth and wisdom.

Life often involves tensions between important values. This can mean difficult choices. However, we must find ways to harmonize diversity with unity, the exercise of freedom with the common good, short-term objectives with long-term goals. Every individual, family, organization, and community has a vital role to play. The arts, sciences, religions, educational institutions, media, businesses, nongovernmental organizations, and governments are all called to offer creative leadership. The partnership of government, civil society, and business is essential for effective governance.

In order to build a sustainable global community, the nations of the world must renew their commitment to the United Nations, fulfil their obligations under existing international agreements, and support the implementation of *Earth Charter* principles with an international legally binding instrument on environment and development.

Let ours be a time remembered for the awakening of a new reverence for life, the firm resolve to achieve sustainability, the quickening of the struggle for justice and peace, and the joyful celebration of life.

This document, the Earth Charter, *along with relevant information relating to it, can be found in English at the following URL: http://www.earthcharter.org. It has been translated into thirty languages and these are also accessible at the main portion of the Web site.*

Index

About the Contributors

Bosselmann, Klaus

Klaus Bosselmann was born in Germany. He studied political sciences, sociology, and law at the universities of Tübingen, Lausanne, and Berlin. After completing his Ph.D. in legal history and constitutional law at the Freie Universität in Berlin (1979), he was appointed a judge with secondment to the Federal Administrative Court of Germany where he specialized in administrative and nuclear energy law. He then helped pioneer the field of environmental law. He co-founded Germany's first Institute for Environmental Law in Bremen. In 1988 he was appointed Law Professor at the University of Auckland. He is founding director of the New Zealand Centre for Environmental Law. His special interests are in the interface between environmental ethics, legal theory, law, and governance.

Brown, Donald A.

Don Brown was born in the United States. He is Director of the Pennsylvania Consortium for Interdisciplinary Environmental Policy, an organization comprising fifty-six colleges and universities in Pennsylvania, as well as the Pennsylvania Departments of Environmental Protection and Conservation and Natural Resources. He has worked for most of his career as an environmental lawyer or in policy for the States of New Jersey and Pennsylvania, and the United States Environmental Protection Agency, Office of International Environmental Policy. In the fall of 2007, he assumed a new position as associate professor of environmental ethics, science, and law at Penn State University. He has written and spoken extensively on the need to integrate environmental ethics, science, economics, and law.

Brown, Valerie A.

Val Brown took her first degree in one of the earliest ecology programs at the University of Queensland, Australia in the 1950s. She worked alternately on the social implications and on the environmental implications of social change, until bringing the two together in a Ph.D. in human sciences at the Australian National University in 1980. After this, she worked in policy development, teaching, and research in that emerging field in Australia, Nepal, Malaysia, and China. She was awarded an Order of Australia for this work in 1999. Her current research interests are in whole-of-community change toward sustainability, and her most recent book is *Leonardo's Vision: A Guide to Collective Thinking and Action* (2007).

Burkhardt, Helmut

Helmut Burkhardt was born in Romania, educated in Germany, and lives in Canada. He has a doctorate in physics. His early research was on thermonuclear fusion, and on magneto-hydrodynamic energy conversion at the University

449

of Stuttgart, at the Institute for Mathematical Sciences, New York University, and at the University of Quebec. He taught physics at Ryerson University in Toronto, and was director of the Ryerson Energy Centre. Later in his career he became interested in a full spectrum, wide-angle scientific view of the world and in scientific ethics. He is a life member and past president of Science for Peace Canada, member of the International Network of Engineers and Scientists for Global Responsibility, and member of the Canadian Pugwash Group.

Crabbé, Philippe

Philippe Crabbé was born in Belgium, where he studied history, law and economics. He studied quantitative economics in Paris and at Harvard, where he worked on the economic value of human life with T.C. Schelling. His initial work in Canada was with the National Energy Board as energy economist, and then with the University of Ottawa as natural resources and environmental economist, and systems scientist, including the history of these subjects. He was coeditor of one of the first books on Natural Resources and Environment in Canada. He became First Director of the Institute of the Environment, where he led large community-based multidisciplinary projects on water quality and on climate change.

De Leo, Giulio A.

Giulio De Leo was born in Italy where he obtained his first degree in environmental engineering and natural resource management. After completing his Ph.D. in applied ecology in 1993, he worked as a post-doctoral fellow for three years in the United States, first at Cornell University, New York, and then at the Princeton Environmental Institute, Princeton University, New Jersey. In 1996, he returned to Italy and, since 1998, he has worked at the University of Parma, where he is full professor in applied ecology. His research activity is mainly in the area of environmental impact assessment and, especially, on the relationship between energy and the environment. Since 1999, he has been working on the cost-benefit analysis of the Kyoto protocol's ratification.

Dellapenna, Joseph W.

Joe Dellapenna was born in the United States and has taught law there and abroad for thirty-seven years. His work focuses on water issues. He has been a consultant to governments on three continents regarding water law. In a 2002 legal case, he persuaded the Connecticut Supreme Court to adopt a significant reinterpretation of Connecticut water law. He is director of the Model Water Code Project of the American Society of Civil Engineers. As rapporteur of the Water Resources Committee of the International Law Association, he led the revision of the *Helsinki Rules,* the generally recognized summary of the customary international law on water resources, resulting in the Association's approval in August 2004 of the *Berlin Rules on Water Resources.*

Dolderman, Dan C.

Dan Dolderman was born in Canada. He trained as a social psychologist, receiving his Ph.D. from the University of Waterloo (2003). His early research on trust and prejudice in interpersonal relationships expanded to examine integrity in human and environmental systems. At the University of Toronto since 2002, he has collaborated with the University's Sustainability Office to develop and evaluate community based social marketing programs for promoting more sustainable behavior practices in home and workplace settings. Working with *Free The Children*, an international children's charity, he has developed educational materials and research programs related to youth empowerment and civic engagement. His research examines the determinants of pro-environmental behaviors. He is interested in the connections between meditation, personal well-being, and sustainable living.

Döring, Ralf

Ralf Döring was born in Germany where he trained as an environmental and resource economist. In 1996 he received a scholarship from the Deutsche Bundesstiftung Umwelt to work at the Department of Landscape Economics, University of Greifswald, on small-scale fisheries at the German Baltic Sea coast. After obtaining his Ph.D. from the University of Greifswald in 2000 he worked for the German Council of Environmental Advisors. There he was responsible for agriculture and fisheries policies and for developing a basic position of the council on sustainability (with Konrad Ott). After returning to the Department of Landscape Economics, he now works on policy changes for sustainable fisheries, capital theory and natural capital, and a sustainability theory.

Dyson, Rose A.

Rose Dyson was born in Canada. Her background in psychiatric nursing informed her subsequent studies in general arts, adult education, counseling, and applied psychology. Her qualitative, participatory research interests led to her doctorate on violence in the media, with over fifty-five recommendations on cultural policy. Her book *MIND ABUSE, Media Violence in an Information Age* followed. She is president of Canadians Concerned about Violence in Entertainment; co-sponsor of the 1996 Founding Convention for the Cultural Environment Movement; chairperson of the Media Working Group, Science for Peace; and editor of The Learning Edge, Canadian Association for the Study of Adult Education. Other involvements include countless media interviews, and consultation to governments, nationally and internationally. She is also a mother and grandmother.

Engel, J. Ronald

Ron Engel was born in the United States. A Unitarian-Universalist minister, he was active in the civil rights movement, co-founding the first neighborhood development corporation in Chicago. As professor of social ethics at

Meadville/Lombard Theological School, and lecturer at the Divinity School, University of Chicago, he was a pioneer in the fields of environmental theology, history, and ethics. As founder of the World Conservation Union's Ethics Working Group, he helped draft Caring for the Earth, the Draft International Covenant on Environment and Development, and the *Earth Charter*. He is currently Senior Fellow at the Marty Center for Religion and Public Life at the University of Chicago, and Senior Research Consultant for the Center for Humans and Nature.

Gatto, Marino

Marino Gatto was born in Italy. He graduated in Engineering from the Politecnico di Milano in 1972. Since 1987, he has been full professor of ecology at the same institution. He has authored or coauthored more than 150 scientific papers, half of which have appeared in peer-reviewed journals. He is an editor of *Theoretical Population Biology, Ecology and Society*, and also of *Biologia e Conservazione della Fauna*. His current research interests include: dynamics and management of marine resources, models of fragmented populations, extinction risk assessment of wildlife populations, climate change ecology, parasite ecology, and ecological economics.

Goodland, Robert

Robert Goodland was born in Guyana and raised in Canada. After his Ph.D. from McGill University on Brazilian ecosystems, he environmentally assessed large infrastructure projects in Brazil and elsewhere. He served the World Bank between 1978 and 2001, where he wrote and persuaded the Bank to adopt most of its "Environmental and Social Safeguard Policies," such as on Indigenous Peoples, Biodiversity, and Environmental Assessment. He was elected President of the International Association of Impact Assessment, and Metropolitan Chair of the Ecological Society of America. He has helped several commissions, including the Extractive Industry Review, and the World Commission on Dams. His two latest books are on the impacts of pipelines (2006), and human rights in India's bauxite mines (2007).

Huynen, Maud M. T. E.

Maud Huynen was born in Heerlen, the Netherlands. After obtaining her master's degrees in environmental health science and epidemiology at Maastricht University, she started her Ph.D. research in 2002 at the International Centre for Integrated assessment and Sustainable development (ICIS). This project ("Future health in a globalizing world") explores possible global health futures by means of the health transition theory, scenario analysis, and an integrated framework for globalization and health. Other research in which she has been involved over the past five years concerned the health impacts of climate change and biodiversity loss. After finalizing her Ph.D. thesis (end 2007) she will continue working at ICIS as a research fellow on topics related to global and environmental health.

Karr, James R.

Jim Karr was born in the United States, where a fascination with nature led to his career in ecology and environmental policy. After completing his education at the University of Illinois, he held postdoctoral appointments at Princeton University and the Smithsonian Tropical Research Institute, Panama (where he later became deputy and acting director), and faculty positions at several U.S. universities: Purdue, Illinois, Virginia Tech, and Washington. Over time, his research expanded from basic ecology to environmental policy, and from natural ecosystems to human environmental impacts. He developed the first ecological multimetric index to evaluate the effects of human actions on the health of living systems. His present concern is how to incorporate biological information into societal decision-making.

Kay, James J. (Deceased)

James Kay died in 2004, just short of his fiftieth birthday. He had reinterpreted the second law of thermodynamics, applying it to understand how exergy gradients induce self-organizing structures, and how living systems organize so as to destroy exergy gradients at the fastest rate possible. His 1994 paper with Schneider was recently identified as one of the twelve most important papers in ecology in the 1990s. He advised the Ontario Ministry of the Environment on how to develop indicators of ecological integrity. As a member of the United States National Science Foundation Advisory Committee on Environmental Research and Education, he profoundly influenced its ten-year outlook with *Complex Environmental Systems: Synthesis for Earth, Life and Society in the 21st Century* (2003).

Kotzé, Louis J.

Louis Kotzé was born in South Africa where he trained as a lawyer. His doctoral thesis at North West University focused on mechanisms to improve the sustainability of environmental governance efforts in South Africa, the Netherlands, and Finland. He has published extensively in national and international journals and textbooks, and presented papers at national and international environmental law conferences. He is a member of the IUCN Commission on Environmental Law, the IUCN Academy of Environmental Law, the IUCN Specialist Group on Governance, and the national secretary of the South African Environmental Law Association. He currently concerns himself with issues of South African, regional, and international environmental law, including the effect of good governance.

Krewski, Daniel

Daniel Krewski was born in High River, Alberta, Canada, and grew up in Edmonton. He subsequently moved to Ottawa, and completed his Ph.D. in statistics at Carleton University in 1977. He then worked with Health Canada until 1997, when he joined the University of Ottawa, where he holds the Natural Sciences and Engineering Research Council/Social Sciences and Humanities Research Council/McLaughlin Chair in Population Health Risk Assessment, with academic appointments in the Department of Epidemiology and Community Medicine, the Department of Medicine, and the Department of Mathematics and Statistics. He also serves as Scientific Director of the Pan American Health Organization/World Health Organization Collaborating Centre in Population Health Risk Assessment at the University of Ottawa. His professional interests include epidemiology, biostatistics, risk assessment, and risk management.

Ladd, Brian D.

Brian Ladd was born in Canada and studied psychology and natural resources management before moving to Boulder, Colorado, where he worked first for the National Audubon Society's Migratory Bird Conservation Program, and then for Eco-Cycle, a non-profit recycling and environmental education and advocacy organization. He returned to Canada in 2003 for master's-level study in epidemiology at the University of Alberta. His research interests include the ethical, scientific, and legal aspects of children's environmental health protection, and the relationship between global change processes and human health.

Mackey, Brendan G.

Brendan Mackey was born in Australia. He has worked as a research scientist with the Australian Commonwealth Scientific and Industrial Research Organisation (CSIRO), and the Canadian Forest Service. He is an environmental biogeographer, with special interest in ecosystem dynamics and connectivity conservation. His work with the International Union for the Conservation of Nature (IUCN) Ethics Specialist Group, the Global Ecological Integrity Group (GEIG), and the Earth Charter Initiative, has led to significant and ever-growing involvement in issues of environment and sustainability from both the scientific and public policy perspectives.

Manno, Jack P.

Jack Manno was born in the United States. His career has focused on protecting and restoring the Laurentian Great Lakes. He has worked to understand the economic and social forces that undermine sustainability and distort human and social development. He received his Ph.D. in interdisciplinary social science from the Maxwell School of Citizenship at Syracuse University. For twenty years he was executive director of the New York Great Lakes Research Consortium and is currently Associate Professor of Environmental Studies at the State University of New York College of Environmental Science and Forestry. His current research focuses on sustainability theory and governance, and institutional means to improve science-based decision-making. He authored *Privileged Goods: Commoditization and Its Impacts on Society and Environment*.

Manuel-Navarrete, David

David Manuel-Navarrete was born in Spain where he trained as an environmental scientist and ecological economist. His initial work focused on multicriteria assessment of development projects in Spain and Mesoamerica. His doctoral research at the University of Waterloo, Canada, analyzed ecological integrity discourses in the Mayan forest of Guatemala and Mexico. Most recently, he worked at the Sustainable Development Division of the UN Economic Commission for Latin America and the Caribbean (ECLAC). At ECLAC, he collaborated with the universities of Chiang Mai, Harvard, and Stanford in the study of knowledge systems for sustainable development. He also assessed environment and development policies in the Argentine pampas and the Brazilian Amazon. His current research analyzes adaptations to climate change in the Gulf of Mexico.

Martens, Pim

Pim Martens was born in Heerlen, the Netherlands. After obtaining his master's degrees in environmental and biological health sciences at Maastricht University, he worked at the Dutch National Institute of Public Health and the Environment (RIVM). In 1997, he obtained his Ph.D. at Maastricht University and his thesis was pioneering in modeling climate change. Currently, he is Director of the International Centre for Integrated assessment and Sustainable development (ICIS), where he holds the chair in "Sustainable Development."

McDowell, Ian

Ian McDowell was born in Northern Ireland, but raised in England, where he obtained his Ph.D. in epidemiology from the University of Nottingham. He is a professor in the Department of Epidemiology and Community Medicine at the University of Ottawa where he coordinates a component in the medical curriculum entitled Individual and Population Health; he also teaches courses in the M.Sc. program in epidemiology and in the Ph.D. program in population health. His research interests include health measurement (author of *Measuring Health: A Guide to Rating Scales and Questionnaires*, 2006); the epidemiology of cognitive impairments and dementia (principal investigator of the Canadian Study of Health and Aging, 1989–2006), and the manner in which social factors influence health.

McMichael, Anthony J.

Tony McMichael was born in Australia where he trained in medicine and subsequently in epidemiology. His epidemiological research contributions have spanned the fields of occupational diseases; diet, nutrition, and disease; and environmental influences on health. He currently directs the National Centre for Epidemiology and Population Health at the Australian National University (ANU). Previous to this, he was Chair of Epidemiology at the London School of Hygiene and Tropical Medicine. He has been an international leader in developing research and forecasting methods for the health risks of climate change, contributing centrally to the UN's Intergovernmental Panel on Climate Change (IPCC) assessment of health impacts. Through his pioneering international research and scientific assessments, he has developed a growing interest in how population health relates to sustainability.

Oke, Yemi

Yemi Oke is a Nigerian-born lawyer and scholar. He obtained his LL.M and Ph.D. degrees from the Osgoode Hall Law School, York University, Canada; his LL.B from the University of Ilorin, Nigeria; and his B.L. from the Nigerian Law School, Abuja. He is a barrister and solicitor of the Supreme Court of Nigeria. His law practice, consultancy, and research interest is in energy, natural resources, and environmental law.

Ott, Konrad

Konrad Ott was born in Germany. He studied philosophy and history at the University of Frankfurt. He completed his Ph.D. under the supervision of Jürgen Habermas on the origins and discursive logic of the historical disciplines. In the 1990s, he worked at the universities of Tübingen and Zürich. Since 1997, he has been full professor of environmental ethics at the University of Greifswald. The chair for environmental ethics is integrated with the interdisciplinary "Landscape Ecology and Nature Conservation." study program. His fields of research are discourse ethics, environmental ethics, justification of nature conservation, theories of sustainability, ethical aspects of climate change, and the history of nature conservation. Since 2000, he has been a member of the German Environmental Advisory Council.

Pimentel, David

David Pimentel is professor of ecology and agricultural science at Cornell University. His Ph.D. is from Cornell University, followed by postdoctoral studies at Oxford University and the University of Chicago. His research spans the fields of sustainable agriculture, ecological, and economic aspects of pest control, biological control and biotechnology, land, water and energy conservation, natural resource management, environmental policy, and basic population ecology. He has published more than six hundred scientific papers and twenty-four books. He has served on many national and government committees including the National Academy of Sciences; President's Science Advisory Council; U.S. Department of Agriculture; U.S. Department of Energy; U.S. Department of Health, Education and Welfare; Office of Technology Assessment of the U.S. Congress; and the U.S. State Department.

Pimentel, Marcia

Marcia Pimentel is a senior lecturer in the Division of Nutritional Sciences, College of Human Ecology, Cornell University. Her B.S. and M.S. degrees are from Cornell University. She is a nutritionist specializing in foods and nutrition, world food supplies, human ecology, and the environment. She has published more than sixty scientific papers and two books: *Food, Energy and Society* (1996), and *Dimensions of Food* (2006).

Rainham, Daniel G.C.

Daniel Rainham was born in Canada and is completing his Ph.D. in population health at the University of Ottawa. His academic interests are focused at the intersection of population health, ecological sustainability, and health geomatics. He teaches courses at Dalhousie University in human health and sustainability, and in geographic information systems within the Environmental Science program.

Rajepakse, I. Ruana

Ruana Rajepakse was born in Sri Lanka where she has been a practicing lawyer. Her higher education was from London University, the Inns of Court in England, and the Sri Lanka Law College. Her professional practice is mainly focused on the environment, fundamental rights, and administrative law. She served two five-year terms as a member of the Law Commission of Sri Lanka, and she is a member of the IUCN Commission on Environmental Law, Sri Lanka chapter. She has written and presented a number of papers at local, regional, and international nongovernmental conferences on the relationship between human rights jurisprudence, the rules of the World Trade Organization, and the sustainable use of natural resources in "Third World" countries.

Rees, William E.

Bill Rees was born in Manitoba and grew up in Montreal, Toronto, and rural Ontario, Canada. Fascinated by the life sciences, he ultimately obtained his Ph.D. (population ecology) from the University of Toronto. Currently a professor in the University of British Columbia, Vancouver, Canada, he teaches human ecology, ecological economics, and the policy and planning implications of human-induced global change. He is perhaps best known for pioneering "ecological footprint analysis," now arguably the world's best-known indicator of (un)sustainability. His current research focuses on the roles of biological and cultural factors in the evolution of human societies and on the vulnerability of urban-industrial civilization to global change. He was elected to the Royal Society of Canada in 2006.

Soskolne, Colin L.

Colin L. Soskolne was born in South Africa. He was educated at the University of the Witwatersrand in Johannesburg where he trained in applied mathematics. His initial work in South Africa was with the Human Sciences Research Council, and then with the Medical Research Council as biostatistician. His early career focus was on occupational cancer, both in toxicological and human studies. After obtaining his Ph.D. from the University of Pennsylvania in Philadelphia in 1982, he moved to Canada. His research interests expanded from the occupational environment to include the broader environment, the need for professional ethics, and then, through work with the World Health Organization, to global change drivers of health and well-being. He is interdisciplinary and concerned about expanding the methods of epidemiology to measure health impacts from global change.

Taylor, Prue E.

Prue Taylor was born in New Zealand. She received her legal qualifications from Victoria University, New Zealand, and Tulane University, in the United States. She has been teaching law at the University of Auckland since 1995. Prior to her academic appointment, she worked as a commercial lawyer. She currently teaches environmental and planning law to graduate and undergraduate students. She became the Deputy Director of the New Zealand Centre for Environmental Law in 2003, and is a member of the IUCN Commission of Environmental Law and its Ethics Specialist Group. Her specialist interests are in the areas of climate change, human rights, biotechnology, environmental governance, ocean law and policy, and environmental ethics.

Vo, Thanh

Thanh Vo is from Vietnam where he was trained as a forestry engineer. Throughout his career, he has always worked to bridge science, policy, and public involvement in development processes. He has worked for the Department of Science and Technology of Thua Thien Hue province and was the regional advisor of Sida (Swedish) Environmental Fund in Vietnam. He founded the Green Volunteer Network and the Nature Care Association in Thua Thien Hue Province. His research interests focus on sustainability and resilience of linked social-ecological systems, particularly local livelihoods and natural resources, under global change processes. He received his master's degree from the State University of New York where he is currently a Ph.D. candidate.

Westra, Laura

Laura Westra was born in Trieste, Italy. Moving to Canada, she raised her three children, subsequently receiving her Ph.D. in philosophy from the University of Toronto (1983). She then taught in the United States, returning to Canada to teach at the University of Windsor until 1999. From 1992 through 1999, her research on ecological integrity was supported by the Social Sciences and Humanities Research Council, allowing her to assemble the group of scientists and ethicists that became the Global Ecological Integrity Group (GEIG). Recognizing the need to know law, she returned to Osgoode Hall Law School in Toronto, to prepare her for her fifteenth book, which became her second doctoral thesis in 2005. Her current focus is on the human rights dimensions of environmental harm.

Westra, Richard

Richard Westra received his Ph.D. from Queen's University, Kingston, Canada in 2002. He has taught at universities and colleges around the world, including The Royal Military College of Canada, Queen's University, the International Study Centre in East Sussex, UK, and the College of the Bahamas, Nassau. Currently, he is assistant professor in the Division of International and Area Studies, Pukyong National University, Pusan, South Korea. His work has been published in numerous international scholarly refereed journals and books. His contribution to this volume draws upon his abiding interest in the political economy of social change.

Witbooi, Emma V.

Emma Witbooi was born in Scotland, moving to Cape Town, South Africa, before her first birthday, where she grew up and was educated. She trained in law, specializing in environmental and marine law. Her career path has been largely academic, lecturing and researching at the University of Cape Town and later, tutoring at University College London, where she obtained her Ph.D. in 2007. Her initial research focused largely on the role and development of South African environmental law. It subsequently evolved to include an increasing focus on the broader challenge of sustainable marine fisheries management and development, particularly in the context of European-African fisheries relations.